Readings in Economic Geography

Readings in

ECONOMIC GEOGRAPHY

Edited by

HOWARD G. ROEPKE
Professor of Geography
University of Illinois

with the assistance of

THOMAS J. MARESH
University of Illinois

John Wiley and Sons, Inc.   New York • London • Sydney

Library of Congress Catalog Card Number: 67-19451
Printed in the United States of America

To Ruth,
who did much to bring order out of chaos

PREFACE

Those who teach economic geography face a great many problems. Many of these result from the variety and complexity of the economic activities which must be described and interpreted for their students. Even the best textbook, facing practical limitations of length and weight, can go little beyond a generalized description and explanation of spatial variations. These generalizations need further development and exemplification if beginning students in geography are to grasp them. Such expanded treatment is particularly important if we wish the students to develop the ability to reason independently from the generalizations and to apply their conclusions to current world affairs.

There is a growing recognition that additional reading assignments to supplement textbook materials are desirable. Making such reading assignments, however, creates serious problems for instructors in most colleges and universities. Potentially valuable material may be found in a tremendous variety of publications. Even if the library is large enough to have most of them in its collection, these publications will be scattered and difficult of access for students. Just making reading assignments in familiar and readily accessible geographical publications can create major problems when large numbers of students are involved.

This book brings together in convenient form a collection of supplementary readings for use in an introductory course in economic geography. It is designed to be useful with any of the widely adopted textbooks in economic geography now available. If combined with an economic atlas, this collection of readings could itself be used as the basis for a one-quarter course. Additionally, the variety of articles included is such that the book will be a useful supplement to text materials in introductory world regional geography courses, some advanced economic geography courses, and courses in such related fields as regional economics.

The selection of articles for this book was very difficult. The problem was mainly one of elimination from the multitude of possibilities. The articles included were chosen after an examination of nearly one thousand which seemed potentially useful. (Practical problems and the wide choice available limited consideration to articles published in English.) Many more than the final number of articles would have made useful supplementary reading, but problems of space and cost severely limited the number which could be included. The primary criterion in the selection of articles was that they provide greater depth on topics of importance to economic geography than is possible in a textbook. Some of the articles are conventional "case studies," but many were chosen because they more broadly illuminate a principle or a generalization than is possible in a detailed study of a single occurrence of some type of economic activity.

Several additional considerations helped to guide the final selection. It is desirable that students in introductory courses become acquainted with the research being done by geographers and with some of the important geographical journals. Therefore, nearly half of the articles are taken from familiar journals of the profession. On the other hand, students should realize the wide range of publications in which material relevant to economic geography can be found, so 28 different publications are represented. In some cases it was necessary to sacrifice additional excellent articles on a particular topic to ensure that as many as possible of the subjects usually included in an introductory economic geography course be represented by at least one article each.

The selection of articles for a book such as this can never achieve all the desirable objectives nor satisfy completely all who may use it. The first edition particularly inevitably reflects my own preferences and prejudices. Many desirable articles were omitted because of space limitations, but some may simply have escaped my attention. Suggestions of articles for possible inclusion in future editions will be welcomed.

If the book is found useful, revisions will be made necessary by changes both in the facts pertaining to the subject matter and in the techniques of the field. The articles here included bear various dates, but an attempt was made to select material which was both broadly useful and still representative of the contemporary situation.

Two particular questions of emphasis which may be raised can be explained here. This first selection may contain fewer examples of the use of quantitative techniques than some would prefer. The presentation of research techniques, however, is only a secondary objective of the book. As more of the substantive results of applying quantitative techniques are reported in a fashion comprehensible by students in an introductory course, such articles will certainly be included. Also, it might have been expected that more articles describing the relationships of economic activities to urban areas would be included; it was felt that the several recent collections of readings concerning urban areas adequately covered this aspect.

The physical form of the book was dictated by the effort to keep the cost down to a level at which many students could afford their own individual copies. This was judged more important than uniformity of type style or margin width.

My greatest debt, of course, is to those who performed the research and wrote the articles here included. Also the cooperation of publishers and authors in allowing the use of the material must be acknowledged. My gratitude is extended to all, but special mention must be made of the role played by <u>Economic Geography</u> and its long-time editor, Dr. Raymond Murphy. The function of this journal in providing an outlet for reporting the results of research in economic geography and Dr. Murphy's constant encouragement of such research and reporting cannot be overestimated. Without the solid core of articles available from this source, compiling a book such as this would have been much more difficult and the result less useful.

Many people's work, suggestions, and criticisms have assisted in the preparation of this book. They cannot all be recognized here, but if the book contributes to a more effective teaching and realistic presentation of economic geography I hope they may feel amply rewarded.

February 1967   *Howard G. Roepke*
Urbana, Illinois

CONTENTS

INTRODUCTION

Economic geography is the field of study which seeks to understand the areal patterns of man's economic activity. This seems to be the common denominator of the variety of definitions offered by writers in the field. Each author of a textbook defines his field in his own words, and in no two economic geography textbooks have the authors chosen precisely the same words and phrases to describe the field. An examination of the contents of a number of the major textbooks, however, reveals a greater consensus on the focus of the field than the varying statements of definition would suggest.

In part, this multiplicity of definitions simply mirrors the situation in the field of geography as a whole. There, too, a widely accepted concern with areal patterns has frequently been obscured by different ways of verbalizing that focus of interest. Whether they define geography as the study of "areal differentiation" or of "differences and similarities between places" or of "spatial interaction," geographers work on similar problems and communicate effectively with each other. In the same fashion, whatever the words they choose to define the field, economic geographers all concern themselves with the areal patterns of economic activity.

Another reason for the varying definitions of economic geography stems from the fact that authors of textbooks, faced with limitations of space, choose to emphasize differ-

ent aspects of the subject.[1] For example, some authors choose their material to emphasize the theme of economic development.[2] This leads to an examination of the reasons for differences in the level as well as the kind of economic activity in various parts of the world. Other authors, following a very old geographic tradition, choose to emphasize man-earth relationships.[3] These books frequently give particular emphasis to the physical environment. Still other authors may phrase their definitions so as to allow them to include or exclude certain activities. For example, some authors deliberately exclude personal and professional services from the scope of the subject,[4] whereas others are concerned that patterns of consumption be explicitly included.[5] It should be stressed again, however, that in spite of these differences in emphasis the various authors utilize most of their space in the discussion of a common group of economic activities. It is work on

[1]The footnotes in this introduction are intended to include most of the textbooks now commonly used in introductory economic geography courses. Therefore, each book has been referred to only once, although many of them fit several of the categories discussed.

[2]LAWRENCE A. HOFFMAN, Economic Geography (New York: The Ronald Press Company, 1965).

[3]C. LANGDON WHITE, PAUL F. GRIFFIN, and TOM L. McKNIGHT, World Economic Geography (Belmont, California: Wadsworth Publishing Company, 1964).

WILLIAM VAN ROYEN and NELS A. BENGTSON, Fundamentals of Economic Geography (5th ed.; Englewood Cliffs, N.J.: Prentice-Hall, 1964).

[4]CLARENCE FIELDEN JONES and GORDON GERALD DARKENWALD, Economic Geography (3rd ed.; New York: The Macmillan Company, 1965).

[5]JOHN W. ALEXANDER, Economic Geography (Englewood Cliffs, N.J.: Prentice-Hall, Inc., 1963).

this common core which allows this book of readings to supplement effectively all the widely adopted textbooks.

There are at least two related fields of study which, though differently defined and focused, share many of the topics of their concern with economic geography. Both regional economics and regional science are concerned with certain aspects of the interrelationships of the activities dealt with in economic geography. The result of this is relatively free exchange of concepts and conclusions to the benefit of all the fields.

The appearance of diversity among textbooks in economic geography is further enhanced by the different approaches they take to the presentation of the subject matter. These differences in organization stem both from the authors' differing definitions of the field and from their different views on the most effective means of presenting the material to students. Areal economic patterns are most often exemplified by discussing man's occupations,[6] types of economic activity,[7] or the production of important commodities.[8] Each of these varying approaches will result in a table of contents which appears much different from that of a book organized in another fashion; however, the difference is more apparent than real.

As an example, we may take a discussion of the mining of copper. In one case it might appear as representing the occupation of mining; in another, it might be offered as representative of the mineral industries; alternatively, it might be included simply because copper is an important commodity in the economic life of the world. In each case, although the emphasis may be different, many of the same facts will be presented and many of the same conclusions will be drawn.

There are two other quite distinctive approaches to the study of economic geography and to the presentation of the results of such study. One of these, the use of a framework of economic regions, was formerly very common; now it is used in only a few textbooks or for only certain types of economic activity. One text follows a systematic treatment of economic activity with a discussion of the major economic regions of the world;[9] several texts use a regional format to discuss the distribution of manufacturing industry.[10] The other approach now being taken to the study of economic geography has not yet been used in an introductory text. Much interesting research in economic geography is now involved in attempts to construct mathematical models or to apply game theory to the distribution of economic activity. Thus far these techniques have not been applied broadly enough to provide the material necessary for a basic undergraduate textbook.

For those just beginning to study economic geography, a series of questions may be suggested to guide their approach to this new material and to the viewpoint of geography.

[6]HANS BOESCH, A Geography of World Economy (Princeton, N.J.: D. Van Nostrand Company, 1964).

[7]RICHARD S. THOMAN, The Geography of Economic Activity (New York: McGraw-Hill Book Company, 1962).

[8]RICHARD M. HIGHSMITH, JR. and J. GRANVILLE JENSEN, Geography of Commodity Production (2nd ed.; Philadelphia: J. B. Lippincott Company, 1963).

[9]LESTER E. KLIMM and OTHERS, Introductory Economic Geography (3rd ed.; New York: Harcourt, Brace and Company, 1956).

[10]LOYAL DURAND, JR., Economic Geography (New York: Thomas Y. Crowell Company, 1961).

These questions should be raised in regard to each activity or commodity to be studied. In fact, if the students could be trained habitually to ask these questions — to make geographic analysis a regular part of their thinking — most instructors would consider their introductory economic geography courses a success.

The first question to be asked in any geographic analysis is, "Where?" Contrary to popular opinion, this is not the central interest of geographers, but no geographic analysis is possible until the details of the distribution of the phenomenon have been established. This is the least interesting and most difficult part of any introductory geography course. As in an introductory course in any subject, there is no substitute for a considerable amount of memorization. A variety of devices — maps and others — may help, but the student must learn the locations of the major coal deposits of the world before he can use these facts in further analysis.

The next question to be asked is, "Why There?" Once the details of a distribution have been clearly established, the real enjoyment in learning economic geography begins. Most of the activities of interest are unevenly distributed over the earth, and simple explanations of their location seldom suffice. Economic geography may call on any other discipline or body of knowledge to provide information which will contribute to the understanding and explanation of locational patterns.

This attempt to explain the location of economic activities is the heart of most introductory econom-ic geography courses. It is an attempt in which the instructor is constantly engaged along with his students. Our knowledge of the reasons for the location of most economic activities is still imperfect and incomplete, and research is constantly providing new evidence to improve and refine our explanations. Even if we could completely explain the reasons for the location of all economic activities, our questioning would not be finished. In many cases an activity has been located in a particular place for a long time; in other instances the locational pattern may be changing rapidly. Even if we can explain clearly the reasons for the original choice of the site, we may face equally great complexities in understanding its survival on that site through a long period of changing conditions. Changing conditions are the constant preoccupation of the economic geographer. He is interested not only in explaining present locations but in predicting future ones. While the basic principles may remain the same, no pattern of distribution of economic activities is static for very long. The work of the economic geographer, like that of the housewife, is never done.

The last question to be asked by the student of economic geography is, "So What?" As some of the modern textbooks are beginning to emphasize,[11] the study of distribution and causation does not end the task of an economic geographer. He must seek to understand the consequences of the distributions he has been trying to explain; he must try to understand the spatial interrelationships among various kinds of economic

[11]D. W. FRYER, World Economic Development (New York: McGraw-Hill Book Company, 1965).

activities and between economic activities and other physical and human phenomena. It is this attempt which adds real depth to economic geography, for it is an understanding of these consequences and inter-relationships which makes economic geography truly operational in helping to solve major local, national, and world problems. Obviously the extent to which this complex understanding has so far been achieved is limited; even more limited is the extent to which it can be transmitted in an introductory course. Nonetheless, if students are to recognize the full dimensions of the field, the attempt must be made.

Just as it was earlier suggested that evidence useful to economic geography may come from any field of study, so any conceivable research technique may be employed if it promises to provide useful information. The articles in this book of readings illustrate some of the variety of techniques in frequent use. In common with all of geography, the map is the economic geographer's most characteristic tool.

The economic geographer's interest in the spatial patterns of economic activity leads to the use of maps in a variety of ways. Most directly, he may map the distribution of the activity in which he is interested and use this map as a direct research tool. Mental or physical comparison of the map of his activity with maps of other distributions may provide useful hypotheses for the researcher to investigate. In some cases, a variety of factors thought to be associated with an activity may be mapped so that their distributions may be compared with each other and with the map of the activity itself. Whatever maps may

have been used in the research, however, the article frequently will contain one or more maps designed specifically to illustrate the conclusions. Although evidence may be drawn from fields not spatially oriented, it is the spatial variation of phenomena in which the geographer is interested, and that spatial variation usually is expressed in map form.

Quite recently statistical techniques have been used more widely in geographic research than has traditionally been the case. These techniques promise to make possible the measurement of geographic associations which in the past have only been described in qualitative terms. It is further hoped that greater precision of expression, the development of common measures, and the use of model-building techniques may assist in the formulation of more generally applicable principles than have been achieved thus far. It should be strongly emphasized, however, that the focus of interest, the objectives, and the questions asked by geographers remain exactly the same. Further, the statistical techniques supplement rather than replace traditional means of geographic research. The essential elements in geographic research continue to be a spirit of curiosity about spatial patterns and the imagination to design research projects which will help to explain these patterns.

Certainly the general categories already described — cartographic and mathematical — do not convey an adequate idea of the range of techniques used in geographic research. Economic geographers use any appropriate method of gathering information, from interviews to the study of aerial photographs. A basic problem in research in economic geography stems from the fact that many of the data published by public and private bodies are not collected for areas sufficiently small to make feasible the accurate discovery and depiction of spatial patterns. A further research problem arises from the lack of agreement on the best measures for displaying the spatial patterns of widely differing phenomena. By devising new statistical measures, by counseling with the Bureau of the Census, and in other ways, geographers are constantly seeking means to portray more accurately the spatial patterns of the phenomena with which they are concerned.

Economic geography, like the field as a whole, has many applications which make it a valuable part of every student's education. Perhaps the two most important values relate to the student's roles as an educated person and as a citizen. The purpose of attending a university is to acquire a liberal education. A liberal education is designed to make one aware of the world in which he lives, and it is obvious that spatial patterns of economic activity play an important role in shaping that world. Similarly, many of the decisions which must be faced by this country — and by the individual as an intelligent voter — directly involve areal variations in economic activity.

In a more directly vocational sense, economic geography has many applications in activities of business and government. Such activities as industrial location, area development, marketing, and planning benefit from the insights of economic geography as well as provide career opportunities for those trained in this discipline.

The primary purpose of this book of readings is to provide greater depth and interest for the topics included in introductory economic geography courses. It is hoped, however, that it will also serve the wider purpose of conveying the scope and the fascination offered by further work in the field. All who are interested are welcome.

Population and Resources

One of today's harsh realities is that a land mass of fixed size is inhabited by a population that is rapidly increasing its numbers. Having doubled its size since the turn of the century to the present some 3.3 billions, this population is expected to double again within 30 years. Yet, neither total population figures nor growth-rate figures are in themselves adequate for a thorough understanding of the pressures, problems, and patterns of this population increase.

Commonly, population is measured in terms of the physical base — that is, the ratio of people to land (density). By mapping densities we portray the manner in which this ratio of man/land varies from place to place. In explaining these variations in population densities, the economic geographer may need to interpret the impact of differences in the physical environment. Even more important, however, is the realization that differences in patterns of livelihood and differences in income and productivity frequently can only be explained by the cultural, political, economic, and technical systems under which people operate.

The problem of understanding existing differences in standards of living and productivity is one of understanding differing values, differing desires, and differing abilities. As our population increases we face the challenge of both re-evaluating existing resources and developing new ones, of overcoming both the problem of human numbers and of educational and technological inadequacies.

It is proper that in these readings on economic geography we begin with three articles concerned with those factors contributing to the formation of the resource base and the inequalities in it, as well as with the related disparities in levels of production and income. The first article, by Duncan, discusses the dynamic nature of resources, their use, and their conservation. This article points out the combination of factors necessary to bring a material into use as a resource. In logical succession, Fryer's article is concerned with the types of economies built on differing resource bases. He discusses problems and methods of economic development, as well as the implications and results of development. Duncan discusses the many factors influencing resource formation, whereas Fryer considers the complexities and multitudinous factors affecting development and growth. He then systematizes and classifies various types of economies. The third article, by Joosten, briefly presents statistics of food production and consumption throughout the world. Not only does the available food supply differ from place to place, but within an area there may be inequalities of distribution due to internal frictions. An understanding of these three articles and their implications will lead to a better understanding of the geography of specific economic activities.

7

RESOURCE UTILIZATION AND THE CONSERVATION CONCEPT

Craig Duncan

Dr. Duncan is Senior Lecturer in Geography at the University of Queensland. His article is based on a paper read before the Australian and New Zealand Association for the Advancement of Science in June, 1961.

RESOURCES and the conservation concept are intimately associated. Because changing functions in the use of resources are so closely tied to the conservation concept, any attempt at definition is particularly difficult. In this paper, it is proposed to examine the nature and implications of this relationship in so far as they contribute to a definition of the conservation concept. It will be a basic contention that the conservation concept is a part of the total economic fabric in which resources have a fundamental role, contributing to want-satisfying processes; that conservation, therefore, cannot be studied in isolation, but must be seen in relation to this role. It will be a further contention that conservation practices must be identified with a stage in the process of economic growth before they can be imposed on the use of resources.

LABOR AND CAPITAL CONSERVATION

Although the word "conservation" does tend to evade final definition, its use implies a managing of resources in such a way as to maximize the satisfaction of human wants. Early conservationists were concerned only with the part that "land" played in contributing to this end; but it is legitimate to speak also of the conservation of labor and capital.

In the developing economies of southern and eastern Asia, the conservation of the three factors of production, individually and collectively, receive considerable attention. Industrialization is seen as a means of providing employment, increasing the return from the country's resources, and accumulating capital with which to further production and provide necessary social services. Because capital, in these countries, is in short supply, it has to be accumulated painstakingly and utilized sparingly. J. E. Orchard, in a study of industrialization in Japan, China Mainland, and India, has examined recently published material of the United Nations Economic Commission for Asia and the Far East, which relates to this subject.[1] He suggests that capital formation is well nigh impossible where people are on marginal subsistence levels. He notes that Japan has obviously been the most successful in rising above these levels, achieved largely through the taxation of agricultural effort, and the diversion of accumulated capital to more remunerative industrial activities.

[1] John E. Orchard, "Industrialization in Japan, China Mainland, and India—Some World Implications," *Annals Assn. Amer. Geogrs.*, Vol. 50, 1960, pp. 193–215.

"Resource Utilization and the Conservation Concept" by Craig Duncan. Reprinted from Economic Geography, *Vol. 38 (April 1962), pp. 113-121, with permission of the editor.*

In India and China opposing viewpoints are expressed in the reactions to labor surplus and capital shortage. On the one hand, India is trying to reduce population increase and through the operation of five-year plans, to build up a core of capital-intensive industries which will eventually absorb some labor, raise per capita income, and make best use of natural resources. China, on the other hand, is trying to absorb her embarrassingly large population in predominantly labor-intensive industries. As a result, Chinese are mass-employed more or less gainfully in the fields, on public works projects, and in various handicraft industries such as the home-smelting of iron ore.

It soon becomes evident in a study of the situation in that country, that labor cannot unequivocally be regarded as a resource. Labor demands transport, organization, and minimum food and social services. Without these, diminishing returns are soon operative.

L. A. Hoffman has interpreted the conservation of man to mean "the avoidance of waste in reproduction and in rearing and educating youngsters, together with the maintenance at minimum cost of good health and high productivity in the adult working population and the aged."[2] While such a definition may be a satisfactory one in occidental economies like that of the United States, its use in labor-surplus situations is economically untenable. In the continuing absence of either compensating capital, or natural resources, labor can never hope to become a real resource. The recent famine in China is a tragic witness to the determined attempt to improve land, labor, and capital relationships in the face of locally insurmountable odds.

[2] L. A. Hoffman, "The Conservation of Man," *Conservation of Natural Resources* (2nd edit.), Guy-Harold Smith, ed., New York, 1958, p. 403.

The need to evaluate the degree of interdependence of the factors of production is an obvious and impelling corollary to the true functioning of an economic system. Conservation measures must then be applied, when and where an element of scarcity becomes apparent. It follows that conservation of the natural resources cannot be considered in isolation, but must be related to the general economic situation.

THE NATURAL RESOURCES

Land has been defined as space equipped with varying kinds and amounts of natural forces, processes, and resources.[3] Forces and processes are ubiquitous in their occurrence, but the unique location, the varying quality, and the limited quantity of the natural resources render them of critical importance in most economic situations. It is, therefore, not surprising that conservation practices have been directed mainly towards the conservation of natural resources.

Natural resources have been defined as ". . . all the freely given material phenomena of nature within the zone of men's activities. . . ."[4] The material phenomena consist of the physical resources such as soils, water, rocks, and minerals; and the biotic resources which include natural vegetation, native wild life, and marine life. As the definition suggests, resources necessarily reflect human needs. Erich W. Zimmermann would suggest that the word resource, "does not refer to a thing or a substance but to a function which a thing or a substance may perform. . . ."[5] The function, of course, is as a raw material

[3] George T. Renner, *Conservation of National Geography*, New York, 1954. p. 18.
[4] Norton S. Ginsburg, "Natural Resources and Economic Development," *Annals Assn. Amer. Geogrs.*, Vol. 47, 1957, p. 204.
[5] Erich W. Zimmermann, *World Resources and Industries*, New York, 1951, p. 7.

for industry or, in the case of the soil, in providing the media in which to produce either the raw material for industry or the commodity for consumption.

An important characteristic of resources relates to their degree of expendability. Economists speak of fund and flow resources. An elaboration of this classification has been suggested by Renner.[6] He writes of six classes of resources which range from the "inexhaustible and immutable" flow resources, a renewable asset, to the exhaustible one-use fund resources, a wasting asset. The implications of such a classification will be a major factor in attempting to formulate conservation measures.

Fund resources can be used only once; so, if we consider them as part of our national heritage, we have a right to demand that they be used wisely. Flow resources are renewable, provided the resource base is adequately maintained. Again we have a right to demand that this be done—that reafforestation schemes accompany the depletion of forest areas; that accelerated soil erosion be minimized, especially in the more productive soil areas; that reproduction be maintained at an adequate level in the fishing areas.

THE CHANGING VALUE OF RESOURCES

A number of factors contribute to the "becoming" of resources, and these must be considered before attempting to impose conservation measures on their use. Among the more important, is the dependence of resource values on the stage of technological development of the society using the resources. The native African iron worker, for example, draws on limited but high-quality supplies of bog iron, shells, and charcoal for the raw materials for his

[6] George T. Renner, *Conservation of National Resources*, New York, 1942, p. 50.

smelter. But the large steel mill owner of the United Kingdom must look to overseas supplies of high-grade hematite, or local supplies of beneficiated taconite. He must have access to large deposits of good quality coking coal, and limestone obtained, preferably, from the local area.

Both the African smelter and the steel mill owner use resources, but these are not interchangeable and must be strictly related, the one to a handicraft activity, the other to a major industrial enterprise. Quantity and quality are factors to be considered in the location and use of these resources.

Geologic and geographical considerations may, under many circumstances, determine resource values. Coal which is located in deep and badly fractured seams, as for example, in the eastern Appalachian Mountains of Pennsylvania, has an economic decrease in its resource values (the result of decreasing markets) further depressed by the resulting difficulty of access to only limited quantities of the resource. High extraction costs of this very good-quality coal have practically precluded its use for all major purposes.

The remote location of resources may also detract from their value. Fertile bottom lands in the isolated Ord River area of northwestern Australia are only now being brought into production. Petroleum and iron deposits, recently discovered in Canada's vast Arctic wastes, are not being used. Industrial establishment costs and extraction and transportation costs are at present too high to allow their use while other sources of these materials are more readily available. Only when the element of scarcity is interposed between the resource and its use, will these distant materials assume real resource value.

Bauxite, the crude ore from which

aluminum is made, did not become a resource until Henri Ste. Claire Deville recognized in the "red soil" of Les Baux, in the south of France, a material from which he could extract alumina. Following discovery of an inexpensive method of alumina extraction by Karl Bayer, Charles M. Hall, and Paul Héroult, in 1886, made a major contribution when they electrolytically reduced alumina to aluminum. Those bauxite deposits which were located near large sources of inexpensive hydroelectric power supply, and those which had ready access to water transport facilities between mine and smelter, became particularly valuable resources. Because economies of scale result, in this industry, from the building of large plants (the largest at Arvida in Quebec has a capacity of 350,000 tons per annum), and because these have large annual intakes, large deposits have added resource value.

One of the world's largest deposits of bauxite has recently been discovered in Australia. Its location on the lonely coast of the Cape York Peninsula makes for difficulties in development and exploitation. To the high establishment costs associated with the isolation of the area, must be added the lack of a reliable source of water.[7]

The slightly depressed nature of the aluminum industry in the world today has been a further factor in assessing the value of this resource. Two major companies, the Consolidated Zinc Corporation and British Aluminium Limited planned to develop the resource; but, with the acquisition of British Aluminium by the Reynolds Metals Company

of the United States, it soon became evident that developmental capital was not readily available from this company. Without access to large supplies of capital, such a resource had no value, and it was only as a result of the withdrawal of British Aluminum from the holding company, and the advent of the Kaiser aluminum interests (Kaiser Aluminum and Chemical Corporation), presumably with available developmental capital, that the resource value has been maintained.

At a stage when all these factors are impinging on the desirable use of a resource, conservation measures, except in their broadest application, are not readily accepted. What, one might also ask, would become of a conservation program if a resource like bauxite were superseded? Research into the use of high-quality clays is being undertaken in the United States,[8] while ilmenite and rutile, sources of the lightweight metal, titanium, await only lower costs from smelting to make them strong contenders for aluminum's superior economic position.

RESOURCES AND CONSERVATION

Natural resources are subject to fluctuations in value, the amount of change being primarily related to the predictable function of the particular resource. Under such circumstances, the writing of effective conservation measures becomes an extremely complex exercise. The effectiveness of the exercise is a direct reflection on the accuracy of prediction of human wants, coupled with the accuracy of estimate of the extent of the resource base. The

[7] Expensive capital works on the Wenlock River are required in order to obtain storage for industrial use. The alumina, processed at Weipa, is to be shipped to New Zealand for smelting. See C. Duncan, "The Aluminum Industry in Australia," *Geogr. Rev.*, Vol. 51, 1961, pp. 21–46.

[8] Anaconda Aluminum Company has built a 50-ton-per-day pilot plant for testing an acid process for recovering alumina from Idaho clays. North American Coal Corporation is seeking to recover alumina from low grade ores and coal mine wastes. *Mineral Facts and Problems*, 1960 ed., U. S. Bureau of Mines, Bulletin 585, Washington, D. C., 1960, p. 24.

framer of the conservation measures must attempt to comprehend all of the factors involved, if his conservation program is to attain the degree of preciseness which would be required for the satisfactory implementation of a conservation program.

A further factor requiring resolution is the conflict between commercial and community interests. Because commercial interests are designed to obtain a maximum return from investment, blatant exploitation of resources may have to be discouraged. It must, however, be pointed out that a large company with a heavy investment in the use of a particular resource will tend to treat it with respect, extracting efficiently, processing with the minimum of waste, and continually seeking to expand the resource base through prospecting and the use of suitable substitutes. Incipient forms of conservation are introduced in an endeavor to maintain the raw material supply to the industry.

But it is suggested that true conservation must go much further than this. If we regard the natural resources as a part of our heritage, then the protection of that heritage assumes something of an ethical quality. True conservation policies are, therefore, designed to make a greater provision for the future than the market mechanism or any procedure based on the imputation of market values would allow. It is in order to insure this degree of protection that the State often formulates policy to be followed in the extraction and use of resources. "The essence of conservation," to quote the assessment of a well-known American economist, "is the sacrifice of present economic interests on behalf of posterity."[9] It would be a rare thing for

[9] Erich W. Zimmermann, *op. cit.*, p. 810.

commercial interests alone to assume such a role.

CONSERVATION AND THE ECONOMIC FRONTIER

It remains now to consider the stage in an evolving economic system when true conservation measures may, most opportunely, be introduced. It has been suggested that abundance or scarcity of any of the factors of production is liable to influence conservation policies. For this reason, "stage" must ultimately be defined largely in terms of land, labor, and capital relationships.

A primitive subsistence economy, lacking capital and the technical knowledge which goes with it, has but little command over its environment. The primitive society readily adopts conservation measures because resources are limited to the more obvious means of subsistence, and on these the group presses. Conservation measures have an urgent appeal, and are often a part of the social mores of the group. With but limited ability to expand, conservation of the few resources has an impelling urgency, and is readily accepted and universally practiced. An advanced commercial economy, on the other hand, assured of the means of subsistence, introduces conservation measures in order to maintain the input of raw materials to the manufacturing industries, the basis of its wealth. The desire, at first, is to protect the investment in manufacturing rather than to conserve the resources as a part of the heritage. Emphasis is shifted from the natural resources to the skills utilized in manufacturing industries as the key factor in the economy. Raw materials are assumed to be available. A wealth of resources is also assumed, through ignorance, or through an optimistic faith in the inventive genius of the group, to support raw material supply. Whatever the reason, conservation has no compelling urgency.

While disjunctive resource frontiers in foreign lands were wide open, countries like the United Kingdom and the United States assumed an ability to obtain resources, limited only by their ability to obtain political or economic suzerainty over the areas from which the resources were to be obtained. Any concern over domestic resource use was related primarily to strategic resources, or to those local flow resources which were being misused. One writer has suggested that a growing trend towards conservation of mineral resources in hitherto backward countries and their utilization for national benefit will be the most significant development in the coming decade.[10] If this is so then the disjunctive frontier may no longer be unconditionally available for exploitation.

Canada's economic predicament at the present time is, in part, a result of the persistence of a resource-exporting stage in the economy. In order to protect the investment in manufacturing, the United States, Canada's most important customer, has traditionally imposed selective tariffs on semi-fabrications and manufactured goods. As a result, Canada has been forced to export raw, or partly-processed raw materials, and has thus lost the income to be derived from adding value in manufacturing. In seeking to speed up the transition from a colonial, to a more mature type of economy, conservation measures, where operative, will have to be adapted to the change in stage.

Stage, in any situation, may be defined in terms of the accumulation of capital and the attraction of labor, through the utilization of natural resources. Frederick Jackson Turner saw the stage of development of a country as part of the frontier process,[11] the spread of the edge of settlement away from a settlement nucleus or core area until it embraced the whole of the sovereign territory. A later writer described the frontier as "the geographic area adjacent to the unsettled portions of the continent in which a low man-land ratio and abundant natural resources provide an unusual opportunity for the individual to better himself economically and socially without external aid."[12]   (See Figure 1.)

Over the horizontal frontier of the land, capital accumulated through the undisciplined exploitation of resources. More capital was attracted from the distant metropolises which supplied the frontier with labor. In furthering the satisfaction of human wants, and as part of the process of economic growth, manufacturing industries were established. Although at first elementary in form, they did represent the beginnings of what might be called a vertical frontier, based on the earnings of manufacturing.

On the open horizontal frontier, man was a waster, basing his whole economy on exploitation and replacement through new discoveries, rather than on the conservation of natural resources. It has been pointed out that early settlers on the North American continent sought to conserve labor and capital rather than land and in doing so they naturally turned to the exploitation of the land and all its resources in order to

[10] D. N. Wadia, "Metals in Relation to Living Standards (in industrially under-developed countries)," *Proceedings of the U. N. Scientific Conf. on the Conservation and Utilization of Resources*, Vol. 1, Plenary Meetings, United Nations, New York, 1950, p. 113.

[11] Frederick Jackson Turner, *The Frontier in American History*, New York, 1920, 1947.
[12] Ray A. Billington, *The American Frontier*, American Historical Association, 1958, p. 9.

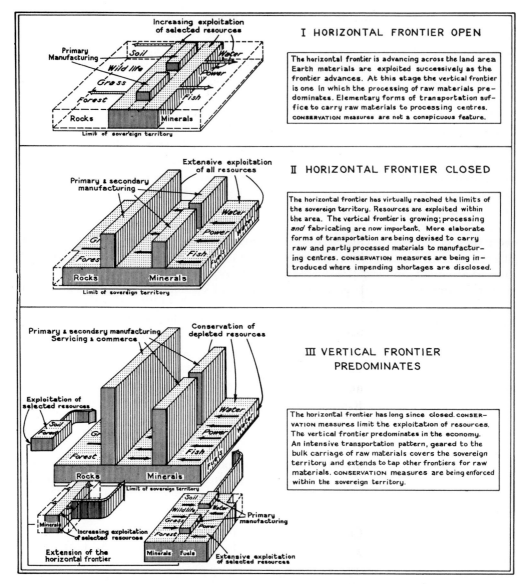

Increasing exploitation of selected resources

I HORIZONTAL FRONTIER OPEN

Primary Manufacturing — Soil — Water — Power
Wild life
Grass
Forest — Fish
Rocks   Minerals
Limit of sovereign territory

The horizontal frontier is advancing across the land area Earth materials are exploited successively as the frontier advances. At this stage the vertical frontier is one in which the processing of raw materials predominates. Elementary forms of transportation suffice to carry raw materials to processing centres. CONSERVATION measures are not a conspicuous feature.

Extensive exploitation of all resources

II HORIZONTAL FRONTIER CLOSED

Primary & secondary manufacturing — Water
Power Water
G
Fores   Fish Fuels
Rocks   Minerals
Limit of soverdign territory

The horizontal frontier has virtually reached the limits of the sovereign territory. Resources are exploited within the area. The vertical frontier is growing; processing *and* fabricating are now important. More elaborate forms of transportation are being devised to carry raw and partly processed materials to manufacturing centres. CONSERVATION measures are being introduced where impending shortages are disclosed.

Primary & secondary manufacturing
Servicing & commerce

Conservation of depleted resources

III VERTICAL FRONTIER PREDOMINATES

Exploitation of selected resources
Soil Forest — Water
G
Forest — Power Water
Fish
Fuels
Rocks   Minerals
Limit of sovereign territory
Minerals
Increasing exploitation of selected resources
Extension of the horizontal frontier
Soil
Wildlife
Water
Grass — Primary manufacturing
Forest
Minerals Fuels
Extensive exploitation of selected resources

The horizontal frontier has long since closed. CONSERVATION measures limit the exploitation of resources. The vertical frontier predominates in the economy. An intensive transportation pattern, geared to the bulk carriage of raw materials covers the sovereign territory and extends to tap other frontiers for raw materials. CONSERVATION measures are being enforced within the sovereign territory.

FIG. 1. Schematic representation of the development of the horizontal and vertical frontiers; and a comment on the relationship this development bears to conservation concepts.

accumulate capital.[13] As long as the frontier remained open, they could justify their exploitation in terms of the apparent unlimited supply coupled

with the evident prosperity. But, as exploitation continued, new names were added to the language. The "land of stumps" replaced virgin forest around the Great Lakes, "ghost towns" remained as relics of former lusty mining centers, "badlands" spread over areas where once the soil was productive.

[13] Alfred J. Wright, "The Development of Conservation in America," *Conservation of Natural Resources* (2nd edit.), Guy-Harold Smith, ed., New York, 1958, p. 4.

The frontier moved to the limits of the sovereign territory, and only then was a note of caution engendered by the imminence of its closing. The assumption of abundance was no longer tenable. Conservation was needed to replace wasteful exploitation if maximum returns were to be obtained from the use of resources.

Impending scarcity, in the face of continuing demand, gave a higher value to resources. When it became apparent that there was a need to protect the growing investment in manufacturing industries, conservation measures had a more urgent appeal. It was realized that the whole fabric of the economy was threatened by the imminence of raw material shortage, and incipient forms of conservation, often resulting in the postponement of profits, were introduced. Capital was diverted to seek new sources of the resource; extraction was made more efficient; processing was accomplished with a minimum of waste and uses were sought for by-products. As conditions of scarcity became more apparent, and only then, did true conservation measures, arising from the demands of an informed public, begin to appear.

The interplay of many interests and forces are involved in determining how well a country's resources are used and how long they will last. When all are conscious of the need to sacrifice present economic interests and show some concern for the future, then the conservation measures are more readily accepted. The more fortunate country is that in which the closing of the frontier has been anticipated, and conservation measures gradually introduced. The community has accepted responsibility, and has sought to ensure for future generations the benefits which it has received from the use of natural resources. In this situation the ethic of true conservation has been achieved.

CONCLUSION

W. K. Hancock has pointed out that, in the expansion of the frontier, "modern historians have revealed the deep significance of the economic impulse."[14] Although such an impulse is surely self-evident, hardly requiring revelation but rather demanding elaboration, Hancock would rightly add the investors' frontier to those of the trader, the rancher, miner, planter, and farmer. An awareness of this heterogeneous sequence of occupance which contributes to the total development of an economy is a necessary factor in understanding the resource utilization pattern. The sequence must play a part in modifying the conservation concept. While most contribute their labor in the expansion of the frontier, the investor, whether long term or speculative, local, regional, or remote, provides capital. Because of the risk involved, he demands a good return for his investment. Both labor and capital in concentrating their productive potential on the exploitation of resources invariably receive an ample reward. Thus it follows that conservation measures may most propitiously be applied only when labor and capital are satisfactorily available, or when the combined adequacy of the resource base is jeopardized.

European countries generally accept conservation as a factor in the use of resources. Within the United States, the turn of the present century saw the first real demands for conservation. In Canada and Australia conservation has local implications only. The frontiers are still wide open, tempered only by

[14] W. K. Hancock, "Problems of Economic Policy, 1918–1939," *Survey of British Commonwealth Affairs*, Volume II, Part I, London, 1940, p. 6.

the reduced value, through intense cold in the one area, and extreme aridity in the other, of the basic resources.

In Australia it is this inferior quality of the land resource which provides the key to an understanding of the frontier process. In the extensive areas of mallee, mulga scrub, and grassland which reach toward the interior, the maximum return, limited only by some minimum improvement in the resource base, is generally acceptable. Ignorance and accident have combined to discourage any more rigorous imposition of conservation measures, and governmental policy has been directed more towards the extension of the resource base than to the demand for its better use. In other words a *stage* has not been reached when the imposition of conservation measures, in their general application, would prove beneficial to the total economy of the country.

Between resources and their utilization, conservation measures cannot be interposed *per se*. Cognizance must be taken of the total geographic situation. Conservation, in a positive form, is generally applicable only when the maintenance of production becomes of greater importance than the continued unrestricted acquisition of wealth. Consistent with an awareness of future needs, optimum benefits may then continue to be derived from the use of the natural resources.

WORLD INCOME AND TYPES OF ECONOMIES:
THE PATTERN OF WORLD ECONOMIC DEVELOPMENT

D. W. Fryer

Mr. Fryer, Senior Lecturer in Economic Geography in the University of Melbourne, has been working for some time on an approach to economic geography through the concept of "the level of development" and national income analysis. He plans to publish this material eventually in book form as "The Geography of World Economic Development."

IN what may perhaps be regarded as the Old Testament of economists, his *Principles of Economics*, Alfred Marshall commenced to define his subject as "a study of mankind in the ordinary business of life . . . the attainment and use of the material requisites of well being." But what is this ordinary business of life? It is obvious that the ordinary business of life means one thing in the Red Basin of Szechwan in Western China, another in the mining valleys of South Wales, and another still on the farms of Iowa. To some extent differences in the natural environment help to explain such contrasts, but of much greater significance are the dissimilarities in the social and cultural superstructures erected on the framework provided by nature. Essentially similar environments can be used in very varying ways; the same environment has different significance for human activity at various points of time. Only the most primitive people, moreover, are unable to effect some change in their environment. It may indeed be doubted if there is any sizable portion of the globe,

apart from the Polar Regions and the great seas and oceans, that remains in a state of nature, while the changes wrought by highly organized and technologically advanced peoples are immense.

"The material requisites of well-being," or the level of material welfare, is very closely linked to the general way of life. From a world standpoint it appears that economists have mostly been concerned in the analysis of a particular type of economic society which embraces only a small proportion of the world's inhabitants. Recently there has been a great deal of interest in the problems of economic development in the poorer nations of the world, but in the main it is the economics of the wealthy and industrialized nations that are the principal fields of study. The poverty that Marshall so deplored in western industrial society has now been greatly reduced, in part through a better understanding of how our economic system works and how maladjustments can be corrected, but western poverty might be judged modest opulence by the standards of Asia or Africa.

"World Income and Types of Economies: The Pattern of World Economic Development" by D. W. Fryer. Reprinted from Economic Geography, *Vol. 34 (October 1958), pp. 284-303, with permission of the editor.*

Here the battle against poverty has hardly been joined.

There is overwhelming evidence that the traditional way of life of the great majority of the world's population inevitably results in a low, static, or declining level of productivity per worker, and this in turn leads to low incomes and deplorably low standards of living which the West, to its credit, now recognizes some responsibility for improving. Of course this interest in improving the living standards of others is not entirely altruistic, and the possible implication of political advantage has rendered much western aid less effective than it might have been. Nevertheless, it represents a momentous step forward in improving human relations.

It is a very difficult matter to make international comparisons of economic welfare; in fact it cannot strictly be done at all, as welfare is impossible to measure. Some approximation, however, can be made through comparisons of *per capita income* (i.e., the arithmetic result of dividing the estimated total national income by total population), though such figures must be used with extreme circumspection. Countries which have overwhelmingly subsistence economies are inevitably undervalued, because it is impossible to make an accurate assessment of the money value of all the goods and services that subsistence farmers and their families provide for themselves or for their neighbors. Moreover, figures of per capita income suggest a degree of precision which is quite unmerited, as the difficulties of estimating and translating all the various components of national income into common monetary terms (United States dollars) are very considerable for a wide range of countries and often have to be settled by approximations on the best of the limited evidence available. Nevertheless, despite these drawbacks, per capita income is a

useful index of the level of economic progress, but to avoid any implication of a direct correlation of per capita income and welfare the Economics Division of the United Nations in revising its well-known estimates of national per capita income in 1949, used the neutral "per capita net national product" for an international comparison based on the years 1952–54.[1] These estimates are the basis of Figure 1.

Some changes have taken place since these estimates were made; Western Germany and Japan, for example, would certainly rank higher at present, but the general picture would not differ greatly. The inequality is most striking; the United States with about 6 per cent of the world's population enjoys over 40 per cent of world income. Southern and Southeast Asia on the other hand, containing about 30 per cent of world population, receive only about 4 per cent of world income. From the evidence of the few countries for which figures are available the Middle East appears to receive a higher per capita income than the rest of Asia with the exception of Malaya and Japan, and as its income from oil mounts the disparity should further increase.[2] Latin America in

[1] U.N. Statistical Office, *National and Per Capita Incomes in 70 Countries in 1949*, Statistical Papers, Series E., No. 1, New York, 1950; *Per Capita Net National Product of 55 Countries in U.S. Dollars, 1952–54*, Statistical Papers, Series E., No. 4, New York, 1957. The change in nomenclature has no practical significance apart from that stated. Net national product may be defined as the total value in monetary terms of all goods and services consumed privately and by government, plus net investment during the period under review.

[2] The dangers of attributing conceptions of welfare to estimates of per capita income are nowhere better displayed than in the oil-rich shiekdoms of the Middle East with their large incomes in oil royalties and scanty populations. Qatar, with a population of 20,000, received oil royalties amounting to 42 million dollars in 1956 and had the highest per capita income in the world. Its inhabitants continued however to live poverty-stricken lives. Though changes in patterns of living have undoubtedly occurred

(*Continued on next page*)

general seems to be better off than Asia, and the effects of huge oil royalties can be seen in the high ranking of Venezuela. Many countries of eastern and southeastern Europe stand at approximately the same level of per capita income as those of Latin American countries; the countries of the Iberian peninsula, generally considered part of western Europe, have per capita incomes which are markedly lower than those of their western European neighbors.

It is apparent that a high per capita income is not a prerogative of countries of large size or diverse resources; tiny Switzerland and Denmark, with small populations and limited resources, appear to receive higher per capita incomes than some other European countries with a much larger volume of industrial production. The dominance of Anglo-Saxon countries in the higher per capita income groups is very striking; the Soviet Union, which ranked second to the United States in total national income, occupied only a modest position on a per capita basis, as the national income (rather less than one-third of that of the United States in 1949) is shared between over 200 million people.

Nevertheless, wide regional variations in per capita incomes are concealed in the national average. Even the richest countries have areas of per capita income well below the national average. Thus the inhabitants of the Ozark Mountains of Arkansas, or the hill people of the Appalachians receive incomes which are little, if at all, above those of the poorer parts of western and central Europe; California and the Pacific Coast receive incomes well above the national average. Many similar contrasts suggest themselves—the North

in other parts of the Middle East as a result of oil production, a rigid social structure has greatly hindered the downward percolation of this enhanced income.

Italian Plain and the poverty stricken *Mezzogiorno*, Ontario and French Canada, Ulster and Connaught, and numerous others.

The high level of incomes in the richest and economically advanced nations is due primarily to their great productivity per worker, which in turn is due to the number of machines or "inanimate slaves" at the disposal of each worker. Buck estimated that the Chinese farmer produced on the average only one-fourteenth of his American counterpart. In 1948 the average American worker produced twice as much as the worker in western Europe, and over three times as much as the average for workers in Europe as a whole. Moreover, productivity per worker is increasing much more rapidly in countries with high per capita incomes than in countries with low, though here the very rapidly increasing productivity in the "planned economies" of Eastern Bloc countries needs to be noted as an exception. In other words, the rich are becoming much richer and the poor are often finding it difficult to resist further impoverishment; at best the gap is widening, for despite considerable progress in raising the total national income through its First Five Year Plan, India is farther behind the United States at present than when it began. But even the poorest nation can have substantial economic progress and higher standards of living, provided that it is prepared to make the inevitable social and cultural adjustments that are involved. No nation is so poor in resources that it could not be better off by making alternative use of those it already has.

TYPES OF ECONOMIES

Several attempts have been made to classify the many economic systems found in the world, and most of these have attempted to see an evolutionary

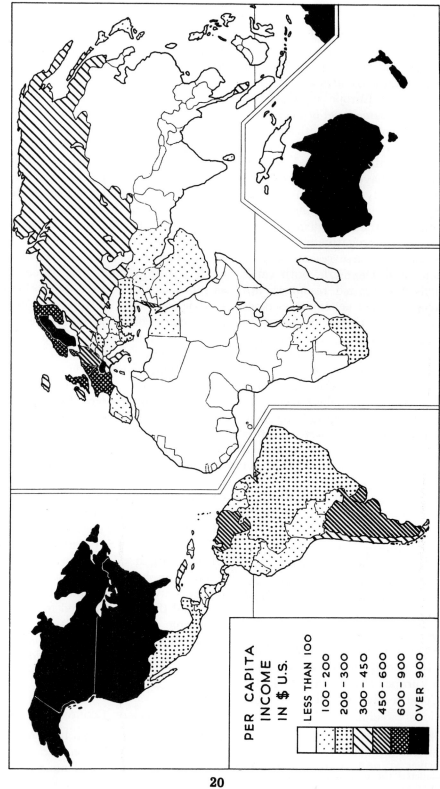

FIG. 1. Per capita income in United States dollars. The map shows the average situation for the years 1952–54 and is largely based on U.N. Statistical Papers Series E, No. 1, 1950 and No. 4, 1957 with other estimates.

PER CAPITA
INCOME
IN $ U.S.

LESS THAN 100
100 – 200
200 – 300
300 – 450
450 – 600
600 – 900
OVER 900

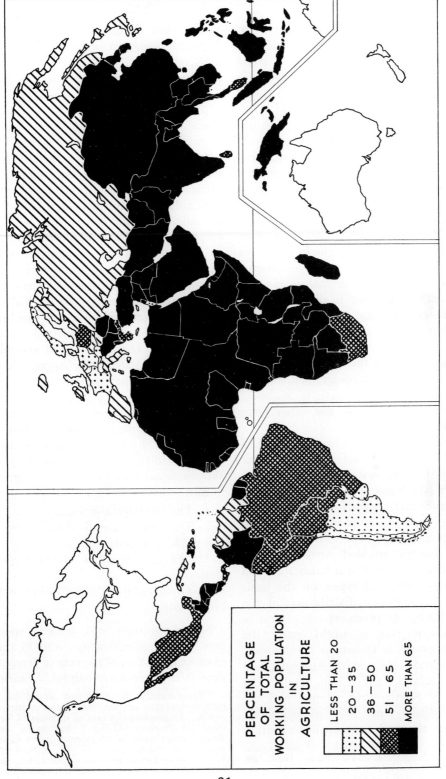

FIG. 2. Working population in agriculture. Source: F.A.O. Yearbook, 1956, Vol. 1.

PERCENTAGE
OF TOTAL
WORKING POPULATION
IN
AGRICULTURE

LESS THAN 20
20 – 35
36 – 50
51 – 65
MORE THAN 65

succession from relatively simple to successively more complicated economic patterns. Many countries do show evidence of such successions, but in others "simple" and "advanced" stages may occur side by side with little interaction. Such "dual economies," to use the nomenclature of the Dutch colonial economist Boeke, are a distinctive feature of many countries with very low per capita incomes. Yet it has been shown that even countries with high per capita incomes show marked regional disparities in income, and in fact "economic dualisms" occur in countries at every level of economic development. Economic activity, nevertheless, is overwhelmingly organized in distinct political frameworks, and in some countries considerable progress has been achieved in raising the general level of incomes in depressed parts of the national territory up to the national average. In a world survey statistical limitations make it virtually impossible to use other than national units.

Various suggested classifications of world economic patterns and their distribution are reviewed in the Woytinskys' monumental survey, *World Population and Production*.[3] The authors suggest a major division between subsistence and money economies, the latter being further divided into primarily agricultural, agricultural-industrial, and primarily industrial types, on the basis of the occupational distribution of the labor force. It produces some strange companions; on a world map the United States is shown as "industrial-agricultural" along with Australia and New Zealand, but Chile, Italy, the Union of South Africa, Japan and the Soviet Union are also so classified. Even on the authors' own basis neither

[3] W. S. and E. S. Woytinsky: *World Population and Production*, New York, 1953, pp. 415–439.

[4] *Ibid.*, pp. 416 and 436.

the United States, nor Australia and New Zealand, can in fact be described as "industrial-agricultural." The map is supplemented by another to show "levels of well-being" based on per capita income, and illustrates the authors' contention that "the richest countries of the world are 'agricultural-industrial' rather than 'primarily industrial.'"[4] More recent figures of occupational distribution than those available to the authors clearly illustrate the falsity of this contention, but it is surprising that it should have been made at all as it follows an analysis which examines agriculture's share of national income and clearly demonstrates that per capita incomes in the agricultural sector of a national economy are lower than in the non-agricultural sector. Woytinskys' classification of economic systems (Fig. 5) hardly appears compatible with the real world or the authors' own analysis.

A more realistic picture of the varying levels of economic development throughout the world can be obtained by using criteria additional to those used by the Woytinskys. Four criteria are suggested in all:

1. The per capita income.

2. The occupational distribution of the working population.

3. The age structure of the population.

4. The geographic distribution of the population.

Some countries still present special problems of classification, and in these cases examination of the rate of economic growth is particularly helpful.[5] Statisti-

[5] Theoretically the best test would be the rate of increase of Net National Product *per capita*. In practice the rate of increase of Gross National Product (G.N.P.), has to be used, though this should be considered in the light of population movements. G.N.P. differs from N.N.P. in including *gross* investment; i.e., there is no allowance for capital consumption or depreciation.

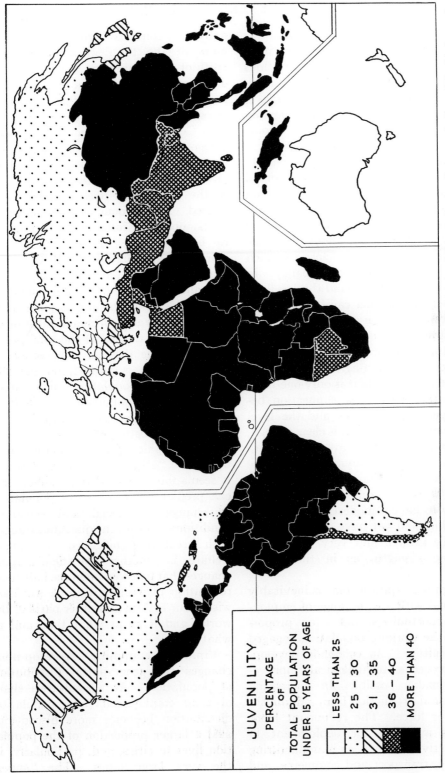

JUVENILITY

PERCENTAGE
OF
TOTAL POPULATION
UNDER 15 YEARS OF AGE

LESS THAN 25

25 – 30

31 – 35

36 – 40

MORE THAN 40

Fig. 3. Juvenility. The effect of the post-war increase in birth rates in North America is clearly visible, as is also the great decline of the birth rate in Japan. Source: U. N. Demographic Yearbook, 1955.

cal information of this nature is, however, extremely limited, while most countries show considerable variations in the rate of growth over time. Nevertheless, the rough estimations available are of considerable value. Occasionally the distribution of the national income between major occupations is useful in deciding marginal cases, particularly when compared with the occupational distribution of population. The share of agriculture in national income, for example, is always lower than its share of total national employment. But the difference can vary from a close approach to parity to a very wide discrepancy. In Australia and New Zealand there is little difference between per capita incomes in agricultural and non-agricultural activities, but in Peru the per capita income in agriculture appears only about one-fourth of that in non-agricultural activities, and in Indonesia it is only one-fifth.

That there is a close connection between per capita income and the level of economic development is clear enough, but for the reasons stated per capita income is not synonymous with the general level of welfare, or "standard of life." It is also quite possible for a country to have a modest or low standard of life, and yet have a high rate of economic growth and very substantial economic strength, as in the Soviet Union.

A high per capita income is inevitably associated with a wide range of employment opportunities, and a low proportion of the working population engaged in agriculture. As economic development proceeds, technological improvements make possible an increasing agricultural production from a diminishing labor force. The redundant labor is thus available for deployment in other activities, such as manufacturing industry, transport and commerce, and as the economy grows these latter activities come to employ more and more of the total work force. The truth of this contention was first clearly demonstrated by Colin Clark, who pointed out that it had in fact been recognized by Sir William Petty in the 17th Century. The effects of economic development are much more far reaching however; not only the occupational distribution, but the whole structure of the population itself is profoundly altered. As economic development proceeds, powerful influences are brought to bear on the factors determining mortality and natality. Birth rates, death rates, and, in particular, infant mortality rates, are profoundly changed. The expectation of life is increased. These changes are reflected in substantial movements in the size of the total population, and, as the age composition of the population is altered, on the size of the working population. From studies of the effect on population caused by economic change, some observers have been led to postulate a general picture of demographic evolution characterized by certain "stages" of growth, although it seems fairly clear that no simple law can predict the response of population to changes in social and economic conditions. One of the questions fraught with greatest significance for human welfare is whether the demographic changes that followed upon the industrial revolution in western Europe will likewise occur in Asia and other parts of the world, and if so at what time and at what pace.

Finally, economic development changes the geographical distribution of population. As agriculture's share of total employment falls, population distribution becomes more discontinuous; a larger proportion of the population lives in cities, and, particularly, in the very large cities. The "supergiant" city, or "Megalopolis" to use

Mumford's term, is a very distinctive feature of countries at a high level of economic development.

On the basis of these criteria it is possible to make a fourfold division of types of economies (Fig. 6):

(a) *highly-developed*, or predominantly industrial-commercial, economies. Economies of this type support only about 8 per cent of world population.

(b) *semideveloped*, or mixed industrial-agricultural economies, supporting about 12 per cent of world population.

(c) *underdeveloped*, or predominantly agricultural, economies. These economies are very widespread and support almost 45 per cent of world population.

To these may be added:

(d) *planned economies*, which are essentially either of type (b) or (c) above but which, nevertheless, have some of the characteristics of type (a), and have so many other special features of their own that they are best considered as a separate category. The planned economies at present probably include about 30 per cent of world population.

The Highly-Developed Economies

Nations with highly-developed economies are the economic aristocrats of the world. Not only are they the richest nations but they also show the highest rates of economic growth, and are therefore tending to leave the poorer countries farther and farther behind. Of course, this wealth is not spread evenly throughout the whole of the community, and even the richest nation in the world, the United States, can show plenty of poverty; 27 per cent of American families received total annual incomes of less than $2000 per annum in 1948, and had a standard of living which was well below socially acceptable standards. But inequality of wealth is relatively less in the highly developed countries than in the underdeveloped and the semideveloped, and there has been a marked improvement in the fortunes of the lowest paid workers in western industrialized countries since the second World War.

The highly-developed countries all have very low proportions of their working populations engaged in agriculture. These proportions may still nevertheless be too high, as in the United States, and this is true even for countries like Australia and New Zealand which depend in large measure upon their agricultural and pastoral exports for their economic well-being. All, on the other hand, have a large proportion of the working population in manufacturing and commercial activities, though these proportions may differ appreciably between various countries. Their productivity per worker, both in agriculture and manufacturing industry, is very high, and while it is certainly not constant, the annual increase in productivity is also considerable. The reason for the high and increasing productivity is clear: it is a consequence of the very much higher rate of capital formation and investment in the highly-developed countries. They save proportionally much more of their national income than poorer countries, and what is equally important, invest a greater proportion of their savings in productive enterprises, which in turn augment further the size of the national income, enabling a still higher rate of saving, and so on. Hence a high level of economic development leads in turn to a high rate of growth; "Nothing succeeds like success."

There are, nevertheless, wide disparities in the wealth even of the highly-developed countries. There is apparently only one really rich country—the United States. Canada, a clear second in per capita income, owes a great deal to its proximity to the United States, and is by far the largest recipient of United States foreign investment. The highly industrialized countries of Europe have a considerable way to go to reach the American level of per capita income, which stands relatively as far ahead of theirs as theirs does above that of the greater part of the world. Their rate of economic advance as indicated by the proportion of the national income saved is much lower than in the United States, so that the gap is widening.[6] But it will be relatively much easier for them to raise their proportion of national income saved to the present American level than it will be for the underdeveloped countries to achieve western European rates of saving. Moreover, disparities at the upper end of the scale of wealth are much less significant in terms of health, nutrition, expectation of life, education, and most other aspects of material welfare than those at the lower extremity.

It cannot be said, however, that the highly-developed countries have already utilized a large proportion of their resources and that, therefore, their rate of economic progress must eventually slow up. True, diminishing returns may appear in some lines of production, but

[6] This is not true of Western Germany or of Australia or New Zealand, however, which in recent years appear to have been saving about 25 per cent of their national incomes. The United States has averaged about 19 per cent, but the United Kingdom only 16 per cent. The increased pace of economic development in France, also, since 1950 is reflected in a present rate of saving little inferior to that of the United States. However, investment in housing and other largely non-productive ends which do not contribute much to the capacity for growth has to be considered in relation to these figures, and this has been proportionately higher in the United Kingdom.

this view rests on a misunderstanding of the nature of resources. Resources arise from the application of technological, managerial, and financial skills to the handiwork of nature, and while some resources are being used up or destroyed many more new ones are continually being created. Culture, operating on the background of nature, produces resources; hence an expanding cultural equipment broadens the resource base of the economy and makes possible increasing productivity and incomes.

In the highly-developed countries the cultural equipment is expanding rapidly. Firstly, there are powerful influences tending to accelerate technological progress, and foremost among these is the pressure of competition. A large modern corporation in the United States or Great Britain may spend 2 per cent or more of its gross sales on research in an effort to keep ahead of competitors. But competition itself is a reflection of the "acquisitiveness" and dynamism that are the mainsprings of modern industrial society. Attitudes of mind are more important than technologies. It has been frequently pointed out that an industrial establishment in the United States will generally achieve higher productivity than one in Great Britain with identical equipment and under the same management; although few American manufacturers realize American levels of productivity in Britain, British manufacturers have no difficulty in reaching American productivity in their plants in the United States—the psychological "climate" is more favorable. This observation, however, is by no means true of all industries.

Secondly, while changes in the social and institutional framework take place much more slowly than changes in technology, they are nevertheless brought about more easily in highly-developed countries than in underdeveloped ones.

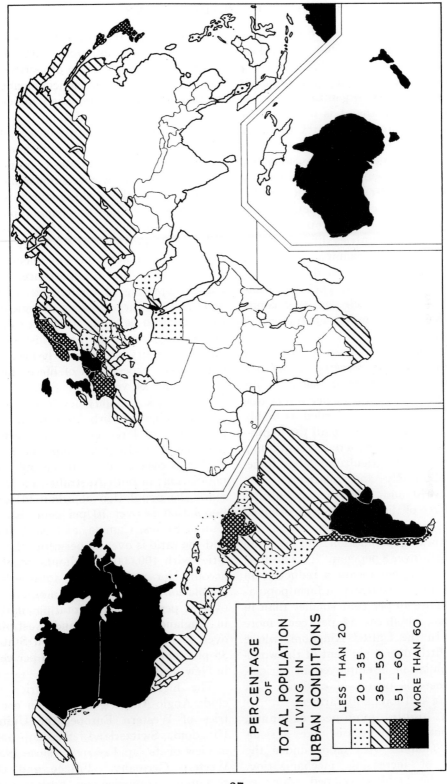

FIG. 4. World urbanism. Urban populations are variously defined so comparisons are only approximate. Source: U N. Demographic Yearbook, 1955.

PERCENTAGE
OF
TOTAL POPULATION
LIVING IN
URBAN CONDITIONS

LESS THAN 20
20 – 35
36 – 50
51 – 60
MORE THAN 60

New machines or new processes may impoverish a certain class of workers or a region, but no Gandhi preaches a return to hand tools and a self-sufficient type of economic organization. Ultimately the adjustment is made. Generally, the poorer the country the more massive the obstacles to a social change, and therefore to economic development.

In a sense, even the richest nations can be regarded as "underdeveloped," as the scope for economic development is infinite. Many recognize the potentialities of countries like Australia and Canada for example, but they exist equally in the United States and the United Kingdom. They will cease only when cultural change itself comes to a halt and the social framework congeals.

In a highly-developed country *the proportion of the working population engaged in agriculture is below 20 per cent;* countries with a higher proportion should not really be regarded as highly developed. Moreover, in all the highly-developed countries there is a continuing decline in the agricultural labor force, both absolutely and relatively. Between 1940 and 1950 the agricultural work force of the United States declined from 19 per cent to 12 per cent of the total working population and by 1956 was a little over 8 per cent. This decline, however, has not meant a reduction in output; on the contrary, a farm population almost 40 per cent smaller than in 1930 now produces 54 per cent more food. In the United Kingdom, where only a little over 4 per cent of the working population is employed in agriculture, there is plenty of evidence that there are still too many farmers.

In a highly-developed economy, manufacturing industries like agriculture economize with labor under the impact of increasing mechanization. In all the highly-developed countries employment in tertiary industries substantially exceeds employment in manufacturing industry. The proportion of the total employment in commerce is particularly significant as an indicator of the level of development.

The population structure of a highly-developed country is characterized by a high proportion of adults of working age (15–65) and a low proportion of children. In the 1930's many fears were expressed that the population of the highly-developed countries would fail to replace itself, and that they were therefore in a state of "incipient decline" and eventual disappearance. The marked upswing of birth rates during and since the war has shown such gloomy predictions to be false. Birth rates and death rates are both at a low level; infant mortality is particularly low, and the average expectation of life at birth is more than 60 years.

A hallmark of highly-developed countries is the level of urbanization and the prevalence of large cities. The urban population of England and Wales in 1951 was over 80 per cent of the total population; in both Australia and Denmark the population of urban to total population is over 70 per cent; in the United States, Canada, and New Zealand the ratio is over 60 per cent. Large cities with 100,000 inhabitants or more account for much of the total urban population; cities this size account for over 51 per cent of the total population in England and Wales and Australia, over 43 per cent in the United States, 36 per cent in Canada, and 33 per cent in New Zealand and Denmark.

The highly-developed countries include Anglo-America and certain countries of Western Europe, the United Kingdom, Switzerland, Sweden, and, in view of its rapid recovery since 1950, Western Germany. France and the remaining countries of northwestern

Europe, Norway, Denmark, and the Benelux countries, can be considered as poorer relations. Outside North America and Europe, only Australia and New Zealand can be numbered among the wealthy nations of the world.

The Semideveloped Economies

The semideveloped countries are very widely distributed with representatives in every continent. They form a very diverse assemblage, including countries as varied as Japan, Italy, Argentina, South Africa, Cuba, and Finland, while the more advanced of the Eastern Bloc countries can also be regarded as falling within this category. There are considerable differences in per capita incomes between the uppermost and lowest members of the group, but in all the proportion of the working population in agriculture is much higher than in the highly-developed countries—from 35 per cent to as much as 55 per cent. In the semideveloped countries the contrasts between the industrialized cities and the populous agrarian countryside are very great. Contrasts between cities and rural areas are great in highly-developed countries, but in the semideveloped countries the techniques of agriculture are considerably more primitive. There are few of the machines that give high output with little labor so numerous in the highly-developed countries.

The semideveloped countries, with their lower per capita income, save proportionately less of their national incomes than the highly-developed countries, though for short periods they may be able to equal them. Japan, indeed, at certain periods of its development has shown a faster rate of growth of manufacturing output than the United States, and the Soviet Union still continues to do so, but these are exceptional cases. Generally, the rate of economic advance in the semideveloped countries is very

modest, and some are recipients of economic aid from the highly-developed nations like many underdeveloped countries.

Population pressure in some of the semideveloped countries is severe; the Japanese islands show distinct evidence of overpopulation and it will be extremely difficult to provide sufficient new openings in industrial employment for the present rate of population increase; Japan will have to run very hard in order to remain in the same place. Italy too has shown evidence of overpopulation for a long period, but the apparent potential wealth in petroleum may prove ultimately to be the economic salvation of the country. On the other hand, Argentina, from many points of view, could be regarded as underpopulated, and it is generally unwise to make definite statements about overpopulation in semideveloped countries. Even with existing techniques, changes in social outlook could radically change the picture. A new appraisal of the position and function of the landlord and his position in society could produce very beneficial effects in many semideveloped countries, even in Europe. In Italy and Spain the political and social strength of the large landowners and the wide extent of *mezzadria* (share cropping) and rural indebtedness duplicate some of the worst features of Asian agrarian organization. Again, in Japan, the traditional obligation of the employer to maintain all his workers even when he can no longer find a profitable use for their labor tends to keep costs high and hamper mobility.

Generally, however, the semideveloped countries have already taken the most difficult steps along the road to a high level of economic development. Most have been able, like Japan, the Soviet Union, and other European countries, to accomplish this largely with their own unaided resources; a few, like Argentina, owe their present level of development almost entirely to the investment of foreign capital. But all started from levels of development that were already higher than those at present found in most underdeveloped countries, and even in Japan there had been a long tradition of large scale economic activity in some of the great clans or families—the Zaibatsu have their roots far back in Japanese history. In a few of these semideveloped countries there is almost no branch of modern industrial activity that is unrepresented; many have well established iron and steel industries, chemicals, electric power, cement, and similar types of heavy industry that are essential for further economic growth. Those that do not already possess one or other of these activities are endeavoring to make good their deficiency.

In the semideveloped countries the population structure generally shows a smaller proportion of the total population of working age than in highly-developed countries. Under the impact of economic development and the consequent fall in death rates population continues to expand. However, changes in social structure have already occurred as a result of increased development and its higher living standards, and slowly birth rates move in conformity with falling death rates; Japan's birth rate (19.2 per 1000) is now in fact one of the lowest in the world. Though every semideveloped country has some really large cities the urban population is a smaller proportion of the total than in the highly-developed countries; many semideveloped countries also possess one city of the "super-giant" category.

The Union of South Africa, though anomalous, is perhaps best included among semideveloped countries. Though its white population enjoys standards of living comparable to those of a highly-developed country, its African population is little above the underdeveloped stage. But a great maldistribution of wealth is almost everywhere found in semideveloped countries.

The Underdeveloped Economies

Underdeveloped economies are the most extensive on earth, and support about 70 per cent of world population if the underdeveloped countries of the Eastern Bloc are also included. They include the whole of Africa with the exception of the Union of South Africa, the greater portion of South and Central America, and virtually the whole of Asia outside Soviet Asia, Japan, and Malaya.

Per capita incomes in the underdeveloped countries are very low, though again there are discrepancies, as in the other types of economies. Standing at the lowest level of development is the African continent. Throughout most of inter-tropical Africa economic development is virtually confined to isolated mining and plantation activities which affect a negligible proportion of the indigenous population. In many areas traditional agricultural and pastoral activities, through deforestation, overgrazing, and erosion of the soil, tend to depress further the already low living standards. Moreover, the traditional way of life is such that infection by diseases, such as malaria, framboesia, trypanosomiasis, amoebiasis, bilharziasis, and infestation by helminthic parasites is virtually inevitable. Poor health is a powerful factor in the low productivity of the great majority of the peoples of the underdeveloped countries, while resistance to infection is lowered by poor diet, which may often be a little above starvation level before harvests. Certain of the Pacific Islands and New Guinea have not progressed

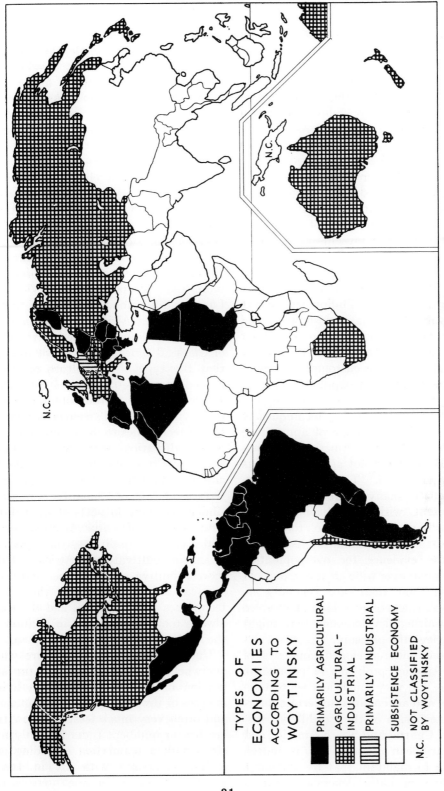

FIG. 5. Types of economies as adapted from W. S. and E. S. Woytinsky, *World Population and Production*, 1953, Figure 139.

above the African level of economic development.

With a level of development appreciably above the average for Africa, but containing by far the world's most extensive deposit of human misery is the great continent of Asia. The enormous rural slums of Eastern and Southern Asia present the most massive and intractable problems of economic development anywhere, though this general pauperization exists alongside fantastic accumulations of individual wealth. Yet Asia presents many variations on the same basic theme of poverty; the problems in the development of Indonesia differ appreciably from those of the Philippines despite an essentially similar environment and pattern of life, and these in turn differ from those of India or Thailand or Saudi Arabia. It is customary to regard Asia as being over-populated in that there are too many people to be supported with the existing techniques to make possible any hope of appreciable progress. But the American agronomist, Buck, could not agree that China is overpopulated. Thailand could accommodate many more people than at present without reducing present standards of living and so, too, could the great island of Sumatra. Nevertheless, the evidence for overpopulation is very great over wide areas of monsoonal Asia, and there are certainly no extensive tracts of good land unoccupied and awaiting development that might help relieve the pressure.

In the underdeveloped countries of Latin America problems of population pressure are very much less acute than in Asia, and are confined to certain intermontane basins in the Cordilleran systems of Central and South America and the Caribbean islands. It is indeed possible to maintain that by and large the whole of Latin America is under-populated even in relation to existing techniques. On the whole, the prospects of speeding up economic development in Latin America appear to be substantially brighter than in Asia.

The underdeveloped countries are essentially agricultural economies though, occasionally, as on the African and Asian grasslands, pastoral activities may almost completely replace agricultural ones. Everywhere, the proportion of the working population in these occupations is very high; about 60 per cent for many of the Cordilleran states of Latin America, 70 per cent for Eastern or Southern Asia, probably more than 90 per cent for Vietnam, Laos, and Cambodia, and still higher proportions in Africa. Techniques are primitive, frequently inferior to those of Classical times. This is not to deny that the type of agriculture practiced in underdeveloped countries may show a nice appraisal of the potentialities of the environment and an effective adaptation of techniques to those potentialities. Rice cultivation with two or three stages of transplanting in Cambodia and Cochin China, the elaborate rice terraces of Java or China, the somewhat similar terracing in parts of the Cordilleran system of Latin America, even, under certain conditions, the activities of shifting cultivators in Africa and the more primitive parts of Asia and New Guinea—are all evidence of this. But techniques are traditional and there are always too many farmers in relation to the land and capital at their disposal.

Underdeveloped countries are thus overwhelmingly rural: generally the proportion of the total population living in cities or towns is less than one-quarter and often very much less. Large cities are few in number: India has only five cities with a population exceeding one million compared with six in Japan which has less than one quarter the population, and 14 in the United States. Even including all cities with a population exceeding 100,000, of which there are 73, large cities accounted for less than 7 per cent of India's population in 1951.

Many underdeveloped countries are faced with a problem of rapid population increase, which greatly outstrips the rate of economic advance. This population increase has come about largely through a reduction in death rates, while birth rates determined by social custom and tradition largely remain unchanged. Even where the rate of increase is not particularly high, as in India at present, the absolute increase is formidable. The effect of the lack of balance between birth rates and death rates is to produce a population structure in which there is a very high proportion of children and young persons. In underdeveloped countries the proportion of the total population under 15 years of age is usually around 40 per cent. The size of the work force in relation to total population is proportionately much smaller than in highly-developed countries, and the very large proportion of children of low or negligible productivity is a great burden on the economy. This burden is enhanced by an expectation of life at birth of about half that of a highly developed country. As Zimmermann says, a ". . . people with a high birth and death rate balance virtually exhausts itself in the biological process of group survival."[7]

In the underdeveloped countries the proportion of the national income that is saved is very low, usually not much more than 1 to 2 per cent. Moreover, little of the income that is saved is invested in productive enterprises that will enlarge the total income—saving is too often for conspicuous consumption

[7] E. W. Zimmermann: *World Resources and Industries*, New York, 1951, p. 110.

at feasts, weddings, etc., while investment is usually in land or in trading, and seldom in manufacturing or productive activities. Some underdeveloped countries do possess a considerable range of industrial development, but activities of this kind are often the preserve of non-indigenous peoples. Manufacturing is restricted to processing of local raw materials, food products, and other articles of wide population consumption and technologically simple industries, particularly cotton textiles. Heavy industries are very poorly developed and are usually the result of foreign investment.

With a low level of saving and capital formation the economy fails to advance or is outstripped by population increase, which is almost always very high, occasionally as much as 3 per cent per annum. Thus incomes remain low, savings are scanty, and the economy stagnates. It is not therefore surprising that many governments of underdeveloped countries have attempted to use some of the techniques of the planned economies to produce a high rate of economic growth. Almost every country of Eastern and Southern Asia has its "Five Year Plan" and it is everywhere recognized that Government investment must be proportionally much greater than in more highly-developed countries.

The central problem facing the undeveloped countries is how to escape from the cycle of low incomes, low savings, low investment, and, in turn, continued low incomes. The answer however will differ considerably from country to country; though the general pattern is familiar the problems in any one underdeveloped country are unique.

The Planned Economies

As indicated above, the planned economies are essentially of the mixed industrial-agricultural or predominantly agricultural type; even the most advanced economically, the Soviet Union, has not yet reached the predominantly industrial stage of the highly-developed countries. However, the Soviet Union is already second only to the United States in total industrial production; its output of coal, steel, and electric power exceeds the combined outputs of the United Kingdom and Western Germany, the two most highly industrialized nations of Western Europe. It will almost certainly become the world's leading producer of coal within a very short period. In the development of atomic energy and other extremely complex and capital intensive technologies the Soviet Union appears to be little if at all behind the United States. Clearly the Soviet Union is very different from other semideveloped countries.

Of the other countries within the Eastern Bloc only Eastern Germany and Czechoslovakia are at approximately the Russian level of economic development. Poland and Hungary before the second World War were primarily agricultural countries though a considerable range of industrial activities already existed. In Yugoslavia, Bulgaria, and Rumania the proportion of the working population in agriculture was quite as high as in the underdeveloped countries of Asia. Each of these countries now has an expanding iron and steel industry. Nor is there any reason for believing that the densely populated China—or indeed any other section of the congested continent of Asia, should it fall into the Eastern Bloc's control—will prove too difficult an economic problem for the Communist planners. China has already achieved considerable industrial progress since 1949: its steel production is already equivalent in fact to that of the Soviet Union in 1928 when that country began

the first of its great Five Year Plans, and it has a commanding lead over India in the race for Asian economic leadership.

In the planned economies, vested interests and all the massive and entrenched obstacles to economic growth are ruthlessly swept aside. Nothing is allowed to stand in the path of economic progress; personal liberty is severely curtailed. The rate of economic progress in the Soviet Union is perhaps the most rapid in the world. Even the United States at its periods of most intense development did not better the average annual increase of industrial production in the Soviet Union in recent years, although Western Germany has maintained an equivalent rate of growth since 1950. This high rate of development is made possible by a very high level of saving. The Soviet Union saves much more of its national income than do either the United States or the United Kingdom; in an economy of the Soviet type the proportion of national income saved can be virtually what the government likes. Moreover, the Soviet Union makes a larger proportion of total investment than highly-developed countries in activities that increase the capacity of the system for further economic growth and increase economic strength—fuel and power, iron and steel, chemicals, cement, communications, etc. Investment in consumer goods industries and housing get merely what is left over. There is some indication that the Soviet Union now feels that it can give the consumer a larger share than he has had in the past of the fruits of Soviet economic expansion. The effect of this must inevitably be to slow down the rate of growth of the economy as a whole, but the dominant importance of heavy capital goods industries has again been forcibly restated.

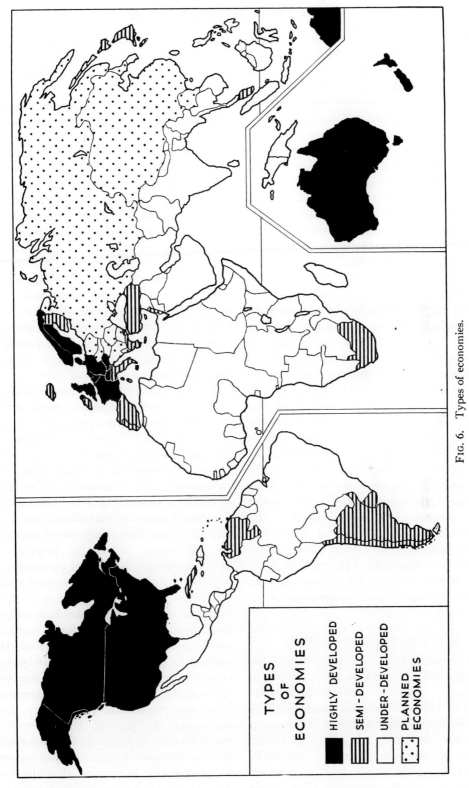

FIG. 6. Types of economies.

TYPES
OF
ECONOMIES

HIGHLY DEVELOPED

SEMI-DEVELOPED

UNDER-DEVELOPED

PLANNED
ECONOMIES

35

In comparison with Northwest Europe or Anglo-America the Soviet Union is still a poor place in that living standards are very much lower. But they are already comparable with those of some countries of western and central Europe, and are better than those of Spain, Portugal, or Italy. So long as the Soviet Union saves more of national income than the highly-developed countries and invests the greater part of its savings in capital good industries it will steadily narrow the gap between them and itself.

There are few studies of economic growth in the "satellite" countries and the evidence is confusing. Almost everywhere, however, it appears that it is the rapid growth of the capital good industries and the deliberate flouting of the needs of the consumer that has produced the great waves of discontent in Eastern Europe that have challenged Soviet domination. It is doubtful if the rates of economic growth in the satellites have matched those of the Soviet Union itself. Nevertheless, it seems best to put all the satellites in the planned economy category.

The planned economies are formidable competitors despite their present lower level of economic development. The latest Soviet Five Year Plan, which will raise coal production to 600 million tons, petroleum to 135 million tons, and steel output to 70 million tons by 1960, is fraught with consequences for the West.

The Economies in Summary

Reviewing this survey of world incomes and occupations the pattern of economic activity appears as follows. In the highly-developed countries the whole economy is integrated in the world market. Agriculture operates at a high level of efficiency with a relatively small labor force, but still receives lower per capita incomes than other activities. In manufacturing, the processing and working up of minerals and metals are extremely well developed and are powerful factors making for further economic growth. The highly organized market is made possible by, and equally has made necessary, an elaborate system of distributive trades, transport, communications, and financial institutions. In semideveloped countries some characteristics of the highly-developed economies are found, but they exist alongside an agricultural organization which in many respects is little altered by the impact of the world market on the rest of the economy. Though technologies may have somewhat improved, the social structure outside the cities is essentially traditional and a powerful obstacle to change. Manufacturing is less concerned with metal and mineral processing and fabrication.

In underdeveloped countries only a very small portion indeed of the economy has experienced the pressures of the world market. These "economic exclaves," as they have been called, are entirely the result of foreign investment, technology, and managerial skills, and resemble a small fragment of a highly-developed economy embedded in a rural and traditional economy based on local self-sufficiency. They are largely devoted to the production of commodities required by the highly-developed countries, and serve needs which are international rather than national in origin. Such economic exclaves have come in for a good deal of hostility with the spread of nationalism and in many countries which have recently achieved sovereignty hindrances and restrictions have been deliberately placed in their way. At the present the immediate result of such negative policies can only be the impoverishment of the country concerned, but it may be that the conduct of the foreign owned and operated enterprises has sometimes hindered the path of economic progress as well. Only the simplest of manufacturing activities are found outside those serving these mainly external interests.

The planned economies do not fit tidily into this pattern, for neither their agriculture nor social structure is traditional. On the contrary, agriculture is the whipping boy of the whole economy and is under the strongest of pressure to provide both the labor for the rapidly growing industries and the food for the expanding urban population. Its depressed state is a direct result of developmental policy. Manufacturing industry is even more specialized on mineral and metal processing and fabrication than in the highly-developed economies. Consumer goods industries, relatively important among manufacturing industries in semideveloped and underdeveloped countries, receive the barest minimum of investment.

Transport and communications, though poor by comparison with those of highly-developed countries, are being vigorously expanded and the extension of the network is strongly influenced by the distribution of fuel and mineral deposits.

In short, the organization of the whole economy is fundamentally different from that of any of the three types found in the rest of the world, and is directed at ensuring the maximum rate of economic growth, with minor consideration for social cost.

Little reference has been made to political organization in this survey of world economies. A high rate of economic development is not a prerogative of any particular type of political organization, nor indeed is economic stagnation. Recent Asian experience shows that democratic forms of government can be successful in underdeveloped as well as highly-developed countries, and it would not be difficult to show that political democracy is far from secure in one of two of the latter. Any form of political organization can have economic progress if it really wants it, and is prepared to make the social readjustments that inevitably arise.

FIGURES AND THE WORLD'S HUNGER

by
*J. H. L. Joosten**
Wageningen (Netherlands)

INTRODUCTION

Undernourishment and malnutrition still prevail in many parts of our world. It was *Sir Boyd Orr,* former Director-General of the Food and Agriculture Organization (F.A.O.), who called the attention of mankind to this urgent problem by declaring that "a life-time of malnutrition and actual hunger is the lot of at least two thirds of mankind."

This statement was based on the food-situation just after the war, and on certain assumptions as to the standards of nutrition.

In the course of the nineteen fifties, however, more knowledge on this subject became available, and gradually the official statement of F.A.O. became less harsh and more modified. This may be evident from the foreword of Dr. Sen, Director-General of F.A.O., to the latest of F.A.O.'s yearly reviews — The State of Food and Agriculture, 1961 —, which opens as follows:

"This year's review of the State of Food and Agriculture again reveals the general pattern which has become familiar during the past decade. There is still an abundance,

often a surplus, of agricultural products in the economically more developed half of the world, side by side with continuing malnutrition and even hunger in many of the less developed countries."

The foreword further states that this is one of the fundamental problems "of much more than purely agricultural significance,[1] which do not permit of any rapid solution. They will remain with us for many years to come."

In his speech recently made at a press-conference at the Hague Dr. Sen said that about 300 to 500 million people have not enough to eat in physical quantities and that another 1200 millions suffer of malnutrition. Based on these facts Dr. Sen launched his Freedom From Hunger Campaign in 1960 which is now picking up momentum in many parts of the world and started not only initiatives to tackle the problem on a world-wide basis, but also initiated studies necessary to place the food problem in its proper place and perspectives.

This article aims at a rough reconnaissance of the field of the

*Professor in rural economics of the tropics, Agricultura University, Wageningen, Netherlands.

[1] F.A.O., The State of Food and Agriculture, 1961.

"Figures and the World's Hunger" by *J.H.L. Joosten. Reprinted from* Tijdschrift voor Economische en Sociale Geografie (*February* 1962), *pp. 42-46, with permission of author and publisher.*

world's hunger, whereby a distinction has to be made between two main types of hunger:

1. the physical hunger, meaning that people do not have enough to eat to meet the quantitative food requirements;
2. the hidden hunger (malnutrition), meaning that people eat enough in quantities of food to meet the caloric requirements, but with inadequate composition of the food to be healthy and to develop sufficient resistance against diseases. The diet in these cases is sufficient in calories but is short of proteins, minerals and vitamins resulting in physical inability, deficiency-diseases such as *beri-beri*, *pellagra*, *kwashiorkor*, *anaemie*, *xerophtalmia*, *rachitis*, *protein-oedemata*, and retarded growth of children.

THE PHYSICAL HUNGER

Undernourishment or physical hunger can be (a) permanent (b) seasonal and (c) occasional. The latter — occasional hunger — better indicated by the word "famine" may occur, when over an extended area the crops fail, because of "Acts of God" such as floods, droughts, pests which destroy the harvest, and wars. In this case there is an acute shortage of food in a specific — mainly limited — area. In former days, with insufficient communications and inadequate governmental and international organization, local famines were occurring from time to time. They took a heavy toll among the hunger-stricken people, but were mainly temporary, as they lasted only till the next harvest.

Nowadays national and international relief is able to act very fast and such famines no longer have their severe character as in former days. To relieve a famine money and organization are all that is needed, as there are big surpluses of food in many parts of the world.

Leurquin[2] puts it this way: "ce n'est pas par hasard que les famines constituent un problème propre aux economies de subsistance." He quotes *Bauer*[3]. The problem of local and seasonal famines in Ruanda Urundi could easily be solved by developing a food-reserve kept by means of a cassava crop by the farmers. Every farmer was more or less compelled to plant a small area of cassava, which crop can be kept in the fields for a few years and can be harvested according to need. More or less the same policy was followed by the British Administration in several regions of Africa. The colonial governments were much concerned with the prevention of local famines in these regions with few transportation, organizational and financial facilities.

In the general frame of the world's hunger, the occurrence of local famines is indeed no longer a problem. The more complicated is the problem of permanent and of seasonal hunger.

Let us first examine the problem of permanent undernourishment, being a permanent shortage of food in physical terms for a large number of the population. Based on theoretical insight in the working of the subsistence-economy it still is in principle improbable that at least

[2]LEURQUIN, PH., Le niveau de vie des populations rurales du Ruanda Urundi. Louvain, 1960.
[3]BAUER, P. T., Economic Analysis and Policy in Underdeveloped Countries. London, 1957.

Table 1: Land in Acres Per Household, Per Member and Per Earner

Size of household	Average no. of earners per household	Land in acres						
		per household		per member		per earner		differ-ence
		owned	cultivated	owned	cultivated	owned	cultivated	
1	0.9	1.1	0.6	1.1	0.6	1.2	0.6	− 0.6
2	1.2	1.8	1.7	0.9	0.9	1.6	1.5	− 0.1
3	1.4	3.2	3.2	1.1	1.1	2.4	2.3	− 0.1
4	1.5	4.2	4.2	1.0	1.0	2.8	2.8	0
5	1.8	4.8	5.2	1.0	1.0	2.7	2.8	+ 0.1
6	1.8	5.1	5.4	0.9	0.9	2.9	3.1	+ 0.2
7	2.2	6.7	7.7	1.0	1.1	3.0	3.4	+ 0.4
8	2.8	6.5	8.3	0.8	1.0	2.4	2.9	+ 0.5
9	3.0	10.4	10.6	1.2	1.2	3.5	3.5	0
10 and above	4.2	21.8	20.1	1.7	1.6	5.2	4.8	− 0.4

the farmer and his family are subject to permanent shortage of food. Basically in these economies the farmer first of all produces the food he requires. For example the size of the farms is related to the size of the family, the number of workers in the family and to the needs of the family. Even in the agriculturally densely populated areas of India this appears to be true. Investigations by the Indian Planning Commission made in the scope of the Community Development Projects, the so-called "Bench Mark Survey Reports" give much evidence on this specific point. To demonstrate this we refer to such a report on Bhadrak block (1956)[4]. In this report we find Table 1.

We would draw attention to three columns: cultivated per member, cultivated per earner and difference between owned per earner and cultivated per earner. Leasing and renting of land adjusts the area cultivated per member and per earner. This is completely in accordance to the theoretical expectations. Also it

is found when studying subsistence-agriculture, that the number of acres under crop is closely related to the size of family, the productivity of the land and the consumption-pattern of the farmers. This is also valid for sparsely populated regions. In the frame of this article it would take us too far to demonstrate this with figures — calculated and found in practice. One point we would like to emphasize in this context: the farmer only sells surpluses. This was subject of discussions at the meeting of the Indian Society of Agricultural economists held at Chandigarh, December 1960[5]. One of the subjects was: Problems of Marketable Surplus in Indian Agriculture. In his paper P. C. Bansil (scientific co-worker of the Planning Commission) — "Problems of Marketable Surplus" — states that the marketable surplus is actually directly related to the size of holdings as shown in Table 2.

The conclusion from the foregoing considerations and data is that, if actually there would be permanent

[4]Indian Planning Commission, Bench Mark Survey Report on Bhadrak district. Delhi, 1956.

[5]Ind. Soc. of Agr. Ec.; Proceedings of the twentieth Conference held at Chandigarh, December 1960. The Ind. Jrn. of Agr. Ec. Vol. XVI (1961), Nr. 1.

Table 2: Distribution of Marketable Surplus by Size Level of Holdings (1953-54) and Distribution of Holdings

Farm size in acres	Marketable surplus as percentage of total produce[6]	Percentage of total land per size-group[7]	Percentage of households per size-group[8]
no land	—	—	6.3
1.25 and less	5.8	1.5	37.0
1.25— 2.50	32.0	4.5	11.5
2.50— 5.00	25.4	10.9	15.9
5.00—10.00	36.4	19.6	14.9
10.00—15.00	34.2	12.6	5.5
15.00—25.00	31.7	17.7	5.0
25.00—50.00	23.9	18.8	3.0
50.00 and more	47.7	14.4	0.9

Sources: see footnotes 5 and 7.

undernourishment, even in densely populated India, this hunger is of a structural nature. Normally the farmer will not be hungry, but the hungry people will be found outside the farmers' community. This conclusion, we think, is valid for all underdeveloped countries, the main reason being, that the millions in the towns and a small portion of the rural population do not have sufficient purchasing power caused by insufficiently gainful employment within and outside agriculture for the landless people.

Within the subsistence-economy seasonal shortages of food are, however, in specific cases not uncommon. In Indonesia for example there are special names for this feature: "lapar biasa" and "patjeklik". With these names the pre-harvest period, in which there is a gradually decreasing supply of basic foodstuffs (rice and/or maize) is indicated. This seasonal shortage can be found in regions with ample land resources, but is also not uncommon in certain densely populated regions of Java and India or other parts of the world. The solution to this problem in rather sparsely populated regions is an agricultural problem, in the sense that the farmer himself can take the necessary measures on his farm, by improving his farming techniques as may be possible under the mainly adverse soil and climatic conditions responsible for too low returns to cover the food-requirements throughout the year. Heavy indebtedness can also lead to seasonal food shortages.

In the other regions such as Java and India, however, the problem is also of a structural nature, related to the lack of sufficient land resources and the lack of employment in agriculture in the off-seasons, in places where the irrigations and/or the rainfall only permit one crop per year.

HOW MANY PEOPLE GO PERMANENTLY HUNGRY?

There is of course no statistical registration of the number of people who are permanently hungry. Only estimates can be made, based on case studies and macro-data, the food balance sheets of the countries involved. These data provide figures regarding the average quantity of food available per head of the population per year and give some indications as to the average composition of the food-supplies. As from such figures it is impossible to conclude as to shortage or abundance a standard has to be applied.

With regard to physical quantity

[6] Ibid.
[7] Ind. Soc. of Agr. Ec.; Cost studies in Agriculture. Seminar Series III —1961.
[8] Ibid.

the calorie-content of the diet is taken as a measure. Although the number of calories in the food can be calculated rather easily, if the composition of the diet is known, not so simple is the application of standards in order to judge in what cases a specific number of calories per head per day is sufficient to maintain health and vigor. When working with national averages matters become still more complicated, and it will therefore not be surprising, that figures for the same country from several sources differ widely. It is beyond the scope of this article to discuss the various methods of calculations. A fair number of publications on this subject is available and we refer only to a few bulletins issued by F.A.O.[9,10]

In 1950 F.A.O. published "Calorie requirements" of which a revised

[9]F.A.O. – Calorie requirements – June 1950.
[10]F.A.O., Nutritional Studies No. 15 and No. 16 (1957).

edition has been made in 1957. In these publications F.A.O. presents calculations for 3 types of regions.

Regions I: Average temperature 25°C; Average male adult weight 50 kg;

Regions II: Average temperature 10°C; Average male adult weight 65 kg;

Regions III: Average temperature 5°C; Average male adult weight 70 kg.

The figures so far calculated for these regions were:

Region I: 1950: 1860; 1957: 1994 calories/head/day

Region II: 1950: 2269; 1957: 2400 calories/head/day

Region III: 1950: 2390; 1957: 2520 calories/head/day

There is still uncertainty in this matter, and when trying to assess the requirements for a specific country wide differences in the results have to be expected depending

Table 3: Average Calorie Content of National Average Food Supplies in Selected Countries (calories per head per day)

	1934–38	1949/50	1958/1959	
Ceylon	2140	1970	2100	(1959)
India	1950	1700	2080	(1958/59)
Pakistan	—	2020	1930	(1958/59)
China	2230	2030	2310	(1959: Taiwan)
Japan	2180	2100	2210	(1959)
Philippines	1920	1960	2010	(1958)
Egypt	2410	2290	2650	(1957/58)
Iran	2010	1820	2040	(1960-USDA)
Turkey	2600	2480	2850	(1958/59)
Belgian Congo	1910	1930	2650	(1960-USDA)
Fr. W. Africa	2030	2070	2450	(1960-USDA)
Tanganyika	1980	—	2175	(1960-USDA)
Brazil	2150	2340	2500	(1958)
Colombia	1860	2280	2170	(1956-58)
Mexico	1800	2050	2330	(1957-59)
Italy	2510	2340	2710	(1959/60)
Portugal	2110	2320	2350	(1959)

Sources: see footnotes 1 and 11. F.A.O Second World Food Survey. 1952.

on the methods used and the assumptions made. The areas of the world said to have shortages in food are confined to those regions which can be classified as region I and others which are intermediary with I and II.

The latest F.A.O. publication: "The State of Food and Agriculture 1961" provides us with the data in Table 3.

These figures show that the average food supply in all these countries is well in accordance with the calculated requirements of the regions I and II, so that the conclusion could be, that in general the average food supply is sufficient in the regions represented by the selected countries of which the actual figures are produced in the foregoing table. However, we are dealing with averages which means that a certain part of the population will get more, but another part will get less. In accordance with the theory of subsistence-farming the suffering part will mostly consist of the landless families which are not taken up in the farmers' households and which find insufficient employment either as share-cropper, or agricultural labourer or outside the agricultural industry, to earn an adequate income. In the end this is a problem of the existing economic and social structure.

The question now arises, how many people are involved? The food production in the under-developed areas still is basically a subsistence-production. The farmer and his family (many times extended families) normally will produce enough to meet the food requirements, especially in the field of basic foodstuffs (cereals and roots). We now estimate the portion of under or unemployed, in the sense as stated above, to vary between 5-15 per cent of the rural population. On the other hand in many under-developed countries a rather large percentage of insufficiently employed persons will be found in the other sectors of the economy. This may be estimated to amount to 20-30 per cent of the non-rural population. Based on these in our opinion rather pessimistic assumptions we made a calculation of the percentage of the world population suffering from

Table 4: Estimate of the Portion of the
World's Population Suffering from Food Shortages

Region	Population of the region in pct. of world population	Pct. of world population suffering from food shortages		
		rural	others	total
S. Asia	19	2,1	1,4	3,5
E. Asia	22	2,5	1,6	4,1
N.E Asia	5	0,2	0,4	0,6
Pacific/Malaya	4	0,1	0,2	0,3
Near East	5	0,2	0,5	0,7
N. Africa	1	0,1	0,1	0,2
C. Trop. Africa	4	0,1	0,2	0,3
Latin America	6	0,4	0,5	0,9
	67	5,7	4,9	10,6

physical undernourishment. The out-comings of these calculations are given in Table 4.

This estimate reveals that still nearly 11 per cent of the world pop-ulations does not get enough to eat, that is about 300 million people, a figure which is well in line with the most recent estimate of Dr. Sen (300 to 500 million). Fortunately the problem is not as serious as pre-viously stated and as advertisements made us believe, but it is still se-rious enough and a challenge too. In our opinion the solution has to be found in a structural change of the economies.

THE HIDDEN HUNGER

Much more serious for the world's health and economic growth, however, is the hidden hunger, the widespread malnutrition. Dr. Sen estimates that about 1200 million people having probably enough calo-ries suffer from malnutrition: un-balanced diets considerably short of proteins, vitamins and minerals. It is an established fact that the protein-content of the diets varies widely, while the figures of animal protein intake vary much more. This is demonstrated by the figures in Table 5.

In the matter of protein-require-ments, because of controversial opinions of experts, established standards do not exist. F.A.O.[11] put the average minimal protein-re-quirements for adult males at 0.35 g per kg body weight, in terms of a "reference protein" of ideal amino-acid composition. Allowing for poor composition of the foodstuffs this

should be multiplied by 2.25 to ar-rive at the total requirements, termed the "safe intake". This im-plies a total requirement of 40 grams per caput per day for re-gions type I and of 52 grams for re-gions type II.

Table 5:   Protein Intake of Selected Countries

| Country | Protein per caput/day (grams) | |
	total	animal protein
Netherlands	80	45
Brazil	62	20
Mexico	65	20
Japan	68	18
India	56	6
Egypt	79	13
Ghana	50	10
(B.) Congo	42	6
Madagascar	60	24

Sources : Congo and Madagascar, F.A.O., Second World Food Survey, 1952; Ghana, see footnote 11; others, see footnote 1

Oomen[12] refers to some striking examples of low total protein intake by Bantus and Papuas, while no de-ficiencies could be found clinically. *Bailey*[13] observed also very low protein intakes in the cassava-area Gunung Kidul (Java).

In his conclusion Bailey states: "The fact that the majority of the population maintain the appearance of good physical health despite the extremely low intakes requires closer scrutiny of existing stan-dards of caloric, protein and amino acid requirements, on the one hand, and a closer assessment of the evi-dence of caloric undernutrition and

[11]Foreign Agr. Service — Food balances in foreign countries — Part IV — Estimates for 28 countries of Africa and Western Asia. U.S.D.A. No. F.A.S. M-108 — Febr. 1961.

[12]OOMEN, Dr. H. A. P., Armelijke voeding in tro-pische gebieden. Groningen — 1960.
[13]BAILEY, K. V., Rural nutrition studies in Indo-nesia. I. Background to nutritional problems in the cassava area. Trop. Geogr. Medicine (in print).

protein malnutrition, on the other hand."

In Ghana the total amount of protein in the average diet is approximately 50 grams, of which 10 are animal protein per caput per day. That is more or less of the same order as is common in India, but in the African cassava-region kwashiorkor is not uncommon and in India and Java, mainly grain areas, this child disease is almost unknown. The disease is found in restricted densely populated cassava areas and only rarely in overpopulated grain areas.

Terra[14] recently drew attention to typical features of food patterns, the apparent relations between the agricultural environment and the tradition still in vigour, especially in dietary habits and the preparing of food. These dietary habits are mainly responsible for an uneven distribution of the available proteins among the various members of the family. In consequence of this the young children beyond the sucking-age in many parts of the world become victims of serious malnutrition especially in cassava areas. Here the problems are mainly educational; home-economists and nutritionists have to disseminate knowledge and skill, and agriculturists have to promote diversification of crops, especially the development of kitchen-gardens and the raising of fowl. This is the basic idea behind the program of the Netherlands in the scope of the Freedom From Hunger Campaign. It is extremely difficult to assess, how far spread malnutrition is. When travelling for instance in Central Africa one is surprised to observe the strong and well-built bodies of the adults. Also in the rural areas of India adult people do not look malnourished on the average. Bailey[15] states that, at first sight, the general appearance of the population of the cassava-area Gunung Kidul (Java) is sturdy, despite the obviously poor hygienic, dietary, and agricultural conditions.

It is as yet not clear on what information the figure of 1200 million malnourished people — besides 300 to 500 million undernourished people — is based. Probably too much emphasis is laid on the low animal protein intake in many parts of the world.

But let us assume that *all* children in the underdeveloped areas of the world from 1 year up to 12 years of age are malnourished, then about 600 million are involved ($0.3 \times 0.7 \times 3000$ million). The other half of the 1200 million constitute about 45 per cent of *all* adults, from 12 years and older, and this apart from the already counted 300 million who probably are physically underfed.

It seems to us a grave exaggeration of an in fact serious situation, which is not helped by exaggerations, but needs exact assessment in order to enable mankind to acquire a just and balanced insight in its consequences and to plan and to execute the measures needed to solve the problems involved.

[15]BAILEY, op. cit.
Further Literature F.A.O./W.H.O., Fifth Report of the Joint F.A.O./W.H.O. Expert Committee on Nutrition, Rome, 1958.

[14]TERRA, G. J. A., Food patterns in Indonesia. Proceedings of the 3rd International Congress of Dietetics, London 1961.

The Exploitation of Biotic Resources

The activities involved in the utilization of biotic resources are often classified into two major groups — the hunting and gathering industries, and the pastoral industries. The former includes such activities as hunting, trapping, fishing, forest gathering, lumbering, and the production of forest products. Pastoral industries include nomadic herding and commercial ranching, both involving the grazing of animals with primary dependence on natural vegetation.

These industries range in size from small-scale subsistence activities to large-scale commercial organizations such as major timber companies or ranches. All these activities, at large or small scale, rely on the extraction and/or processing of naturally occurring animal or plant life.

Another characteristic of these activities is that they take place in many parts of the earth. Fishing is done on all major water bodies, grazing occurs in the arid and semiarid zones on all continents, and forestry activities range from equatorial tropical forests to the far northern coniferous forests. In most instances these activities occupy land which, due to physical or locational restrictions, is not now profitable to cultivate intensively. If properly practiced, all of these activities share the advantage of a renewable resource base. Unfortunately, due to overfishing, excess cutting, or overgrazing, this base is sometimes severely weakened or destroyed.

The following articles deal with several aspects of commercial fishing and with the production of forest products. Both the Helin and Sommers articles deal with commercial fishing in Northern Atlantic fishing grounds. Together these articles provide an insight into the magnitude of the industry, its importance as an employer, and its importance as a source of food. The articles suggest some of the economic, political, and physical factors influencing the industry, and they indicate possible future trends in this activity.

The two articles dealing with forest products are both concerned with the large-scale commercial aspects of utilizing this group of resources. The Thomas article examines the financial implications to the industry of changing markets for forest products. Stafford, using a basic statistical test, evaluates several possible factors influencing the location of paperboard plants.

SOVIET FISHING IN THE BARENTS SEA
AND THE NORTH ATLANTIC

RONALD A. HELIN

FISHERY products provide the average Soviet citizen with one-third of his total consumption of animal protein. Some reports place the figure as high as 40 percent.[1] In recognition of this contribution, Soviet planners have invested heavily in state fishing fleets and bases ever since the inauguration of the five-year plans. National landings have doubled since 1950 and tripled since 1930, but fishermen have yet to satisfy government demands. The national diet is in need of more protein, and planners continue to find the fishing industry a most convenient medium through which to meet this need. Its commendable record of plan fulfillment contrasts sharply with the consistent failure of the livestock industry to reach predetermined goals.

The increased landings recorded by the Soviet fishing industry reflect mainly a more intensive exploitation of maritime fisheries. Seven-eighths of the 1,020,000 tons[2] of fish landed in 1913 were obtained from domestic lakes, rivers, and inland seas; the remainder came mostly from the shallow waters close to the Arctic and Pacific shores. Today maritime waters contribute about three-quarters of the 3,250,000-ton annual catch, and national vessels regularly visit banks far from Soviet coasts. Significantly related to the successful exploitation of high-seas fisheries is the northern coast of European Russia. In 1913 this region sheltered subsistence fishermen dependent on handlines and canvas craft; today it harbors highly mechanized fishing fleets and specialized labor from all parts of the Union. Annual landings have increased more than twenty times, and the port of Murmansk has evolved from a tiny settlement into the largest industrial fish harbor in the Soviet Union. Americans commonly associate the Soviet Barents Sea coast either with interventionist troops in World War I or with lend-lease in World War II. Few realize that this coast is the home of one of the world's great fishing fleets and industries. Information in English on the Barents Sea fisheries is scarce, dated, and perfunctory. The present paper attempts to fill, at least partly, this gap in the literature.

---

[1] Morton J. Garfield: High Seas Fisheries of the U.S.S.R., *U. S. Dept. of the Interior, Fish and Wildlife Service, Fishery Leaflet 482*, Washington, 1959.

[2] The tonnages cited in this paper are metric.

➤Dr. HELIN is assistant professor of geography, California State College at Fullerton.

"Soviet Fishing in the Barents Sea and the North Atlantic" by Ronald A. Helin. Reprinted from Geographical Review, *Vol. LIV (July 1964), pp. 386-408, with permission of the editor.*

THE PHYSICAL AND HISTORICAL SETTING

The Barents Sea is the westernmost link in the chain of waters along the northern perimeter of the Soviet Union. Soviet frontage on this sea comprises the abrupt, linear Murman Coast[3] on the west and the subdued, embayed shore of the Great Russian Lowland on the east (Fig. 1); separating the two is the White Sea, which introduces maritime water southward into the Karelian A.S.S.R. Novaya Zemlya virtually isolates the Barents Sea from Arctic waters to the east.

The Murman and Spitsbergen Currents, two branches of the North Atlantic Drift, carry warm Atlantic water far into the Barents Sea. The Murman Current sweeps round the North Cape, passes close to the Finnmark and Murman coasts, and then veers toward the northeast and Novaya Zemlya to mix with cold Arctic water; the Spitsbergen Current passes directly from the northwestern coast of Norway to Spitsbergen and on into the Arctic Sea. The warmth and turbulence associated with the two flows keep much of the southern and western Barents Sea ice-free throughout the year, and combine with a shallow continental shelf to create an environment especially favorable for the growth of plankton and other fish nutrients. As a result, the southern and western sectors of the sea provide rich feeding grounds for large numbers of cod, sea perch, and other species of demersal fish.

A short growing season and a barren, glaciated landscape pose formidable obstacles to settlement along the Barents Sea littoral, and residents traditionally have depended on fishing for their livelihood.[4] The economy of Russians living along this coast on the eve of World War I hinged closely on the capture of cod in spring and summer, when the fish feed in offshore waters. A dependence on handlines and on archaic, oar-powered craft confined operations to banks within twenty or thirty miles of the shore. An Arkhangel'sk entrepreneur introduced the first Russian steam trawler into the southern Barents Sea in 1906, but he had little success and few immediate successors. Shore facilities proved woefully inadequate, and the highly efficient Norwegian fishermen provided severe market competition. Only four

---

[3] The designation "Murman" refers to the northern shore of the Kola Peninsula. Some authorities maintain that the term originated in the early Middle Ages, when Russians referred to the White Sea and shores along the northern coast of European Russia as *Murmanskiy*, "Norman" or "Norwegian." See N. Karamsin: Histoire de l'empire de Russie (translated from the Russian by MM. St. Thomas and Jauffret; 11 vols.; Paris, 1819–1826), Vol. 1, p. 412, note 23.

[4] In the words of a visitor to the area in the sixteenth century, ". . . the country would not be habitable for Christians were it not that the catch of fish is so plentiful as to attract people to settle down there" (Erik Valkendorf, a visitor to Finnmark in 1511, cited in Frank N. Stagg: North Norway: A History [London, 1952], p. 75).

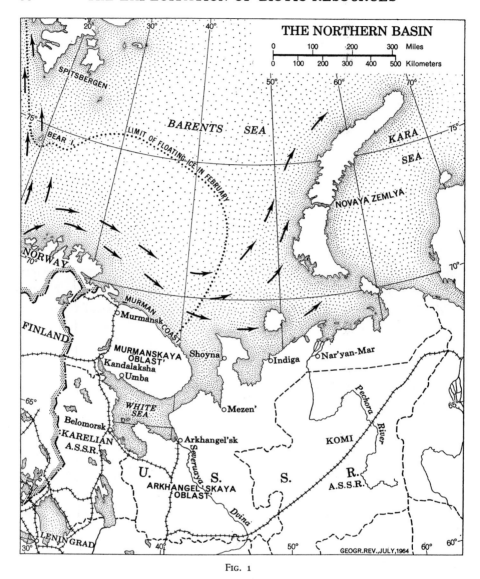

FIG. 1

Russian steam trawlers were operating in the Barents Sea in 1913. All worked out of Arkhangel'sk, and their annual catch amounted to only 512 tons. During the same year resident fishermen depending on more traditional craft caught thirteen times as much fish along the north Russian shore.[5]

<hr>

[5] Leonid Breitfuss: Die Erschliessung des eurasiatischen hohen Nordens, *Petermanns Mitt. Ergän-zungsheft No. 207*, 1930, pp. 26–27. Instrumental in attracting the industrial vessels into the Barents Sea was investigatory work by the Scientific Murman Expedition, a government undertaking initiated to help establish and advance Russian fishing and sea-animal industries in the Barents Sea. The expedition functioned from 1898 to 1908, and its scientists during this time firmly established the presence of numerous untapped fishing banks in the southern sector of the sea.

Since 1913 the nature and magnitude of fishery endeavor along the northern coast of European Russia have altered considerably. Acute food shortages induced the new Soviet government to invest in a northern fishing fleet soon after the Revolution, and subsequent economic success and continued market demands have led to heavy and systematic state invest-

TABLE I—NORTHERN BASIN, LANDINGS OF FISH
(*In thousands of metric tons*)

YEAR	MURMANSKAYA OBLAST'	ARKHANGEL'SKAYA OBLAST'	KARELIAN A.S.S.R.	TOTAL	% OF NATL. TOTAL
1913	17.6[a]	8.0[c]	4.1[d]	29.7	2.8
1928*	45.7[a]	6.0[c]	7.2[d]	58.9	7.0
1940	178.3[a]	7.7[c]	8.0[d]	194.0	14.8
1945	76.0[a]	11.3[c]	8.4[d]	95.7	8.5
1950	223.9[a]	44.4[c]	10.6[d]	278.9	17.1
1955	631.9[a]	130.4[c]	33.5[e]	795.8	31.9
1958**	510.0[b]	106.7	34.4[f]	651.1	24.8
1965**	830.0[b]	171.8	46.5[f]	1,048.3	22.6

*For Murmanskaya Oblast', 1927–1928.
**For Arkhangel'skaya Oblast', estimate based on figures cited for the Karelian A.S.S.R. and Murmanskaya Oblast'.

[a] Narodnoye khozyaystovo Murmanskoy Oblasti: Statisticheskiy sbornik [National Economy of Murmanskaya Oblast': Statistical Compendium] (Murmansk, 1957), p. 27.

[b] Borisov, Technicheskiy progress . . . [Technical Progress . . .] [see text footnote 20 below], p. 3.

[c] Narodnoye khozyaystvo Arkhangel'skoy Oblasti: Statisticheskiy sbornik [National Economy of Arkhangel'skaya Oblast': Statistical Compendium] (Arkhangel'sk, 1957), p. 23.

[d] 40 let Karel'skoy ASSR: Statisticheskiy sbornik [40 Years of the Karelian A.S.S.R.: Statistical Compendium] (Petrozavodsk, 1960), p. 34.

[e] Valentik, Kareliya v shestoy pyatiletke [Karelia in the Sixth Five-Year Plan] [see text footnote 44 below], pp. 25 and 27.

[f] S. K. Koryako: Rybnaya promyshlennost' Karelii v semiletke [The Karelian Fish Industry during the Seven-Year Plan], Rybnoye khozyaystvo, Vol. 35, No. 8, 1959, pp. 64–66, reference on p. 64; Morozov, Ekonomika, organizatsiya i planirovaniye proizvodstva v rybnoy promyshlennosti [Economy, Organization, and Planning Production in the Fish Industry] [see text footnote 13 below], p. 7; A. A. Ishkov: Razvitiye rybnoy promyshlennosti za 40 let Sovetskoy vlasti [Development of the Fish Industry over 40 Years of Soviet Rule], Rybnoye khozyaystvo, Vol. 33, No. 11, 1957, pp. 9–19, reference on p. 14; United Nations Statistical Yearbook 1962 [see text footnote 6 below].

ment in the north Russian fishing industry ever since. Local fishermen now belong to collectives, and their traditional equipment has given way to motor craft and complex gear. State employees manage large modern fishing fleets, with diesel and steam trawlers capable of operations the year round on fishing grounds thousands of miles from home ports. Regional landings have increased spectacularly (Table I). In 1913 fishermen in the Northern Basin (Murmanskaya Oblast', Arkhangel'skaya Oblast', and the Karelian A.S.S.R.) landed a mere 29,700 tons of fish. But by 1955 the catch had increased to 795,800 tons, and vessels working out of the basin in 1965 are "scheduled" to land about 1,000,000 tons, a volume equal to the current national production of countries such as Canada and the United Kingdom.[6]

---

[6] United Nations Statistical Yearbook 1962, Vol. 14, Department of Economic and Social Affairs, New York, 1963, pp. 127–128.

Barents Sea Fisheries

Organized state activity in the Barents Sea region dates from 1920, the year interventionist troops withdrew from Murmansk and Arkhangel'sk and Communist administrators first gained control over the northern coast of European Russia. Immediate nationalization brought into government hands twelve small minesweepers already rigged for trawling by former White Russian owners. Authorities in the old, well-established port of Arkhangel'sk received administrative control of this fleet, and operations soon began in the White Sea and on grounds flanking the Murman Coast and the Kanin Peninsula.[7] An embarrassing problem developed almost immediately. Ice blocked Arkhangel'sk to water traffic for half of the year, and regional rivalry caused officials in Murmansk to refuse Arkhangel'sk fishermen the privilege of wintering in ice-free harbors along the Murman Coast.[8] As a result, the new state fleet sat idle throughout most of the winter. Incensed central planners responded in 1924 by assuming direct administrative control over the entire northern fishing industry. They also transferred its headquarters to Murmansk, the one site in north European Russia that possesses not only a deep and well-protected maritime anchorage and an outlet to an ice-free sea but also a railroad connection with the national ecumene.[9]

The initiation of full-scale collectivization paved the way for the ascent of Murmansk to national industrial importance. Soviet agricultural production fell disastrously after 1928, and authorities responsible for supplying cities with food turned with new appreciation to fisheries within and outside the country. The Barents Sea attracted special interest because research and the success of foreign trawlers clearly indicated huge schools of fish in areas accessible to, but unvisited by, the Murmansk fleet. Planners outlined ambitious forecasts, administrators issued appropriate decrees, and party cadres received explicit instructions. The gears of the state-controlled econ-

---

[7] The central government, to help guarantee successful catches in these areas, reduced foreign competition by establishing a twelve-mile limit for territorial waters in the White Sea and in the Arctic Sea in 1921 (R.S.F.S.R.) and in 1927 (U.S.S.R.) (T.A. Taracouzio: The Soviet Union and International Law [New York, 1935], p. 63). A fascinating discussion of the precedents and consequences of this legislation is, included in an article by Bohmert, "Die russische Fischereigrenze (I)," *Zeitschr. für Volkerrecht*, Vol. 21, 1937, pp. 441–495.

[8] Vladimir V. Tchernavin: I Speak for the Silent (translated from the Russian by Nicholas M. Oushakoff; Boston, 1935), pp. 14–15. See also I. N. Arnol'd: Rybnyye promysly nashego Severa [Our Northern Fisheries] (Leningrad, 1928), pp. 56–58.

[9] The natural setting of Kola Inlet and other potential commercial harbors along the northern shore of the Kola Peninsula is discussed in M. Liinaharja: Murmanin rannikon satamista, *Teknillinen aikakauslehti*, Vol. 10, No. 1, Helsinki, 1920, pp. 63–69.

omy turned inexorably, and the Murmansk fishing industry began to exploit increasingly large expanses of water. By 1939 its captains had conquered virtually every offshore bank between the North Cape and southwestern Novaya Zemlya, and the decade after World War II brought the mastery of shallows off Bear Island and Spitsbergen, the second of the great Barents

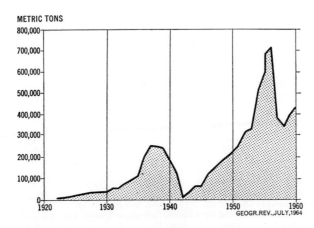

FIG. 2—Landings of the Soviet trawler fleet in the Barents Sea, 1922–1960. Sources: V. N. Travin: Promysel morskogo okunya v yuzhnoy chasti Barentseva morya i rayone Kopytova (see text footnote 19 for full reference), p. 163; *Bull. statistique des pêches maritimes,* Conseil Permanent International pour l' Exploration de la Mer, Copenhagen, 1955–1960, Table 2.

Sea fishery regions. Accompanying areal expansion were developments that promoted a more rational and intensive use of fishing grounds: engineers designed more-efficient gear; captains and crews accumulated experience at sea; research scientists conducted numerous fishery investigations; and shipwrights constructed larger and swifter craft. The cumulative effect of these developments increased landings substantially (Fig. 2). Few areas of the Barents Sea known to contain commercial concentrations of fish remain unexploited by the Soviet fleet today.[10]

The high point of success came when the fleet obtained some 725,000 tons of fish from the Barents Sea in 1956. Landings dropped sharply in the following year, and fishermen have yet to equal or exceed that peak. Overfishing of demersal stocks and a drop in water temperatures in the southern Barents Sea have been given as reasons for the persistent depression.[11] In compensation, local planners have placed more emphasis on selective fishing. Moreover, the Soviet Union signed in 1958 the Northeast Atlantic

---

[10] For a map of the principal Soviet fishing regions in the Barents Sea see "Karta promyslovykh rayonov Barentseva morya [Chart of Bering Sea Fishing Grounds]," *Trudy Polyarnyy nauchno-issledovatel' skiy institut morskogo rybnogo khozyaystva i okeanografii,* Vol. 10, Murmansk, 1957, p. 281.

[11] K. K. Sarakhanov and G. Ya. Schulman: Murmanskiy ekonomicheskiy administrativnyy rayon [Murmansk Economic-Administrative Region] (Murmansk, 1959), p. 19; V. M. Shparlinskiy: Rybnaya promyshlennost' SSSR [Fish Industry of the U.S.S.R.] (Moscow, 1959), p. 31; and "Stocks Reduced in Barents Sea," *Fishing News,* London, July 25, 1958, p. 1.

Fisheries Convention. Signatories of the agreement pledge to abide by its regulations concerning mesh size, minimum size of fish landed, closed fishing seasons and areas, and other conservation measures in North Atlantic fishing grounds between Novaya Zemlya and the eastern coast of Greenland.

TABLE II—LANDINGS AT LEADING FISHING PORTS OF THE WORLD*
(*In metric tons*)

PORT	1955	1960
Murmansk, U.S.S.R.[a]	631,900	700,000 (est.)
Bremen, Germany[b]	297,400	258,600
Hull, England[c]	270,000	233,600
San Pedro, United States[d]	160,800	170,900
Boulogne, France[e]	118,900	120,500
Chimbote, Peru[f]	20,600	926,500
Callao, Peru[f]	16,100	1,324,300

*For Murmansk, fish landed in Murmanskaya Oblast'. Vessels working out of other ports probably caught between 5 and 10 percent of the volume indicated for each of the two years.

[a] Narodnoye khozyaystvo Murmanskoy Oblasti: Statisticheskiy sbornik [National Economy of Murmanskaya Oblast': Statistical Compendium] (Murmansk, 1957), p. 28; "Briefs on U.S.S.R. Fisheries" [see text footnote 25 below], Apr. 16, 1962, p. 2.

[b] *Statistisches Jahrbuch für die Bundesrepublik Deutschland,* 1956, p. 162, and 1961, p. 186.

[c] *Sea Fisheries Statistical Tables,* London, Ministry of Agriculture, Fisheries and Food, 1955 and 1960.

[d] E. A. Power: Fisheries of the United States, 1960, Preliminary Review, *U. S. Dept. of the Interior, Fish and Wildlife Service, Fishery Leaflet 393,* 1961; personal communication with Mr. E. A. Power, U. S. Department of the Interior, Fish and Wildlife Service, Office of Statistics, Dec. 20, 1962.

[e] *Annuaire Statistique de la France,* 1955 and 1961.

[f] *Anuario Estadístico del Perú,* 1955; "La pesca peruana en 1960," *Serie de Divulgación* No. 15, Peru, Ministerio de Agricultura, Servicio de Pesquería, p. 16.

About four hundred vessels work out of the Murmansk harbor.[12] Of these, roughly a third belong to the Murmansk herring fleet, the remainder to the Murmansk trawler fleet. The Murmansk *sovnarkhoz,* a regional economic council subordinate to the central government, directs and finances both fleets. In addition, it administers units responsible for fish packing, ship construction, harbor improvement, and the various other services associated with the operation of the industry.[13] The two fleets consistently catch more than three-quarters of the fish landed in the Northern Basin; by 1952 their product had become large enough to make Murmansk the leading fishing

[12] Estimates range from 300 to 500 vessels. See, for example, Wilhelm Blanke: Seefischerei und Fischereipolitik im nordatlantischen Raum (Hamburg, 1959), p. 206; Georg Borgström: The Atlantic Fisheries of the U.S.S.R., *in* Atlantic Ocean Fisheries (edited by Georg Borgström and Arthur J. Heighway; London, 1961), pp. 282–315, reference on p. 298; and Evg. Dvinin: Port chetyrekh okeanov [Port of Four Oceans] (Murmansk, 1957), p. 79.

[13] Sarakhanov and Schulman, *op. cit.* [see footnote 11 above], pp. 16–19. For a comprehensive discussion of the administrative organization of the Soviet fishing industry as a whole see M. V. Morozov: Ekonomika, organizatsiya i planirovaniye proizvodstva v rybnoy promyshlennosti [Economy, Organization, and Planning Production in the Fish Industry] (Moscow, 1960).

port in the world. However, the past eight years have witnessed a phenomenally rapid exploitation of anchoveta (*Engraulis ringens*) fisheries off the coast of Peru, and since 1959 Callao and Chimbote have exceeded the Soviet port in volume of fish landed annually (Table II).[14]

THE CATCH

Cod (*Gadus morrhua*) and haddock (*Melanogrammus aeglefinus*) regularly constitute about three-quarters of the Barents Sea trawler catch. Current Soviet statistics lump both species under the heading "cod," but prewar data indicate clearly that annual landings of cod exceeded those of haddock.[15] Two varieties of cod frequent the Barents Sea: Murmansk cod are commercially insignificant because of small numbers; Atlantic cod form the staple of the trawling fleet.

Atlantic cod begin their lives as spawn deposited in the vicinity of the Lofoten Islands during the winter. The spawn drift toward the north and northeast in the North Atlantic Drift, and by the time they reach the North Cape they have developed into small fry. The Murman Current sweeps part of them into the southern Barents Sea, and the Spitsbergen Current carries others toward Bear Island and Spitsbergen. Millions of the young cod perish. Some become food for other fish; others die from starvation. Small fry washed into the southern Barents Sea appear off the Finnmark coast in the early spring; here they are joined by mature fish that have returned from the Lofoten spawning grounds and by immature fish that have wintered in offshore waters. The cod now begin a seasonal food migration. Drifting with the temperate Murman Current and keeping to banks and shallows along the southern Barents Sea shore, the fish move eastward in search of plankton, bottom life, and the young of other fish. By summer the migrating cod are feeding in the shallows that bound the northern shores of Arkhangel'skaya Oblast', and by early autumn they have reached broad underwater pastures off western Novaya Zemlya. The onset of cold water temperatures in late autumn leads the immature cod to swim to wintering grounds in waters north of the Murman Coast. Mature cod retrace their path first toward the grounds in the southern Barents Sea and then to spawn-

---

[14] Peruvian refineries transform most of this catch into fish meal, whereas factories in Murmansk specialize in products for human consumption. Murmansk therefore retains its primacy only if judged according to its output of edible fish.

[15] See N. A. Maslov: Promyslovyye donnyye ryby Barentseva morya [Demersal Fisheries of the Barents Sea], *Trudy Polyarnyy nauchno-issledovatel' skiy morskogo rybnogo khozyaystva i okeanografii*, Vol. 8, 1944. pp. 1–186; reference on p. 25.

ing grounds in the Lofoten area. Here, with the onset of spring, the cycle begins again.[16]

Small fry swept northward toward Bear Island by the Spitsbergen Current participate in a seasonal migration that carries them north and south rather than east and west. The fry, along with their elders, spend the summer in search of food on the banks around Spitsbergen. Autumn signals a retreat toward the south and warmer water. Young fish winter in the Bear Island area, and adults move on to the spawning grounds off the Lofoten Islands. Both age groups, along with new small fry, slowly wend their way back toward the Spitsbergen feeding grounds during the following spring and summer.[17]

These migration patterns determine to a large extent the distribution of the Murmansk fleet in the Barents Sea throughout the year. The annual fishing season begins in late winter when vessels gather on banks off the northern coast of Norway and south of Bear Island to await schools of cod about to start their annual migration. Fishing begins in April, and for the next six months the fishermen follow and exploit the schools as they migrate either north toward Spitsbergen or east toward shallows off southwestern Novaya Zemlya. Early autumn marks the end of the peak season. The cod during late autumn and winter are widely spread throughout the Barents Sea, and catches drop considerably in volume.

The life habits of cod and haddock are roughly similar, and both are found in about the same areas at the same times of the year. Catches of haddock approach or exceed those of cod only in the eastern third of the Barents Sea. The haddock gather here in large numbers during the summer and autumn in order to bask and feed in the warm shallows that flank the coast of the Kanin Peninsula and the southwestern shores of Novaya Zemlya.[18]

Murmansk fishermen also exploit sea perch (*Sebastes marinus, S. mentella*) in the warm waters of the western Barents Sea. Vessels out of Murmansk first sought the fish on a commercial scale in 1948. Operations since then have proved eminently successful, and sea perch now make up about one-sixth of the annual Barents Sea catch. The sea perch was originally by-passed in favor of cod and haddock because of its tendency to concentrate

---

[16] N. A. Maslov: Puti treskovykh kosyakov [Cod Shoal Routes], *in* Na tralerakh v Barentsevom more (Leningrad, 1946), pp. 173–176.

[17] G. C. Trout: The Bear Island Cod: Migrations and Movements, *Fishery Investigations,* Ministry of Agriculture, Fisheries and Food, Ser. 2, Vol. 21, No. 6, London, 1957, pp. 46–47.

[18] Maslov, Promyslovyye donnyye ryby Barentseva morya [see footnote 15 above], p. 176.

TABLE III—MODELS OF FISHING VESSELS

CLASS AND MODEL	FULL-LOAD DISPLACEMENT(MT)	OVERALL LENGTH(m)	FREIGHT CAPACITY	MOTIVE POWER(hp)	SPEED (knots)	CRUISING RANGE($days$)	CREW
Seiner[a]	—	33.4	50MT	300	14	.0	15
Small fishing trawler (MRT)[b]	—	—	—	150	11	—	12
Medium fishing trawler (SRT)							
Standard[c]	—	39.1	65MT	300–400	9.0–9.5	30	22
Refrigerated[c]	—	50.5	160MT	600	10	40	28
Fishing trawler (RT)							
Steam[a]	—	59.2	280MT	1,000	12	18	—
Diesel *Pioner*[a]	—	58.0	223MT	1,100	12	45	44
Kreml'[a]	—	73.6	830MT	1,080	12	90	56
Large ocean fishing trawler (BMRT)							
Pushkin[a,d,e]	3,700	84.8	1,666 m^3	1,900	12.5	65	100
Mayakovskiy[d,e,f]	3,658	84.7	1,543 m^3	2,000	13	80	102
Leskov[e]	—	85.2	1,780 m^3	2,000	12.5	—	—
Refrigerated transport							
Tavriya[g]	5,215	99.3	3,200 m^3	4,000	13.6	60	82
Aktyubinsk[h]	10,250	130.9	—	1,800	17.8	—	—
Factory ship							
Severodvinsk[d]	17,140	155.1	—	5,000	13	60	—
A. Zakharov[d,i]	15,300	162.1	—	4,000	12.7	75	640

[a] Sarakhanov and Schulman, Murmanskiy ekonomicheskiy administrativnyy rayon [Murmansk Economic-Administrative Region] [see text footnote 11 above], pp. 25–33.

[b] Dvinin, Kray v kotorom my zhivem [The Region in Which We Live] [see text footnote 31 below], p. 210.

[c] V. D. Alimov: Puti povysheniya effektivnosti raboty srednikh rybolovnykh tralerov [Increasing the Efficiency of the Medium Fishing Trawler], *Rybnoye khozyaystvo*, Vol. 33, No. 9, 1957, pp. 10–14; reference on p. 11.

[d] "Novyye suda rybnoy promyshlennosti" ["New Vessels of the Fish Industry"], *ibid.*, Vol. 37, No. 1, 1961, pp. 54–61; reference on pp. 54–58.

[e] Kamenskiy and Muragin, Novaya seriya rybolovnykh tralerov [A New Series of Fishing Trawlers] [see text footnote 24 below], pp. 43 and 49.

[f] S. A. Minovich: Promyslovyye ispytaniya BMRT "Mayakovskiy" [Test Runs of the BMRT "Mayakovskiy"], *Rybnoye khozyaystvo*, Vol. 35, No. 3, 1959, pp. 32–38; reference on p. 33.

[g] S. S. Vershinin: Proizvodstvennoye refrizheratornoye sudno [Refrigerated Factory Ship], *ibid.*, Vol. 36, No. 10, 1960, pp. 38–42; reference on p. 41.

[h] V. P. Pomukhin and A. P. Bochek: Dizel'-elektrokhod: "Aktyubinsk"—flagman refrizheratornogo flota [Diesel-Electric Movement: "Aktyubinsk"—Flagship of the Refrigerator Fleet], *ibid.*, Vol. 32, No. 11, 1956, pp. 8–11.

[i] S. S. Vershinin: Plavuchiy rybokonservnyy zavod [Floating Fish Cannery], *ibid.*, Vol. 37, No. 7, 1961, pp. 17–22; reference on p. 22.

on grounds whose depth and irregular terrain made trawling difficult, but it has come into its own with the construction of powerful fishing craft and gear. The persistent national shortage of meat has also helped stimulate its exploitation. The largest catches are presently taken during the spring on banks north of western Finnmark; a second peak comes in late summer in the same region and on the banks in the vicinity of Bear Island and Spitsbergen.[19]

THE VESSELS

Steam- and diesel-powered fishing trawlers, RT's, dominate the branch of the Murmansk fleet responsible for exploiting the cod, haddock, and sea-

[19] V. N. Travin: Promysel morskogo okunya v yuzhnoy chasti Barentseva morya i rayone Kopytova [Sea-Perch Grounds in the Southern Part of the Barents Sea and the Kopytova Region], *Trudy Polyarnyy nauchno-issledovatel'skiy institut morskogo rybnogo khozyaystva i okeanografii*, Vol. 10, 1957, pp. 161–171.

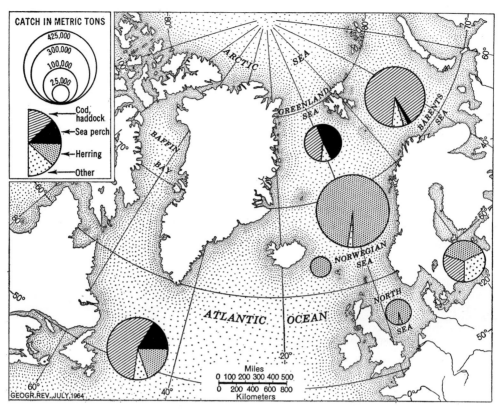

Fig. 3—Landings of fish by Soviet fleets in the northwestern (1961) and northeastern (1960) sectors of the Atlantic Ocean, by area of origin.

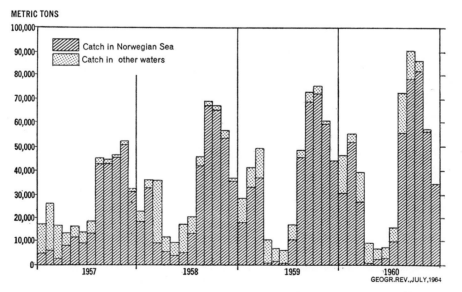

Fig. 4—Soviet herring catch in the eastern North Atlantic Ocean, 1957–1960, by months. The eastern North Atlantic Ocean, as defined here, comprises the Norwegian Sea, the North Sea, the Barents Sea, and the waters around the Faeroe Islands. Source: *Bulletin statistique des pêches maritimes,* Conseil Permanent International pour l'Exploration de la Mer, Copenhagen, 1957–1960, Table 11.

perch fisheries of the Barents Sea. Steam RT's ruled before World War II, and similar craft, many of them constructed in Polish, Swedish, or Finnish shipyards, continued to be introduced after 1945. Table III gives specifications of a model purchased from Poland soon after the war. State planners introduced diesel RT's into the Murmansk fleet about 1950. The new vessels represented an improvement over their steam-powered competitors in their compact engines, which displaced less room, and in their use of oil instead of coal, which permitted longer voyages on the same amount of bunker space. These advantages proved economically decisive, and since 1950 steam RT's have lost much of their relative economic significance.[20] Fishermen now use them mainly to exploit banks in and around the southern Barents Sea, which are within economic sailing distance of home port and sources of coal.

The method of fish preservation used on both steam and diesel RT's depends largely on the distance of the fishing grounds from port. Ice-cooled fish, even under ideal handling conditions, seldom keep longer than ten days, and fishermen normally resort to ice cooling only when working grounds three to four days out of Murmansk. Fish taken in more distant waters are generally salted and packed in barrels. Fishermen on *Pioner*-model RT's can also freeze or can their catch.

North Atlantic Fisheries

Before 1939 Soviet catches in the North Atlantic amounted to only a few thousand tons annually. Commercial operations began in the summer of 1949 when twenty-eight vessels, twelve from Murmansk and the others from Kaliningrad, caught 4500 tons of herring in the Norwegian Sea and the waters off Iceland.[21] Planners moved quickly to expand the scope of operations, and Soviet catches in the North Atlantic since 1960 have reached about 900,000 tons a year. Herring obtained from grounds in the eastern North Atlantic make up about three-fifths of this total; the remainder consists largely of demersal fish (cod, haddock, and sea perch) from banks off the Canadian coast (Fig. 3). Soviet sources fail to specify the proportion of the catch taken by fishermen working out of Murmansk, as distinguished from vessels working out of Soviet ports on the Baltic Sea.

Murmansel'd', the administrative branch of the Murmansk fishing industry responsible for exploiting the herring fisheries of the eastern North

---

[20] A goal of the current Seven-Year Plan in Murmanskaya Oblast' is to convert RT's still burning solid fuel over to liquid fuel (A. G. Borisov: Technicheskiy progress v rybnoy promyshlennosti Murmanskogo basseyna [Technical Progress in the Murmansk Basin Fish Industry], *Rybnoye khozyaystvo*, Vol. 36, No. 5, 1960, pp. 3–9; reference on p. 4).

[21] Sarakhanov and Schulman, *op. cit.* [see footnote 11 above], p. 29.

Atlantic, controls more than a hundred vessels, which at last report (1959) were catching about 100,000 tons of herring annually.[22] Basic to this fleet are SRT's, medium-sized trawlers (Table III) equipped with drift nets and, in some cases, with variable-depth trawls. Drifting accounts for most of the medium-trawler catch; variable-depth trawling has graduated only recently from an experimental stage. The herring are frequently salted directly into barrels, by hand labor on standard SRT's, through an automatic salting line on refrigerated SRT's. Or a crew may transfer its unprocessed catch to large factory ships, which accompany fleets of SRT's to the high seas. The factory ships also supply the trawlers with provisions, fuel, and services (medical, recreational, and so on). In addition, tankers and maritime repair tugs accompany SRT's into distant waters.

A flotilla of SRT's complete with a complement of tenders can spend as much as four months away from home port, and Soviet herring fleets may range widely. Indeed the Murmansk herring fleet now competes with vessels from Norway, England, and other northwest European fishing powers in waters from the Faeroe and Shetland Islands in the south to Jan Mayen in the north and from Iceland in the west to Norway in the east. One or another part of the fleet is at sea during every month of the year. Its largest landings come in autumn and winter when the SRT's exploit the prolific herring fisheries off the western coast of Norway (Fig. 4).[23] Fisheries around Iceland, the Faeroe Islands, and the British Isles have proved of less commercial importance to Soviet fishermen.

The Murmansk Trawler-Fleet Administration, the administrative unit once responsible for operations solely in the Barents Sea, now controls vessels working off the northeastern coast of North America as well. Planners paved the way by providing the Trawler-Fleet Administration with BMRT's, large stern trawlers with engines and storage facilities sufficient to permit trawling on fishing grounds three to four thousand miles away from home port.

---

[22] N. A. Dmitriev: Murmanskaya Oblast' v poslevoyennyye gody [Murmanskaya Oblast' during the Postwar Years] (Murmansk, 1959), p. 42; and Borisov, *op. cit.* [see footnote 20 above], p. 5.

[23] The Norwegian-Soviet fisheries agreement that went into force on August 1, 1962, grants Soviet fishermen permission to operate inside Norwegian territorial waters in a zone six to twelve miles from shore. In return, Norwegian fishermen obtained special rights in Soviet territorial waters between six and twelve miles from shore in the Varanger Fjord area and between eight and twelve miles from shore along other parts of the northern Soviet coast. The latter privilege holds as long as Soviet vessels are allowed to to load and unload at a distance of four miles off Jan Mayen. The agreement terminates on October 31, 1970 (*News of Norway*, June 28, 1962, and Aug. 23, 1962).

The *Pushkin,* a stern trawler constructed for the Soviet Union in West Germany in 1954, has received considerable publicity.[24] A 1900-horsepower engine enables the 280-foot vessel to brave high seas at any season of the year; capacious fuel tanks hold enough diesel oil for some ten weeks of continuous operation; and canning and refrigeration facilities eliminate danger of spoilage. Sonar and various electronic and radio navigation aids facilitate the finding of fish at sea. A hundred or so men and women staff the ship. Many work on a factory deck, where they receive, kill, and eviscerate the daily catch. Mechanized equipment permits the complete use of raw material. Offal and small fish pass through machines that yield fish-meal briquettes; livers pass through an oil reduction machine and into a cannery. Large fish are canned or routed through a filleting machine, frozen into blocks, and stored in refrigerated holds. From a trip lasting about two months a successful trawler will land about 650 to 700 tons of frozen fillets in addition to 200 tons of canned products and considerable fish meal. The *Pushkin* was the earliest model of BMRT introduced into the Murmansk trawler fleet. Successors with slightly greater hold capacities and longer cruising ranges have since appeared.

BMRT captains first trawled off the northeastern coast of North America in 1956. Their earliest runs covered banks near northern and eastern Newfoundland, and substantial success encouraged them to begin operations in the waters off New England, Nova Scotia, Labrador, and western Greenland (Davis Strait). In all these areas the BMRT's now share traditional fishing grounds with ships from many other countries. In most of the areas they also work grounds heretofore almost untouched because of depths too great for all but the most modern and powerful trawlers. Other types of Soviet fishing craft have followed the BMRT's into these fisheries. Diesel RT's and tankers trawl for demersal fish off the eastern coast of Canada; flotillas of 100 to 150 SRT's (and associated mother ships) drift for herring off New England; and refrigerated transports shuttle between both regions and Murmansk. The transports, by carrying home much of the catch, permit the BMRT's and other fishing vessels to function as floating factories unrestricted by their carrying capacity. The catch of the various Soviet craft working the western North Atlantic in 1961 totaled about 350,000 tons. Cod represented slightly less than half the catch; the rest consisted of roughly

---

[24] See, for example, "German Built Factory Trawlers for the U.S.S.R.," *Fishing News,* London, Jan. 27, 1956, p. 4; and Ye. V. Kamenskiy and F. P. Muragin: Novaya seriya rybolovnykh tralerov [A New Series of Fishing Trawlers], *Rybnoye khozyaystvo,* Vol. 37, No. 3, 1961, pp. 42–50.

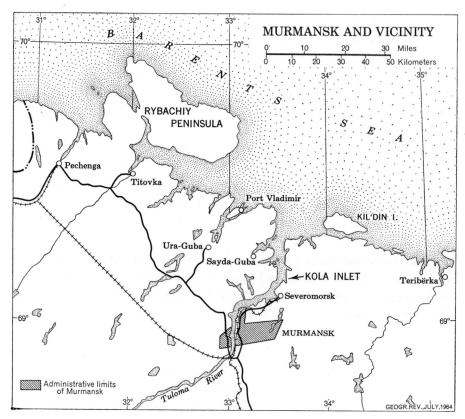

FIG. 5—Murmansk and a part of the Murman Coast.

equal parts of herring, sea perch, and other fish (Fig. 3). The 1962 catch is reported to have been at least as large.[25]

THE PORT OF MURMANSK

Murmansk, like many another industrial center in the Soviet Union, is a product of the Soviet era: in 1917 its population was about 1500; today it exceeds 245,000. The city dates from World War I and the decision of the beleaguered Tsarist government to improve its access to Allied supply lines by completing a rail link between St. Petersburg and the ice-free Murman Coast.[26] Engineers selected the then unoccupied site of Murmansk as the

---

[25] "Briefs on U.S.S.R. Fisheries," unpublished news notes, U. S. Dept. of the Interior, Fish and Wildlife Service, Bureau of Commercial Fisheries, Branch of Foreign Fisheries and Trade, Division of Industrial Research, Washington, D. C., Jan. 16, 1963, p. 1.

[26] The line from St. Petersburg to Petrozavodsk had already been completed before the war. Construction between Petrozavodsk and Murmansk began in January, 1915, and the line was ready for service by the end of 1916 (Leonid Breitfuss: Die Erforschung des Polargebietes Russisch-Eurasiens, *Petermanns Mitt. Ergänzungsheft No. 188,* 1925, p. 19).

maritime terminal for their track. A deep and spacious anchorage ensured access for large craft,[27] a topographically subdued hinterland guaranteed easy approach by rail, and a swath of coastal plain offered room for expansion. A thin sheet of ice covered Kola Inlet during severe winters, but the mouth of the inlet remained ice-free throughout the coldest of years. The site was selected in February, 1915; construction followed; and an imperial decree declared the new settlement a city in October, 1916. Originally called Romanov-na-Murmane, the city received the name Murmansk in the spring of 1917.[28]

Murmansk has grown so much that it now occupies about twelve miles of shore on the eastern side of Kola Inlet (Fig. 5). Industrial enterprises dominate the waterfront, and docks, rather than parks and boulevards, line the shore. The situation is similar along the one or two miles of developed waterfront on the opposite side of the inlet. The fish harbor commands about a mile and a quarter of piers on the eastern shore. Piers, railroad sidings, warehouses, tugs, and ships cluster in a hub of activity. Vessels clutter the harbor, floating idly as they await their turn in overcrowded berths. The postwar growth of the fishing fleet has outstripped by far the construction of new port facilities, and moorage is at a premium.[29] Especially acute is the shortage of deepwater berths for large BMRT's and supply tenders. The imbalance of investment has overburdened local ship repair yards, and planners, to provide partial relief, now stress the increased use of secondary yards elsewhere along the shores of Kola Inlet and in Teribërka.[30]

The city performs a variety of functions. It services ships plying the Northern Sea Route, harbors the northern branch of the Soviet naval fleet, and receives vessels engaged in international commerce. Above all, it commands two state fishing fleets and the largest fish-processing combine in the Soviet Union. The industry employs half of Murmansk's labor force and accounts for three-quarters of its gross industrial product.[31] The captains and

---

[27] The channel of the inlet leading to Murmansk has a depth of about fifteen fathoms. Berths can accommodate vessels with draft up to thirty feet (Sir Archibald Hurd, edit.: Ports of the World [17th edit.; London, 1963], pp. 1473–1474).

[28] Dvinin, op. cit. [see footnote 12 above], pp. 69–71; and Charles Steber: La Sibérie et l'extrême-nord soviétique (Paris, 1936), pp. 146–152.

[29] The decade following 1945 saw 800 million rubles spent on the local fishing fleet but only 150 million rubles spent on the local fishing harbor (Dmitriev, op. cit. [see footnote 22 above], p. 52).

[30] O. S. Bolotnova: The Soviet Herring Fisheries in the North Atlantic, Problems of the North, No. 2, 1958 (translated from the Russian by the National Research Council, Ottawa, Canada), pp. 239–251; reference on pp. 248–249.

[31] Evg. Dvinin: Kray v kotorom my zhivem [The Region in Which We Live] (Murmansk, 1959), p. 230; and "Murmansk," in Bol'shaya sovetskaya entsiklopediya (2nd edit.; 50 vols; Moscow, 1950–1958), Vol. 28, p. 570. The fishing industry in 1957 accounted for 64.5 percent of the gross industrial product of the Murmansk sovnarkhoz (Sarakhanov and Schulman, op. cit. [see footnote 11 above], p. 16).

crews of fishing boats tread the sidewalks; prominently posted placards urge residents to catch and process more fish for the motherland; virtually every page in local newspapers contains information of some kind concerning the industry; and the sounds and odors of the processing plants fill the air.

Fishing vessels docking in Murmansk land fish that is frozen into blocks, salted in barrels, or chilled on ice. Cranes and mechanized unloading lines transfer the cargoes into dockside sorting houses. From there fish already finished at sea (about 20 percent of the catch) passes straight into storage warehouses or waiting railroad cars; salted herring and blocks of frozen cod and sea-perch fillets probably constitute the greater part of the transfer. Partly finished and unfinished fish passes into the Murmansk Fishery Combine, an agglomeration of factories occupying about a hundred acres along the Murmansk waterfront. The combine comprises two salting factories, an establishment for the mechanical slicing of fillets, a freezing plant with a refrigerated warehouse, several canneries and a tin-can factory, a smokehouse, a fish-meal factory, and a plant for rendering medicinal and industrial fish oils. These enterprises employ altogether about 5500 people.[32]

In 1960 the combine produced some 300,000 tons of fish, and planners forecast an output of 340,000 to 350,000 tons by 1965.[33] Data for Murmanskaya Oblast' indicate that salted and frozen fish made up respectively about one-half and one-third of the combine's production in the middle 1950's (Table IV). Since that time technicians have stressed the production of frozen fish, on the basis of evidence which indicates that salting, in spite of its relative simplicity, demands more space and more man-hours than freezing does.[34] It appears likely, therefore, that frozen fish by now constitutes at least half the production of the combine. Nevertheless, salted fish undoubtedly continues to retain its market appeal for the many customers still unable to afford—or to find—the refrigeration facilities needed to preserve frozen food in their homes. Canned fish has yet to acquire large-scale importance in the Murmansk industrial scene. However, the renovation and expansion of canning facilities in the combine and the continued introduction of small canneries on BMRT's and factory ships indicate a growing interest in the commercial possibilities. The combine presently handles about 10,000 tons of canned fish a year. Half is packed locally, the remainder in the holds of factory ships and BMRT's.[35] Both the combine and the ships also process

---

[32] Borgström, *loc. cit.* [see footnote 12 above].

[33] "Briefs on U.S.S.R. Fisheries" [see footnote 25 above], Apr. 16, 1962, p. 2.

[34] Borgström, *op. cit.* [see footnote 12 above], p. 305.

[35] Calculated from data in Borgström, *loc. cit.* [see footnote 12 above].

considerable volumes of fish oil, and Murmansk reputedly is the prime source of medicinal fish oil in the Soviet Union.

Whether frozen, salted, or canned, fish from Murmansk is destined almost entirely for domestic consumption. The combine sells its products to a state marketing organization for distribution locally and to points as far distant

TABLE IV—OUTPUT OF PROCESSED FISH, MURMANSKAYA OBLAST'
(*In thousands of metric tons*)

	1940	1950	1956
Total landings	178.2	223.9	684.7
Consumable product	92.7	148.7	443.5
Salted fish	46.3	75.2	250.6
Frozen fish	33.2	46.6	140.3
Smoked fish	0.6	4.8	21.6
Fish oil	1.7	4.3	5.7
Other	10.9	17.8	25.3

Source: Narodnoye khozyaystvo Murmanskoy Oblasti: Statisticheskiy sbornik (Murmansk, 1957), p. 24.

as the Kuznetsk Basin and the northern shores of the Black Sea.[36] Railroad cars, refrigerated when necessary, bear the fish to its destination. Dispatchers now route more than 100 cars loaded with fish out of Murmansk on an average working day, and 250 during the peak of the spring fishing season.[37]

OTHER SOVIET FISH HARBORS ON THE BARENTS SEA

Soviet fishing operations from Barents Sea ports other than Murmansk are managed by fishing *kolkhozy* and state fishery bases. The kolkhozy are fishing collectives, imposed on resident fishermen by the government in the 1930's.[38] The fishery bases process the kolkhozy catch, and some also own a small fleet. At least eleven such bases occupy the southern Barents Sea shore. Three are on the western Murman Coast, four on the shores of the White Sea, and four between the mouth of the White Sea and Novaya Zemlya.

Vessels at the disposal of *kolkhozniki* and employees of the fishery bases include motorboats for service along the coast, small trawlers (MRT's) for banks farther offshore, and seiners for the more distant reaches of the Barents Sea (Table III). Motorboats were in use by the kolkhozy fleets before

[36] Dvinin, Port chetyrekh okeanov [see footnote 12 above], p. 230.

[37] Borgström, *loc. cit.* [see footnote 12 above].

[38] The kolkhozy in the Northern Basin contained about 5700 fishermen in the middle 1950's (Ye. A. Prudnikov: Tekhnicheskiy progress—put' k uvelicheniyu ulovov rybolovetskikh kolkhozov [Technical Progress: The Way to Increase Kolkhozy Catches], *Rybnoye khozyaystvo*, Vol. 33, No. 10, 1957, pp. 19–43; reference on p. 40).

World War II, MRT's first came into use in 1949, and seiners appeared in the middle 1950's. The occasional SRT's that now carry kolkhozniki into the North Atlantic are an innovation of the current planning period. The sail- and oar-powered craft common among the kolkhozy until about 1950 have disappeared from the scene—or at least from the literature.[39] Mechanically operated trawls and drift nets have replaced hand nets and lines in bank and open-sea fisheries, though the traditional equipment probably continues to see service in local bays and inlets.

Until 1959 kolkhozniki rented both their vessels and their gear from motor-fishery stations. These stations were under the direct control of the central government and served largely as channels through which planners directed collectivized fishing operations. However, the attendant division of responsibility engendered chronic administrative inefficiency, and in 1959 the government disbanded the stations and sold their equipment to the kolkhozy originally dependent on their services. It hoped to increase efficiency in this way and to improve the incentive of the fishermen. Newly established ship-repair technical stations, managed by the state, service the vessels and gear sold to the kolkhozy.

Fleets attached to the kolkhozy and fishery bases in the Northern Basin presently land between 150,000 and 200,000 tons of fish a year. Vessels based on the Murman Coast account for perhaps one-third of this total, and most of the rest is landed by craft working from ports along the White Sea.

MURMAN COAST

The western half of the Murman Coast contains the heart of its collectivized fishing industry; little information is available on operations east of Teribërka. About 800 fishermen are engaged in the collectivized fishing.[40] Some of them are descended from families that have lived in the area for centuries; others are the product of government resettlement programs. Central authorities sponsored several such programs near the end of World War II in order to reactivate kolkhozy abandoned because of military maneuvers. Cod from banks immediately off the Murman Coast constitute the bulk of the catch, but the increased use of long-distance vessels is expanding the operational sphere, and demersal fish from the open Barents Sea and

---

[39] The number and types of craft used by fishermen belonging to kolkhozy and state fishery bases in Murmanskaya Oblast' for selected years between 1940 and 1953 are given in M. A. Sonina: Pribrezhnyy promysel na Murmane v 1953 i 1954 gg. [Coastal Enterprise on the Murman in 1953 and 1954], *Trudy, AN SSSR, Kol'skiy filial, Murmanskaya biologicheskaya stantsiya*, Vol. 3, 1957, pp. 159–168; reference on p. 160.

[40] Dvinin, Port chetyrekhokeanov [see footnote 12 above], p. 230.

herring from the North Atlantic should soon vie with local cod for predominance in the annual catch.

The state fishery bases that serve the Murman Coast are in Teribërka, Sayda-Guba, and Port Vladimir (Fig. 5). Before 1917 all three, along with numerous neighboring settlements, functioned primarily as spring and summer fishing sites for migrant fishermen who arrived from Karelia and elsewhere on the White Sea to seek cod feeding in coastal waters. In winter the fishermen returned home, and the settlements were virtually deserted. But times have changed. Teribërka, Sayda-Guba, and Port Vladimir each contain several thousand permanent residents, and their fishery bases function throughout the year. Karelian and other fishermen also migrate to the area in winter in order to take advantage of ice-free harbors. To judge from Port Vladimir, each of the settlements possesses facilities sufficient for processing about 15,000 tons of fish a year, largely salted cod and herring. Mechanized cranes for loading and unloading vessels have recently become available in Port Vladimir, and at least some of the processing lines in its fish factory are mechanized.[41] Finished products are transported to market on the Murmansk–Leningrad railroad.

WHITE SEA AND ARKHANGEL'SKAYA OBLAST'

Fishermen belonging to kolkhozy and fishery bases along the shores of the White Sea operate both in local offshore waters and in the Barents Sea and the North Atlantic. Fish taken in the White Sea are commonly obtained close to shore in stationary nets and traps placed at or near the mouths of gulfs and bays, primarily in summer and autumn. Herring and cod make up about half of the annual catch; the remainder comprises a wide range of other species.[42]

Commercial long-distance fishing began with the introduction of MRT's into kolkhozy and fishery-base fleets in the early 1950's, and seiners and SRT's have since appeared. Fishermen once confined to the White Sea by their archaic craft began gradually to visit the rich and extensive fisheries of the Barents Sea and the North Atlantic. Some now work these waters the year round by shifting to the Murman Coast during the winter. Planners sponsor the seasonal migration with enthusiasm. Teribërka becomes a home-away-from-home for vessels from the Karelian A.S.S.R., Murmansk for

---

[41] N. I. Dyagilev: Mekhanizatsiya priyemki i transportirovki ryby na Port-Vladimirskom rybozavode [Mechanization of Fish Reception and Transport in the Port Vladimir Fish Factory], *Rybnoye khozyaystvo*, Vol. 36, No. 5, 1960, pp. 51–53; reference on p. 51.

[42] Borgström, *op. cit.* [see footnote 12 above], p. 292.

vessels out of Arkhangel'sk.[43] The employees of state fishery bases constitute the bulk of this migrant labor force; the kolkhozniki are more likely to spend their winters at home. The White Sea has lost much of its relative importance as a commercial fishery since the introduction of these long-distance operations. For example, Karelian fishermen obtained 50 percent of their catch from the Barents Sea and the North Atlantic in 1950 and 83 percent in 1955, and planners hope to increase the figure to 92 percent by 1965.[44]

Fishery bases along the White Sea shore include small establishments at Umba and Kandalaksha (Fig. 1), both of which service neighboring kolkhozy. Larger and more active bases are in Arkhangel'sk and Belomorsk. Arkangel'sk has harbored a commercial fishing industry since the sixteenth century, and was Russia's principal Barents Sea fishing port until Soviet officials moved the headquarters of the northern fleet to Murmansk in 1926. Planners have since reintroduced a fleet, but the offhand manner in which it is treated in the literature leads to the conclusion that it numbers relatively few vessels.[45] The fishery base contains processing establishments that produce salted, canned, and frozen fish, fish meal, and fish oil.[46] Vessels from kolkhozy scattered along the western shores of Arkhangel'skaya Oblast' complement the local fleet in providing the catch. Figures giving the volume of fish landed and processed in Arkhangel'sk are unavailable.

Belomorsk, the fishery center of the northern Karelian A.S.S.R., derives regional significance from its location on the White Sea at the junction of the Leningrad–Murmansk railroad and a branch of the Vologda–Ark-hangel'sk railroad (Fig. 1). The White Sea–Baltic Canal also debouches at Belomorsk. The fishery base serves fishermen based all along the north Karelian shore, and landings have recently reached 30,000 tons a year, 90 percent of the landings recorded for the entire A.S.S.R.[47] Processing facilities

---

[43] A. A. Grigor'ev and A. V. Ivanov, edits.: Karel'skaya ASSR [Karelian A.S.S.R.] (Moscow, 1956), p. 205; and V. F. Ovchinnikov: O razvitii tralovogo flota na Severe [Concerning the Development of the Trawler Fleet in the North], *Rybnoye khozyaystvo*, Vol. 31, No. 3, 1955, pp. 36–37.

[44] I. Ya. Valentik: Kareliya v shestoy pyatiletke [Karelia in the Sixth Five-Year Plan] (Petrozavodsk, 1957), p. 25; and S. K. Koryako: Rybnaya promyshlennost' Karelii v semiletke [The Karelian Fish Industry during the Seven-Year Plan], *Rybnoye khozyaystvo*, Vol. 35, No. 8, 1959, pp. 64–66, reference on p. 64.

[45] The most informative source notes that the fleet contains a variety of vessels which return to port with salted and frozen fish, cod-liver preserves, fish oil, and fish meal (D. Podoplekin: Novatory rybo-promyslovogo dela [Innovators in the Fishing Business], *in* Na promyslakh v Barentsevom more [n.p., 1956], p. 6).

[46] A. L. Garf: Sever [North] (Moscow, 1948), pp. 80–81; and Borgström, *loc. cit.* [see footnote 12 above].

[47] Personal estimate based on data in Valentik, *loc. cit.* [see footnote 44 above]; and Koryako, *loc. cit.* [see footnote 44 above].

include a freezing plant, a cannery, a cooperage, factories for salting and smoking fish, and assorted warehouses. The freezing plant and a large part of the cannery are products of the current Seven-Year Plan; the salting and smoking factories date from an earlier period. Salted fish probably dominates the present output, but the current plan stresses an expanded and improved freezing chain, and the traditional predominance of salted fish seems fated to disappear in the relatively near future.[48]

Fishing operations based on Barents Sea ports east of the White Sea receive scant mention in the literature. A small and collectivized native population filling primarily subsistence needs appears characteristic of the area. Mezen', Shoyna, Indiga, and Nar'yan-Mar provide fishery bases. Three factors help explain the lack of commercial fishing: ice restricts large-scale operations to the warm half of the year; climate makes the area unattractive to settlement; and isolation makes the distribution of products both difficult and expensive.

PROSPECTS

The Soviet diet, as was noted earlier, requires additional animal protein, and the planners ask ever more of the fishing industry. Of the fishermen in the Northern Basin they have asked a 400,000-ton increase in landings between 1958 and 1965 (Table I). Stress is on a more intensive use of lightly fished grounds off western Greenland and eastern North America, a more well-rounded seasonal effort in the herring grounds of the eastern North Atlantic, and an initiation of activity in waters as yet unexplored by the Soviet fleets. The recent establishment of a Soviet-Cuban fishing base in Havana Bay reveals—among other things—an interest in grounds off the southeastern United States,[49] and long-distance trawlers have now begun to exploit tuna, sardines, and pilchard off the trade-wind coasts of northwest and southwest Africa. Planners find prospects in the heavily exploited Barents Sea less enchanting. Vessels are already working the traditional fisheries in the southern and western sectors to full capacity, and the northern and eastern sectors offer little commercial promise. The exploitation of heretofore unutilized species presents one hope for the future. More visionary are current schemes to revitalize herring and salmon stocks by transplanting varieties

---

[48] Planners foresee a 6.5-fold increase in the production of frozen fish in the Karelian A.S.S.R. between 1958 and 1965. Refrigerated SRT's and transports now being introduced into the Karelian fleet are to play a major role in achieving this goal (A. V. Kudryavtsev: Karel'skiy ekonomicheskiy rayon [Karelian Economic Region] [Petrozavodsk, 1958], p. 35).

[49] The Soviet Union is constructing a fishing base that will include a fishing terminal, a new boatyard, and a fish-processing plant. Soviet vessels began using Havana as a base in 1962 ("Briefs on U.S.S.R. Fisheries" [see footnote 25 above], Feb. 18, 1963, p. 1).

from the Pacific coast. Ice blockage ruins prospects in the Arctic waters east of Novaya Zemlya.[50]

Murmansk continues to handle three-quarters of the fish landed in the Northern Basin, and signs that the city may decline in regional importance have still to appear. Winter ice precludes a serious challenge from ports such as Arkhangel'sk and Belomorsk, and the ice-free harbors along the Murman Coast lack processing facilities or adequate transport links with the national ecumene. Future competition, if any, seems likely to emanate from the Baltic ports. Kaliningrad, for example, has already captured part of the investment that would probably have accrued to Murmansk had the war not brought territorial annexations. But this race has yet to be run, and for the present Murmansk continues to reign supreme.

---

[50] These waters contributed about 1 percent (25,970 tons) of the total Soviet catch of fish in 1954 and 1955 ("Fisheries in the Soviet Arctic, 1954 and 1955," *Polar Record,* Vol. 9, 1958–1959, pp. 578–579; from a paper by S. V. Mikhaylov in *Problemy Severa,* No. 2, 1958, pp. 238–252, translated by the National Research Council, Ottawa, Canada, in *Problems of the North,* No. 2, 1958, pp. 253–269).

COMMERCIAL FISHING IN NORWAY

by
*LAWRENCE M. SOMMERS**
East Lansing, Mich. (U.S.A.)

The mountainous interior and limited land based resources have resulted in many Norwegians looking seaward for food and an economic livelihood throughout recorded history. The long, fjorded and island dotted coastline and the numerous offshore banks possess advantages for commercial fishing despite Norway's northerly latitude (Figure 1). The many coastal indentations provide excellent harbors to base fishing operations, the continental shelf has excellent spawning grounds as well as suitable bottom conditions for net and trawl fishing, the mixing of cold and warm currents and the water from coastal rivers provide abundant nourishment for plankton on which the fish feed, the moderate climate facilitates fish preservation and ice free ports the year around, and a location accessible to other fishing grounds of the North Atlantic as well as the markets of populous western Europe are among the factors leading to the importance of fishing to Norway.

The extensive coastal nature of the Norwegian fisheries and the short distances between the fishing

*Chairman, Department of Geography, Michigan State University, East Lansing, Michigan.

grounds and the bases of the fishing fleet and processing centers have resulted in numerous small-scale fishermen (many part-time) and many small fish processing enterprises in the hands of private individuals, cooperatives and companies along the entire coast. Due to the seasonal nature of the catch, most of these enterprises of necessity usually depend on more than one species of fish for successful operation. About 71 percent of the 76,000 Norwegians engaged in fishing are also involved in farming, forestry, manufacturing, or some other activity in order to make a living. The independent fishermen who have been largely responsible for the development of the Norwegian fishing industry have resisted changes that have threatened their livelihood such as efficient large trawlers and other modern gear. This has been a major political and economic issue particularly in North Norway and the government has taken action in the past to protect the small fisherman against threats to his traditional occupation. However, during the present century, especially the postwar period, the fishing industry has been gradually changing from its tradi-

"Commercial Fishing in Norway" by Lawrence M. Sommers. Reprinted from Tijdschrift voor Economische en Sociale Geografie *(November* 1962), *pp.* 237-242, *with permission of author and publisher.*

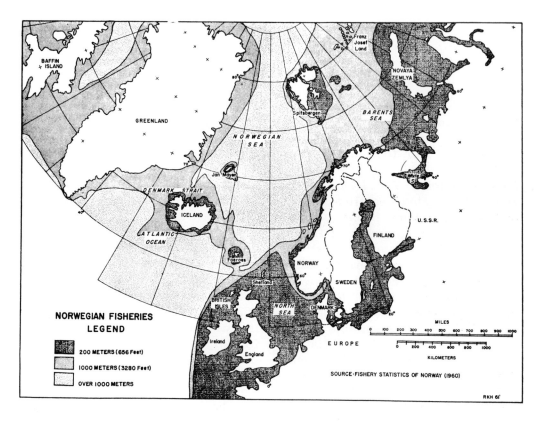

Figure 1

ditional character but nevertheless is destined to play a decreasing role in Norway's evolving industrial economy. The purpose of this paper is to evaluate the impact of some of these changes on the geography of the Norwegian fishing industry.

FISHING IN THE ECONOMY OF NORWAY

The 1,260,000 metric tons of fish landed in Norway in 1960 with a raw material value of $90 mil. represented only 1.8 percent of total national product. This value is doubled by fish processing and trade.[1] Fish and fish products accounted for 13.5 percent of the value of Norwegian exports which represents a proportional decline from nearly 20 percent in most years since World War II. Almost 90 percent of the fish landed are sold in foreign countries so the industry is highly dependent upon world market conditions. About four percent of the gainfully employed of the country are engaged in fishing and another 40,000 are

[1]SØMME, AXEL (ed.), The Geography of Norden, J. W. Cappelens Forlag, Oslo, 1960, p. 251.

involved in processing and associated activities.

Fishing is much more important to certain areas in Norway than others, although Norwegians engage in commercial fishing to some degree along the entire 1,300 miles of coastal waters. The principal banks are off the west coast with latitude of Trondheimfjord separating the predominantly herring fishery to the south from the cod fishery to the north. Fishing is far more significant in the economy of the cod areas of North Norway where 29 percent of the population received all or a portion of their income from fishing.[2] If employment in fish processing and other associated industries is included the percentage dependency increases significantly. Only in the outer seaward districts along most of the coast is the fishing industry still dominant as a livelihood for the people. Industrialization and diversification of the economy have lessened the reliance in many coastal districts, decreased catches of herring and cod have affected others, and the impact of technological change within the industry is significant in still others.

TWENTIETH CENTURY CHANGES AND PROBLEMS

Despite man's attempt to overcome variations in the annual catch, the cyclical nature of the landings of the herring and cod remains a major problem. This is particularly serious because herring and brisling (small sardine-like fish) normally account for 70 percent of the total

catch and cod 15 percent (Figure 2). Since 1957 the herring catch has been declining precipitously. In 1961 the landings were the smallest in 27 years and resulted in a raw material loss of $36 million and a reduction of Norway's gross national product by $70 million as compared to the last good year of 1957.[3]

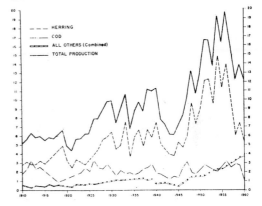

Figure 2: Norwegian Fish Catch Tonnage, 1910-1960

During the period of generally rapidly increasing herring catches from 1947-57 many coastal processing plants were built to handle the large tonnage. The herring meal and oil factories are especially hard hit in lean years as for example in 1961 when plants received 7,000 tons as compared to 700,000 tons during a similar time period in 1958.[4] The section of the coast with the largest landings also shifts materially (Figure 3). The loss has been offset to some extent by much more efficient use of the smaller quantities of herring landed which results in a greater average profit per pound. This is illustrated by the fact that the value of the catch decreases

[2] ANGERMAN, HAAVARD, LUND, OLAV, and RASMUSSEN, BIRGER, "Norway's Fishing Industry" in: BORGSTROM, GEORG and HEIGHWAY, ARTHUR J. (eds.), Atlantic Ocean Fisheries. Fishing News Books Ltd, London, 1961, p. 84.

[3] News of Norway, Vol. 18, No. 8, March 9 (1961), Norwegian Information Service, Washington, D. C., p. 33.
[4] Ibid., p. 33.

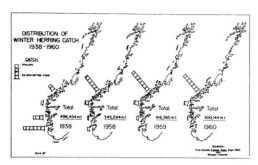

Figure 3

relatively less in poor years than does the tonnage (Figure 4). Also partially responsible for the smaller decline in value is the lower price of herring per ton than cod and other species due normally to the conversion of large quantities of herring into low value per unit weight oil and meal.

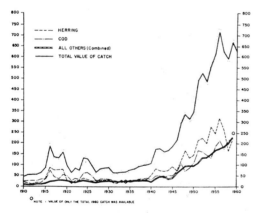

Figure 4: Value of Norwegian Fish Catch, 1913-1960

The catch of other species shows less fluctuation than herring and cod and the steady rise in landings of these fish has helped to partially offset the cyclical nature of the two leading species. These other species such as halibut, haddock and coalfish are more important in the herring regions than to the North Norway cod districts. Considerable

quantities are caught by trawlers and other larger vessels based in the ports south of Trondheim.

The failures in the herring fishery affect most of the coast from Trondheimfjord to the southwest near Stavanger. The losses are particularly serious in such ports as Aalesund, the herring capital, and surrounding Sunnmøre, long a leading district in Norwegian fishing. The adverse impact is lessened by the development of industries other than those dependent upon fish such as furniture, aluminum, and shipbuilding. Individual enterprises and fishermen are hard hit, however. The drop in catch from about 1.4 mil. metric tons of herring and brisling in 1954 and 1956 to half this amount in 1960 and even less in 1961 represents a tremendous fluctuation in the income of fishermen, the raw materials for factories, and fish products for exports. In 1960 only 9 of 450 boats utilizing purse-seines managed to catch the 1,000 ton minimum for profitable operation. The number of purse-seine vessels in operation decreased from 600 in 1959 to half this number in 1961.[5]

The variation in cod catch has been much less pronounced than herring but a bad year has more impact on North Norway than a poor catch has on the South because of the greater relative dependence upon fish as a resource in the North and the predominance of cod in their catch. A government sponsored development scheme for North Norway since World War II which terminated in 1960 had as its objective the diversification of industry including the modernization and enlargement

[5]News of Norway, Vol. 17, 9, March 3 (1960), and Vol. 18, 3, January 26, (1961).

of fish processing plants and the attempt to eliminate or resettle many of the small-scale marginal fishermen to larger settlements. Several large new freezing plants were built as was a new integrated government iron and steel plant at Mo i Rana. Overall results of the plan have not been as successful as anticipated partly due to the smaller cod catches and partly to the resistance of the traditional fisherman to change. The decreased cod catch has also affected the Sunnmøre coast to the south as this is a major center of klipfish production depending largely on surplus Lofoten (North Norway) cod for raw materials.

GREATER DEPENDENCE UPON DISTANT FISHERIES

One obvious means of offsetting the declining catches in coastal waters is to fish more intensively on distant banks such as Iceland, Jan Mayen, North Sea, Barents Sea, Faeroes, Svalbard (Spitsbergen), and the Davis Strait off western Greenland. The tonnage from these sources has increased from about 50,000 tons to nearly 135,000 tons in the decade from 1948 to 1958 (Table 1). During this same period the value of the catch from these waters has tripled. In 1958 fish from distant waters represented 11 percent of Norway's total tonnage and 16 percent of the total value. Herring (35,000 tons in 1958) from Iceland and cod (28,000 tons) from the Davis Strait represent the principal species brought back to Norway. Undoubtedly fish from these sources could be increased if a freer policy for the development of large trawlers and well equipped floating factories existed in Norway.

TECHNOLOGICAL DEVELOPMENTS IN EQUIPMENT AND THEIR IMPACT

Modernization has been slow in certain segments of Norwegian fish-

Table 1: Norwegian Fishing in Distant Waters

	1939	1958
North Sea	2,000[1]	30,246
Iceland	21,157	41,339
Faeroes & Hebrides	314	4,103
Norwegian Sea	—	11,347
Barents Sea	—	198
Bear Island & Spitsbergen	8,554	10,545
Greenland-Newfoundland	7,086	30,378
Unspecified	11,763[2]	7,195
Total[3]	50,874	135,351

[1] In metric tons.

[2] Fish caught by trawling in various waters but primarily the Norwegian Sea.

[3] The total average for 1910-19 was 11,093 tons, for 1920-29 was 11,725 tons and for 1930-39 was 24,268.

Source: Norges Offisielle Statistikk, Norges Fiskerier 1958, Fiskeridirektøren, Bergen, 1960.

ing but gradual improvements have inevitably changed many aspects of the industry. The motorization of the fishing fleet was well developed by the 1930's. Nevertheless, the number of vessels without motors dropped still further from 2700 in 1940 to 203 in 1960. In the late 1930's diesel motors were introduced with their smaller fuel requirements and increased carrying capacity of vessels for fish and made more feasible trips to distant fishing banks such as West Greenland. Since World War II most of the larger vessels have been equipped with echo sounders and asdics,[6] radio telephones, and radio navigation aids. Electricity has been installed in the majority of fishing craft. Better navigation charts, more accurate weather forecasting, and an improved system of navigation lights along the coast have improved the efficiency and safety of the fleet. Five government fishing schools train personnel in the technicalities of navigation, fishing and fish processing.

In 1959 there were 28,118 open motorized fishing vessels in operation totaling 79,430 gross tons and 12,692 decked motor craft totaling 309,979 gross tons.[7] In the last decade the number of open vessels has increased; since 1938 the number has doubled while the number of decked vessels has remained almost constant. The average size of the fishing vessels has increased as has the number of small trawlers and purse seiners attempting year around fishing. The largest vessels, trawlers over 300 tons, are based

primarily in Aalesund and Bergen, the most important ports in the herring fishery areas. The number of vessels in proportion to fish tonnage landed is much greater in North Norway than to the south of Trondheimfjord. The proximity of fishing banks to ports along the entire coast and the seasonality of the catch with two-thirds of the annual catch landed during the period from January to April has tended to keep the vessels small. Also the opposition of the small fisherman to large trawlers as a menace to his livelihood and strict government control over the licensing of these craft have prevented the anticipated increase in vessels of this type. Only 11 large trawlers were licensed in the immediate postwar period but increased to 30 with 27 vessels actually participating in 1958 (Table 2). The tonnage sold as fresh fish tripled from 1953 to 1958 but the total trawler catch fluctuated considerably.[8] The more progressive fishermen of the herring district favor increasing the licensing of large vessels, while those in the North Norway cod area are opposed. The fishing gear has not changed in type as much as in efficiency during the recent decades. Schools of fish can now be located as much as 100 miles offshore and with larger ships, echo sounders and mechanical equipment, significant catches can be obtained in these waters, especially of herring. Purse-seines have become very important in the herring fishery and were utilized experimentally in the Lofoten cod fishery but outlawed in 1960 as a result of pressure by small-scale fishermen. Other types of nets have been im-

[6]Equipment to detect location, direction of movement and depth of fish.

[7]Statistisk Aarbok for Norge 1960. Statistisk Sentralbyraa, Oslo, 1960, p. 72.

[8]MOLLESTAD, SVERRE, Stortraalernes Fiske i 1958, Fiskets Gang, November 26 (1959), p. 650.

Table 2: Norwegian Large Trawler Fishing
(Vessels over 300 gross tons)

	1953	1954	1955	1956	1957	1958
No. of Vessels	15	16	17	23	26	27
Average Vessel Size (Gross tons)	473	473	450	413	410	406
Crew Members	423	448	479	624	711	708
Total Catch (tons)	21,164	27,312	28,740	34,763	26,975	25,703
Total Value of Catch (1000 kr)	12,267	17,202	20,442	24,141	20,108	18,570

Source: MOLLESTAD, SVERRE, Stortraalernes Fiske i 1958. *Fiskets Gang*, No. 48, November 26, (1959), p. 650.

proved by using artificial fibers which are lighter and longer lasting.

The impact of improvements in equipment and vessels has been to decrease the number of marginal fishermen especially in the southern west coast district, increase the efficiency and total catch when the runs are heavy during the short cod and herring seasons, concentrate the major commercial efforts in larger ports like Aalesund, Bergen, Kristiansund, and Bodø, and to increase the range of the larger vessels. The rapidity of change is retarded by the opposition of the small-scale fishermen and the organizations that represent them.

CHANGES IN PROCESSING, MARKETING AND USE

The distribution of the catch amongst various kinds of uses depends upon the total catch and the market conditions for a given year (Table 3). The amount used for fish meal and oil varies from 60 percent of the total catch in 1956 (a good herring year) to 43 percent in 1958 (a poor herring year). The process-

ing of frozen fish on a significant scale has developed after World War II and the amount so used has steadily increased, particularly since the early 50's, and in fish other than herring. Frozen fish are now even sold widely in Norway especially the populous southeast. Large freezing plants have sprung up along the coast, several of which are run by fishermen's organizations and the government. The trend toward larger factories with their increased needs for raw materials to meet the market for canned fish, meal and oil, frozen and fresh products has helped to concentrate the processing in the larger fishing ports. Even the salting and drying of stockfish and klipfish,[9] traditionally dried on racks or rocks along several sections of the coast, are being increasingly artificially dried in the processing plants.

Another major change in this century has been the development of fishermen organizations (cooperatives) for the sale of fish as they are landed, for the export of fish and in-

[9]Stockfish are dried cod and klipfish are dried salted cod.

Table 3: Use of Norwegian Fish Catch by Per
Cent of Total Catch for Selected Years

	1948	1955	1956	1957	1958
Fresh.	20	12	8	10	12
Frozen	4	6	6	6	9
Salted	19	16	15	15	17
Dried (stockfish)	3	7	8	10	14
Canned	4	3	2	4	3
Meal & oil	49	55	60	54	43
Bait	1	1	1	1	2
	100	100	100	100	100
Total (Metric tons)	1,318,000	1,646,872	1,986,300	1,573,892	1,238,851

Source: Norges Offisielle Statistikk, Norges Fiskerier 1958. Fiskeridirektøren,
Bergen, 1960.

creasingly for processing. The first organization, the Norges Sildesalslag (Norway's Herring Sales Association), was founded in 1929. Many others for various kinds of fish sprang up in the 1930's and subsequent years. Now the landings of fish are almost completely sold by these organizations. Major accomplishments have been the stabilization of the price paid the fisherman for fish, protection of the rights of the fishermen, and in general making the occupation a more stable but more socialized occupation.

EXPORT TRENDS

The proportional value of fish and fish products has declined steadily from 25 percent of the total export value in the 1930's to 13.5 percent at present. The total value in Norwegian kroner however, during the period from 1938-1958, increased more than 6 fold. The relative importance of the export of the various fish products from year to year depends greatly upon variations in the catch and the market (Table 4). Herring and other fish meal and frozen and fresh herring fluctuate the greatest. There has been a steady increase in the amount of frozen fish and frozen fillets as well as stockfish. Salted and canned fish have remained relatively constant and klipfish have declined with the smaller cod catches. In 1960 the following were the leading fish exports by value: stockfish 20 pct., klipfish 12.6 pct., canned products from the sea 12.2 pct., herring meal 8.4 pct., frozen fillets 7.8 pct., fresh or iced fish 6.0 pct. and shellfish 5.1 pct. The major ports from Trondheim south to Stavanger are by far the principal export centers and this will continue if not increase if Norway develops greater dependence upon larger vessels and in general a larger scale type industry.

Western Europe and the U.S. continue to be the major consumers of Norwegian fish exports except for klipfish and stockfish which are sold

Table 4: Norway's Exports of Fish and Fish
Products by Types and Value
(1000 Norwegian kroner)

	1938	1946	1950	1956	1960
Fresh herring			34,771	26,558	17,135
Frozen herring	13,035	18,697	6,035	26,701	28,362
Fresh fish & fillets			30,858	44,560	65,357
Frozen fish & fillets	16,117	28,854	16,057	43,659	78,809
Round-frozen fish			9,819	32,522	44,198
Stockfish	18,918	29,301	54,528	149,075	201,549
Klipfish	22,136	60,816	116,126	177,620	126,852
Salted & spiced herring	7,917	63,529	47,363	84,924	38,719
Other salted fish (incl. roe)	3,431	46,531	12,184	10,841	16,492
Smoked fish	505	3,444	3,939	5,698	8,338
Shellfish fresh & frozen	4,119	7,588	14,330	25,161	51,436
Canned fish products	30,106	63,767	129,355	137,559	178,248
Fish meal	15,902	4,846	63,423	220,331	99,805
Herring oil	2,169	2,614	1,009	2,871	
Liver oil	14,001	44,559	55,542	39,593	46,183
Refined fish oil	—	—	32,931	4,919	
Other fish products	370	1,467	3,311	9,681	18,579
Total	148,726	375,473	616,140	1,042,273	1,020,032[1]

[1]Preliminary figure based on calculations from *Maanedsstatistikk over Utenrikshandelen*, December (1960) Statistisk Sentralbyraa, Oslo.

Source: Norges Fiskerier 1938-58. Fiskeridirektøren, Bergen

to sub-tropical or tropical and catholic countries. The Soviet Union is the major market for salt herring with East Germany and Czechoslovakia also significant buyers of fresh and frozen herring.

CHANGING FISHING LIMITS IN COASTAL WATERS

Norway's fishing limits in the coastal waters have been a most controversial question as they have in Iceland, the Soviet Bloc countries, and a number of other countries, in the postwar period. Norway followed Iceland's example in establishing a limit of four nautical miles and this was measured from a line connecting the mouths of fjords. The further extension of this limit has been favored by the North Norway fishermen whose livelihood is largely based on the resources of coastal waters where catches have been very unreliable in recent years because of the changing habits of fish due to changing biological conditions in the waters. They wish to eliminate the competition of other nations for the declining numbers of fish. The fishermen of South Norway, the herring district, favor the narrow limits as they are increasingly dependent upon distant waters and are fearful of reprisals.

This question has been under international study for a number of years. In the United Nations Conference on the Law of the Sea, Norway supported the Canadian proposal of a six-mile territorial limit and that an additional six miles be reserved for fishing. When this failed the Norwegians passed a law providing a 6 mile fishing limit effective April 1, 1961 and a 12 mile limit effective September 1, 1961. Norway then signed a bilateral agreement with Great Britain, the principal nation frequenting the Norwegian coast for trawling. This agreement provided a 6 mile limit effective September 1, 1961 and special privileges for British trawlers in the 6 to 12 mile area for the ten year period ending October 31, 1970. Vessels of Sweden, Denmark and the Faeroe Islands will be permitted to operate within the 6-12 mile limit, subject to Norwegian law. This does not solve the problem of the interests of West Germany, Poland, the U.S.S.R. and other nations in this zone. Six armed craft of the Norwegian Navy have been assigned to guard infractions of the 12 mile zone in the coastal waters from Cape Lindesnes on the extreme southwest coast.

The Norwegians themselves have been split over whether their own trawlers should be permitted in the 4-6 mile zone. Exceptions will be made to permit their operation in specified waters and at certain times of the year. In fact, as mentioned previously, there is considerable opposition to the licensing of large trawlers, those over 300 tons, for operation anywhere along the coast.

FUTURE

It appears inevitable that the role of fishing in the economy of Norway will continue to decrease in relative importance. The decline of the cod and herring catches seems destined to continue. Herring have disappeared in large quantities from the Norwegian coast for 35 to 70 years at a time in the past and the present trend may be the beginning of such a herring drought period.

The conservative small-scale fishermen have opposed modernization such as the increased use of large trawlers. Thus Norway has fallen behind other nations such as West Germany and the U.S.S.R. who are making elaborate plans for exploiting the world oceans with large mechanized fleets including well equipped processing ships. Increased control of larger areas of their coastal banks does not provide the answer. The Norwegians did carry out experiments with seven fishing vessels, a mother ship and a research vessel off West Africa from October-December, 1960. The results were only fair but indications are that Norway will undoubtedly widen the scope of her future fishing efforts to include new areas.

Norwegian fishing has undergone changes in modernization, in emphasis and distribution in this century but this traditional industry as a livelihood is destined to play a declining role in the total economy as industrialization and diversification increase. However, fish as a raw material for some of the coastal factories, as a domestic food, as an export product, as a full-time occupation for the more specialized and a part-time way of life for others will continue to be significant in the geography of Norway.

MONEY DOES GROW ON TREES

by
DANA L. THOMAS

A few months ago, Kroehler Mfg. Co. added a bit of spice to the goings-on at Chicago's International Home Furnishings Show. Taking an ordinary looking coffee table, the company subjected it to everything from glowing embers and scalding liquids to scuffing, nail polish and other abrasive elements. Lo and behold, it emerged from the torture chamber in tip-top shape. The secret: a manufacturing process, the likes of which no lumberman had ever seen before.

According to a Kroehler spokesman, the process is a multi-step affair which begins when the air is drawn from the pores of the wood and replaced with liquefied plastic. The table then is placed in an atomic reactor and bombarded with gamma rays, a procedure which causes the plastic to solidify. What emerges is a piece of furniture that combines the warmth and beauty of wood with the toughness and flexibility of plastic. While the process still is experimental, Kroehler feels that it is loaded with promise. So, apparently, does the Atomic Energy Commission, which recently asked Vitro Corp. to design a plant that will delve deeper into the subject of atomically treated woods.

SPACE AGE TECHNOLOGY

Striking as all this sounds, the idea of nuclear-powered furniture is merely one of the many exciting new concepts that have emerged of late from the country's lumber camps. Hard hit by the synthetics, plastics and wonder metals, the industry found itself in a profit skid. To get back to the right side of the ledger, it has turned to mergers, automation programs and new selling procedures, while at the same time, lashing back at its new competitors, it has reached into its labs and come up with some space age technology of its own.

From deep in the woodlands, for instance, the lumbermen have extracted wonder drugs, fertilizers, livestock feeds and a host of other by-products. Utilizing high-energy physics, polymer chemistry and high-speed computers, they have developed a dazzling array of prefinished panels, sidings and laminates, high fashion veneers and fire-retardant products, all of which are cutting a wide swath in a variety of new fields. To be sure, some of the industry's new products and processes are laboratory curiosities that have yet to prove themselves

"Money Does Grow on Trees" by Dana L. Thomas. Reprinted from Barron's *(November* 1, 1965), *p.* 3ff, *with permission of the publisher.*

in the marketplace. Still, most are promising, so much so that many a once-cautious insider sees big potential profits in the woodwork. As one recently put it: "Strange as it seems, this is beginning to look like a real growth industry."

Indeed it does. Last year, the nation's forest product companies shipped $2.7 billion worth of lumber, plywood, hardboard, pulp, paper and allied items. Over the past five years, their volume has been growing at an annual rate of 4.5%. Of the product they take each year from the tree, some 60% winds up at the paper and pulp mills. Three-quarters of the remainder — lumber, plywood, hardboard and particle-board — goes into residential and commercial construction. The rest is employed in furniture, automobiles, toys and the like.

PUBLICLY OWNED FIRMS

By and large, the business of producing these goods is dominated by publicly owned concerns. Among them are Weyerhaeuser, Georgia-Pacific, U.S. Plywood, International Paper, Crown Zellerbach, St. Regis Paper, Rayonier, Boise Cascade (which was listed on the NYSE this year), Pope & Talbot, Masonite, General Plywood, Potlatch Forests, E. L. Bruce (which announced plans last week to sell some of its operations to Armour & Co.), Carolina Pacific Plywood, Pacific Lumber, Edward Hines Lumber, Medford, Atlas General Industries and Evans Products. A number of non-lumber firms make specialty items for the wood industry. This group includes Koppers, National Starch & Chemical, Reichhold Chemicals and American Cyanamid.

Of late, sales and earnings of most of the woodworkers have been moving upward (see table). Last year, for instance, firms like Weyerhaeuser and Masonite chalked up record results. This year, business remains brisk and the reports impressive. In part, current gains reflect an increase in prices for West Coast lumber in August. The recently passed $7.5 billion housing bill, moreover, promises to give a lift to the construction business, still the largest single user of lumber and plywood.

Yet the strongest plank in the lumberman's success story comes from their own labs. Wood's position in the American scheme of things reached an all-time peak in the early 1900s, when lumber production rose to 45 billion board feet. Then came an outpouring of competitive materials and, by the end of World War II, wood had lost almost half of its potential market.

VANISHING MARKETS

To some extent, the decline was not the industry's fault. New concepts in home building virtually did away with front porches and substantially reduced the size of attics. The emergence of aluminum, plastics and the synthetics — i.e., asphalt for shingles, vinyl for floors, formica for table tops — added to the pressure. The industry, in the face of vanishing markets, seemed at loose ends. Promotional efforts were scant, research meager. And timberland resources, once seemingly limitless, began to dry up. As a result, from 1948 through 1960, after-tax earnings of the wood products industry — figured as a percentage of sales — plummeted from 9.9% to 1.7%.

Earnings of Selected Firms

	Revenues (In Millions)		Net Per Share	
	1965	1964	1965	1964
Boise Cascade				
9 mos. to Sept. 30	$306.98	$271.7	$2.61	$2.18
Evans Products				
9 mos. to Sept. 30	157.8	135.8	2.94	2.45
General Plywood				
9 mos. to July 31	9.7	a15	0.40	c0.08
Georgia-Pacific				
9 mos. to Sept. 30	426	401	2.45	2.24
Masonite				
Yr. to Aug. 31	92.6	94.8	2.70	2.92
Potlatch Forests				
6 mos. to June 30	98.5	90.8	0.83	0.81
Seaboard				
6 mos. to July 31	7.2	6.6	0.25	0.18
U.S. Plywood				
3 mos. to July 31	131.4	121.9	0.94	0.83
Weyerhaeuser				
9 mos. to Sept. 30	526.5	498.2	b1.94	1.70

a-Including operation of Kochton division sold in 1964;
b-0.14 a share attributable to change in accounting method;
c-deficit.

During the past few years, however, the decline has been checked and a comeback launched. First of all, the industry set out to broaden its capabilities. Companies like U.S. Plywood, that started out as distributors and later branched out into production, have been integrating backward by acquiring their own timberland. Firms like Weyerhaeuser, once mainly concerned with lumber, now are upgrading into finished products. As a result, today's major woodworkers own everything from timberlands to, in some cases, their own consumer outlets.

Hand in glove with these moves, the woodworkers have undertaken a massive plant modernization. Over the past five years, Masonite has doubled its investment in plant and equipment (from $89 million to $180 million), changing itself from a maker of unfinished hardboard into a firm which specializes in more profitable prefabricated lines. Weyerhaeuser also is spending heavily on new facilities: this year, capital outlays will climb over $120 million. Over the next three years, Weyerhaeuser expects to plunge another $275 million into capital improvements. Says George H. Weyerhaeuser, executive vice president, operations: "We are in the midst of a growth program which overshadows in size and scope anything this company has undertaken in its 65 years of existence."

FRESH LOOK AT MARKETING

In the process of upgrading itself, the industry also has taken a fresh look at marketing. At one point, the typical lumber firm simply made and shipped its products and left the selling to the retailer. Not any longer. Weyerhaeuser, for one, is adding dealers, providing architectural services, and even arranging consumer financing on new homes. Boise Cascade has acquired its own retail outlets; it now operates 100 Bestway Building Centers, each of which offers the amateur handyman and the housewife a complete home remodelling and improvement service. Boise also owns Kingsberry Homes, a prefab builder it acquired in 1964. U.S. Plywood, meanwhile, which just purchased a Hawaiian builder, also is participating in several West Coast real estate projects, in order, the firm says, to learn at first hand the problems of builders.

In the final analysis, however, an industry's fortunes depend on its products. And, in the lumber business, the major reason for the spirited comeback has been a renaissance in technology. A spokesman for one leading company notes: "Our competitors did us a great favor by awakening us not only to the threats of their products but also to modern concepts of research and technology." Says another: "We no longer consider ourselves in lumber, but rather in wood cellulosics." To ram home the point, scientists in dozens of fields — plastics, chemistry, atomic physics and computer mathematics, to name but a few — are pooling their skills these days and producing research breakthroughs in every phase of the business.

Their work begins in the forest. In the old days, when America's timberlands were virgin and no one worried about scarcities, trees were chopped down recklessly. Today, forests are looked upon as crops to be carefully harvested and replanted. Moreover, through a greater understanding of genetics, scientists are manipulating hereditary characteristics and actually controlling the growth of trees. And since trees are the slowest growing of all crops — they take 60 years and more to mature — research is stressing the breeding of faster growing specimens.

RADIOACTIVE SEEDLINGS

In Weyerhaeuser laboratories, for example, radioactive materials are being injected into seeds before they are put in the ground. Every 30 days they are checked by a geiger counter (which locates them easily enough: the seed triggers an electric buzz) and examined to determine which types are taking root successfully, which have been destroyed by animals or insects, and which have the best chance of growing into superior trees. Formerly, several years were necessary to determine whether a particular tree would be a slow or rapid grower. Now this can be foretold virtually from the start. Moreover, if a tree is doing poorly, scientists can use hormones to alter its characteristics.

To guarantee a supply of raw timber in perpetuity — which is the goal of every major firm — the industry is turning to computers. Using data assembled from the growth rates of thousands of trees, the electronic brains are telling management exactly how many trees to plant per acre, and where and how to plant them. There is a new look, too, in the harvest. Ingenious equipment has been developed to eliminate human labor. The day of the high climber, picturesquely topping a spar tree, is rapidly becoming a thing of the past.

MECHANIZED MONSTER

Among the new equipment is a Swiss unit that spirals up the trunk of a tree like a mechanical monkey, cutting off dead and dying branches with a chain saw. The industry also sports mechanical sky cars with diesel engines and winches, remote-controlled from the ground, that lift, hoist and carry logs in midair, much like a cable car hauls skiers over the Alps. International Paper has a mechanized monster that in one continuous operation fells a tree, delimbs it, cuts the trunk into five-foot lengths and loads them onto a truck for haulage to the lumber mill. The job, which is supervised by a single man, formerly required the services of at least six husky individuals.

Meanwhile, the traditional process of storing felled logs in ponds and floating them to the mill rapidly is becoming obsolete. To cut heavy losses from sinkage, lumber firms have been switching over to dry logging methods. Weyerhaeuser has a 60-ton mechanical behemoth that lifts a pile of logs 20 feet into the air, then drops it onto a freight car or a trailer. Lumberjacks used to

take more than a day to load a string of freight cars. Using the new methods, they now do the job in an hour.

HEADING OFF TERMITES

Once a tree has been felled and lugged to the mill, the wizardry of science takes over and transforms it into a host of wondrous products. One of the disadvantages of lumber — compared, that is, to aluminum and plastic — has been its age-old susceptibility to termites and fungi. To ward off such attackers, scientists typically inject chemicals into the wood. Unfortunately, while the chemicals have added 30 years to the life of the average plank, they give off an unpleasant odor and turn the wood an ugly brown, making it extremely difficult to paint.

However, Koppers, the leading name in the chemical preservation of wood, is exploiting a process that eliminates these headaches. Under its method, logs are rolled into huge steel cylinders, from which the air is removed to make the wood fibers more penetrable. Next a chemical, pentachlorophenol, is forced into the wood under heavy pressure. The gas is then permitted to escape, but the "penta" remains as a solid preservative, rendering the wood odorless and giving it an affinity for dazzling hues.

Poles that have been treated in this way are finding a thriving new use in the utility business. For years, the utilities have been fighting community pressure groups which complain about the unsightliness of overhead poles and attempt to drive them underground. Since underground installation entails greater costs, Koppers' poles, which can be dyed to conform to the aesthetics of virtually any community, are just what the doctor ordered. The colored poles have caught on in the South, and many of the big industrial cities of the North are beginning to express interest.

One of the big handicaps of lumber in the construction field has been its inflammability. However, a "wonder drug" has been developed that makes wood fire-resistant. A compound of ammonium salts, which is injected under pressure into the lumber, it gives off a carbon and water vapor that retards burning.

FIRE-RESISTANT STUDS

This ingenious "shot in the arm," combined with its low installation costs, has catapulted wood back into many markets that had been lost to steel and concrete. Fire-resistant wood studs are beginning to crop up in high-rise buildings, and insurance firms and local building codes which once used to insist on steel, concrete or masonry, now are giving their blessing to wood in one community after another.

Morton Salt recently replaced the concrete flooring in one plant with specially treated wood. Morton's insurance company decided, that since the wood was fire-resistant, it wouldn't demand a sprinkler system. As a result, the company was able to save over $1 per square foot.

Koppers also is pushing preserved woods into other fields and with some success. Washington, D.C., officials turned their backs on concrete and chose wood for the stadium constructed last year. Its chemically treated seat sections are color-matched to tickets, enabling patrons easily to find their way around the stadium. As an indication of this growing popularity of wood, Koppers reports that sales of its forest products division have doubled in the last 10 years.

In the battle with rival materials, wood always has suffered from a major liability: unlike plastics or metals, natural wood is not uniform. No two trees are exactly alike. Nor, for that matter, is any portion of a tree exactly like another. Owing to such unpredictability, woodworking for centuries has remained a handicraft.

SANDWICH OF WOOD

To lick the problem, scientists set out to develop man-made wood that could be machined to close tolerances. The first big breakthrough was plywood, a multiple deck sandwich of thin wood slices, which are peeled from a log like the skin of an apple. Glued together in alternate layers, with the grain in one running at right angles to that of the next, plywood is rigid, yet easily shaped, and, relative to its weight, actually structurally stronger than steel.

Yet, while demand for plywood has soared, not all producers have found it particularly profitable. The difficulty is basic. On the one hand, only Douglas fir, which grows on the West Coast, is fashioned easily and economically into plywood. On the other, the major markets are in the East. Thus transportation costs historically have eaten into profits.

Within the past 18 months, however, a technological advance has been scored that conceivably could revolutionize the profits picture. A commercially feasible way has been found to make plywood out of pine from the South. Though the Southern pine is far different from the Douglas fir, industry scientists have developed equipment capable of peeling the smaller logs (their diameters are less than a third those of the Douglas fir) and new adhesives that work with the heavily resined trees from the South.

The economic benefits could be substantial. For one thing, Southern pine has a fast growth rate and is more abundant than Douglas fir. Labor rates in the South are relatively low. And freight charges on goods shipped to the big consumer markets on the Eastern Seaboard will run about half the cost of plywood hauled from the Coast.

As might be expected, the wresting of plywood from pine has opened up vast new economic vistas for the South. Farmers are rushing into timber growing, lured, among other things, by the tax benefits. (It is possible to get capital gains treatment on timber profits.) Almost two million Southerners currently are growing trees. And the nation's major lumber firms have embarked on an active program of plant construction: at latest count, over 25 plywood plants are being planned or erected in Dixieland.

The pioneer, Georgia - Pacific, built its first plant in Arkansas as early as January 1964. Since then, business has been so good that the company already has enlarged the facility and started construction of a second. U.S. Plywood has three plants underway, while Weyerhaeuser, which has a facility in Plymouth, N.C., recently announced plans for a second.

UNUSED POTENTIAL

Still, the new versions of lumber and plywood, for all their techno-logical ingenuity, fail to utilize the full potential of the tree. For years, the industry pondered what to do about the chips and shavings that filled the sawmill floors. The pioneering achievement was that of William Mason, founder of Masonite Corp., who discovered a way to explode wood chips into their component fibers and then, by applying high temperatures and pressure, to reform the fibers into an extremely hard, dense board that had no grain or knotholes, took paints easily and could be machine-fabricated into any desired form.

While the first hardboards were relatively crude affairs, the industry has become conspicuously adept at turning the wastes into saleable products. Moreover, in recent years wood technologists have gone far beyond the original Mason process and are working with a wider variety of wastage than previously thought possible. For example, particleboard, a "homogenized" wood, is nothing more than slivers and flakes that have been rebound into sheets of board and processed much like paper.

To finish their reconstituted wood as inexpensively as possible, whole new groups of equipment have been designed, including infrared ovens for high-speed drying of freshly painted and enameled boards; to keep the wood from blistering, new high-velocity fans are employed. Using the infrared lamps, furniture parts and panellings can be dried in one-tenth the time it previously took.

As for the appearance of the man-made wood, industry researchers have turned their ugly duckling into a thing of beauty. Thanks to offset printing, they can simulate expensive wood grains and make cheap panelling look as though it has been inlaid with exquisite veneers. The industry also is using plastic and metal overlays to revolutionize the feel and appearances of surfaces. Embossed products are turned out by Masonite, for instance, which simulate travertine marble and other rare textures that once could be afforded only by the wealthy connoisseur.

Owing to this marriage with plastics and metals, wood is cropping up in many an industrial area, so many, in fact, that the industry's classic quip — "When home building sneezes, the lumber business gets pneumonia" — no longer holds water. U.S. Plywood, for one, is doing a thriving business with wood it has joined with aluminum for railroad piggyback containers. Recently, when the Association of American Railroads asked the company to develop a shipping container for radioactive materials, the firm came up with a plywood unit that survived 30-foot drops and passed the fire-resistant test with flaming colors.

METAL-LIKE WOOD

Masonite has introduced "Bene-lex," a wood that performs like metal but can be machined at a lower cost with woodworking tools. Used as a top for operating tables, the radiologically penetrable material facilitates the taking of X-rays during surgery. Another version replaces steel as insulating material in pipe organ consoles. Still another is used as a neutron shielding to enclose the gate of reactors in atomic energy plants.

Other man-made woods, decked out in new laminated combinations and finishes, are going into interior panelling of kitchen cabinets, television sets, furniture and toys. Weyerhaeuser has developed a molded wood — "Pres-Tock" — that serves as door panels, package trays and interiors in automobiles. U.S. Plywood has come up with Flexwood, a cloth-backed wood veneer found in the instrument panel and doors of the luxurious Chrysler Imperial.

Aided by these new markets, wood makers have been able to cut their dependence on new home building. The results make pleasant reading. For the last four years, U.S. Plywood's earnings have climbed steadily, even though the housing business has been erratic. Similarly, in these years, Masonite's sales have grown 13% faster than new home construction.

This is not to say that the industry is neglecting the construction market, which after all provides the major sources of its business. Indeed, working with Reichhold Chemicals, American Cyanamid, National Starch and others, the lumbermen have developed glues which retain their strength even in freezing weather. With them, the wood workers are able to laminate short lengths of cheap lumber together to form larger trusses and beams that, pound for pound, are actually stronger than some steels and can be bent, curved or arched into virtually any shape.

SOARING FREE

As a result, structural wood, hitherto hidden as sheathing underneath other materials, now is being displayed boldly as architectural ornamentation in schools, churches and office buildings. Parabolas, free-soaring cantilevers, winding staircases are highlighting this renaissance of wood as an aesthetic material — the first major resurgence since the Middle Ages. In fact, a whole new industry has mushroomed to deal in laminated beams and arches — the so-called "Glulam" industry. Not only are the new products ringing up brisk sales in the U.S., but also they are going in growing quantities to Western Europe and Japan.

FEWER CARPENTERS

Yet for all these advances, the industry still has its share of headaches. The aluminum, steel and plastic producers are continuing to wage a fierce battle for the consumer dollar and woodworkers will have to devote increasing sums and ingenuity to broaden their market position. At the same time, there is a growing shortage of carpenters and other craftsmen, on whom the wood industry relies. Then, too, wages are rising on every front. Just recently, the House Labor Committee voted to eliminate the minimum wage law exemption that had applied to 12-man forestry and logging operations.

To this and other problems, industry leaders have one answer — research. The potential, they maintain, merely has been scratched. Fully half of the log still is carted away as waste. Accordingly, wood people are busily enlarging their laboratories and bolstering their technical staffs. Masonite, which has opened a research center at St. Charles, Ill., is plowing $1 million annually into R&D. St. Regis, which built a technical center at West Nyack, N.Y., three years ago, already has doubled its size.

Among others, the industry is counting on success in the area of chemical by-products. Tree scientists long have studied lignin, the mysterious substance nature uses as a binder in a natural wood. Out of lignin, a whole new field — the silvicultural chemical industry — is springing up. Weyerhaeuser and Georgia Pacific, among others, have developed an extract that is used as a mud additive in oil well drilling. Others have discovered that the lignin, which combines readily with minerals in the soil, provides superior nourishment for plants and makes a red-hot fertilizer.

SUGAR AND EXPLOSIVES

Meanwhile, through a special percolating process, wood chemists have extracted from chips a sticky molasses-like substance which, when fermented, yields a glycerine that can be used in the manufacture of cosmetics and explosives. Masonite has been experimenting with a way of producing sugar out of waste chips. At Weyerhaeuser, the "men in white" have come up with a technique to extract acetic acid from the residue of pulp mills; the firm plans to build a $1 million plant to make the acid for the plastics industry.

Perhaps the most publicized by-product of all is Crown Zellerbach's DMSO, a drug which, because of its unusual ability to penetrate the skin, was thought to be useful in the treatment of bursitis, arthritis and burns. After several years of research, the company recently ended clinical studies following termination of its FDA authority. At the moment, it is studying the compound's action in the control of plant diseases.

EYE ON THE BALL

While some enthusiasts prophesy that chemical by-products eventually will bring in high profits, the main focus of the industry's research still is on wood, and here the most ultra-sophisticated research techniques are under development. Scientists are bringing the mysteries of the laser, maser and cobalt to wood. In U.S. Plywood's lab at Brewster, N.Y., where once only woodworking specialists toiled, experts in over a dozen different fields of science have gathered to pool their knowledge. Their most recent breakthrough: new accoustical properties for wood, a discovery they hope soon to turn to commercial use. Earlier, they had scored with a siding for home construction, PF-L, which, laminated with Du-Pont's Tedlar, a tough plastic, reportedly need never be painted.

Another "first" recently was scored by Georgia-Pacific, which fabricated a sheet of plywood that was as high as a 20-story building to be used as a floating walkway from shore to a deep-water float in Puget Sound. Usually, plywood is extended by joining standard panels. Georgia-Pacific technicians tried another tack and turned out a mammoth continuous sheet. For good measure, they coated it with synthetic rubber, to form a non-slip walking surface. To transport it, the owners took possession at the mill and simply towed the 200-foot walkway to the docksite.

BRIGHT PROSPECTS

In short, prospects for wood are brighter than ever. Thanks to the magic of technology, the industry is beginning to free itself from the erratic profit swings of the past. Part of its success comes from its own resourcefulness, part from the inimitable qualities of the material with which it works. As one spokesman has put it: "If scientists had invented the tree, they would have called it the miracle of the ages."

FACTORS IN THE LOCATION OF THE
PAPERBOARD CONTAINER INDUSTRY

Howard A. Stafford, Jr.

Mr. Stafford is a candidate for the Ph.D. degree at the State University of Iowa.

THE manner in which an industry responds to locational stimuli depends in large part on the nature of the industry, a situation which gives rise to a considerable element of uniqueness in the locational patterns of various industries. Unfortunately, there exists no general theory in which all locational patterns may be considered simultaneously. Therefore, partial analyses, each concerned with a particular industry, are desirable. The purpose of this study is to analyze the locational pattern of a specific industry, the paperboard container industry. The analysis involves three kinds of operations: (1) definition of the phenomenon to be analyzed, (2) identification of the locations in which that phenomenon appears, and (3) accounting for the existence of the locational pattern.

DEFINITION AND LOCATION

Descriptions employed by the United States Bureau of the Census are used to define the paperboard container industry. The census industrial classification number is 267 (which includes subclasses 2671 and 2674). The descriptions are as follows:[1]

> 267—Paperboard Containers and Boxes: Paperboard boxes (folded, set-up and corrugated), fiber cans, tubes, drums, and similar products.

[1] U. S. Department of Commerce, Bureau of the Census, *Census of Manufactures*, 1947, Vol. II, *Statistics by Industry* (Washington: U. S. Government Printing Office, 1949), p. 332.

> 2671—Paperboard Boxes—Folded, Set-up and Corrugated: This industry comprises establishments primarily engaged in manufacturing paperboard containers or boxes from paperboard or fiber stock. The chief products of this industry are folding paper boxes and cartons, set-up boxes and corrugated and solid fiber shipping containers from paperboard or fiber stock.

> 2674—Fiber Cans, Tubes, Drums, and Similar Products: This industry manufactures fiber cans, cones, cores, mailing cases, ribbon-blocks, spools, tubes, drums, and similar products from paperboard.

At the outset it was thought desirable to restrict the analysis to the continental United States. The reasoning involved in the construction of the hypotheses accepts the premises of the American economic system and is not necessarily applicable to other parts of the world. The hypotheses apply to the United States as a whole and they contemplate the use of counties as areal statistical units. Unfortunately, however, county data are not available for the entire United States, nor are data available for the whole of the industry under consideration. Mapping and testing are, therefore, limited to such figures as are presented for the 471 "large" counties

"Factors in the Location of the Paperboard Container Industry" by Howard A. Stafford, Jr. Reprinted from Economic Geography, *Vol.* 36 *(July* 1960*), pp.* 260–266, *with permission of the editor.*

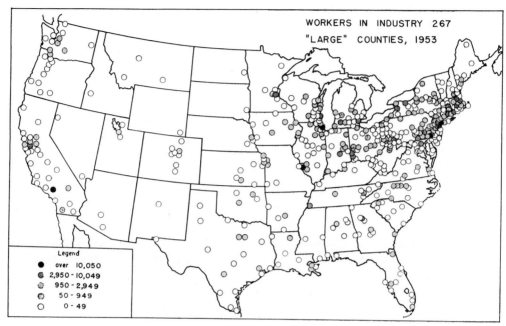

FIG. 1.

for which data are presented in *County Business Patterns for 1953*.[2]

The magnitude of an industry can be measured in a number of ways that are familiar to all students of economic geography. For this study the number of workers employed in Industry 267 is used.[3] Spatial variations in the location of workers in the paperboard container industry in 1953 (for those 471 counties for which data are available) are shown graphically on Figure 1.

Since these 471 "large" counties include about 92 per cent of all workers in the industry in 1953, it is assumed that the distribution depicted by Figure 1 is representative of the industry as a whole. All of the more important concentrations are shown.

The literature of industrial location theory states that three major types of cost factors generally determine industrial location. These are the costs of (1) obtaining materials, (2) hiring labor, and (3) marketing the products.[4] Transportation costs are of great importance in the locational process; but they are not considered as independent variables in the present hypotheses, which are expressed primarily in terms of nearness rather than cost. It is desir-

[2] U. S. Department of Commerce, Bureau of the Census, and the Department of Health, Education, and Welfare, Bureau of Old-Age and Survivors Insurance, *County Business Patterns, First Quarter, 1953* (Washington: U. S. Government Printing Office, 1955). The "large" counties are chosen primarily on the basis of a large number of reporting units. A reporting unit is, generally, a single establishment or a group of similar establishments of one employer. A complete description can be obtained from the "General Explanations" section of any volume. The actual number of "large" counties listed is 480. However, in order to keep the universe on a somewhat comparable scale throughout, certain combinations of counties are not included in this study, thus reducing the number to 471.

[3] Workers are classified in regard to their place of employment rather than to their place of residence.

[4] Other cost factors, for example power costs, could be mentioned. The three cited seem to be, however, the most important in a general sense and are those most often mentioned in the literature. Two excellent references on locational factors are Melvin L. Greenhut: *Plant Location in Theory and in Practice* (Chapel Hill: The University of North Carolina Press, 1956) and Walter Isard: *Location and Space-Economy* (New York: The Technology Press of M.I.T. and John Wiley and Sons, Inc., 1956).

able to establish the manner in which variations in these three major types of costs may affect locational patterns.

DEVELOPMENT OF THE GENERAL HYPOTHESIS

Nearness to markets appears to be of greatest importance in the location of the paperboard container industry. Establishments are said to seek market locations for two reasons: (1) to minimize transportation costs on shipping the finished products, and (2) to provide better service to customers.

Location theory, especially as advanced by Weber, indicates that high transportation costs are an important locational determinant for the set-up container segment of the industry. According to Weber's analysis, the increase in bulk (of the finished product over the materials) is tantamount to an increase in weight, thus increasing the relative importance of marketing costs and forcing firms to locate near their markets in order to minimize total outlays for transportation.[5] The hypothesis, therefore, may be advanced that the set-up-box segment is positively associated, in space, with the markets for its products.

It also appears that savings in transportation costs will be realized by the shipping container segment of the industry if it locates near its customers. Such an orientation would not be due to an appreciable increase in bulk, since shipping containers are transported "knocked down"; but the savings would accrue from locations near markets because of a rather unique system of pricing the major raw materials used in making shipping containers. These materials are virgin kraft and corrugat-

ing papers. Ninety per cent of the cost of materials for shipping containers lies in the purchase of virgin kraft and corrugating papers; and the *delivered prices for these materials are maintained at the same level throughout the United States, regardless of distances from the mill.*[6] It is, therefore, impossible for the manufacturer of paperboard shipping containers to effect any savings in transportation costs by moving closer to his supplier. Since the other materials he uses, such as cornstarch, stitching wire, cloth and paper tape, ink, and twine are of minor importance in his operations, the only significant savings he can make in terms of transportation costs must be in terms of minimizing his marketing costs. Under these conditions, a market orientation hypothesis, already advanced for the set-up container segment of the industry, seems also to be applicable to the knocked-down container segment.

The second major reason for the paperboard container industry locating near its markets arises out of its function as a "service industry." As with nearly all services, such an industry would tend to locate near its markets in order to serve its customers better. Fast, efficient, competent service would seem to be quite advantageous in this highly competitive field. Two aspects of this service feature are worth noting. First, most users of paperboard containers do not keep large stocks on hand, mainly because of the large space requirements they entail. Box makers often must supply customers on short notice; and distance from those customers is often a critical element in their ability to serve those customers promptly. Secondly, further service features arise from the fact that each producer has his own relatively unique

[5] For a detailed discussion of "transport orientation" see C. J. Friedrick (ed.): *Alfred Weber's Theory of Location of Industries* (Chicago: The University of Chicago Press, 1929).

[6] This statement has been verified by interviews with industry executives.

packaging problems. The paperboard container industry has been characterized as a job-order business.

In summary, it appears that a market orientation for the major segments of the paperboard container industry in the United States can be rationalized in terms of profit maximization to the entrepreneures through savings in transportation costs and also in terms of faster, more personalized service to customers. The general hypothesis may be formally stated as follows: The magnitude of the paperboard container industry will vary directly with variations in the magnitude of its markets.

TESTING OF THE HYPOTHESIS

Now that the operation of the mechanism which determines locational patterns in the paperboard container industry has been hypothesized, it is desirable that the hypothesis be subjected to tests which will give some quantified measure of its validity. "The proof of a hypothesis is the testing of the hypothesis."[7]

There is, of course, no body of data that can be used to measure directly the importance and location of the markets simply because these kinds of information are regarded as confidential in the United States and are almost never released for public use. It is, therefore, necessary to discover substitute measures that are acceptable.

A large percentage of the goods consumed by the general public are packaged in paperboard containers, but it is not correct to assume orientation with respect to a general consumer market; practically all of the purchasers of the products of this industry are other manufacturers including, of course, those who produce consumer goods. When a

search is made for variables that will best measure the markets for the paperboard container industry, it is not surprising that employment data for the major groups of manufacturing industries seem best suited to the task.

Six separate industry groups comprise major markets for the products of Industry 267: Food (Standard Industrial Classification Number 20); Textiles (No. 22); Apparel (No. 23); Furniture (No. 25); Machinery, except electrical (No. 35); and Machinery, electrical (No. 36).[8] There are, of course, many other industries which constitute markets of varying magnitude. Furthermore, other segments of our economy, such as retail and wholesale trade, purchase new paperboard containers. But to include all of these is not practicable, and therefore the original test of the hypotheses is restricted to measurements of spatial variation among the above mentioned industrial groups. If the association between Industry 267 and its major markets tends to substantiate the general hypothesis, the inclusion of more variables can only serve to make the statistical association more intense. While such a consequence is not at all undesirable, it is considered desirable to keep the analysis as simple as possible. The remainder of manufacturing industries cannot be ignored entirely, however, and a single additional variable, total workers in manufacturing, is included in the analysis. Its inclusion recognizes, in a general way, the fact that almost all industry uses paperboard containers in one way or another.

A more specific subhypothesis may be set up, therefore, to permit a more precise test of the general market orientation hypothesis: the areal distribution of Industry 267 will vary

[7] J. W. Mayne: "Role of Statistics in Scientific Research," *Scientif. Monthly*, January, 1957, p. 28.

[8] "End Use Distribution of Selected Containers," *Modern Packaging, Encyclopedia Issue, 1956* (Bristol, Conn.: Packaging Catalog Corp., November, 1955), p. 47.

TABLE I

Mean and standard deviations (in hundreds of workers) of the variables used in the analysis of locations of industry 267 (1953)

Variable	Mean ($\bar{x}$)	Standard deviation (σ)
Food (No. 20)	23.83	65.72
Textiles (No. 22)	16.72	45.34
Apparel (No. 23)	22.50	166.82
Furniture (No. 25)	6.00	18.65
Machinery, except electrical (No. 35)................	33.70	93.62
Machinery, electrical (No. 36)	21.43	81.58
Total Workers in Manufacturing...................	30.90	81.88
Paperboard Containers (No. 267)...............	2.78	9.10

directly with the number of workers in Food (No. 20); Textiles (No. 22); Apparel (No. 23); Furniture (No. 25); Machinery, except electrical (No. 35); Machinery, electrical (No. 36); and Total Workers in Manufacturing. Data for the variables for each of the counties in the universe can be obtained from the same source as the data for the dependent variable.[9] From these data the mean and standard deviation have been computed for each variable. These arithmetic averages and their measures of dispersion are presented in Table I.

Simple coefficients of correlation (r) have been computed to measure the degree of association between Industry 267 and the seven independent variables. These coefficients are listed in Table II. Coefficients of determination (r²) also have been computed to indicate what portions of the variations in the paperboard container industry can be related statistically to variations in each of the independent variables. It appears that approximately 81 per cent of the spatial variation in Industry 267 can be "explained," in terms of concomitant occurrence, by variations in the location of the food industry (No.

[9] U. S. Department of Commerce, Bureau of the Census, and the Department of Health, Education and Welfare, Bureau of Old Age and Survivor's Insurance, *op. cit.*

20). Approximately 77 per cent also can be "explained" by the variations in total workers in manufacturing.

Even though the simple coefficients of correlation between the paperboard container industry and both the food industry and total workers in manufacturing are relatively high, it is felt that a more accurate description of the spatial variations in the location of the paperboard container industry in terms of concomitant occurrence with other phenomena can be obtained by taking all seven independent variables into account simultaneously.

To perform this task a system of multiple correlation has been employed. A multiple coefficient of correlation (R) can be found and a test of statistical significance applied to the independent variables. The 95 per cent confidence level has been used, and those variables not significant eliminated. However, the insignificant variables have been eliminated one at a time beginning with the lowest, since it is possible that a variable which is not significant in a certain combination may become significant after one of the insignificant variables has been dropped. In this system, if two variables measure essentially the same thing, only one appears as significant. (It should be mentioned that such variables are labeled "not significant" only in a statistical sense and only at the chosen level of confidence.)

TABLE II

Coefficients of correlation and determination between locational data for industry 267 and various other industries (1953)

Variable	r	r²
Food (No. 20)......................	.900	.810
Textiles (No. 22)....................	.473	.224
Apparel (No. 23)....................	.748	.558
Furniture (No. 25)..................	.814	.662
Machinery, except electrical (No. 35)..	.654	.427
Machinery, electrical (No. 36)........	.820	.673
Total Workers in Manufacturing......	.878	.771

Final results of the multiple correlation are summarized in Table III.

These computations make it possible to eliminate three variables from the analysis without reducing to any great extent the amount of statistical explanation afforded by the combination of the eight variables of the hypothesis. The variables excluded from the analysis are Furniture (No. 25), Machinery, except electrical (No. 35), and Total Workers in Manufacturing. The coefficient of multiple correlation (R) for all eight variables is .941, and the explained variance is almost 89 per cent. After dropping the three above mentioned variables the "R" declines only to .940 and the explained variance declines only two-tenths of one per cent.

The coefficient of multiple correlation (R = .940) is higher than any of the simple coefficients. The explained variance of 88 per cent indicates a high degree of relationship between the industry and the variables which are thought to measure the existence of markets for paperboard containers. This result tends to substantiate the general hypothesis of market orientation.

The multiple regression equation for the dependent variable and four independent variables is:

$$Y_c = .0601(X_1) + .0219(X_2) + .0154(X_3) + .0313(X_4) - .0400$$

where Y_c is the estimated number of workers employed in Industry 267 and the symbols in parentheses refer to the industries for which actual numbers of workers are substituted in predicting for each statistical unit. The numbers preceding the parentheses are weights applied to the number of workers in each of these industries in order to predict most accurately on the average. In the equation, (X_1) refers to Food, (X_2) to Textiles, (X_3) to Apparel, and (X_4) to Electrical Machinery.

TABLE III

RESULTS OF MULTIPLE CORRELATION AND REGRESSION ANALYSIS (5 VARIABLES)

Variable	Beta	t	Significant*
Food (20)	.4343	12.5520	yes
Textiles (22).............	.1092	6.3121	yes
Apparel (23)............	.2825	14.1250	yes
Machinery, electrical (36)	.2811	9.3700	yes
R = .940			yes**
R² = .884			

*The least significant value of t is 1.965.
**The least significant value of R with N = 471 and m = 5 is .145.

An estimate for each of the 471 counties in the universe can then be made from the regression equation. Deviations of the predicted values from the actual values are noted $(Y_c - Y)$. The standard error of estimate $(S_{y.1234})$ has been computed and found to be substantially lower than the standard deviation of the distribution of the dependent variable. The standard deviation of Industry 267 is 9.10 (00's) while the standard error of estimate is only 3.09 (00's). In other words, on the average better predictions can be obtained from the regression equation than from the mean of the dependent variable.

Deviations of the actual values from the predicted values $(Y_c - Y)$ have been placed in their respective counties as shown on Figure 2 (Accuracy of Estimate Map). Those counties of over- or under-prediction of more than one standard error are specifically noted. The chief purpose of mapping the performance of the regression equation is to gain an insight into some other relevant variables that might further explain the distribution of Industry 267.

A comparison of Figures 1 and 2 reveals that the regression equation predicts well for those counties with very few workers in the paperboard container industry. A cursory examination reveals that, for the most part, these counties have very little manufacturing of any kind. These observations seem to strengthen the hypothesis that there

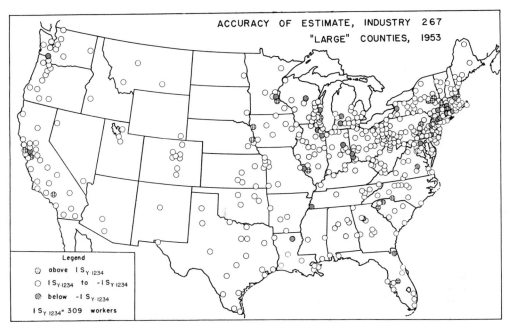

ACCURACY OF ESTIMATE, INDUSTRY 267
"LARGE" COUNTIES, 1953

Legend
$\oplus$ above $IS_{Y\cdot 1234}$
$\bigcirc$ $IS_{Y\cdot 1234}$ to $-IS_{Y\cdot 1234}$
$\circledast$ below $-IS_{Y\cdot 1234}$
$IS_{Y\cdot 1234}=$ 309 workers

FIG. 2.

will not be many workers in Industry 267 in those areas that do not provide markets. Areas of extreme over- or under-prediction are generally counties of moderate to heavy concentrations of workers in the industry. There are, of course, counties that have many workers in Industry 267, such as those in Chicago and New York City areas, which are very well predicted.

To obtain a complete analysis of any particular county requires a detailed study of that area and consideration of many more variables. However, to increase the ability to predict more accurately for the industry as a whole, attention should be directed primarily to those variables which appear to be of importance in those counties of extreme over- or under-prediction.

The inability to estimate well in certain counties may not be due to deficiencies in the market orientation hypothesis or in the variables used in the statistical analysis. The poor estimations may stem from the fact that mar-

ket areas for paperboard container plants do not necessarily follow county boundaries. It is quite possible that a container producer may be located immediately adjacent to his market, but be separated from it by a county boundary, leaving the association completely unmeasured by the data. It appears that such situations might actually exist in several cases where counties of over- and under-prediction are adjacent. Prominent examples appear in certain counties just outside New York City, in Connecticut and Massachusetts, and in the St. Louis and San Francisco areas.

Problems and procedures involved in the analysis of the paperboard container industry resemble closely those that appear in many aspects of research in economic geography. Progress in that discipline has often been said to depend on the discovery of generalizations that can be elaborated only after many studies of these types have been made.

The present study may constitute a small contribution to that end.

Intensive Subsistence Agriculture

Extending in an arc from India to Japan, and including many of the world's regions of the densest and least economically developed population, is an area where intensive subsistence agriculture is the dominant rural occupation. This is a region of small, fragmented land holdings, with parcels of less than an acre being common. It is a region of primitive farming devices and essentially noncommercial systems, where the use of labor-saving, capital-intensive technology common in Western agriculture is restricted by the farmer's lack of purchasing power and scale of operation. Highly inefficient by the measure of output per worker, it is effective in feeding large numbers by maximizing the most abundant (and least costly) input — labor. This type of agriculture may, under ideal conditions, be considered efficient if measured by the yield of food per acre.

This type of subsistence agriculture is characterized by the dominance of rice and a sparsity of livestock. Although other crops are also important, rice is the agricultural mainstay, with most of it being consumed within the region. Although termed "subsistence," much of the rice and other products of this system enters into trade, at least locally. Several producing nations export surpluses, primarily to neighboring areas with a food deficit.

Measured by volume produced, the products of subsistence agriculture make up a significant portion of the world's total agricultural output. Intensive subsistence agriculture is especially important when measured by the number of people supported. Moreover, this region of subsistence agriculture is an important segment of that portion of the world which is struggling to rise to a higher level of economic productivity.

The objective of the following articles is to aid in an understanding of the importance of the various subsistence crops and the processes and systems under which they are produced. Barton presents a fine statement of the processes and techniques involved in the various rice growing systems. There is significant variation in the productivity of differing systems, as well as in the amount of land occupied by each. Complementing this is Bennett's article which discusses the relative importance of the several commodities which the intensive systems produce. Both papers relate the impact of physical and cultural features on the technical system. When reading these two articles, the student is urged to recall the related ideas contained in the first section, "Population and Resources."

GROWING RICE IN THAILAND*

THOMAS FRANK BARTON

Indiana University

Relative Importance

IN THAILAND one of the morning greetings is *Ghin kao laael yung*. Translated, this greeting means "Have you eaten rice?" or "Have you had something to eat?" And in Thailand if you are an Asian and you have eaten, you have had rice.

On the average, a Thai consumes about 1.2 pounds of rice per day.[1] Perhaps it is more meaningful to say that in four months a Thai eats a quantity equivalent in weight to that of his body. In a year the rice he consumes will amount to about three times that of his body weight.

Although Thailand is one of the largest export rice producing countries in Asia, so much is consumed within the country that only about one and one-third million tons are available for export.[2] Yet between 40 and 50 per cent of the country's total income from export is from the sale of rice.

Throughout its written history, Thailand has always had an agricultural economy. About 80 per cent of Thailand's working population is engaged in agricultural activities, and, according to the latest surveys, more than four-fifths of the Thai farmers own their own farms. These contain approximately nine-tenths of all the cultivated land in the country,[3] and *paddy*[4] is the principal cash crop on most of these farms. (Nearly all farmers raise the rice they eat.)

Rice Producing Areas

In spite of the emphasis on production and the intensive use of land, most of the rice areas are comparatively small, vary in size, and are scattered throughout the country (Fig. 1). Even the largest and most wide-spread farm areas occupy clearings in the forest and jungle. In 1950 land held in farms amounted to less than one-fifth of the entire domain. The country's total area is approximately 198,000 square miles or about 127 million acres. Of this, only about 23 million acres are classified as "farm holding land" (land held in farms).[5] As late as 1950

---

* Most of the basic concepts in this paper are a part of an illustrated lecture entitled "The Rice Industry of Thailand" which was presented as the National Council for Geographic Education banquet address at St. Louis on November 29, 1957.

Through the courtesies received from President Saroj Busari, the College of Education, Krung Thep, Thailand, and many other Thai, this article is based on seasonal field observations made in 51 of Thailand's 71 changwats during a two year period (June, 1955 to May, 1957).

[1] Ladejinsky, W. I., "Thailand's Agricultural Economy," *Foreign Agriculture*, VI (1952), 169.

[2] Between 1949-1956 the average annual production amounted to about 7.1 million metric tons and the annual export was 1.3 million metric tons.

[3] Three general references printed in English by the Thailand Ministry of Agriculture, Division of Agricultural Economics are: (1) *Areas of Thailand by Province and Region, 1950;* (2) *Thailand Economic Farm Survey, 1953;* and (3) *Agricultural Statistics of Thailand, 1955.*

[4] In Thailand *paddy* refers to rough, unhulled rice (grains) and to the small diked fields in which lowland irrigated rice is grown. Also in Thailand, paddy is spelled *padi. Padi* fields are small diked fields.

[5] Thailand Ministry of Agriculture, Division of Agricultural Economics, *Areas of Thailand by Province and Region, 1950.*

"Growing Rice in Thailand" by Thomas Frank Barton. Reprinted from Journal of Geography, *Vol. LIX (April 1960), pp. 153–164, with permission of author and editor.*

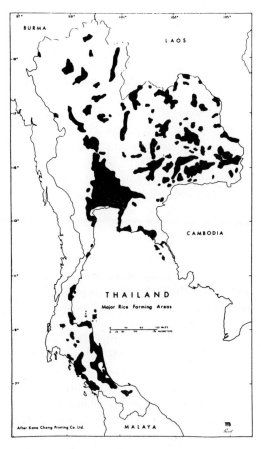

BURMA

LAOS

CAMBODIA

THAILAND
Major Rice Farming Areas

MALAYA

After Kona Chang Printing Co. Ltd.

FIG. 1

nearly three-fifths of the country was still a part of the public domain and classified as "forest land."

About 64 per cent (about 15 million acres) of the land held in farms is planted to paddy. This means that in the entire country less than one acre in eight produces rice. In contrast upland crops and tree crops occupy less than 4 per cent of the total area of the country.

The most extensive and productive rice producing region is found on the delta and flood plain of the Chao Phraya River in the southern part of the Central Plain Region. This alluvial plain, which is sometimes called the Bangkok Plain, is just north of the mangrove swamps which border the seaward and salty margins of the delta.

Types of Rice Cultivation

The Thai raise three general types of rice, namely (1) garden (in small plots), (2) floating or deep-water, and (3) upland. Methods of rice cultivation vary according to established customs and to the amount and availability of water. The latter in turn varies because of differences in rainfall (and other weather conditions), topography, and soil.

Sometimes the term wetland and dryland are applied to rice production. Wetland rice requires natural flooding and/or irrigation. Most varieties of rice grown in irrigated fields need about 70 inches of water to make a good yield, yet most changwats (provinces) receive less than 60 inches of rainfall. Consequently, wetland rice fields must receive water from the run-off of non-cultivated land in addition to direct rainfall. Both garden and floating rice are types of wetland cultivation. Dryland, or upland, rice is not irrigated; the crop must develop on the limited amount of water which falls as rain.

Three methods are used to plant this crop. Upland rice is usually planted by dibbling. The broadcasting method is used for both floating and garden types. Only the garden rice is transplanted. Statistics are not available concerning the number of acres planted to each of these three types or the relative number of acres planted by each of these methods. However, it is estimated that the upland type totals less than ten per cent (perhaps as low as five per cent) of the entire yield and that about 80 per cent of the wetland rice is transplanted.

Upland Rice[6]

Upland rice is grown by hill people

[6] Any crop grown in Thailand without the aid of irrigation is called an upland or dryland crop. The terms "dryland rice" and "upland rice" are used interchangeably.

and by pioneers who are making permanent clearings in the forest. Thus this type is found on the margins of wetland rice areas. More specifically, it is grown: (1) in the hills adjacent to the floodplains; (2) along new transportation lines where the forests are being cleared and the land occupied permanently; (3) in temporary clearings which have been cut in the forest and jungle which border all wetland rice producing areas, and (4) in wooded areas near rather extensive grazing lands. Some farmers in Northeast Thailand make a living primarily by raising livestock and enough rice in small paddies for family use. Nearly all of the crop grown by this method is used for subsistence or as seed.

The upland fields are found interspersed in the forests and not in grassy areas. With their simple tools, the farmers can remove the forest vegetation but not cogan grass. In addition, the surrounding forest and jungle reduce the wind velocity and protect the crop and field from excessive evaporation. The farmers believe that in these clearings the humidity is higher.

Regardless of the site selected, the fields for the growth of upland rice are prepared in the same general way. The farmer selects his potential fields early in the dry season after he has harvested his previous year's crop. At this time the vegetation is not dripping wet and some of the trees and vines will be without their leaves. Insects and disease are less prevalent. Trees are "ringed." Some of the trees which die and dry out more quickly than others are cut.[7] Brush is chopped down with a sturdy short-bladed knife used as an ax. It is then piled haphazardly in wind rows or around fallen trees to facilitate burning.

At the end of the five or six months' dry season, the vegetation and jungle floor are extremely dry and the clearing is burnt in April or May just before the rains come. The plant nutrients in the wood ash plus the nutrients stored in the ground from the decay of leaves prove sufficient for one good crop and perhaps a poorer second crop.

Either just before[8] or after the early rains moisten the soil, the farmer plants the newly cleared land by using a pointed bamboo stick or an iron-tipped tool. Holding the stick in one hand, he jabs it into the ground, making holes about an inch deep. With his other hand, he drops a few unsprouted rice seeds in it and closes the hole with his foot. Upland rice requires only a four month, or less, moist growing season.

Perhaps twice during the growing season the farmer weeds and pulls up or cuts down the tree suckers. This removal conserves the limited moisture for the grain and keeps the rice plants from being choked out. After the first or second year, the field is abandoned unless it is to become a permanent clearing where paddy fields are constructed by building dikes to hold the water. When the former practice is followed, this method of regularly abandoning fields is called "shifting cultivation." This type of farming is: (1) very destructive to forests and is the antithesis of proper forestry management; (2) produces sheet, rill and gully erosion; and (3) contributes to the erratic flow of the rivers.

Often the cultivator lives some distance from his small clearings. The fields require little labor. Once the land is cutover, it only takes a few days to burn the slash. Later, a few days at a time with long intervals between are spent in planting, weeding, cutting and threshing. Some build a temporary shelter adjacent

[7] In new clearings along a new highway leading to the Chainat Dam which is only about 165 miles north of Krung Thep, I saw gasoline-motored chain saws in operation during the dry season of 1957.

[8] Thailand Ministry of Agriculture, *Agriculture in Thailand*, Bangkok, Thailand, 1957, 5.

to or in the field. However, this is seldom occupied for more than a few weeks during the year.

Wetland Rice

Plowing. Whether the rice is planted by broadcasting or transplanting, the first step is to plow the land as early as possible in the rainy season. With the exception of peninsular Thailand, the rainy season starts in May or June. Cultivation begins several weeks after the rains come. The first precipitation is absorbed quickly by the parched and baked earth. During the dry season, often lasting five to seven months, the fields can become so dry and hard that it is nearly impossible to sink a mattock in the ground. The water table drops and deep cracks appear. Most of the buffalo mud wallows, ponds, intermittent lakes and swamps, ditches and small canals are dry. Some types of fish burrow down into the ground to find moist conditions where they can stay alive. Consequently the first rains do not make the ground soft enough to plow unless the fields also receive run-off. Moisture from the first rains runs into the cracks; the soil swells and the ground becomes water tight again. Then the water from later rains, and/or irrigation ditches, standing in the fields a few days or weeks softens the ground and kills the weeds.

As a rule plowing does not start until June, and most of it takes place in early July or later if the rains do not start in May or are inadequate in amount. Some plowing is done during the cool season of December, January, and February if irrigation water is available in sufficient quantity to permit the growing of two crops per year or where on-shore winds of the winter monsoon bring rains to the eastern part of peninsular Thailand.

Nursery beds. The farmer selects one of his most accessible and fertile fields near his compound (farmstead) or at the edge of the village as the site of his nursery bed. This field must be strategically located so that the first rains may be supplemented by surface run-off from other fields or from irrigation ditches. It should also be accessible to the compound to receive the buffalo, oxen and poultry manures or commercial fertilizers. If these are used anywhere on the farm, the nursery bed is favored.

As soon as fresh rain water (in contrast with stagnant water with less oxygen) is available, it is let into or pumped into this bed. When the ground becomes soft, it is plowed and cross-plowed. The home-made wooden plow has a pointed share usually tipped with iron, but it has no moldboard. The soil is stirred, not turned over. Water buffaloes are used where the mud is deep, sticky and primarily clay in nature. In the lighter soils containing more sand and/or silt, bullocks are used. After the field is plowed several times, water is allowed to stand and the land is permitted "to weather." The water helps rot the vegetable matter; it penetrates the clods, and it may settle below the plow line, softening the ground to a greater depth.

Planting time varies in different parts of the country, but the farmer generally plans to sow his nursery bed about 25-30 days before his first field is ready for transplanting.[9] The number of superior nursery bed sites is so limited that the preparation and use of these are often a cooperative undertaking. One farmer may contribute the land. Another will plow it. Still another may harrow it. They may divide the field into several plots, each one planted to a different type of rice, such as short, medium, and long maturing varieties. Rice maturing in a short growing period is placed on land farthest from the irrigation supply where water will stand for the shortest time. The yield here will not be as high;

[9] *Ibid.*, 8.

the crop may fail; and, in some dry years, these plots are not even planted.

The farmer sprouts the seeds before they are sown. They are first soaked in water overnight and then scattered on split bamboo trays or other containers permitting adequate drainage. The seeds on the trays are covered with wet straw to hasten germination. These are sprinkled at least twice daily to prevent overheating, and, after being covered in this way for forty-eight hours, the sprouted seeds are ready to plant.

While they are sprouting, the plot is harrowed several times and the ground thoroughly puddled. Soil, water and air are so well blended that the mixture resembles a well-beaten cake batter. All clods and trash are removed. Next the plot is drained and the mud leveled with a piece of wood or a large banana stalk pulled by one or more persons (only hand labor is used in the final stages of preparing this bed).

After leveling, the mud is left for a few hours to set so that the sprouted seeds, when sown, will not sink too deeply. Young plants from seeds which settle too far into the mud will become too tightly set. And when they are uprooted for transplanting, too high a percentage of the root system will be lost. When too many roots are broken off, the plant will not grow or produce well.

When the bed is ready and the seeds sprouted, they are sown broadcast. The sowing takes place in the morning, and afterwards this bed is carefully guarded. A temporary bamboo fence is built around it to keep out buffaloes and bullocks. If located near the village, a bamboo lattice is put around the field to keep out chickens and ducks. For the first few days after the sowing, either someone stays near the field to shoo away the birds, or scarecrows are set up.

Fortunately, the nursery is planted early in the wet season before the rains become too frequent and heavy. After sowing, the bed is left to dry for a week. Then water is let in a little at a time, and the height of the seedlings is determined by controlling the water. In some parts of Thailand where water is scarce and the fields are covered with only a few inches, short seedlings are preferred. These are also desirable where the fields are least accessible to water.

Field preparation. While the seedlings are growing, the farmers quickly prepare the fields for transplanting. Often the plots are plowed only one way and then harrowed. This latter process both puddles the soil and levels the ground. Trash (such as undecayed stalks, roots of weeds, and leaves) is removed and placed on termite hills or paddy dikes (sometimes called bunds).

Ordinarily a single buffalo, usually driven by man, is used in plowing. Sometimes on the Bangkok delta plain two buffaloes in double harness are used for deeper plowing in the sticky clay. Often women or older girls may be seen plowing, especially on the delta where labor is in short supply and where there is less exchange of local help.

Two buffaloes are used to harrow the field. The harrow is heavier than the plow. The teeth stick down deep into the mud, and it takes strength to pull it as it churns the soil, water and air into the right mixture and texture. Guiding the harrow is heavy work carried on by men. In the clay soils, such as those in the Bangkok plain, about one-third of the water required for the crop is used in wetting and puddling the soil.

Plowing and harrowing are done in the morning between the hours of six and ten and in the evening between three and six. Buffaloes are not worked during the intense heat of the day. The animals rest in shallow water or in mud wallows. The field workers bathe, eat, and then rest in the shade.

The last harrowing is done just before the transplanting. Often the two processes are carried on in the same paddy field at the same time.

Transplanting

Careful preparation is made in advance for the uprooting, bundling and transportation of the seedlings. A small bamboo shelter, thatched with leaves or straw, is often built to protect the bundled seedlings and the bundler from the hot sun. Thin bamboo strips are cut for tying the bundles.

In order to protect the rice stalks, whose root system is partially broken off when uprooted, transplanting is usually carried on in the afternoon and early evening before dark. If the stalks were transplanted during the hottest part of the day—between 10 A.M. and 3 P.M.— they would wilt, be severely damaged, or even die. Moreover, persons planting the rice bend over nearly double. During the middle of the day, the sun's rays come down on them almost at right angles. The heat is less intense and the glare from reflected sunlight is also less in the late afternoon.

Only the most experienced persons, usually the older women, uproot the plants. Several seedlings are pulled up at one time with the arm moving in an arc. The roots of the plant may be hit against the foot and/or washed to remove all the dirt which otherwise would hasten evaporation, make the bundles too heavy, and interfere with replanting. Leaves may be cut back in order to reduce the amount of transpiration and make the plants more uniform. After several hundred stalks have been uprooted, they are placed, roots down, on a stand and tied into a bundle. These are then placed upright on the ground with the roots in the water. Later, after being carried to the field, they are again placed in the water, and the stalks are kept moist by sprinkling.

The means of transporting the plants to the fields vary in different parts of the country. The bundles may be threaded on a long bamboo pole; placed in baskets at each end of a "carrying pole"; floated down deep ditches; carried in boats; pulled on earthern sleds and even stacked in buses and trucks. Sometimes a combination of these methods is used before the plants reach the fields.

If more than one person is planting, the workers form a line. They take a bunch of stalks in one hand and select two, three or four with the other hand and push them down in the mud. The workers move backward as they plant. Generally the larger the number of stalks planted in one hill, the farther the hills are apart. Although the ground is not cultivated between these rows, this checkerboard pattern facilitates weeding.

The operator decides how many stalks should go into a hill and the width of the space between the hills. These are not easy decisions because so many variables are involved. Operators know the fertility of their soils. They know when the rains usually come and the amount of water they can generally rely on from irrigation. However, they know, too, that the amount of rain and irrigation water varies greatly from year to year. Consequently, if they are too conservative, they may lose an opportunity for a large crop. If they are too optimistic and put too many plants in a hill and place the hills too close together, then the rains may be light and the yields greatly reduced. In addition, operators must decide what maturing varieties of rice should be planted and whether the fields should be planted or left fallow.[10] After the field is planted, a few extra seedling are heeled in some corner to be used later in re-

[10] In areas where such major decisions must be made and where so much depends upon the whims of nature, should one be surprised to find the "Mother Earth God" respected; Spirit Houses in the compounds; and Buddhas in wats cast in the position of asking for rain?

placing plants which die.

In rice cultivation, transplanting is the hardest and most exhausting work. It is always monotonous, back-straining, wet and sloppy. The task goes on rain or shine. The planters may get drenched in a tropical downpour one hour and feel the almost blistering heat the next. Clothes also get wet from body moisture because of the high humidity in the growing season. The skin on the hands, forearms, feet and lower legs wrinkles from long hours of exposure to mud and water, and often leeches cling to the planters' limbs. In spite of all these inconveniences, if a large crew works together, there are often humor and pranks to help break the monotony.

After the transplanting, the fields are kept well supplied with water, if this is possible. If the rains should stop, the water in the fields and smaller ditches dries up; the earth cracks open; and the rice stalks start to turn yellow. If it does not rain soon again, the yield is reduced and all the plants may die.

In some instances, farmers drain their fields in order to fight an invasion of land crabs. This draining permits the rice stalks to harden and pass the tender stage when crabs are most liable to attack.

Broadcasting

The broadcasting method is used for two types of wetland rice—floating rice and ordinary garden rice.

Floating rice. In the commercialized agricultural areas of the Bangkok delta plain, large areas of rice grow in deep water. Here sprouted seeds are broadcast. The young stalks of floating rice are too long, brittle and too fragile to be uprooted.

Many steps in broadcast planting are the same as those in transplanting. The fields are prepared in about the same way, but they require less plowing and harrowing. The rice seeds are sprouted, but they are sown directly on the field rather than in a nursery bed. After puddling the soil, the sediment and other foreign matter in the water is given time to settle. Otherwise the suspended material might settle down on the young seedlings and cut them off from sunlight. If this should happen, the sprouts would rot.

Timing in the planting is all important. It is best to broadcast the sprouts in shallow water (about two feet is a maximum). When the sprouts send up stalks, the upper part must remain above the surface of the water to secure oxygen. If the rains come at the usual time, mid-May, broadcasting must be completed by June or July. If not sown by then, the water may become so deep that the fields cannot be planted or the water may rise faster than the stalks can grow causing the plants to drown. The plants must be well established before their stalks start growing several inches a day to keep ahead of the rising water.

Garden rice. The oxygen factor limits the amount of land which can be sown to garden rice. The water must contain enough oxygen to supply the young sprouts until they reach the surface of the water. This may require several days. The processes of preparing the fields, sprouting, and broadcasting the seed are the same for both types of wetland rice. The primary difference is that garden rice can only be sown in fields watered by large rivers or canals (water that has a high oxygen content), or in fields where the rain and irrigation water is frequently changed or moved in such a way to add oxygen. The young sprouts need sunlight; they must not be smothered in mud or by stagnant or salty water. Moreover, the plants sown by the broadcast method develop an extensive root system near the surface of the soil. This system requires greater amounts of oxygen because not as much air has been worked into the soil by puddling.

Sometimes garden rice is sown broadcast directly on the ground without sprouting the seed. (About 65 to 100 pounds of rice is sown per acre.) The seeds are covered by cross-plowing. The advantages and limitations of this method depend on the amount and distribution of rainfall and the texture of the soil. Covering the seeds by plowing protects them from birds and rats. The young sprouts are also protected from the drying effect of direct sunlight and strong winds. The seedlings become anchored in the soil from the start, and the plants do not suffer much during short droughts nor do they lodge so easily at maturity. This method is used widely in Northeast Thailand.

However, covering broadcast unsprouted seeds by cross-plowing can be disastrous. If the rains are too heavy and come too soon after plowing, several things may happen. (1) The lumps of plowed soil may be completely broken down and the seeds may be buried too deeply. (2) A crust may form and keep the sprouts from pushing their way to the surface after germination. Or, the opposite extreme may take place. It may not rain for 15 or 20 days after the plowing, and, consequently, (1) the seeds may rot; (2) not enough seeds may sprout or reach the surface; and (3) the stand may be so thin that reseeding is necessary.

The texture of the soil is an important factor in limiting the use of cross-plowing. The soil should be well floccuated and should break up into large pieces. If the soil contains too much sand and is too friable, a small amount of rain will cause the particles to break down and smother the seeds. If the soil is poorly drained, and too wet and sticky, it is best not to cover the seeds.

Transplanting vs Broadcasting

Technically, the transplanting method is simpler than broadcasting. It involves less risk of loss of rice seed, time, and perhaps a crop. The transplant method requires more labor, time and back-bending work. It is believed that the economic unit of a farm family in areas where commercial rice is grown by transplanting is from 7.5 to 10 acres, whereas a farm to be as productive by the broadcasting method of planting should contain double the acreage.

Where physical conditions do not permit broadcasting, transplanting is a necessity. Although flood, delta, and coastal plains may appear level, comparatively small topographic variations help create habitat differences which are significant in land use. Transplanting is superior to the broadcasting method in the following physical habitats: (1) in depressions or on land too level to have adequate drainage and/or where the rain water tends to stagnate for long periods of time early in the growing season; (2) on soils which contain comparatively large quantities of soluable salt, such as areas near the sea on both the deltas and the old abandoned soil-filled lagoons;[11] and on (3) level land which is too high for inundation by the annual floods and too far from the rivers or canals for irrigation. In this last habitat the rice has to depend primarily on rainfall but may receive some water from surface or subsurface drainage which originates on waste or forest land at higher levels. Broadcasting would not be desirable in the habitats just described because too much seed would be wasted; the plants would not be evenly distributed for the most efficient soil water utilization and too many seeds may sprout and too many plants die later for lack of moisture.

Between Planting and Harvesting

The tempo of farm work slows down

[11] On this type of soil, the planting must be postponed until late in the wet season because the water from the early rains is needed to dissolve and wash away the salt which has accumulated during the hot dry months. If rice were planted too soon, the high concentration of salt would kill the plants.

between planting and harvesting, but the farmers are not idle. Farmers cannot be considered seasonally unemployed during the rice growing season. Through careful management, field preparation and planting are extended over several weeks if not two months. Then the fields must be tended, preparations made for the harvest, and secondary crops, fruit trees and gardens, cared for. The growing rice must be protected from land crabs, rats, stray livestock and birds. Plants in some hills may need to be replaced. Dikes may need to be repaired, widened, and built higher. Weeds must be controlled. If the rains are too heavy, it may be necessary to cut outlets in the dikes and let the water slowly out without damaging the plants or the dikes.

Between planting and harvesting, the farmers must construct or repair the vehicles needed to transport the bundles of rice to the compound (farmyard) or field stack and the threshed grain to market. Other tools used in harvesting must be made or repaired. The granaries are constructed or cleaned and repaired. Everything is made ready for the increased work tempo of harvest time.

Harvesting and Threshing

Harvest time varies from region to region and from field to field within regions according to the time of planting and the type of maturing varieties grown. It is impractical for the farmer either to plant or to harvest all his fields at one time. In most of Thailand the harvest generally starts in late November and December at the beginning of the dry season. However, in parts of the Central Plain where the water cannot be drained from the fields until the water in the rivers falls, harvesting may take place as late as mid-February. Fortunately the farmer can rely on four very dry months for harvesting and threshing in all parts of the country except peninsular Thailand.

If the farmer can control the water in his paddy fields, about ten days or two weeks before cutting the grain he cuts off the water supply and drains the field because: (1) it is much easier for the harvesters to work on dry land; (2) there is less danger of the stalks breaking and the heads dropping into the water and spoiling; and (3) not as much care is necessary in drying the stalks nor in bundling the cut grain. In fact, if the stalks are dry enough, the cut grain will not need to be placed on the stubble of the rice plants to dry. However, if the ground is wet or the stalks are too green, the stems are scattered to dry on the stubble of the rice plants.

Most of the grain is cut several stalks at a time with the women and men working in the field together. The reaper bends over, grasps several stalks in one hand, and cuts them with a curved sickle held in the other. These sickles are about 15 inches long and have an 11-12 inch serrated-edged blade fastened to a hollow pipe-like handle. In some provinces of peninsular Thailand such as Trang, stalks of rice are cut one at a time with a homemade knife.

In the geographic regions of North Thailand and Northeast Thailand the grain is usually stacked in the fields. In the North the stacks are built in an arc and resemble an amphitheater with the threshing floor in the center. In the Northeast stacks are arranged in square or oblong shapes and are often covered by a straw- or leaf-thatched roof supported by a bamboo framework. The family lives in a small temporary shelter built near the stack for protection from the cold rather than rain. Most of the cooking is done in front of this temporary shelter. This camping near the stack and the threshing floor saves time which would otherwise be wasted going a long distance to the compound. In this way it is possible for one to guard his crop 24 hours a day. Moreover, only the grain

FIG. 2. Notice that the water level has dropped drastically and that the sides of the klong (ditch) are drying and cracking open. The trees on the horizon indicate the location of a permanent water course.

will need to be transported.

Great care is taken in cutting the grain so that none, or as few as possible of the seeds, shatter out. Cutting starts in the morning after the sun has dried the dew from the stalks. The cutters work about four hours and stop for lunch. Often they lunch in the fields in the shade of a near-by tree or bamboo clump. After a respite of about an hour, cutting goes on again until dark.

In the Central Plain Region of Thailand, various means of transportation move the sheaves to the compound. In some areas the grain is carried on bamboo sleds pulled by buffaloes or these sleds are used to move the sheaves to the edge of a waterway where the grain is then carried by boat (Fig. 2). In some areas the sheaves are hauled in ox carts pulled by bullocks, and if the fields are dry enough and the earth will support a truck, these modern vehicles are pressed into service. In the North and the Northeast, if the trip is not too long, the sheaves are often carried on a pole to the stacks and sometimes to the compound.

The threshing floor is prepared while the grain is going through a sweat in the stack. "Going through a sweat" refers to the process whereby heat is generated by the grain itself and the heads become brittle. In the Central Plain, the threshing floor is near the center of the com-

pound and located midway between the stacks of grain. In North Thailand the floor is within the arcs formed by the stacks. A space about 30 to 50 feet in diameter is flattened and hardened with heavy wooden mallets or paddles. In some places these floors are plastered with buffalo dung, and in others the floor is covered with large closely woven, split-bamboo mats.[12]

After the grain goes "through the sweat" threshing starts. In the North, the Northeast and peninsular Thailand, the grain is beaten from the heads. The thresher takes the bundle in his hands or wraps a thong fastened to two sticks around the bundle and hits the heads against: (1) the sides of large bamboo baskets or boxes; (2) split bamboo mats held vertically by stakes; or (3) over planks or on mats placed on the threshing floors. The "thong and hand sticks" enable the worker to hit the short-stemmed sheaves against the planks or mats without bending over so far.

In the Central Plain Region, animals are used for threshing. Men and women working together take the bundles from the stack, cut the bamboo strings and scatter the grain to a depth of about a foot (Fig. 3). Then three or four buffaloes or bullocks, harnessed together side by side, are driven round and round (Fig. 4). When the grain is separated from the straw, the straw is stacked around a bamboo pole (Fig. 4). The grain and chaff is piled to one side. Then more bundles of grain are cut and scattered on the floor, and the process is repeated.

Winnowing practices do not vary much in Thailand. The grain and chaff are tossed into the air with flat wooden shovels resembling long-handled paddles or with large bamboo trays (Fig. 5). If there

[12] Sometimes a post is placed in the center of the floor on which offerings to "Mother Earth" may be hung. In other places small banners are placed on the stacks of bundled grain in respect to the spirits of the harvest.

FIG. 3. A bamboo rake rests against the oblong stack of sheaves. Using a bamboo pitchfork, a man throws the sheaves onto the threshing floor.

FIG. 5. Hand tools are more common than machines in Thailand. Much of the grain is still winnowed in the same way it was done centuries ago. Many compounds are lined with bamboo clumps and "rain trees." Note the farm and household utensils under the lean-to of the house.

is little or no wind, large round bamboo fans about 18 inches in diameter with short foot-long handles are used to set up an air current. In the Bangkok delta plain the more prosperous farmers have hand-operated winnowing machines; however farmers with this mechanized device are the exception rather than the rule (Fig. 6).

After the winnowing, the grain is stored or taken to market. The rice threshed in the fields is taken to the compound in baskets on carrying poles, in wooden boxes on carts, or in huge, tightly-woven split-bamboo beds placed on ox carts.

In the subsistence rice producing areas, nearly all the grain is stored for food and the next year's planting. The more

FIG. 4. Notice the stack's cone shape. The ladder, long-handled pitchfork and stake at the center of the straw stack are made of bamboo.

FIG. 6. The winnowing machine, the iron shovel head, the clothing and the artistic split bamboo basket indicate a prosperous family.

FIG. 7. Grain is carried up the gentle incline of the log rather than up the steep ladder (Courtesy of FAO Office, Krung Thep).

FIG. 8. A humble farmstead. The granary made of split bamboo rests on bamboo poles. Both the granary and the house to the right are thatched with yaka grass (Photo by Robert L. Pendleton).

prosperous farmers have large oblong granaries made of solid wood and divided into several bins. These granaries have long eaves extending over the sides; are set on teak pillars about six feet above the ground; and have clay tile roofs (Fig. 7). These are the most weather proof, fireproof and vermin-proof of all the granaries in Thailand. Other granaries are made of woven split bamboo and plastered with mud and/or buffalo dung and thatched with leaves or straw. These granaries are: (1) more or less cylindrical or cone-shaped; (2) built on a platform set on stilts; and (3) are covered with a roof which may be a lean-to fastened to one side of the house (Fig. 8).

In the commercial rice producing areas, the grain is rushed to market almost directly from the threshing floor (Fig. 9).

Summary

Growing rice in Thailand involves hard work, technical know-how, keen evaluation of the natural environment, and action based on practical guesswork. The biggest conservation problem facing the country is a more efficient use of land and water. After the crop is threshed, the Thai have time to relax, and many of their holidays and festive traditions are observed in the dry season.

FIG. 9. Rushing the grain to market in small klong boat. A typical farm scene along a large klong (Courtesy of W. J. van der Oond, ECAFE, Krung Thep).

THE BASIC FOOD CROPS OF JAVA AND MADURA

Don C. Bennett

Dr. Bennett is an Assistant Professor of Geography at Indiana University. He spent the period 1953–1955 in the Netherlands and Indonesia on research grants from the Ford Foundation.

THE diet of the people of Java and Madura is composed very largely of foods derived from seven basic crops: wet rice, corn, cassava, soybeans, dry rice, peanuts, and sweet potatoes. No attempt has been made to bring up to date our knowledge of the distributional aspects of these crops since the work of Van Valkenburg in the mid 1930's.[1] That discussion was largely concerned with describing individual crops and did not attempt to show crop association patterns. Later studies having to do with Javanese agriculture have described the distribution of these crops with a broad brush, never below the provincial level.[2] This article is an attempt partly to fill in these gaps, namely: (1) to determine and describe the variety and patterns of basic food crop combinations, and (2) to examine in detail the distributions of the individual crops as they are a part of the total crop association.[3]

The territorial unit used is the *kabupaten*, of which there are 86 in Java and Madura. Six of these are primarily urban areas: the kabupatens of Djakarta, Bandung, Jogjakarta, Surakarta, Semarang, and Surabaja (Fig. 1). Even though some of the kabupatens are large enough to include significant land use diversity, they are generally of a size to provide a rather detailed distributional picture and, with the exception of the urban areas, do not vary greatly in size.

Cultivated land, as used in this paper, includes the *sawah* (irrigated) and *tegal* (unirrigated) open fields but excludes the garden areas that are closely associated with dwellings. Normally, the seven basic crops are not planted in the gardens. It should also be remembered that these crops do not occupy all of the cultivated land, since such crops as tobacco and sugar cane are widely grown. However, known conditions in East Java indicate that the seven major food crops do occupy the overwhelming proportion of the total cultivated area since the subsidiary crops are grown on less than 6 per cent of the total.[4] Leased tree plantation areas are also excluded from the data on native cultivated lands.

A significant distinction in Javanese agricultural land use is that between the sawah and tegal lands, since the sawah lands are considerably more

[1] Samuel Van Valkenburg: "Agricultural Regions of Asia, Part IX: Java," *Econ. Geog.*, Vol. 12, 1936, pp. 27–44.
[2] Java is divided into three provinces: West, Central, and East.
[3] All data used in this paper refer to 1953 statistics gathered at the Central Statistical Office, Djakarta. This research was made possible by grants from the Ford Foundation although they are in no way responsible for any statements in the paper.
[4] Don C. Bennett: *Population Pressure in East Java*, Ph.D. Dissertation, Syracuse University, Syracuse, N. Y., 1957, p. 42.

"The Basic Food Crops of Java and Madura" by Don C. Bennett. Reprinted from Economic Geography, *Vol.* 37 *(January* 1961), *pp.* 75–87, *with permission of the editor.*

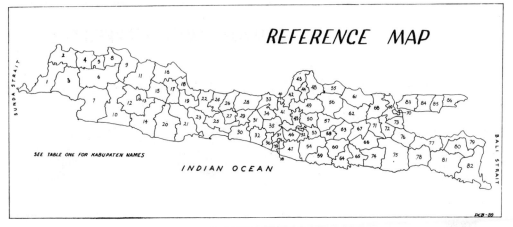

FIG. 1.   Reference map.   Numbers refer as follows:

Map Number	Kabupaten	Map Number	Kabupaten	Map Number	Kabupaten
29	Bandjarnegara	46	Klaten	84	Sampang
12	Bandung	9	Krawang	41	Semarang
13	Bandung City	44	Kudus	40	Semarang City
83	Bangkalen	36	Kulonprogo	2	Serang
25	Banjumas	19	Kuningan	73	Sidoardjo
82	Banjuwangi	68	Lamongan	37	Sleman
39	Bantul	3	Lebak	50	Sragen
8	Bakasi	78	Lumadjang	11	Subang
74	Blitar	63	Madiun	7	Sukabumi
56	Blora	17	Madjalenka	52	Sukohardjo
62	Bodjonegoro	35	Magelang	15	Sumedang
6	Bogor	58	Magetan	86	Sumenep
45	Bojolali	75	Malang	69	Surabaja
80	Bondowoso	72	Modjokerto	70	Surabaja City
22	Brebes	67	Ngandjuk	51	Surakarta City
42	Demak	57	Ngawi	20	Tasikmalaja
5	Djakarta City	85	Pamekasan	24	Tegal
43	Djapara	79	Panarukan	34	Temanggung
81	Djember	1	Pandeglang	4	Tengerang
71	Djombang	76	Pasuruan	18	Tjeribon
14	Garut	48	Pati	21	Tjiamis
49	Grobogun	59	Patjitan	10	Tjiandjur
47	Gunungkidul	28	Pekalongan	23	Tjilatjap
16	Indramaju	26	Pemalang	64	Trenggalek
38	Jogjakarta City	60	Ponorogo	61	Tuban
53	Karanganjar	77	Probolinggo	65	Tulungagung
30	Kebumen	27	Purbolinggo	54	Wonogiri
66	Kediri	32	Purworedjo	31	Wonosobo
33	Kendal	55	Rembang		

productive than the tegal and are the only areas on which wet rice can be grown. The sawah area accounted for 42 per cent, or 34,334,000 hectares, of the cultivated land area in 1953.

Multiple cropping is widespread in Java and Madura and significantly enlarges the harvested area as opposed to the cultivated land area. Practiced predominantly on sawah, multiple cropping means the equivalent of 39 per cent more sawah land on which the basic food crops are grown, indicating a high intensity of use. The areal importance of the basic food crops, in all cases, has been evaluated in relation to the *harvested* area rather than to the *cultivated* area.

Multiple cropping on sawah lands is most important in eastern Java,

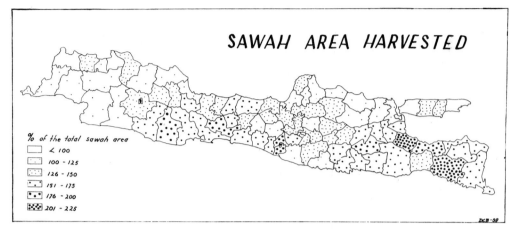

FIG. 2.

where several regions record a harvested sawah area which is at least 175 per cent of the sawah land area (Fig. 2). At the other extreme, there are several areas where the rate of multiple cropping of sawah is no more than 125 per cent. These are located west of Djakarta-Bandung, along the northern coast from Japara to Surabaja, in a few scattered areas of central Java, and on Madura Island.

The intensity of cultivation of the basic food crops on tegal is much lower than that on sawah although the distributional patterns of intensity are similar. In general, the tegal areas having the lowest intensity of use are in the west and increase toward the east.

CROP COMBINATIONS

A knowledge of the particular combination of crops and the relative importance of each in an area, i.e., the crop combination, can be very useful in understanding aspects of the economic and social geography of an area. Weaver lists three directions in which crop combination information may have significance. He points out that they are essential to an adequate understanding of the individual crop geography; that the crop combination region, itself, is an integrative reality that requires definitions and distributional analysis; and that such regions are essential for the construction of the still more complex structures of

TABLE I

THE MAJOR FOOD CROPS OF JAVA AND MADURA IN 1953

	Wet rice	Corn	Cassava	Soybeans	Dry rice	Peanuts	Sweet potatoes
Sawah Harvest (100 ha)....	37,421	4,248	635	3,318	464	1,038	809
Tegal Harvest (100 ha).....	......	10,738	8,034	924	2,524	1,355	1,365
Total Harvest (100 ha)...	37,421	14,986	8,669	4,242	2,988	2,393	2,174
% Sawah Harvest.........	78	9	1	7	1	2	2
% Tegal Harvest.........	0	44	32	4	10	5	5
% Total Harvest.........	51	22	12	6	3	3	3
% Sawah................	100	28	7	78	15	43	37
% Tegal................	0	72	93	22	85	57	63

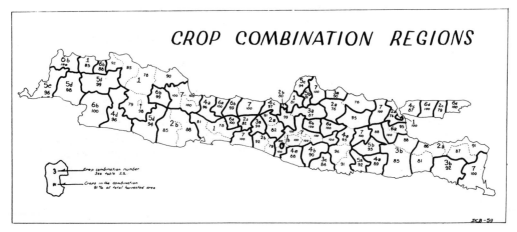

CROP COMBINATION REGIONS

FIG. 3.

agricultural regions.[5] In addition, crop combination regions may be used to evaluate such conditions as dietary adequacy and labor under- or unemployment in essentially agrarian economies. The crop combination regions depicted in Figure 3 are those that show the smallest deviation from theoretical model curves using the formula:

$$\delta = \frac{\Sigma d^2}{n}$$

where:

δ = deviation
d = difference between the actual crop percentage in an area and the theoretical curve
n = number of crops in a given combination

The 21 crop combination regions shown on Figure 3 indicate the number and kind of crops composing the region and the percentage of the total harvested area that these occupy in that area. Figure 4 indicates the areally most important crop, the percentage of the total harvested area it occupies, and the crop diversity or specialization of each kabupaten.

A striking feature of Javanese agriculture as shown by Figure 3 is the areal variety of crop combinations.

[5] John Weaver: "Crop Combination Regions in the Middlewest," *Geogr. Rev.*, Vol. 44, 1954, p. 176.

The distribution of the 21 recognized combinations present few examples of large clusters of kabupatens. The coherent area having the largest number (seven) of similar kabupatens is a 7-crop region (the least specialized) in the vicinity of Jogjakarta-Surakarta. There is also a large 1-crop wet rice area (six kabupatens) along the northern coast eastward from Djakarta. Other groupings include the 2-crop corn-wet rice area at the eastern end of the island and a 4-crop wet rice-corn-cassava-soybeans region that extends north

TABLE II

CROP COMBINATION REGIONS

1   Wet rice
2a Wet rice—corn
2b Wet rice—cassava
2c Corn—cassava
3a Wet rice—corn—cassava
3b Wet rice—corn—soybeans
3c Wet rice—cassava—dry rice
4a Wet rice—corn—cassava—soybeans
4b Wet rice—corn—cassava—dry rice
4c Wet rice—corn—cassava—sweet potato
4d Wet rice—cassava—dry rice—sweet potato
4e Corn—cassava—dry rice—peanuts
5a Wet rice—corn—cassava—soybeans—dry rice
5b Wet rice—corn—cassava—soybeans—sweet potato
5c Wet rice—corn—cassava—dry rice—peanuts
5d Wet rice—corn—cassava—dry rice—sweet potato
5e Wet rice—cassava—soybeans—dry rice—sweet potato
5f Wet rice—cassava—dry rice—peanuts—sweet potato
6a Wet rice—corn—cassava—soybeans—peanuts—sweet potato
6b Wet rice—corn—cassava—dry rice—peanuts—sweet potato
7   All crops

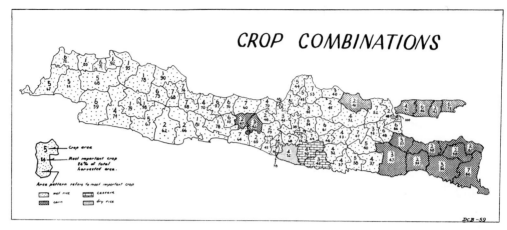

FIG. 4.

and south of Madiun. Elsewhere there are a few locations where the same combination is found in two or three adjacent kabupatens, but on the whole one is struck by the fractured nature of the distributions, the relative absence of extensive areal similarity, and the scattered nature of kabupatens having similar conditions.

A second important feature of Javanese crop combination regions is the relative dominance of the particular combination crops in any area. In the 1-, 2-, 3-, and 4-crop areas the areal importance of these crops is very high, generally over 85 per cent of the total, indicating the specialized nature of these regions.

The dominant position of wet rice in Javanese agricultural land use is clearly shown by Figure 4. In all, it is areally the most important crop in 68 of the 86 kabupatens, giving way to corn, cassava, and dry rice in local areas. Thirteen kabupatens are 1-crop wet rice areas; it is the only crop that so dominates as to be a 1-crop region. Four of the 13 are urban areas, reflecting the insignificant development of market gardening around the large Javanese cities. Throughout the rural 1-crop wet rice regions the harvested

area of wet rice varies from 78 per cent (Subang, Banjumas) to 95 per cent (Krawang) of the total harvested area. There is a marked concentration of the rural 1-crop areas along the northern coast of western Java from Tangerang to Tjeribon, mentioned above. In the interior, Bandung Kabupaten in the west and Demak, Banjumas, and Tjilatjap Kabupatens in central Java are 1-crop wet rice areas. With the single exception of Surabaja City there is no area in eastern Java where wet rice so dominates. Again, this extraordinary position is substantiated by the large number (34 per cent) of 1- or 2-crop kabupatens in which wet rice is represented.

All 2-crop regions, of which there are three types, are some combination of wet rice, corn, and cassava. Ten of the sixteen 2-crop kabupatens are combinations of wet rice and corn, five of wet rice and cassava, and one of corn and cassava. Thus, wet rice figures in all but one of these regions. It should be noted that corn becomes increasingly important toward the east and, in fact, occupies a larger harvested area than wet rice in six of the ten wet rice and corn areas, especially those farthest east.

In contrast to the 1-crop areas, the

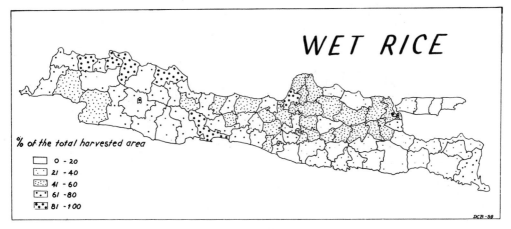

% of the total harvested area

☐ 0 - 20
☐ 21 - 40
☐ 41 - 60
☐ 61 - 80
☐ 81 - 100

FIG. 5.

2-crop areas are largely located in central and eastern Java. The wet rice-corn combination is the only 2-crop combination found east of a meridional line through Semarang and also occupies the three interior central Java 2-crop kabupatens. A wet rice-cassava combination occurs at two separated locations along the southern coast from Tasikmalaya to Kulonprogo. Semarang City is also a wet rice-cassava area. Pamekasan, on Madura Island, is the only kabupaten where a corn-cassava combination prevails.

The same three crops—wet rice, corn, and cassava—figure strongly in the 3-crop combinations; in addition, soybeans are prominent and dry rice is locally important. There are two major 3-crop combinations, wet rice-corn-cassava and wet rice-corn-soybeans, and three minor combinations. The distribution of 3-crop combinations is confined to an area east of a meridional line through Wonosobo. The wet rice-corn-cassava combination is found in four disconnected kabupatens in central Java. The wet rice-corn-soybean regions lie adjacent to the 2-crop wet rice-corn areas in the far eastern part of Java. Wet rice occupies more area than corn over most of the wet rice-

corn-cassava regions while corn dominates wet rice throughout the wet rice-corn-soybean areas. A cassava-wet rice-dry rice area is confined to Patjitan Kabupaten, along the hilly southern coast.

All seven major food crops are represented in each of the 4-, 5-, 6-, and 7-crop combinations. There are five 4-crop combination types, six 5-crop combination types, and two 6-crop combination types. Wet rice is absent from only one of these fourteen combinations. This is at Gunungkidul Kabupaten in the hills south of Jogjakarta-Surakarta.

There are only two 6-crop combinations: (a) without soybeans and (b) without dry rice. Soybeans are insignificant in the area west of Tjeribon and dry rice is similarly of little importance in the area east of Ngawi.

The areas having the least crop specialization, the 6- and 7-crop areas, represent a third of the total kabupatens (29). They are distributed widely from west to east and north to south but lie principally in the central and eastern sections of Java. There is an evident tendency toward rather large clusters separated from each other. The largest nonspecialized zone (includ-

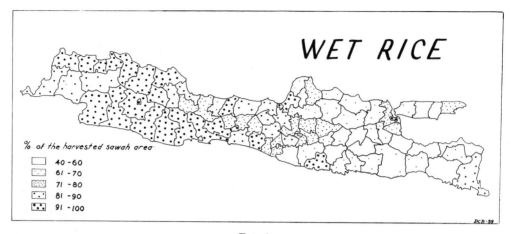

FIG. 6.

ing 13 kabupatens) extends with only small interruption from Bantul eastward to Surabaja and Sidoardjo. A second zone (five kabupatens) extends across the island from Tegal-Wonosobo on the Java Sea to Kebumen on the Indian Ocean. The third large region lies between Bandung and Tjeribon and includes four kabupatens. The remaining five nonspecialized kabupatens are widely dispersed.

WET RICE

The paramount position of wet rice in the food crop picture of most of Java and Madura has been partially described. It occupies more land than any other crop in no less than 68 of the 86 kabupatens. There are only two kabupatens that utilize less than half (44 per cent and 49 per cent respectively) of the total sawah harvested area for wet rice production. The median wet rice harvested acreage is 78 per cent and there are 19 kabupatens (22 per cent) in which over 95 per cent of the harvested sawah area is with wet rice. Notwithstanding its predominant role, there exists a considerable areal variation in the degree of importance that wet rice has. In Gunungkidul Kabupaten only 4 per

cent of the harvested area is wet rice; in Surabaja Kabupaten it approaches 100 per cent. The median value for all kabupatens is 53 per cent. Figure 5 shows the percentage of the total harvested area occupied by wet rice. West from a meridional line through Tjeribon it generally occupies 60 per cent or more of the harvested area with most of this area having values over 70 per cent; between Tjeribon and a meridional line through Semarang values between 20 and 81 per cent occur with most of the area under 70 per cent; east of Semarang wet rice values generally vary between 20 and 70 per cent with most of the area having values under 50 per cent. Banjuwangi, the easternmost kabupaten on Java, with 66 per cent, shows an especially high intensity of wet rice for this part of the island. Madura Island is exceptional in that it has the only extensive area where wet rice is less than 20 per cent of the harvested acreage, with values about 10 per cent.

Wet rice is, of course, grown only on sawah lands, the fields that can be irrigated. The relative position of this crop is better understood if we examine its importance on just these lands. The distributional pattern, as shown by

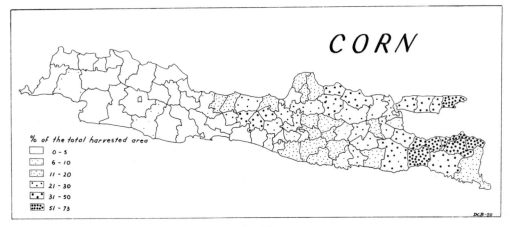

FIG. 7.

Figure 6, may be summarized as follows: West from Tjeribon it occupies 86 per cent or more of the harvested sawah area; between Tjeribon and Semarang is a zone in which the importance of wet rice varies between 60 and 100 per cent; east of Semarang values between 60 and 70 per cent are most common, and in several kabupatens wet rice occupies less than half of the harvested sawah. The low position of wet rice on Madura Island and Gunungkidul Kabupaten is due not only to the relative absence of sawah lands but also to a preference for other crops.

CORN

Corn is the second most important food crop. In 1953, it occupied 22 per cent of the major food crop acreage. It is grown on tegal as a wet season crop and on sawah as a dry season crop. The areal importance of this crop is explained in part by the relative predominance of sawah or tegal lands. There are very few areas in Java in which corn equals wet rice in harvested land acreage. The median value of the corn harvest relative to the total harvested area is only 12 per cent. This rises to 26 per cent on just the tegal lands and declines to only 5 per cent on just the sawah lands. In almost 40 per cent of the kabupatens, 5 per cent or less of the harvested area is in corn; it exceeds 50 per cent in only five kabupatens.

The areal pattern of the corn harvest is almost the reverse for that of wet rice (Fig. 7). The areas of greatest corn intensity, where it occupies more than half of the cultivated land, are confined to the eastern tips of Java and Madura. In addition, there are important zones near Rembang-Tuban along the northeastern coast and again in central Java at Bandjarnegara-Temanggung-Wonosobo, where 30 to 50 per cent of the harvested area is in corn. In almost all of the area west of Tjeribon and in a zone extending east of that city along the southern coast to Jogjakarta the harvested acreage of corn is less than 5 per cent of the total.

Seventy-two per cent of the corn harvest is from tegal lands. Indeed, corn occupies over half of the tegal acreage in a continuous zone from the Strait of Bali westward through Malang Kabupaten and then along the north coast to Rembang. A similar area of intensity exists between Bandjarnegara and Magelang in interior central Java. In general, harvest values of corn on

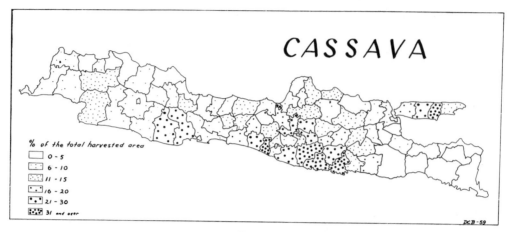

FIG. 8.

tegal are 20 per cent or more north and east of a line between Tjeribon and Jogjakarta while south and west of this line values are everywhere less than 20 per cent and predominantly less than 10 per cent.

The areal pattern of corn intensity on sawah lands is very similar to that on tegal. The same diagonal line between Tjeribon and Jogjakarta neatly separates the western half, where less than 1 per cent of the sawah is planted to corn, from the eastern half where upwards of 33 per cent is so planted. The most important sawah-grown corn area extends from Rembang to the Strait of Bali.

The relatively important position of corn in eastern Java results first from its dominant position on the tegal lands and, second, from its high status as a sawah-grown crop in this area. Generally, less than 10 per cent of the local corn comes from sawah lands in the west of Java; in many areas in the eastern part of the island, 50 to 80 per cent is sawah-grown.

Cassava

Cassava, harvested from 12 per cent of the total harvested area, is the third ranking food crop in Java and Madura and owes this position largely to its cultivation on tegal lands. Grown extensively, it occupies at least 1 per cent of the total harvested area in all but two kabupatens although the median harvest area value is only 10 per cent. In 80 per cent of the kabupatens, cassava represents less than 20 per cent of the total harvested acreage. Consequently, cassava is a part of the land use pattern in virtually all areas although it assumes major significance in only a relatively small area (Fig. 8). It has greatest areal importance in a triangular area bounded by Purworedjo, Patjitan, and Sragen in south central Java, where it generally accounts for over 20 per cent of the harvested area. A second important region includes Tasikmalaya and Tjiamis, also along the southern coast. On the other hand, there are two widely separated large areas in which cassava is very minor, less than 5 per cent: along the northwestern coast from Tangerang to Brebes and in the area east of Surabaja-Malang.

Cassava is overwhelmingly a tegal crop, 93 per cent of its harvested area, and as such it figures far more prominently in the tegal harvested acreages than in the total harvested acreages.

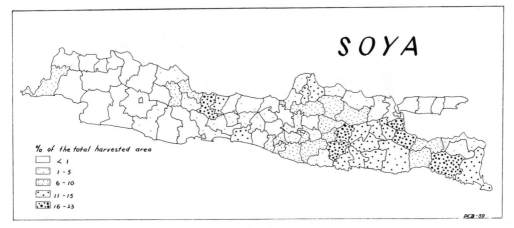

SOYA

% of the total harvested area
- ☐ < 1
- ☐ 1 - 5
- ☐ 6 - 10
- ☐ 11 - 15
- ☐ 16 - 23

FIG. 9.

The median harvest of cassava on tegal is 36 per cent of the total tegal harvested area. In 22 kabupatens it exceeds 50 per cent and in only 14 kabupatens is it harvested from 20 per cent or less of the tegal harvested area. With few exceptions, the areas in which cassava occupies more than 50 per cent of the harvested tegal area extend along the south of Java from Bandung to Madiun. It is least important, less than 20 per cent of the harvested tegal area, east of Surabaja-Malang. A point of interest is that cassava has a greater importance in the urban areas of Djakarta and Semarang than in their immediate hinterlands, although the opposite condition prevails with respect to all other major cities.

The long-maturing requirements of cassava are primarily responsible for its insignificant occupance of sawah lands. Only four kabupatens record a cassava harvest greater than 5 per cent of the total harvested sawah area. The median sawah occupance is only 1 per cent. The distributional pattern on sawah is in three large compact blocks: In the central area, Tjeribon to Surabaja, cassava occupies from 1 to 5 per cent of the harvested sawah acreage while in the two zones on either side the values are less than 1 per cent.

Over 90 per cent of the harvested cassava is from tegal lands throughout the major part of Java. Two exceptions are a rather large interior region which lies between meridional lines through Semarang and Surabaja, and a much smaller region along the northern coast from Krawang to Tegal.

SOYBEANS

Soybeans are the fourth most important food crop and are harvested from 6 per cent of the total harvested area. They are cultivated mainly as a second crop on sawah but are also grown on tegal. Although occupying a greater area than either dry rice, peanuts, or sweet potatoes, soybeans are the most areally restricted of the major food crops. They are entirely absent from five urban and four rural kabupatens.

The greatest cultivation of soybeans, by far, occurs in the area east of Semarang-Jogjakarta (Fig. 9). Within this large region the crop is extensively cultivated and reaches its maximum concentration in a compact area between Ponorogo, Surabaja, and Malang,

FIG. 10.

where the harvested area of soybeans is between 10 and 23 per cent of the total harvested area. Lesser values, from 1 to 10 per cent occur extensively along the northern coast. West of Semarang-Jogjakarta to Tjeribon is a transition zone with a few important soybean areas but many kabupatens which, with the areas west of Tjeribon, have less than 1 per cent of their harvested area in soybeans. The one area of significant concentration west of Semarang is along the northern coast between Tegal and Brebes. Almost no soybeans are grown on Madura Island.

The geographic distribution of the soybean harvest from either sawah or tegal lands individually is very similar to that for the total harvested lands. The maximum cultivation on sawah is 32 per cent while the median is only 3 per cent. On tegal the maximum and median are 16 and 1 per cent, respectively.

DRY RICE

Unirrigated, or dry rice, occupies only 8 per cent as much of the total harvested area as wet rice and only 70 per cent as much as soybeans. About 85 per cent of the dry rice is harvested from tegal lands at the close of the wet season. Altogether it represents only 2 per cent of the harvested area of the major food crops.

There are two areas of major concentration. The largest of these extends through 18 kabupatens along the southern coast from Sunda Strait to Kuningan (Fig. 10). In this area dry rice accounts for over 6 per cent of the harvested area of the major crops and in the extreme western part exceeds 10 per cent. The second areal nucleus, though less extensive, is also located along the southern coast, from Patjitan to Blitar. Here, the intensity of cultivation ranges between 6 and 10 per cent of the harvested area. Small discontinuous areas in which dry rice has greater than average importance are found at Djepara-Kudus, Lamongan-Surabaja, and again at Pamekasan-Sampang on Madura Island.

Although considered a minor food crop in general, dry rice attains major importance on tegal lands areally. The median value is only 5 per cent on these lands, yet throughout the greater part of the area west of Bandung it accounts for between 30 and 50 per cent of the harvested tegal area. Elsewhere, tegal-grown dry rice has greater areal importance along the southern coast than

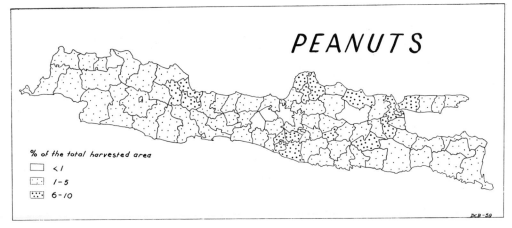

FIG. 11.

in the interior or northern coastal areas.

On sawah, the median harvest figure is only a fraction of 1 per cent of the total sawah harvest. Indeed, 58 kabupatens record no dry rice harvested from sawah lands. The major area of sawah-grown dry rice is in a broad central zone bounded by Semarang-Surabaja-Madiun-Jogjakarta.

PEANUTS

Peanuts occupy relatively small acreages in all parts of Java and Madura. Nowhere are they harvested from more than 10 per cent of the total harvested area and the median harvested area is only between 2 and 3 per cent of the total. On the other hand, there are no rural areas in which peanuts are entirely absent. They are of greatest local importance in a zone bounded by a line connecting Semarang-Jogjakarta-Surabaja and again near Tjeribon where they occupy between 6 and 10 per cent of the total harvested land in several kabupatens (Fig. 11).

The distributional pattern of peanut cultivation on sawah lands is broadly similar to that for the total peanut harvest. This crop is seldom grown on the sawah lands west of Tjeribon.

In urban areas, too, peanuts are not popular.

The pattern of peanut cultivation on tegal, on the other hand, is quite different. On these lands, median cultivation is 5 per cent of the tegal total. They reach their greatest intensity as a tegal crop in Tjeribon and Madjalenka where 22 and 25 per cent, respectively, of the tegal is in peanuts. A somewhat less intense cultivation occurs along the northern coast on either side of Djakarta and again just west of Surabaja.

Although the total peanut harvest shows them to be grown about equally on sawah and tegal, local patterns show wide variations. They are predominantly a sawah crop (over 80 per cent) in very limited areas: at five kabupatens near Jogjakarta and at Panarukan Kabupaten in the east. On the other hand, there are 27 kabupatens in which 80 per cent or more of the peanuts are grown on tegal. These are largely concentrated west of a meridional line through Tjeribon with secondary areas on Madura Island and the adjacent northern coast from Surabaja to Tuban. Elsewhere, peanuts are harvested about equally from sawah and tegal.

% of the total harvested area
☐ < 1
☐ 1 - 5
☐ 6 - 10
☐ 11

FIG. 12.

SWEET POTATOES

In 1953, sweet potatoes were harvested from approximately the same acreage as peanuts, 2,174,000 hectares. Almost two-thirds are grown on tegal and they account for 5 per cent of the harvested tegal acreage whereas they represent only 3 per cent of the total harvested area of the major food crops (Fig. 12).

In 22 of the kabupatens, over 80 per cent of the sweet potatoes are grown on tegal. As a tegal crop they are areally most important west of a meridional line through Pekalongan and assume greatest importance along the northern coast where they occupy between 11 and 20 per cent of the harvested tegal area. Very few sweet potatoes are grown in the vicinity of Bandung. East of Pekalongan, they represent 10 per cent of the harvested tegal area in large sections of the northern coastal plain and less than 5 per cent south of the plain.

As a sawah crop, the median harvested area of sweet potatoes is only 1 per cent of the total. The areas of greatest intensity are found in the extreme west near Lebak and Bogor, somewhat east at Kuningan, and on Madura Island, where they form between 6 and 10 per cent of the harvested sawah acreage. Interestingly, the northern coastal plain of western Java is a major tegal-grown sweet potato region and a very minor region of sawah-grown potatoes.

SUMMARY

This examination of the distributional qualities of the seven major food crops of Java and Madura has been focused on the distinctive combinations of crops that exist and on the areal significance of each crop as a part of the total. This method of geographic investigation has shown Java to have a highly diversified crop pattern. Even wet rice does not figure importantly in all areas. To what extent this pattern of crops is related to climate, soil, water availability, market, population density, or custom would make fruitful lines of investigation. There is also a need for comparable studies of other predominantly wet rice areas.

Middle-Latitude Mixed Farming

This group of articles includes discussions of several important agricultural systems characteristic of the middle latitudes, primarily in the United States and Europe. These systems involve the production of both crops and livestock for commercial marketing. Two general systems of agriculture are especially characteristic of middle-latitude mixed farming: crop-livestock farming and dairying. These two categories show some similarities, but there are sharp distinctions as well. Moreover, within each system there are significant regional variations.

Crop-livestock farming and dairying are both characterized by year-round labor requirements; however, dairying is far more labor intensive, and its demands on labor are less seasonal. Both systems are highly mechanized and represent a large capital investment in land, buildings, machines, and livestock. Both systems typically produce a high standard of living and involve the use of modern, scientific agricultural methods. Crop-livestock farming, however, usually has fewer owner-operated units than does dairying, and the land values are higher. Dairying generally occupies smaller farms where more land is devoted to animals and less to crops than in crop-livestock production.

The fact that each of these systems may vary regionally can be seen by contrasting two major areas of crop-livestock farming: the Corn Belt of the United States and the mixed-farming region of northwest Europe. Both areas produce a variety of field crops and livestock, both are significant meat producers, and both have similar farming systems. Farms in Europe, however, tend to be smaller and less mechanized than their United States counterparts, with higher production per acre but lower production per worker. Moreover, there are climatic and other physical variations between the two areas.

The first two articles in this section deal with the crop-livestock system, particularly with the Corn Belt. Many of the generalizations formulated by these articles, however, may be extended not only to other areas of crop-livestock production but also to some dairying activity. Hidore's article is primarily concerned with the relationship between the production of field crops (for sale rather than on-farm feed) and physical features. He measures the apparent correlation between landforms and cash grain activities. Complementing this is Roepke's article which illustrates the changing limits of the Corn Belt in response to technological change — a variable which may modify the location of any economic activity. The third article, by Durand, concerns the major dairy areas of the United States Northeast and is especially useful in understanding the diversity of factors which may lie behind regional patterns and variations.

THE RELATIONSHIP BETWEEN CASH-GRAIN FARMING AND LANDFORMS

John J. Hidore

Dr. Hidore is an instructor in the Department of Geography, University of Wisconsin.

IT may be hypothesized that the distribution of cash-grain farms in the Midwest is largely associated with the distribution of level land. Such a hypothesis is derived from the known spatial distribution of cash-grain farms and a knowledge of the farming methods associated with this type of farming. Cash-grain farming in Midwest United States is completely mechanized from initial plowing to planting and harvesting. Flat land is necessary in a mechanized agricultural system both for efficient machine operation and for the maintenance of minimum rates of erosion.

There are, of course, many other factors in addition to flat land which help to explain the distribution of cash-grain farming. Some are physical, some economic, and still others are of a cultural nature. Relief, however, is believed to be one of the more important variables. It is the purpose of this paper to investigate the hypothesis that the pattern of cash-grain farming in the Midwest is spatially associated with the flatness of land. Since this paper is an examination of only one of the independent variables in what is certain to be a multi-variate relationship, it is not expected that this single independent variable will explain the entire spatial distribution of cash-grain farming.

The area selected for this study consists of eight states: North Dakota, South Dakota, Nebraska, Kansas, Minnesota, Iowa, Missouri, and Illinois. These states were selected for two reasons. First, within their boundaries occur portions of the largest contiguous concentrations of cash-grain production in the United States, and, second, of the total acreage in the United States planted to corn, oats, wheat, and barley, at least 45 per cent of each is within these eight states.[1]

DEFINITION AND DISTRIBUTION OF CASH-GRAIN FARMS

A cash-grain farm is defined by the United States Census of Agriculture as being one on which at least 50 per cent of the value of all farm products sold off the farm comes from the sale of specified grains.

Two measures of the distribution of cash-grain farms may be used. They are percentage of total farms classified as cash-grain and percentage of total farm area in cash-grain farms. The computed distributions are presented in Figures 1 to 3.

The first map shows the distribution of the percentage of total farms classified as cash-grain on a county basis. In order to graphically emphasize the areas of high and low values the isopleths are based upon the mean and standard deviation of the distribution. The use of the value of the mean as the primary

[1] U. S. Bureau of Census, United States Census of Agriculture, Vol. 1, 1954, U. S. Government Printing Office, Washington, 1956.

"The Relationship Between Cash-Grain Farming and Landforms" by John J. Hidore. Reprinted from Economic Geography, *Vol. 39 (January 1963), pp. 84–89, with permission of the editor.*

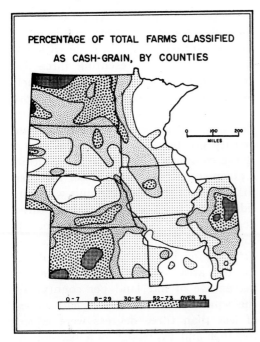

PERCENTAGE OF TOTAL FARMS CLASSIFIED AS CASH-GRAIN, BY COUNTIES

0-7   8-29   30-51   52-73   OVER 73

FIG. 1.

The maps show three areas of relative concentration of the dependent variable. They are essentially East Central Illinois, Northwest North Dakota, and Western Kansas. Each of these areas is in part two standard deviations above the mean.

DEFINITION AND DISTRIBUTION OF FLAT LAND

The concept of flat land is one that has been discussed and debated for many years. Technically, flat land would be a perfectly flat, horizontal surface, but for farming purposes land areas with gentle slopes are as good as, or better than, a horizontal plane would be. The question then is, if the land does not have a horizontal plane surface, what degree of sloping land can be classified as flat for the practical purposes of farming, and for cash-grain farming in particular?

With the very rapid increase in mechanization of cash-grain farming, it

isopleth and the standard deviation as the interval places the majority of the area which has values near the mean of the distribution in one category, while the areas which depart most from the mean are more clearly indicated. The second distribution is also percentage of total farms classified as cash-grain but based upon state economic areas as the areal unit.[2] The third distribution is based on percentage of total farm area in cash-grain farms by state economic areas. The second and third distributions are quite similar having equal or nearly equal ranges, means, standard deviations, and a coefficient of correlation between the two sets of data of $+.855$. These similarities suggest that as the percentage of cash-grain farms varies, so also does the percentage of area in cash-grain farms.

[2] The state economic areas used are those established by the Bureau of Census. They are basically defined as "—single counties or groups of counties which have similar economic and social characteristics."

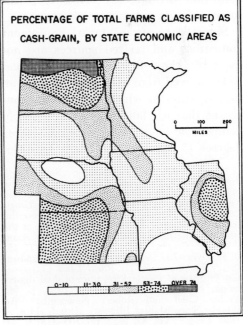

PERCENTAGE OF TOTAL FARMS CLASSIFIED AS CASH-GRAIN, BY STATE ECONOMIC AREAS

0-10   11-30   31-52   53-74   OVER 74

FIG. 2.

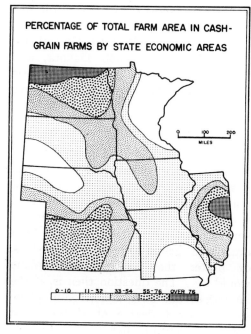

PERCENTAGE OF TOTAL FARM AREA IN CASH-GRAIN FARMS BY STATE ECONOMIC AREAS

0   100   200
MILES

0-10   11-32   33-54   55-76   OVER 76

FIG. 3.

appears as though the efficient limits of machine operation should be the most logical factor in determining the definition of flatness. However, this information is not easy to obtain.

Since data from farm equipment companies and related sources are not available, the definition of flat land had to be derived from existing literature, an investigation of which indicates a consensus that flat land may be acceptably defined as land with slopes of three degrees (5 per cent) or less.[3]   In order

[3] V. C. Finch: "Geographic Surveying," Bulletin No. 9, Geographic Society of Chicago, 1933, p. 5; Erwin Raisz and Joyce Henry: "An Average Slope Map of New England," *Geogr. Rev.*, Vol. 27, 1937, pp. 467–472; G. T. Trewartha and G. H. Smith: "Surface Configuration of the Driftless Cuestaform Hill Land," *Annals Assn. of Amer. Geogrs.*, Vol. 31, 1941, pp. 25–45; D. R. Dyer: *The Development of the Geographical Survey Techniques for the Rural Land Classification Program of Puerto Rico*, unpublished dissertation, Northwestern University, 1950, p. 96; Wesley Calef and Robert Newcomb: "An Average Slope Map of Illinois," *Annals Assn. of Amer. Geogrs.*, Vol. 43, 1953, pp. 305–315; R. D. Young: *A Geographic Classification of the Land-*

to determine areas having slopes of three degrees or less, topographic maps were consulted. Using a scale with the contour density representing three degree slopes, each square mile of each topographic sheet available for the eight states was checked for land area with slopes of over three degrees, or a contour density greater than that of the scale.[4] If the contours at any one place within a given square mile were closer together than those of the scale the unit was considered to have slopes of over three degrees. This method was used on all topographic maps with a scale of 1:62,500 or larger that were available for the area. To obtain a figure for percentage of flat land per county, all the square mile units that had slopes of less than three degrees were added together and expressed as a percentage of the total number of square miles in the county.

The entire Midwest, unfortunately, is not covered by topographic maps at the desired scale. Only Illinois and Missouri have nearly complete coverage. The other states have lesser degrees of coverage ranging down to a low of about one-fourth for Minnesota.

The existing topographic maps do provide a good sample representation, however, of the different types of land-forms found in the study area. Through the use of this sample coverage, together with information on landforms from available maps of geology, glaciology, slope, and erosion, a fairly accurate estimate was made of the percentage of flat land in the areas for which large-scale topographic maps were unavailable. The resultant distributions by county and economic area are shown in Figures 4 and 5.

forms of Puerto Rico, unpublished dissertation, University of Wisconsin, 1954, p. 75.
[4] A. N. Strahler: "Quantitative Slope Analysis," *Bull. Geol. Soc. of Amer.*, Vol. 67, 1956, pp. 571–596.

CORRELATIONS

After all percentages were derived for both flat land and cash-grain farms, a series of areally weighted product moment correlations were computed between the two distributions.[5]

The correlations are based on two sizes of areal units, the county and the state economic area. The universe contains 730 counties and 72 economic areas. The coefficients of correlation (r) and determination (r^2) for the universe between percentage of flat land and percentage of total farms classified as cash-grain are:

(1) by counties $r = +.667$ and $r^2 = .445$.
(2) by state economic areas $r = +.743$ and $r^2 = .552$.

The value of the coefficients of determination indicate that the variation in

[5] A. H. Robinson: "The Necessity of Weighting Values in Correlation Analysis of Areal Data," *Annals Assn. of Amer. Geogrs.*, Vol. 46, 1956, pp. 233–236.

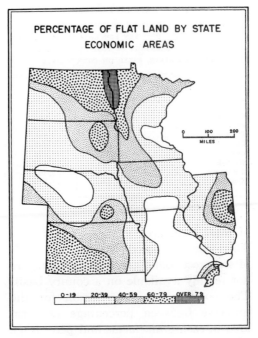

FIG. 5.

flat land "explains" about one-half of the variation in cash-grain farming.[6]

Tables I and II present the coefficients for individual states, based on county data and state economic area data respectively. The coefficients for South Dakota in Table II are the highest obtained for any state with either of the two dependent variables. In this case, the distribution of flat land "explains" 95 per cent of the variation in the distribution of cash-grain farming in the state.

The second variable correlated with percentage of flat land is the percentage

[6] The coefficient of correlation (r) is a dimensionless number which indicates the direction and degree of association between two variables. A value of zero indicates no association and the more nearly the value approaches ± 1 the closer the relationship between the two variables. The + or − serves to denote whether the association is a direct or inverse relationship. The coefficient of determination (r^2) when multiplied by *100* indicates the percentage of variation in the distribution of the dependent variable (cash-grain farming) which may be attributed to the variation of the independent variable (flat land).

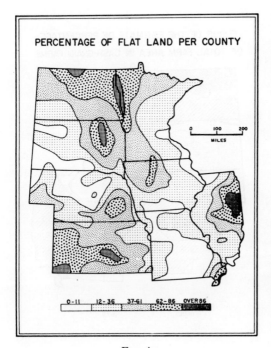

FIG. 4.

TABLE I

VALUE OF COEFFICIENTS OF CORRELATION AND
DETERMINATION BETWEEN PERCENTAGE OF FLAT
LAND AND PERCENTAGE OF CASH-GRAIN FARMS
FOR EACH STATE, BASED ON COUNTY DATA

State	r	r^2
North Dakota	+.971	.943
South Dakota	+.874	.764
Illinois	+.749	.561
Kansas	+.726	.527
Iowa	+.637	.406
Nebraska	+.585	.342
Minnesota	+.554	.307
Missouri	+.386	.149

TABLE II

VALUE OF COEFFICIENTS OF CORRELATION AND
DETERMINATION BETWEEN PERCENTAGE OF FLAT
LAND AND PERCENTAGE OF CASH-GRAIN FARMS
FOR STATES, DATA BY STATE ECONOMIC AREAS

State	r	r^2
South Dakota	+.974	.949
Illinois	+.926	.857
North Dakota	+.850	.723
Iowa	+.805	.648
Kansas	+.782	.612
Minnesota	+.730	.532
Nebraska	+.668	.446
Missouri	+.408	.166

of total farm area in cash-grain farms. This was computed only at the scale of state economic areas as the data are not readily available on a county basis. The coefficient of correlation for the universe between percentage of farm area in cash-grain farms and percentage of flat land is $r = +.746$ and $r^2 = .561$. These two variables show the highest correlation for the universe as a whole. In this case the amount of flat land accounts for about 56 per cent of the variation in distribution of farm land in cash-grain farms.

The residuals map, obtained by plotting the error of the estimate for percentage of total farm area in cash-grain farms, suggests that the general tendency was to underestimate the amount of cash-grain farming in the areas of existing high density of cash-grain farms, and to overestimate in areas of lowest density of cash-grain farms (Fig. 6).[7] The residuals map also indicates where other independent variables may be more significant, as, for example, in northeastern Minnesota and southeastern Missouri. Both areas are over two standard errors from the mean.

[7] The error of the estimate is the difference between the actual percentage of area in cash-grain farms and a percentage estimated from the amount of flat land in each economic area. Where the differences between the two values are greatest the association between the two variables is poorest.

In Minnesota the Laurential Upland provides an area of poor soils and poor drainage which has practically no cash-grain farms. Flat land is present but the periods of glaciation have left much of this land covered by thin soils or virtually no soil at all.

The Mississippi flood plain of southeastern Missouri is another area with very poor association between flat land and cash-grain farming. The climate

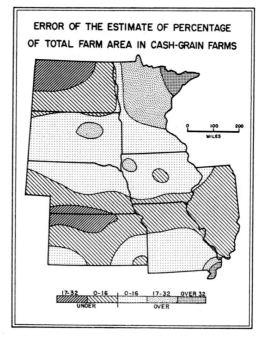

ERROR OF THE ESTIMATE OF PERCENTAGE
OF TOTAL FARM AREA IN CASH-GRAIN FARMS

FIG. 6.

TABLE III

VALUE OF COEFFICIENTS OF CORRELATION AND
DETERMINATION BETWEEN PERCENTAGE OF FARM
AREA IN CASH-GRAIN FARMS AND PERCENTAGE
OF FLAT LAND, DATA BY STATE ECONOMIC AREAS

State	r	r^2
South Dakota	+.938	.880
North Dakota	+.894	.799
Illinois	+.860	.740
Iowa	+.771	.594
Minnesota	+.758	.575
Nebraska	+.712	.507
Missouri	+.682	.465
Kansas	+.681	.464

here favors a mid-latitude subtropical type of agriculture. Here, as in north-eastern Minnesota, is an area of flat land but with little grain produced.

CONCLUSIONS

The results of this study support the hypothesis that the pattern of cash-grain farming in the Midwest is spatially associated with the flatness of the land. The graphic and statistical analysis suggests that the variation in the distribution of flat land "explains" up to 56 per cent of the variation in the distribution of cash-grain farming for the eight-state area as a whole and up to 95 per cent of the dependent variable in individual states.

Changes in Corn Production on the Northern Margin of the Corn Belt

Howard G. Roepke

Since the 1930's an almost complete change has been brought about in the type of corn grown commercially in the United States. In 1930, all the corn planted, except for experimental fields, was of the open-pollinated variety. At present, more than 90 per cent of the corn planted is hybrid seed of one sort or another. The early adoption was rather slow and confined to limited areas, so in order to illustrate the changes after it ceased to be a novelty this paper deals with the period from 1940, when less than one-third of United States corn was hybrid, to 1954, when nearly 90 per cent of the corn in the United States and 97 per cent of that grown in the North Central states was of hybrid varieties.[1]

Probably the most important consequence of hybridization is the increase in yield it has made possible (estimated at 20 per cent on a national basis),[2] but other desirable characteristics have also been obtained. Much of the efficiency of mechanical corn pickers, for example, is due to the breeding of corn varieties with improved standability.

The characteristic of hybrid corn with which this paper is concerned is rapid maturity and its consequences. Most of the old open-pollinated varieties took 140 days or longer to mature. Through hybridization, varieties have been developed which mature in as little as 90 days—although at some sacrifice in yield. (In passing it may be noted that some breeding has aimed at the opposite result—slower maturity in order to take maximum advantage of the long growing season in some areas.) The quick-maturing hybrids make it possible to grow corn for grain in areas where the short growing season formerly made this impossible.

There has been much speculation as to the effect of hybrids on the areal extent of corn production, and there have been tentative statements that the corn-growing area and perhaps even the Corn Belt[3] was being extended northward. Two types of areas might be expected to show agricultural change if there had been an extension of the corn-growing area; first, those areas which were formerly marginal for the growing of corn for grain but which can now count on maturing the crop each year; second, those areas where, because of the short growing season, little or no corn was formerly grown but which have now become at least marginal for corn. Any northward extension of the complex, multifactor region known as the Corn Belt would have to be revealed by coincident changes in other characteristics—livestock production, for example—and not by corn production alone.

The first set of maps[4] (Figs. 1 & 2) shows a change which has taken place within the heart of the corn-growing area as well as on its northern margin. Throughout the whole area there has been a general increase in the proportion of cropland planted in corn. In 1940 only three small areas had more than 40 per cent of their cropland in corn, while in 1954 these had expanded into two large sections covering much of the heart of the corn-growing area. In these areas of corn dominance the increased intensity of corn growing is probably not directly related to the introduction of hybrids, but rather reflects the decreasing number of work animals which has freed for corn land formerly devoted to the cultivation of oats for animal feed. Fig. 3, which shows the northern boundaries of the regions of various intensities for the two years, better illustrates these changes on the northern margin of the corn-growing area. On this northern margin the percent change in crop land planted in corn was even greater

---

[1] U. S. Department of Agriculture, *Agricultural Statistics, 1955* (Washington: Government Printing Office, 1956), 31.

[2] A. P. Grotewold, "Regional Changes in Corn Production in the United States from 1909 to 1949," Univ. of Chicago, Dept. of Geography, *Research Paper No. 40* (Chicago, 1955), 19.

[3] For a discussion of the general adoption of this term see: William Warntz, "An Historical Consideration of the Terms 'Corn' and 'Corn Belt' in the United States," *Agricultural History*, 31 (no. 1): 40–45 (January, 1957).

[4] Data used in compiling all the maps were taken from the 1954 *Census of Agriculture*.

"Changes in Corn Production on the Northern Margin of the Corn Belt" by Howard G. Roepke. Reprinted from Agricultural History, *Vol. 33 (July 1959), pp. 126–132, with permission of the editor.*

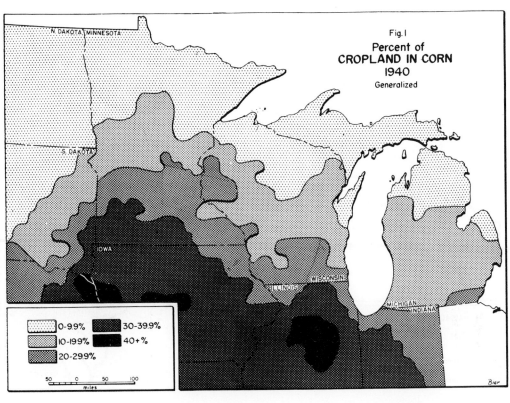

Fig. 1
Percent of
CROPLAND IN CORN
1940
Generalized

N. DAKOTA | MINNESOTA
S. DAKOTA
IOWA
WISCONSIN
ILLINOIS
MICHIGAN | INDIANA

0-9.9%		30-39.9%	
10-19.9%		40+%	
20-29.9%			

50 0 50 100
miles

Bier

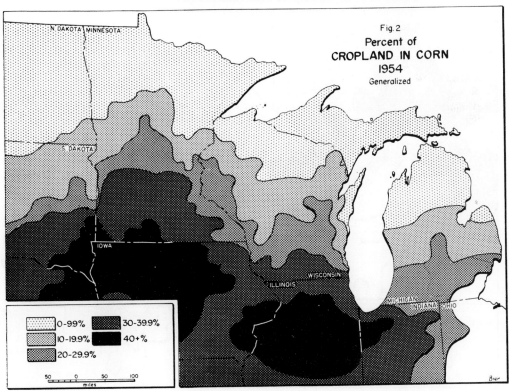

Fig. 2
Percent of
CROPLAND IN CORN
1954
Generalized

N. DAKOTA | MINNESOTA
S. DAKOTA
IOWA
WISCONSIN
ILLINOIS
MICHIGAN | INDIANA | OHIO

0-99%		30-39.9%	
10-19.9%		40+%	
20-29.9%			

50 0 50 100
miles

Bier

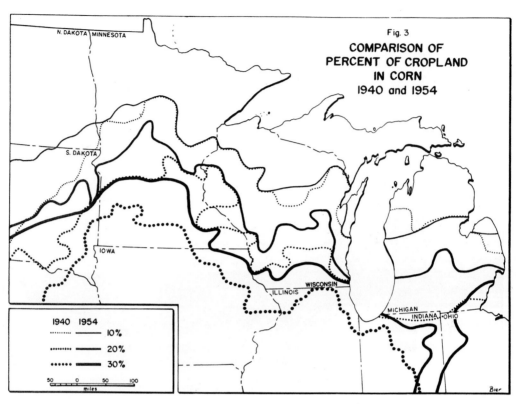

Fig. 3
COMPARISON OF
PERCENT OF CROPLAND
IN CORN
1940 and 1954

1940	1954	
....	———	10%
●●●●●●●	———	20%
●●●●●●●	———	30%

50 0 50 100
miles

Bier

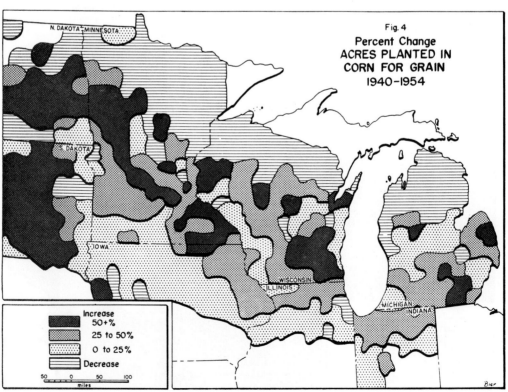

Fig. 4
Percent Change
ACRES PLANTED IN
CORN FOR GRAIN
1940-1954

Increase
50+%
25 to 50%
0 to 25%
Decrease

50 0 50 100
miles

Bier

134

than in the heart of the corn-growing area and undoubtedly reflects at least in part the availability of quicker-maturing hybrid corn. In areas formerly marginal for corn growing the boundaries have been displaced considerably northward. This is particularly apparent in the 20 per cent and 30 per cent lines and has occurred in Minnesota, Wisconsin, and Michigan. In contrast, the 10 per cent line has shifted very little in these states during the 1940-54 period. From this measure, then, it is indicated that there has been a considerable change in the intensity of corn growing in the areas formerly marginal for corn but relatively little change in areas where corn maturing has now become a marginal possibility.

Another method of discovering the areas in which the greatest change in corn growing has occurred is to examine directly the changes in the amount of land planted in corn. Since we are interested here particularly in the possibility of maturing corn, that planted for grain is probably the best indicator. Fig. 4 shows the per cent of change in the acreage planted to corn for grain between 1940 and 1954. Several things are apparent from this map. First, nearly the whole formerly-marginal area shows a marked increase in the acreage planted to corn for grain. Second, especially large increases—those amounting to 25 per cent or more—occur in Minnesota, Wisconsin, and Michigan in approximately the same areas which showed the greatest change on the previous maps. Third, there has been an actual decrease in the acreage of corn for grain in the northern parts of these states in the area presumably newly marginal for corn.

Much of the area shown on Fig. 4 as having less corn planted for grain in 1954 than in 1940 has an average frost-free period of about 120 days—which is very near the minimum for 90-day corn with the present imperfect weather forecasting techniques. While small amounts of corn were actually involved, it is interesting to speculate as to what kind of optimism led to the planting of corn for grain with the varieties available in 1940.

A much more widespread pattern of increase is shown on Fig. 5 which illustrates the change from 1940-1954 in the acreage of corn planted for silage. Some of the areas in Minnesota, Wisconsin, and Michigan which showed the greatest increase in corn for grain show decreases in corn for silage. This probably reflects the increased certainty of maturing the crop resulting from the use of hybrids. It should particularly be noted that the sizable areas of decrease in the southern portion of this map lie within the areas which were marginal for corn in 1940.

Changes in the actual production of corn are shown on the next series of maps. The measure of bushels per square mile was chosen because it probably best reflects the actual intensity of production by including the effect of variations in proportion of land in farms and in crops, differences in yield, etc. For whatever reasons, this is the production which has been attained. Fig. 6, showing production in 1940, illustrates the rapidity with which corn production decreased to the northward of the main producing area. (If the isopleths for quantities greater than 1000 bushels per square mile were shown, the close spacing would continue southward to a peak of 12 to 13 thousand in northern Illinois and central Iowa.). The major exception to the rapid decrease northward was in Western Michigan where the rate of change was less rapid. By 1954 (Fig. 7) this anomaly was no longer present. In 1954 the isopleths in Minnesota and Wisconsin had moved northward from their 1940 positions and showed a less rapid rate of decrease from the central area of high production. In Michigan the 1000 bushels per square mile line was in almost exactly the same position in 1954 as in 1940, while the isopleths of lower value were actually well south of their 1940 positions. The positions of the isopleths in the two years are compared in Fig. 8. Incidentally, the 1000 bushels per square mile line corresponds quite closely with the line of 4 bushels of corn per acre of farmland used by the United States Department of Agriculture as one of the criteria for the margin of the "commercial corn producing area" in establishing acreage allotments under the price support program.[5]

If space permitted, a similar series of maps could be shown to illustrate changes in the several factors which together may be used to

---

[5] The U.S.D.A., of course, uses a 10-year average production figure and includes the criterion of an average production in a county of 450 bu. or more per farm.

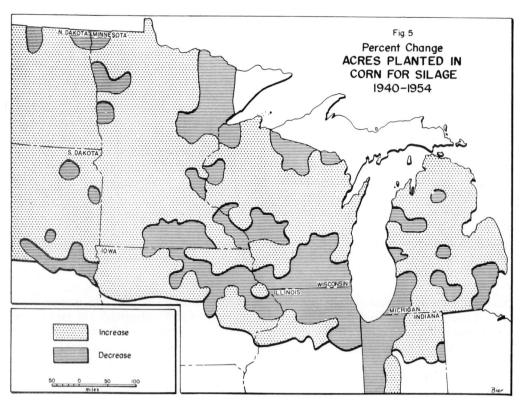

Fig. 5

Percent Change
ACRES PLANTED IN
CORN FOR SILAGE
1940-1954

Increase

Decrease

50   0   50   100
miles

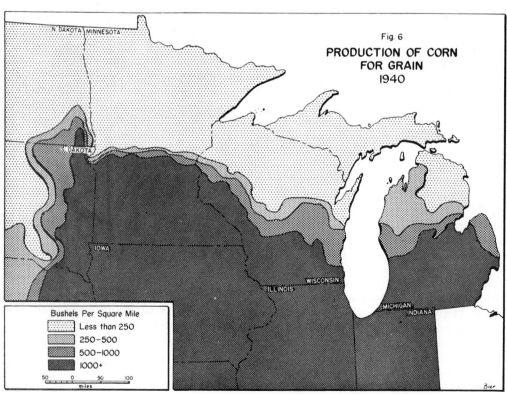

Fig. 6

PRODUCTION OF CORN
FOR GRAIN
1940

Bushels Per Square Mile
Less than 250
250-500
500-1000
1000+

50   0   50   100
miles

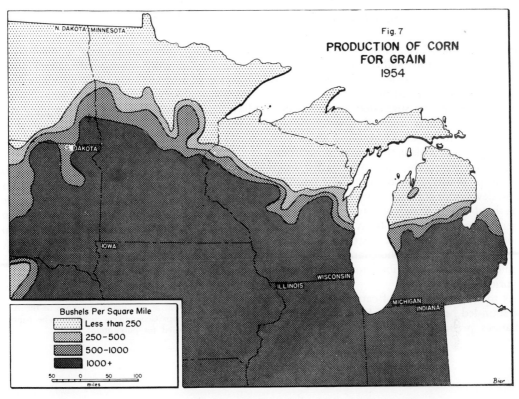

Fig. 7
**PRODUCTION OF CORN
FOR GRAIN
1954**

N. DAKOTA MINNESOTA

S. DAKOTA

IOWA

ILLINOIS   WISCONSIN

MICHIGAN
INDIANA

Bushels Per Square Mile
Less than 250
250-500
500-1000
1000+

50   0   50   100
miles

Bier

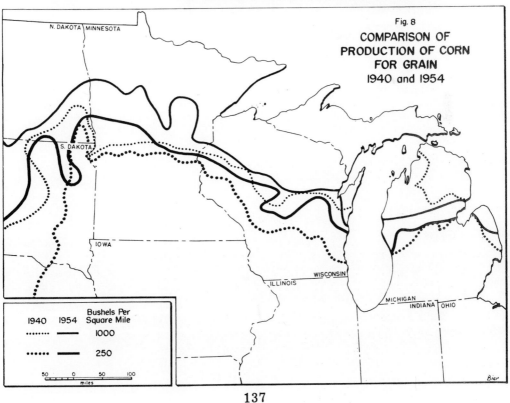

Fig. 8
**COMPARISON OF
PRODUCTION OF CORN
FOR GRAIN
1940 and 1954**

N. DAKOTA MINNESOTA

S. DAKOTA

IOWA

WISCONSIN

ILLINOIS

MICHIGAN
INDIANA   OHIO

1940   1954   Bushels Per
Square Mile
....   ————   1000
••••••   ▬▬▬▬   250

50   0   50   100
miles

Bier

137

define the Corn Belt. A summary of the results, however, must suffice. The patterns of change are much less clear than those already shown for corn production. Employing the multi-factor criteria suggested by de Laubenfels,[6] it is possible to find only one area which seems now to be acquiring true Corn Belt characteristics. This is the district in southern Wisconsin which showed up on earlier maps so conspicuously as increasing the amount of land devoted to corn for grain and decreasing the land devoted to corn for silage. Here there seems to be a shift from dairying to the Corn Belt crop-livestock system. It is quite certain, however, that the change in this area cannot be wholly ascribed to the impact of hybrid corn.

A more general note of caution should also be sounded here. This analysis has described changes probably attributable to the use of hybrid corn, but it by no means follows that these changes were the inevitable result of the introduction of the new varieties. The areal impact of these genetic improvements might have been quite different had the adoption of hybrids come under different market situations than have actually prevailed.

The introduction of quick-maturing and reliable varieties of hybrid corn, then, may be suggested to have had the following results: (1) a significant increase in grain corn production in areas formerly marginal for corn; (2) no significant extension into newly marginal areas; and (3) perhaps some part in the extension of the Corn Belt crop-livestock system into certain areas of southern Wisconsin.

---

[6] In a paper read at the annual meetings of the Association of American Geographers in 1955. The paper is now being prepared for publication.

THE MAJOR MILKSHEDS OF THE NORTHEASTERN QUARTER OF THE UNITED STATES

Loyal Durand, Jr.

Dr. Durand is Professor of Geography in the University of Tennessee. He has published widely on the geography of dairy farming in the United States.

THE production of fluid milk (market milk) for the densely inhabited and urbanized northeastern quarter of the United States is one of the most widespread activities within this portion of the nation. Although the broad American Dairy Region, from Maine to Minnesota with its southward extension in the Appalachian valleys and on the plains of southeastern Pennsylvania and Piedmont Maryland, is the chief contributor of the daily supply of milk to hundreds of cities, large and small, the existence of major cities in the heart of the Corn Belt, or on the Ohio and Missouri Rivers, and at the fringes of the region of intensive dairying has resulted in market-oriented dairy districts developing in their environs. Thus, there is hardly a county in the northeastern quarter of the nation that does not contain farms producing "Grade A" or city market milk—that destined for direct human consumption.[1]

The milksheds of the many major cities of the northeastern portion of the United States, from the Atlantic Ocean to the plains border, are competitive with one another. Milksheds of the

major cities usually overlap. They also surround, impinge upon, and compete with the milksheds of cities of small and medium size. Along transitional borders where two, three, or more major cities compete for milk, the individual farmer, the cooperative to which many farmers may belong, and the receiving station or the country pool plant to which whole milk is delivered each has a choice of market. When the milksheds of the hundreds of cities of medium and small size are added to the economic scene, the over-all American Dairy Region and the adjacent types-of-farming regions to its south become areas of severe competition among the dairy distributors for market milk. A few random examples will illustrate this. Milk from southwestern Vermont is directed to New York and Boston. Dairy districts in New York State west of the Catskill Mountains ship to New York City, Philadelphia, and to Connecticut markets. New York and Philadelphia compete in southeastern Pennsylvania and in the Appalachian valleys of the state, and these two cities, with Baltimore, Wilmington, and Washington added, draw milk from Delaware and the eastern shore of Maryland. The Cleveland milkshed overlaps on the east those of both Pittsburgh and New York; it also overlaps on the west the milksheds of both Chicago and Detroit, and over-

[1] Manufactured milk is Grade B. The differences are mainly ones of market, and of certain inspection items, rules, and regulations, as set up by the dairy inspections and health departments of the cities. If the city market is available and the price is attractive, most dairy farmers can make the capital investment to meet the Grade A regulations.

"The Major Milksheds of the Northeastern Quarter of the United States" by Loyal Durand, Jr. Reprinted from Economic Geography, *Vol. 40 (January 1964), pp. 9–33, with permission of the editor.*

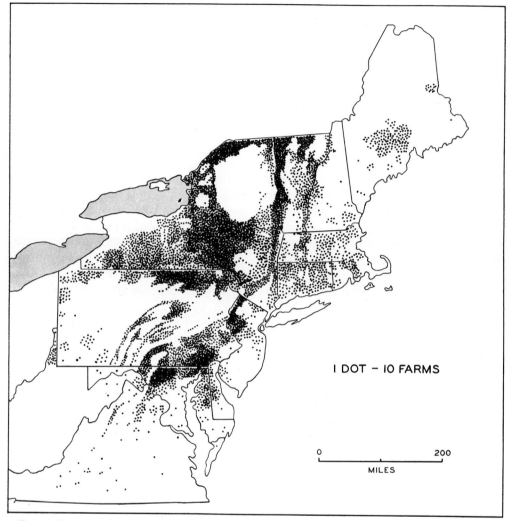

1 DOT – 10 FARMS

0   200
MILES

Fig. 1. Farms in the major milksheds of the northeastern United States, 1962. Each dot depicts ten farms.

laps on the south those of Cincinnati, Columbus, Dayton, and Indianapolis. Several counties in northeastern Indiana are in seven major milksheds. The Milwaukee milkshed is competitive everywhere with that of Chicago; even in the small and almost-completely urbanized County of Milwaukee, of 41 dairy farms remaining in 1962, only 25 shipped to adjacent Milwaukee, despite propinquity to the twelfth city in size in the nation; 16 farms (all less than ten miles from Milwaukee) shipped to the Chicago market. The Chicago milkshed, in addition, overlaps those of St. Louis, Indianapolis, Detroit, Minneapolis–St. Paul, and Duluth. Farmers in southwestern Missouri supply milk to the cities of St. Louis, Kansas City, Dallas, Fort Worth, Oklahoma City, and San Antonio.

Milksheds may become complicated by certain market factors. An 1800-mile long milk route transports fresh milk in cartons from Minneapolis to Phoenix, Arizona. This milk from the milkshed of

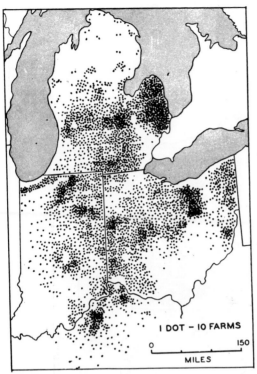

FIG. 2. Farms in the major milksheds of the eastern portion of the middle western United States, 1962. Each dot depicts ten farms.

the Twin Cities has originated both in east-central Minnesota and in northwestern Wisconsin, and yet is delivered to a consumer in Arizona. The bottling of milk in a city of the northeastern United States, and its sale in a nearby city, or the shipment of milk in bulk from one city to an adjacent one, is not unusual. Milk delivered to Dayton, Ohio, is bottled and marketed in part in Columbus; milk from Lansing, Michigan, is shipped in part to Grand Rapids, although each city has its own major area of supply; these examples could be multiplied many times. And the New England milk producers maintain a general supply plant in Springfield, Massachusetts, from which milk can be directed, when needed, to any market in southern New England. Thus a portion of the final market for milk may not be in the original milkshed of pro-

duction or city of receipt, even though market milk is bulky and relatively costly to transport.

ORGANIZATION OF MILKSHEDS

The *major* milksheds, here mapped, are defined by the writer as milksheds on which there are more than 1000 separate producing farms and for which there is reliable data. Milksheds, in organization, may be: (1) under Federal Order and control, (2) under state control, or (3) unregulated—the latter meaning, in effect, that neither the federal nor state authorities are involved in regulation. In all cases, however, every urban milkshed is subject to city control through health department regulations and inspections. Data vary among the control agencies and health departments. In some few cases there is none: even field trips fail to disclose adequate information; some states collect no data; in certain cities only the retail distributors may have information on their sources, information they may refuse to disclose. However, the 26 major milksheds mapped (those for which the writer has adequate information) provide a pattern for the northeastern quarter of the United States. The theoretical "circular" milkshed rarely occurs: Minneapolis–St. Paul, Omaha, and Columbus, Ohio, are the closest examples, and even in these certain segments of the circle are more productive than others. The usual milkshed is highly irregular in shape. A few are oval rather than circular. Many contain outlying non-contiguous producing areas.

Federal Orders

The Federal Order Markets originated pursuant to the provisions of the Agricultural Marketing Agreement of 1937. These orders, as now amended, are administered by the Agricultural Stabiliza-

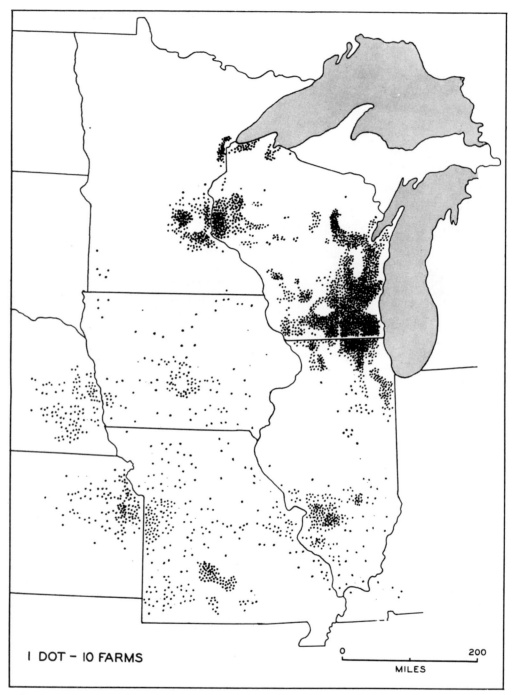

FIG. 3. Farms in the major milksheds of the western portion of the middle western United States, 1962. Each dot depicts ten farms.

1 DOT – 10 FARMS

0   200
MILES

FIG. 4. Major milksheds and competitive overlaps in the northeastern United States, 1962. The numbers are explained in Appendices A and B.

tion and Conservation Service (ASCS), Marketing Agreements and Orders, United States Department of Agriculture. Each specific order is administered by a Market Administrator and his staff, the office for each being located in the central city of the particular Federal Order. There are 83 Federal Order milk marketing areas (early 1963), and others are added almost annually.

Some 90 million people, or about 53 per cent of the 1960 population of the United States, now are subject to the federal milk orders. These orders now cover the marketing of milk for three-quarters (73.5 per cent) of the urban and suburban residents of the nation. And 45.1 per cent of all milk delivered to all plants and dealers in the conterminous United States in 1961 was federally regulated. Nine of the ten largest Federal Order Markets are located in the area mapped.

The Market Administrator, through the use of a formula, determines the monthly minimum price to be paid by the *handlers* (milk distributors) to the *producers* (farmers) for market milk. Federal Orders are operative, also, in the admission of new *country pool plants* (milk receiving stations) to the milksheds; thus, they affect the marketing directly and the extent of the milkshed indirectly.

The minimum price to be paid by the handler to the producer is a *blended price*. It is a blend of the higher price paid for milk consumed as whole milk, skim milk, cream, and half-and-half and of a lower price paid for surplus milk not needed at the time. All farmers on the milkshed share in the price differential and receive the blended price. Thus, a farmer who delivers directly to a bottling plant (and knows that all of his production has been marketed in bottles or cartons) has his check reduced in proportion to the amount of surplus of the *entire milkshed*. A widespread formula in use for the determination of payment for surplus milk in the blended price is the Wisconsin-Minnesota monthly price of manufactural milk; this reflects the fact that nearly half of all the milk used in dairy manufacture originates and is processed in these two states. The amount of surplus differs greatly among milksheds during the course of a year; some have very little, some are plagued by the problem of surpluses. Nearly all possess a seasonal surplus during the spring—the "spring flush" from April to June when cows are first on pastures. The surplus is manufactured: Federal Order Markets alone, from coast to coast, supplied 57 per cent of the cottage cheese, 40 per cent of the ice cream, 21 per

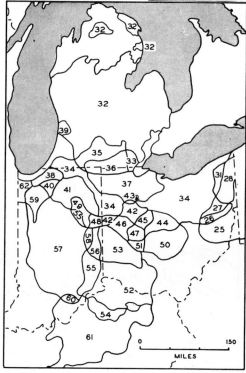

FIG. 5. Major milksheds and competitive overlaps in the eastern portion of the middle western United States, 1962. The numbers are explained in Appendices A and B.

cent of the evaporated and condensed milk, 16 per cent of the butter, and 15 per cent of the cheese of the nation in 1961.

State and Local Control

Several states or parts thereof have state milk control agencies, and these set minimum prices and promulgate other regulations concerning marketing. California is the largest state-controlled market. In the northeastern quarter of the United States, some cities in New York State, Pennsylvania, and New Jersey beyond the metropolitan areas have state control. Pittsburgh and Buffalo are the largest of the state-controlled markets in the northeast. By contrast, in this section, New England producers are subject to the highest percentage of federal control, 90 per cent of the milk produced being so regulated.

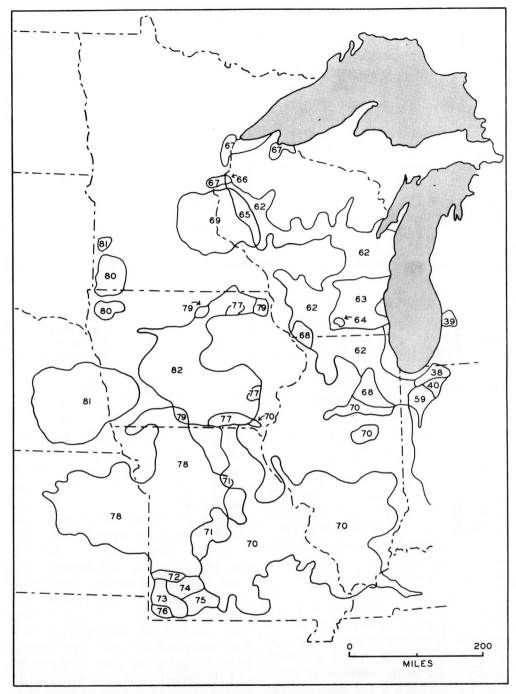

FIG. 6. Major milksheds and competitive overlaps in the western portion of the middle western United States, 1962. The numbers are explained in Appendices A and B.

The local health authorities in all cities have control of inspection and health services. They may be important in helping determine the outer boundary of milksheds by refusing inspection of farms beyond an arbitrarily-set mileage. Or, in cases of perennial shortages of milk, they may expand milksheds by granting inspection or by allowing milk from distant milksheds to enter their market if the inspection has been made by sister health authorities.

Milk Collection Patterns

Milk in major milksheds is now usually collected from bulk tanks, installed in a milkhouse, or in a sealed milk room in the dairy barn.[2] There is still some collection in cans, but this is passing from the scene rapidly; over 93 per cent of Chicago's milk was assembled in bulk tanks in early 1963, whereas in 1954 this percentage was less than five. On some milksheds all producers are equipped with bulk tanks which require a capital investment of from $3,000 to $5,000, or more, dependent upon the size of the herd.

There is direct delivery by tank truck from the farm to the city milk distributor on small (in area) milksheds and from close-in portions of large milksheds. Springfield, Massachusetts, for example, has all direct delivery from producer to handler.

The country pool plant on Federal Order Markets or a country receiving station on other milksheds assembles the milk for forwarding by rail or truck. These plants are located in a village or town, not in the open countryside. The number of country plants varies

[2] The milk passes from the milking machine through pipes to the cooler and bulk tank. It is cooled almost immediately to a temperature of a few degrees above freezing. When the tank truck arrives for collection, the milk is pumped to it from the bulk tank. The truck is unloaded by pumping at the country pool plant or at the plant of the city distributor. Railroad tank cars are handled the same way.

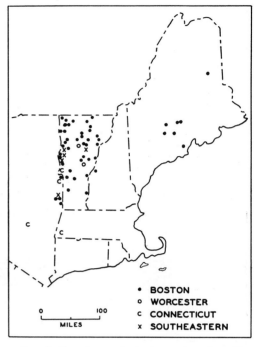

- • BOSTON
- ○ WORCESTER
- c CONNECTICUT
- × SOUTHEASTERN

FIG. 7. Country pool plants serving the milksheds of New England cities, 1962.

with respect to the size of and distances within the milkshed. The Connecticut milkshed, a Federal Order and state-wide one, has direct delivery from all nearby portions of New York, Connecticut, and Massachusetts; it is in addition served by four country pool plants, located at Smith's Basin and Prattsville, New York, Great Barrington, Massachusetts, and Benson, Vermont. Large milksheds have many country plants, some of them as distant as 300 or more miles from the market. The milkshed of Metropolitan New York contained 443 country pool plants in 1958, some as far away as the outlet of Lake Ontario, and in extreme northwestern Pennsylvania, near Lake Erie. Many country plants are now being consolidated in response to excellent highways, bulk tank receipts from farms, and longer truck hauls in larger trucks. The Boston milkshed was served by 50 country plants in 1962, a reduction from the 84 of 1958; of those remaining, the greatest concentrations are in the most distant portions of the milkshed, in northern Vermont and central Maine.

Country plants (or creameries, cheese factories, and condenseries) located within a Federal Order area, but whose milk is not shipped to an "order city" are said to be "unregulated" and non-pool plants. They must find a market for their receipts of milk in a "non-Federal Order" city or town, or else use the milk in dairy manufacture. Under complicated rules, they may qualify for the milkshed and thus are potential sources of supply if needed.[3]

The Farms

The farms that produce milk for the many cities of the northeastern quarter of the United States are almost entirely *family farms*. Thus, large numbers of farms on a major milkshed are usual. The milksheds mapped contained, collectively, a total of more than 155,000 farms in 1962. Some 48,000 farms supply the New York–New Jersey (metropolitan New York) milk. There are 20,000 farms in the Chicago milkshed, 10,000 in that of Detroit. Milwaukee and Minneapolis–St. Paul, located in the heart of the Dairy Region, are supplied by 2300 and 3700 farms, respectively, all located within a 100 miles of the cities. St. Louis, in a generally non-dairying agricultural region, has to obtain milk from 4700 farms in five states—Missouri, Illinois, Iowa, Wis-

[3] The requirements for admission to the milkshed vary from Order to Order. For example, on the Chicago Order a country pool plant, to qualify, must ship 30 per cent of the butterfat (cream) in milk, or 30 per cent of the volume of milk to handlers in the Chicago market in July and December, 40 per cent from August through November, and 15 per cent in January and February. By so doing, it attains pool plant status from March to June and rounds out the year of qualification, and is on the market. Farmers delivering milk to the plant are now producers for Chicago. Procedures differ on different orders, and are amended from time to time.

consin, and Kentucky. At the western margin of the Corn Belt, Kansas City and Omaha have little nearby urban competition for milk. But they lie in the heart of the livestock-rearing countryside where dairy farms are few; this results in areally enlarged milksheds, considering the size of the markets. Thus, not only do nearby portions of Missouri and Kansas, and Nebraska and Iowa, respectively, contribute milk to these cities, but each obtains some from Minnesota; Kansas City reaches also to portions of Iowa.

Negatively, the feedlot-type of dairy farm, conspicuous in warmer regions, such as in southeastern Florida, near some cities of Texas, in southern Arizona, in the environs of Los Angeles and San Diego, and in Hawaii, is virtually absent from milksheds of the northeastern quarter of the United States.[4] A few such are located near eastern cities; custom-milking occurs in a few isolated places—the cows of several owners being fed and milked at one central farm by an operator hired for the purpose.

BROAD CLASSIFICATION OF NORTHEASTERN MILKSHEDS

A broad or gross twofold classification of the milksheds of the northeastern quarter of the United States is suggested: (1) those entirely in the type-of-farming region characterized by dairying—the American Dairy Region; and (2) those within other types-of-farming regions, where the market-oriented dairy farm has developed in response to the urban demand and the attractive prices and steady monthly income that it provides.

[4] Examples of the feedlot-type of milk production for city markets are discussed in: Loyal Durand, Jr., "The Dairy Industry of the Hawaiian Islands," *Econ. Geog.*, Vol. 35, 1959, pp. 228–246; and in Gordon J. Fielding, "Dairying in Cities Designed to Keep People Out," *Professional Geogr.*, Vol. 14, 1962, pp. 1–5.

Milksheds in the Dairy Region

Milksheds in the Dairy Region are in the area where dairying is the major rural enterprise, where its existence has been traditional for a hundred years or more in response to many human and environmental factors, where the monthly income from milk sales has been regular and expected, and where the farm population has generally been trained or brought up in dairying. Cattle densities are high, cows are productive, milk production per cow or per farm is large. With the growth of cities in or near this region, the use of milk for manufacture has declined with respect to its use as market milk, especially in the eastern states.[5] Because many city markets are located within the southern portion of the Dairy Region, or immediately south of it, shipments of milk move generally in a southerly direction throughout large areas.

Many major cities receive their entire supply of milk from the Dairy Region. Among these are: Boston and the cities of New England; those of upstate New York such as Syracuse, Rochester, and Buffalo; and the cities of Detroit, Chicago, Milwaukee, Minneapolis, and St. Paul. Nearly all of the milk for Metropolitan New York is from the Dairy Region. Much of Cleveland's milk originates in this type-of-farming area.

Some milksheds within the Dairy Region terminate sharply at the Canadian border. The Boston supply area terminates abruptly at the northern boundary of Vermont, and the New York–New Jersey milkshed ends at the 45th parallel and the St. Lawrence River. The Detroit milkshed spreads westward and northward of the city, even to the Straits of Mackinac, but does not cross the Detroit or St. Clair Rivers or Lake St. Clair into Canada, even though there are Canadian dairy farms within a few miles of downtown Detroit. At present, under federal regulations, imported fluid milk must pass through a milk-import station; none have been built.

There are, no doubt, southward extensions of the American Dairy Region that have developed or intensified in response to market orientation. One such extension is, in all probability, the extreme southeast of Pennsylvania together with Piedmont Maryland and the extreme north of Virginia. But detailed work has disclosed that some of these so-cited extensions were dairy areas in the past and engaged in the manufacture of dairy products: the Pennsylvania German communities engaged in dairy manufacture almost from their inception, and a large area in southeastern Pennsylvania north and northwest of Philadelphia contained numerous creameries and some cheese factories as late as the 1910's; there was also an important manufacture of butter in Maryland, just northwest of Baltimore. Another example is northeastern Illinois (north and northwest of Chicago in the young Wisconsin Drift); long before the Chicago milkshed expanded to this area it was important in the manufacture of butter, and Elgin was the quotation center for national butter prices.[6]

---

[5] The use of milk for manufacture in New York State is now confined mainly to the St. Lawrence Valley and a few scattered locations. Even in the St. Lawrence Valley, the principal manufacture of cheese in the remaining cheese factories is during the spring flush. In Pennsylvania, less than 5 per cent of the milk production enters manufacture. In general, most Eastern manufacture is now only of surplus in the milksheds.

[6] V. C. Finch and O. E. Baker, *Geography of the World's Agriculture*, Washington, 1917. (Maps, pp. 118 and 119). See also Loyal Durand, Jr. "Dairy Region of Southeastern Wisconsin and Northeastern Illinois," *Econ. Geog.*, Vol. 16, 1940, pp. 416–428. (Illustration and map, p. 422).

Milksheds Outside of the Dairy Region

The milksheds that are not within the major American Dairy Region, or extend into it only in part, are basically those of the cities located within the livestock-farming area of the Corn Belt, the cash-grain farming portions of the Corn Belt, and in the general farming regions to the south of it. On the Atlantic side of the Appalachian divide, a large part of the milkshed of Washington, D.C., lies well south of the Dairy Region and extends into several types-of-farming areas. In all of these milksheds, the original market-oriented dairy farm or dairy district is near or even adjacent to the city. But the rapid growth of the cities has resulted in an expanding market as well as the loss of local dairy farms to suburbanization; therefore, through the years, the milksheds have enlarged into livestock-farming areas not formerly engaged in serving the milk market. This is in contrast to the milksheds of the Dairy Region. The New York milkshed expanded into the cheese-manufacturing regions of the Mohawk Valley, and eventually over most of the state. Cleveland expanded to the cheese regions of northeastern Ohio, Detroit and Toledo to the former Lenawee cheese area of Michigan and to condensery districts, Chicago and Milwaukee to regions of dairy manufacture.

The enlargement of the non-Dairy Region milksheds has not necessarily resulted in the displacement of the former type of farming. Dairy farms are established among the original types; individuals shift to a dairy enterprise; younger farmers, if they have the capital to invest, engage in dairying from the start as the regularity of income is attractive in meeting mortgage payments; displaced dairymen from the urban fringe buy farms and shift the location of their operations. Many farmers—the majority in nearly all cases—continue with their livestock, tobacco, or other income-producing activity. The choice is up to the individual. And in these latitudes the farm operator has more alternative choices than his counterpart in the American Dairy Region in general, or the more northern, cool-summer portion of it in particular.

The major milksheds outside of the Dairy Region proper are *larger in area*, considering the *size of the city market* they supply, than those of the American Dairy Region. They are *less intensive* in milk production *per unit area*. The dairy farms are scattered among other types; there are few districts of marked concentration of dairying. Collection routes from the country pool plant or city handler are longer in order to obtain an adequate supply. The actual dairy farm may ship as much milk as its Wisconsin or New York counterpart, but the distances between such farms are longer; instead of 300 to 1000 farms per county in a milkshed (common in the Chicago and New York supply areas), figures of 20 to 50 for an equivalent-sized county are more usual. In some of the milksheds of the cities of the western Corn Belt, west of the Mississippi River, and in considerable portions of the central Virginia section of the Washington milkshed, fewer than ten farms per county are in the milkshed—fewer than five in many areas.

The less intensive production of milk per unit area in the milksheds located outside of the Dairy Region proper is evident in many ways; among these are the landscape features such as the more widely dispersed dairy farms and dairy herds, the areal extent of the milksheds themselves, and the relatively large numbers of farms in the milkshed in proportion to the size of the market (as compared with numbers in milksheds within the Dairy Region). For example, the Indianapolis milkshed, with 3800 producers, covers nearly all of Indiana except the southwest; it is three times larger in area than the Milwaukee milkshed, and supplies a market whose predominant urban county contains 700,000 people, as against the more than a million inhabitants in metropolitan Milwaukee, whose milk originates on 2300 farms. St. Louis and its suburbs receive milk from 4700 farms located in a milkshed highly irregular in shape, fragmented in form, and with outliers of production. Some of the farms are almost as distant from the city in airline miles as the outer limits of the 48,000-farm New York–New Jersey milkshed, and farther than the outer border of that of Philadelphia. In contrast to the St. Louis situation, in the intensive dairy region of extreme southeastern Wisconsin, within a semicircle of a radius of 60 miles from Milwaukee (Lake Michigan precludes a full circle), there are 4500 farms serving the Chicago market and 1500 in the Milwaukee milkshed; also, within the northwestern arc of this semicircle there is manufac-

ture of dairy products.[7] If St. Louis were close to this area it could obtain its entire milk supply from it.

A further feature of several of the milksheds that are not in the Dairy Region proper is that *more than 100 per cent* of the *census-classified dairy farms* are on the urban market. This is particularly true of the northern two-thirds of Indiana and of western Ohio; it is also a feature of the Omaha milkshed. This seeming anomoly is the result of the fact that many a livestock farmer maintains a small dairy herd as a supplementary source of income. They ship to a country pool plant. Thus, when these producers are added (in milkshed farm totals) to the specialized dairy farms, the figure exceeds one hundred. The widespread prevalence of this type of livestock-dairy farm in western Ohio and Indiana reflects the fact that this area is one of very severe competition

[7] Dodge County, Wisconsin, manufactured more cheese in 1961 than any state but five, and in this county in the same year 896 farms shipped market milk to Chicago, 246 to Milwaukee.

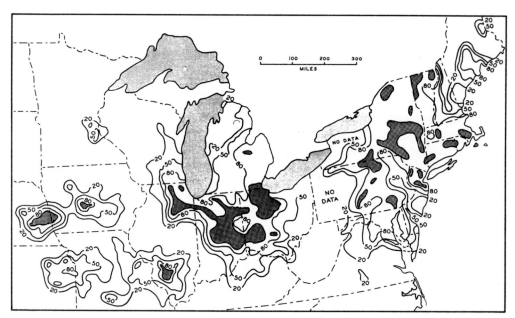

Fig. 8. Percentage of census-classified dairy farms in major milksheds, 1961.

for milk. The explanation of this anomoly in the Omaha milkshed, one of little urban competition from elsewhere, is in part the same. It is also related to the fact that many of the livestock-dairymen possess large farms and are major feeders of western beef cattle during the winter; their sales of finished cattle to stockyards are of such magnitude that their enterprise (even if quite significant in dairying) is census-classified on an income basis in the livestock-farm category.

GENERAL REGIONAL DISTRIBUTION PATTERNS

New England

The milksheds of New England lie largely within the six states of the section, and in that part of New York State between the Hudson River and the eastern border of the state. Farther north, Lake Champlain is the western limit of milk destined for the cities of New England, except for an extension of the Boston milkshed almost to the Canadian border in northeastern New York. These milksheds are thus generally concentrated regionally except for a few Mohawk Valley farms and an outlier of the Connecticut milkshed in New York state west of the Catskill Mountains.

Nearly all of the farming districts of New England produce market milk. The pattern of agriculture is reflected in the over-all production of milk. Even the islands in Lake Champlain and farms on Martha's Vineyard Island in the Atlantic are in major milksheds.

The Boston milkshed of 10,000 farm producers funnels northwestward from the city to its chief source region in Vermont and northeastward to a secondary source in south-central Maine, jumping the milkshed of Portland. Sixty per cent of the farms in the milkshed are in Vermont, nearly 20 per cent

in Maine. Only a small area west of the city and the extreme northeast of Massachusetts are included in the milkshed, and Boston has only 450 producers of milk in this state, a smaller number of Massachusetts farms than in the milksheds each of Springfield, of Worcester, or of Fall River–New Bedford. Expansion through the years has been to the former dairy manufacturing area of northern New England, and into Washington County, New York, west of southern Vermont, one of the three most intensive county-producers. In several districts of Vermont the milkshed overlaps with outlying producing-areas of the milksheds of the other Massachusetts cities. The most distant supplier of Boston is Aroostook County, Maine, separated from the principal source region in Maine by forest-farm country; the country pool plant in this county is 329 road-miles from Boston.

The milksheds of the other cities in Massachusetts are smaller in area, and more compact. Each, however, obtains some milk from New York and from every New England state except Maine (and Rhode Island in two cases). Massachusetts producers are dominant in each.

The Connecticut milkshed is a state-wide one under Federal Order. Two thousand farms in the state and over 1000 in the Hudson River counties of New York, other farms west of the Catskills, plus producers in Rhode Island, Massachusetts, and Vermont supply the handlers. The most intensive production is in the Litchfield area of northwestern Connecticut and in the Hudson River counties of New York to its west.

Milk production in New England is almost entirely organized around the fluid market. Prices of milk are high, usually $1.50 to $2.00 per hundredweight above the Middle Western price, more than that above the Wisconsin-

Minnesota manufactured price. Regional effort in pricing systems, methods of payment, and in other forms operate to keep "New England markets for New England (and Hudson Valley) producers" and "outside milk" out; the fear is of the attraction of New England prices to New York State producers, and to the Middle West, especially Wisconsin.[8]

New York

The 48,000 dairy farms of the New York–New Jersey (Metropolitan Region) milkshed are located in six states. The milkshed includes nearly all of the farming areas of New York State except for the Rochester-Buffalo-Niagara frontier area. The producers are in the southern plateau of the state, the Mohawk Valley, the central counties, and as far west as the state extends; they surround the non-agricultural Adirondack Mountains, the rougher portions of the Catskills, and the Tug Hill Plateau. County after county in New York contains more than 500 farms in the milkshed; a dozen counties have more than 1000, some over 2000, one nearly 3000. In all, some 32,000 separate farms in this intensive dairy state ship milk to New York; other farms supply the considerable quantities of milk consumed in Buffalo, Rochester, Syracuse, and the host of smaller cities.

The portion of the New York milkshed contiguous with New York State includes the northern tier of counties of

[8] In June, 1962, the Federal Government lost the Lehigh Case in the courts. A cooperative in Pennsylvania had challenged the compensatory payment provision, a method of payment used in certain Federal Orders (including all in New England) whereby differential prices for milk used as cream and as whole milk were paid into a producer settlement fund (the pool). The object was to keep out outside or non-pool milk (called "riding the pool" in the industry). As of the time of writing, the New England Orders had appointed committees to study the situation and to recommend changes that would be within the policy expressed by Congress in the law, and yet operate toward the same result.

Pennsylvania westward almost to the Ohio line, southwestern Vermont, and the Appalachian valleys of northwestern New Jersey; it thence extends southward in the Delaware River area to within 40 miles of Philadelphia.

The New York milkshed has several outliers, major ones in southeastern Pennsylvania, the Appalachian valleys of the state such as the Kishacoquillas (Big) Valley, and a minor one on the Delmarva Peninsula—part of the eastern shore of Maryland and central Delaware. In total, there are more than 12,000 Pennsylvania farmers shipping milk to New York; a quarter of the milk production of the state reaches this market.

The New York milkshed partially blocks Philadelphia in southeastern Pennsylvania. Lancaster County, although a leading supplier of milk for Philadelphia, has more farms shipping milk to New York. Chester County, just west of Philadelphia, contains over 250 New York producers, and 700 in the Philadelphia milkshed. Westward and northward, in York, Adams, and Lebanon counties, New York producers dominate; more than 85 per cent of the producers for these two markets ship to New York. Still farther west, in the Appalachian valley counties just north of the Maryland line, Philadelphia is virtually supreme, its milkshed extending to the base of the Allegheny Front. Thus, this milk, destined for Philadelphia, is hauled through the southeastern Pennsylvania portion of the New York milkshed; and milk from more than 2500 farms that are closer to Philadelphia than to New York passes through (or near to) that city en route to the more distant market. Early trade and business connections, rail (now usually truck) transport, and other competitive factors help explain this; when the Philadelphia milkshed expanded westward it was "forced to jump" this region, or the handlers would have found it necessary to offer higher prices to divert the supply. The New York milkshed dominates, too, in the Appalachian valleys of central Pennsylvania, in some areas by well over 90 per cent.

Philadelphia

The traditional source of Philadelphia's milk supply has been to the north and northwest of the city, and immediately to the west. The present milkshed has expanded northward to the Appalachian foothills in the Delaware Valley, and up the Susquehanna Valley into the wide lowland tributary at right angles to the main river, an area where Philadelphia producers are dominant. Westward, even in Chester County, there is now competition with New York. The competition continues westward, as noted. Beyond this competitive area the Philadelphia milkshed widens, not only in Pennsylvania, but southward of the Mason-Dixon Line into the Great Valley in Maryland, and the Valley counties in the Eastern "panhandle" of West Virginia. Philadelphia now receives milk from dairy farms in western Pennsylvania, on the Appalachian Plateau, in the broad Pittsburgh region. These more distant districts, of recent advent in the milkshed, are easily accessible to market by the route of the Pennsylvania Turnpike.

The entire Delmarva Peninsula lies within the Philadelphia milkshed. Farms in the milkshed are not only in Maryland and Delaware; there are also a few in the outlying counties of Virginia, at the southern tip of the peninsula, between Chesapeake Bay and the Atlantic. With some small areas in extreme southern New Jersey in the milkshed, and a small detached Philadelphia producing district west of the Catskills in New York, the more than 6000 farms of the milkshed are in six states, although five out of every six are in Pennsylvania; 17 per cent of the state's milk production reaches this market, a lower percentage than that marketed in New York.

Baltimore and Washington

The Mason-Dixon Line is virtually a northern boundary of the compact Baltimore milkshed. Only a few more than 200 farms are north of it in Pennsylvania, and more than a hundred of these are located in southern York County. More than 1700 of Maryland's 2000 producers in the milkshed are located in five counties near the city, from the northeastern corner of the state westward to the base of the Blue Ridge. From this area, Baltimore handlers receive most of their milk; only on the west, in Frederick County, is there major competition from Washington. The expansion of the milkshed has been "around" the head of Chesapeake Bay into the Eastern Shore counties of Maryland and to Delaware, where Baltimore, New York, Wilmington, and Philadelphia compete. Expansion westward has been to a small area in extreme northern Virginia, and through the water gap in the Blue Ridge at Harpers Ferry to the Great Valley in West Virginia.

The rapid growth of Washington and its suburbs during the days of the Depression, the New Deal, World War II, and since—and the resulting expanded market—is reflected in the shape and extent of the present milkshed. The original market-oriented supply area in immediately adjacent Maryland and Virginia is still the heart of the capital's milkshed. But hundreds of farms have been lost to suburbanization, governmental installations, airports, country estates, and fox-hunting establishments; the traditional and rooted Baltimore milkshed, with its long-established trade contacts, blocks expansion on the north. Only in Frederick County east of the Blue Ridge is there major overlap, and in this county alone nearly 600 farms shipping to Washington constitute 60 per cent of Maryland producers in the milkshed. Fewer than 50 farms north of here in Pennsylvania ship to Washington.

Expansion has been southwestward. The Washington supply area now extends almost throughout Piedmont Virginia, and into the Shenandoah Valley and its continuation (the Great Valley) to beyond Roanoke. In these areas, specializing in types of farming other than dairying, the dairy farms are few and far between. In a third of these Virginia counties, there are five or fewer Washington producers; several have but one Washington supplier. Some of the dairy farms are almost as far south as the North Carolina border.

Westward expansion of the Washington milkshed has been modest; it is to the Great Valley in the West Virginia eastern "panhandle" and to the Appalachian Valley counties of the state southwestward of this. A more important expansion to a Pennsylvania district at the base of the Allegheny Front and west of it on the Plateau has produced an outlier of the milkshed, one involving more farms and production than the small overflow into Pennsylvania north of Frederick, Maryland.

Pittsburgh and the Western Slopes

The milksheds of the western slopes of the Appalachian Highlands, in the dissected hill lands of southwestern Pennsylvania and the glaciated hill lands of extreme western New York, northwestern Pennsylvania, and northeastern Ohio lie in existing dairy regions; they have, in addition, the advantage of relative nearness to Pittsburgh, Erie, Cleveland, Canton, Akron, Youngs-

town, and the urbanized Mahoning Valley. This region, particularly on the glaciated lands of the uplands south of Lake Erie, has long been important in dairying; the Western Reserve of Ohio was nicknamed "Cheesedom" a hundred years ago; the Grove City area of Pennsylvania and Cattaraugus and adjacent counties in western New York were important in cheese production.[9] In other words, the urban market has grown in an existing dairy region, one that has long been included in the southern portion of the American Dairy Region. The growth of the nearby urban markets has not resulted in shifts in the type of agriculture, but in a change from manufacture of dairy products to the marketing of fluid milk in reponse to this growth. Pittsburgh (*for which there is not adequate data for mapping the farm locations*) obtains its milk supply from this area.[10] The Youngstown milkshed is competitive throughout with Pittsburgh and Cleveland. The most intensive portion of the Cleveland milkshed lies in the glaciated hill lands of northeastern Ohio. New York City taps the region in western New York and northwestern Pennsylvania. And, from the southern, unglaciated portion, some milk is directed across the Appalachian divide to Philadelphia and Washington. Far-

[9] Loyal Durand, Jr., "The Migration of Cheese Manufacture in the United States," *Annals Assn. of Amer. Geogrs.*, Vol. 42, 1952, pp. 263–282. A map of cheese production in this area in 1849 appears on page 269.

[10] The Pittsburgh milkshed is in Pennsylvania, eastern Ohio, and in a small neighboring district of West Virginia. Fig. 9 shows the country plants serving the Pittsburgh market. Deliveries to these plants originate beyond their location in most cases. In the close-in portions of the milkshed there is direct delivery to handlers— all West Virginia milk is in this pattern. Figures for the *entire state of Pennsylvania* are: 25 per cent of the milk produced in the state is shipped to New York City, 17 per cent to Philadelphia, 17 per cent to Pittsburgh, 6 per cent to Washington, Wilmington, Youngstown, Cleveland, and other out-of-state cities, 30 per cent to cities in Pennsylvania other than Philadelphia and Pittsburgh, and 5 per cent enters manufacturing.

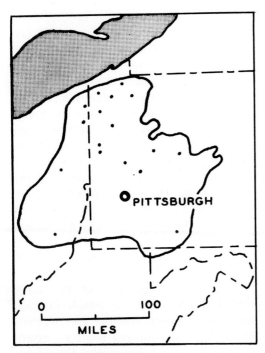

FIG. 9. The distribution of country pool plants in the Pittsburgh milkshed, 1959.

ther south, in the unglaciated hill lands of southeastern Ohio, West Virginia, and Pennsylvania, a compact milkshed is the source region of milk for Wheeling.

Ohio, Indiana, and Louisville

Western Ohio and eastern Indiana, whose rural districts are engaged principally in livestock farming, is an area of many cities and of severe competition among milksheds. Note from Appendix B that Cleveland has 21 separate competitive (overlapping) areas, Cincinnati 12, and Indianapolis 10. The relatively few dairy farms are generally market-oriented. Nearly every county is included in at least three major milksheds, large numbers are in four, and considerable areas in five. Peaks of six and seven are reached in northeast-central Indiana. Yet, not as many farms are involved per unit area as in the American Dairy Region to the north; in effect, the competition is among the

handlers from Cincinnati and Louisville on the south, Indianapolis to the west, South Bend, Fort Wayne, and Toledo to the north, Cleveland to the northeast, and Columbus and Dayton to the east. The individual farmer, the farm cooperative, the country pool plant, and the private receiving station each enjoys a considerable choice of market.

The milkshed of Cincinnati stretches from northwestern Ohio to northern and central Kentucky, and into eastern Indiana. Just under half of the nearly 4000 producers are Ohio farmers, who contribute somewhat more than half of the supply. The Kentucky portion of the milkshed, except for the few counties immediately south of Cincinnati, has the lowest daily average per producer; more than a third of the milkshed farms are in Kentucky, but they yield only a quarter of the supply. Cincinnati's milkshed overlaps that of Dayton and Cleveland to the north, Indianapolis to the west and northwest, and Columbus to the northeast.

The milk supply of Columbus is entirely from Ohio, but except on the east and south the producing area is one of considerable competition. Some milk destined for Cleveland is produced just north of Columbus. The same is true

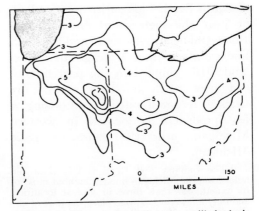

FIG. 10. The number of major milksheds in northern Ohio and Indiana, and southern Michigan, 1961.

north of Dayton, whose milkshed over-laps others in all of its portions in both Ohio and Indiana.

The milkshed of Louisville has the least areal competition. Its most con-centrated producing district, east and northeast of the city, overlaps the south-western portion of the Cincinnati area in part of northern Kentucky, and it meets competition from Indianapolis northward in southern Indiana. Ken-tucky production, for both Louisville and Cincinnati, is more dominant in the hilly regions of the northern part of the state than in the rolling and rich Blue Grass Basin where livestock farming and tobacco culture offer superior economic opportunities on larger farms.

Cleveland

The Cleveland milkshed stretches 350 miles from east to west, from north-western Pennsylvania to northwestern Indiana, where its westernmost pro-ducers are within 50 miles of the center of Chicago and 20 miles of Gary. It bends northward west of Lake Erie to include districts in the southern counties of Michigan. The chief production of milk in the western part of the milkshed is from the Dairy Region-Corn Belt transi-tion in the Indiana-Michigan state line countryside, with an intensive spot east of South Bend. This entire area is along or near the high speed Indiana Toll Road–Ohio Turnpike route and the main line railroads from Chicago to Cleve-land. Milk shipped in the past by rail can now reach handlers rapidly by truck.[11] A small outlier comprising a few producers is located in western Michigan, near the shore of Lake Michigan.

[11] The Indiana Toll Road is less than ten miles from the Michigan line throughout most of its extent, less than three in several localities, and only a few yards at one place. As part of the Chicago–New York toll road system, it offers direct connection to the Ohio Turnpike and its exits for Cleveland.

The eastern portion of the Cleveland milkshed lies in the glaciated uplands of northeastern Ohio and adjacent Penn-sylvania, in the American Dairy Region. The largest concentration of producers is on the westward margins of the Allegheny Plateau, south and southwest of the city; these producers are not therefore far removed from the market. Southward expansion from this district has now resulted in the entrance of the milkshed into the Swiss Cheese manufac-turing area of Holmes and adjacent counties. Although nearly 1000 dairy-men have shifted to the urban market, the manufacture of cheese has been maintained to date.

The southern portions of this large milkshed are in the livestock farming areas of northern Indiana and western Ohio. Milk is collected from an exten-sive territory. Consequently, the Cleve-land milkshed here overlaps with those of Toledo, Columbus, Dayton, Cincin-nati, and Indianapolis. Westward, the overlaps are with the milksheds of Chicago, Detroit, and Toledo (in Mich-igan), eastward with Akron, Youngs-town, Erie, and Pittsburgh. In fact, the Cleveland milkshed, as shown in Appen-dices A and B, has more overlaps than any other *major milkshed* in the north-eastern quarter of the United States.

Toledo

The Toledo milkshed encompasses a relatively compact tri-state area in Ohio, Indiana, and Michigan. Areally and in total production, the flatlands of the Maumee Plain in Ohio constitute the heart; the largest number of farms per unit area, and the most intensive production, however, is northwest of Toledo in the dairy area of the old Adrian (or Lenawee) cheese-manufac-turing region of southeastern Michigan. The milkshed includes, also, the dairy counties of extreme northeastern Indiana. The milkshed overlaps with that of Cleveland throughout most of its extent, and with Detroit in its northern portion.

Detroit

The Lower Peninsula of Michigan, in its market orientations in the fluid milk industry, is in many ways like an island. Or it might be compared to the situation in the milksheds of New England. The milk consumed in the state is produced almost throughout the agricultural regions of the Lower Peninsula, and Michigan farmers supply Michigan urban markets. Only 82 farms in extreme northwestern Ohio and seven in extreme northeastern Indiana ship market milk into Michigan; all of these are in the Detroit milkshed.

The competition offered by out-of-state milksheds is confined to the two southern tiers of counties—the overlap area with Toledo and Cleveland—and to the small district in western Michigan located in the "gap" between the southern and northern portions of the Lake Michigan Fruit Belt; from this area, milk is directed to both Chicago and Cleveland, as well as to Detroit and to nearby Grand Rapids, and in it some manufacture of dairy products still persists.[12] Competition for milk in the Lower Peninsula is thus mainly among the numerous cities of southern and southeastern Michigan. Each has its own supply area, city health inspection, rules, and regulations. But all the southeastern cities, *collectively*, are included under a single Federal Order Market. Nearly 10,000 producers are in the milkshed of Detroit; more than 4000 others supply the milk for the smaller cities of the southeast.

The Detroit milkshed includes all of

[12] Loyal Durand, Jr., "The Lower Peninsula of Michigan and the Western Michigan Dairy Region: A Segment of the American Dairy Region," *Econ. Geog.*, Vol. 27, 1951, pp. 163–183.

the agriculturally-used portions of the Lower Peninsula except the southwestern three counties and the northern counties of the Lake Michigan shore. It extends as far north as Ludington on the Lake Michigan side of the state, to the sandy High Plains of Michigan in the northcentral part of the peninsula, and through the agricultural areas east of the sand country—that is, the farm territory along the Lake Huron shore almost to the Strait of Mackinac. Thus, virtually all farming districts are included. The largest number of farms in the milkshed are in the major agricultural districts—southeast of a line from Saginaw Bay to Muskegon. The most intensive production is in the area north of the city to the Thumb of the state and northeastward along the St. Clair River and Lake Huron to the Thumb.

The Southeastern Michigan (total Federal Order) milkshed differs in pattern from that of Detroit only in that it surrounds the sandy High Plains on all margins. It, too, does not include southwestern Michigan, mainly a fruit belt, or the narrow fruit belt from Ludington north to Traverse City. This milkshed differs in detailed pattern from Detroit in that districts near the other Michigan cities—Kalamazoo, Battle Creek, Jackson, Lansing, Grand Rapids, Flint, and others—contain more, or as many, farms oriented to the local market as to the Detroit handlers.

Dairying in Lower Michigan is now organized principally around the urban fluid markets, as in New England. Until February, 1962, payment for surplus milk on most Federal Orders west of the Appalachians was made on the so-called Midwest Condensery price for manufactured milk. Originally, 18 condenseries reported their price. By late 1961, all but eight had closed because of competition in price with city market milk. Only two reporting condenseries remained in Michigan, and their prices were forced to a competitive situation. Therefore, the Wisconsin-Minnesota manufacturing price was substituted, in Michigan and elsewhere. This illustrates the rapid reorientation in the destination and use of milk from Michigan dairy farms.

Chicago-Milwaukee-Minneapolis-St. Paul

The key word to describe the milksheds of Chicago, Milwaukee, and the Twin Cities might be "Wisconsin." The more than four million inhabitants of the Chicago Metropolitan Area, the more than a million of the Milwaukee Area, and the million and a quarter of the Twin Cities Area obtain the bulk of their supplies from this leading dairy state. And, over and above these and the production for smaller cities in the state, about 45 per cent of all milk used in the manufacture of dairy products in the United States originates in Wisconsin and Minnesota. During the entire year of 1962, 72.7 per cent of Chicago's milk came from more than 14,000 farms in Wisconsin, 23.8 per cent from northern (mainly northeastern) Illinois, and 3.4 per cent from the portion of the milkshed in Indiana and Michigan combined. All of Milwaukee's milk is from southeastern Wisconsin. Nearly half of that of the Twin Cities is from the 1700 producers in northwestern Wisconsin. Portions of other out-of-state milksheds—St. Louis, Davenport, Dubuque, Duluth, and the cities of the Upper Peninsula of Michigan—extend into the state as well.

The Chicago milkshed funnels northward and northwestward from the city. As recently as 1940, the chief producing district was in the dairy region of northeastern Illinois and adjacent southeastern Wisconsin; Illinois farms then produced 60 per cent of Chicago's milk, Wisconsin only 28 per cent. Now the greatly expanded milkshed semicircles that of Milwaukee, is aligned along the shore of Lake Michigan even into the Door Peninsula, and extends north and northwest of Green Bay to the forest border of the Superior Highland Cut-Over and Forest countryside; westward from here, the milkshed crosses north-central Wisconsin between the Central Sand Plain (on its south) and the Northern Forest (on its north) to the northwestern portion of the state. The "funnel" extends, also, northwestward from Chicago to southcentral Wisconsin and into the hill lands of the Driftless Area of southwestern Wisconsin, where it reaches the Mississippi River. The most distant source is in northwestern Wisconsin, in an area competitive with the Twin Cities and with Duluth-Superior, where some producers are more than 400 miles from Chicago, and the pool plant forwarding their milk is 370 miles from that city. The largest quantities of milk originate in a semicircle in Wisconsin, from 145 to 190 miles distant from the Chicago City Hall.

The Illinois portion of the Chicago milkshed is the intensive dairy area of the northeast—the counties north and northwest of Chicago. The milkshed has expanded, since the 1940's, westward to the Mississippi River, in extreme northern Illinois, into the Swiss-cheese manufacturing region of the state. Because of the urban competition, one of the large American dairy companies shifted the location of one of its major factories to northeastern Wisconsin, but many rural cheese factories have been maintained to date (as in southwestern Wisconsin to the north).[13]

The Indiana portion of the Chicago milkshed is now and always has been virtually confined to the rolling and

[13] Loyal Durand, Jr., "Cheese Region of Northwestern Illinois," *Econ. Geog.*, Vol. 22, 1946, pp. 24–37.

rough Valparaiso Moraine south of Lake Michigan. South of this the rich flatlands of the prairie of northwestern Indiana is cash-grain (corn) country. Only a few scattered dairy farms are interspersed with cash-grain enterprises, as is true also in the cash-grain area south of Chicago. In these flat, rich lands the sale of corn, or the livestock enterprise, is usually more remunerative than dairying and requires far less labor; and—equally important—it does not require the daily regularity of labor, every day in the year. The Michigan outlier of the milkshed, also stationary, is the Dutch-settled area of Ottawa and Allegan counties, where long-time connections of the receiving station with Chicago handlers is operative.

Throughout the Wisconsin portion of the Chicago milkshed, manufacture of dairy products persists, except in the extreme southeastern part of the state, where nearly all dairy factories (mainly condenseries in this former "outer ring" of the milkshed) have ceased operations, having been unable to compete with Grade A prices. In more distant portions of the milkshed, dairy factories have been able to maintain production; individual farmers prefer the manufacturing market—whey returned from the manufacture of cheese, or skim milk from butter manufacture, provides these farmers with supplementary feed for swine and poultry. Their transport charges to market are less.[14] Elsewhere, Chicago's competition is with the large, centralized dairy factory—many now owned by nationwide corporations, which capitalize upon the advertising value of the name "Wisconsin," especially in the cheese industry.

The Milwaukee milkshed, in its ex-

pansion, has shifted northward, into districts of less competition with Chicago, whose milkshed extends even into southern Milwaukee County. The expansion of the milkshed of the Twin Cities has been eastward, across the St. Croix River into Wisconsin, and this milkshed now approaches the theoretical shape of a circle surrounding the market. Minneapolis and St. Paul do not have to transport milk long distances. The intensive dairylands of eastern Minnesota and northwestern Wisconsin do not only supply the market; there are dairy factories inside the circular border of the milkshed of the Twin Cities.

The "go north" aspect of the expansion of the milksheds of Chicago and of Milwaukee is an expectable relationship to the existence of the intensive dairy farming in much of Wisconsin. Economically, it reflects the financial ability of milk distributors to divert manufactural milk to market milk, the financial ability of the dairy farmer to make the capital investment to meet health regulations, and the price attraction of the urban market (even with large surpluses—quite usual on these milksheds—and the resulting blended price). But the "go north" pattern is usual, too, on the smaller milksheds of the region; this is related to competition with Chicago. For example, the minor milkshed of Madison, at one time entirely local and in a single county, has "gone north." Milk for Chicago is produced in all directions now from Madison; this city's milkshed now receives milk from localities a hundred miles or more to its northwest, near LaCrosse.

St. Louis

The type-of-farming map of the United States depicts a general-farming region in southern Illinois, east of St. Louis, entitled "St. Louis Milk-

[14] Loyal Durand, Jr., "The Cheese Manufacturing Regions of Wisconsin, 1850–1950," *Trans. Wisconsin Academy of Sciences, Arts and Letters*, Vol. 42, 1953, pp. 109–130.

shed.''[15] The milkshed is now far larger areally than this, and it covers more territory in Missouri than in Illinois. But the Illinois portion contains the largest concentration of producers, even though there are only a few more than 2000, and is the most intensive in milk production of any part of the far-flung milkshed. Actually, there are two Federal Order Markets in the metropolitan region—St. Louis and suburban St. Louis. These are mapped as one, even though there is overlap between them particularly in southern Illinois. This producing area east of the Mississippi River extends northeast, east, and southeast of the city. Semicircling this intensive area some additional producing farms lie as far east as the counties on the Indiana line, and as far south as western Kentucky.

The second core of the St. Louis milkshed is in south-central Missouri, on the Salem Platform of the Ozark Plateau, west of the roughest portion of the Ozarks. Here a concentration of some 1000 producers are farther removed from the market than any of the farms in southern Illinois. Westward from this core, the milkshed receives supplies from the dairy districts of the Springfield Structural Plain, even to the southwest corner of Missouri. The relatively recent rise of dairying on the Salem and Springfield Platforms of the Ozarks has attracted not only the St. Louis market, but fringes of the Kansas City milkshed, and the handlers of milk in the cities of Oklahoma and Texas, as well as dairy manufacturers.

The farming regions north of the Ozarks, in the eastern half of the Missouri Valley in the state, and the eastern half of northern Missouri (north of the River), with a contiguous area in south-

[15] "Generalized Types of Farming in the United States," *Agricultural Information Bulletin*, 3, United States Department of Agriculture, 1950.

eastern Iowa, comprise the rest of the odd-shaped conterminous milkshed; it is one of few producers per unit area over most of its extent, except in the twin-cores.

Five outliers of the St. Louis milkshed lie in four states: two small ones are in eastern Iowa; one is in western Kentucky (separate from the Kentucky district that is contiguous to the southern Illinois portion of the producing region); one is partly in southwestern Wisconsin and partly in adjacent Illinois; and the largest is located in northern Illinois south and southwest of Chicago. From this last, milk produced from within 30 miles of Chicago is marketed in St. Louis, 200 miles southwestward.

The St. Louis milkshed covers the largest total area, considering the size of the market and number of producers, of all of the milksheds in the northeastern quarter of the United States. It is, in addition, the most irregular in shape, has the largest area that is characterized by twenty or fewer producers per county, and is the only one with twin cores whose numbers of milk producers is not as large per unit area as extensive districts in the milksheds of the cities located in or near the American Dairy Region. The St. Louis milkshed also surrounds a farming district of size from which no milk is obtained, and contains indentations explainable by natural settings and by cultural and economic conditions.

Kansas City–Omaha–Des Moines

The major milk supply for Kansas City originates south of the latitude of the two Kansas Cities, and south of the Missouri and Kansas Rivers. Some six counties in Missouri and a wider area (twice the size) to their west in Kansas constitute the heart region. This oval to elliptical-shaped heart is thus mainly south, southwest or due west of the market in these state-line cities. Beyond this, milk is supplied in lesser quantities from other parts of northeastern Kansas, and from much of the western half of northern Missouri. The northern edges of the milkshed extend into southwestern Iowa.

The Omaha milkshed, one of little urban competition from elsewhere, is almost circular, but it centers not on the city, but to its southwest, near Lincoln. Thus, the producing area is more extensive in Nebraska than in Iowa.

The largest quantity of milk for Des Moines is from a circular area within a radius of about thirty miles from the city—a theoretical and actual core. Expansion has been in two arcs to northeastern and to southeastern Iowa. Thus, a C-shaped, or crescent-shaped, milkshed results, the horns pointing eastward. At one locality in the northern crescent a few producers in Minnesota are included on the Des Moines market. The northern horn of the crescent extends into districts where there are a few producers in small outliers of the St. Louis and Kansas City milksheds, the southern horn into an overlap area with St. Louis.

Milk-receiving plants in southwestern Minnesota and northwestern Iowa are suppliers of three distant markets—Kansas City, Omaha, and Des Moines. This compound or triple-outlier involves relatively few farms, but these are on the respective milksheds. Within this same region, however, most farms engaged in the production of market milk are suppliers of the minor milkshed of Sioux City.

AFTERVIEW

The twenty-six major milksheds mapped depict the irregular pattern of milk production for the residents of the major urban centers of the Manufactural Belt of the United States, and the commercial cities to its west. Nine of the ten largest Federal Order milksheds are included. Pittsburgh, the largest state-controlled market in the northeast, is represented only on the overlap maps, not on the farm location map.

The theoretical circular, market-oriented milkshed does not exist in fact. Competition among the handlers of cities is keen; throughout large areas the dairy farmer and country pool plant enjoys a choice of alternative markets—even more than here mapped because of the existence of hundreds of cities of medium size.

Milk production per cow has increased enormously during recent years, from 5000 pounds annually per animal in 1947 to 7200 by 1961; in much of the American Dairy Region proper the average now exceeds 9000 pounds. Numbers of dairy cows in the United States have declined from 21 million in 1954 to about 17 million. However, total milk production, nationwide, has increased by nearly a billion pounds in ten years. Fewer farmers on the major milksheds now ship more milk to market. Conversely, the per capita consumption of fluid milk has increased at a slower rate than that of the growth of population. The result of these marked changes may be (at least for a time) relatively stationary milksheds, except in regions of unusual growth of the urban market.

APPENDIX A

THE COMBINATION OF NUMBERS LISTED DEPICTS THE MILKSHEDS OF THE NAMED CITY,
THE NUMBERS REFER TO FIGURES 4, 5, AND 6

Boston 1, 2, 7, 8, 9
Southeastern New England 2, 3, 5, 8, 11
Connecticut 4, 5, 8, 9, 10
New York 6, 7, 8, 9, 10, 11, 12, 13, 14
Philadelphia 12, 13, 14, 15, 16, 17, 18, 19

Baltimore 13, 16, 17, 20, 21
Washington 17, 18, 21, 22, 23
Pittsburgh 14, 19, 23, 24, 25, 26, 27, 28, 29
Wheeling 25, 26
Youngstown 14, 28, 29, 30, 31
Cleveland 14, 26, 27, 28, 31, 34, 35, 36, 37, 38, 39, 40, 41, 42, 43, 44, 45, 46, 47, 48, 49
Detroit 32, 33, 35, 36, 39
Toledo 33, 36, 37, 43
Indianapolis 40, 41, 48, 49, 55, 56, 57, 58, 59, 60
Cincinnati 42, 43, 45, 46, 47, 48, 49, 52, 53, 54, 55, 56
Columbus 44, 45, 47, 50, 51
Dayton 46, 47, 48, 51, 53, 56, 58
Louisville 54, 60, 61
Chicago 38, 39, 40, 59, 62, 63, 64, 65, 66, 68
Milwaukee 63, 64
Minneapolis-St. Paul 65, 69
Duluth 66, 67
St. Louis 64, 68, 70, 71, 72, 73, 74, 75, 76, 77
Kansas City 71, 72, 78, 79, 80
Des Moines 77, 79, 82
Omaha 80, 81
Dallas (part) 72, 73, 74
San Antonio (part) 74, 75
Oklahoma City (part) 76

APPENDIX B

MILKSHED OVERLAPS ARE INDICATED WHERE THE NUMBERS ARE INDENTED; WHERE THERE IS NO INDENTION THE NAMED CITY IS SUPREME IN THE MAJOR MILKSHED. THE NUMBERS REFER TO FIGURES 4, 5, AND 6

Milkshed	Number of separate locations on maps	Location
1. Boston...........................	4	Northern New England
2. Boston–Southeastern New England..........	4	Western Vermont, Northern Connecticut Valley in Vermont and New Hampshire, Southeastern Massachusetts
3. Southeastern New England....................	1	Southeastern New England
4. Connecticut...............................	1	Connecticut, Southwestern Massachusetts, New York State east of the Hudson
5. Connecticut–Southeastern New England......	1	Eastern Connecticut
6. New York................................	3	New York State–Northern Pennsylvania–Northern New Jersey, Appalachian Valleys in central Pennsylvania
7. New York–Boston.........................	2	Eastern Mohawk Valley in New York State, Northeastern corner of New York State
8. New York–Boston–Southeastern New England–Connecticut..............................	1	Vermont–New York border
9. New York–Boston–Connecticut..............	1	Eastern New York–Southwestern Vermont
10. New York–Connecticut....................	2	West of Catskills in New York State, Hudson River Valley
11. New York–Southeastern New England.......	1	Northwest of Catskills in New York State
12. New York–Philadelphia....................	6	Southeastern Pennsylvania, Appalachian Valleys–Pennsylvania, Southwestern New Jersey, Western New Jersey, Northeastern New Jersey, West of Catskills in New York State
13. New York–Philadelphia–Baltimore..........	1	Delaware–Eastern Shore of Maryland
14. New York–Cleveland–Philadelphia–Pittsburgh–Youngstown.............................	1	Northwestern Pennsylvania
15. Philadelphia...............................	7	Eastern Pennsylvania, five locations in Appalachian Valleys–Pennsylvania, Southern Eastern Shore of Maryland and Virginia
16. Philadelphia–Baltimore	2	Southeastern Pennsylvania–Northeastern Maryland–Northern Delaware, Southern Delaware
17. Philadelphia–Baltimore–Washington..........	2	Western Maryland–Northern Virginia–Eastern West Virginia, Eastern Shore of Maryland
18. Philadelphia–Washington..................	2	Western Maryland–Eastern West Virginia, Southwestern Pennsylvania
19. Philadelphia–Pittsburgh...................	1	Southwestern Pennsylvania
20. Baltimore................................	1	Northeastern Maryland–Southeastern Pennsylvania
21. Baltimore–Washington.....................	2	Central Maryland, Northeastern Maryland–Southeastern Pennsylvania
22. Washington...............................	9	Northeastern West Virginia–Western Maryland, Northern Virginia–Southern Maryland, Shenandoah Valley–Great Valley, six locations in Piedmont and Coastal Plain Virginia
23. Washington–Pittsburgh....................	1	Southwestern Pennsylvania
24. Pittsburgh................................	1	Western Pennsylvania–edges of plateau Maryland and West Virginia

APPENDIX B—Continued

Milkshed	Number of separate locations on maps	Location
25. Pittsburgh–Wheeling......................	1	Pennsylvania–West Virginia–Eastern Ohio
26. Pittsburgh–Cleveland–Wheeling..............	1	Eastern Ohio
27. Pittsburgh–Cleveland.....................	1	Eastern Ohio
28. Pittsburgh–Cleveland–Youngstown...........	1	Northwestern Pennsylvania–Northeastern Ohio
29. Pittsburgh–Youngstown....................	1	Northwestern Pennsylvania–Northeastern Ohio
30. Youngstown.............................	1	Northwestern Pennsylvania
31. Cleveland–Youngstown....................	1	Northeastern Ohio
32. Detroit................................	4	Lower Peninsula of Michigan
33. Detroit–Toledo.........................	1	Southeastern Michigan
34. Cleveland..............................	2	Northern Ohio, Southwestern Michigan–Northeastern Indiana–Northwestern Ohio
35. Cleveland–Detroit......................	1	Southern Michigan
36. Cleveland–Detroit–Toledo.................	1	Southern Michigan–Northeastern Indiana–Northwestern Ohio
37. Cleveland–Toledo.......................	1	Northeastern Indiana–Northwestern Ohio
38. Cleveland–Chicago	1	Northwestern Indiana
39. Cleveland–Chicago–Detroit.................	1	Western Michigan
40. Cleveland–Chicago–Indianapolis.............	1	Northwestern Indiana
41. Cleveland–Indianapolis...................	1	Northern Indiana
42. Cleveland–Cincinnati....................	2	Western Ohio
43. Cleveland–Cincinnati–Toledo...............	1	Northwestern Ohio
44. Cleveland–Columbus..	1	Central Ohio
45. Cleveland–Cincinnati–Columbus.............	1	Western Ohio
46. Cleveland–Cincinnati–Dayton..............	1	Western Ohio
47. Cleveland–Cincinnati–Columbus–Dayton......	1	Western Ohio
48. Cleveland–Cincinnati–Dayton–Indianapolis....	1	Northeastern Indiana
49. Cleveland–Cincinnati–Indianapolis..........	1	Northeastern Indiana
50. Columbus.............	1	Central Ohio
51. Columbus–Dayton.......................	1	Western Ohio
52. Cincinnati..............................	1	Southwestern Ohio–Southeastern Indiana Northern Kentucky
53. Cincinnati–Dayton......................	1	Southwestern Ohio–Eastern Indiana
54. Cincinnati–Louisville....................	1	Northern Kentucky
55. Cincinnati–Indianapolis...................	1	Southeastern Indiana
56. Cincinnati–Dayton–Indianapolis.............	1	Eastern Indiana
57. Indianapolis............................	1	Indiana
58. Indianapolis–Dayton.....................	1	Eastern Indiana
59. Indianapolis–Chicago....................	1	Northwestern Indiana
60. Indianapolis–Louisville...................	1	Southern Indiana
61. Louisville...............................	1	Kentucky–Southern Indiana
62. Chicago................................	1	Wisconsin–Northern Illinois–Northwestern Indiana
63. Chicago–Milwaukee......................	1	Southeastern Wisconsin
64. Chicago–Milwaukee–St. Louis..............	1	Southern Wisconsin
65. Chicago–Minneapolis–St. Paul..............	1	Northwestern Wisconsin
66. Chicago–Duluth.........................	1	Northwestern Wisconsin
67. Duluth.................................	3	Wisconsin–Minnesota border, Lake Superior Lowland
68. Chicago–St. Louis........................	2	Northeastern Illinois, Southwestern Wisconsin–Northwestern Illinois
69. Minneapolis–St. Paul....................	1	Northwestern Wisconsin–Eastern Minnesota
70. St. Louis................................	4	Southern and Eastern Missouri–Southern Illinois–Western Kentucky, Southeastern Iowa, two in eastern Illinois
71. St. Louis–Kansas City.....................	2	West Central Missouri, North Central Missouri
72. St. Louis–Kansas City–Dallas..............	1	Southwestern Missouri
73. St. Louis–Dallas........................	1	Southwestern Missouri
74. St. Louis–San Antonio–Dallas..............	1	Southwestern Missouri
75. St. Louis–San Antonio....................	1	Southwestern Missouri
76. St. Louis–Oklahoma City..................	1	Southwestern Missouri
77. St. Louis–Des Moines.....................	3	Southern Iowa, Southeastern Iowa, Northeastern Iowa
78. Kansas City.............................	1	Eastern Kansas–Western Missouri–Southwestern Iowa
79. Kansas City–Des Moines..................	3	Southwestern Iowa, Northeastern Iowa, Northern Iowa
80. Kansas City–Omaha......................	2	Northwestern Iowa, Southwestern Minnesota
81. Omaha.................................	2	Eastern Nebraska–Western Iowa, Southwestern Minnesota
82. Des Moines.............................	1	Crescent Northeastern through Central to Southeastern Iowa

Tropical Commercial Agriculture

Tropical commercial agriculture — including the production of such crops as bananas, coffee, rubber, sugar cane, tea, and cacao — involves the production of crops in tropical areas for sale outside the tropics, usually in markets of the industrialized and urbanized countries of the Northern Hemisphere. These tropical crops, which must be high in value to justify the cost of long-distance transport, are produced on both small holdings and plantations. Although farmers on small holdings are increasingly important producers of certain crops, the plantation still remains as a distinctive operating unit.

Tropical commercial agriculture is widespread throughout the tropical areas of the world. Even though individual plantations may be quite large, the production of commercial tropical crops occupies only a small proportion of the earth's cultivated lands.

Certain generalizations can be made about the production of tropical crops. Traditionally, tropical commercial agriculture has been a monocultural system, with each plantation or farm specializing in the commercial production of a single crop. Capital and management for the plantation have, in the past, come from outside the tropics, usually from the countries which form the major markets for the tropical crops. Also characteristic of tropical production has been the intensive use of local labor, with only modest mechanization. This has been true on both plantations as well as on small holdings. Still another characteristic is the tendency for the production of tropical crops to be located at coastal sites or along waterways, thus facilitating shipment of crops to market and importing of supplies. Although individual crops have specific physical requirements, there is a tendency for production to locate in areas of year-round rainfall and warmth. Since soil depletion is rapid under such conditions, cultivation frequently shifts to new sites as soil productivity declines.

The first article in this section considers various characteristics of plantation agriculture, including those just mentioned, and discusses ways that the complexion of the plantation is being altered by political, economic, and corporate actions. The remaining four articles deal with the production of specific tropical crops.

THE CHANGING PLANTATION

HOWARD F. GREGOR

University of California, Davis

ABSTRACT. The usual classification of plantation farming as a tropical institution can no longer hold in the face of continued agricultural rationalization. Characteristics long considered essential to the plantation, such as crop specialization, advanced cultivation and harvesting techniques, large operating units, management centralization, labor specialization, massive production, and heavy capital investment, are also being increasingly associated with more extratropical farms. Other traditional marks of the plantation have been altered. Monoculture has declined and cooler-zone crops have gained in importance. Domestic markets are beginning to challenge foreign outlets. Administrative structures now range from the individually owned to the state-controlled type. Entrepreneurs are ethnically more diverse but often are of the same group as their workers. Labor is scarcer but better trained and is more imbued with the attitudes of an industrial worker. Rapid expansion of the modern plantation has also made for a richer typology than has heretofore been presented.

Classification of agricultural systems, the ways in which farmers make their living and alter the landscape accordingly, has long been a popular activity for agricultural geographers, agricultural economists, and culture historians. Eduard Hahn, Leo Waibel, Erich Otremba, and Derwent Whittlesey have been only some of the more notable geographers in this effort.[1] More recently, a special commission on agricultural typology was created within the International Geographical Union. Such efforts are understandable, for the agricultural variations of the landscape are the most obvious, widespread, and often the most complex. Furthermore, if geographers are to consider not only the areal uniqueness of things but the

reasons for that uniqueness, they must "seek to generalize, to define categories in terms of selected criteria, to formulate classifications."[2] Also, information on the different forms of agricultural activity and their distribution is becoming ever more necessary as the need for agricultural improvement in the face of burgeoning populations increases. An increasingly complicating element in classification efforts, however, is the quickening spread of modern farming technology among farmers of all cultural and economic levels. The result in some cases has been significant modifications of the original agricultural system and the blurring of boundaries between it and other systems. Nothing illustrates this problem of coordinating classification with economic change as well as plantation farming, a system which is not only undergoing changes itself but is apparently becoming the direction in which other systems are evolving.

Agricultural classification schemes, however, have traditionally restricted plantation farming to comparatively small, scattered, and predominantly tropical areas. And more recent political events have convinced many that even in several of these areas the plantation is disappearing. Yet the Agricultural Revolution continues to favor on a growing scale most or all of those characteristics long con-

[1] E. Hahn, "Die Wirtschaftsformen der Erde," *Petermanns Mitteilungen*, Vol. 38 (1892), pp. 8–12; E. Otremba, *Allgemeine Agrar- und Industriegeographie*, Vol. 3, 2d ed. rev., of *Erde und Weltwirtschaft*, Rudolf Lütgens (Ed.), 4 vols. (Stuttgart: Franckh'sche, 1950–1960), pp. 213–29, 343–51; D. Whittlesey, "Major Agricultural Regions of the Earth," *Annals*, Association of American Geographers, Vol. 26 (1936), pp. 199–240. L. Waibel did not actually set up a classification scheme of agricultural systems, although he did develop a firm conceptual basis for one in his article, "Das System der Landwirtschaftsgeographie," *Wirtschaftsgeographische Abhandlungen*, Nr. 1 (1933), pp. 7–12. N. Helburn followed somewhat the same tack in his proposal for a comprehensive classification of world agriculture; see "The Bases for a Classification of World Agriculture," *The Professional Geographer*, Vol. 9 (March, 1957), pp. 2–7. Otremba and Waibel also give excellent summaries of previous attempts by geographers to formulate agricultural classification systems.

[2] P. E. James, "The Field of Geography," *American Geography: Inventory and Prospect*, P. E. James and C. F. Jones (Eds.) (Syracuse, N.Y.: Syracuse University Press, 1954), Chap. 1, p. 8.

"The Changing Plantation" by Howard F. Gregor. Reprinted from ANNALS — *Association of American Geographers, Vol. 55 (June 1965), pp. 221-238, with permission of the Association of American Geographers.*

sidered typical of the plantation, *viz.*, crop and areal specialization, highly rationalized cultivation and harvesting techniques, large operating units, management centralization, labor specialization, massive production, and heavy capital investment. Thus many farms have been rapidly acquiring plantation characteristics and in areas well beyond the low latitudes. Nor have all the newly independent countries in the old plantation areas been so anxious to eliminate the system as they have been to modify some of its features; indeed, many governments are encouraging the further spread of the plantation system. Why should there be this lag of recognition behind the actual event? It would seem that the principal reason has been too rigid a definition of the plantation system, one that has not been flexible enough for the dynamic nature of the plantation and, therefore, only too accommodating to those who would consign the plantation to decline as soon as it deviates from classification criteria set up during a particular historical period. Although there has never been complete agreement on a definition of the plantation, there are several commonly held biases. Their analyses provide an opportunity to suggest those modifications needed for a more realistic idea of the plantation system and its changing nature. By the same token, the use of a more liberal definition requires consideration of a plantation typology, for the increasing expansion of the plantation has inevitably created more regional variations than have heretofore been presented in farming classifications.

CLIMATIC AND CROP BIASES

Perhaps the oldest of definitional biases is the view of the plantation as a solution by the white man to his supposed inability to do manual labor in the tropics. The cultural roots of this belief go deep. European philosophers of the eighteenth century were impressed by the increasing efforts of the naturalists to explain the many areal differentiations among the world's peoples and their types of economic activity on the basis of natural history. People and their activities were to have their explanation in the laws of nature just as was the case for all other organic life. It is not surprising, then, that the philosophers expressed a great skepticism on settlement pos-

sibilities in areas other than Europe and with strange climates. Their views, in turn, were enhanced by the post-Renaissance preeminence of Europe in modern thought and were readily accepted and preserved for a long period by the elite.[3] Not until the last world war was "tropical determinism" seriously opposed by a mass of scientific research that indicated that most whites can acclimatize themselves to tropical climates and that the main reasons for settlement difficulties would have to be sought elsewhere.[4] Nor do past and present distribution patterns of plantations show a strict correlation with tropical climates, or for that matter, any climate. Plantations were first developed in Iran, Iraq, and the Mediterranean Basin, and are not unimportant there today. Plantation farming also is a thriving occupation in southwestern and southeastern United States and in certain sections of Australia, Chile, and the Republic of South Africa. Plantations have been recorded for areas well beyond the subtropics, such as Iceland, Ireland, and parts of colonial New England and New Jersey. Today many fruit, vegetable, sugar beet, and tobacco farms in northern United States and sugar beet farms in northwestern Europe display marked plantation characteristics. Certain Soviet *kolkhozes*, specializing in crops like sugar beets and cotton, are about the nearest equivalent to the California "factory farm." Furthermore, as the plantation has spread, it has become less and less precisely an institution of the European entrepreneur, as the growing number of Asian entrepreneurs strikingly shows.

Another climatic bias, but more influential indirectly, is the common restriction of the plantation classification to those large-scale farms producing tropical or subtropical crops. Nor have all crops raised in these latitudes been considered plantation crops. Many agricultural scientists and a not insignificant number of geographers have excluded those farms which, although in practically every respect plantations, grow perennial (i.e., woody) and

---

[3] J. Gottmann, *La Politique des États et leur Géographie* (Paris: Armand Colin, 1952), p. 35.

[4] P. E. James, "Man-Land Relations in the Caribbean Area," *Caribbean Studies: A Symposium*, V. Rubin (Ed.) (Seattle: University of Washington Press, 1960), p. 15. See also D. H. K. Lee, "Physiological Climatology," *American Geography: Inventory and Prospect, op. cit.*, footnote 2, pp. 470–83.

not annual plants. Further, they have usually been quite specific as to what perennials should be included.[5] Some, however, would exclude only the fruits but include other crops, whether woody or grassy, although even here individual definitions can be restrictive.[6] Others would bar from plantation consideration all plants that are not planted or tended individually.[7] But the crop restriction that has probably had the most influence on plantation students is that of Leo Waibel's. In his search for the *reinen und typischen* plantation, Waibel believed he had found the ultimate index: a complex industrial processing of the product, this being necessary to preserve highly perishable tropical commodities for their long trip to the middle latitudes and through hot and humid climates.[8] Thus, though not so explicit in crop specifications as other plantation definitions, Waibel's criterion still asserted a close correlation between plantations and tropical crops.

However, the rapidly evolving agricultural economy and its accompanying technology have invalidated most of these crop criteria in the plantation definition. Nothing has prevented entrepreneurs from importing middle-latitude crops into warmer areas and incorporating them into a plantation system, as with potatoes and sugar beets in California;[9] nor have entrepreneurs hesitated to apply plantation methods to such crops in their more common and cooler locales, as in northern United States and northwestern Europe. Simultane-

ously, improvements in crop selection have also made possible advances of normally tropical or subtropical crops into the cooler margins. Plantation operations, in the forms of Russian *sovkhozes* and *kolkhozes*, have accompanied the poleward movement of cotton, citrus fruits, tea, and vineyards. Cotton in the U.S.S.R. had, by 1950, penetrated as far north as 47°.[10] Major developments in agricultural chemistry promise even further expansion of warm-latitude crops into cooler climates as scientists learn more about the chemical content of plants and how to alter it so as to "substitute" for the natural growth stimulants, sunshine, rainfall, and soil.[11] Clearly, developments such as these no longer allow us to limit the distribution of so complex a farming system as the plantation solely on the basis of certain low-latitude crops, confined within certain climatic boundaries.[12]

Economic and technological expansion also continues to make ever more tenuous the association by Waibel of complex processing with only low-latitude location of plantations. Complex processing methods, ranging from canning and drying to pickling and distilling, are being applied to a growing number of crops heretofore not considered the plantation type and not necessarily located in the low latitudes. Nor do all crops raised in the plantation manner need complex processing, as testified by the growing shipments of fresh fruits and vegetables from the large specialized farms in southern United States, the Mediterranean area, and elsewhere. Actually, technological improvements have been so pervasive that they are making academic any ef-

---

[5] C. R. Fay stated that ". . . today plantation denotes not only a system of agriculture but a system which chiefly grows plants from wood as opposed to plants from grass: tea, coffee, rubber, cocoa, coconut, cinchona." Quoted from "Plantation Economy," *Economic Journal*, Vol. 46 (1936), pp. 622–23.

[6] Sugar, tea, coffee, cocoa, spices, tobacco, and rubber were listed by the Commonwealth Economic Committee in 1960 as appropriate to plantations; see *Plantation Crops* (London: H. M. Stationery Office, 1960), p. 1. S. Passarge provided an example of this plant particularism in practice in his book, *Südafrika* (Leipzig: Quelle & Meyer, 1908), p. 275, when, under the paragraph heading of *Plantagenprodukte*, he listed the tobacco areas of Cape Province but omitted those sections in the province where fruit is raised under the same farming system.

[7] Waibel, *op. cit.*, footnote 1, pp. 15–16, citing A. Reichwein, *Die Rohstoffe der Erde* (Jena: 1924), p. 22, and others.

[8] Waibel, *op. cit.*, footnote 1, p. 18.

[9] H. F. Gregor, "The Plantation in California," *The Professional Geographer* Vol. 14 (March, 1962), p. 2.

[10] T. Shabad, *Geography of the USSR* (New York: Columbia University Press, 1951), p. 60.

[11] P. Fabrizius, "Farming on the Factory Plan," *Science Digest*, Vol. 40 (November, 1956), pp. 13–16.

[12] Although crop bias has been the most influential in encouraging undue restriction of the total plantation area, it has also promoted overemphasis of plantation extent in those low-latitude areas where small farmers raise the same crop as do nearby plantations and then send it to the larger organizations for processing and marketing. Such farms have commonly been called "small plantations," "native plantations," or "smallholdings," despite their having little in common with their big neighbors except crop type and marketing arrangements. A better term for these small farms, and one indicating its commercial relations with the plantation, such as Waibel's *Pflanzung*, is still wanting in the English-language plantation literature.

fort to differentiate between plantations and nonplantations solely on the basis of any one level of processing complexity.[13] On the one hand, farms which do not completely transform their product more than maintain their industrial character by employing a vast array of machines for such different purposes as waxing, dyeing, bathing, sterilizing, cooling, dehydrating, freezing, packing, hastening ripening, and imparting odor. On the other hand, plantations that do produce crops undergoing complex processing are increasingly surrendering their control of this last step in favor of bigger, more efficient, and more centrally located plants serving a greater number of farms (refineries, canneries, distilleries, and wineries).

Crop biases in previous agricultural classification schemes have also encouraged the underestimation of the changing nature of the plantation and its areal extent. Engelbrecht's "Die Landbauzonen der Erde," which has strongly influenced German and American geographers to this day, emphasized crop regions, not agricultural systems, and restricted plantation activity to those crops which were thought typical of plantations, i.e., low-latitude crops.[14] Whittlesey's "Major Agricultural Regions of the Earth," still considered by most American geographers as the definitive agricultural classification, was based on more criteria; yet it, too, assigned plantation farming mainly to tropical crops ("Plantation Crop Tillage").[15] Curiously enough, two of the most ardent and influential plantation scholars, Waibel and Hahn, although much more system-oriented than either Engelbrecht or Whittlesey with respect to the plantation, were also more restrictive in the areal delimitation. Hahn, in his "Die Wirtschaftsformen der Erde," maintained that the tropical zone location was the single most important characteristic of the

plantation.[16] Waibel also implied as much, although his concept of an agricultural system, as represented by his *Landwirtschaftsformation,* was even more comprehensive than that of Hahn.[17] More recently, Prunty has set up criteria aiming at a more comprehensive and less commodity-influenced view of the plantation, but he has applied them only to the American South.[18]

English geographers and economists, in their emphasis on commodities, have also heavily contributed to the tradition of associating only certain crops with plantations. Most influential among geographers has been *Chisholm's Handbook of Commercial Geography,* still the most popular economic geography text in Britain and one that has preserved its almost exclusively commodity organization through sixteen editions.[19] Also of no mean influence is *Plantation Crops,* one of the many authoritative and regularly revised monographs on various agricultural commodity groups put out by the Commonwealth Economic Committee in London.[20] Although the committee now qualifies the title of this monograph in the introduction, it does so by referring to the increasing number of small farmers raising the same crops produced on the plantations. Nothing is said of the increase in the crop types, especially the extratropical crops, raised by the plantation.

ECONOMIC BIASES

Traditional plantation concepts in need of reassessment are also to be found in the more

---

[13] For an excellent and succinct discussion of the nature of the boundary between crops undergoing industrial processing and those not so affected, see W. Wirth's "Über den Anteil industrielle verarbeiteter Nahrungsmittel an der gegenwärtigen Ernährung in der Bundesrepublik Deutschland," *Berichte über Landwirtschaft, Neue Folge,* Vol. 40 (1962), pp. 845–46.

[14] H. Engelbrecht, "Die Landbauzonen der Erde," *Petermanns Geographische Mitteilungen, Ergänzungsband 45* (1930), pp. 286–97.

[15] Whittlesey, *op. cit.,* footnote 1.

[16] Hahn, *op. cit.,* footnote 1.

[17] Waibel, *op. cit.,* footnote 1, p. 11. Waibel never applied his concept to a worldwide classification system of plantations, although he did so for the coffee plantations in "Die Sierra Madre de Chiapas," *Mitteilungen der Geographischen Gesellschaft zu Hamburg,* Vol. XLIII (1933), pp. 102–44. Otremba, however, did apply the idea in his *Wirtschaftsformation* typology, although he referred to plantations only indirectly and then consigned them mainly to the tropics. See Otremba, *op. cit.,* footnote 1, pp. 347–48.

[18] First stated by M. Prunty in "The Renaissance of the Southern Plantation," *The Geographical Review,* Vol. 45 (1955), pp. 459–91, reference on p. 460; and restated in "The Woodland Plantation as a Contemporary Occupance Type in the South," *The Geographical Review,* Vol. 53 (1963), pp. 1–21, reference on p. 2.

[19] L. D. Stamp and S. C. Gilmour, *Chisholm's Handbook of Commercial Geography* (16th ed. rev.; London: Longmans, 1960).

[20] Commonwealth Economic Committee, *op. cit.,* footnote 6.

strictly economic realm. Probably the most tenacious concepts are those which emphasize the dependence of the plantation on cheap labor, cheap land, and the inflexibility of the system in terms of monoculture and dependence on world (i.e., foreign) markets. Both views must be increasingly qualified and, for many plantation areas, completely changed.

If the land and labor of plantations are still to be considered cheap, then they are also undoubtedly becoming much less so as competition for these two resources becomes keener. Small-farm economies are drawing a growing number of rural people who would formerly have continued to supply the plantations with labor. Increasing mining activity is another detractor. Both of these developments have been particularly strong in the low-latitude plantation areas. City jobs, on the other hand, have noticeably reduced the potential plantation labor supply in both low- and higher-latitude zones, although the repellent aspects of the rural economy have been at least as powerful in the rural exodus from the underdeveloped areas, especially in the low latitudes.

Governmental action has also fostered higher land and labor costs. New and higher taxes on land have been imposed to provide for expanded governmental programs. Competing economies have been encouraged in order to provide more jobs and an expanded economic base, a policy that puts a special burden on plantation in areas where the frontier of cheap land is nearing exhaustion, as in parts of southern Brazil. New and more direct labor costs have been imposed on plantations in such forms as wage minimums and social security compensation. Finally, international flows of migrant workers have been severely restricted by governments anxious to develop their own economies more fully.

But increasing land and labor expenses have not brought about a decline in the plantation. Increased rationalization of farming operations has not only helped the plantation to weather these two problems, but has given it an even greater scope in production level, production variety, and area of distribution. Such a reaction is not too surprising. With its large area and other extensive capital resources, its concentration on only a few products, and the complex handling or processing required of those products, the plantation has always been particularly receptive to technological advances.

Of special interest geographically are the ways technology is being employed to compensate for a less effective growing season, thus encouraging the spread of plantations into cooler latitudes. By extensively mechanizing the planting, cultivating, and harvesting procedures, planters have added several vital days, and sometimes weeks, to the growth period. The time saved has then also allowed the planter to expand his crop area. More fertilization, better crop varieties, and other improved cropping practices also have made crops more adaptable to shorter and cooler growing seasons, as well as greatly increasing crop yields per acre. In addition, a reciprocal and spiraling effect obtains between increased yields and mechanization. Increased yields strongly encourage mechanization since machine costs stay the same, whereas hand labor costs commonly increase with yield. Mechanization in turn encourages increased yields since write-off costs can be paid more rapidly. Machines can be used only at certain times, so that interest costs and other kinds of costs are long-term costs.

Mechanization has also promoted the more recent poleward push of the plantation in other ways. With reduction of the need for labor, the plantation operator is no longer so critically dependent on finding a crop that will provide employment opportunities for the longest period possible. Seasonal, rather than long-term, labor contracts have also eased the problem of unused labor capacity. Thus, planters are finding not only new extratropical areas open to their operations, but a far greater choice of crops. A wider choice of crops, in turn, offers planters still another opportunity to capitalize on the improved farming practices they have introduced. This crop variety continues to grow as mechanized procedures are increasingly applied to plants long assumed to be inaccessible to anything but hand labor. Tea, notorious for its exacting labor demands, is now largely machine picked in the Soviet Union. Tree crops, until recently considered incapable of machine picking, are being subjected to "tree shakers" in California. In the same state, prototypes of machines designed to pick such "unassailable" crops as grapes and tomatoes have also been developed. Mechanical cultivators and tree trimmers are becoming commonplace on many Brazilian coffee plantations. Sugar beet and potato harvesters already prevail in the United States and Canada and are now gaining popularity in Europe.

Mechanization and other technological measures imply an abundance of capital, and here, too, the extratropical areas seem to be favored in the matter of plantation growth. The middle latitudes have long been the centers of both capital formation and investment. That capital need not necessarily flow in greatest amounts to underdeveloped areas, but to areas that are already well advanced economically is now being vividly demonstrated in the widening gap between these two sections. Capital is also especially critical for plantation owners in higher latitudes, since it is in precisely those areas where land and labor costs have been the most onerous. By the same token, these cost increases have done more to promote the growth of the large-scale farm at the expense of the small than has been true for most lower-latitude areas. The fact that these and other incentives to plantation farming are so marked in more economical advanced areas also qualifies considerably the frontier hypothesis of plantation origin, i.e., that plantations develop only in sparsely populated and economically virgin areas. Economic frontiers are not always coincident with geographical or environmental frontiers. An economic frontier is an area which offers opportunity to a more efficient economic organization, and this can be true of any environment, well populated or otherwise, economically advanced or not. Thus, for example, large fruit and vegetable farms have grown rapidly in California and New Jersey, despite the fact that small farms are both numerous and proficient in both states.[21]

Technological meliorations have also benefited the low-altitude plantation. With the longer growing season, better farm practices and more machines bring even better results than in higher latitudes. Machine capacity can be used more fully and good machine operators can be retained more easily since they can be paid for a longer period of work. New methods of extending the harvesting season, such as planting at different times, and either staggering or concentrating ripening by the application of chemicals, have greater scope. Even the great extent of empty spaces, the most formidable barrier to plantation expansion in the tropics, now appears to be turning into an invitation as mechanization of hand procedures continues and labor switches from tenant to seasonal wage-labor status. But, as already noted, capital sources for these various improvements are less plentiful than in cooler latitudes, although surplus capital seeking new investment areas should continue to increase.[22] Perhaps, then, one may expect future plantation growth to be especially vigorous in the subtropics, since it is here that the best compromise between length of growing season and availability of capital is achieved (U.S.A., Australia, South Africa, and similarly situated countries). Certainly, one can no longer view the plantation as an institution that is inherently unsuited to extratropical areas without ignoring the present industrialization of the plantation and unduly restricting the plantation definition.[23]

Waibel, "The Climatic Theory of the Plantation: A Critique," *The Geographical Review*, Vol. 32 (1942), pp. 307–10.

[21] Waibel had already attacked the frontier hypothesis of the plantation in 1942 by pointing out the lack of correlation between plantations and sparsely populated areas of southeastern Asia. His other objection, that associating the plantation with a frontier, hence dynamic, institution would belie its "extremely stable and conservative" nature, is more debatable. Certainly the plantation has been anything but conservative in its record of economic innovation and aggressiveness. Ignored by Waibel in his objections were the locations of middle-latitude plantations in areas that were both well populated and economically advanced, e.g., sugar beet plantations in northwestern Europe. See L.

[22] On a major instance of the role of capital in the spread of the plantation, see W. Gerling's discussion of the sugar cane plantation in *Die Plantage* (Würzburg: Stahel'schen Universitätsbuchhandlung, 1954), pp. 5–13.

[23] The negative conclusions of some plantation scholars on the expansion capabilities of plantations have a strange ring today in view of the recent technological advances and their effect on the plantation economy. Waibel maintained in 1941 that industrialization was "unsuited by its very nature to the agriculture of the temperate zones." See "The Tropical Plantation System," *Scientific Monthly*, Vol. 52 (1941), p. 156. R. O. Buchanan apparently little foresaw, in 1938, the potentials of mechanization and of alternatives in labor contracting when he asserted that because labor peaks could be more easily eliminated in the tropics through year-round planting, "it would seem that plantation agriculture in the future is likely

Growing land and labor costs have not only strongly influenced, through technological countermeasures, the plantation distribution pattern, they have also played a large part in the increasing efforts of the plantation toward greater market flexibility. Squeezed between rising competition and increasing land and labor charges, the planter has begun to diversify his production on an ever-widening scale. Some of the new crop additions are sold directly, as is done with peanuts on African cotton farms; others are capitalized indirectly, as is done on the plantations in the South where legumes are fed to cattle. Many of these additions have been introduced via rotation systems or as permanent cover crops, thus reducing soil depletion as well. Subsistence crops are also being raised in larger amounts and, where possible, incorporated into rotation schemes. Although these crops are not immediate additions to the plantation income, they provide ultimate benefits in the form of a more satisfied and efficient labor supply. Another improvement of labor efficiency effected through crop diversification has been a more even distribution of the work period. Mechanization, surprisingly enough, has also favored, to a point, a diversity in crops. Although one of the most potent forces favoring one-crop cultivation, mechanization also makes available more area and cultivating time, not all of which necessarily has to be given to one and the same crop. How much more rapidly machinery costs can be amortized by the addition of new crops will naturally depend on the degree of specialization demanded of the machine.

Not all motivations for diversification have stemmed directly from concern over the price–cost squeeze, of course. Some of the governments heavily dependent on the plantation economy have begun to insist on more production variety. Diseases, which thrive and spread quickly over extensive and uninterrupted areas, have been another spur. Unusually good market prices for one or more additional crops have also been at times the overriding stimulant for diversification. Droughts, destructive

storms, and other vagaries of the physical environment have been still other catalysts.

An almost bewildering variety of crop combinations now characterizes many a plantation cropping system. Such traditional plantation crops as rubber and bananas have begun to be paired in Haiti. Cocoa, however, has become the companion of rubber in Ceylon, and bananas are being combined with both cacao and oil palms by the United Fruit Company in Central America. Citrus fruit, sugar cane, and rice are raised by the same operator on some of the new plantation lands in South Africa, whereas on the other tracts citrus fruit and bananas have been planted together. Mulberry trees, fruit trees, and vines are frequent partners on the cotton plantations in the U.S.S.R. Rubber–tea and coconut–tea combinations are now common in Ceylon. Potatoes and tomatoes now supplement bananas on plantations in the Canaries. Sugar cane, citrus fruit, and cattle are additional bulwarks for the large vegetable grower in Florida. Cotton, sugar cane, and coffee are raised by the same producer in West Africa. Even more inclusive is the combination of coffee, cacao, oil palm, and coco palm of São Tomé plantations. But it is the subtropical plantation in the United States that most spectacularly exemplifies the lengths to which plantations can capitalize on a situation in which markets are abundant and capital and technology easily available. The Southern plantation now concentrates on groups of specialties, with such new combinations as cattle–cotton, pecans–dairy products, and rice–soybeans.[24] One 38,000-acre plantation draws its income from sales of cotton, corn, rice, soybeans, spinach, wheat, cattle, and pulpwood. Millets, sorgho, alfalfa, and oats are raised for the livestock.[25] The typical Imperial Valley plantation in California produces for sale cotton, sugar beets, alfalfa, flax, barley, and a wide variety of vegetables.

This growing variety of crops has been complemented by the steadily expanding markets of the plantation. Much of this market

[24] Prunty, op. cit., 1955, footnote 18, pp. 462–63.

[25] M. Prunty, Jr., "Deltapine: Field Laboratory for the Neoplantation Occupance Type," Festschrift: Clarence F. Jones, M. Prunty, Jr. (Ed.) (Evanston, Ill.: Northwestern University Studies in Geography No. 6, Northwestern University Department of Geography, 1962), pp. 151–72, reference on p. 165.

to be more and more closely associated with the Equatorial Belt." See "A Note on Labour Requirements in Plantation Agriculture," Geography, Vol. 23 (1938), p. 164.

extension has gone unnoticed because of its recency, or because attention has been attracted more by the increasing competition of small-farm producers than by the continuing growth of the plantation economy. A more deliberate myopia, however, has hindered recognition of a particularly impressive development in the plantation market situation, the growth of the home market for plantation products. This has been the view that the plantation economy is primarily dependent on markets that are distant and are commonly in foreign countries. Many plantations in former colonies have now begun to cultivate the domestic market in an attempt to meet the growing competition of other plantation areas and to gain favor with the new governments. Some have even shifted completely to supplying home demands, as have several Indonesian plantations. Numerous plantations have always been mostly dependent on home demands, of course, and there, too, growth has been impressive. One thinks of such enterprises as the sugar plantations in Australia or Argentina; the fruit, cotton, and sugar plantations in the Soviet Union or the Republic of South Africa; or the large fruit, sugar, and vegetable plantations in the United States. Nor are distance and regional competition, the two problems implied in the foreign-market qualification of the plantation, necessarily absent from a plantation economy oriented mostly to home consumption. Thus, although fruit and vegetable plantations in California, on the Gulf Coast, and in Florida have greatly increased their shipments to the Northeast within the last thirty or forty years, and particularly since the last world war, they have had to do so through a program carefully designed to minimize the difficulties of thousands of miles of transportation and of heavy competition from a major fruit and vegetable industry in the market area.[26] In fact, some of the plantation farms in the Northeast have significantly extended their market area well beyond their own regions.

One of the more impressive examples is that of the 19,000-acre Seabrook Farms Company in New Jersey. Although its chief market has always been New England and the Middle Atlantic states, its sales area has now been extended as far west as Texas, Oklahoma, and Missouri, and south to Florida.[27] Soviet plantations are even more dependent than American plantations on distant markets within the home territory, although associated marketing problems have become, since the Revolution, more a problem of the planner than of the entrepreneur.[28] One can go back as early as the reign of the Tsarina Elizabeth to find fruit being shipped from the Black Sea and Lower Volga areas to Moscow and St. Petersburg by special services of fast *telegas*.[29]

POLITICAL AND SOCIAL BIASES

To speak of certain kinds of Soviet collective farms as plantations goes against another time-honored conviction about what the plantation should always be. This is the view of the plantation as primarily an imperialistic weapon, designed for ruthlessly exploiting the natural resources and population of one country for the benefit of another. The plantation thus is seen more as a particular political and social, rather than economic, institution, despite the fact that the primary purpose of the plantation has always been economic, but not always necessarily and purposely imperialistic. Also ignored in this comparative de-emphasis of the economic motive are the universality of

---

[26] On the reverse problem of the Northeastern fruit and vegetable farms, that of adjusting to increased production from areas with more favorable climates, see the detailed treatment by M. Biehl, *Der Obst-, Gemüse-, und Gartenbau im Nordosten der Vereinigten Staaten von Amerika unter der Konkurrenz subtropischer Landesteile* (Kiel: Forschungsberichte des Instituts für Weltwirtschaft an der Universität Kiel: Kieler Studien, Vol. 43, 1958), 235 pp.

[27] Anonymous, "This is Seabrook Farms," *Quick Frozen Foods*, Vol. 19 (1956), p. 190.

[28] Because domestic markets are protected to some degree by governments, P. George would sharply differentiate those speculative farming operations largely dependent on domestic demand from those speculative types dependent mostly on foreign demand. *Précis de Géographie rurale* (Paris: Presses universitaires de France, 1963), p. 262. But protectionism, as already implied, need not stifle intensive intraregional competition; it may even promote it, although such stimulation may sometimes be of doubtful benefit to the overall national economy (e.g., southeastern vs. southwestern cotton areas in the United States). Furthermore, protectionism in the form of cartels and international conferences of producer nations has become an increasingly important adjunct of those speculative operations heavily dependent on foreign markets.

[29] G. Jorré, *The Soviet Union* (2d ed. rev.; translated and revised by E. D. Laborde; New York: John Wiley & Sons, Inc., 1960), p. 147.

technology and the desire for economic advancement, both of which are now promoting the increasing adoption of the highly rationalized methods of the plantation by peoples of widely diverging political and social orientations. And with this spread of the plantation has come a decided amelioration of those conditions that have encouraged many to link indissolubly the plantation system to social degradation but to ignore its potentials for economic, and therefore social, betterment.

No better example of the primacy of economic motives is the way large farm size, an indispensable qualification of the plantation, has been favored in one degree or another by governments of widely contrasting political philosophies. In countries where free economies hold sway, properties have been expanding at a phenomenal rate. Forces contributing to growth of property size, such as rural exodus and competition between small and large farmer, are given full play. An impressive variant of this last development, farmer competition, has been the consolidation of older, individually owned plantations into larger units operated by corporations. Several sugar cane plantations in Brazil and Peru, for example, have increased their average size to anywhere from 50,000 to 70,000 acres.[30] Leasing has also been extensively resorted to in some areas; some California cotton plantation operators have expanded their holdings by as much as eight or nine times through this method. Fiat has replaced individual economic decisions in the state-controlled economies, but the end result in terms of large farms has been no less impressive, particularly in the Soviet Union and China. The cotton *sovkhoz*, that type of Soviet state farm that most closely approaches the free-economy plantation in extensiveness of operations and complexity of crop processing, now averages approximately 32,000 acres in size.[31] The cotton *kolkhoz*,

smaller in size but more numerous, may sometimes be as large as 25,000 acres or more.[32] Consolidation of smaller properties has also been a prominent part of cotton *kolkhoz* history. Like all other *kolkhozes*, cotton *kolkhozes* have been reduced in number but considerably increased in size by the government since the 1930's. Chinese farms have gone through two consolidation periods. The first involved a reorganization based on the *kolkhoz* system; the second, in 1958, featured a regrouping into 25,000 "communes."[33]

Large farm size would seem to have little future in countries with strongly socialistic economies, and where major programs have been started in order to increase the number of small landholders. Yet an increasing practice for many of these governments is to maintain administrative control of the expropriated property, while allowing operations to continue in much the same way as before or dividing the land among tenants. The product continues to be sold on the open market. The majority of the vast estates in Sumatra have been little disturbed by the Indonesian Government, although 101 out of 217 had been nationalized by 1959.[34] The Gezira cotton plantations in the Sudan are well-publicized examples of the tenancy, or "partnership," approach. Schultze notes one of these plantations as including almost 98,000 acres.[35] Nor are

tural Economists, 19–30 August 1961 (London: Oxford University Press, 1962), p. 313. Cotton *sovkhozes* and *kolkhozes* on new cotton land in the Uzbek Republic average between 8,000 and 10,000 acres in size, according to K. M. Djalilov in "Agriculture in Economic Development: Country Experiences (Uzbek S.S.R.)," *Proceedings of the 11th International Conference of Agricultural Economists, 19–30 August 1961* (London: Oxford University Press, 1962), pp. 239–40.

[32] S. R. Sen, "Technical Change in Different Environments (Asia)," *Proceedings of the 9th International Conference of Agricultural Economists, 19–26 August 1955* (London: Oxford University Press, 1956), p. 54.

[33] B. Kayser, *L'économie de plantation et les problèmes du développement,* Part II of *Économies et Sociétés rurales dans les Régions tropicales* (Paris: Centre de Documentation universitaire, 1963), p. 133.

[34] W. A. Withington, "Changes and Trends in Patterns of North Sumatra's Estate Agriculture 1938–1959," *Tijdschrift voor Economische en Sociale Geografie,* Vol. 55 (1964), p. 12.

[35] J. H. Schultze, *Der Ost-Sudan* (Berlin: Abhandlungen des 1. Geographischen Instituts der Freien Universität Berlin, Vol. 7, 1963), p. 117.

[30] T. L. Smith, *Brazil: People and Institutions* (Baton Rouge: Louisiana State University Press, 1946), p. 525; T. R. Ford, *Man and Land in Peru* (Gainesville, Fla.: University of Florida Press, 1955), p. 57. Ford gives one extreme example of plantation consolidation by noting that the holdings of the Empresa Agricola Chicama, Ltd., owned by the firm of Gildemeister and Company, comprised more than sixty former holdings.

[31] I. S. Kuvshinov, "The Experience of Large-Scale Collective and State Farms of the U.S.S.R.," *Proceedings of the 11th International Conference of Agricul-*

restrictions on large private properties by land-reform programs always necessarily extreme. In Mexico, for example, owners of "henequen *haciendas*" in Yucatan are still allowed a maximum 1,000 acres apiece[36] and a growing number of families in the northwest have been able to increase their properties to as much as 3,000 acres.[37] Even larger holdings have been amassed in the Philippines, despite an early American land policy restricting an owner to 2,500 acres being still in force.[38] Italian land-reform laws exempt farms as large as 750 acres from expropriation and partitioning if management is efficient and a sizable labor force is employed.[39]

The inner spatial patterns of the plantation also reflect the superiority of economic to political or social motivation. Plantation operators the world over have paid increasing attention to the need for spatial subunits as management problems multiply with the increasing amount and complexity of plantation operations. The details of this subdivisioning vary considerably from place to place, but few of these variations correlate with regional differences in political or social philosophies. Some plantations have accomplished this subdivision in the process of expansion. The amalgamated plantations then become managerial units. "Group *kolkhozes*" in the Soviet cotton areas, "estate groups" in the Indian and Ceylonese tea areas, *usina* plantations in the Brazilian sugar cane areas, and the "factory unit systems" of the Louisiana sugar cane plantations are more prominent examples of this method of compartmentalization. Still other plantations form their managerial units by simply subdividing their original areas. Increasing variety in crops and machinery may eventually encourage a reorganization of an earlier structural network, with units becoming smaller and more numerous, as detailed by Prunty in his description of the Deltapine "plantation units" in Mississippi.[40] The relative importance of the managerial units within a plantation also varies. Some plantation operators concentrate most of the capital equipment and administrative and processing activities on one or at least a minority of the units; the remaining units then assume "crop-feeder" roles. The Louisiana cane plantations and the Indian and Ceylonese tea plantations offer just a few of the examples of this procedure. On some plantations, however, managerial units are given equal responsibilities, with each unit specializing in production of a certain product. These units have become completely self-sufficient communities on some of the larger Brazilian plantations.[41] Between these two extremes of responsibility assignments to the managerial units come such plantations as the group *kolkhozes* and the neoplantation of the Cotton Belt. Sizes of managerial units also differ considerably from plantation to plantation, but again owing largely to economic considerations. Labor demands of a crop are a primary consideration. Thus a tobacco farmer in Southern Rhodesia usually limits the amount of acreage under one supervisor to 200,[42] but a cotton planter on a Southern neoplantation, even with many additional crops, often can set his acreage minimum at 1,000 or more.[43]

---

[36] R. E. Chardon, "Hacienda and Ejido in Yucatan: The Example of Santa Ana Cucá," *Annals*, Association of American Geographers, Vol. 53 (1963), p. 178.

[37] Large families have been able to amass sizable amounts of land, since each member of a family upon reaching majority is entitled to as much as 250 acres. Adjacent *ejido* lands are also often, and illegally, rented. The composite is then operated as one unit. See C. L. Dozier, "Mexico's Transformed Northwest," *The Geographical Review*, Vol. 50 (1963), p. 562. R. Dumont gives a critical account of these developments in *Terres Vivantes* (Paris: Librairie Plon, 1961), pp. 101–04.

[38] The same process of land acquisition as in Mexico (footnote 37) has taken place, each individual of the family claiming the maximum 2,500 acres. Personal communication from J. E. Spencer. See also Chap. 16 of his book, *Land and People in the Philippines* (Berkeley and Los Angeles: University of California Press, 1954), pp. 196–208.

[39] G. Kish, "Italy," *Focus*, Vol. 3 (May, 1953), p. 2. Only four per cent of the Po Delta land-reform area, which includes the greatest concentration of Italy's "industrialized" plantations, had been expropriated by July of 1952, compared with twenty to ninty per cent for other areas; noted by R. E. Dickinson, "Land Reform in Southern Italy," *Economic Geography*, Vol. 30 (1954), p. 163.

[40] Prunty, *op. cit.*, 1962, footnote 25, pp. 168–70.

[41] Comments by H. W. Hutchinson on the article by E. T. Thompson, "The Plantation as a Social System," *Plantation Systems of the New World* (Washington, D.C.: Social Science Monographs, VIII, Pan American Union, 1959), pp. 26–41, reference on pp. 38–41.

[42] D. Whittlesey, "Southern Rhodesia—An African Compage," *Annals*, Association of American Geographers, Vol. 46 (1956), p. 89.

[43] Prunty, *op. cit.*, 1962, footnote 25, p. 169.

Degree of mechanization also makes for variations in acreage minima for managerial units. It is certainly one major reason for the gap between the acreage-limit estimates of the cotton neoplantation operator and the limits of 375 to 500 acres determined by Soviet experts for their cotton farms.[44]

Trends in settlement patterns on the plantation are no less striking evidences of the general urge to economic rationalization. That plantation operators have long recognized the advantages of concentrating processing facilities and personnel in one spot is shown by the traditional nucleated plantation settlement. Increasing magnitude and complexity of plantation operations have put an even greater premium on compact settlement. Some of these agglomerations approach city size, as on the more specialized Soviet farms or many of the corporate plantations. One tobacco *sovkhoz* has a population of over 27,000.[45] On just two of the Firestone plantations in Liberia, populations now total 72,000.[46] The industrial aspect of the settlements has also become more prominent. Processing plants are larger and more numerous. Just one freezing plant on a vegetable plantation in New Jersey covers twenty-three acres and is four stories high.[47] Smith describes some of the bigger sugar plantations near São Paulo as having on the same property one or more sugar mills, paper plants, and distilleries, besides those facilities for processing food for the plantation population, such as macaroni plants and slaughterhouses.[48] Shops for repairing, or even manufacturing, processing machinery and farming equipment have multiplied and added to the industrial complex. Sheds and fenced yards house tractors and other farming machinery. Tractors, understandably, have become key machinery as field mechanization has progressed. They and their allied farm equipment and housing facilities, as well as repair shops, have become a pole of activity second only to the processing center. Where processing is done on another of the plantation subunits or elsewhere, the "tractor station" becomes the activity focus. Prunty's term for this concentration, although applied to the mechanized Southern plantation,[49] also recalls the more spectacular examples of Soviet "machine tractor stations."[50]

The move toward even greater settlement concentration on plantations has its regional variations. Where governments are attempting to settle tenants on the land of former privately owned plantations, as in Sudan, dispersed settlement becomes important, although processing centers are also commonly expanded and even new ones created. Small agglomerated settlements may be established as headquarters areas for the various managerial subunits of a plantation, their function being secondary only to the headquarters area of the overall plantation. Many plantations in Brazil are just beginning to shift into the *usina* type of operation, the smaller size of their settlements and the general lack of machine shops, equipment sheds, and yards clearly reflecting the older *fazenda* plantation form. No such lag is to be found in the Soviet Union, where headquarters settlements are the case for all large farms, plantation or otherwise, and where an ambitious program for establishing *agrovilles* continues to be pushed. These agricultural cities would become the functional centers of the more recently formed group *kolkhozes*.

Worldwide changes in the management and labor structure of plantations are, no less than changes in their spatial structure, convincing answers to those who would view the plantation more as a political and social institution than as an economic one. The shift of ownership control from the individual owner to a larger and more impersonal body, the rise of the manager as principal plantation administrator, the industrialization of the workers, and the blurring of ethnic lines between all three of these groups, all these are changes that can be found to one extent or another in all countries where a plantation economy is practiced.

[44] Djalilov, *op. cit.*, footnote 31, pp. 242–43.

[45] R. Dumont, *Sovkhoz, Kolkhoz, ou le Problématique communisme* (Paris: Éditions du Seuil, 1964), p. 143.

[46] G. Kunke, "Gummi aus Liberia," *Zeitschrift für Wirtschaftsgeographie*, No. 8 (1962), p. 225.

[47] Anonymous, *op. cit.*, footnote 27, p. 181.

[48] Smith, *op. cit.*, footnote 30, p. 62.

[49] Prunty, *op. cit.*, 1955, footnote 18, pp. 485–86.

[50] Now being disbanded in favor of similar machinery complexes on the *kolkhozes*. Dumont gives several excellent firsthand descriptions of the magnitude of these "tractor complexes" on some of the larger Soviet grape and cotton farms (*op. cit.*, 1964, footnote 45). No less impressive are the "equipment yards" on the larger California cotton farms, Gregor, *op. cit.*, footnote 9, p. 2.

More and greater administrative problems and increased demands on capital resources are making the position of the individual plantation owner always more precarious. Many plantation families in Latin America have sought the needed capital, managers, and technicians by incorporating themselves and then soliciting outside investment. But this tactic is proving inadequate compared with the efficiency gained by the acquisition of individually owned plantations by corporations. Capital resources for the corporate enterprise may come partly from local sources, but the larger enterprises depend on foreign capital. Governments have also taken over both privately and corporately owned plantations, to be sure, but economic motives have been paramount in the efforts of many of these governments to maintain, and often expand, the former plantation economies, as we have seen. Actually, governments of all political bent are becoming, through publicly supported agricultural and business schools, the principal sources of a growing class of experts capable of managing, or advising the management of, large farming operations. Nor has government enlistment of such personnel seriously altered that distinct division of functions between managers and labor which is such an important criterion of the plantation. Managers are often installed directly by the state, or, if elected by the workers, are frequently, in fact, appointed. This last procedure is typical of the installation procedure for the *kolkhoz* chairman.[51]

Increasing managerial administration implies an accompanying industrialization of labor. Only through closer supervision and greater specialization of the worker can the manager hope ultimately to increase productivity, reduce inefficiency, and thereby justify his role. Wages have been a prime tool in this production and efficiency drive; they can be used far more easily as a production incentive than land or produce. Wages also help to satisfy better the increasing demands of plantation labor for consumer products, particularly those produced off the plantation. The decline of rented land or crop shares as production incentives in favor of a basic wage

can be observed in practically all major plantation areas. In the South, the wage system is crowding out the traditional share arrangements; in the American Southwest, its rise has been coincident with the beginnings of large-scale agriculture; in Latin America, it has made less progress against the extensive *hacienda* and *fazenda* systems of tenancy, but the rate of advance is increasing; in Africa, Asia, and Australia, wage systems have long been standard; in the Soviet Union, *kolkhoz* workers have received a basic wage since 1958.

Job specialization, primarily in handling of machinery, has been another mark of labor industrialization on the plantation. The most thorough and extensive examples of this specialization are on plantations of the United States and the Soviet Union, where technical progress is rapid and agricultural labor is becoming increasingly dear. The modern Southern cotton plantation has a detailed hierarchy of machine operators, beginning with a few specialists, notably mechanics, at the top; followed by operators of cotton pickers or self-propelled combines; then tractor drivers; and finally, at the bottom of the scale, those using just hand tools.[52] Utmost efficiency in the use of machines and implements is also the primary reason for the Soviet practice of dividing workers into "brigades" and "squads." This similarity in labor rationalization between state-controlled and capitalistic plantations is not coincidental. Whereas the drive toward agricultural development on an industrial scale has advanced, at best, under only indirect encouragement of governments in capitalistic countries, the Soviet Government has done all it can, directly and indirectly, to promote the movement. Marxian doctrine calls for the disappearance of differences between the worker and the peasant, this to be effected by the machine.[53] Even prerevolutionary cultural legacies have supported the Leninist program for farm labor industrialization, notably the collectivist organization of the *mir*.

---

[51] K. Mehnert, *Soviet Man and His World* (translated by M. Rosenbaum; New York: Frederick A. Praeger, 1961), pp. 81–82.

[52] Prunty, *op. cit.*, 1962, footnote 25, pp. 164–65.

[53] D. Faucher, *La Vie rurale vue par un Géographe* (Toulouse: Institut de Géographie, 1962), p. 304. H. Haushofer provided an interesting explanation of the similarity of Soviet and capitalistic motives for developing an industrialized agriculture based on division of labor to the ultimate degree, in "Typen agrarischer Lebensformen," *Studium Generale*, Vol. 8 (1958), pp. 473–80.

If political and social differences seem not to have hindered attempts to transform the plantation worker into a technician, the transformation itself has had important effects on the political and social attitudes of the workers. Undoubtedly, mechanization of labor has reduced the rural proletariat and enhanced the prestige of the new plantation worker, although it has also created a social hierarchy of its own, as already implied for the Southern cotton plantation. In fact, where tenants are involved, the shift from hand to machine cultivation can reduce the status of tenants to that of laborers, as observed on those Southern plantations where tractor drivers now do a major proportion of the work formerly done by croppers with mules.[54] Growing political awareness, and its concomitant, unionization, have been additional consequences of the impact of industrialization on plantation labor. Demands for unionization have matched the rise of the corporate plantation. In Latin America, they have become the psychological substitute for claims on the paternalism of the old *hacienda* or *fazenda* planter. Unionism on plantations is much less developed in Africa, but it is strongly entrenched in many parts of southeastern Asia (e.g., Indonesia and Malaysia). Plantation unionism in the United States is just now beginning to become an important movement on the mainland, but it has become so important in Hawaii that unions are already beginning share plantation control with companies. This has occurred where plantation workers cannot afford the capital for mill machinery.[55] Unions on Soviet plantations are naturally quite another story, although their existence is enough indication of how important the government considers them as outlets for, and barometers of, labor feelings.

Another powerful influence of plantation industrialization on worker attitudes has been the stimulation of desires for urban amenities. Part of this influence has been through the intensified dealings of the plantation with the outside areas, with contacts between

its workers and those of the cities then also becoming more intimate. Where cities are close enough, workers may choose to live there and commute to the plantation, an arrangement particularly suited to the part-time laborer who prefers not to migrate during the plantation slack season but is therefore dependent on a city job. Day-haul plantation labor is already well established in such diverse plantation areas as California, Mississippi, Brazil, and the Sudan. It is also important on the Soviet *kolkhoz*, although for different reasons.[56] A more direct influence of plantation industrialization on worker preferences for urban amenities has been the efforts of unions, governments, and plantations to ensure better living and working conditions in the plantation community. Better homes, more schools and hospitals, newer and bigger stores, theatres, and clubs now give some plantation settlements many of the aspects of a modern city. Soviet authorities also have made major efforts to provide urban amenities to all its *kolkhoz* workers, far more than they were accustomed to in the *mir*. A great gap still exists between the conditions of workers on the various plantations, as between American workers on the one side and Peruvian workers on the other, but it is also a gap that is narrowing. As plantations continue to industrialize, the old view of synonymity of labor exploitation and plantation economy will have to be increasingly qualified.

Still another traditional view of the plantation that is coming more into question is that foreign whites control the supervisorial and most other high-level positions and give a nonwhite indigenous population what is left. Increased capital accumulation by local entrepreneurs and nationalization of plantations have helped expand the number of nonwhite plantation owners. Indians in India, creoles and mestizos in tropical America, and Ceylonese in Ceylon are a few examples of this upsurge. Ceylonese already controlled the ma-

---

[54] A. L. Bertrand and F. L. Corty, *Rural Land Tenure in the United States* (Baton Rouge: Louisiana State University Press, 1962), p. 222.

[55] E. T. Thompson, "The Plantation Cycle and Problems of Typology," *Caribbean Studies: A Symposium*, V. Rubin (Ed.) (Seattle: University of Washington Press, 1960), pp. 29–33, reference on p. 33.

[56] The superposition of *kolkhoz* farming on the old *mir* village pattern, established when farming was largely extensive cereal cultivation with fallow, has made truck hauling of farm workers to and from the fields a well-established practice. Elimination of much of this transportation by reducing the number of villages has been one of the main goals of the *agroville* program. Dormitories have also been constructed in some areas to house temporarily those workers living farthest from the fields.

jority of the plantations on the island by 1952, although the proportion was lower for the larger plantations than for the smaller ones. Owners comprised both companies and wealthy individuals.[57] Even where ethnic differences between owner and operator personnel do occur, there need not necessarily be a capping layer of foreign white nationals, as illustrated by the growing number of plantation owners of Chinese and Japanese descent in Southeast Asia. However, even where the cleavage in occupational responsibilities is both ethnic and nationalistic, the divide is lowering. Plantation companies, in particular, are making serious efforts to assign the indigenous groups to more advanced jobs. Examples abound of Africans being assigned to as many mechanizable operations as possible.[58] The United Fruit Company, long held by many to be the prototype of plantation imperialism, has a policy of replacing Americans with native labor wherever possible.[59] For many plantations, such steps are deliberately planned transitional stages to positions of full management responsibility. There are also many large and expanding plantation areas in which foreign control and exploitation has not been a factor for a long time, even though ownership has been white.[60] Southern and eastern United States, northern France, and Soviet Middle Asia are good examples. Labor on many of these plantations is also white, although not always necessarily of the same ethnic groups as those of the owners. The progress of these workers to positions of responsibility has been notable, although uneven areally.

Political and social improvements such as these still have not erased all the resentment of former colonial areas over past exploitation by plantations, of course. But the growing awareness of the economic advantages inher-

ent to the plantation organization and the desperate need for capital, nevertheless, have encouraged an increasing number of governments to take various measures fostering plantation growth. The establishment of government plantations on a tenancy, or partnership, system has probably been the most significant of these actions. Other examples besides the Sudanese Gezira cotton plantations and those sugar plantations operated by the Indonesian Government are the cooperative cacao farms in Nigeria; the factory units specializing in tea in Kenya, Uganda, and Tanganyika; the government corporations producing abacá and coconut in the Philippines; and the state sugar, rubber, and tea plantations in Ceylon. Foreign investment in plantation expansion also has been encouraged. Nigeria has exempted approved rubber plantations from governmental action designed to help peasant farmers.[61] Ceylon in 1958 forbade the fragmentation by sale of estates of over 100 acres in size,[62] and in 1961 promised not to nationalize them for at least ten years.[63] In some cases, governments have offered to sign partnership agreements with private firms, as in Nigeria, where several rubber plantations of 20,000 acres each have been set up under this arrangement.[64] Many governments have observed how plantations and their supporting and consuming industries (fertilizer companies, coffee plants, and the like) stimulate each other's development, and have established agricultural schools and research laboratories to strengthen this combination.

Even the old plantation imperialism has taken a new twist. To preserve their supply sources and maintain their power position in the international arena, mother countries are now courting their former colonies with additional economic aid. A major part of this effort is increased support of the plantation economy, in many cases the only significant means by which the newly independent countries can obtain badly needed capital. Power politics has also encouraged those countries not considered former colonial powers to aid

[57] B. H. Farmer, "Peasant and Plantation in Ceylon," *Pacific Viewpoint*, Vol. 4 (March, 1963), p. 9.

[58] G. T. Kimble, *Tropical Africa*, 2 vols. (New York: The Twentieth Century Fund, 1960), Vol. 1, p. 575.

[59] J. P. Augelli, "Bananera: A Tropical Plantation on the Pacific Lowlands of Costa Rica," *Focus on Geographic Activity*, R. S. Thoman and D. J. Patton (Eds.) (New York: McGraw-Hill Book Company, 1964), Chap. 6, pp. 30–36, reference on p. 33.

[60] Including here regional exploitation within a country, as in prerevolutionary Russia where the central government conducted a more or less exploitive program with regard to the cotton lands and other areas more distant from the population core in Europe.

[61] Commonwealth Economic Committee, *op. cit.*, footnote 6, p. 180.

[62] Commonwealth Economic Committee, *op. cit.*, footnote 6, p. 178.

[63] Farmer, *op. cit.*, footnote 57, p. 16.

[64] Commonwealth Economic Committee, *op. cit.*, footnote 6, p. 180.

plantation economies, to the point where we have such economic incongruities as the United States and the Soviet Union, both leading synthetic rubber producers, guaranteeing Indonesia a certain part of its needed market for natural rubber.

HISTORICAL BIASES

But such artificial measures are viewed by many as only temporary halts to the inevitable decline of the plantation. Increased rationalization and distribution are, also from this point of view, not so much evidences of a vigorously expanding plantation form as they are of the plantation giving way to newer economic forms. All of this is quite understandable if one recalls that the plantation had its first major expansion during the eighteenth and nineteenth centuries, and that, therefore, it was from this period that the popular image of the plantation was derived. But if this aspect of history encourages the formulation of a plantation pathology, then other aspects effectively challenge it.

Modern deviations from the plantation prototype of the colonial era have not been without precedent, both in that period and the several prior centuries during which the plantation was developing. As early as Roman times, free, and white, workers were being used in harvesting, crop diversification was beginning to be practiced, and plantation outposts were being located in such extratropical areas as the Rhineland and the interior of the Balkan Peninsula.[65] During the very flowering of the traditional plantation, crop rotation was a typical part of the plantation system in Brazil.[66] Plantation operations in New Jersey, by the middle of the eighteenth century, were foreshadowing several subsequent plantation developments: expansion of plantation operations in cooler latitudes, crop diversity, and emphasis on both local and distant markets.[67]

Current changes in the plantation also have precedent in the historical pattern of development of economic forms in general. This pattern has not been a constant succession of separate and distinct forms, but one of forms being constantly modified as methods are refined and tools are improved. Borrowings from other economic forms also have increased. It is instructive that those who would see in these economic changes the demise of the plantation define it more as a political and social, rather than simply an economic, institution. With this priority of criteria, it is easy to see how Edgar Thompson, the foremost of American sociologist students of the plantation, could conclude that such economic criteria as unionism and division of labor marked not an improvement of the plantation, but its final stage.[68] Actually, increased economic rationalization has been encouraging a return to some of the most salient cultural characteristics of the traditional plantation. Expanded mechanization on the neoplantations of Southern United States has been at least partly responsible for a growing reversion to antebellum days by encouraging the formation of community villages, reduction of tenants, and institution of more direct owner control.[69] Somewhat the same thing has been happening in Brazil, where the

---

[65] K. Ritter, "Geschichte der Landwirtschaft der Welt," Part I of *Wirtschaftslehre des Landbaues*, Vol. I of *Handbuch der Landwirtschaft*, Fr. Aeroboe, J. Hansen, and Th. Roemer (Eds.) (Berlin: Paul Parey, 1928), p. 37.

[66] M. Diegues, Jr., "Land Tenure and Use in the Brazilian Plantation System," *Plantation Systems of the New World* (Washington, D.C.: Social Science Monographs, VIII, Pan American Union, 1959), p. 119.

[67] For the details of New Jersey plantations during

colonial times, see C. R. Woodward's *Ploughs and Politicks* (New Brunswick, N.J.: Rutgers University Press, 1941), especially p. 230.

[68] Thompson detailed his "plantation cycle" in "Population Expansion and the Plantation System," *American Journal of Sociology*, Vol. 41 (1935), pp. 314–26.

[69] Prunty argued that forces outside of the rural economy, and not mechanization, have been largely responsible for the rural exodus and its effect on the Southern plantation; "Land Occupance in the Southeast: Landmarks and Forecast," *The Geographical Review*, Vol. 42 (1952), p. 447. The "pull" forces outside the economy should not be maximized at the expense of the "push" forces of mechanization, however. Farm workers, particularly those on large plantations engaged in extensive experimentation with field machinery, are becoming increasingly aware of the imminence of full-scale mechanization. This consciousness may be at least one of the prods to seek work outside of agriculture while conditions for non-farm employment are favorable. Transitional tenure arrangements also indicate that the "push" of mechanization on Southern farm population is already well underway in areas where partial mechanization had previously little displacement effect; see J. H. Street *The New Revolution in the Cotton Economy: Mechanization and Its Consequences* (Chapel Hill: University of North Carolina Press, 1957), pp. 222 and 247.

growing consolidation of *fazendas* into the larger *usinas* represents a trend back to the very earliest colonial times when large land grants still had not been split up into *engenhos* (called *fazendas* after 1889).[70] Nor do all sociologists and anthropologists agree with Thompson that social and political changes have been drastic enough to obliterate the plantation's identity. In this view, the more industrialized plantation is simply another developmental stage, or "subculture," of the plantation.[71]

The most impressive precedent for a vigorous and dynamic plantation form, however, is in the present agricultural revolution, a process that is spurring all agricultural forms to acquire many of the characteristics already considered most typical of the modern plantations. So well recognized has this process become, that several scholars have formulated steps in its operation. Herlemann and Stamer propose a three-stage sequence for agricultural industrialization, the sequence varying between countries of high and low population density but the outcome being the same: a massive shift of emphasis from land and labor to capital, and in particular, to mechanization.[72] Andreae deals with another major trend in agricultural modernization that is already widespread among plantations: specialized production.[73]

Again a three-stage sequence is proposed, although exceptions for certain countries are admitted. But specialization is still held to be inevitable. Haushofer stresses the growing emphasis on division of labor, leading to an ultimate stage that is even now practiced by many plantations, the contracting of people in nearby cities and towns for various farming operations.[74] The conclusion that Haushofer draws from this movement also has favorable implications for the continuing expansion of the plantation form. This is the opinion that labor division pushed to the ultimate can lead to the elimination of all differences between agricultural economic forms.[75] Since intensive labor specialization in agricultural operations cannot be divorced from the many other highly rationalized practices so typical of the modern plantation, it would seem reasonable to conclude, then, that the standardization of economic forms would usher in a plantation millenium, or at least a time in which all agricultural forms would have a certain resemblance to the plantation. Worldwide uniformity of agricultural systems is obviously still some time off, but the convergence of forms in the direction of the plantation already seems close at hand in some areas, notably in the Soviet Union and in the United States.[76]

---

[70] H. W. Hutchinson, *Village and Plantation Life in Northeastern Brazil* (Seattle: University of Washington Press, 1957), p. 43.

[71] More prominent supporters of this view are C. Wagley and M. Harris, "A Typology of Latin American Subcultures," *American Anthropologist*, Vol. 57 (1955), pp. 428–54; S. Mintz, "The Culture History of a Puerto Rican Sugar Cane Plantation: 1876–1949," *Hispanic American Historical Review*, Vol. 33 (1953), pp. 224–51; and V. Rubin, "Cultural Perspectives in Caribbean Research," *Caribbean Studies: A Symposium*, V. Rubin (Ed.) (Seattle: University of Washington Press, 1960), pp. 114–15. But also in this last publication is a defense by E. Thompson of his cyclical theory in "The Plantation Cycle and Problems of Typology," pp. 29–33.

[72] H. H. Herlemann and H. Stamer, *Produktionsgestaltung und Betriebsgrösse in der Landwirtschaft unter dem Einfluss der wirtschaftlichtechnischen Entwicklung* (Kiel: Forschchungsberichte des Instituts für Weltwirtschaft an der Universität Kiel: Kieler Studien, Vol. 44, 1958), 147 pp.

[73] Andreae defines specialized production in the more modern plantation sense: the raising of one crop for sale, but accompanied by "potential-sale" crops which are used to improve the soil or spread out the work period; *or* the raising of several crops

for sale, but of which one brings in at least fifty per cent of the total revenue. B. Andreae, *Betriebsvereinfachung in der Landwirtschaft* (Hamburg and Berlin: Sonderhefte der Berichte über Landwirtschaft, Nr. 169, Neue Folge, Verlag Paul Parey, 1958), 86 pp.

[74] Haushofer, *op. cit.*, footnote 53.

[75] Haushofer, *op. cit.*, footnote 53, p. 479: "Die bis zum aüssersten getrieben Arbeitsteilung kann also zur völligen Aufhebung von selbständigen Typen agrarischer Lebensformen führen."

[76] Exactly how far convergence between the American family farm and the plantation has progressed is still much debated. Edward Higbee is perhaps the most forceful exponent of well-advanced convergence in his application of the term *hacienda* to all farms with a production value of $40,000 or more; see his *Farms and Farmers in an Urban Age* (New York: The Twentieth Century Fund, 1963), 182 pp. This criterion would apply to about four per cent of all American farms. But the plantation definition is loose, at best, because it comprises farms of all sizes and types of production. Nor can the traditional *hacienda* be considered the equivalent of the modern plantation. A much slower rate of convergence may be hypothesized on the basis of R. Nikolitch's criterion of man-years of hired labor; *Family and Larger-Than-Family Farms*, United States Department of Agriculture, Agricultural Economic Report No. 4 (Washing-

TECHNOLOGY AND TYPOLOGY

Once the revolutionizing effect of agricultural technology on plantation growth is recognized, it also becomes apparent that there cannot but be many more regional variations than was the case for the period of the traditional plantation. But technology being what it is, it is a regionalization based not on the peculiarities of geographic regions, but on the scale and complexity of plantation operations. A cotton plantation is much the same all over the world in the processing of its product and in the installational complex needed for its operation, but no one can confuse a cotton plantation with a tea plantation in these two aspects! Nor can even crops be considered absolutely reliable indices of certain levels of processing complexity, for the same crop may be treated in a variety of ways, ranging from the superficial to the intricate (e.g., fresh and dried bananas; fresh, frozen, dehydrated, and canned vegetables; copra and coconut butter).

Walter Gerling (*Die Plantage*, 1954) has been the first to construct a plantation typology based on processing complexity. He ranked seventeen plantation types on the basis of a threefold division of complexity, *viz.*, plantations with only minor (*geringfügigen*), a few but indispensable (*unentbehrlichen*), or extensive (*umfangreichen*) processing installations.[77] Gerling failed to include, however, such major plantation types as the vegetable plantations in the United States, the sugar beet plantations in this country and northwestern Europe, the rice plantations of the United States and southern Europe, and the several varieties of forest plantations scattered over many parts of the earth. Technological advances have also continued at a rapid rate since Gerling's writing, so that even more plantation types would now have to be added. These additions have resulted from both new crops being processed in the plantation manner and new types of preparation being applied to crops that have already been contributing to plantation production (e.g., freezing). Also, certain technical innovations have begun to provide a few exceptions to the direct relationship implied between the degree of processing and the magnitude of the installations. The most obvious deviation is probably that found on some of the large vegetable plantations, where the installations of a food-processing plant may surpass a ginning complex in size and number, yet involve a processing method that is much simpler. Deviations like these, however, still provide no clue to any other criterion that might differentiate plantations more clearly than does the extent and intricateness of their operations.

QUASI-PLANTATIONS

A typology of any agricultural forms must necessarily exclude many closely related, or modified, versions, and that for the plantation is no exception. In certain cases, only the lack of some sort of specialized handling of the product during or immediately after harvesting prevents one from including in the plantation classification such mammoth enterprises as those Soviet *kolkhozes* specializing in crops other than those already mentioned in connection with those farms. Insufficient acreage or excessive fragmentation can also prevent an otherwise extraordinary productive and rationalized farm from being properly labeled a plantation. Vertical haciendas, as Higbee calls them, have especially proliferated around cities and in irrigated areas of the United States.[78] Far-flung fragmentation is particularly characteristic of those large Midwestern farms specializing in corn and soybeans for sale. In still other situations, it is the specialization in animals or animal products, rather than crops, that furnishes the basis for a differentiation between the plantation and other large-scale, intensive agricultural forms.[79] Some of the most extensive and industrial types of farming operations can be found on livestock farms such as some of the

ton: U.S. Government Printing Office, January, 1962), 44 pp. Using this measurement, Nikolitch found that only slightly more than half of all farms in the highest production-value category used labor beyond that furnished by the family. Furthermore, as with Higbee, no attempt was made to exclude farms of small size or certain production types which would not be classified as plantation enterprises (e.g., cattle ranches).

[77] Gerling, *op. cit.*, footnote 22, p. 27.

[78] Higbee, *op. cit.*, footnote 76, pp. 91–92.

[79] P. S. Taylor, an economist, disregarded even this differentiation and applied the plantation term to large-scale commercial livestock farms (e.g., Western ranches). "Plantation Agriculture in the United States: Seventeenth to Twentieth Centuries," *Land Economics*, Vol. 30 (Feb.–Nov., 1954), pp. 141–52.

larger American dairy farms or the Australian air-beef stations.[80] The question of plantation suitability becomes more involved, however, when one considers those large farms that produce a sizable variety of both plant and animal products for sale, none of which forms an outstanding part of the total farm income. An excellent example is one of the *grandes fermes* in the vicinity of Paris, and described by Phlipponneau: 1,500 acres; barns for 100 cows; chicken houses; a dairy for pasteurizing and bottling of milk; a distillery for processing of potatoes; a cannery for fruit and vegetables; and quarters for workers.[81] The large version of the American general farm in the Southern states would also be a good example, an increasing number of which are coming from the former cotton plantations now in the process of diversifying.

Quasi-plantations, like the true plantations, can be expected to increase in number and variety. Even more than the plantation, they show how widespread agricultural industrialization has become, a process that is narrowing the gap between the plantation and other farms, as well as between the plantation and its industrial counterpart, the factory.

---

[80] A more recent development in Australia, in which cattle are slaughtered in the interior and the carcasses then shipped by air to the ports. The largest of the dairy quasi-plantations are in the United States, especially in the subtropical and tropical parts. Higbee describes one in Florida, *op. cit.*, footnote 76, pp. 40–42; L. Durand describes them in Hawaii in "The Dairy Industry of the Hawaiian Islands," *Economic Geography*, Vol. 35 (1959), pp. 228–46; and H. F. Gregor details some of the farmsteads of these operations in California and Hawaii, in "Industrialized Drylot Dairying: An Overview," *Economic Geography*, Vol. 39 (1963), pp. 299–318.

[81] M. Phlipponneau, *La Vie rurale de la Banlieue parisienne* (Paris: Librairie Armand Colin, 1956), pp. 177–79.

TOP BANANAS

by
PHILIP CORWIN

Within the next six months, lawyers for United Fruit Co. will show up in federal court with a plan to slice off a big chunk of its banana empire. Bowing to the terms of a 1958 consent decree, United must get rid of assets accounting for almost 30% of its current domestic business in the yellow fruit. While not effective until 1970, the move will mean the loss of roughly 15% of the company's present revenues.

SEVERAL PLANS

United has several ways to satisfy the consent decree. It can set up a subsidiary and spin it off by distributing the shares to its own stockholders; it can sell the new business to any individual or firm other than its major rival, Standard Fruit & Steamship Co.; or it can combine the first two plans by selling part of the assets of the new firm (for not less than $1 million) and then parcelling out the remaining shares among its shareholders. In any case, the latter will not be hurt: they will get a pro-rata share of any distribution or benefit indirectly from a cash sale, since the money, of course, would end up in the company treasury.

While scarcely happy about the upcoming divestment, United feels the long-term impact may not prove too painful. For some time, the company has wanted to broaden its operations and cut its dependence upon bananas, which now contribute over 80% of its revenues. In fact, President John Fox says that he hopes within five years "at least half of earnings" will come from other sources.

NEW MARKETS

Nonetheless, even though domestic demand for bananas has levelled out at 17-18 pounds per capita and growing world supplies have put pressure on prices (the latter now average 10% below a year ago), United has no desire to abandon the business. It has spent a lot of money during the past few years to revamp its banana operations, cutting costs, improving plantation yields and developing new disease-resistant trees. At the same time, the company is busily tapping new markets in Europe. These measures are beginning to pay off.

United and Standard Fruit (84.4% owned by Castle & Cooke, Inc.) dominate the banana market in the U.S. and Canada; between them, they slice up about 75% of the total. Standard, which has been boosting its share steadily, commands nearly

"Top Bananas" by Philip Corwin. Reprinted from Barron's *(December* 13, 1965), p. 11ff, *with permission of the publisher.*

25%, compared with 16% five years ago. The two firms are the only domestic suppliers growing their own fruit; the others usually buy bananas from independent plantations in the tropics, mainly in Ecuador.

Both companies are enjoying sharp gains in profits this year, though in each case, third-quarter results were aided by a strike that kept the ships of competitors tied up in port. In the 36 weeks ended September 11, Standard scored a 25% jump in net, to $4.07 a share. Earnings for the full 12 months apparently should run substantially ahead of the $2.92 a share in 1964; sales may exceed $93 million, up from $84.6 million.

NET SOARS

United fared even better: nine-month net soared to $1.65 per share, from 26 cents a year earlier. What's more, the company expects to be "in the black" in the last quarter, whereas during October-December 1964, a 17-cent deficit was incurred; thus, for all of 1965, profits should be dramatically above the nine cents a share of last year. Revenues for the nine months, meanwhile, rose 12% to $286.1 million, and for all of 1965 are likely to exceed last year's $334.1 million by a comfortable margin. Prospects for 1966 also appear promising, and United recently resumed dividends with a 15-cent quarterly payment — the first since November 1964.

While a half dozen or so independents supply 25% of the domestic banana market, none approaches the annual volume of either United or Standard. For example, Pan American Fruit Co., one of the largest, estimates its 1965 sales at around $23 million. Another prominent supplier, West Indies Fruit Co., does a somewhat smaller yearly business.

Both United and Standard have received a shot in the arm from new management or controlling interests. At United, John M. Fox, one of the founders of Minute Maid Corp. (now part of Coca Cola) took over as chief executive in April. Fox, who came to United in 1961, largely has been responsible for revamping the company's entire banana operation over the past few years. In particular, Fox automated production processes and streamlined an administration that had ballooned into a minor bureaucracy. Moreover, his know-how with citrus fruits and frozen foods figures to be extremely useful in the future as United explores acquisitions in those fields. Castle & Cooke, on the other hand, acquired a majority position in Standard last year. The Hawaiian food processor is best known for its Bumble Bee seafoods and Dole pineapple operations.

OTHER STAKES

At the end of 1964, United operated 94,336 acres of banana plantations, mostly in Costa Rica, Honduras and Panama. In addition, the company has bananas in three other countries and Jamaica, and buys bananas from growers in Ecuador. Although this fruit, as noted, accounts for 80% of United's revenues, the company also has substantial stakes in several other agricultural products, including cacao, oil palm and sugar cane. Most of its sugar-producing properties went down the drain after Fidel Castro took over in Cuba, but the firm still owns cane plantations in Jamaica and a sugar refinery in Massachusetts run by a subsidiary, Revere Sugar Refinery.

Another subsidiary, Tropical Radio Telegraph Co., operates a wireless communications business in Central and South America, the West Indies, and in the U.S. Finally, United owns a fleet of 46 ships and 1,133 miles of railway in Central America. Under the aforementioned 1958 consent decree, the company sold its 39% interest in International Railways of Central America (IRCA). However, IRCA is suing United for $500 million, claiming that the latter, while controlling the railroad, charged itself unduly low rates. United contends that the allegations are unfounded.

Standard boasts much larger banana properties, or around 626,000 acres — all in Costa Rica and Honduras — and, in addition, buys from independent growers in Ecuador. Unlike United, it charters its ships instead of owning them. The company also operates a 305-mile railroad in Honduras, and has other agricultural activities including the coconuts and citrus fruits. Finally, Standard has interests in a Honduran firm making beer and soft drinks and in one turning out soap and vegetable oil products.

United, too, has branched out modestly into other fields. In 1960, it acquired Liana, Inc., a Texas firm which freeze-dries shrimp and other items. Between 1964 and June 1965, United bought about 15% of the common stock of Gorton's of Gloucester, a leading seafood packer; in addition, United acquired a one-third interest in a Peruvian subsidiary of Gorton's, which processes meat and fish oil. Finally, in July, the company acquired Numar, S.A., a Costa Rican processor of edible oils.

The most noteworthy developments in the past few years at both United and Standard, however, center around two major improvements in their banana operations — both pioneered by Standard. The first was the evolution of a new high-bearing and disease-resistant banana tree. The second was the decision to pre-package the fruit in the tropics before shipping, instead of transporting it in the traditional stem form.

THE BIG MIKE

Until 1950, all bananas grown in Central America and sold in the U.S. were of the Gros Michel — Big Mike — variety. The Big Mike, however, is susceptible to Panama Disease, a lethal plant fungus. Once soil is infested, it can never again grow bananas. During the 'forties, this fungus swept through the plantations on the eastern side of Central America, prompting Standard to develop in 1950 a new disease-resistant banana, the Giant Cavendish. United soon followed suit with a variety called Valery.

Both types possess other significant advantages. They grow to a height of only 15 feet — half that of the Big Mike — and hence are more resistant to tropical wind storms that have leveled thousands of acres of the old variety. Even more important, the Giant Cavendish and Valery bear twice as much fruit, or between 18 and 20 tons per acre. Today, Standard concentrates its production entirely in the Cavendish; approximately 40% of United's output is in the Valery.

BOXING BANANAS

However, the new types have two other distinctions — thinner skins and weaker stalks — which make them more perishable when handled extensively. Hence, in 1959, Standard began to box its bananas in the tropics before shipping them, in order to provide better protection; United soon followed suit. Today, over 95% of the bananas imported into the U.S. arrive in boxes.

Pre-packaging in the tropics eliminates a great deal of work in warehouses here, including cutting, packing in boxes and stem disposal. Moreover, there are no difficulties with broken stalks or loose "fingers" on the banana "hand." At the same time, producers are now able to market more of the crop. When bananas were shipped in stems, uneven sizes or missing hands might cause a whole stem to be rejected.

Finally, pre-packaging provides better quality control of fruit. As a result, United is able to label its best bananas and charge premium prices for more of its output than previously. Today, its premium Chiquita brand accounts for well over three-fourths of its domestic sales.

Boxing bananas also has eliminated most of the tedious hand work at the plantations and docks from the time when they were shipped in stem form. Nowadays, fork-lift trucks, conveyor belts and other mechanized equipment handle the job swiftly. As a result, Standard says that its total number of processing operations has been slashed from 17 to 4.

RISE OF ECUADOR

However, pre-packaging also has been adopted extensively in Ecuador, the banana capital of the world. Plantations there supply the independent rivals of the two industry leaders and the new mode of shipping has enabled the country to boost its exports sharply. This, in turn, has brought a substantial rise in global supplies of bananas.

As a result, Standard and United have been forced to develop new markets outside the U.S. They have been quite successful in fostering a taste for bananas in West Germany; indeed, per-capita consumption there is now as high as it is in this country. Italians also have upped their demand. In addition, both companies are eyeing the growing Japanese market, now largely supplied by Taiwan.

Ecuador's stepped-up invasion of the world market also has forced the two industry giants to streamline drastically their banana operations in order to remain competitive. All phases have been revamped, from agronomy and accounting, to land ownership. In 1960, United, for instance, instituted a policy of selling or leasing banana lands to individual growers. Called the Associate Producers Program, the project not only is an incentive to local farmers but also presumably gives them an interest in opposing possible nationalization.

PRO AND CON

Furthermore, the program frees United from the cost of providing homes, schools, hospitals, and the like for its employes, which it is obligated to supply when the land is company owned. True, there are also drawbacks: once the land is leased or sold, United relinquishes control over the quality of the products; and in the case of a sale, has no way of preventing the owner from reselling it to someone unreliable. In the main, however, the benefits outweigh the disadvantages. At any rate, Standard has set up a similar plan.

Another significant stride in cutting handling costs has been for both companies to invest in their own boxing plants. United now operates such stations in Costa Rica, Honduras and Panama, and estimates that the plants will save some $6 million in operating costs in 1965 alone.

Further economies also have been achieved. Sigatoka, a leaf disease, is now largely controlled by spraying chemicals via planes; previously, thousands of people were required for the job, walking through the fields with sacks over their shoulders and spreading the pesticide manually. Fertilizer, too, is sprayed from a plane instead of being spread manually, and herbicides are used to kill weeds, instead of hacking through them with a machete.

In short, the banana business has jumped from the nineteenth century to the twentieth in just a few short years. While it has lost some of its easy-going tropical glamor in the process, it has gained in efficiency which already is being translated into better profit margins.

COFFEE: CASH CROP OF THE TROPICS

by
WILLIAM H. HESSLER*

Our land rover swung 'round a curve of the red dirt road, lurched into a narrow lane, passing a field of bright green coffee trees, and stopped on the neatly kept lawn before a modest brick farmhouse.

"Now you'll have a chance to meet a first-rate African farmer, one of the best in this area," I was told by my guide and counsellor for the day, the British district officer for that section of south-central Kenya. He hopped out and introduced me to the farmer, waiting for us at his front door, and to his wife and two small grandchildren.

So began a visit that was to confirm once more why coffee is a world crop of immense political significance. The lesson wasn't altogether easy, for there were language barriers. Benjamin Kithorne, the farmer, spoke only the dialect of the Kamba tribe, so he talked to our native driver. The driver repeated in Swahili to the district officer, who in turn gave me the word in English — with a strong Scottish accent. But we managed, with some confusion and much good humor.

Gray-haired and aging, but erect and spry, Benjamin Kithorne is a living symbol of what has happened to Africa in 50 or 60 years — and of the role that coffee has played in that transformation. He was born

into a rude, primitive society, before white men came to Kenya as administrators and settlers. But he has done well for himself and his family by listening closely to the government agricultural agent. He has only a small farm, thirteen acres. But he grows good corn, keeps three milk cows, has a generous banana patch, and each year a larger planting of coffee trees.

This would be just another subsistence farm, merely keeping a single family alive — like hundreds of thousands of farms through Africa — save for the coffee. It provides a cash crop — for Benjamin, and a rapidly growing number of native farmers throughout much of sub-Sahara Africa. It is coffee, nothing else, that puts East African shillings into Benjamin's pocket and pays for the amenities that lift his family well above the level of subsistence. He lives in a fairly modern brick house with wood floors and carpets on them. Without his coffee income, he would still be in a round mud and wattle hut with a conical thatched roof, with an earthen floor and no windows.

We spent an hour wandering over Benjamin's farm, looking at everything, asking about everything. What interested me most was the coffee, for by that point in my African trav-

*WILLIAM H. HESSLER is foreign news analyst for the Cincinnati Enquirer.

"*Coffee: Cash Crop of the Tropics*" *by William H. Hessler. Reprinted from* Farm Quarterly, *Vol. 18 (Summer 1963), pp. 50-51ff, with permission of the editor.*

els I had come to realize what an extraordinary part coffee has had in reshaping the economies and the political fortunes of large segments of tropical Africa. Coffee in fact has had a pivotal role in modernizing some exceedingly primitive countries, in both hemispheres.

Benjamin's coffee trees, still quite young and mostly eight to ten feet high, were bent nearly double with the weight of the still-green cherries.

"How many acres do you have in coffee?" I inquired through my two interpreters. And the word came back circuitously, "Nearly five acres."

"And how much coffee did you harvest last year?"

That took some searching of memory and calculation.

"Around 4,000 pounds." It was a good yield, well above the world average per tree or per acre. And it made a very good living indeed for an illiterate African who started life in a barbaric society before Kenya had even become a British crown colony.

Benjamin was lucky in some respects. His land, quite rich red soil, and rolling but not rugged, was near a range of high hills that insured him more rain than most of arid Kenya gets. And from a mission station close by, he got piped water. So he and his wife were spared the toilsome daily task of most native farmers in Kenya — carrying water in drums on their backs from a stream or communal well. Nor did he have to drive his animals through the blazing sun to a water point. Besides being lucky, however, Benjamin was intelligent and patient. His steeper slopes were painstakingly terraced, to hoard water and check

erosion. The youngest coffee trees, seedlings ten inches high, had their individual shelters of sticks and brush, to fend off the hot sun. Coffee is a demanding crop.

Farther north, is the higher country of the Kikuyu tribe, better farmers than the Kamba; and the greater altitude gives better quality coffee. In most years, coffee has been Kenya's most valuable export crop. And fully half of all Kenya's coffee is grown, not on the big farms of the white settlers, but on the family-size farms of native Africans.

FROM ISTANBUL TO BRAZIL

Benjamin is just one of millions of people who live chiefly by growing coffee. They are spread over the tropical areas of three continents, with the greatest concentration in Latin America. Rice and wheat, of course, are the world's great food crops. They feed most of the three billion people who clutter our ever more crowded globe. Coffee, by contrast, does not have a calory in a carload. All the same, coffee feeds some millions of people in 40-odd countries — the people who grow it for the breakfast tables of the United States and Europe. It might even be argued that coffee is today the most politically significant crop in world agriculture. It is the chief cash crop of two dozen countries or colonies. Those countries are all underdeveloped, many of them in political or social revolution, teetering between a backward feudalism and a new way of life that may be capitalist democracy or may be communism. Conceivably, the price of green coffee in New York could ordain the fateful choice between these alternatives for a score of nations.

The coffee tree came to Latin America by way of Istanbul, Paris, and the island of Martinique in 1723, and spread quickly through the West Indies and onto the mainland. For 200 years, Latin America had a near monopoly of coffee production for export. It brought high prices in Europe, in the early period, and this led to the enormous expansion of plantings from Mexico to south-central Brazil. Soon it became the main reliance of numerous countries.

Colombia today is the extreme case. Coffee exports in recent years have provided 71 to 78 percent of its foreign exchange earnings. That is a lot of eggs in one basket — and a highly unreliable basket. In tiny El Salvador, coffee has been 60 to 72 percent of exports. In Guatemala, known for its fine mountain coffees, the figure has run from 58 to 72 percent, and in Haiti it has been as high as 70 percent. Brazil has long been the giant in the coffee industry, sometimes producing well over half the world crop. But so big and diverse a country has many other resources also. Even so, coffee has been providing 50 to 60 percent of Brazil's foreign exchange earnings. In Costa Rica, the figure is 54 percent.

Those are the half-dozen countries for which coffee provides half to three-quarters of all export revenue. Eight other Latin American countries, notably Mexico and Venezuela, produce coffee in substantial quantity for export, as do ten countries in Africa and several in Asia. For Latin America as a whole, coffee ranks after petroleum as the most valuable export product. And far more people live by coffee production there than by an other cash crop or by exploitation of any mineral resource.

But coffee growers are gamblers, inescapably. For in the realm of world prices, coffee is a bad actor. In 1921, with the postwar slump, it dropped in price from 23 cents to 9 cents. In the good years around 1928-29, it held firm at 23 cents to 25 cents. But with world depression (and larger plantings) it fell to 8 cents. (That means the annual yield of one coffee tree might bring the grower less than a dime in U.S. currency.) Recovering after the worst depression years, coffee brought good returns for a time; and then Adolf Hitler and Joe Stalin invaded Poland. Instantly, the whole European market was closed. Coffee plummeted to 7 cents.

While in the heart of the Brazilian coffee country at about that time, I walked through warehouses in which bagged green coffee was stacked thirty feet high, in masses two city blocks long.

"What will you do with all this coffee?" I asked of my host.

"Maybe the price will be better next year, or the year after," he said hopefully. "Coffee will keep for years." But then he added with a wry smile: "Most of this may be burned."

In Brazil, coffee is really big business. And consequently, Brazil has taken the main responsibility for efforts to stabilize world prices. Growers and government authorities together destroyed 11 million bags in 1931-32, and 13 1/2 million bags in 1933. In 14 years of surpluses, they removed from the market a total of 78 million bags — almost two years' world production. (Bag = 132 pounds.) Farmers in that period abandoned millions of trees, turning to other crops. Then frost and drouth ravished Brazil's great *fazendas*. Meanwhile, during World War II, Americans really learned to drink coffee. *Per capita* consumption in the U.S.A. rose from 13 1/2 pounds a year to 17 pounds. The natural result was a world shortage, and the price of Santos jumped from 27 cents to 52 1/2 cents. In 1954, production was off and demand was rising. Coffee sold at 80 cents for mild; 79 cents for Brazils. But that didn't last long. Overproduction is the normal pattern.

THE BIG BUYER

In terms of *production*, then, coffee is extremely important to about two dozen countries. On the *consumption* side, the picture is truly startling. There is *only one* truly important consumer country. Americans have become a race of inveterate coffee-drinkers. Some major countries — Russia, China, Great Britain — are tea-drinkers. Germany and Italy would be big coffee consumers, only they have tariff and excise taxes, ranging up to 160 percent, which hold down consumption. Scandinavians are the heaviest coffee-drinkers; but there aren't many Scandinavians.

The upshot is that the United States uses about 22 million bags of coffee a year, or in round numbers over half of the total export production of the world. By the usual rule of thumb, that is *120 billion* cups of coffee a year. America spends more coffee — about $1 billion a year — than for any other single commodity it imports. U.S. imports of coffee are more than six times those of either of the next-largest importers, West Germany or France. For a

time, late in World War II, the United States actually consumed 79 percent of the world's coffee. With a proper impartiality, the U.S.A. imports coffee from 40 to 45 countries (or colonies) in a rough proportion to their exportable production. From 45 to 50 varieties are used in blending in America. The two really meaningful categories, however, are "Brazils" and "milds" — which mean low-altitude and high-altitude coffee. There's a marked diversity also in roasts, from "cinnamon" to "Italian" — from light to very dark brown, that is to say.

Besides having only one king-size customer, the coffee industry has another peculiarity, an unfortunate one. It has no secondary uses whatever. Growers' associations have had scientists at work to find new uses. But coffee beans are stubborn. They won't turn into plastics, won't make good cattlefeed, won't serve as insulation. So, with too much coffee grown, the producer countries have no choice but to limit their exports.

Except for a small amount of superior coffee grown in Hawaii, the United States does not grow a single pound. (Puerto Rico, to be sure, if included, grows 220,000 bags a year.) Even if the necessary low-cost hand labor were available, we still could not grow coffee anywhere in the continental United States, save a small corner of southern California. Nowhere else is there the required combination of altitude, soil, rainfall, and freedom from frost. In coffee, America is destined to be the Great Consumer.

BERRIES ARE CHERRIES

Coffee is an exacting crop. Left to itself, the tree grows to perhaps

30 feet, but it usually is pruned back to 12 or 15 feet, for easier picking. An evergreen, it looks a little like a holly tree, has nicely scented small white flowers, followed by berries that start green, turn yellow and orange, and cherry-red — but not all at once. The berries — more commonly called cherries, in the trade — ripen unpredictably, so that a tree may have to be picked, selectively, three or four times in a season. In some places, the harvest is almost a year-round enterprise. Even so, the yield may be no more than one pound of beans (green weight) per tree. That is a typical yield, although it varies greatly.

Hand labor, consequently, is a key factor in coffee-growing, no mechanical picker having been contrived. In addition, constant cultivation is required — mechanical, on the big *fazendas* of Brazil, but with backbreaking hand labor on the smaller holdings in the hill country of Colombia or El Salvador or Guatemala. One hears of "great coffee plantations." There are such, especially in Brazil, with one million trees or more. But the vast bulk of the world crop — five billion pounds in a normal year — is grown on family farms with no hired hands — just a farmer and his family.

For an acceptable crop, coffee requires a quite rich, well-drained soil; abundant water (50 to 70 inches of rain a year does it); freedom from frost at all times; and, most surprisingly, a very limited amount — one or two hours — of direct sunlight each day. There are two usual ways to get "limited sunshine." One is to plant bananas, or cocoa trees, or some other tree crop, between the rows of coffee trees, giving partial shade. The other way is to plant the coffee trees in rugged mountain country, where high hills cut off the sun for long periods of the day. That is part of the secret of Colombia's immense crop of high-grade coffee. As a special case — unique, so far as I know — the superior coffee grown in Hawaii is the result of peculiar cloud formations, which provide a cloud cover most of each day and give shade automatically.

The quality, meaning the flavor, of coffee depends directly, and very largely, on the altitude above sea level at which it is grown. I have visited large *fazendas* in Brazil, north of Sao Paulo, where the trees stretch in well-planned rows to the horizon. It is a gigantic business. But that coffee grows at 1,500 to 2,000 feet, and commands in the world market only the standard price for Santos — 36 cents average for 1961. In Guatemala, on the other hand, I have seen small, rather slovenly patches of coffee, a few acres here and there on steeply rolling plateau land, on family-size farms under open shade at 5,000 to 6,000 feet. These meager plantings are not impressive. They look a bit amateurish. And the crop is smaller, per tree and per acre. But these are the so-called "mild" coffees, the product of altitude; and they bring premium prices in New York — 39 cents average in 1961. The same is true in Colombia, biggest producer of "milds" — 44 cents average in 1961.

COFFEE AND STABILITY

Now we can come back to Africa, the first home of the coffee tree and in recent years the chief convert to coffee-growing. When they moved into Africa, the British, French, Belgians and Portuguese found either primitive herding societies, or else an inefficient form of subsistence agriculture. Typically, an African farmer would clear a few acres of hill land by cutting and burning, and then put in bananas, manioc, and a few vegetables. New soil, tropical sunshine, and fair rainfall gave relatively good crops despite primitive methods. But in three or four years, drenching rains would leach out the minerals and wash away some topsoil, and the land would become barren. The African simply moved a half mile, built a new mud and wattle hut, cleared a new patch of land, and started over. But such slash-and-burn agriculture is wasteful of the land, and provides only the barest subsistence. But how to persuade the African native to take care of his land and stay with it?

In the Kenya highlands, the Kikuyu learned by working on the white settlers' farms, and then launching their own farms on the best land they could get. In Ruanda-Urundi, the Belgians faced a formidable problem when they took over from the Germans in 1918. The people were near the starvation line, for this was and still is the most densely settled part of Africa. It is only two degrees south of the Equator, but it is so high it seems like Switzerland in Spring — the year 'round. It is rugged country, but every slope is farmed, either in plow crops or for grazing herds, from the narrow valleys to the crests of the hills. Belgian agricultural experts helped the people with contour plowing and terracing, and also in the search for new crops suited to the high tropics.

Even so, Ruanda-Urundi remained perilously close to mass starvation. The land simply would not produce enough food for so dense a population, especially when so much was grazed and there still was too much shifting agriculture. Finally, the Belgian administrators hit on coffee. At Usumbura, a Belgian official told me how it was done.

"The African farmers weren't responsive to the idea of growing coffee," he said. "So we told the kings of Ruanda and Urundi the problem. The kings passed the word down the echelons of their tribal organization: 'Plant coffee trees.' And the farmers did as they were told."

It takes a seedling coffee tree six to eight years to bear. Instead of clearing a patch and then moving on to another, the farmers had to stay on the land and take care of it, nursing the seedlings, keeping them sufficiently shaded and cultivated. Then they had to stay on to get successive crops. And coffee began to provide them with money — the first money most of them had ever seen.

In this fashion, coffee as a crop did two things. It cut down on the wasteful practice of shifting agriculture — slash-and-burn farming. And it created the foundation of a cash economy, in lieu of a mere subsistence economy. For coffee-growing, Ruanda-Urundi had two advantages, one natural, the other political. The altitude, much of the land being 5,000 to 7,000 feet above sea level, made for good-flavored beans. And there were the Belgian technicians, to see to it that every last bean went to the central processing station near Usumbura, to be correctly graded and labeled for export. As a result, some of the best coffee reaching the United States has been coming from Ruanda-Urundi.

It is much the same story on the high, well-watered land of Kenya and across Uganda — and also in the upland of Tanganyika. In the former Belgian Congo and Portuguese Angola, and likewise in various states of French West Africa, coffee is a major crop. But this is new. As recently as the 1920's, Africa produced only 2 percent of the world's coffee supply. At the beginning of World War II, it provided 7 percent. In the latter 1950's, Africa's share had risen to 18 percent. By 1961 it reached 26 percent and it may go higher since some of the African areas have preferential access to European markets, giving them a marked advantage over Latin American competitors. The European Common Market will give the African "insiders," at least the French Community countries, a 16 percent tariff preference.

There is one fly in the coffee ointment, however. Coffee can play its rightful part in the underdeveloped countries only if world prices can be kept reasonably stable. The range from 7 cents to 80 cents is far too great. Some major growing countries have been trying for many years to maintain acceptable prices by holding back surplus production and at times by destroying surpluses. The effort has been only partly successful. A new and far-reaching attack on the problem was undertaken in 1962, at an international coffee conference in which all significant growing countries *and major consumer countries* have

been represented. The effort this time is to limit exports realistically, in line with consumption, and to tax coffee exports to get the revenue for technical research and enforcement of the agreement. Consumer countries are included for the first time. This is to insure against any world monopoly to gouge the coffee-drinkers of North America and Europe. To be sure, this seems now a remote danger, for the world carryover stock at present is estimated at 78 million bags, or nearly two years' world consumption. The agreement also should enable the consumer countries, chiefly the United States, to ride herd on the producers, buying selectively so as to make sure producer nations live up to their agreements.

It seems unlikely that there will be a problem of growing enough coffee to meet world demand. But if that ever does become a problem, there are ready solutions. Yields per tree and per acre could be increased by better farming methods. There is more land at 4,000 to 6,000 feet for growing mild coffee, and limitless additional land at lower altitudes throughout the tropics for growing *Robusta* and *Liberica*, which are good enough for the instant coffee that now represents 18 percent of U.S. consumption.

The only really challenging problem is to keep world prices reasonably stable, which means keeping production and consumption in line. And every farmer knows this is the toughest problem in all agriculture.

ESTATES AND SMALLHOLDINGS: AN ECONOMIC COMPARISON*

by
D. H. Penny and M. Zulkifli
University of North Sumatra

Many countries are faced with the problem of choosing the best form of agricultural production organization for economic development. Where there is more than one existing type, e.g., estates and smallholdings, consideration is often given to choosing or at least favoring one over the other(s). It is difficult, however, to make appropriate policy decisions if no suitable basis exists for comparing the economic performance of the different types of production organizations.

This paper provides, with Indonesian data, a direct economic comparison of estates and smallholdings. In this way the respective advantages (and disadvantages) of estates and smallholdings can be more meaningfully discussed. It is shown that the efficiency differential in favor of the estates is probably less than generally believed. The paper concludes with a brief discussion of some policy implications suggested by the analysis.

THE NEED FOR A COMMON BASIS OF COMPARISON

It is commonly believed in Indonesia that estates are more efficient than smallholdings; estates develop and adopt improved practices; estates are orderly, e.g., the trees are in rows; estate managers are well-educated, have cars and live in big houses; estates use large scale modern methods, and estates have profit maximization as their goal and therefore must make more economic use of resources than peasant farmers producing for subsistence with traditional methods.

If the problem of estates versus smallholdings is looked at in this way, one might almost inevitably draw the conclusion that estates are, and will probably continue to be,

*This is an abridgement of the original paper. A copy of this paper with its fuller bibliography and description of research methods used may be obtained on request from D. H. Penny, Warren Hall, Cornell University.

more efficient than smallholdings. To rely on such arguments, plausible though they seem, may still provide a distorted picture of the true relative economic efficiencies of the two types of farm organization — when economic comparisons are made between one type of agricultural enterprise and another, one must be sure that a suitable common basis for making such comparisons has been used.

The fact that proponents of peasant farming often rely largely on noneconomic criteria is further evidence of the need for using a common economic basis for comparison.

In the example that follows, *value added*, i.e., value of production less value of purchased inputs and excluding direct payments to factors of production, has been related to two major resources employed in each enterprise, land and labor. In this way the income produced in each enterprise may be compared with the resources employed, and direct comparisons of the economic performance of two quite different types of production organizations might be made. Only two measures of efficiency have been used, value added per hectare and value added per man employed, since it was difficult to get an adequate comparable measure of capital.

ARE ESTATES MORE EFFICIENT THAN SMALLHOLDINGS — AN INDONESIAN EXAMPLE

Background. The east coast of Sumatra in Indonesia is a major plantation area in Southeast Asia. When the estates were established (the majority from 1900 to 1920), there were few smallholders in the area. A great expansion in the number of smallholdings occurred during and immediately following World War II.

The data. The data on estate operation are for two large foreign estate companies operating about one-quarter of the area under estate rubber in the east coast region. Rubber is the dominant estate crop.

The data on village agriculture are for a total of 45 farms from three villages each situated close to sea level within 20 miles of the provincial capital, Medan. Two of these villages adjoin rubber estates. All but one of the farmers surveyed was a new settler, i.e., took up land in the area within the last 20 years; three-quarters of the total were explantation laborers. All of them were subsistence farmers, i.e., grew food crops in traditional ways for their own consumption selling only the surpluses.

A note on prices. No market in Indonesia is exempt from government intervention. This is particularly true of the market for foreign exchange, though government intervention in the markets for imported production requisites, basic food commodities and labor is also considerable. Thus two independent calculations of the efficiency indicators were made, the first in rupiah (local currency) terms, which reflects the actual situation faced by estate and farm managers and the second, in dollar terms, which shows what might have been earned if sales and purchases could have been made at world market prices. Only the calculation in rupiah terms is presented in detail here.

Value added by estates. In 1960-61, the average production of rubber per tappable hectare was 526 kilograms. For the total area used, i.e., tappable rubber, areas under replanting, and roads, housing lines, factories, etc., it was 392 kilograms per hectare. The gross value of production per hectare was Rp 8,820 at an average rupiah price for all grades of Rp 22.50. Since purchased inputs were 15 percent of the value of production, the value added per hectare was Rp 7,500. The average labor force per hectare was 0.45 persons; this included both permanent and casual *(borongan)* labor, and covers field laborers, factory workers and office personnel on the estate. Value added per worker was Rp 16,700.

Value added in village agriculture. For the villages, average gross value of production per hectare was Rp 10,100 for the same period. Average farm size was 1.87 hectares. Annual value of purchased inputs was 3 percent of total value of production, thus value added per hectare was Rp 9,800. There was an average of 2.06 adult male equivalents per farm, all but 2 1/2 percent of which was family labor; thus value added per worker was Rp 8,900 (based on data from [1] and [3]).

Summarizing:

	Estates	Small-holdings
Value added per hectare	Rp 7,500	Rp 9,800
Value added per man employed	16,700	8,900

The efficiency indicators when calculated in dollar or world market terms are as summarized below.

	Estates	Small-holdings
Value added per hectare	$183	$149
Value added per man employed	407	134

NOTES ON THE CALCULATIONS AND THEIR INTERPRETATION

Since the generally held view was that estates were much more efficient than smallholdings, it was decided to confine the study to a comparison of estates and subsistence farms only.

It is recognized that the data on which this comparison is based are probably not as complete as one would wish. The importance of the question and the paucity of data on the economics of smallholder agriculture in Indonesia justify making the comparison, however.

The differences in per family incomes are less than the data for value added per man employed would indicate, since smallholdings had more "breadwinners" per family of the same size. The wages of estate laborers are, of course, lower than the value added per man employed figures would indicate.

It is not surprising to find that subsistence farms have a relative advantage in value added per hectare, i.e., when compared with value added per man employed, since rubber production is labor extensive compared with rice production.

The efficiency indicators show that estates are somewhat more efficient than subsistence smallholdings. The indicators also suggest that the arguments on behalf of the estate, as indicated earlier are rather overstated.

CONCLUDING NOTES

The economic scales have traditionally been weighted in favor of the estates. Such advantages have included: (1) estates have had the sympathy and understanding of government, particularly during the colonial period; (2) estates have monopsony power and/or preference in the purchase of many commodities, e.g., imported production requisites, and in the purchase of price-controlled consumption goods; (3) estates also have the ability to import cheap labor — indeed if local labor had had to be employed there is some doubt that the plantations would have been vi-

able; (4) estates have access to research information denied to smallholders.

While it is true that estates have been hampered in their post-independence activity by government policy inimical to foreign enterprise and estates generally, all the advantages listed above are still available to them.

It is interesting to speculate how estates would compare with smallholdings if the latter were operated by men who were somewhat less subsistence oriented, had better access to the markets for fertilizer, etc., and were served by research and extension services. It seems clear from other work done that the interest of small farmers in increasing productivity is much greater than is generally realized [2, 3]. It is probable, however, that if given the chance, estates could increase production more rapidly than smallholdings since the institutional changes necessary to provide adequate agricultural services for smallholders are much greater than for estates.

Estates are much more effective than smallholdings, as presently operated, as a source of foreign exchange and taxes and thus play an important role in the generation of funds for economic development.

On the other hand, the fact that smallholdings can produce approximately the same real value per hectare of food crops might be regarded as all-important in a country such as Indonesia where there is a food deficit and arable land is scarce.

The preceding discussion has been based on a general comparison of large modern rubber estates and typical subsistence farms. No consideration has been given to the question of the relative production efficiencies of rubber estates and rubber smallholdings, or of rubber estates and modern smallholdings producing commercial crops. Some crops grown by estates may not feasibly be grown by smallholders and vice versa. It was for this reason that the performance of the most common type of estate was compared with the most common type of smallholding.

In conclusion, the use of simple indicators provides a rather different picture of the relative efficiencies of estates and smallholdings than the generally accepted one. The measures used should be such that direct and relevant comparisons might be made.

[1]ZULKIFLI, M., "The Agricultural Economic Situation in Three Villages in North Sumatra," Medan, Faculty of Agriculture, 1962 (Indonesian).

[2]PENNY, D. H., "The Role of the Farmer in the Economic Development Process in Indonesia," Ekonomi, December 1960 (Indonesian).

[3]PENNY, D. H. (ed.), "The Farm Management Class" Smallholder Agriculture in North Sumatra, Medan, Faculty of Agriculture, December 1962 (mimeo, introduction in English, text in Indonesian).

RECOVERY OF THE SUGAR INDUSTRY IN INDONESIA

D. W. Fryer

Mr. Fryer is Senior Lecturer in Economic Geography at the University of Melbourne, Australia. He spent several months in the field in Indonesia in 1956 under the auspices of the University's Department of Indonesian Studies.

VICISSITUDE and catastrophe have been of fairly frequent occurrence in the world sugar industry, whose history has seen many remarkable fluctuations of fortune. Indonesia, successor to the Netherlands Indies, has been a sugar producer of the first importance for a considerable time, a low cost producer whose efficiency made it a strong competitor in the contracting "free" market of the interwar period. But not even its efficiency could protect it from the Great Depression, the planted area of estate cane falling catastrophically from 200,000 hectares in 1931 to 27,600 in 1935. By 1939 the planted area had climbed again to 94,900 hectares; then in the Second World War, Indonesia, the second largest cane sugar exporter in the world, was eliminated, together with a large part of the European beet industry, and the way was open for the enormous expansion of cane sugar production in the western hemisphere, an expansion which continued in most producing countries of that part of the world until 1953. In this post-war phase of expansion Indonesia was denied a part, for what remained of the sugar industry after the Japanese occupation was largely destroyed in the struggle for independence in 1948 to 1949.

Though the time is long distant when sugar provided almost a quarter of the export income, as it did before 1930, the destruction of the sugar industry would have been a heavy blow to the new Republic had it not been for the boom in rubber prices with the outbreak of the Korean War. In the period between the post Korean drop in prices and the great resurgence of American business activity in the latter half of 1954, a period during which rubber never rose above 22–24 cents a pound, the real nature of Indonesia's economic position became obvious. For a country with problems of development as great as those anywhere in Asia, and faced with chronic balance of payments difficulties, the resuscitation of the sugar industry, which had exported well over a million tons of sugar annually before the war and contributed almost 7 per cent of the export income, was an obvious and desirable course of action. Moreover, though cane is grown in almost every part of Indonesia, the sugar industry is confined to Java, an island which, while absorbing the greater part of the national income, earns only about one quarter of the foreign exchange; Java needs to expand its foreign earnings to help refute the charge which is frequently made in the other islands that it is a parasite which is appropriating the national resources for its own exclusive benefit. The Indonesian Government, however, has taken little positive action itself to assist the recovery of the sugar industry.

The difficulties confronting the reestablishment of the industry after 1949

"Recovery of the Sugar Industry in Indonesia" by D. W. Fryer. Reprinted from Economic Geography, *Vol. 33 (April 1957), pp. 171-181, with permission of the editor.*

TABLE I

AREA AND PRODUCTION OF ESTATE SUGAR IN JAVA

Year	No. of estates	Harvested area (1000 ha.)	Sugar production (1000 metric tons crystal)		Sugar yield per ha. (quintals crystal)
			From estate cane	From cane purchased from smallholders	
1930	179	193.7	2915.7		152
1938	97	84.8	1400.3		162
1950	...	30.3	277.1	....	91
1951	54	44.2	414.1	8.5	97
1952	54	46.6	434.1	22.3	93
1953	54	44.9	552.6	62.8	123
1954	55	48.9	.589.7	115.7	120
1955	55	.....	851 (est)		...

Source: Statistik Perkebunan; Statistik Pertanian Rakjat; N.I.V.A.S.

were very great. The general uncertainty over the future of the foreign enterprise in Indonesia was a considerable deterrent to European companies faced with the necessity of rebuilding burnt-out mills; the situation regarding leases and rents of sugar land was obscure; the delivery of new equipment was tardy; and in many parts of Java bandit gangs continued to make depredations on company property and on growing cane. In addition to these internal difficulties the rapidity with which world sugar production had expanded was threatening to glut the market; by 1953 the familiar pre-war situation of mounting surpluses and the prospect of a substantial fall in price led to attempts at international control of sugar marketing and the International Sugar Agreement. The Agreement attempted (so far without much success) to stabilize prices, allotting "free market" quotas to its producing signatories. The sugar industry of the Netherlands Indies was always based on export markets and the likelihood of Indonesia regaining a substantial share of former markets did not therefore appear very strong; though refusing to be a party to the Agreement Indonesia has nevertheless on balance benefited by it, and has provided a further example

of the tendency for restrictive agreements to benefit outsiders. However, as Java carried an enormous burden in the pre-war restriction schemes of the 30's—a policy in which few Indonesians were consulted—Indonesia can fairly claim a measure of economic justice. In the face of declining or restricted production of most other cane producers Indonesian output has increased rapidly. By 1955 the pre-war sugar output had not been regained, but its realization did not appear far distant, as can be seen from Tables I and II. The present level of sugar production is still less than one-third of the 2.9 million tons produced in 1930, the high water mark of the industry, and room for further expansion

TABLE II

SMALLHOLDER CANE IN JAVA

Year	Harvested area (1000 ha.)	Sugar production (all kinds) (1000 metric tons)	Sugar yield per ha. (quintals crystal)
1931	8.7	53.8	62
1938	12.1	91.2	76
1950	8.5	.....	..
1951	16.5	117.2	71
1952	21.6	182.2	68
1953	22.3	202.8	75
1954	27.7	198.4	72

Source: Statistik Perkebunan; Statistik Pertanian Rakjat; N.I.V.A.S.

is therefore considerable, though it would not appear that an output of this magnitude is at all probable in the foreseeable future.

STRUCTURE AND LOCATION OF THE SUGAR INDUSTRY

There are a number of very distinctive features in the Indonesian sugar industry which contrast markedly with those of other cane producers and also with other large scale agricultural activities in Indonesia itself. The most important section of the industry by far is that of the so-called "estates" (Perusahaan Perkebunan) though in fact the estates own no land. Indigenous farmers' and small landholders' cane (Tebu Rakjat) has always made a small contribution and in recent years small holder cane growing has expanded considerably; nevertheless it accounted only for one-fifth of centrifugal sugar production in 1954. The estate industry is entirely non-indigenous in ownership and management, but while other estate industries such as rubber, copra, palm oil, tea, etc., include considerable British and occasionally American and other foreign capital investment as well as Dutch, the foreign sugar companies are virtually entirely Dutch owned. The balance of the estate industry which is not Dutch controlled is solidly in the hands of the Chinese. The Chinese have been engaged in the production of sugar in Java from the earliest years of the Dutch East Company, and can be regarded as the founders of the industry. The Chinese have never been entirely displaced by the European companies, and at present with the destruction of many Dutch owned mills the Chinese share of the industry is somewhat greater than in 1939. Largest of the Chinese sugar interests is the Kian Gwan Company which operates ten mills on the north Java plain, and is part of the Oeei Tiong Ham concern which has wide ramifications throughout Southeast Asia in trade, shipping, and banking.

The location of the industry is also in striking contrast to that of other estate industries in Indonesia. Of the 1.8 million hectares of all estate land in Indonesia only about one-third is located in Java, and of this almost one-half is located in the Residencies[1] of Djakarta, Bogor, and Priangan in the Province of West Java (Fig. 1). But apart from 5000 hectares in Tjirebon Residency in West Java the 49,000 hectares of estate sugar in 1954 were entirely confined to the Provinces of Central and East Java. Climate largely dictates this pattern of sugar cultivation in Java; sugar requires a definite dry season and thus does not extend into West Java, where, though the months from April to October receive distinctly less rainfall than the rest of the year, a dry season can scarcely be said to exist; the Tjimanuk is thus the effective western limit of cane cultivation, though at present very little cane is grown west of Tjirebon city itself. Even in central Java the dry season is not really strong; it is strongest in the north coast plain. Only in East Java is the dry season well marked, its severity generally increasing eastwards, being of as much as six months' duration on the coast of Besuki north of the Idjen. East Java, including the Residencies of Madiun, Kediri, Malang, Surabaja, and Besuki, is thus the most important by far of the three Provinces for sugar production and in 1954 accounted for 65 per cent of the estate output compared with 27 per cent

[1] The old Residencies have no real administrative function, though statistics on a Residency basis are still collected. The units of Local Government are the Kebupaten (Regencies) and the Propinsi (Provinces). The whole structure of Local Government is still confused and obscure; some parts of Java are administered as Special Territories (Daerah Istemewa), e.g., Jogjakarta.

for Central Java, the balance coming from Tjirebon. These proportions do not differ greatly from those of 1930 or of 1938, so that the fluctuating fortunes of the sugar industry have not affected the three Provinces very differently.

Nevertheless, there have been considerable changes in the location of the industry which are concealed in the above statement; the present distribution of commercial cane cultivation is determined by the survival or reconstruction of mills. In those parts of Java where the fighting in the war of independence was severe the gutted shells of former mills are a common sight. Other dilapidated and overgrown ruins can be seen throughout central and east Java, their former nature being indicated by the remains of *djalan lori* (Decauville track) used for cane transport; these represent mills abandoned in the great depression of the 30's. Outstanding is the daerah of Jogjakarta, the seat of the Republican Government during the revolution. In the fighting every mill in the Jogja area was destroyed. In 1931 there were 17 in operation; by 1938 their number was reduced to ten of

which seven were actually in operation. The evidence of this long decline and fall is to be clearly seen in both the countryside and in the city of Jogjakarta itself, where the wrecked equipment of the former mills now constitutes the raw material of state-owned Pedjebit ironworks, one of the largest in the country. This works was originally constructed to service the sugar mills in the Jogja area; now the heavy lathes that were installed to deal with the massive rollers of the mills are used to produce metal household utensils, vises, presses, rubber mangles, and other metal equipment for migrants to Sumatra. The renewal of commercial cane cultivation on a large scale in the Jogja is thus dependent on the completion of a new mill now being built for the Sultan of Jogjakarta with equipment and technicians from Eastern Germany. In Madiun and Surabaja there was also considerable physical destruction, but in these areas recovery has been fairly rapid. Another area from which the industry has disappeared is south central Java; i.e., Banjumas and Kedu, but here it never recovered from the depression

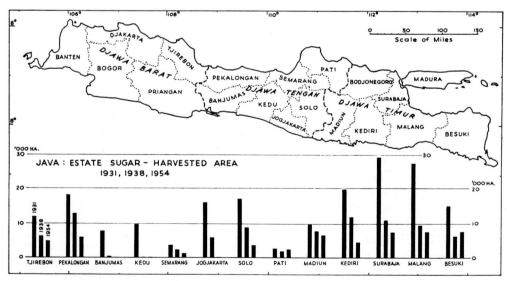

Fig. 1.

and the pre-war production was small; moreover the lack of a well-defined dry season made the area climatically marginal. Where there was comparatively little fighting in 1948–49 and where civil disturbance has since been slight the industry has made the greatest recovery; thus in Malang and Besuki estate production in 1954 exceeded that of Surabaja Residency which before the war was always the leading producer. In only two Residencies is estate production now above the level of 1938. These are Pati (formerly Japara-Rembang), now close to the 1931 peak, where there has been a considerable extension of cane growing in the plains south of the Murjo volcano, in which the enterprising Kian Gwan Company has taken a major part; and Besuki, where isolation brought freedom from disturbance and an opportunity to benefit by the elimination of other producing areas.

The organization of the estate industry is not significantly different from that of the days of the Dutch administration, the most important changes being in sugar disposal. The most distinctive feature is that the Companies, or "Estates," own no land, a consequence of the Agrarian Law of 1870 and the Land Rent Ordinance, which while prohibiting the sale of land to non-indigenes made provision for the leasing of land to Europeans and others under certain safeguards. In the lightly populated Outer Islands unoccupied land was made available to estate companies by the Government on long leases (erfpacht) and concessions, but in densely populated Java this was not possible. Sugar companies thus make contracts for the hire of village lands, which may be of short or long duration. Short contracts may run for up to 3½ years and long contracts for up to 21½ years; short contracts cannot be made more than 15 months ahead of the proposed commencement of cultivation and long contracts not more than 30 months ahead. The purpose of this regulation is to discourage villagers from using the rentals from estates as a form of credit, a difficulty with which the Netherlands Indies Government struggled without success. In the past estates undoubtedly obtained land at low rentals by exploiting the *tani's* chronic shortage of cash—the further ahead the lease was negotiated, the lower the rent.[2] Otherwise there is complete freedom for both parties in negotiating rents for short term contracts but minimum rents are laid down by the Government for long contracts, and these are subject to periodic review—rent regulations have been made annually in recent years.

A further provision of the former Dutch administration which has been preserved arises from the fact that all estate cane is grown on sawah (padi) land, but rice is Java's principal crop, of which it has never really had enough; accordingly not more than one-third of the total village sawah land may be planted to sugar at any one time. As cane is in the ground for a period of a year to 18 months it thus forms part of a three-year rotation with rice, and other crops such as sweet potatoes, cassava, ground nuts, soy beans, etc., collectively known as *polowidjo*. By this means competition for land between sugar and food crops is minimized. The cycle of cultivation involving the rotation of crops and the virtual absence of ratooning makes Indonesia unique among cane producers.

During any wet season two-thirds of the sawah land is under rice. Unlike the "colono" system of the Caribbean, or the tenant cultivation in the Philip-

---

[2] For a discussion of this point *vide* J. H. Boeke, *Structure of the Netherlands Indies Economy*, 1942, p. 80, also K. J. Pelzer, *Pioneer Settlement in the Asiatic Tropics*, 1945, p. 172.

TABLE III

THE CYCLE OF CULTIVATION IN THE JAVANESE SUGAR INDUSTRY

(Village Sawah Land)

	First	*Second*	*Third*
Dry Season—1956..............	Planting of cane (May–July)	Harvest of old cane (June–November)	Polowidjo
Wet Season—1956/57............	Cane	Rice	Rice
Dry Season—1957..............	Harvest of old cane (June–November)	Polowidjo	Planting of cane (May–July)
Wet Season—1957/58............	Rice	Rice	Cane
Dry Season—1958..............	Polowidjo	Planting of cane (May–July)	Harvest of old cane (May–July)
Wet Season—1958/59............	Rice	Cane	Rice
Dry Season—1959..............	As for 1956		

pine industry, the estates produce sugar themselves on the rented land, and employment is available for individual owners, or villagers where the land is communally held, as cultivation hands. In effect the "tenant" thus becomes the landlord. The system is undoubtedly open to abuse, but it is extremely efficient and yields of sugar per hectare are very high. Before the war Java had the highest yield of sugar per unit area of any cane producer, and even at present it is exceeded only by Hawaii and Peru. The length of time cane is in the ground depends upon the variety planted and upon weather conditions;

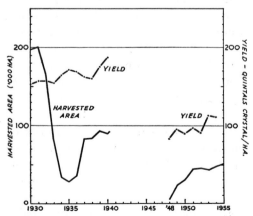

FIG. 2. Harvested area and yield of estate sugar in Java, 1930–1955.

12–14 months is a common duration but high yielding varieties like the famous P.O.J. 2878 may be in the ground for 16 months or longer. A selection of varieties maturing at different periods enables a longer crushing season and lowers costs, and estates therefore plant up to three or four varieties where possible; resistance to pests and infection is also minimized.

Smallholders' cane can be divided into cane grown under contract for processing at a company mill and cane processed in simple domestic equipment. Non-centrifugal sugar of this type, or *gula Java*, is confined to local consumption and competes with a number of other sources of sugar such as the Palmyra palm (Borassus flabellifer). Owing to the different periods of time that cane and padi occupy the ground and their different water requirements smallholders have usually found the growing of cane on sawahs difficult. Where smallholders grow cane on sawah land it is planted in the dry season for cutting the following year, followed, if the harvest is early enough, by polowidjo, and in the following wet season by padi. In the past, therefore, most smallholder cane was produced by dry fields (tegalan), leaving the sawahs for food crops. But in some areas the capacity of reconstructed mills exceeds estate production and smallholder cane is now eagerly sought after, though its sugar content is considerably below that of estate cane. Political changes, too, have favored the expansion of smallholder production. Thus since 1950 there has been a considerable expansion of smallholder cane on sawahs; in 1954 almost 16,400 ha. of sawah land was planted to smallholder cane, almost double the pre-war area, while the 11,500 ha. of dry field also exceeded that of 1939. The total area of sugar cane grown by Indonesian farmers is almost certainly much larger than these figures indicate, but though grown by every Javanese village for chewing, smallholder cane for crushing at a modern mill is quite restricted in distribution. In 1954 the Residencies of Madiun, Kediri, and Malang accounted for 62 per cent of the smallholder sawah cane (cf. 38 per cent of estate cane), while Kediri alone possessed 67 per cent of the dry field cane.

The conflict of land use, though reduced by the lease system, is nevertheless a real one. Despite the upward trend in rice production since 1950 to a level now well above that of 1939, there is a chronic rice shortage in many parts of the country and Government refusal to make available foreign exchange for rice imports while permitting importation of many semi-luxuries is a source of continued irritation to many Indonesians.[3] For the first time since 1950 rice output in 1955 showed a decrease on the preceding year of some 7 per cent due to unfavorable weather. The 50,000 hectares of estate cane represent only about 1.3 per cent of the total sawah area of Java and Madura, but the productivity of these sawahs is considerably above

the national average, and it is in the local rather than the national setting that the issue should be judged. As Robequain has pointed out, sugar cultivation has affected all the best sawahs in that part of Java suitable for cane growing.[4] An official of a large company interviewed expressed the view that the operations of the companies involved no conflict of land with food crops, but that this was true of smallholders whose productivity was much lower and who employed a two- as opposed to a three-year rotation. It was added, moreover, that because of the heavy use of fertilizers on cane grown by the companies and their exacting standards of cultivation, the productivity of sawahs leased for sugar was greater than if rice alone were grown. The considerable growth of smallholder production suggests that cane growing is a profitable operation at present, but whether the tani who leases his land to a company would be better off if he could afford to forego the rent payment and cultivate the land himself (which was frequently the case before the war) the writer found difficult to decide; not unexpectedly it is denied by the companies, on arguments similar to the above.

Inseparable from the conflict of land use is the conflict for water; both rice and cane need irrigation water, for though not essential for cane it is an important factor in the high yields obtained by the estate industry. In the early stages of growth, water is often poured over the plants by hand; later it is distributed over the field by a system of rectilinear ditches (got mudjur and got malang) which are made during the preparation for planting. Estates pay for irrigation water while farmers do not, its cost being included in the land

---

[3] Foreign exchange for the import of 500,000 tons of rice is to be made available in 1956.

[4] C. Robequain: Le Monde Malais, 1946, p. 368, translated E. D. Laborde, as Malaya Indonesia and the Philippines, 195.

tax, and, in the past, estates have attempted to claim a priority when water has been short. However, the *waduk* or reservoirs which were constructed before the war to serve the sugar areas have a capacity much in excess of the demands of the industry at present, and in recent years Java, like much of Asia, has experienced an excess rather than a deficiency of rain. However, population pressure and a run of drier years could make the problem a serious one. Water is divided between the various sawah crops in some predetermined proportions, usually in the ratio of 4 : 2 : 1 for padi, cane, and polowidjo respectively, though varying to 2 : 1 : 1 according to local conditions and practice.

PRODUCTIVITY AND EFFICIENCY

The productivity and efficiency of the Java sugar industry has for long been very high, a necessity since the island, unlike other important cane producers, has never had a large protected or reserved market, and has had to compete on the "free" market for the disposal of the greater part of its output. Costs of production before the war were among the lowest in the world; unfortunately for Java, costs of production are of relatively little significance in the chaos of economic contradictions and anomalies that constitutes the world sugar industry. Output per man, the real test of economic efficiency, is at present below that of before the war. Indonesian competition would become acute if the opportunities for cost reduction which undoubtedly exist were realized. However, many of these opportunities depend on changes in the political and social environment over which the industry has no control.

In 1938 Java had the highest yield of sugar per unit area of cane harvested in the world; the average of over 160 quintals per hectare (6.4 tons per acre, approximately) represented a tenfold increase in productivity over that of a century earlier, when the introduction of the Culture System marked the beginning of the modern industry. Yields of estate cane are at present much below those of before the war; up to 1953 yields did not rise above 100 quintals per hectare harvested, i.e., about the same as in the first decade of this century; but since 1953 there has been a marked improvement (Fig. 2). In the meantime Hawaii, with only slightly inferior yields to pre-war Java, has stepped up productivity per acre by over 40 per cent. It is extremely doubtful if Indonesia can match this performance unless there is some considerable change in the social and political climate, which seems improbable in the immediate future.

Nevertheless, Indonesia's present yield is considerably higher than most other cane producers; many of these, too, have only recently regained pre-war yields (Philippines, Formosa, Brazil), while others show no appreciable advance or even a decline on pre-war productivity (Puerto Rico, South Africa, Fiji, U.S.A.). The high yields in Indonesia are due to the use of irrigation, heavy application of fertilizers, and the use of high-yielding varieties. The work of the Dutch plant breeders at the famous Pasuruan research station in producing new varieties with a higher sucrose content and resistance to disease was of profound importance, not only to Java but to the cane sugar industry everywhere in the world. Smallholder cane for crushing averaged only 74–76 quintals of crystal sugar production per hectare harvested before the war, but there has been no subsequent decline and present yields are well up to the former level.

The sugar estates have always been the largest consumers of fertilizers in the Netherlands Indies and Indonesia, the only other important consumers being the tobacco estates, which in Java likewise lease land from villages. Upwards of 100,000 tons were used annually before the war, principally the nitrogenous fertilizers; sulphate of ammonia and sodium nitrate. Three applications of ammonium sulphate around each plant at successive stages of growth, totalling 4–5 quintals per hectare, is the usual practice. But costs of imported fertilizers are heavy (virtually none are produced in Indonesia itself) and the pre-war fertilizer consumption has not been regained. Other inorganic fertilizers are little used; cane unlike rice shows limited response to phosphatic fertilizers. When used, double super-phosphate is applied at the time of planting. Smallholders make negligible use of inorganic fertilizers, an important factor in their lower productivity. Buffalo manure is the principal fertilizer used, but a large application is necessary for a high return and buffalo, likè most other livestock, are still below pre-war numbers. Green manuring is also practiced by smallholders, legumes such as chickpea (Cajanus cajan) being sown on the ridges between the young cane plants, and turned in when the cane is earthed up.

The introduction of progressively higher-yielding varieties of sugar cane was of great importance in maintaining the industry in a strong competitive position in the days of the Dutch administration. Thus the replacement of the widely grown variety Tjirebon Hitam (Black Cheribon) by the Pasuruan bred P.O.J. 100 raised yields from a little more than 50 to nearly 80 quintals per ha. between 1880 and 1890; the introduction of B 247 lifted sugar yields to over 100 quintals by 1910; and E.K. 28 and B.I. 52, to almost 125 quintals per ha. harvested by 1925. Resistance to disease, particularly attack from the

Fig. 3.   Cane fields and irrigation channel. Kediri, East Java.

parasitic plant *serai*, was a characteristic of the new cane P.O.J. 2878. Shortly after its appearance in 1927 this famous variety revolutionized the Javanese industry, and by 1929 occupied over 90 per cent of the estate sugar area. But in turn it tended to become superseded by still newer varieties and by 1939 its proportion of the total estate plantings had fallen to 70 per cent. In addition to the variety 2878, estates at the present plant the newer P.O.J. varieties 2967, 3016, and 3067 and H.V.A. 124. But like many other of the specialized scientific services in Indonesia, the Pasuruan station has virtually ceased to function since 1950, and Java is out of the running in the constant search to reduce costs through the activities of the plant breeder.[5] It is vitally necessary if the Indonesian sugar industry is to regain its former competitive position that research services with an adequate budget and sufficient trained personnel be provided for the industry. The same could be said, however, for all the other plantation industries of Indonesia.

The lower productivity per hectare harvested in the estate industry at present can be partly explained by

[5] For some unexplained reason there is also a tendency in many parts of the world for the yields of a variety to decline with the passage of time; a high turnover of varieties is thus often desirable.

unfavorable seasons, but in the main is undoubtedly due to the changed social and political environment. This problem is common to other estate industries of the country, all of which have lower output and productivity than before the war. Estate labor is highly unionized, in itself a desirable development, but Communist influence is strong and labor too often works hours which are insufficient to keep processing machinery operating at full efficiency. Output per man is difficult to estimate with a large number of seasonal workers, but the output per man in Javan sugar mills is probably no more than one-tenth that of Australian mills in Queensland. While the unions continue to regard themselves as in the vanguard of the fight against the vestiges of "colonialism," i.e., the foreign companies, it is unlikely that efficiency can be greatly increased.

Sugar Disposal

Like most cane producers, the bulk of the pre-war production of Javan sugar was destined for the export market; domestic consumption was only a little over 200,000 tons and per capita consumption was one of the lowest in the world, only 4.5 kg. per annum. Unlike that of most other producers Javan sugar was exported in the refined as well as the raw state, although at present this practice is becoming increasingly common. Asian countries have always been the best markets for Javan sugar, though small amounts reach Europe from time to time. At present the industry is still mainly dependent on the domestic market, though exports have increased rapidly. Up to 1953 exports were small. Indonesia refused a quota of 150,000 tons offered by the International Sugar Council, and requested a quota of 450,000 tons on the basis of its pre-war export of over one million tons. This was rejected by the Council and Indonesia has, therefore, failed to join the International Sugar Agreement which is to operate until 1959. By rationing home consumption in conjunction with the growth of output, substantial quantities of sugar were made available for export while other producers have accepted quota reductions. In 1953 exports rose from less than 2000 tons to over 100,000 tons; in 1954 there was a further increase to over 220,000 tons, and for 1955 exports are estimated at over 400,000 tons. Brazil, another non-signatory, has also managed to increase its exports substantially. Japan has been the largest buyer of Indonesian sugar and has negotiated for the purchase of 200,000 tons of Java raws for 1956. Other important buyers have been Burma, India, and Thailand. A significant development has been the purchases of Eastern Bloc countries, particularly China, which was the largest buyer after Japan in 1955. A not unlikely development is the purchase of Indonesian sugar by the U.S.S.R., which has recently been a substantial buyer on the world market. Increased trade with the Communist world seems inevitable, however, and the present Prime Minister, Ali Sastroamidjojo, has already stated its desirability. Since 1954 the export trade to Asia, as well as the domestic trade, has been reserved to Indonesian nationals, which has meant in practice that the Chinese dominance of the sugar trade has increased substantially.

Indonesian domestic consumption while absorbing rather more than half of the current output is still very low, and the pre-war per capita consumption has only very recently been regained. Allocations to the home and export market are made by the sugar producers' syndicate N.I.V.A.S. (Netherlands Indies Sugar Producers Syndicate) which acts as the agent of the Government.

There is undoubtedly scope for a very substantial increase in the domestic consumption. This largely arises from the very high internal price of sugar in Indonesia, 3.3 Rp per kg. (about 15 cents per lb.), which is very substantially above the world price; a reduction in the various taxes on sugar could bring about a substantial increase in local demand.

PROSPECTS

The sugar industry in Indonesia has recovered at a rate that hardly appeared possible in 1950, and at the present Indonesia does not find it difficult to dispose of the whole of its expanding output. But Indonesia cannot hope to enjoy immunity from the world problem of overproduction forever. Opportunities for a reduction of costs exist, though it may not be possible to realize them; unfortunately the balance of cost advantage is seldom a telling factor in the world sugar trade. With the increasing tempo of economic development in Asia and an increase in Asian incomes there should, however, continue to be a strong demand for Javan sugar, and the geographic advantages of the island are considerable. It is highly probable, however, that if Indonesia became burdened with a large sugar surplus the interest of Communist buyers would be sharply heightened. In such a situation Indonesia could act no differently than other Asian countries already faced with this problem.

Specialized Farming

Outside the tropics, where we have already seen certain distinctive examples of specialized agriculture, a number of crops are characteristically grown on farms which produce only one crop or a limited number of related crops. The products differ widely, the farms range greatly in size, and many regions contain examples of this type of agriculture. For convenience, a number of these crops which form the basis for a high degree of specialization are included together in this section. One common characteristic of the various examples of this type of agriculture is that the products usually are of major importance in international trade.

In many respects, there are wide variations in the characteristics of the systems under which these crops are grown. Wheat and other cereals are typically extensive crops occupying large acreages near the dry margins of cultivable land. Irregular rainfall, government controls, available transport facilities, and the demands of a worldwide market are but a few of the factors influencing grain farming. Jackson's article discusses the attempts of the Soviet Union to expand its area of wheat production and suggests various problems involved in such expansion. Bitting and Rogers describe the several types of wheat and areas of production important in the United States.

Tobacco, unlike wheat, is grown intensively. This is partly a response to government controls, but it also reflects the high labor requirements of the crop. It is a major item in international trade and is thus affected both by national and world market conditions. The McMurtry article discusses current problems of tobacco production in the United States and illustrates the complexities involved in formulating a production program. The final two articles in this section deal with fiber crops. Large examines the impact of government controls on cotton production and indicates the importance of labor, water, and other variables to the geography of this crop. Puterbaugh discusses the increased competition from synthetic fibers — still another variable affecting cotton production in the United States.

THE RUSSIAN NON-CHERNOZEM WHEAT BASE[1]

W. A. DOUGLAS JACKSON
University of Washington

THE publicity surrounding recent attempts to expand crop production in the Soviet Union, such as the ploughing of virgin and idle lands in the eastern regions of the country, the sowing of corn for livestock in seemingly almost all parts of the cultivated area, and the development of irrigation in the moisture-deficient regions of the south, should not be permitted to obscure the efforts which the Soviet regime has made over the past quarter of a century to create a commercial wheat base in the non-chernozem or podsolic soil zone of European Russia.

Until the early 1930's when the drive to expand the cultivation of wheat in that part of the union began, the non-chernozem zone had never been an important producer of wheat. Prior to World War I, in an area where the total land in crops amounted to somewhat less than 50 million acres, that sown to wheat represented less than a million acres. Indeed, in peasant agriculture, rye, oats, and barley were the standard grains, with potatoes and flax contributing to the general pattern of land utilization. Throughout the decade following the Bolshevik Revolution, some years showed an increase in wheat acreage above that of the pre-revolutionary period, but there was no strong upward trend. Certainly, in 1928, on the eve of collectivization, the non-chernozem zone with its large

and expanding cities relied almost entirely on imports from the wheat-producing steppe regions to the south and southeast.[2]

The Stalinist goal, the building of socialism in one country through the erection of a mighty industrial fortress, required that bread be made available to the workers attracted to the cities that would mushroom in the future. Consequently, the decision was shortly thereafter made that a commercial wheat base be established in the non-chernozem zone. This was designed to increase the supply of white bread (in preference to rye or black bread) to the cities of the Central Industrial Region, and would lessen dependence on, and length of haul from, other regions of the country.[3]

Such a drive would inevitably arouse peasant opposition; in part because it would run counter to traditional peasant attitudes and experience, but also because, as an outcome of collectivization, it would constitute along with other controls immediate state direction

[1] Research on this topic was undertaken in the summer of 1957 supported by a grant for Slavic and East European Studies from the Social Science Research Council. The manuscript was completed while the author was on leave during the autumn quarter, 1958, as a Research Fellow at the Harvard Russian Research Center, the facilities of which are gratefully acknowledged.

[2] By 1928, the chief source of wheat for the non-chernozem zone was the South, including the Ukraine, North Caucasus and Crimea. The Volga Basin was of secondary importance, as were the Asiatic regions. The latter, however, had become more important during the mid-1920's. The central chernozem zone supplied only small quantities. See: Vladimir P. Timoshenko, *Agricultural Russia and the Wheat Problem* (Stanford: Stanford University Press, 1932), pp. 468–9.

[3] Timoshenko points out that during the mid-1920's the sources of supply for the cities, particularly of the non-chernozem, were very unstable. In 1928–29, for example, the South had practically no surpluses of wheat (in part due to climatic conditions) and the Asiatic regions provided about 60 percent of the total. Thus, the length of haul of grain stuffs, and of wheat in particular, by the end of the decade had increased substantially. *Ibid.*, p. 429.

"The Russian Non-Chernozem Wheat Base" by W. A. Douglas Jackson. Reprinted from ANNALS — *Association of American Geographers*, Vol. 49 (*June* 1959), *pp.* 97–109, *with permission of the Association of American Geographers.*

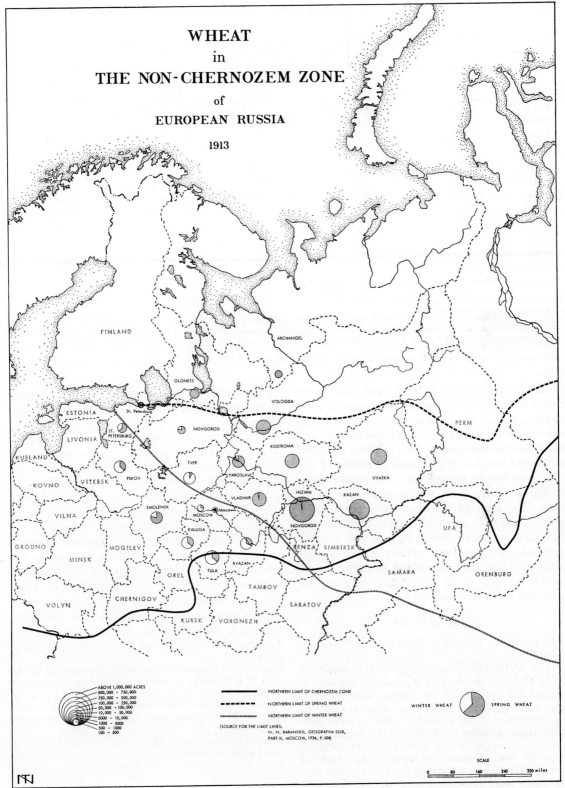

WHEAT
in
THE NON-CHERNOZEM ZONE
of
EUROPEAN RUSSIA
1913

FINLAND

ARCHANGEL

OLONETS

VOLOGDA

St. Petersburg

ESTONIA

ST.
PETERSBURG

NOVGOROD

LIVONIA

KOSTROMA

KURLAND

TVER

KOVNO

VITEBSK

PSKOV

YAROSLAVL

VYATKA

VILNA

SMOLENSK

VLADIMIR

NIZHNI

KAZAN

MOSCOW   Moscow

GRODNO

MOGILEV

KALUGA

NOVGOROD

UFA

MINSK

PENZA   SIMBIRSK

RYAZAN

OREL

TULA

SAMARA

ORENBURG

CHERNIGOV

TAMBOV

VOLYN

KURSK   VORONEZH

SARATOV

PERM

ABOVE 1,000,000 ACRES
500,000 - 750,000
250,000 - 500,000
100,000 - 250,000
50,000 - 100,000
10,000 - 50,000
5000 - 10,000
1000 - 5000
500 - 1000
100 - 500

NORTHERN LIMIT OF CHERNOZEM ZONE

N ORTHERN LIMIT OF SPRING WHEAT

NORTHERN LIMIT OF WINTER WHEAT

(SOURCE FOR THE LIMIT LINES:
        N. N. BARANSKII, GEOGRAFIIA SSSR,
        PART II, MOSCOW, 1934, P.104)

WINTER WHEAT   SPRING WHEAT

SCALE

0   80   160   240   320 miles

FIGURE 1.   1913

215

TABLE 1.—TOTAL CROP, GRAIN, AND WHEAT ACREAGES IN THE NON-CHERNOZEM ZONE FOR SELECTED YEARS
(in millions of acres)

Year	Total crop sown	Grain	Wheat	Wheat as a percent of all grain sown	Grain as a percent of total crop sown
1913[1]	32.6 (50.2)	25.6 (43.5)	.7 (1.0)	2.8 (2.1)	78.3 (86.2)
1926[2]	55.8	44.7	1.0	2.3	80.4
1928	56.8	44.5	.9	2.0	76.9
1930[3]	61.3	45.7	1.1	2.3	74.5
1932	64.0	44.7	1.6	3.4	69.4
1934	67.4	46.5	4.4	9.4	71.7
1937[4]	66.0	47.0	7.2	15.3	71.0
1938	66.0	45.0	7.4	16.5	68.4
1940[5]	65.2	44.7	6.4	14.3	68.5
1950[6]	60.8	41.8	4.8	11.4	68.7
1952	62.3	43.2	6.8	15.5	67.4
1954	63.0	43.5	9.2	21.2	69.0
1956	64.7	38.0	6.7	17.5	59.0

[1] *Sel'skoe Khoziaistvo Rossii v XX Veke.* Sbornik statistiko-ekonomicheskikh svendenii za 1901–1922 gg. (Moscow, 1923), pp. 78–89. The second set of data are from *Narodnoe Khoziaistvo RSFSR.* Statisticheskii sbornik (Moscow, 1957), pp. 165–70. The first set of data are for districts which existed as of 1913 and thus are not comparable with the latter set which are based on districts as constituted in 1956.
[2] *Statisticheskii Spravochnik SSSR za 1928* (Moscow, 1929), pp. 160, 178–79, 186–87.
[3] *Sotsialisticheskoe Stroitel'stvo SSSR:* Statisticheskii ezhegodnik (Moscow, 1935), pp. 334–37, 342–45.
[4] *Posevnye Ploshchadi SSSR 1938 g.* Statisticheskii spravochnik (Moscow and Leningrad, 1939), pp. 41, 43, 53, 74.
[5] *Narodnoe Khoziaistvo RSFSR,* pp. 165–70.
[6] *Posevnye Ploshchadi SSSR.* Statisticheskii sbornik (2 vols., Moscow, 1957), Vol. 1, pp. 174–82, 200–08, 274–82, 338–46.

of land utilization. Wheat had not been grown extensively in the non-chernozem zone in the past simply because the peasants had not found it profitable under prevailing soil and climatic conditions. Much better adapted to the wet, acid soils and cool summers of the zone was hardy winter rye, the staple grain of the northern and northeastern European plain. The attempt to introduce wheat culture widely into the non-chernozem zone would, therefore, to some extent negate the idea of regional specialization, which requires that crops and livestock be raised in areas where conditions are more favorable, making the activities most economical.[4]

AREA OF STUDY

In order to permit a better understanding of the history and nature of the Soviet drive to create a commercial wheat base in the non-chernozem zone, the present study has been restricted to an area embracing 19 oblasts and 7 autonomous republics in the central and northern part of European Russia (Fig. 1). These provinces were selected on the basis of available and workable data. Excluded from consideration were the Baltic Republics, Belorussia, and the non-chernozem oblasts of the Urals, since administrative boundary changes with respect to those territories have made the pertinent data difficult to assess and correlate with any exactitude over a period of time. Northern Siberia did not figure to any extent in the program and therefore has not been included. Nevertheless, the area thus delimited for the purposes of this study constitutes

---

[4] The XVIth Party Congress in 1930 charged the Lenin All-Union Academy of Agricultural Sciences to examine the question of the rational distribution of crops and branches of agricultural activity, involving the substitution of less profitable crops for more profitable crops, assuring the USSR of the possibility of a sufficient supply of the basic food and technical crops, etc., etc. Certainly, in view of the supply of lime and fertilizers available to the farms of the non-chernozem zone, the attempt made within a few years to expand significantly the acreage in wheat would seem to contradict the directive of the Party. Balzak, writing at the end of the 1930's, nevertheless cites

examples of progress in this task: the increase in the area in grain crops in the eastern and non-chernozem regions; the spread of wheat northward; the creation of new cotton and sugar-beet regions; etc. S. S. Balzak, V. F. Vasyutin, and Ya. G. Feigin, *Economic Geography of the USSR* (New York, 1950), p. 355. However, according to Obolenskii, the Academy "did not fulfill its important task . . ." and "for many years entirely ignored the introduction of economic considerations into agriculture." K. P. Obolenskii, "Problema ratsional'nogo razmeshcheniia i spetsializatsii sel'skogo khoziaistva v SSSR," in *Voprosy Razmeshcheniia i Spetsializatsii Sel'skogo Khoziaistva* (Moscow, 1957), p. 23.

the bulk of the European Russian non-cherno-zem zone.

THE DRIVE FOR A WHEAT BASE

Although the First Five Year Plan (1928–32) and the collective re-organization of agriculture that accompanied it brought an increase in wheat acreage (Table 1), the concerted drive for a northern wheat base began officially with the Second Five Year Plan (1933–37).[5] Surveys and studies of northern climatic and soil conditions were organized and carried out in the summer of 1933,[6] and ambitious goals for sowing wheat were established. It was proposed to expand acreage during the plan period by more than seven times, raising the total area under wheat in the zone to more than ten million. By 1937, therefore, the wheat acreage of the non-chernozem zone would represent about ten percent of the total Soviet wheat area. Indeed, the non-chernozem zone was to become, if goals were fulfilled, a secondary producer of wheat, a development which would involve a marked change both in the traditional position of wheat among other northern grains as well as in the relationship of the non-chernozem zone to other regions of the country in marketability of wheat.

Much of the planned increase in acreage was to be achieved through the cultivation of virgin and little-used land, the reported estimates of which were considerable (Table 2). In fact at the XVIIth Party Congress in 1934, where the plan to create "a steady wheat base in the central and northern regions" of European Russia was reaffirmed,[7] Stalin indicated that about 12 million acres of virgin bush land in the non-chernozem zone could be utilized immediately for wheat.[8] Thus, the initial drive to expand the sowing of wheat in the north was intended to come not at the expense of other agricultural land uses, but rather through the occupation of new land. The collective farms would continue to grow

TABLE 2.—ESTIMATES OF ARABLE LAND SUITABLE FOR WHEAT IN THE NON-CHERNOZEM ZONE[1]
(in millions of acres)

Province	Total area of crop and unim-proved land suitable for wheat	Crop land suitable for wheat with-out liming	Crop land suitable for wheat after liming
Northern Krai	n.d.	1.5	1.0
Leningrad Oblast	14.8	2.4	1.2
Western Oblast	11.9	2.7	2.1
Moscow Oblast	22.9	8.6	2.0
Ivanovo Oblast	12.1	1.9	1.5
Gorki Oblast	24.2	11.0	1.7
Tatar ASSR	15.6	7.7	n.d.
Total	101.5	35.8	9.5

[1] *Severnaia Pshenichnaia Baza* SSSR (Leningrad, 1934), p. 68.

rye and other traditional crops, but in addition they would assimilate new land for wheat.

By 1937, to all outward appearances, considerable progress had been made (Table 1, Fig. 2). Within the study area, the planting of wheat had grown to more than seven million acres, with wheat constituting about 15 percent of all grains sown. However, in spite of Stalin's statement at the XVIIth Party Congress, the increase in wheat came not so much through the use of virgin land; rather, wheat was sown on pasture and meadow lands requiring little initial investment.[9] To some extent also, wheat replaced winter rye and oats. While the prewar edition of the Soviet agricultural encyclopedia revealed that more than six million acres of land had been reclaimed in the non-chernozem zone from 1933 to 1936,[10] it seems doubtful that such land contributed significantly to the increase in the wheat area. Actually, the total sown area of the non-chernozem zone increased during the Second Five Year Plan by only two million acres, thus falling far short of the original goal. Nevertheless, it was this dramatic expansion in wheat acreage that led Balzak, Vasyutin and Feigin to state in their prewar *Economic Geography of the USSR* that "a new wheat base has been created in the non-chernozem zone . . . a reliable wheat base which provides the country with supplemen-

[5] *Vtoroi Piatiletnii Plan Razvitiia Narodnogo Khoziaistva* SSSR (1933–1937 gg.) (Moscow, 1934), pp. 15–81; *Severnaia Pshenichnaia Baza* SSSR (Leningrad, 1934), p. 3.

[6] *Pochvovedenie*, 1934, No. 2, p. 265.

[7] A. K. Shevliagin, *Kul'tura Iarovoi Pshenitsy na Severo-Vostoke* (Moscow, 1953), p. 5.

[8] V. E. Pisarev, "Iarovaia pshenitsa v nechernozemnoi polose," *Sovetskaia Agronomiia*, 1948, No. 5, p. 42.

[9] "Soviet Agricultural Reorganization and the Bread–Grain Situation," in *Wheat Studies of the Food Research Institute*, Vol. XIII, No. 7 (April, 1937), pp. 340–41.

[10] *Sel'skokhoziaistvennaia Entsiklopediia* (2nd ed., 4 vols.; Moscow and Leningrad, 1937–1940), Vol. 4, p. 490.

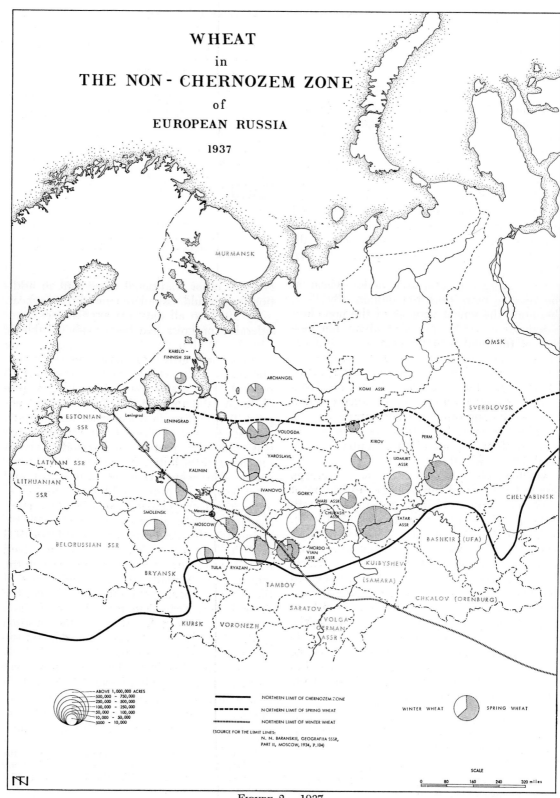

FIGURE 2. 1937

TABLE 3.—Changes in Wheat Acreage for Given
Provinces in the Non-Chernozem Zone, 1937–40
(in acres)

Province	1937[1]	1938	1940[2]
Gorki Oblast	609,600	663,700[1]–651,800[2]	504,100
Kirov Oblast	279,500	301,700 –298,500	271,600
Leningrad Oblast	444,300	384,700 –375,800	272,800
Moscow Oblast	345,400	310,400 –262,700	183,300

[1] *Posevnye Ploshchadi SSSR 1938 g.*, pp. 53, 74.
[2] Naum Jasny, *The Socialized Agriculture of the USSR*
(Stanford: Stanford University Press, 1949), p. 724, quoting
S. F. Demidov, in *Socialist Agriculture* (Sotsialisticheskoe
Zemledelie), 1942, No. 2, p. 21.

TABLE 4.—Wartime Decline in Spring Wheat
Acreages on Kolkhozes for Given Provinces
in the Non-Chernozem Zone[1]
(in acres)

Provinces	1940	1946
Veliki Luki Oblast	66,500	14,800
Mari ASSR	74,100	39,500
Yaroslavl Oblast	126,000	81,500
Moscow Oblast	150,000	89,000
Tatar ASSR	1,499,900	894,500

[1] I. Benediktov, "Za moshchnyi pod'em zernovogo khozi-
aista," *Sotsialisticheskoe Sel'skoe Khoziaistvo*, 1947, No. 2, p.
12.

tary resources of commercial grain to meet the needs of the cities of the Central Industrial Region. . . ."[11]

The upward trend in wheat acreage continued in some non-chernozem oblasts into 1938 but thereafter came to a general halt (Tables 1, 3). The Third Five Year Plan (1938–42) had directed the kolkhozy in the non-chernozem zone to assimilate six million acres of virgin land. However, no major increase in the wheat area was called for.[12] On the other hand, the regime relaxed its drive and offered, by the decree of December 28, 1939, some choice to the collective farmers as to the grains they were to grow; those in the non-chernozem zone responded by returning to traditional crops.[13] The approach of World War II may have dictated concessions to the collective farms. In the non-chernozem zone, however, serious difficulties must have become readily apparent as a result of the relentless drive for wheat in the mid-30's. In the haste to reach the goals assigned, sound agronomic practices, including the introduction and maintenance of proper crop rotations, were largely ignored. At the same time, the

reduction in pasture land and, to some extent, in feed grains, could not but have an adverse effect on livestock-raising already reeling under the impact of collectivization. Reflecting the response to the change in policy, the sowing of wheat in the non-chernozem in 1940 declined to scarcely more than six million acres.

During the war, when part of the non-chernozem zone, i.e., to the west of Moscow, fell to invading German armies, the cultivation of wheat continued to decline (Table 4), reaching by the end of the conflict probably about half of the seven million acres sown in 1938.

The immediate postwar period saw the Soviet regime again turn its attention to the northern wheat base in an effort to recover the losses endured during the war. In February, 1947, the Plenary Session of the Central Committee of the Communist Party directed the collective farms in the non-chernozem zone to increase the sowing of spring wheat by 500,000 acres and raise by 1948 total spring wheat acreage to more than four million.[14] Moreover, since much land, including that reclaimed during the 1930's, had gone back into bush and had been unattended during the war, it was recommended that it be put immediately into use.[15]

Recovery, however, was slow. It was not until 1950, and particularly after the XIXth Party Congress in 1952, that a significant increase in wheat acreage again occurred. By 1954, the wheat base in the non-chernozem consisted of 9.2 million acres, a record year in

[11] Balzak, *op. cit.*, p. 374.

[12] *Tretii Piatiletnii Plan Razvitiia Narodnogo Khoziaistva Soiuza SSR* (1938–42 gg.) (Moscow, 1939), p. 70. By 1941, ameliorative work had been carried out on some three million acres of virgin land, but much of this land served to strengthen the feeding of livestock. See: *Sel'skokhoziaistvennye Melioratsii v Nechernozemnoi Polose* (Leningrad, 1949), p. 12.

[13] Pages 723–24 of Jasny cited in Table 3, fn. 2. Jasny writes that the kolkhozy replaced with oats part of the spring wheat planned for them, and with winter rye part of the planned winter wheat, although in this action they were handicapped by the obligation to deliver to the government all of the wheat required of them in the 1940 delivery plan, and wheat was not replaceable by any other crop in obligatory deliveries to the government.

[14] Pisarev, *op. cit.*, p. 43.

[15] *Sel'skokhoziaistvennye Melioratsii v Nechernozemnoi Polose*, p. 14; A. G. Trutnev, *Obrabotka Tselinnykh i Zalezhnykh Zemel'* (Moscow and Leningrad, 1954), p. 55. The use of such land was still being recommended as late as 1954.

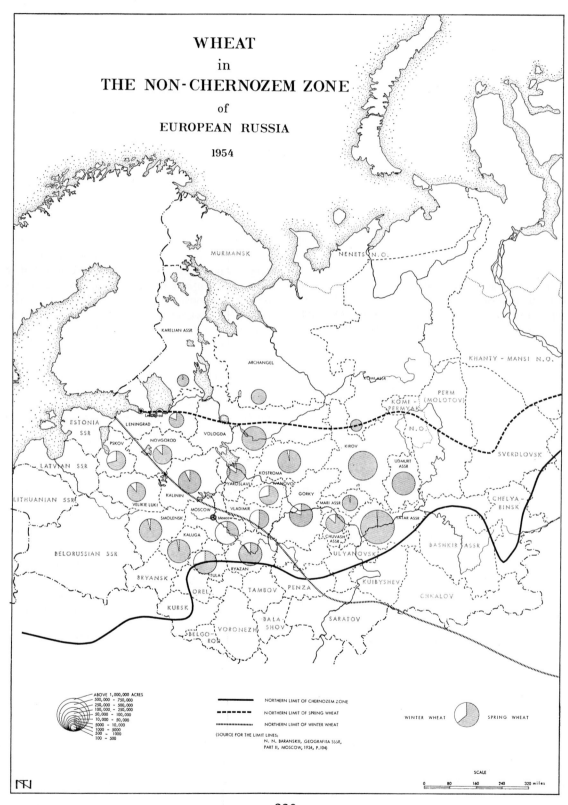

WHEAT
in
THE NON-CHERNOZEM ZONE
of
EUROPEAN RUSSIA

1954

ABOVE 1,000,000 ACRES
500,000 - 750,000
250,000 - 500,000
100,000 - 250,000
50,000 - 100,000
10,000 - 50,000
5000 - 10,000
1000 - 5000
500 - 1000
100 - 500

NORTHERN LIMIT OF CHERNOZEM ZONE

NORTHERN LIMIT OF SPRING WHEAT

NORTHERN LIMIT OF WINTER WHEAT

(SOURCE FOR THE LIMIT LINES:
N. N. BARANSKII, GEOGRAFIIA SSSR,
PART II, MOSCOW, 1934, P.104)

WINTER WHEAT   SPRING WHEAT

SCALE
0   80   160   240   320 miles

220

acreage, and this represented about 21 percent of the grain area compared with 15 percent in 1937–38 (Table 1, Fig. 3). Since the area in grains grew by only 1.7 million acres from 1950 to 1954, the 4.4 million-acre wheat increase during the same period was achieved largely at the expense of other crops, notably rye and oats.[16]

However, in 1955 decline set in again. The remarkable expansion in wheat acreage resulting from the ploughing of virgin and idle lands in the eastern regions of the country undoubtedly had repercussions on the non-chernozem wheat base.[17] At the same time, the persistent problems associated with wheat culture in the non-chernozem zone may also have again dictated a shift in emphasis, as in the latter part of the 1930's. Nevertheless, by 1956, the sowing of wheat in the non-chernozem had fallen below the 1937–38 level, although wheat continued to constitute a much larger portion of the grain sown than in the prewar years.

THE PROBLEMS OF WHEAT CULTURE IN THE NON-CHERNOZEM ZONE

Although the Soviet regime has claimed that it has been successful in pushing the limits of wheat cultivation northward far beyond that achieved before the revolution,[18] the non-chernozem wheat base involves essentially the southern part of the zone, roughly south and southeast of Leningrad. In European Russia, the northern limit of steady wheat cultivation marches closely with the 60th parallel east of the latter city, but dips southward to the neighborhood of Perm (Molotov) as the Urals are approached. This line represents the thermal limit of wheat which, according to Soviet agronomists, totals about 1600 Centigrade degrees of summer heat (i.e., the sum of the mean daily temperatures for days with aver-

age temperatures above 10° C.).[19] Wheat may be sown farther north, but such fields are essentially oases of cultivation found mainly in protected river valleys.

Southward from Leningrad to Moscow the frost-free season lengthens from 110 to 130 days, and normally is of sufficient duration for wheat to mature.[20] Since climatic conditions in winter throughout much of the non-chernozem zone are severe, a large portion of the wheat must be sown in spring. Yet, for spring wheat the danger of an early autumn frost is real, especially if the spring is late and/or delays occur in sowing or in harvesting. On the other hand, not only low winter temperatures but an uneven and unreliable snow cover may present considerable risks in the cultivation of winter wheat.

While total precipitation throughout the non-chernozem zone totals on the average about 20 inches or slightly more, dry periods in spring are not infrequent, especially in Moscow Oblast, and in the provinces along the Volga to the east. The drought, if accompanying late sowing, may significantly retard growth. On the other hand, when summers are cool and damp, the Swedish fly may cause considerable damage. Swedish fly infestations are particularly heavy also in the central chernozem zone to the south.[21] Because of the prevalence of the fly, losses in yields of spring wheat during the 1930's were considerable, ranging from four to 20 percent of the wheat sown. Indeed, losses have been reported up to 50 percent of the sowings! Largely because of the fly, therefore, spring wheat acreage in the central oblasts of the non-chernozem zone has declined significantly since the early 1930's, and the regime has given considerable

[16] The decline in rye and oats amounted to nearly three million acres.

[17] W. A. Douglas Jackson, "The Virgin and Idle Lands of Western Siberia and Northern Kazakhstan: A Geographical Appraisal," *Geographical Review*, Vol. XLVI, No. 1 (1956), pp. 1–19.

[18] K. A. Fliaksberger, *Pshenitsy* (Moscow and Leningrad, 1935), pp. 160–62.

[19] G. T. Selianinov, "Spetsializatsii sel'skokhoziaistvennykh raionov po klimaticheskomu priznaku," in *Rastenievodstvo SSSR* (2 vols., Leningrad and Moscow, 1933–34), Vol. 1, pp. 1–16.

[20] V. P. Kuz'min, "Nechernozemnaia polosa," in *Rastenievodstvo SSSR*, Vol. 1, pp. 99–237.

[21] Pisarev, *op. cit.*, pp. 44–48. The Swedish fly, Pisarev writes, is not only a hindrance to the successful cultivation of spring wheat in the central non-chernozem oblasts, but also to the south, in Ryazan, Tula, Orel and Kursk Oblasts, which fall in part or entirely within the central chernozem zone. The problem is less serious to the east, where the climate is more continental and wheat is sown earlier. Nor does the fly seem to be a problem in the western districts. Spring wheat also suffers periodically from the *Fuzarium* blight, which is more pronounced on heavier soils, particularly when spring wheat is sown late as temperatures are rising. See also: *Sel'skokhoziaistvennaia Entsiklopediia* (3rd ed., 5 vols., Moscow, 1949–56), Vol. 5, p. 291.

TABLE 5.—COMPARATIVE LOSSES OF WINTER WHEAT AND WINTER RYE FOR GIVEN DISTRICTS IN THE NON-CHERNOZEM ZONE[1]
(percent of total sowings)

District	1926–34 Winter wheat	1926–34 Winter rye	1935–38 Winter wheat	1935–38 Winter rye
Leningrad Oblast	2.8	2.9	4.4	2.9
Smolensk Oblast	1.8	4.4	3.4	3.4
Kalinin Oblast	4.5	3.2	5.6	1.9
Moscow			10.4	2.4
Gorki Oblast	11.8	4.5	2.5	0.6
Kirov			26.3	3.1
Tatar ASSR	16.4	3.2	28.5	6.0

[1] M. Lapin, "Itogi i perspektivy prodvizheniia pshenitsy na sever," *Sotsialisticheskoe Sel'skoe Khoziaistvo*, 1939, No. 6, pp. 70–87. The author also gives losses in hectares for winter wheat and winter rye.

TABLE 6.—SOWN AREAS OF SPRING AND WINTER WHEAT IN THE NON-CHERNOZEM ZONE FOR SELECTED YEARS (1913–56)
(in millions of acres)

Year	Spring wheat	Winter wheat	Spring wheat as percent of total wheat
1913[1]	.6	.1	90.6
1926[2]	.8	.2	79.0
1928	.7	.2	78.2
1930[3]	.8	.3	69.7
1932	1.2	.4	77.0
1934	3.0	1.4	68.0
1937[4]	5.0	2.2	69.7
1938	5.0	2.4	67.8
1940	nd	nd	nd
1950[5]	4.4	.4	86.7
1952	6.0	.8	88.6
1954	8.0	1.2	86.6
1956	5.3	1.4	78.7

[1] *Sel'skoe Khoziaistvo Rossii v XX Veke*, pp. 78–89.
[2] Pages 186–89 of source cited in fn. 2, Table 1.
[3] Pages 342–45 of source cited in fn. 3, Table 1.
[4] Pages 53, 74 of source cited in fn. 4, Table 1.
[5] Pages 274–83, 338–47 of source cited in fn. 6, Table 1.

attention to the sowing of winter wheat instead. Because of the unhappy situation with respect to the cultivation of spring wheat throughout parts of the zone, the regime, in its drive to create a wheat base, has made a vigorous attempt to push the limits and extent of winter wheat culture northward.[22]

In this endeavor Moscow Oblast has received much of the attention. As a result, 90 percent of the oblast's wheat is fall-sown. However, in 1956 winter wheat totalled only 313,000 acres, approximately 20 percent of all winter wheat sown in the non-chernozem zone. Losses due to winter killing have been high; east of Moscow, where the winters are more severe, losses have been phenomenal.

The western districts of the non-chernozem zone, because of their relatively milder winters, have been described by Soviet writers as offering the best opportunity for expanding the cultivation of winter wheat.[23] However, losses have also been incurred due to late sowing and early autumn frost, or as a result of inadequate snow cover in mid-winter.[24]

Winter rye may also succumb, but losses normally are lower than for winter wheat (Table 5). At any rate, in spite of efforts to expand winter wheat in the western districts, about three-fourths of the wheat in Leningrad Oblast is spring-sown, and the situation in adjacent oblasts, as well as in the Baltic Republics, is comparable.

Throughout the non-chernozem as a whole, the ratio between spring and winter wheat may fluctuate markedly from year to year. In 1913, for example, spring wheat constituted about 90 percent of all wheat sown in the non-chernozem zone; in 1937, it was approximately 70 percent; and in 1954, 87 percent (Table 6). Spring wheat, though more demanding on the soil than winter wheat, continues to constitute the bulk of sowings. Winter wheat lacks the hardiness of winter rye, but with survival yields have generally been higher than those for winter rye or spring wheat (Table 7). This factor accounts for much of the rationale behind the continuing effort to expand the sowing of winter wheat in the non-chernozem zone.[25]

More basic problems confronting the Soviet regime in the non-chernozem zone pertain to the nature and management of the soils. Wheat prefers a well-drained loamy soil, of

[22] E. K. Alainis, "O prodvizhenii ozimoi pshenitsy na sever," *Sotsialisticheskoe Rekonstruktsiia Sel'skogo Khoziaistva*, 1933, No. 6, pp. 90–100; P. F. Sekun, *Ozimaia Pshenitsa v Nechernozemnoi Polose* (Moscow, 1953), p. 119.

[23] *Sel'skoe Khoziaistvo SSSR*, 1935 (Moscow, 1936), p. 37.

[24] For a description of the general climatic conditions of the non-chernozem zone, with respect to crop cultivation, see G. T. Selianinov, "Klimaticheskoe raionirovanie SSSR dlia sel'skokhoziaistvennykh tselei," in *Pamiati Akademika L. S. Berga*, ed. E. L. Pavlovskii (Moscow and Leningrad, 1955), pp. 215–16.

[25] M. Lapin, "Itogi i perspektivy prodvizheniia pshenitsy na sever," *Sotsialisticheskoe Sel'skoe Khoziaistvo*, 1939, No. 6, p. 73.

TABLE 7.—COMPARATIVE YIELDS OF WINTER WHEAT, SPRING WHEAT, AND WINTER RYE[1]
(centners per hectare)

District[2]	Winter wheat 1928–35		Spring wheat 1928–35		Winter rye 1928–35	
Northern Krai	n.d.	12.3	n.d.	10.3	8.9	12.3
Leningrad Oblast	9.3	10.3	8.3	8.5	8.8	10.5
Kalinin Oblast	10.0	10.6	7.9	9.3	8.7	11.0
Moscow		10.4		9.8		10.0
Western Oblast	8.9	9.5	8.5	9.4	8.3	9.0
Ivanovo Oblast	9:6	12.0	7.5	9.9	8.9	11.3
Yaroslavl		10.1[3]		8.9		11.4
Gorki Oblast	9.1	10.8	7.9	9.9	8.2	11.5
Kirov		8.8		8.9		10.4
Tatar ASSR	n.d.	9.9	n.d.	9.9	7.3	9.9

[1] Pages 74–75 of source cited in fn. 1, Table 5.
[2] Within administrative districts as of 1935.
[3] 1935 only.

neutral reaction. In general, the podsolic soils of central and northern European Russia are noted for their high acidity (pH values range from 6.5 to 4 or less), low organic content, stoniness, and poor drainage.[26] Since the territory is vast in extent, considerable variation obviously exists from place to place. Directives of the party and government have, over the past two decades, repeatedly urged the reclamation and use of virgin land as well as improvement of land already cropped or pastured, but there is little evidence to support a contention of substantial progress. Much of the non-chernozem remains in forest or bush. This is essentially true of the taiga of the north-central and northern districts; but even in the south-central and southern districts, anywhere from 10 to 40 percent of the land is wooded.[27]

A region of relatively recent glaciation, central and northern Russia contains large stretches of poorly drained and marsh land. One of the more extensive areas of wet land, for example, is east of Moscow, in the Meshchora Lowland. It extends over five million acres, primarily in Ryazan, Moscow and Vladimir Oblasts. Special attention was given to

[26] *Ob Uluchshenii Sel'skokhoziaistvennogo Ispol'zovaniia Zemel' Nechernozemnoi Polosy Evropeiskoi Chasti SSSR*, pp. 42–67. Smirnov in his handbook on crops states that wheat requires a neutral or slightly alkaline soil with a pH from 6 to 8. A. I. Smirnov, *Rastenievodstvo* (5th ed.; Moscow, 1952), p. 39.

[27] *Ob Uluchshenii Sel'skokhoziaistvennogo Ispol'zovaniia Zemel'* . . . , pp. 68–9, 72–4.

reclamation in the Meshchora at the XIXth Party Congress in 1952 and reclamation is already under way. But, according to all reports, the problems are immense.

In general, in the eastern districts of the non-chernozem zone, drainage improvement is needed on six percent of the plough land and 25 percent of the pastures and meadows. In the western districts, the ratios are approximately 17 percent and 33 percent, respectively.[28] As has already been suggested, however, the cultivation of reclaimed land, especially virgin land, tends to trail at some considerable distance the actual process of reclamation, if indeed much of the land is ever cropped.[29]

As a result of surveys made in 1933, Soviet writers claimed optimistically that more than 100 million acres of land, then either in use or unimproved and unused, could ultimately be sown to wheat (Table 2). Of this, slightly more than a third or some 35 million acres of crop land could be sown to wheat without the need of applications of lime; an additional 10 million acres would be suitable only after liming. Altogether the 45 million acres of potential wheat land were equal in 1933 to about three-fourths of the sown area of the non-chernozem zone, the sown area being only a small fraction of the reputed total available area, some 70 percent of which was in meadows and pasture.[30] The remainder of the 100 million-acre fund, approximately 55 million acres, consisting of marshes, bush and forest land, could be sown to wheat only after considerable expenditure for improvement. Undoubtedly the 12 million acres which Stalin indicated at the XVIIth Party Congress were to be reclaimed during the First Five Year Plan represented the more readily assimilable portion of the above land fund. In any one year, of course, only a relatively small part of the fund could be sown to wheat, since consideration had to be given to the maintenance

[28] *Ibid.*, p. 109.

[29] M. Neznaev, "Ob osvoenii novykh zemel' v nechernozemnoi polose SSSR," *Sotsialisticheskoe Sel'skoe Khoziaistvo*, 1947, No. 12, pp. 52–6. Neznaev states that, in 1946, of 330,000 acres reclaimed in the northern oblasts of the non-chernozem zone, 28 percent remained *unused*. In Gorki Oblast, of 50,000 acres reclaimed, more than 80 percent remained unused.

[30] *Ob Uluchshenii Sel'skokhoziaistvennogo Ispol'zovaniia Zemel'* . . . , p. 180.

of correct crop rotations, to pasture and feed stuffs for livestock, and the demand for other grains, vegetables, and industrial crops, such as flax.

The estimate of crop land suitable for wheat without liming seems altogether too generous. A recent Soviet publication reveals that in the non-chernozem zone from 50 to 60 percent of the crop land (which tends to remain at about 65 million acres) normally requires liming, while in some districts the ratio might rise to 90 or 100 percent.[31] During the 1930's, liming was done on a negligible scale. Indeed, as late as 1954, it is reported that no more than 120,000 acres in the non-chernozem zone were limed, although applications of lime were required on many million more.[32] Unquestionably, liming could raise yields from 2 to 5 centners per hectare in spring wheat and from 3 to 7 centners in winter wheat, as tests on experimental farms in the non-chernozem zone have indicated.[33] However, adequate supplies of lime have not been available to the collective farms as a whole.

Similarly, extensive applications of manure are also needed. But in this connection it should be remembered that the drive for a northern wheat base got under way at a time when livestock were being depleted in great numbers in protest against collectivization. Thus, throughout the 30's, manure was in short supply throughout much of the zone. Peat, though abundant, has not been used widely nor extensively; nor have commercial fertilizers been available in sufficient quantities.[34] At the same time, other difficulties exist which have hampered work in the fields. In the party magazine *Kommunist*, the Minister of Agriculture of the RSFSR revealed that "the organization work behind the application of manure and peat on the fields of the kolkhozes of Ryazan and Tula Oblasts, Mari and Mordvin ASSR's, in 1957, was especially unsatisfactory. There, on one hectare of ploughed land in 1957, only 1.1–2 tons of organic fertilizer were applied. Somewhat better was the situation on the kolkhozes of Moscow, Briansk and Vladimir Oblasts, where 3–4 tons were applied to one hectare of ploughed land."[35]

On the whole, throughout the 1930's, wheat yields in the non-chernozem were low (Table 7).[36] In general, they may still be low. Inadequate or incorrect crop rotation practices seem to be chronic. Underlying this situation may well be peasant stubbornness to change, implicit in the "scornful attitudes of the kolkhozy toward the question of agrotechnics and their failure to accept scientific advances in cultivation."[37]

For their work in developing and adapting new strains and varieties of wheat and other grains, both Tsarist and Soviet agronomists have gained international repute. Yet, despite the success achieved in raising yields and improving quality in experimental fields, the distribution of new varieties to farms throughout the non-chernozem zone, as well as throughout the union as a whole, has tended to lag. During the 1930's, the planting of improved varieties of wheat in the non-chernozem zone probably reached 30–40 percent or more of all wheat sown, although the proportion fell behind the exceptionally high norms established by the Second Five Year Plan.[38] Actually, the area sown to improved varieties has tended to fluctuate markedly from year to year, often due to failure of the

[31] *Ibid.*, p. 103.

[32] N. Avdonin, "Vashnye voprosy povysheniia kul'-tury zemledeliia v nechernozemnoi polose," *Kommunist*, 1954, No. 9, p. 46.

[33] N. Avdonin, *O Pod'eme Zemledeliia v Raionakh Nechernozemnoi Polosy* (Moscow, 1953), p. 9. Avdonin points out that K. K. Gedroiz, the Soviet soil and agricultural specialist, states that up to 8 and more tons of lime per hectare are required on the soils of the non-chernozem.

[34] *Ibid.*, pp. 54–5. In discussing a system of agriculture for the non-chernozem zone, Fredin states that about two tons of manure and peat, and about 22 kgms. of mineral fertilizer per hectare are needed on ploughed land in the non-chernozem zone. See: A. Fredin, "Tvorcheski razrabotat' sistemy zemledeliia," *Ekonomika Sel'skoe Khoziaistvo*, 1957, No. 2, pp. 8–26.

[35] I. Benediktov, "Maksimal'no ispol'zovat' rese·vy sel'skokhoziaistva," *Kommunist*, 1957, No. 18, p. 48.

[36] V. V. Gritsenko, *Agrotekhnika Iarovoi Pshenitsy v Nechernozemnoi Polose* (Moscow, 1955), p. 5.

[37] N. V. Kotel'nikov, "Osvoenie sevo-oborotov v kolkhozakh nechernozemnoi polosy," *Zemledelie*, 1953, No. 6, pp. 15–19.

[38] *Semenovodstvo i Sortosmena Zernovykh Kul'tur: 1933–1937 gg.* (Leningrad, 1934), p. 27.

kolkhozy to set aside sufficient improved seed for planting the following year.[39]

CONCLUSION

Wheat *can* grow in the non-chernozem zone, and it would not have been unreasonable to assume, say in 1927, given the "normal course of events," that the acreage in wheat might have increased in the years to come in response to general improvements in agricultural techniques. Climatic conditions from year to year do present risks; but such difficulties may be offset somewhat by flexible farm management, as well as by the development and cultivation of hardy varieties of winter wheat and early-maturing varieties of spring wheat. Non-chernozem soils do not constitute the best medium for wheat, but drainage, systematic applications of lime and manure, as well as careful cropping, can make some areas productive. Indeed, under such conditions wheat might overtake winter rye in yield and productivity.

The drive for a northern wheat base, however, got under way during a period of revolutionary change and disorder. An ambitious program, it was instituted under the most inauspicious circumstances. Collectivization was imposed and, in the non-chernozem zone, on a peasantry noted for its adherence to traditional and backward ways and methods. The result, if not open opposition, was sullen noncooperation — and the slaughter of livestock by the thousands! Dramatically and suddenly, the non-chernozem zone, where fertilization is imperative, lost a supply of manure at a time when other fertilizers were not readily available.

Under these conditions, the program could not have been assured success. Nevertheless, with considerably expanded acreage, wheat production in the non-chernozem zone by the end of the 1930's must have increased markedly, though falling far short of the regime's expectations.

The rationale for establishing a commercial wheat base in the non-chernozem zone, while not necessarily creating regional self-sufficiency, was undoubtedly valid in the eyes of Soviet planners in the early 1930's. As the regime anticipated, the development of a mighty industrial fortress would necessitate a great movement of surplus laborers from the countryside to the cities; the expansion of the urban population in the non-chernozem zone would require that more grain and wheat be made available. Wheat grown in the non-chernozem for market would tend to lessen the length of haul from other regions to the south and east. Moreover, as experience had shown in the past, parts of the steppe region, especially in the Ukraine, could not always be counted on to produce a surplus for shipment to the northern cities. Such a surplus might disappear for some time, too, as a result of black-earth peasant opposition to collectivization. Hence, a supplementary supply of wheat from non-chernozem fields would lessen the dependence on other regions of the country.

However, as Professors Vol'pe and Klupt point out in their *Lectures on the Economic Geography of the USSR* (1957), the average length of haul of grain stuffs in the USSR has tended over the decades to increase, rather than to decrease. From 544 km. in 1913, the length of haul by rail increased to 736 km. in 1940, and to 997 km. in 1954.[40] It may now be significantly higher, due to the eastward movement of the Soviet wheat belt consequent on the ploughing of more than 70 million acres of virgin and idle steppe lands east of the Volga.[41] In view of the low yields and poor quality of non-chernozem wheat, and as a result of the sharp growth in urban population, the dependence of the non-chernozem zone on imports of grain from the steppe regions, relatively speaking, probably has not lessened to any marked degree.

Vol'pe and Klupt point out that the interests of Soviet national economy demand a significant increase in grain production in the non-chernozem zone, a huge possibility which up to now has not been fully utilized, because

[39] An illustration of this problem is found in the following reference: A. A. Ukolov, "Mezhsortovoe skreshchivanie ozimoi pshenitsy," *Agrobiologiia*, 1954, No. 4, p. 26. Ukolov reports that winter wheat variety *Moskovskaia 2453*, widely sown in Moscow Oblast in the past, has been declining in acreage in recent years, in spite of the fact that its quality is superior to other winter wheat varieties. No one, he points out, has worked at maintaining a supply of seed.

[40] V. M. Vol'pe and V. S. Klupt, *Lektsii po Ekonomicheskoi Geografii SSSR*, Part I (Leningrad, 1957), p. 202.

[41] Jackson, *loc. cit.*

yields have been low! An increase is possible, they state, through a sharp improvement in agricultural techniques.[42] In view of what must be a very large and ever-growing demand for meat and dairy products in the industrial cities, we might expect that the Soviet regime will give not less but greater attention to the problems surrounding the grain economy of the non-chernozem zone. However, it is difficult to conceive of a further attempt to expand wheat culture there; indeed, one might expect that, in view of the sharp increase in commodity wheat production in Siberia and northern Kazakhstan, non-chernozem wheat will cause less concern and investment than before 1954. Certainly, by all Soviet accounts, the wheats of the Ukrainian and Siberian steppes are of considerably better quality and are less costly to produce than the wheats of the non-chernozem zone.[43]

At the same time that the need for a greater output of meat and dairy products has increased, so too has the demand for vegetables and potatoes. The supply of vegetables and potatoes to the state stores of the cities leaves much to be desired,[44] and without access to the collective farm market, the workers would be severely rationed. Indeed, so great is the problem of supply that in the latter part of 1958, the Central Committee of the Communist Party ordered 35 sovkhozy in Moscow Oblast to shift to potato and vegetable growing.[45] In addition, Tula, Briansk, Riazan and Kaluga Oblasts were similarly obliged to intensify land utilization on some of their sovkhozes in order to supply the needs of Moscow.

The key to future land utilization and agricultural production in the non-chernozem zone may already be apparent. The virgin and idle land program in the eastern regions, the corn–livestock program especially in the south, and the ever-increasing demand for meat and dairy products, potatoes and vegetables in the non-chernozem zone, to provide a more varied and substantial diet for the urban population, may weaken substantially the case for a commercial wheat base. Indeed, the XXth Party Congress in 1956,[46] stressing the need for "specialization" and "the rational distribution" of agricultural activities throughout the USSR, undoubtedly had these considerations in mind. Improved agricultural techniques may bring greater productivity to non-chernozem wheat culture, but the activity may no longer be "rational."

---

[42] Vol'pe, loc. cit.

[43] Sel'skoe Khoziaistvo SSSR (Moscow, 1958), p. 131; R. Kartashov, "Voprosy razvitiia zernovogo khoziaistva," Sotsialisticheskoe Sel'skoe Khoziaistvo, 1956, No. 2, p. 34.

[44] Pravda, August 20, 1958; Pravda notes that the vegetable stores in Tula and other workers' settlements, for example, are uninspiring at any time of the year. The late summer offers no more than green onions, cabbages, and cucumbers, and those not of the best. In 1958, there were no cabbages for sale (from anywhere) as early as March, and no potatoes as early as May. Ordinarily, there are no onions, garlic, parsley, lettuce, peas, or beans for sale. For a thorough discussion of the problems of suburban truck farming see: N. V. Vasil'ev, Razvitie Prigorodnogo Sel'skogo Khoziaistva (Moscow, 1954), 142 pp.

[45] Sovetskaia Kirgiziia, November 4, 1958.

[46] L. M. Sal'tsman (ed.), Voprosy Rashmeshcheniia i Spetsializatsii Sel'skogo Khoziaistva (Moscow, 1957), pp. 3–4.

UTILIZATION OF WHEAT FOR FOOD

by

H. WAYNE BITTING and ROBERT O. ROGERS

Raw materials used in the food processing industry must have specific properties for specified end uses. As specialization of food processing increases and as new food products are developed, the raw materials used in producing these food products are less easily substituted. The following article illustrates how this trend affects wheat utilization. This has implications in agricultural policy, marketing, and research. A lack of recognition of product properties can lead to loss of export markets, reduced farm income, and a continued decline in per capita consumption of wheat products. Economists often are unaware of product properties. As a result, some food consumption data include food items within a group which require different agricultural raw materials. In this paper an attempt is made to separate wheat foods according to the types of wheat required to produce them. While this research relates to wheat utilization in the domestic market, it has significance to markets for other agricultural commodities as well as wheat exports.

Wheat is one of the oldest and most important food crops. The ability and capacity of the American wheat farmer to produce exceed our domestic market needs. Wheat production efficiency and know-how have outpaced the development of new markets. How can the markets for wheat be expanded? What can research do to help expand these markets? Utilization research has obtained information which should be useful in answering some of these questions.

All types of wheat cannot be used to make all kinds of wheat foods. For example, the following wheats possess specific properties: *Hard red spring and hard red winter* (high in protein and strong in gluten) — essential for quality yeast breads and hard rolls; *white and soft red winter* — necessary for good cakes and crackers; and *durum* — a special type used for good macaroni and spaghetti. For certain food uses, one type of wheat may be partially or completely substituted and still a quality food product can be made. For other food uses, different types of wheat cannot be substituted. As a result, there are certain years when there is a surplus of one and a shortage of another kind of wheat.

Getting the desired wheat properties for specific food uses is even more an exacting process than the selection of wheat on the basis of

"Utilization of Wheat for Food" by H. Wayne Bitting and Robert O. Rogers. Reprinted from Agricultural Economic Research, *Vol. 15 (April 1963) pp. 61–69.*

class. During the growing season the amount of moisture affects the properties which a given variety of wheat will have in any particular year. Even with the same variety, a wet season, accompanied by high yields, lowers the protein level as compared with a dry year and low yields. Likewise, the same variety produced under irrigation, versus nonirrigation, produces different properties. Location also affects wheat properties. A hard red winter wheat grown in a soft red winter area yields dissimilar properties from the same variety grown in a hard red winter area. In addition to the difference in properties, associated with the conditions under which wheat is grown, there are also variations in the properties demanded in wheat flour due to the baking methods used and the management skills of the baker. Add to these variations the fact that a desirable bread in one country may not be considered preferable by consumers in another country.

Despite all of these problems, it is essential that wheat growers endeavor to produce wheat which has the properties needed to make acceptable food products in the markets where the wheat is to be sold. If this is not done, wheat will suffer severe price discounts in the market place. Growers will plan their production more intelligently if they know which wheat varieties in their particular location produce suitable properties for specific food uses, and how many bushels are needed to satisfy these markets at home and abroad.

DOMESTIC FOOD MARKET

In examining the domestic food market for wheat, it is essential to consider the end uses and the wheat properties desired for each use. Since commercial bakers are the primary users of wheat flour, the demands of the baking industry largely determine the flour characteristics for each end-product use.

As a first approximation, the amount of flour required for products purchased by consumers in retail stores has been divided among hard, soft, and durum wheats. Hard wheat (hard red winter and hard red spring) accounts for 66.2 percent of the total domestic food usage; soft wheat, 29.4 percent; and durum, 4.4 percent. How are these classes of wheat used?

Hard wheats are used for the yeast-leavened products — primarily bread, rolls, and sweet goods. For the chemically leavened products — cakes, pies, cookies, doughnuts, biscuits, some pastries, and crackers — flour from soft wheat is used. The relative importance of each end-product use of wheat flour and the amounts of hard, soft, and durum wheats used by each food product are shown in Table 1. Of the wheat used for food in 1961, wheat flour constituted 97.8 percent of the total, and wheat cereals the remaining 2.2 percent.

CAN RESEARCH EXPAND THE MARKET FOR WHEAT?

Research can help the wheat farmer by lowering marketing and production costs and developing new or improved wheat products. A reduction in marketing or production costs, or both, could lead to increased returns to growers without changing the demand for wheat products. On the other hand, the development of new or improved wheat products could expand the demand

Table 1: Domestic food use of wheat, by type,
United States, 1959-1960[1]

Product	Wheat (million bushels)			
	Hard	Soft	Durum	Total
Bread.	200.15	—	—	200.15
Rolls	10.27	—	—	10.27
Biscuits and muffins	—	2.87	—	2.87
Crackers	3.40	18.53	—	21.93
Cakes.	—	6.11	—	6.11
Pies.	—	2.52	—	2.52
Other sweet goods	11.38	8.10	—	19.48
Alimentary paste products	8.20	—	22.00	30.20
Flour:				
All purpose	85.57	72.33	—	157.90
Whole wheat	2.38	—	—	2.38
Cake.	—	12.21	—	12.21
Prepared mixes	—	22.34	—	22.34
Wheat cereals	9.65	1.99	—	11.64
Total.	331.00	147.00	22.00	500.00

[1] Robert J. Lavell, formerly with Economic Research Service, developed the estimates of flour consumption for individual States, based upon the consumption data from the 1955 Household Food Consumption Survey and related demographic data. Robert E. Post, formerly with ERS, provided corresponding data for total wheat disappearance by hard, soft, and durum types. The breakdown by type of flour for each of the major food product categories was developed by the following committee: Robert J. Lavell; Robert E. Post; Lawrence Zeleny, Chief, Standardization and Testing Branch, Grain Division, Agricultural Marketing Service; Philip Talbott, Executive Secretary, Grain Defense Planning Committee, Grain Division, Agricultural Stabilization and Conservation Service; Edward F. Seeborg, Cereal Technologist, Grain and Feed Division, Foreign Agricultural Service; Robert O. Rogers, Assistant Director, and H. Wayne Bitting, Staff Specialist (Food), Product and Process Evaluation Staff, Office of Administrator, Agricultural Research Service. These estimates were based upon the percentage composition of the several types of flour normally used in each food item of the product food group. The flour consumption data, by States, and end-product uses were adjusted to fit the total wheat disappearance, by class of wheat.

for wheat. With expansion in demand, consumers would be willing to buy more wheat at the same price or pay more for a given quantity of wheat. Both the possibilities of reducing marketing costs and expanding the demand for wheat need to be explored for domestic and foreign markets.

Research may contribute to lowering marketing costs, primarily by reducing transportation costs. If wheat were produced and consumed within the same area, transportation costs would be minimized. Is this what we find? Five distinct classes of wheat are grown — hard red spring, hard red winter, soft red winter, white, and durum.

We know from our domestic utilization pattern that local wheat under present milling and baking practices does not always produce all the wheat foods consumed locally (Table 1). For example, in the soft wheat regions, hard wheats or hard wheat flours are imported to produce bread, rolls, general-purpose, and whole-wheat flour. In the hard wheat regions, soft wheats or soft wheat flours are imported for cakes, cookies, crackers, and soft-wheat flours. To the extent that air classification of wheat flour enables local wheats to be used for a wider variety of baked products, a savings in transportation costs could result. With air classification, high protein-low starch fractions of flour can be separated from low protein-high starch fractions by use of air streams. Conceivably, this would enable flour millers consistently to tailor-make flours for specific end uses without blending wheat varieties to obtain the desired protein-starch combinations as practiced under conventional methods. However, the potential savings in transportation are limited because 80 percent of the population resides in areas where only 30 percent of the wheat is produced. To examine this situation more specifically, see Figure 1 — a map showing the production and utilization of hard wheat, by individual States.

Note that hard wheat must be transported to the East, Northeast, Southeast, and Southwest to meet utilization requirements. The States shown in solid black indicate a production in excess of utilization of more than 5 million bushels. The striped areas show the States producing more hard wheat than they utilize, but under 5-million-bushel excess. Similarly, the deficit States are shown in white and in dots. The figure for each State indicates the amount of excess or deficit in terms of million bushels.

Figure 2 shows soft wheat, by States, in relation to domestic utilization. Note that in this case soft wheat must be moved into the States producing hard red spring and hard red winter wheat, as well as the Northeast, South, Southeast, and California. While deficits are not large, transportation costs are involved.

Figure 3 shows total wheat production in relation to domestic utilization. This is the picture if any kind of wheat could be used for any type of end-use product. The significant item to be noted from this map is that wheat still would have to be moved to the East, Northeast, Southeast, and Southwest. Only four States east of the Mississippi River produce more total wheat than they consume. These are Illinois, Indiana, Michigan, and Ohio.

With the exception of Iowa and Wisconsin, all States in the hard wheat region produce more wheat than they consume. Despite the large surplus production in the hard wheat region, it is a deficit region so far as soft wheat flour requirements are concerned. It would seem that air classification offers a possibility for reducing transportation costs in the hard wheat region insofar as it enables bakers to use hard wheats for more of their end-product requirements.

Under conventional milling procedures some of the hard wheats produced in the Southwest are not used alone in making bread flour. Some wheat with higher protein con-

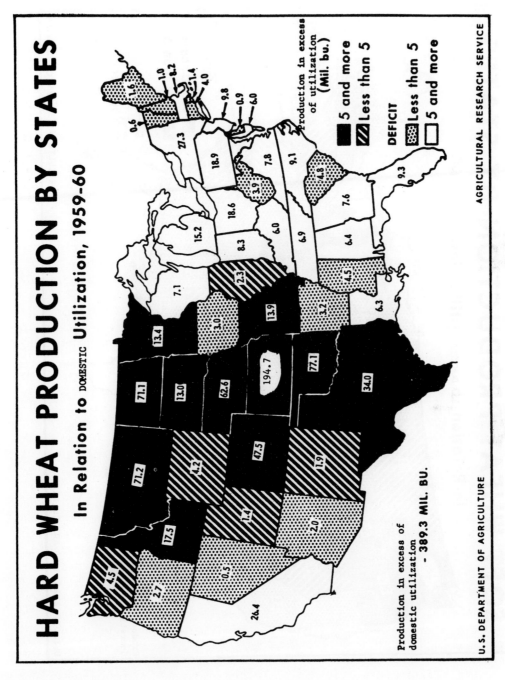

HARD WHEAT PRODUCTION BY STATES

In Relation to DOMESTIC Utilization, 1959-60

Production in excess of utilization (Mil. bu.)

■ 5 and more
▨ Less than 5

DEFICIT

▦ Less than 5
□ 5 and more

Production in excess of domestic utilization - 389.3 MIL. BU.

U.S. DEPARTMENT OF AGRICULTURE

AGRICULTURAL RESEARCH SERVICE

Figure 1

231

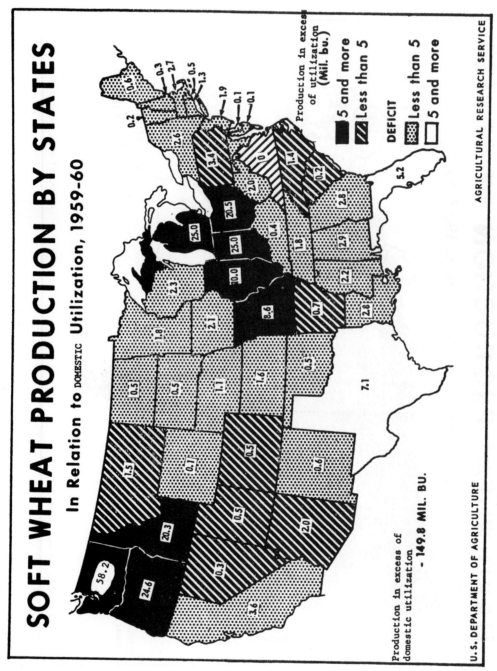

Figure 2

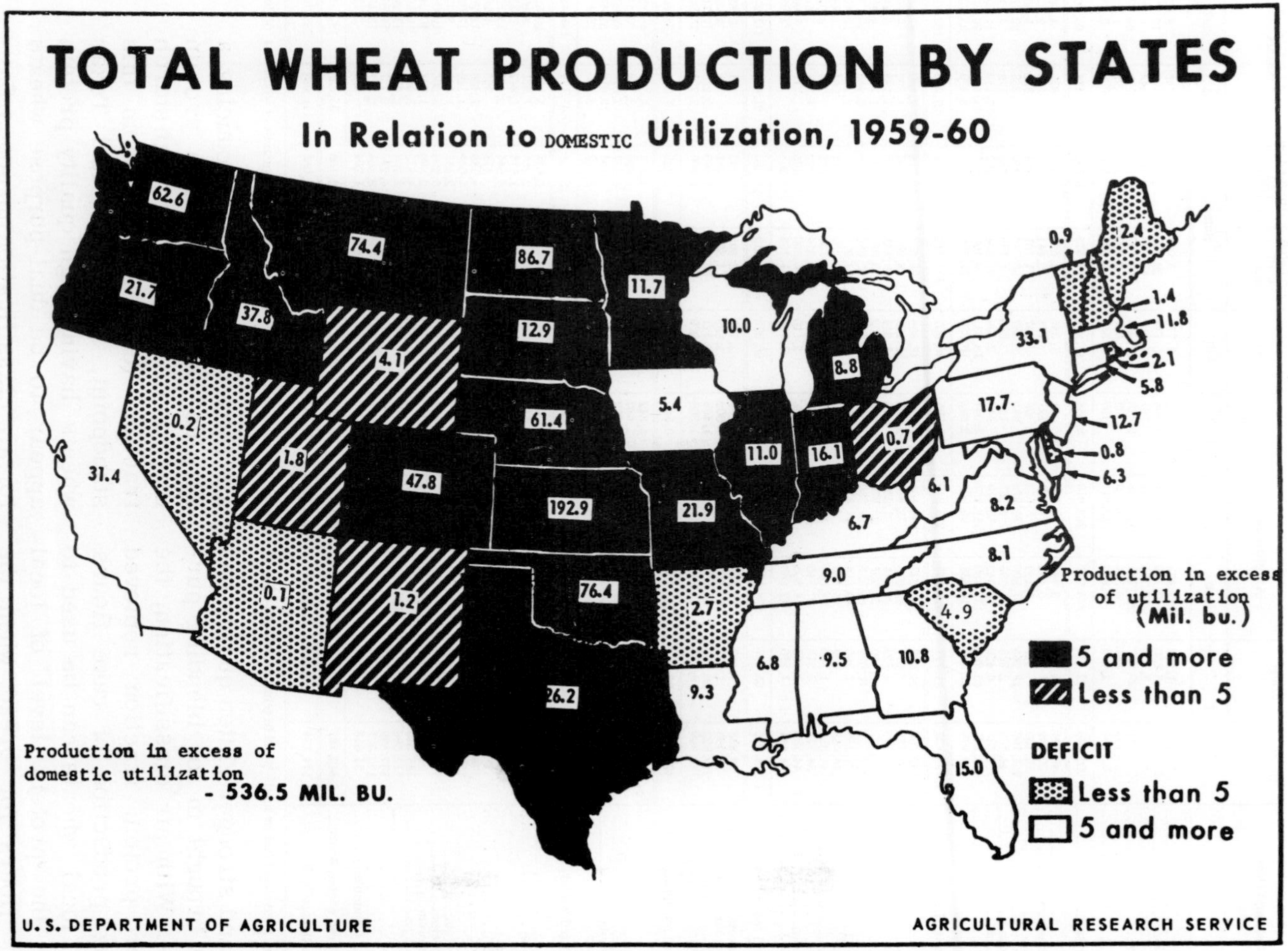
TOTAL WHEAT PRODUCTION BY STATES
In Relation to DOMESTIC Utilization, 1959-60
62.6
74.4
86.7
11.7
21.7
37.8
4.1
12.9
10.0
8.8
33.1
0.9
2.4
1.4
11.8
2.1
5.8
12.7
0.8
6.3
0.2
1.8
47.8
61.4
5.4
11.0
16.1
0.7
17.7
31.4
192.9
21.9
6.7
6.1
8.2
8.1
0.1
1.2
76.4
2.7
9.0
4.9
26.2
9.3
6.8
9.5
10.8
15.0
Production in excess of utilization (Mil. bu.)
5 and more
Less than 5
DEFICIT
Less than 5
5 and more
Production in excess of domestic utilization - 536.5 MIL. BU.
U. S. DEPARTMENT OF AGRICULTURE
AGRICULTURAL RESEARCH SERVICE

Figure 3

TABLE 2.—*Domestic disappearance of wheat flour,*

[*Thousand*

State and class	Bread	Rolls	Flour, other than mixes				Prepared flour mixes	Biscuits and muffins	Crackers	
			All purpose		Whole wheat	Cake				
	Hard	Hard	Hard	Soft	Hard	Soft	Soft	Soft	Hard	Soft
Idaho	33,192	1,218	12,463	10,540	292	1,776	5,056	241	555	3,020
Washington	142,221	5,550	47,146	39,871	1,104	6,718	20,800	1,204	2,308	12,516
Oregon	88,817	3,452	30,182	25,524	707	4,301	13,096	722	1,448	7,882
California	739,854	29,237	231,231	195,548	5,413	32,949	106,697	6,741	11,932	64,938
Nevada	14,120	541	4,397	3,719	103	627	2,022	144	223	1,216
Arizona	62,286	2,436	19,878	16,811	465	2,833	9,004	530	1,008	5,488
White A	1,080,490	42,434	345,297	292.013	8,084	49,204	156,675	9,582	17,474	95,060
Maine	48,621	2,436	9,445	7,987	221	1,346	4,526	385	839	4,567
New Hampshire	30,232	1,489	5,438	4,599	127	775	2,841	241	528	2,873
Vermont	19,130	947	4,189	3,543	98	597	1,781	144	332	1,805
Massachusetts	251,192	13,265	37,806	31,972	885	5,387	23,785	2,359	4,358	23,721
Rhode Island	44,408	2,369	6,583	5,567	154	938	4,189	433	772	4,199
Connecticut	122,635	6,429	18,942	16,019	443	2,699	11,604	1,107	2,132	11,603
New York	838,237	43,788	132,150	111,757	3,094	18,831	79,108	7,655	14,552	79,215
Michigan	443,970	21,048	114,588	96,905	2,683	16,328	52,578	3,467	6,470	35,236
White B	1,798,425	91,771	329,141	278,349	7,705	46,901	180,412	15,791	29,983	163,219
Texas	382,196	24,297	341,343	288,668	7.991	48,668	38,567	12.712	7,580	41,254
Oklahoma	89,158	5,617	85,628	72,415	2,005	12,202	8,907	2,890	1,800	9,798
Nebraska	78,796	3,722	24,874	21,036	582	3,544	9,341	530	1,184	6,446
Kansas	117,227	5,550	34,267	28,979	802	4,833	13,867	867	1,739	9,466
Missouri	232,517	11,032	67,857	57,386	1,589	9,669	27,589	1,686	3,445	18,748
Iowa	151,159	7,106	49,514	41,873	1,159	7,056	17,011	1,011	2,281	12,413
Wyoming	16,055	609	5,620	4,753	132	801	2,359	144	264	1,437
Utah	44,351	1,760	14,545	12,300	341	2,073	6,500	385	724	8,941
Colorado	84,774	3,316	27,840	23,544	652	3,967	12,374	722	1,381	7,514
New Mexico	44,238	1,692	14,805	12,520	347	2,110	6,500	385	717	3,904
Montana	34,444	1,286	12,280	10,386	288	1,750	5,104	288	562	3,056
Hard red winter	1,274,915	65,987	678,573	573,860	15,888	96,673	149,019	21,620	21,677	117,977
North Dakota	33,933	1,557	12,333	10,430	289	1,757	3,993	193	521	2,836
South Dakota	36,495	1,692	12,905	10,914	302	1,839	4,333	241	555	3,020
Wisconsin	219,862	10,355	64,007	54,129	1,498	9,121	26,048	1,589	3,255	17,717
Minnesota	185,320	8,798	55,863	47,242	1,308	7,960	21,956	1,300	2,761	15,028
Hard red spring	475,570	22,402	145,108	122,715	3,397	20,677	56,330	3,323	7,092	38,601
Illinois	571,615	27,072	142,845	120,811	3,342	20,355	67,699	4,574	8,291	45,121
Indiana	255,633	12,114	71,786	60,708	1,680	10,229	30,286	1,926	3,770	20,516
Ohio	540,871	25,651	139,800	118,226	3,272	19,921	64,086	4,237	7,878	42,874
Pennsylvania	576,796	29,644	97,311	82,294	2,275	13,866	54,120	5,104	10,010	54,477
New Jersey	300,952	15,904	45,300	38,309	1,060	6,455	28,505	2,793	5,225	28,436
Soft red winter, North	2,245,867	110,385	497,042	420,348	11,629	70,826	244,696	18,634	35,174	191,424
Florida	196,535	12,588	161,890	136,908	3,790	23,069	20,078	6,644	3,837	20,885
Mississippi	75,893	4,670	98,924	83,658	2,316	14,096	7,174	2,215	1,651	8,987
Arkansas	64,164	3,993	72,775	61,545	1,704	10,370	6,259	1,974	1,347	7,330
Louisiana	123,888	7,783	119,297	100,887	2,793	16,999	12,374	4,044	2,497	13,592
Delaware	18,447	1,218	15,976	13,510	374	2,276	1,878	578	365	1,989
Maryland	124,173	7,918	104,674	88,521	2,451	14,916	12,615	4,189	2,436	13,260
Virginia	155,999	9,813	150,806	127,534	3,531	21,489	15,000	5,055	3,140	17,091
West Virginia	75,893	4,805	75,689	64,009	1,772	10,785	7,559	2,455	1,543	8,398
North Carolina	168,581	10,490	185,723	157,063	4,348	26,465	16,467	5,296	3,506	19,080
South Carolina	91,493	5,685	96,478	81,590	2,259	13,748	9,004	2,889	1,881	10,240
Georgia	148,540	9,340	147,502	124,740	3,453	21,018	14,782	4,815	3,012	16,391
Kentucky	117,568	7,377	125,932	106,498	2,948	17,945	11,556	3,707	2,430	13,223
Tennessee	132,599	8,257	139,488	117,962	3,266	19,876	13,096	4,237	2,727	14,844
Alabama	120,301	7,512	128,352	108,545	3,005	18,290	11,796	3,804	2,477	13,481
District of Columbia	35,413	2,301	27,320	23,104	640	3,893	3,659	1.204	684	3,720
Soft red winter, South	1,649,487	103,750	1,650,826	1,396,074	38,650	235,235	163,897	53,106	33,533	182,511
Continental U.S.	8,524,754	436,729	3,645,987	3,083,359	85,353	519,516	951,029	122,056	144,933	788,792

NOTE: Conversion factors used: (1) 42.95 pounds of flour/bushel of wheat, or 71.58 pounds of flour/cwt. of wheat; or (2) 139.7 pounds of wheat/cwt. of flour;

tent and stronger gluten quality has to be brought in for blending purposes. With air classification, the higher protein fraction removed during production of cake flours from local wheats can be used to raise the protein level of local wheat flours for bread when the wheat has sufficient gluten strength. Thus the need for importing high protein wheat can be eliminated and local wheats can be used to satisfy all food uses without producing a surplus of either a high protein fraction or a low protein-high starch fraction (cake flour). From this standpoint, Oklahoma and Texas wheats having high quality protein appear to be dual-purpose wheats for air classification purposes. Savings in transportation costs would arise from eliminating the purchasing of high protein wheats as well as importing soft wheats for soft

by type of use, State, and class, 1959–1960

pounds]

Cakes	Pies	Other sweet goods		Alimentary paste products (macaroni, spaghetti, noodles)		Wheat cereals		Total		Total
Soft	Hard	Soft	Hard	Hard	Durum	Hard	Soft	Hard	Soft	Hard, Soft
819	578	1,692	1,204	1,262	3,470	2,287	456	52,961	23,690	76,651
3,804	2,600	7,445	5,296	5,195	1,429	9,582	1,907	220,551	94,716	315,267
2,311	1,589	4,636	3,298	3,270	8,997	6,012	1,197	138,524	59,920	198,444
20,511	13,771	39,152	27,854	26,558	73,098	49,359	9,825	1,132,736	478,834	1,611,570
385	241	778	554	506	1,395	943	188	21,611	9,096	30,707
1,685	1,156	3,282	2,335	2,250	6,191	4,167	830	95,772	40,672	136,444
29,515	19,935	56,985	40,541	39,041	94,580	72,350	14,403	1,662,155	706,928	2,369,083
1,733	770	2,775	1,974	2,767	7,581	2,572	512	69,676	23,800	93,476
1,059	530	1,726	1,228	1,739	4,770	1,583	315	42,862	14,461	57,323
674	289	1,083	770	1,069	2,929	1,031	205	27,879	9,808	37,687
9,438	4,670	14,991	10,665	14,795	40,546	12,901	2,568	350,193	114,565	464,758
1,685	819	2,673	1,902	2,619	7,175	2,275	453	61,853	20,185	82,038
4,574	2,263	7,275	5,176	7,202	19,734	6,316	1,257	171,374	56,302	227,676
31,153	15,311	49,608	35,292	49,098	134,546	43,264	8,612	1,173,791	386,934	1,560,725
10,786	3,467	28,628	20,366	16,080	44,239	22,439	4,467	655,906	243,600	899,506
61,102	28,119	108,759	77,373	95,369	261,520	92,381	18,389	2,553,534	869,655	3,423,189
13,241	4,045	18,239	12,976	12,125	33,142	12,654	2,519	806,425	462,650	1,269,075
3,081	915	4,230	3,009	2,844	7,774	2,974	592	194,256	113,809	308,065
1,781	530	4,974	3,539	2,832	7,787	4,282	852	121,246	47,599	168,845
2,744	867	7,478	5,320	4,226	11,626	6,188	1,232	177,477	68,175	245,652
5,441	1,685	14,822	10,545	8,381	23,054	12,267	2,442	351,910	135,191	487,101
3,370	1,011	9,509	6,765	5,421	14,907	8,328	1,658	234,477	93,068	327,545
433	289	812	578	596	1,638	1,089	217	25,177	11,011	36,188
1,204	819	2,335	1,661	1,614	4,445	2,983	594	68,653	29,477	98,130
2,311	1,541	4,467	3,178	3,088	8,499	5,703	1,135	131,221	56,286	187,507
1,156	819	2,301	1,637	1,620	4,461	2,986	594	68,706	29,625	98,331
866	578	1,792	1,276	1,288	3,543	2,352	468	54,292	23,772	78,064
35,628	13,099	70,959	50,484	44,035	120,876	61,806	12,303	2,233,840	1,070,663	3,304,503
722	193	2,132	1,517	1,210	3,329	1,949	388	53,924	22,029	75,953
770	241	2,267	1,613	1,303	3,583	2,073	413	57,592	23,384	80,976
5,152	1,589	14,009	9,967	7,927	21,798	11,587	2,306	332,460	127,618	460,078
4,285	1,300	11,776	8,378	6,673	18,352	9,895	1,970	282,394	109,419	391,813
10,929	3,323	30,184	21,475	17,113	47,062	25,504	5,077	726,370	282,450	1,008,820
14,011	4,573	36,954	26,289	20,728	57,029	28,560	5,690	839,407	309,123	1,148,530
6,067	1,925	16,344	11,628	9,228	25,387	13,300	2,647	383,855	145,932	529,787
13,145	4,236	34,854	24,797	19,590	53,896	27,326	5,444	799,242	296,966	1,096,208
21,089	10,157	33,738	24,002	33,497	91,789	29,972	5,971	813,243	271,080	1,084,323
11,315	5,584	17,935	12,759	17,721	48,562	15,543	3,076	419,640	137,232	556,872
65,627	26,475	139,825	99,475	100,764	276,663	114,701	22,828	3,255,387	1,160,333	4,415,720
6,789	2,167	9,407	6,693	6,198	16,936	6,455	1,285	400,700	224,518	625,218
2,696	578	3,452	2,456	2,488	6,810	2,627	523	192,021	122,383	314,404
2,263	578	2,978	2,119	2,075	5,676	2,181	434	151,217	92,872	244,089
4,285	1,252	5,888	4,189	3,954	10,806	4,134	823	270,234	158,445	428,679
626	193	890	626	584	1,594	609	121	38,453	21,797	60,250
4,285	1,348	5,922	4,213	3,923	10,719	4,088	814	255,585	144,161	399,746
5,393	1,589	7,377	5,248	4,979	13,611	5,207	1,037	340,852	200,036	540,888
2,648	770	3,587	2,552	2,431	6,642	2,543	506	168,263	99,682	267,945
5,922	1,541	7,851	5,585	5,439	14,875	5,710	1,137	391,648	238,556	630,204
3,178	867	4,298	3,057	2,939	8,038	3,082	613	208,115	125,186	333,301
5,152	1,493	7,005	4,983	4,749	12,986	4,971	990	328,572	194,364	522,936
4,141	1,107	5,516	3,924	3,782	10,346	3,969	790	269,522	162,891	432,413
4,622	1,252	6,226	4,430	4,261	11,653	4,467	889	301,291	181,208	482,499
4,237	1,156	5,651	4,020	3,870	10,585	4,059	808	275,227	166,137	441,364
1,204	385	1,692	1,204	1,112	3,036	1,156	230	70,318	38,603	108,921
57,441	16,276	77,730	55,299	52,784	144,313	55,258	11,000	3,662,018	2,170,839	5,832,857
260,242	107,227	484,442	344,647	349,106	945,014	422,000	84,000	14,093,304	6,260,868	20,354,172

and (3) 2.328 bushels of wheat/cwt. of flour.

wheat food uses.

It may be of interest to know how air classification of soft wheat flour is working in Australia. Soft wheat flour of 9-10 percent protein is being reground and classified; the high-protein fraction (17-18 percent) is blended with the coarse residue to give an excellent bread flour (12.5-14.0 percent). The low protein fraction (5-6 percent) is sold to bakers as cake flour, to wet processors for prime starch, to manufacturers of soups and other canned foods as a thickener, and to adhesive producers. Excellent markets are reported for the fortified bread flour, but some difficulty is encountered in disposing of all the low protein fraction.

We do not yet know what advantages, if any, air classification offers in the export markets. Where countries prefer to do their own processing, air classification of flour for exports may be limited even if there were a potential savings in transportation costs from the United States.

EXPANDING THE DEMAND FOR WHEAT

Marketing economists do not provide much encouragement for expanding the demand for wheat foods in the domestic market. Wheat as food has a relatively inelastic demand. This is another way of stating that lowering the retail price of bread will not result in increased bread consumption. We must do something more than just lower the price. In a few cases companies have carved a niche for themselves by providing higher priced products which are sold on the basis of better quality; for example, certain frozen cake and pastry products. A quality bread also is produced by a Nevada bakery which sells for 39 cents per pound loaf along the Pacific coast. This illustrates the fact that consumers will pay for quality products from wheat.

If research leading to new or improved wheat food products could merely stem the decline in per capita flour consumption, it would be the equivalent of finding a new market for over 8 million bushels of wheat each year. An additional 8-million-bushel increase is normally picked up yearly from the increase in population of approximately 3 million people. Up to the present time this increase from population growth has been offset by the average annual decline in per capita flour consumption. If wheat were $2 per bushel, stemming the decline in per capita consumption would add

$32 million a year to the wheat farmers' market. Can the air classification of wheat flour contribute to new or improved wheat food products?

New wheat products are a major field of inquiry at the Western Utilization Research and Development Division of the U.S. Department of Agriculture. For example, bulgur, or parboiled wheat, either cracked or in whole-kernel form, is well suited for use in many recipes — soups, main courses, and desserts. New, inexpensive, and convenient ways have been developed to make this product more attractive and useful to domestic and foreign consumers. New or improved wheat foods, many of which are still in the development stage, may help to maintain per capita consumption in the domestic market and expand exports.

On the basis of the calorie and protein needs in many of the countries throughout the world, it would appear that a great potential export market for wheat does exist. We need to know more about these markets — not so much what the needs are, but rather what these countries will accept and pay for. Questions for which we need answers are what it takes to make wheat products desirable in terms of the tastes, customs, and traditions of consumers in specific countries, and what quality specifications and processing requirements are essential for our wheat to meet the demands of specific importing countries. USDA research groups are working with private industry to give the wheat industry the products needed to develop markets abroad as well as at home.

Table 2 summarizes the domestic

disappearance of wheat flour, by type of use, State, and class, 1959-60. While these data do not adequately describe the wheat or flour properties required by bakers to produce specific end-use food products, they represent a step toward the recognition of differences between end food use requirements. The data do not illustrate why a shortage of bread type wheats could exist with a large carryover of hard wheats; however, they do reflect differences between regional consumption patterns of wheat foods as well as differences between urban and rural population consumption patterns within regions.

Estimates of flour consumption for individual States are based on consumption data from the 1955 Household Food Consumption Survey and related demographic data. (Conversion factors from product weight to flour equivalent are those used in the 1955 survey.) Total consumption of flour in a State was estimated by combining separate estimates for farm households and nonfarm households, using different consumption rates for each group and matching population estimates. Total flour was then distributed to the types of flour on the basis of the considered judgment of Department specialists and trade information. The same distribution was used for all States.

The Farm Population Branch, Economic Research Service, supplied unofficial estimates of farm population, by States, as of April 1959. Nonfarm population was estimated by subtracting farm population from total population, by States, July 1, 1959, as reported in Series P-25, No. 210, of the Current Population Report, U.S. Bureau of the Census.

State consumption rates for flour and flour products, for lack of other data, are estimated to be the same as rates for the same population group (i.e., farm and nonfarm) for the region as a whole in which the State is located.

Table 3: Estimates of flour composition of food groups, 1959-60

Product	Wheat flour		
	Hard	Soft	Durum
	Per-cent	Per-cent	Per-cent
Bread.	100	—	—
Rolls	100	—	—
Biscuits and muffins	—	100	—
Crackers	15	85	—
Cakes.	—	100	—
Pies.	—	100	—
Other sweet goods . .	58	42	—
Alimentary paste products	26	—	74
Flour:			
All purpose	54	46	—
Whole wheat. . . .	100	—	—
Cake.	—	100	—
Prepared mixes. .	—	100	—
Wheat cereals	83	17	—

Source: See footnote 1, table 1.

Further breakdown by type of flour was done by estimating the overall flour composition of each product group based upon estimates of the several types of flour normally used in each food item of the product mix of these groups (Table 3). Finally, minor adjustments of consumption by type of flour were made using a constant factor for each flour type to make the total of consumption in individual States agree with U.S. consumption.

TOBACCO: AN INDUSTRY IN TRANSITION

by
GENE McMURTRY*

The winds of change are blowing across the tobacco fields of Virginia and the industry finds itself in the greatest period of transition since, perhaps, the early days of the colonies. The questions of health, loss of export markets, the mounting surplus, and the acreage-poundage program have resulted in widespread awareness that the tobacco industry is in transition. The exact shape and outcome of this transition, however, is yet to be determined.

The tobacco crop contributes over $100 million to the Virginia farm economy and is the State's number one cash crop. It is the mainstay of the economy in Southside Virginia and to a lesser extent in Southwest Virginia. Tobacco processing and manufacturing has been the number one employer in the Richmond area.

Government programs born of the 1930's are undergoing change. An acreage-poundage program was approved by the flue-cured tobacco farmers by nearly a three to one margin in May 1965. Not since the 1938 referendum had flue-cured growers been given a choice other than (1) a continuation of acreage-allotments or (2) no controls. The earlier tobacco program with its system of acreage-allotments has been held by many as the "ideal" supply control method. Why, after 25 years, did Congress and the growers vote for a method supply control based primarily on pounds of tobacco sold (within the limitations of allotted acres)? To answer this question, let us look at the tobacco situation. Most growers and others concerned with this crop knew that flue-cured tobacco was in serious trouble. In spite of the 10 percent cut in the 1964 acreage, the crop was 17 million pounds larger than the 1963 crop. Of the 886 million pounds of Stabilization stocks on hand on August 1, 1965, about 80 percent was from the last 3 crop years (see Figure 1).

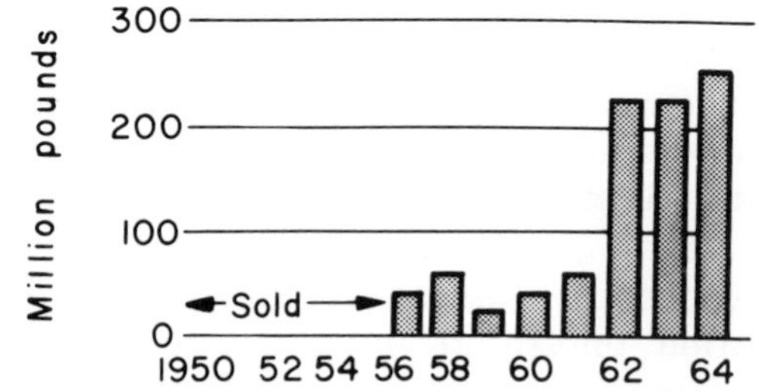

Figure 1. Stocks of flue-cured tobacco (August 1965)

*The author is Associate Extension Economist, Public Affairs, Agricultural Extension Service of the Virginia Polytechnic Institute.

"Tobacco: An Industry in Transition" by Gene McMurtry. Reprinted from University of Virginia News Letter, Vol. 42 (October 15, 1965), pp. 5-8, with permission of author and editor.

Burley production and supplies have literally skyrocketed since 1961 (see Figure 2). In 1964 nearly 18 percent of the burley crop went under loan, with approximately 340 million pounds on hand compared with only 96 million pounds 2 years earlier. Currently, the total stocks of both flue-cured and burley tobaccos are at all-time high levels.

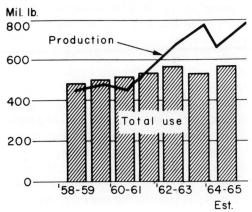

Figure 2. Production and total use of burley tobacco

At one time it would have been possible to adjust supplies by applying acreage-allotment cuts early and with sufficient severity. History has demonstrated the difficulty of this type of action when a program has become immeshed with political considerations.

Flue-cured growers in December 1964 turned out in record numbers and voted overwhelmingly (96.5 percent) for a 19 1/2 percent cut in acreage-allotments. During the months that followed there was much discussion, sometimes heated, of the merits of switching over to an acreage-poundage program as a method of controlling production.

The reduction of 19 1/2 percent for flue-cured tobacco in 1965 would not have reduced substantially the total stocks on hand. The compulsion for even higher yields under the acreage-allotment system would have meant a continued deterioration in the quality of the U.S. leaf, resulting in smaller export sales and having a detrimental effect on the domestic market. Most growers finally realized that another year of large amounts going into loan stocks resulting in heavy government expenditures would, if left unchecked, eventually destroy the tobacco program.

THE ACREAGE-POUNDAGE PROGRAM

In May 1965 the acreage-poundage program by a margin of almost 3 to 1 was approved to become effective for the 1965, 1966, and 1967 crops. Only in Virginia and North Carolina did the vote exceed two-thirds in favor of the acreage-poundage proposal. In Georgia, fewer than 14 percent of the flue-cured growers voted for the program in May in contrast with the 81 percent in the December 1964 referendum. North Carolina cast more than half the total ballots in the May referendum.

A number of growers, especially in South Carolina, Georgia, and Florida, apparently did not clearly understand the provisions of the acreage-poundage program nor what it would mean to them. There developed a strong feeling among some growers that this program would jeopardize their position in terms of Type 14 tobacco, and any change in the program would be to their disadvantage. In contrast, growers in the Middle and Old Belts felt that the acreage-poundage program would give them a somewhat greater advantage than the current acreage-allotment program.

Farm organizations play a major role in the failure or passage of a program or referendum. In the two states where the referendum carried, Farm Bureau and Grange leadership actively supported the program, although there was some Farmers Union opposition in Virginia. In the three states where the referendum failed to receive the necessary two-thirds "yes" votes, the Farm Bureau opposed the acreage-poundage program. A part of this opposition was "on principle." It was felt that this type of control was bad, rather than that acreage-poundage legislation was bad.

Under the acreage-poundage program, farm marketing quotas are stated in pounds along with matching acreage allotments. This differs from the acreage-allotment program where there is no limit on the quantity a grower can market with price support, so long as he complies with his farm acreage allotment. Most growers recognized that under an acreage-allotment and price support program, higher yields meant larger income. Thus, the growers were faced with a pocketbook dilemma in choosing between growing a crop of "quality" tobacco or a crop of "high yield" tobacco on their restricted acres. The income opportunity from continued cuts in allotments nudged the majority of growers toward the "high yield" decision.

Under the acreage-poundage program the emphasis has been shifted from extremely high yields to more moderate yields of quality tobacco, in an effort to obtain the greatest return per pound sold rather than per acre. Determination of farm yields was dependent upon the individual grower's yields during a five-year period, as well as those of his neighbors. Each grower selected his best three out of five years (1959-63). Then adjustments were made on the basis of community yields.

A grower under the acreage-poundage program can market up to 110 percent of his quota if he has been within his acreage allotment. There is no penalty except that his next year's quota will be reduced by the amount overmarketed in 1965. One of the most emphasized features of this program is the under-marketing provision under which tobacco not produced in 1965 may be added to the total allotment for 1966. This provides a type of insurance against crop damage, drought, insects, hail, fire, etc., and can be of special benefit to the smaller grower or part-time farmer because it allows a full crop to be produced every other year. The program reduces the insecurity of small crop yields, and has an advantage over the old acreage-allotment system where the action of other growers could substantially affect the size of allotment (via average cuts) that a farmer could plant the following year.

DOMESTIC AND WORLD CONSUMPTION

The storm cloud of the Surgeon General's Smoking and Health Report is still on the horizon, although most American consumers are once again picking up their packs, pipes, and cigars. Cigarette consumption was off three and one-half percent in 1964 but today cigarette consumption is at record levels (see Figure 3).

The newly passed cigarette labeling and advertising act will take effect on January 1, 1966. This act requires a conspciuous label on every cigarette package reading as follows: "Caution: Cigarette smoking may be hazardous to your health." This warning statement will not apply to newspaper, TV, and radio advertising.

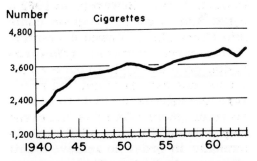

Figure 3. Per capita cigarette consumption, 1940-65

From 1955 to 1963 cigarette consumption grew faster than the population. There was a switch, however, to filter cigarettes which accounted for only 1.5 per cent of the cigarettes sold in 1952 as against 61 percent in 1965. It is obvious, though, that total sales in the years ahead would have been higher if there had been no health scare.

The percentage rise in world consumption of cigarettes averaged five percent annually during most of the 1950's. Recently, there has been a slowing of this annual rate of increase. Even with a smaller rate of increase, however, by 1975 world consumption of cigarettes is likely to be nearly one-third larger than in 1964.

World consumption of the blended cigarette, developed in the U.S., continues upward. The main constituents of the blended cigarette have been and still are flue-cured and burley tobaccos. The high accep-

tance has been caused by good smoking qualities, including flavor and aroma.

Although there has been a rise in domestic cigarette consumption, there has been a downward trend in the amount of leaf tobacco per thousand cigarettes manufactured. Total production of cigarettes was 541 billion pieces in 1964, but the manufacturers used about the same amount of leaf as was required to produce 436 billion pieces in 1952. The introduction of new manufacturing techniques and the increased proportion of filter tip cigarettes will continue to hold domestic leaf usage considerably below what would be expected from any increase in cigarette consumption. The consumption of cigars and smoking tobacco greatly increased in 1964.

EXPORTS OF U.S. LEAF

U.S. tobacco exports, including both manufactured and unmanufactured tobacco products, have in recent years totaled nearly one-half billion dollars per year. This is about 10 percent of the value of all agricultural shipments. Eighty-two percent of all tobacco exported was sold for dollars. The future of U.S. exports will depend to a large extent on the trend in world cigarette output.

Flue-cured exports have maintained a nearly constant poundage total over the last several years but have failed to share in the increasing overseas market. Our competitors — Rhodesia, Canada, and India — have increased their production and are also improving quality. At the same time, U.S. tobacco export prices are increasing. Burley exports are expected to reach an all-time high in 1965. However, about 40 countries are growing burley for export compared with half that number a decade ago.

Western Europe has traditionally been the best market for our tobacco, absorbing nearly three-fourths of our exports. The United Kingdom is our largest market for flue-cured tobacco. Per capita consumption in most West European countries is increasing. As incomes rise, it appears that sales of cigarettes made of flue and burley tobaccos will increase at the expense of cigarettes made mostly of dark tobaccos. This will provide a larger market for U.S. leaf. The U.S. has not shared in the expansion of this market, however, even though our total pounds exported has remained nearly constant (see Figure 4).

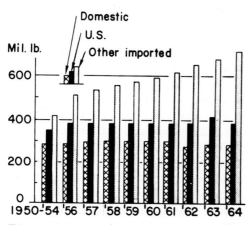

Figure 4. Use of leaf tobacco in Western Europe, 1950-64

A tobacco allotment is the legal right to produce and market tobacco. As such it has a value to the buyer or seller of a tobacco farm. The sale price attributable to the allotment represents a payment for a part of the benefits to be derived in future years from the tobacco program. Currently, the value of an allotment is between $1,500 and $4,000 per acre depending on the area and yield history. Under the acreage-poundage program the value will be calculated on the basis of so much per pound.

In order for a grower to expand his tobacco allotment, it has been necessary for him to purchase other tobacco farms. However, in 1962 a lease and transfer program came into effect which allowed the renting of flue-cured allotments. (This provision does not apply to burley.) As allotments have been cut, the pressure has increased either to rent to or from others. There is increased emphasis on obtaining additional allotments in order to achieve a unit of economical size. This pressure was quite pronounced in the flue-cured area during 1965 when an acre of allotment rented from $300 to $500.

PRICES AND THE GROWER

The lot of the small tobacco farmers, tenants, and sharecroppers are stitched inseparably to changes in government programs. This not only includes agricultural programs but others as well. The use of minimum wage legislation as it applies to agricultural workers will speed transition in the tobacco area. Since tobacco requires so much labor, a minimum wage of $1.15 per hour will put a squeeze on profits since this is 10 to 30 cents more than is currently being paid. Thus, farmers must increase the productivity of their labor which usually means a need for larger operating units and the attendant problem of obtaining additional allotments and poundage quotas.

Higher production costs will mean

that additional emphasis will be given to the level of support prices. Increases in the "Index of Prices Paid" and the change in the grade distribution under the 10-year moving average has meant a 2.2 cents increase in overall price supports for the years 1964 and 1965. Under the present formula the net change in grade rates, from changes in both loan level and grade distribution, will mean an increase of between one and one and one-half cents per year (see Figure 5).

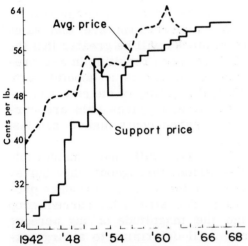

Figure 5. Support price and average price for flue-cured tobacco

These increases will have real meaning in terms of expanding our export markets under our present

levels of price supports. About one-third of our flue-cured tobacco is exported, compared to one-tenth for burley. The difference in price levels between U.S. flue-cured tobacco and that of our major competitors has continued to widen as shown in the accompanying table.

A TWO-PRICE PLAN

In the next few months there will be considerable discussion, and perhaps some new legislation will be submitted which will permit the sale of tobacco at a lower price under a basic two-price plan. Most two-price plans provide that the price to domestic companies would be significantly higher than the price export companies would have to pay. This would be accomplished under several different proposals or formulas, but all would require lowering support prices. This would make our leaf more competitive, with expanded sales to foreign markets. Growers' incomes would depend upon price differentials between domestic and export tobacco, amount of foreign sales, and cost of production. The need is to move more tobacco from the large amounts currently in loan stocks.

The two-price proposal being actively discussed is one similar to

Prices of Flue-Cured Exports from Major Exporting Countries							
Country	1950-54	1955-59	1960	1961	1962	1963	1964*
			(Cents per pound)				
United States	63.4	71.1	77.2	79.4	80.8	82.1	83
Canada	55.6	61.3	71.1	72.9	67.1	71.7	68
Rhodesia-Western Zambia . .	58.1	57.6	57.1	59.2	54.8	63.3	49
India	31.9	32.2	36.6	32.0	30.6	36.1	31

*Estimate

the current wheat program. Under this type of program, new price supports may be at the 43 or 45 cent level. At this level, American flue-cured tobacco would compete favorably with tobacco from foreign exporting countries. All companies, either domestic or export, would purchase tobacco on the auction markets under this set of support prices. However, in addition to purchasing tobacco on the auction market, domestic companies would be required to purchase certificates for tobacco they use. The value of these certificates, perhaps 15 to 20 cents per pound, would be allocated back to the farmer based on pounds marketed. Under the plan, the certificate provision would require domestic companies to purchase their tobacco at significantly higher than present prices. This higher cost to the tobacco manufacturing firm would in all likelihood be passed on to the consumer in the form of higher prices for cigarettes. In effect, cigarette smokers, rather than the general public, would be carrying a larger share of the support program.

VIRGINIA GROWERS FACE THE FUTURE

Until recently, tobacco growers have been able to say the tobacco program has not cost anyone a cent. In order to move crops from inventory, however, some adjustments in price and carrying charges had to be made. Tobacco under loan is collateral for the government loans with which growers are paid. As the collateral becomes less saleable (valuable), losses of taxpayers' monies are inevitable. There were large losses ($80 million) on the

1955-56 flue-cured crop with only nominal losses for burley. There also may be substantial losses on the 1962, 1963, and 1964 crops currently in storage. The cost of the tobacco program has been small, however, when compared with the total price support program on all agricultural commodities.

Even under an acreage-poundage program a period of time will be required for the reduction of present loan stocks. As of August 1965, more than twice as much tobacco has been sold from flue-cured stocks as was sold during all of 1964. Expectations are that sales from stocks will be greater than the 1965 receipts resulting in a net reduction which is a hopeful sign. Also, the quality of the crop has increased and prices paid are currently seven cents higher than last year.

This fall will find considerable discussion throughout the burley area on the acreage-poundage program. The size of the current crop and the magnitude of any acreage cuts will determine to a large extent whether the burley growers will vote for an acreage-poundage program as a method of supply control.

For flue-cured growers the acreage-poundage program must be considered a significant step in the attainment of a more effective method of supply control and the improvement of the overall quality of the crop. The quality advantage of U.S. tobaccos traditionally has allowed us to compete successfully in export trade, as well as in the domestic market. If the American crop is "low in quality," foreign buyers can do just as well or better in other markets. The long-term effect would be detrimental to the U.S. tobacco industry.

The shape of the future will be influenced by our quarter-century of experience with acreage allotments and now with the acreage-poundage program. Although the future of U.S. tobaccos might not appear to be optimistic, neither is it darkly depressing. Maintenance and improvement of our quality are essential. We must continue to be skilled and determined merchandisers, especially in our export markets.

The fund of tobacco knowledge from 350 years of development has made our tobacco the best that is grown, and a recognized standard of quality. However, problems are not new to the tobacco industry. Only with confidence and a determination to make the necessary adjustments will the economic future of the American tobacco industry be secure.

COTTON IN THE SAN JOAQUIN VALLEY

A STUDY OF GOVERNMENT IN AGRICULTURE

DAVID C. LARGE

RECENT studies in agricultural geography hardly accentuate sufficiently the governmental factor in modern agriculture in highly organized states. Dunn's work,[1] for example—an economist's analysis of the problems of agricultural economics, but valuable to the geographer— postulates the normal working of the market as a major factor in location; Weaver's studies of crop combinations in the Middle West,[2] landmarks in the agricultural geography of the United States, are analyses of patterns at a series of points in time. Neither of these writers hints at the great changes and widespread repercussions that result from government intervention in agriculture.

The most spectacular of such changes in the farming pattern of the United States occur when the Secretary of Agriculture is required, by law, to declare a national marketing quota for a given crop.[3] In 1954 "acreage allotments" in cotton planting had automatically to be applied, since the "normal supply" of cotton for the year had been overproduced in the growing season 1953–1954; in consequence, the national acreage of cotton under cultivation in July, 1954, was five and a half million acres less than in July, 1953. A report prepared in January, 1954, for the Giannini Foundation of Agricultural Economics[4] showed how states, and counties within the states, that had only recently increased their acreages of cotton would suffer disproportionately if the impending cuts were to be based on the average of a long period of years. It will be seen from Table I that the states of the West, where cotton is produced entirely under irrigation, did indeed experience generally a greater proportionate cut in acreage than the older-established states of the Cotton Belt, though *production* was not thereby reduced by as large a percentage as the average for the country.

---

[1] E. S. Dunn, Jr.: The Location of Agricultural Production (Gainesville, Fla., 1954).

[2] J. C. Weaver: Changing Patterns of Cropland Use in the Middle West, *Econ. Geogr.,* Vol. 30, 1954, pp. 1–47; *idem:* Crop-Combination Regions in the Middle West, *Geogr. Rev.,* Vol. 44, 1954, pp. 175–200; *idem:* Crop-Combination Regions for 1919 and 1929 in the Middle West, *ibid.,* pp. 560–572.

[3] Agricultural Adjustment Act of 1938 as amended. The specified commodities are now corn, wheat, tobacco, cotton, rice, and peanuts.

[4] T. R. Hedges and C. O. McCorkle, Jr.: Cotton Quotas and Allotments and California Farm Adjustments in 1954, *Giannini Foundation of Agric. Economics Mimeographed Rept. No. 161,* University of California, College of Agriculture, Berkeley, 1954.

➤ MR. LARGE is a Lecturer in Geography in the University of Southampton, England, specializing in the geography of North America.

"Cotton in the San Joaquin Valley" by David C. Large. Reprinted from Geographical Review, *Vol. XLVII (July 1957), pp. 365-380, with permission of the editor.*

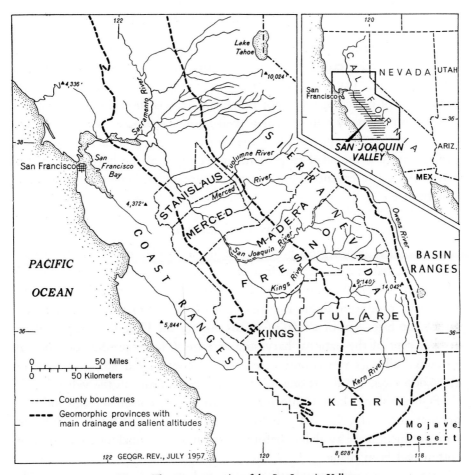

FIG. 1—The cotton counties of the San Joaquin Valley.

TABLE I—ACREAGE, YIELD, AND PRODUCTION OF COTTON IN THE COTTON STATES, 1953 AND 1954*
(*Acreage in thousands. Lint yield in pounds.*
Production in thousands of bales of 500 pounds gross weight.)

STATE	ACREAGE HARVESTED			LINT YIELD PER ACRE		PRODUCTION IN BALES		
	1953	1954	% of 1953	1953	1954	1953	1954	% of 1953
North Carolina	775	545	71.5	278	319	449	364	81.0
South Carolina	1,175	830	70.8	281	288	690	501	72.6
Georgia	1,375	1,025	75.0	262	286	752	612	81.4
Tennessee	950	648	66.7	354	405	702	548	78.0
Alabama	1,620	1,170	72.5	285	298	963	728	75.5
Mississippi	2,490	1,960	78.5	410	384	2,129	1,571	73.9
Missouri	555	450	81.0	386	478	449	450	100
Arkansas	2,070	1,700	68.6	358	380	1,548	1,351	97.6
Louisiana	950	688	72.2	407	399	806	572	71.0
Oklahoma	1,020	930	91.5	205	151	437	293	75.6
Texas	8,900	7,730	84.4	233	244	4,317	3,940	91.0
New Mexico	315	204	65.0	497	743	327	316	96.7
Arizona	690	420	62.0	743	1,039	1,070	911	85.1
California	1,340	883	66.7	632	806	1,768	1,487	94.5
Other States	116	68	59.7	242	367	58	52	89.7
United States	24,341	19,251	78.2	324	341	16,465	13,696	83.1

* Estimates, based on figures supplied by the California Crop and Livestock Reporting Service, California Department of Agriculture, Sacramento, May, 1955.

Such enormous changes, and their ramifying effects on farms throughout the country, may create havoc in the patterns of farming established in "normal" years. Price supports for strategic crops, and consequent government control of acreage, are not new; the artificial boosting of sugar-beet production in many countries is a well-known example. But as we have noted, little has been published on the subject in geographical literature. The present study is intended to provide an example of the effects of a major governmental intervention on a particular area where one crop is of major significance.

COTTON IN CALIFORNIA

Cotton has gained great prominence in California. In 1953 nearly 20 per cent of the state's cash receipts from farm marketings derived from the sale of cotton, which thus ranks first among the crops in value.[5] In that year California produced about 10.7 per cent of the national output of cotton (1,768,000 bales, out of a total of 16,465,000 for the United States) on about 5.5 per cent of the national harvested acreage. Of this production, the San Joaquin Valley (seven counties; see Fig. 1) contributed 86.7 per cent, on 1,176,000 acres,[6] or about one-third of all land in crops in the valley.[7]

Figure 2 shows how California has increased its cotton acreage and production since 1910, the first year for which Bureau of the Census figures on state production are available; before 1910, only occasional attempts to grow cotton had been made.

From 1910 until 1924 both acreage and production were small. The downward trend in yield per acre during this period was associated with unsuccessful efforts to grow long-staple cotton during and after World War I.[8] Almost all of the production, in fact, was long-staple cotton in Imperial and Riverside Counties. By 1925 it had become apparent that an upland cotton, the Acala variety, was best suited to California's soil and climate. The production of long-staple American-Egyptian cotton in California has since been trivial (300 and 200 bales in 1953 and 1954). In 1925 a law was passed by the California Legislature designating the San Joaquin Valley and Riverside County a one-variety district in order to safeguard the quality of the

---

[5] Hedges and McCorkle, *op. cit.* Cotton first gained the lead in 1947.

[6] Figures from California Crop and Livestock Reporting Service, California Department of Agriculture, Sacramento, to whom I am indebted for their assistance.

[7] For a brief account of California agriculture see Michel Tabuteau: Le peuplement rural et l'exploitation agricole en Californie, *Annales de Géogr.,* Vol. 62, 1953, pp. 452–457.

[8] G. J. Harrison: History of Cotton Culture in California, *California Farmer,* San Francisco, Dec. 15, 1951.

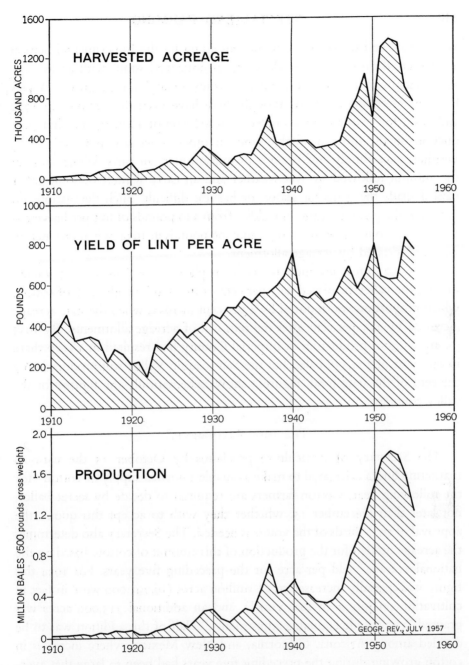

FIG. 2—Cotton in California—acreage, yield, and production, 1910–1955. Sources: California Cotton Statistics, U. S. Dept. of Agriculture (Washington, 1951), and California Crop and Livestock Reporting Service.

Acala strain and to permit constant upgrading by the Experimental Station at Shafter, Kern County. Acala 4-42, an improved strain with an average staple length of $1\frac{1}{8}$ inches, is now the only upland cotton grown. Yields have increased spectacularly, though there have been fluctuations. In 1950 and 1954, for example, yields reflected restriction of acreage, and thus production on the more profitable land; at other times late and cool spring weather, exceedingly hot periods in midsummer, an early killing frost in the autumn followed by wet weather and an early winter, or some other hazard made the growing season or harvest difficult. Such fluctuations do not mask the great increases in yields—from 339 pounds of lint per harvested acre in 1925 to 632 pounds in 1953 and 806 pounds in 1954, when production was concentrated by acreage allotment.

Since 1925 most production has taken place in the San Joaquin Valley. In 1950 the valley furnished 99.3 per cent of the state's production of cotton, which proportion was reduced by 4 per cent in 1951, when the state acreage increased by 115 per cent after the removal of acreage allotments. By 1953 the upswing of production in Imperial County had resulted in a crop there in that year of 174,558 bales, but the San Joaquin Valley still produced 86.7 per cent of the state total. Figure 3 shows schematically the figures for the valley counties.

THE 1954 ALLOTMENTS[9]

The Secretary of Agriculture proclaims by October 15 the national marketing quota calculated to make available a normal supply of cotton[10] for the following year. Cotton farmers are required to decide by secret ballot, not later than December 15, whether they wish to accept this quota; the approval of two-thirds of the voters is needed. The Secretary also determines the acreage needed for the production of this amount of cotton, based on the national average yield per acre for the preceding five years. For 1954 this figure was specially increased to 21 million acres (19,791,000 were in fact in cultivation on July 1 of that year[11]), and an additional 315,000 acres was granted "to provide equitable adjustments." Half of this addition was to be divided among Arizona, California, and New Mexico, where increases in cotton growing during the preceding five years had been so large that averaging would have resulted in excessive reductions in the allotted acreages.

---

[9] Commodity Stabilization Service, "Compilation of Statutes . . . as of January 1, 1955," *U. S. Dept. of Agric., Agricultural Handbook No. 79,* Washington [1955].

[10] Quotas for long-staple cotton are calculated separately from those for upland cotton.

[11] California Crop and Livestock Reporting Service, May, 1955.

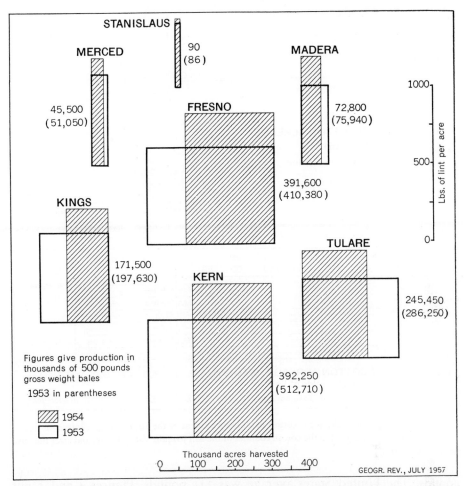

FIG. 3—Changes in acreage, yield, and production of cotton in the San Joaquin Valley counties for 1953 (white) and 1954 (shaded). Horizontal scale indicates acreage, vertical scale yield; blocks are proportionate to production.

Acreages were allotted by county, and then to individual cotton farmers, by a complex system, the net result of which was to reduce the acreage of cotton in the San Joaquin Valley in 1954 by almost a third (to 67.6 per cent of the 1953 total) and production by almost a sixth. However, some land less suited to cotton had been removed from cultivation for this crop, and production was concentrated on the better land, with a resultant increase in per acre yield.[12] The yield of 916 pounds of lint per harvested acre in 1954 in Kern County was exceeded only by the yield in Arizona, 1039

[12] Local conditions during the growing season undoubtedly also had some effect in changing yields. Poor yields in, for example, Mississippi, Louisiana, Oklahoma, and Texas were associated with bad weather; in California growing conditions were favorable.

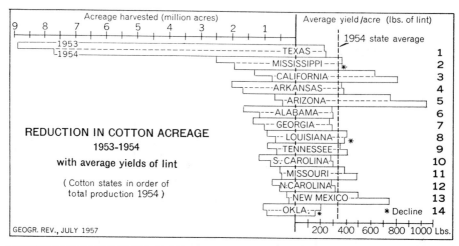

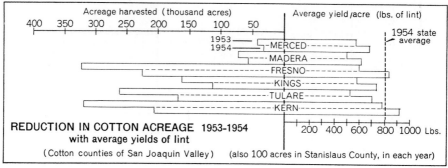

Fig. 4—Acreage and yield in the cotton states before and after the 1954 acreage allotment.

Fig. 5—Acreage and yield in the cotton counties of the San Joaquin Valley before and after the 1954 acreage allotment.

pounds. The United States average was 341 pounds. Figures 4 and 5 put these changes into the national perspective and show details of the San Joaquin counties. It will be seen that in most states and in all the cotton-growing counties of the San Joaquin Valley yields increased (including Stanislaus County, where yield increased by 3 per cent). Compare these yields with the increase in yield in California in 1950, Figure 2, when cotton acreage had been curtailed.

Some 381,000 acres of cotton land in the San Joaquin Valley alone was diverted in 1954 from producing its most profitable crop. California produced about 10.9 per cent of the nation's cotton on 4.6 per cent of the national harvested acreage, as compared with 10.7 per cent on 5.5 per cent in 1953. The cotton farmers of the valley faced a cut of about 14 per cent in their collective income from cotton, assuming stable support prices. What effect did this have on the farms and on the pattern of farming?

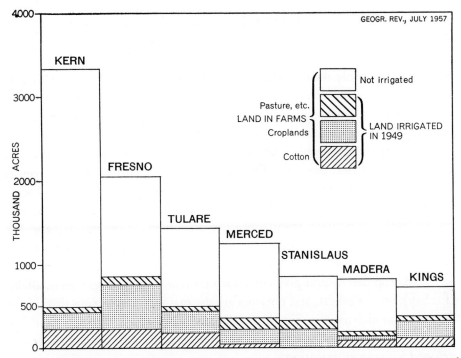

FIG. 6—Irrigated and nonirrigated land in the cotton counties in 1949, showing proportion of irrigated land in cotton and in other uses. Source: Census of Agriculture, 1950.

TABLE II—IRRIGATION IN THE SAN JOAQUIN VALLEY COTTON COUNTIES, 1950*

COUNTY	NUMBER OF FARMS IRRIGATED	PERCENTAGE ON ALL FARMS	FARMS IRRIGATING ALL CROPS	NUMBER OF "COTTON FARMS"	COTTON ACREAGE, ALL IRRIGATED FARMS
Kern	2,156	83.0	1,985	1,498	227,027
Fresno	9,211	90.8	8,209	2,571	226,592
Tulare	6,401	90.6	5,562	2,209	179,678
Merced	3,903	91.1	3,082	225	36,868
Stanislaus	6,100	92.3	4,422	18	1,475
Madera	1,537	80.9	1,273	837	66,327
Kings	1,863	91.6	1,619	884	115,568

* Based on the 1950 Census of Agriculture. "Cotton farms" are those on which cotton amounted in value to 50 per cent or more of the value of all farm products sold. The census material under this class is estimated from a sample that includes all "large farms" and one-fifth of all remaining farms (U. S. Census of Agriculture: 1950, Vol. 1, Part 33, California [1952]).

COTTON AND IRRIGATION

Cotton, which has a high value and gives a good income in all normal years in California, is a strong competitor for irrigated land (Fig. 6). Besides the farms classed by the Census of Agriculture as "cotton farms" (Table II), a large number of other farms produce cotton (a total of 141,000 acres in the San Joaquin Valley in 1949).

Farmland in the San Joaquin Valley is severely limited. Major hazards of slope—and thus of rapid erosion in this semiarid climate—and of poor drainage in the seasonally inundated river lands confine cultivable land to the floor of the valley away from the floodable areas and to the low-lying terraces on its east side.[13] Not all of this land has an adequate supply of moisture for crops,[14] and only the irrigable land is capable of bearing cotton.[15] Climatic factors, in particular excessive precipitation at planting time and early frosts during harvest, make uneconomic the large-scale extension of cotton growing onto suitable land in the northern counties of the valley.[16]

Much of the cultivable land is of course given over to the traditional crops of the district, especially fruit and vegetables; cotton, a field crop, is rarely an alternative to tree or bush fruits, but it may compete for land with vegetable field crops such as tomatoes. On the larger cotton farms there is no effective competition from other irrigated field crops; the demand for high-price fruit and vegetables is virtually inelastic, and land forced out of cotton by the imposition of acreage allotments can seldom be planted with any field crop that would give equal cash returns. Barley, sugar beets, alfalfa (for hay), winter wheat, and potatoes are the main irrigated crops that might be grown as alternatives, but these relatively low-priced products need less irrigation water and thus cannot be grown as profitably on land fully developed for cotton irrigation.[17]

The problem of the alternative use of irrigated land is acute in the newly irrigated areas of the western part of the valley, where "cropland expansion . . . is being accomplished at a very considerable financial outlay, largely for providing irrigation water. A high gross income per acre, such as that from cotton at recent prices and yields, is essential to justify such investments."[18] Even older lands in these areas, where cotton acreage has been expanded at

---

[13] For an earlier study of California soils see H. J. Wood: The Agricultural Value of California Soils, *Geogr. Rev.*, Vol. 29, 1939, pp. 310–313; see especially the map of soil types of the San Joaquin Valley, Fig. 2, on p. 313.

[14] See "The Report of the President's Water Resources Policy Commission," Vol. 2, Ten Rivers in America's Future (Washington, 1950), pp. 79–158 (No. 2, The Central Valley of California).

[15] "Water used by [cotton] plants is around 29 acre inches per acre in the San Joaquin Valley" (A. G. George: Cotton Culture and Costs for Tulare County (University of California, Agricultural Extension Service, Visalia, Calif. [1953]), p. 6.)

[16] For an early mention of the advance of irrigation for fruit and vegetables west of the river in Stanislaus County see S. N. Dicken: Dry Farming in the San Joaquin, California, *Econ. Geogr.*, Vol. 8, 1932, pp. 94–99.

[17] The international repercussions of these changes in the volume and prices of American cotton (and of alternative crops, such as sugar beets, subject to acreage control under the Sugar Act of 1948) are discussed in "Individual Commodity Problems and Policies" in "California Agriculture and International Commodity Developments," *Federal Reserve Bank of San Francisco Monthly Rev.*, January, 1954, supplement, pp. 14–17.

[18] T. R. Hedges and W. R. Bailey: Appraisal of California Agricultural Productive Capacity Attainable in 1955, *Giannini Foundation of Agric. Economics Mimeographed Rept. No. 130*, 1952, p. 10.

the expense of another crop (such as barley, which may be grown on the same farm as an irrigated winter crop), have required supplementary investment in irrigation equipment—equipment surplus to requirements if the cotton acreage is reduced. It may be that the drain on water available for irrigation pumps here is excessive, and that a forced decrease in cotton acreage would indeed be the best thing that could happen if there is to be any hope that water supplies may be conserved.

In 1953 some 450,000 acres in this part of the valley were being irrigated by wells up to 2000 feet deep, and the water table was rapidly dropping.[19] Proposals have been made for bringing in Sacramento River water from the delta in winter and early spring via the Delta-Mendota Canal, at present used in summer and autumn to bring in water to balance the low water of the San Joaquin at this the maximum irrigation season. The water would be stored in a reservoir on San Luis Creek, near Los Banos, which would feed southward for about 120 miles, in already developed land needing additional supplies. A second stage would be a further expansion, with a reservoir at Avenal Gap (Kings County, southwest of Tulare Lake) and a main delivery canal for another 50 miles to a point near Buena Vista Lake. It is unlikely that the cost of water delivered from this proposed extension of the Central Valley Project would be less than the present cost of private pumping.[20] Pending the eventual, and still problematical, arrival of ditch irrigation, the restriction of production of well-water cotton by the imposition of acreage controls is thus genuinely furthering the aims of the 1938 Agricultural Adjustment Act, which in part are the "conserving of national resources, preventing the wasteful use of soil fertility, and of preserving, maintaining, and rebuilding the farm and ranch land resources in the national public interest."

Elsewhere in the valley farmers of course attempted to offset their enforced reduction in cotton income by growing alternative crops, but since they were already growing cotton on all the land they could, it is safe to assume that they had maximized their profits by 1953, and that some decline in income was inevitable in 1954. Some of the land under cotton in 1953 no doubt had been taken from fallow and some from idle land, but most must have been land already irrigated or made available by expansion of irriga-

---

[19] See "The Report of the President's Water Resources Policy Commission" [see footnote 14 above], pp. 125 and 132–133.

[20] Private communication, Regional Office, Bureau of Reclamation, U. S. Department of the Interior, Sacramento.

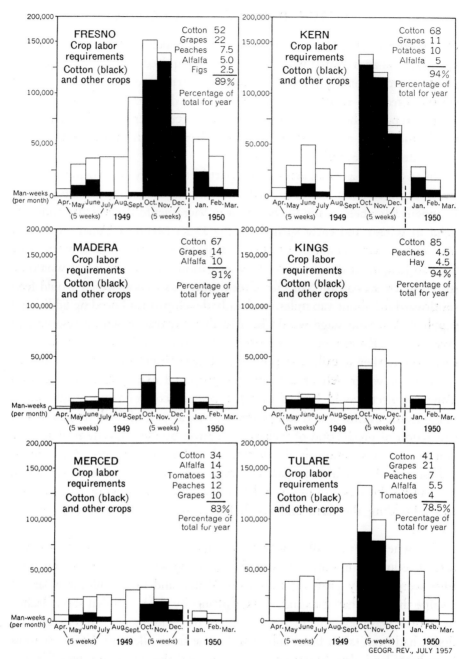

FIG. 7—The seasonal nature of monthly crop labor requirements in each county, based on figures for 1949–1950. Source: Metzler and Sayin, The Agricultural Labor Force in the San Joaquin Valley, California [see text footnote 24].

tion[21]—that is, high-cost land. Continued population growth in the United States will undoubtedly result in a steady increase in the market for California's irrigated foodstuffs, especially fruits and vegetables, and readjustment may be rapid. But large increases in, for example, truck crops can scarcely be expected immediately acreage controls take out of cotton production so extensive an area of land.

Labor Requirements of Cotton

Meanwhile hardships may occur, due, for one thing, to heavy indebtedness incurred in expanding production. It is not likely that these hardships will add to the current decrease in the resident farm population,[22] but since cotton is an intertilled row crop with heavy labor requirements, a decline in planting will have a serious effect on the seasonal demand for migratory labor and/or the demand for labor-saving machinery, whether this machinery is purchased (usually on the installment plan) or is hired from "custom operators."

Figure 7 illustrates the nature of the labor requirements in cotton growing in the San Joaquin Valley at a time when acreages under cotton were roughly comparable with those after the reimposition of control. The dominance of cotton, especially at harvesttime, is seen most markedly in Kings County (85 per cent of the total), but even in Fresno and Tulare Counties, where grapes are a major crop, four or five hours of labor out of every ten were devoted to cotton, with concentration of demand in the three main cotton-harvest months. The labor of both the farmer and the permanent farm workers is included in these figures, which were primarily determined for use by the Farm Placement Service[23] to provide for planned employment of seasonal migratory labor.

A resident farm-labor force is available when there is a long work season, as in cotton (compare raisin grapes, cherries, and peaches, with harvest peaks of perhaps only two weeks), yet there is still a large demand for migratory labor for cotton picking. "In fruit, cotton, and vegetable areas there are

---

[21] The Friant-Kern Canal reached the Kern River near Bakersfield in 1951, and by then some 14 per cent of the distribution channels were in operation.

[22] The decrease in the Pacific States, 1940–1950, was 2.6 per cent, though only 0.3 per cent in California; the United States loss was 18.0 per cent ("Farm Population: Annual Estimates . . . 1920–50," U. S. Dept. of Agriculture, Agricultural Marketing Service, 1953).

[23] "Labor Requirements for California Crops: Major Seasonal Operations, *California Dept. of Employment, Farm Placement Service and Research and Statistics Sect. Rept. 882–No. 3,* Sacramento, 1952. No figures are given for Stanislaus County, which had fewer than 100 hired temporary workers in addition to the regular working force during the peak demand for labor.

three or more farm workers to each farm operator,"[24] and most of these are migratory workers, drawn from all over the state, and from outside, including Mexico.[25] However, increasing mechanization is reducing the demand for labor in some branches of agriculture; in cotton growing the drop is due to the increasing use of machinery in planting, thinning, and picking, and to the decrease in acreage from the 1951–1953 maxima.[26]

Cotton and Mechanization

It is at this point that it becomes difficult to separate the relative importance in the regional economy of the great fluctuations in acreage due to control and of the changes due to technical advances in cotton farming. Enough has been said, however, to show that acreage allotments may change the crop type on a wide margin, necessitating adjustments in water supply and labor demands; repercussions of these adjustments will be widespread, not only within the valley but on the national scene, if increases in alternative crops or changes to livestock farming are involved. But cotton farming is in a dynamic state, both in the West and in the Old South, and with the increase in mechanization basic changes are taking place in harvesting and, to a smaller extent, in hoeing and thinning the seedlings.

In 1950, when only 581,000 acres of cotton was harvested in California, only 34 per cent was mechanically harvested, yet in 1951 of 1,305,000 acres 53 per cent was mechanically harvested (roughly 332,000 bales in 1950 and 935,000 in 1951). Much of the increase was due to lack of suitable hand labor, but it represented a firm movement toward a much higher proportion of machine picking.[27] The quality—and therefore the value—of machine-picked cotton is generally a little lower than that of hand-picked, since it usually includes a large amount of leaves, stalks, and other "trash." Also, machine picking has to await leaf fall or the application of defoliants, whereas

---

[24] W. H. Metzler and A. F. Sayin: The Agricultural Labor Force in the San Joaquin Valley, California: Characteristics, Employment, Mobility, 1948 (Bureau of Agricultural Economics, U. S. Dept. of Agriculture, and Institute of Industrial Relations, University of California, Washington, 1950), p. 6. A peak of about 110,000 hired workers was reached in the valley in October, 1948, which dropped to about 39,000 in March, 1949 (p. 8).

[25] "Wetback" Mexican laborers (illegal entrants to the United States) are less numerous in the migratory cotton labor force in the valley than in some other areas. Recently the Immigration and Naturalization Service has intensified its efforts to control this illegal movement.

[26] In 1952 the demand for labor for the cotton harvest exceeded the supply, but "cotton picking machines have made it possible to increase production during a period of diminishing farm labor supply" (private communication, Farm Placement Service, State of California, December, 1952).

[27] W. R. Bailey and T. R. Hedges: Economics of Mechanical Cotton Harvesting in the San Joaquin Valley, 1949, *Giannini Foundation of Agric. Economics Mimeographed Rept. No. 111, 1951*.

hand picking can usually start earlier and select top-quality bolls. In the 1949–1950 harvest "there was some tendency for the spread between grades of machine-picked and hand-picked cotton to narrow in late season picking."[28] In 1953, the year before acreage control was reimposed, employment in the harvest was higher than in 1952:

the reason was that the 1954 acreage allotment was in prospect and farmers were eager to get as much cotton, and as high grade cotton, as possible off their 1953 acreage. Accordingly, they wanted hand pickers and have kept picking as long as any cotton bolls could be salvaged. Another reason was the use of fewer machines due to reluctance of some farmers to replace old machines or make initial investments in new machines (which cost as much as $16,000) with acreage curtailment in prospect for 1954.[29]

Here, then, is further evidence of the effects of governmental control of acreage.

The high per acre yield of cotton in California, and in other irrigated areas, is sure to result in a continued expansion of machine picking.[30] It was reported in 1952 that an increase in yield of half a bale of cotton per acre (from 375 to 625 pounds) would save $10 per bale in picking costs, by the use of machines, and that a further increase of one bale per acre (i.e. an increase to 1125 pounds) would save an additional $6.50.[31] Despite the premium placed on top-quality hand-picked cotton, some growers are already attempting to pick the entire crop by machine; for, as wages rise, the margin of profit on hand-picked cotton decreases. Many problems still remain to be solved, of course: not every farmer can manage to apply sodium cyanide dust defoliant by airplane![32]

The smaller farms of the east side of the valley, with their mixed economy, will naturally suffer least from the changes brought about by acreage allotments, though their incomes are likely to have been affected by the acreage cuts. More radical adjustments will be necessary on the large cotton farms, both the 5634 "cotton farms" of the 1950 Census of Agriculture and the cotton "ranches" that developed during the three boom years, largely on the

---

[28] *Ibid.,* p. 5.

[29] Private communication, Farm Placement Service, Department of Employment, State of California, March, 1954.

[30] Between 1946 and 1951 the number of cotton-picking machines in California increased from 25 to 3700 and the percentage of the crop picked by machine increased to 54 (T. R. Hedges and W. R. Bailey: Economics of Mechanical Cotton Harvesting, *California Agric. Exper. Sta. Bull. 743,* Davis, Calif., 1954).

[31] H. R. Wellman: Management and Costs in Irrigation Farming, *Cotton Gin and Oil Mill Press,* Vol. 53, No. 23, 1952, pp. 32–35. Note that the *average* yield in Arizona in 1954 was 1039 pounds per acre [see Table I above].

[32] It is interesting to note (George, *loc. cit.* [see footnote 15 above]) that many growers in Tulare County are using geese to control weeds!

west side, with heavy investment in well-drilling and irrigation equipment. On these larger farms the major fluctuations in labor requirements, in acreages planted and fallow, in demand for machinery, fertilizers, and water, will have contributed to cause the greatest changes in the agricultural geography of the San Joaquin Valley. In this aspect of geography California is undergoing dynamic changes as great as the more familiar ones in the fields of population and industry. The national repercussions of the state's rise to a major position in cotton production, though not as widely appreciated, are as important, both to other cotton-farming regions and to other areas affected by marginal shifts in the farming pattern of the San Joaquin cotton counties.

ADDENDUM

Crop figures for 1955 (published in May, 1956, after the preparation of this article) showed a continuation of the trends detailed in the preceding pages. United States cotton acreage fell by nearly 2½ million acres from the 1954 total, while production of lint *increased* by about 1 million bales (1955 harvested acreage, 16,928,000; production, 14,721,000 bales) with an increase of yield per harvested acre (417 pounds, as against 341 pounds in 1954).

Growing conditions were good in the cotton states of the South, and everywhere yields were improved. Increases in production occurred in all southern states except North Carolina and Missouri and were very large in Alabama, Arkansas, and Mississippi. By contrast, yields and production were down in the three western states of New Mexico, Arizona, and California.

COTTON CROP, SAN JOAQUIN VALLEY AND SOUTHERN CALIFORNIA, 1954 AND 1955*
(Lint yield in pounds. Production in bales of 500 pounds gross weight.)

COUNTY	ACREAGE HARVESTED 1954	1955	LINT YIELD PER ACRE 1954	1955	PRODUCTION IN BALES 1954	1955
Fresno	223,500	189,730	838	777	391,600	308,000
Kern	205,000	177,650	916	955	392,250	354,000
Kings	111,000	94,630	739	659	171,500	130,500
Madera	55,200	45,810	631	533	72,800	51,000
Merced	32,000	27,370	681	612	45,500	35,000
Stanislaus	100	....	425	....	90	....
Tulare	165,500	143,730	701	673	245,450	202,000
San Joaquin Valley	*794,300*	*678,920*	*795*	*762*	*1,319,190*	*1,080,500*
Imperial	64,300	45,620	908	917	121,900	87,500
Los Angeles	50	40	664	202	70	20
Riverside	23,660	19,720	909	876	44,930	36,200
San Bernardino	300	160	499	461	310	145
San Diego	290	310	691	432	420	275
Southern California	*88,600*	*65,850*	*906*	*901*	*167,630*	*124,140*
California	*883,000*	*745,000*	*806*	*774*	*1,487,000*	*1,205,000*

* Figures from California Crop and Livestock Reporting Service, May 21, 1956. Figures for California are rounded.

Poor growing weather, especially at planting time, and late ripening seem to account for the general decline in yields, though the continuing rise in Kern County (and in Imperial County) should be noted. The average yield in California is still some 200 pounds per acre higher than in the best southern state (Mississippi, with 570 pounds per acre in 1955). In the San Joaquin Valley, 71 per cent of the crop was picked by machine, partly because of a shortage of hand labor; however, mechanical pickers are still imperfect and skilled operators in short supply, and more hand picking is desired by cotton farmers.

It is reported that reductions in cotton acreage in the San Joaquin Valley have resulted in shifts to corn, alfalfa, alfalfa seed, beans, sorghums, orchards and vineyards, vegetables, and melons; corn registered an increase in production of 84 per cent over 1954.

Preliminary reports (January 18, 1957) indicated that in California average yield for the 1956 cotton crop (harvest to be completed in February, 1957) would be about 900 pounds per acre, a new record. This follows excellent growing and harvest seasons. Total production is estimated to have been 1,445,000 bales on 755,000 harvested acres. Some 73 per cent of the San Joaquin cotton will have been machine-picked; the demand for hand labor was greater than the supply (which included fewer than 400 Mexicans) at the harvest peak.

Plant Fibers—Some Economic Considerations

HORACE L. PUTERBAUGH[1]

Introduction

The problems of plant fibers today are fairly well summed up in one word—competition. The problems of cotton are in many ways representative of those associated with all plant fibers. In terms of quantity and value, cotton is the only plant fiber (excluding wood fiber) of any consequence grown in the United States. A few statistics can serve to give a broad picture of the current cotton situation.

In 1963, per capita mill consumption of cotton was at a record low of 21.6 pounds, down 4% from 1962—yields were at a record high of over one bale per acre. The carryover on August 1, 1964 is expected to be about 13 million bales, up from the 11.2 million bales of a year earlier. Cotton's share of the total fiber consumption declined from more than 59% in 1962 to a record low of less than 57% in 1963. Per capita man-made fiber consumption in 1963 stood at a record high of 14.2 pounds, up 9% from a year earlier. These statistics are indications of trends that have been occurring over a number of years—roughly since the end of World War II.

Broad Economic Developments

The economics of plant fiber production and utilization have been influenced by certain broad developments. The complete list would include about everything of any economic importance over the last 50 years or more but among the most important developments are (1) the increased productivity of labor and resulting higher incomes, (2) changes in methods of living and in the needs and desires for textile products, and (3) the development of new and better man-made

fibers. These developments are, of course, not independent—indeed, they are highly interrelated.

Increased Productivity of Labor. Increased labor productivity and higher incomes generally throughout the United States have resulted in consumers having more money to spend for all consumer articles, including those produced from plant fibers. This development also means that unless production methods for plant fibers can be "automated" at least as fast as those for competing products production costs of plant fibers will be at a disadvantage. Flax production in the United States was a victim of high labor costs and its death serves as a warning for other plant fibers.

High labor costs have influenced consumer's preference for textile materials. Paper products have come to the forefront in certain areas because of high labor costs for competing materials. If, for example, sacks can be re-used enough times, cotton and burlap are cheaper materials than paper. However, it takes labor to re-use articles and labor is a relatively expensive input. (Outside the textile field, the substitution of paper milk cartons for glass milk bottles by many dairies is a prime example of the results of increased labor costs.) The trend toward bulk shipping (again less labor) cuts into all packaging materials.

Changes in Living Habits. Changes in composition of our labor force have affected the plant fiber economy. Increase in the number of working wives has had an impact on the utilization of plant fibers, just as this change has influenced the whole area of household appliances.

Working wives have less time (and energy) to devote to the care and maintenance of clothing, drapes, etc. They tend to demand fabrics that require little or no ironing, that do not soil easily, and that have other easy-care qualities. Family incomes have increased as a result of two family members

[1] Staff Specialist (Textiles), Product and Process Evaluation Staff, Office of Administrator, Agricultural Research Service. Presented to the Fifth Annual Meeting, Society for Economic Botany, Chapel Hill, North Carolina on March 23, 1964.
Received for publication April 8, 1964.

"Plant Fibers — Some Economic Considerations" by Horace L. Puterbaugh. Reprinted from Economic Botany, *Vol. 19 (April 1965), pp. 184-187, with permission of the publisher.*

262

working, and money is available to pay a premium for textiles having the desired characteristics. An increasing proportion of the population works indoors, and lighter weight clothing is preferred. In some cases, this has resulted in a preference for properties offered by man-made fibers.

New and Better Man-Made Fibers. The big competitors of plant fibers are the man-made fibers, both the cellulosics and the non-cellulosics. Following the introduction and acceptance of rayon, many other man-made fibers were developed by the chemical industry. These fibers have been actively promoted and have been accepted in a wide range of textile products, used either alone or in blends with the natural fibers.

Although these fibers were originally priced higher per pound than cotton (and, with the exception of rayon, they still are), inroads were quickly made into the traditional markets of the natural fibers. A vigorous promotion campaign, plus distinctive qualities that for many end uses gave the man-made fibers real advantages, was responsible for this growth. Further, the price per pound of a fiber does not give an adequate basis of cost comparison, since the poundage of fiber required for a given article varies with the type of fiber used and since processing costs and waste at the mill are, in general, higher for the natural fibers than for the man-made fibers. Cotton, for example, has about $0.04 per pound waste costs at the mill compared with $0.005 for rayon.

Nylon's high tensile strength and durability has helped to insure this fiber an important place in the fiber market. Nylon now has the replacement tire market and about 40% of the original passenger-car tires fairly well assured. As soon as the problem of "flat spotting" is solved, nylon expects to capture the entire tire cord market *unless* other synthetics, such as glass-fibers, eliminate both rayon and nylon. This development is no loss to cotton, however, since the tire cord market had been lost to rayon several years ago.

Rayon has a luster and slippery quality that makes it ideal for certain apparel linings, underwear, etc. It is also cheap enough to be practical for this end use.

Rayon staple can be used on the same equipment employed for cotton staple and, largely because it is cheaper than cotton, is often blended with cotton. The objective in such blends seems to be to get the greatest quantity of rayon into the fabric and still have the fabric behave like 100% cotton. Recently, improvements have been made in rayon, and it is now claimed by rayon manufacturers that some basically cotton fabrics are improved by adding rayon.

Cotton's wash-wear characteristics can be improved by blending with synthetic fibers, and Dacron-cotton blends have been accepted in some areas of the shirt market. These examples serve to illustrate a few of the competitive problems of cotton.

There are certain end uses that are still dominated by cotton, however. In 1962, cotton held over 90% of the market in men and boys' shirts, woven sheets, towels and toweling, men and boys' underwear, men and boys' overalls and coveralls, pillow cases, etc. Cotton has a distinct advantage where moisture absorbency and the ability to withstand frequent laundering is of major importance. Work clothes are still predominantly made of cotton.

Price and the Consumption of Fibers

Raw material price is an important aspect of competition among the various fibers, despite the fact that the raw material cost is a small portion of the consumer's cost of a particular article. Cotton farmers, for example, receive about $0.15 of the consumer's dollar spent for cotton products. The farmer's share of a cotton business shirt is approximately $0.20. In contrast, the retailer's mark-up for apparel items may be from 30 to 50% of the price paid by the consumer. Nevertheless, the farm price of cotton is very important in determining what fiber is used for specific end uses.

The decision to use one particular fiber rather than another must, of necessity, be made at the mill where spinning and weaving are performed. Since the difference between profit and loss for a mill operator may be a few cents difference in raw material costs, competition among various fiber producers is intense. Of course, if consumers demand a particular type of fiber (perhaps as a result of a promotion campaign), this preference will be reflected back to the mill operator in terms of a higher price for one type of fabric and that type of raw material will benefit pricewise.

Manufacturers do not shift quickly, however, from one type of fiber to another as a result of small price changes. The manufacturer must consider his equipment set-up, the training and specific knowledge of his personnel, and expectations of future price changes. Thus, changing patterns of consumer demand are reflected, initially, in changing volumes of output on the part of individual manufacturers.

Improving the Competitive Position of Plant Fibers

Efforts to improve the competitive position of plant fibers have taken three general forms: (1) the promotion of plant fibers as superior fibers (and for a good many end uses plant fibers are truly superior products; (2) the development of new and better products from plant fibers; and (3) the lowering of production costs per unit with the aim of an eventually lower raw material cost.

Promotion. Without adequate promotion, few products can hope to survive in modern business competition. It is true that promotion alone will not sell a product for long—the product must have inherent characteristics desired by consumers. On the other hand, no consumer (or manufacturer) will buy a product if he is not aware of its good characteristics.

New Product Development. A lower price for raw plant fibers makes the goal of utilization research easier to attain. Most utilization research efforts have involved additional processing and additional costs. As in any manufacturing process, a lower raw material cost makes the final product more likely to succeed in the market place.

New product development (and this includes improvement of old products) is absolutely essential if plant fibers are to remain competitive with other fibers. Much of this research will be done by governmental institutions and by various associations of producers, ginners, etc., who have vested interests in cotton. Textile manufacturers are not committed to the use of any specific fiber. Their research is oriented toward utilization of the fiber that they believe will meet specific specifications at lowest cost. Nevertheless, textile manufacturers have promoted research beneficial to plant fibers in the past, and more of this may be expected in the future. Considerable progress has been made in utilization research by the United States Department of Agriculture, working in cooperation with others interested in cotton, in developing new and improved cotton products.

Lower Production Costs. A lower price for raw plant fibers would make these fibers more competitive—both at home and abroad. If a lower price was accompanied by a corresponding decrease in production costs, it would seem that fiber producers must gain, since more could be sold at the same profit margin per unit of production. It has been estimated by the National Cotton Council that over a period of years there is a potential of about an $0.11 decrease per pound in farm production costs of cotton through increased farm production research.

Unfortunately, there are some problems associated with the lowering of production costs. Cotton can serve as an example. Much of the production research to date has been of the yield increasing type. Increased mechanization tends to lower the cost of cotton production per unit, *if a large number of units are produced.* Otherwise, mechanization may increase production costs per unit. Mechanical harvesting may also tend to produce a lower quality cotton by increasing the trash content and by increasing the proportion of immature fibers. Mechanization has tended to shift the relative profitableness of cotton from one geographical area to another—from parts of the South where cotton acreages per farming unit are small to other areas, including the West, where acreages per farming unit are large and where irrigation is a factor.

More fertilizer, more and better insecticides, high yielding varieties—all tend to lower per unit costs by spreading a higher total cost over an even higher total production. In an industry that is plagued by production already exceeding utilization, this creates its own problems.

It is possible that yield-increasing and cost-lowering production techniques, followed by corresponding price decreases, would not solve the problem of over production and supply control problems. The increase in cotton production would need to be geared to the increase in cotton markets— domestic and export. The production of cotton could conceivably increase at a much faster rate than additional markets for cotton would develop. This means, of course, that fewer acres would be needed for cotton production. Smaller acreage allotments or increased funds and facilities for storage of an ever-increasing carryover would be a threat.

Nevertheless, there is no alternative to research to lower production costs of cotton. If production costs and prices do not decrease, cotton seems destined to lose disastrously in the fiber market.

If greater supply control problems arise, these problems can, and should, be attacked by increased efforts to expand sales of cotton at home and abroad—by improvements in the properties of the raw cotton fiber, by the development of new and improved cotton products, by increased processing efficiency, and by promotion of cotton's superior qualities.

Metallic Minerals

The impact of metals on the modern world is visible everywhere. Virtually every phase of human life — particularly such economic activities as construction, transportation, agriculture, and manufacturing — is directly dependent on the use of metals.

The list of important metals is long and includes such substances as iron, copper, aluminum, lead, zinc, tin, and their innumerable alloys. Because of their widely variable properties and characteristics, these metals serve vital functions in many occupations and industries. In addition, in terms both of employees and value of production, the extraction and processing of metals are in themselves a major industry which has certain distinctive geographic characteristics.

The following selection of articles emphasizes several of the major aspects of the metallic minerals. For example, the Lounsbury article on aluminum discusses the several phases of processing: extraction and concentration, smelting, and refining. Factors influencing the location of an alumina plant differ from those influencing aluminum refining, causing differing locational patterns for the two activities. Moreover, as Lounsbury indicates, the relative importance of the several factors may change through time and lead to a spatial relocation of the activity. The article also demonstrates the change in transportability of a metal as processing reduces bulk and weight and increases its value.

The articles dealing with copper and lead will suggest some of the factors determining whether or not a given mineral deposit will be exploited. Not only must there be an ore of sufficient quality, but also the quantity must be large enough to warrant the cost of development. Proximity to markets, competition, legal and political restrictions, and numerous other considerations affect the decision. Although moderately technical, these articles illustrate the magnitude and complexity of the mining process, indicating the scope of factors influencing the extraction process alone.

The remaining two articles effectively indicate the impact of technology on the production of minerals. Although metals are an exhaustible resource, technological changes in exploration and processing make previously unuseable materials highly productive and profitable, thus prolonging the supply. Technology frequently provides the metals with competitors — such as plastics — but it also continues to expand many existing markets and open new ones. In addition, secondary recovery now provides a large supply of many metals.

RECENT DEVELOPMENTS IN THE ALUMINUM INDUSTRY IN THE UNITED STATES

JOHN F. LOUNSBURY
Eastern Michigan University

THE aluminum industry of the United States has experienced a spectacular expansion over the last two decades demonstrating a rate of growth appreciably greater than the national economy as a whole. The production of aluminum has now become a major industry second only to iron and steel in the field of metallic minerals. Although the metal was produced commercially as early as 1888, it was not until World War II that the industry experienced a rapid expansion. The light, strong metal was in great demand as a structural material in the aircraft industry. It was anticipated that due to the decrease in the manufacture of military aircraft, the production of aluminum would decline or experience a slow rate of growth in the post war years. Contrary to these predictions, the industry continued to expand rapidly. The 1959 production of 1,953,175 tons in the United States represents over a ten-fold increase in twenty years and an increase of about 295 per cent since 1945 (Fig. 1).

Growth of Industry

The recent growth of the industry reflects new uses other than that of aircraft construction. Its workability and resistance to corrosion and weathering has made it a popular building material. Today, more than one-fourth of the aluminum consumed in this country is used in the construction industry. It is estimated that the average home today contains about 30 pounds of aluminum, and it is anticipated that the use of the metal in the building industry will increase considerably in the near future. About 15 per cent of the aluminum consumed in the United States is used in the transportation industry. Presently, a great deal of the metal is being used in forms of transportation other than aircraft. The automobile industry uses about 60 pounds of aluminum per car today compared to less than 6 pounds per car in 1946, and all indications point to a considerable increase in the next few years. Other forms of transportation such as the railroad and marine industries are increasing their consumption of aluminum annually. The use of aluminum in the manufacture of packages and containers and its use in the electrical industry have increased rapidly. Today, each of these uses consumes over 10 per cent of the aluminum used in the country and it is predicted that these uses will consume considerably more aluminum in the near future. Consumer durables, machine parts, tools and equipment are other major uses of the metal today.

Bauxite Sources

In the last twenty years, several major shifts have occurred in the location of primary aluminum plants reflecting

"Recent Developments in the Aluminum Industry in the United States" by John F. Lounsbury. Reprinted from Journal of Geography, *Vol. LXI (March* 1962), *pp.* 97–104, *with permission of author and editor.*

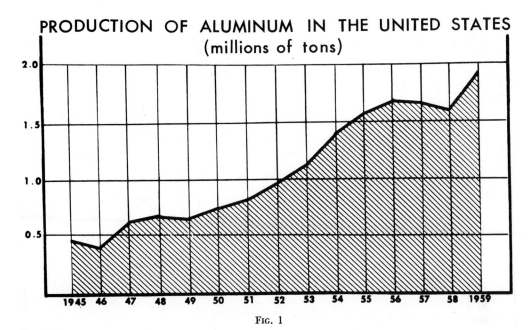

PRODUCTION OF ALUMINUM IN THE UNITED STATES
(millions of tons)

FIG. 1

changing logistical patterns. The location of bauxite reserves, sources of power and markets have been most instrumental in causing these shifts. The first major stage in producing aluminum is the conversion of bauxite into alumina. About two tons of bauxite are required to produce one ton of alumina and, consequently, the location of alumina plants are situated where transportation costs of obtaining bauxite are relatively low. The only domestic source of commercial bauxite is found in Saline and Pulaski Counties, Arkansas. The production of the domestic ore has been well below that of demand and, in recent years, over 85 per cent of the bauxite used has been imported. About 95 per cent of these imports are obtained from Jamaica and Surinam.

Alumina Plants

The eight alumina plants presently in operation or under construction in this country are all located close to the domestic source of bauxite or on the Gulf Coast close to imported sources (Fig. 2). There are now two alumina plants utilizing domestic ore, enriched with foreign imports located at Bauxite and Hurricane Creek, Arkansas. These plants are the only establishments based on domestic bauxite and presently account for about 22 per cent of the alumina production of the country. The three plants located in Louisiana at Gramercy, Burnside, and Baton Rouge account for about 31 per cent of the alumina; the plants at Point Comfort and La Quinta, Texas, account for 28 per cent; and the one plant at Mobile, Alabama, produces about 19 per cent of the country's total. Significantly, the oldest alumina plant in the country, which was located in East St. Louis, Illinois, suspended operations in 1957 reflecting its relative inaccessibility to domestic or foreign bauxite sources.

Primary Aluminum

The second major stage in producing aluminum is the reduction process which transforms alumina into primary aluminum and this operation requires vast amounts of power. It takes about 9 KWH of electrical energy, about two pounds of alumina, and much smaller amounts of petroleum coke, cryolite, aluminum

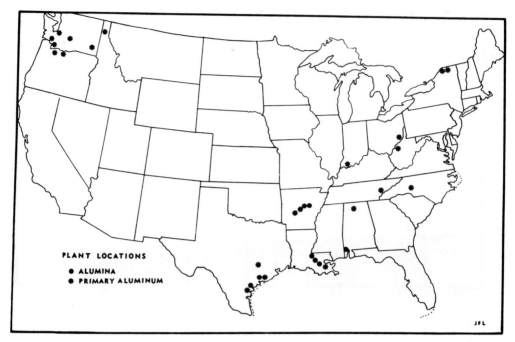

PLANT LOCATIONS
● ALUMINA
✳ PRIMARY ALUMINUM

FIG. 2

fluoride and other materials to produce one pound of aluminum. The most critical locational factors are power and, most recently, accessibility to alumina plants and consuming markets. Hydroelectric power was the only major source of energy used by the industry as recently as ten years ago. Today, coal and natural gas account for about one-half of the energy used by the industry.

Shift of Industry to the Northwest

Previous to 1940, all the aluminum in this country was produced in central Arkansas and the southern Appalachian Mountains using hydroelectric power and small amounts of coal. In 1940, in view of the tremendous hydroelectric developments taking place in the northwestern part of the country, the industry began to shift their expansion facilities to this region. In the next five years, almost 50 per cent of the nation's aluminum was being produced here. By 1950, the demand for water power for home and commercial use increased rapidly in the Northwest and political controversies

over water utilization policies developed, forcing the industry to search for an alternate source of power.

The Gulf States Development

During the 1950-1955 period, another major shift took place as the aluminum industry looked to the Gulf States where electrical energy could be derived from natural gas. By 1955, however, it became apparent that natural gas could not be depended upon for the long range expansion plans of the industry. The widespread use of gas as a source of domestic heating led to the rapid extension of transmission lines and committed large gas reserves to the eastern and midwestern states for a long period of time. The increasing gas rates and potential shortages forced the industry to search again for an alternate source of cheap and abundant power.

The Ohio Valley

At this time, developments in the mechanization of coal mining, construc-

ALUMINUM PRODUCTION CAPACITY, 1960
(by regions)

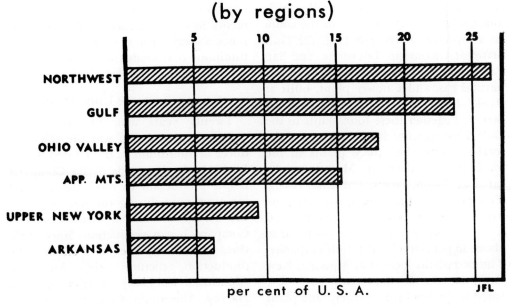

FIG. 3

tion of larger and more efficient coal barges, and innovations in steam generating plants, made it possible to generate a KWH of electricity from as little as 6/10ths of a pound of coal, reducing the cost of coal-generated electricity drastically. The bituminous coal reserves of the country were reappraised upward and estimated to last several hundreds of years at the present rate of consumption. It appeared that coal was the only source of energy that could be depended upon for abundant and cheap power over a long period of time. The major portion of the country's accessible bituminous coal centered on the Ohio Valley. The six states bordering the Ohio River system possessed over 80 per cent of the nation's bituminous reserves of which a substantial portion was near or adjacent to the Ohio River or its navigable tributaries. Further, the uses of aluminum other than aircraft construction had expanded rapidly and about 75 per cent of the total aluminum market now existed in the northeastern manufacturing region of

the country within 500 miles of the Ohio Valley. In relation to the Northwest, the Ohio Valley was 1,000 miles closer to the raw materials and 2,000 miles closer to the major markets which more than offset the now relatively little difference in power costs. As recently as 1957, no aluminum was produced in the Ohio Valley but today this district produces a significant amount of the nation's primary aluminum (Fig. 3).

Location of Aluminum Plants

There are 22 primary aluminum plants in operation or under construction in the United States at present. The eight plants in the Northwest utilizing hydroelectric power located at Vancouver, Longview, Tacoma, Mead, and Wenatchee, Washington; Troutdale and The Dalles, Oregon; and at Columbia Falls, Montana, account for 26 per cent of the nation's total capacity.[1] The three new plants using

[1] Basic Statistical data from Mineral Market Survey No. 3092, 1959, United States Department of the Interior.

coal-generated electricity in the Ohio Valley at Ravenswood, West Virginia, Clarington, Ohio, and Evansville, Indiana, account for 19 per cent of the country's capacity. Three plants in the Gulf States at Chalmette, Louisiana, and San Patricio and Point Comfort, Texas, use natural gas, and a newer plant, built at Rockdale, Texas, uses lignite coal for power. Together these four plants in the Gulf States account for 24 per cent of the total capacity. The three plants in the southern Appalachian Mountains located at Badin, North Carolina, Alcoa, Tennessee, and Lister Hill, Alabama, use hydroelectric power, both private and TVA, and some coal. These plants have about 15 per cent of the nation's capacity. The two plants located at Massena, New York, on the St. Lawrence River are based on hydroelectric power. One plant has just recently been constructed utilizing new power developments associated with the St. Lawrence Seaway. Together these plants account for 9 per cent of the nation's capacity, and the two plants at Arkadelphia and Jones Mills, Arkansas, close to the domestic sources of bauxite, account for 6 per cent (Figs. 2 and 3).

Since 1955, five new plants have been constructed. Only one of these plants was built in the Northwest, close to the company's fabricating mills. This plant uses hydroelectric power. One plant was constructed in Massena, New York, to utilize the new hydroelectric installations associated with the St. Lawrence Seaway. Three plants were located in the Ohio Valley utilizing thermal electric power. In anticipation of future expansion based on coal-generated power, two of the largest companies in the country have acquired control of large coal deposits near Sturgis and Henderson, Kentucky, and also an area of sub-bituminous coal reserves near Lake DeSmet, Wyoming. It is most likely due to the changing uses of aluminum and subsequent shift of the major consuming market to the eastern part of the country that a large part of the future expansion of the industry will take place adjacent to new hydroelectric developments in the east such as the St. Lawrence Seaway, or near easily exploited bituminous coal fields in the eastern interior or Appalachian coal districts.

Companies in the United States

Twenty years ago, the Aluminum Company of America was the sole producer of aluminum in the United States. In 1941, the Reynolds Metal Company began production to meet the demand for aluminum during the war. In 1946, the Kaiser Aluminum and Chemical Company began production. Since 1955, three other companies have entered the production picture: the Anaconda Aluminum Company in 1955, and the Harvey Aluminum Company and the Ormet Corporation in 1959. In 1960, the Aluminum Company of America possessed 38 per cent of the nation's capacity; Reynolds Metal Company, 30 per cent; Kaiser Aluminum and Chemical Company, 23 per cent; Ormet Corporation, 7 per cent; and Anaconda Aluminum and Harvey Aluminum Companies over 2 per cent each (Fig. 4).

Alcoa has two alumina plants located in Arkansas and Texas using domestic and foreign imports from Surinam and one alumina plant in Alabama using bauxite from Surinam. The company has eight aluminum reduction plants in Tennessee, North Carolina, New York, Indiana, two in Texas, and two in Washington. The Reynolds Metals Company has two alumina plants in Arkansas and Texas. The company's seven aluminum plants are located in Alabama, Washington, Texas, Oregon, New York, and two plants in Arkansas. The Kaiser Aluminum and Chemical Company has two alumina plants in Louisiana, using Jamaican bauxite, and four primary aluminum plants located in Louisiana, West Virginia, and two plants in Washington.

The Ormet Company has one alumina plant in Louisiana utilizing bauxite from Surinam and one primary aluminum plant in Ohio. The Anaconda Aluminum Company has one aluminum plant in Montana and, for the present, is obtaining alumina from other companies. The Harvey Aluminum Company with its one recently built aluminum plant in Oregon, is currently using alumina from Japan.

United States and World Production

The United States has played a dominant role in the development of the aluminum industry and its production has been appreciably greater than any other country for many years. In 1959, the country produced over 43 per cent of the world's 4,510,000 tons of aluminum. The world production in 1959 was twice that of 1952. The increase was due to a very large degree to the substantial expansion in United States as well as in the U.S.S.R., several western European countries, and Japan and China. Other major producers at present are: the U.S.S.R. with almost 16 per cent of the world's total production and Canada producing over 13 per cent. The Western European countries produce almost 16 per cent while the Eastern European countries produce less than 6 per cent. The continent of Asia presently produces approximately 5 per cent with Japan accounting for about one-half of the total. Africa produces about 1 per cent while Australia and all of Latin America produce one-half of 1 per cent combined (Fig. 5).

The unequal distribution of potential bauxite sources has influenced American companies to make large financial investments abroad and seek concessions in various parts of the world. To insure alter-

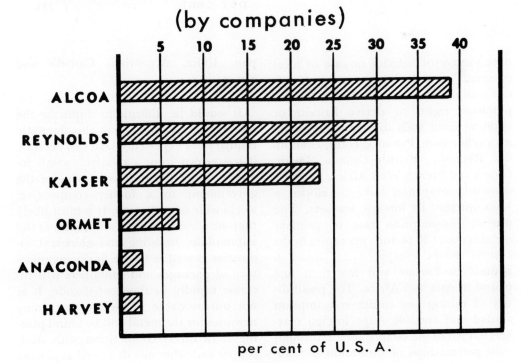

ALUMINUM PRODUCTION CAPACITY, 1960
(by companies)

per cent of U. S. A.

FIG. 4

WORLD PRODUCTION OF ALUMINUM, 1959

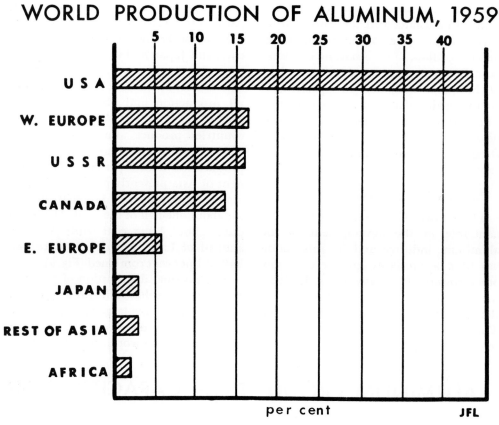

Fig. 5

nate sources of bauxite in case of local economic or political pressures, American companies have concessions and exploration rights or derive bauxite or alumina from such diverse areas as Jamaica, Surinam, Panama, Haiti, Dominican Republic, British Guiana, Japan, Ghana and French West Africa. Recently domestic companies have developed a keen interest in foreign markets. The present consumption rate of primary metal is about 20 pounds per capita in the United States compared to about 6 pounds in Europe and less than one pound in Asia and Africa. The possibilities of raising per capita consumption abroad and creating huge foreign markets has led to the establishment, through joint partnerships, of aluminum and fabricating plants in United Kingdom, Ja-

pan, India, Argentina, Canada and Spain.

Future

It would be difficult to duplicate the remarkable progress that the domestic industry has experienced. In two decades, it has grown from a relatively small industry under the protective wing of the government to a highly competitive, world-wide organization. It is most likely that the consumption of aluminum in the automobile, building and electrical industries as well as its use in the manufacture of packages and containers will increase rapidly in the next decade. It is not unreasonable to assume that many new uses for the metal will be found placing it in direct competition with steel, copper and other metals as well as plastics and wood. The anticipated expansion of the industry should take form in the extension of present facilities and the establishment of new plants primarily in the eastern manufacturing region where coal or new hydroelectric power is available. Barring a technical breakthrough in the economic recovery of low grade, lateritic bauxites in Oregon and Hawaii or submarginal bauxites in Arkansas, the pattern of aluminum is finally established reflecting the geographic factors of markets, power and material flow.

ARIZONA'S NEWEST COPPER PRODUCER —
THE CHRISTMAS MINE

by
AL KNOERR and MIKE EIGO*

Inspiration Consolidated Copper Co.'s intensified development program during the past seven years at the old Christmas property in Gila County Ariz., has revitalized that 50-year-old producer and brought it up to large-scale output.

Two main shafts, a mile-long haulage level, new ventilation workings, a 4000-ton concentrator, a sand fill plant, and all the auxiliary units of a modern mining facility are completed; and 25-ton concentrate trucks are making the haul to the Inspiration smelter at Miami. The "new" project is actually the latest in the long history of the famous property.

CHRISTMAS' PAST

The earliest claims on what is now the Christmas Mine were made about 1880 by Dennis O'Brien and

*Mr. Knoerr is Editor, Engineering & Mining Journal, and Mr. Eigo is Managing Editor.

William Tweed, who subsequently either sold or optioned the property

"Arizona's Newest Copper Producer — The Christmas Mine" by Al Knoerr and Mike Eigo. *Reprinted from* Engineering and Mining Journal, *Vol. 164 (January 1963), pp. 55-67, with permission of the editor.*

to Phelps-Dodge. The locations were proved invalid since they were part of the San Carlos Indian Reservation. Then, in December 1902, the portion of the reservation that included the copper deposits was restored to public domain; on Christmas Day, George B. Chittenden relocated the claims and named the property after the holiday.

Saddle Mountain Mining Co. was then formed to operate the property; and, after successfully fighting a suit by Phelps-Dodge to recover its holdings, the company built a smelter in 1905.

There followed a series of ups and downs, with different operating firms coping with a fluctuating copper price. The first "down" occurred in 1907, when Saddle Mountain failed. Gila Copper Sulphide Co. took over the assets in 1909, and American Smelting & Refining Co. advanced funds, taking over management of the property in 1915. Asarco operated the plant until 1919, when financial troubles arose; and a receiver took over the operation until closing in 1921.

The next "up" occurred four years later when Iron Cap Copper Co. bought controlling interest from Gila Copper Sulphide and moved a 500-ton concentrator from the Globe-Miami area to the newly-named Christmas Copper Co. Some 321,000 tons of ore were treated up to 1932 when the company went bankrupt. It re-formed in 1936 as Christmas Copper Corp. but closed again in 1938 when copper prices dropped.

By 1939, Christmas had reopened again as the Sam Knight Mining Lease Inc. and had begun production of high-lime fluxing ore. Ore shipments, even though limited to

flux requirements of the Asarco smelter at Hayden, had totaled 55-million lb Cu by 1943. The ore averaged 2.16% Cu and about 30% lime.

Through the war years, USBM and USGS, in cooperation with the War Production Board, conducted a diamond drilling and geological mapping program involving more than 10,000 ft of drilling which revealed extensions of the orebody at producing horizons and to considerable depths below the lowest working level of 770 ft.

In 1953, Riviera Mines Co. obtained a lease option from Christmas Copper Corp., Inspiration Copper obtained a lease-and-purchase option in 1955, and since then it has been "up" all the way (see next page).

THE ORE DEPOSIT

The Christmas mineral deposit lies in a thick series of gently dipping Paleozoic limestones, overlain by volcanic rocks; chiefly andesitic tuffs, breccias, flows and conglomerates of Cretaceous age. A generalized stratigraphic series for the vicinity is as follows: 265 ft of Devonian Martin limestone resting unconformably upon Cambrian quartzite. Above the Devonian strata are 550 ft of massive Escabrosa limestone covered by about 1000 ft of Naco limestone of Pennsylvanian and Permian (?) age.

All earlier rocks are cut by generally east-west series of quartz mica diorite dikes. Numerous sills and irregular apophyses which extend into surrounding rocks consist primarily of quartz, feldspar and biotite. In the Christmas mine, narrow post-mineral basalt and andesite dikes cut through Paleozoic sed-

Scope of the Project

Major installations and construction at the Christmas Mine include:

1. Two wells and a pumping station at Dripping Springs Wash which supply water to the 1-million-gal tank at the McDonald Shaft area.

2. A new paved road from Highway 71 to the mine.

3. Three tailings disposal areas north of the McDonald Shaft area.

4. The 16-ft-dia, concrete-lined main service and ore-hoisting McDonald Shaft, 1735 ft deep, servicing the main 1600 haulage level and others.

5. Hoist house enclosing two 600-hp air compressors; a double-drum 10-ft-dia 700-hp service hoist; and a double-drum, 13-ft-dia ore hoist powered by twin 700-hp motors. Hoisting rate is 360 tph.

6. Headframe with dumping gear for 12-ton counterbalanced bottom-dump skips, and gate to divert waste to a conveyor and dump.

7. Two-stage crushing and screening plant at headframe which delivers fine ore via overhead conveyor to a 10,000-ton storage and reclaiming building.

8. A 4000-ton concentrator including rod-mill primary grinding, ball-mill secondary grinding, rougher concentrate regrind, cyclone classification, flotation and filtering units.

9. Other surface buildings at the McDonald Shaft area include mine-dry, office and safety department building; a mechanical and electrical shop; warehouse; and electrical substation and power distribution centers.

10. The 16x7-ft rectangular No. 3 Shaft near Christmas.

11. The No. 6 circular ventilation shaft.

12. A new townsite near the old town of Christmas.

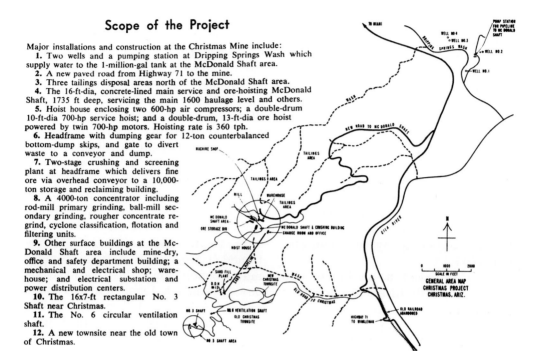

GENERAL AREA MAP
CHRISTMAS PROJECT
CHRISTMAS, ARIZ.

Profile of Progress at the Christmas Mine
1954 to 1962

1954. Ore reserves of the Christmas mine between the 800 and 900 levels were estimated to contain more than 300,000 tons of 3.5% Cu ore. Inspiration also took an option on the claims owned by New Year Mining Co. west of the Christmas project.

1955. Inspiration exercised its option of Feb. 1, 1954, in June 1955 and purchased the property and royalty rights previously held by Riviera Mining Co. An intensified development program revealed an extension of the Christmas orebody 500 ft below lowest workings of the old mine.

1956. The development shaft was deepened from the 900-ft to the 1400-ft level. Reserves were estimated to be 10-million tons of 2% Cu ore. Excavation began at the McDonald Shaft site. A small concentrator on the property was scheduled to operate on development ore, and a new 2500-ton mill was envisioned to handle future production.

1957. Market conditions resulted in a decision to slow development and defer the start of major plant construction. The small mill on the property was refurbished to yield metallurgical data. A new hoist and headframe were installed at the development shaft. Current reserves were estimated to be 20-million tons of 1.83% Cu ore.

1958. The development shaft was deepened to the 1600 level—the main haulage level. Plans called for increasing production capacity to 4000 tpd.

1959. Development work was speeded up, chiefly on the 1300, 1400 and 1600 levels. The pilot plant started operating in July at 100 tpd. Surface construction work was halted for two months by a work stoppage. Construction and installations included a permanent headframe at the McDonald Shaft, a 3000-cfm compressor, warehouse, changehouse, office, and water, power and air lines.

1960. Completed construction included the compressor and hoist building, primary and secondary crushers, conveyor system and mill fresh water supply. Flowsheet design was completed, and mill equipment ordered. Change in Arizona law permits use of diesel equipment underground, and develop-

Expenditures for Development of the Christmas Mine[1]

Year	Development	Plant & Equipment
1954	$ 345,362	—
1955	983,850	$ 278,570
1956	1,187,022	120,281
1957	1,139,976	529,005
1958	713,599	1,796
1959	1,112,572*	1,457,447
1960	2,140,064*	2,871,389
1961	2,567,382*	4,641,285
1962 (9 mo.)	2,549,601	1,169,635
Total	12,739,428	11,069,408

[1]From annual and quarterly company reports
*Includes depreciation

ment plans were revised to include Transloaders. The 12-ft-dia air shaft was sunk to 462 ft. The 18-ft concrete-lined McDonald Shaft was sunk to 1516 ft. Heavy flow of water at the No. 3 Shaft slowed down development progress in that area.

1961. The McDonald Shaft was completed to 1793 ft in April. The 1600 main haulage level, driven simultaneously from the No. 3 and McDonald Shafts, lacked 1379 ft of being completed at the year's end. Heavy water flow requiring grouting delayed progress in the section driven from the No. 3 Shaft. Development advance for the year included 1033 ft at the No. 6 Shaft connecting to the 1600 level and 7281 ft of drifts, raises and other excavations.

1962. The 1600 haulage level was completed by mid-year. Ore hoisting to the mill began on a gradually increasing basis. Heavy water flow in previously opened sections of the mine decreased appreciably, indicating successful lowering of the water table in the orebody. Mill operation yielded metallurgical results somewhat better than indicated by pilot plant work.

iments and diorite intrusives.

The Dripping Springs Range is a faulted anticlinal structure cut by generally trending east-west dikes and a series of northwest trending faults with hanging wall or downthrow sides toward the valleys. At Christmas, the Christmas fault separates the Naco limestone capped by other limestones on the west from andesite which comprises the predominant rock eastward. Surface outcrops of diorite intruding limestone to the west and volcanics to the east form an irregular elliptical outline with long axis trending N 70° E across the Christmas Fault zone.

A second major fault, the Joker Fault running northeasterly, lies between the Christmas Fault and the McDonald Shaft. Both faults are normal post-mineral with indications of pre-mineral movement, and have appreciable shear zones and caused a recognizable displacement of the Christmas orebody on the downthrow side.

Development work underground indicates that the diorite intrusive consists of a central mass which separates into two thick dikes, converging to the west towards the No. 3 shaft and to the east towards the No. 4 shaft with numerous branching

Joy drill mobile at McDonald Shaft is ready for transport on special car to working faces at the Christmas mine.

Miners working from platform on drill jumbo set steel sets and timber lagging in development headings.

Transloader loading-haulage unit, returns to working face. Maximum economy is on 1000- to 1500-ft hauls at Christmas.

Transloader with 5-yd buckets drops 6 1/2- 7-ton load into 15-ton S-D bottom-dump cars at ramp on 1600 level.

sills and interfingering smaller dikes. In the footwall of the Christmas Fault, the great mass of the quartz mica diorite is centered to the east of the No. 3 Shaft between the 500 and 1100 levels where several thick sills and numerous irregular apophyses extend into adjoining limestones.

The Christmas orebody is classified as pyro-metasomatic, occurring as a replacement in metamorphosed limestones of the Naco, Escabrosa and Martin formations. Type and intensity of mineralization varies with distance from the intrusive contacts, with degree of metamorphism, with the physical and chemical properties of the sedimentary rocks, and with the intensity of premineral fracturing and shearing.

Sulphide minerals commonly show a vertical and lateral zonal arrangement. Laterally, mineralization grades from a pyrite-chalcopyrite zone near the intrusive borders to a chalcopyrite-bornite intermediate zone and to a pyrrhotite-pyrite-sphalerite-chalcopyrite outer zone. Vertically in the thicker sections, pyrite, chalcopyrite, sphalerite and sometimes galena generally border a chalcopyrite central zone. Magnetite is the predominant metallic mineral throughout the deposit, comprising 15% to 25% of the total content. Oxidation was almost complete above the 300 level and extends locally to below the 800 level. Supergene ore minerals include chalcocite, native copper, copper oxide and copper carbonates.

The most extensive part of the Christmas orebody is found in the lower part of the Devonian limestones where mineralization extending north and south from main intrusive dikes is flatly dipping, massive and tabular.

Lower limestones developed to the north on the 1300 level and to the south on the 1400 level have proved to be consistently mineralized over an area of 2700 ft in width across the intrusives and 1400 ft in length along the intrusive contacts. Diamond drilling to the east and west indicate appreciable extensions to these dimensions. Currently, development and mining on the 1600 level are revealing additional information on lower extensions of the Christmas ore zone.

DEVELOPMENT WORK

Inspiration started an intensive development program shortly after it concluded its initial agreement with Riviera Mines Co. in 1954. Major workings concluded by the end of 1962 included sinking of the new 18-ft-dia concrete-lined McDonald Shaft to a depth of 1793 ft, sinking the 16×7-ft rectangular No. 3 Shaft to 1735 ft, sinking the circular 12-ft-dia concrete-lined No. 6 Ventilation Raise to the 1600 level, completion of a second ventilation shaft between the 800 and 1400 levels, driving a 5000-ft main haulage level drift to connect the McDonald and No. 3 Shafts on the 1600 level, and other drifts and raises and excavations totaling more than 26,000 ft.

Centennial Development Co. sank the McDonald Shaft and drove 3300 ft of the 1600 level drift upgrade; while Inspiration sank the No. 3 Shaft and drove the remaining portion of the 1600 level drift downgrade to meet the Centennial heading. Two major faults, the Christmas and the Joker, required heavy steel support through 100-ft shear zones on the 1600 level. Trape-

McDonald surface shaft installation includes conveyor to dump at left, headframe, and crushing plant.

Three 600-HP, 900-gpm centrifugal pumps with positive suction head pump mine water via 10-in. line to storage tank.

zoidal steel sets of 8-in. wide flange sections were set on 2-, 3- and 6-ft centers in the shear zones, and in some sections the back had to be spiled. In addition to these delays, the crew at the No. 3 Shaft encountered heavy water flows, chiefly in the quartzite below the Martin limestone, which required installation of much additional pumping capacity together with cementing and grouting in the development headings. Water is still a problem in some of the newer mining openings on the 1600 level, but experience has shown that in time water flow diminishes, and the mine water table can definitely be lowered. After completion of the 1600 haulage drift and the pumping installation at the McDonald Shaft, the volume of mine water decreased from 2500 gpm to 2200 gpm in October 1962.

The McDonald Shaft was sunk with Bain-type slip forms and the three-deck stage equipped with two Cryderman muckers and two winches for elevating and lowering the stage. A 3-ton sinking bucket was used in the sinking of the No. 3 Shaft and two 5-ton buckets for the

McDonald. Concrete and steel were put in place as the sinking progressed.

Centennial used one Machinery Center jumbo with five 9-ft Long Tom feeds mounting four 2 11/16-in. Gardner-Denver drills and one I-R DA 35 for the 2-in. center burn-cut hole to drive the 1600 haulage drift.

A pantograph mounting was used to drill five holes parallel to the center burn-cut hole. Machines drilled nine to ten holes each per round. The average advance per round was 8 ft, and average advance per day was 25 ft. Shifts drilled as many as five rounds per day. When the Joker Fault shear zone was encountered and spiling was required, advance slowed down to 15 to 18 ft per day. A Transloader was used to haul muck for the entire 3300 ft driven by Centennial. At the 2000-ft point, the drift was widened for a distance of 250 ft to accommodate a double track and a ramp loader to cut down uneconomical long hauls by the Transloader. The 2000-ft track section including double track was installed in three weeks. Transloaders at Christmas mark the first use of diesel-powered equipment underground in the state. Approval by the U.S. Bureau of Mines and the state of Arizona was required.

RAISING

The Joy Raise Climbers are used for vertical development. Power has been increased on these climbers to speed travel. Although the climbers can operate in vertical raises up to 600 ft, it has been observed at Christmas that the most economical range is in raises up to 300 ft high. Raises are driven raw in solid ground. In heavy ground, raises are timbered with 6-in wide-flange steel, 6 x 6 ft in the clear. Tracks are mounted within the steel sets.

MINING METHODS AND EQUIPMENT

The Christmas orebody as encountered on the lower levels varies in thickness from 10 to 110 ft and dips about 18°. Final mining techniques have not yet been worked out; but, at this point, it is expected that narrow parts of the orebody will be mined with open stopes and random pillars. In thicker parts of the orebody, a 15-ft cut will probably be taken. After sand-filling, a second 15-ft cut will be taken above the first. The ore tends to be slabby in some places and will require rock bolting. In faulted areas, steel sets will be used. In the thickest parts of the orebody, plans call for slot raises and long-hole drilling.

Drilling equipment under test in the mine includes the Joy Drillmobile mounting three 4-in. rock drills, Joy rotary-percussion drills, and I-R crawlers with 4 3/4-in. drills. A Gardner-Denver crawler jumbo mounting two 4 1/2-in. drills is being used. A Machinery Center jumbo carrying three Gardner-Denver 3-in. drills on Long Tom feeds will also be used. This unit can be picked up by the Transloader bucket and transported to drilling positions. Types of drill thread under test include 400 thread, 600 thread, H thread, 1 1/4-in. rope thread and Hi-Leed thread. The staff expects to standardize on fewer threads as tests proceed.

Two I-R 3184 two-stage compressors powered by 600-hp synchronous motors supply air at 110 psi to mine and plant.

C. Harmon, electrician at mine, calls attention to completely automatic controls installed in hoist house for compressors.

LOADING AND HAULAGE

The Transloader has proved to be efficient in development and mining headings, and mining plans are designed to use this unit for loading and hauling. Maximum grade for the Transloader is 10% loaded and 20% empty. A 20% ramp

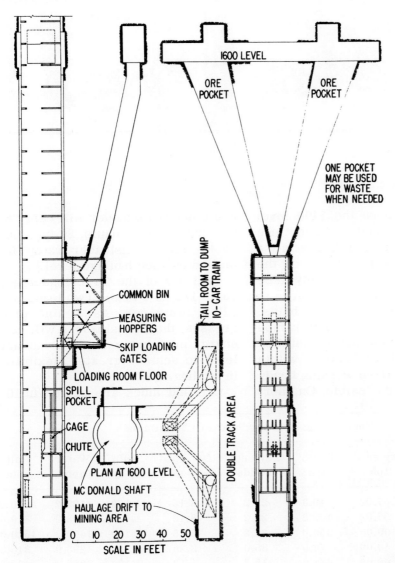

1600 LEVEL

ORE POCKET

ORE POCKET

ONE POCKET MAY BE USED FOR WASTE WHEN NEEDED

COMMON BIN

MEASURING HOPPERS

SKIP LOADING GATES

LOADING ROOM FLOOR

SPILL POCKET

CAGE

CHUTE

PLAN AT 1600 LEVEL

MC DONALD SHAFT

HAULAGE DRIFT TO MINING AREA

TAIL ROOM TO DUMP
IO-CAR TRAIN

DOUBLE TRACK AREA

0 10 20 30 40 50
SCALE IN FEET

Capacity of ore pockets below the 1600-level shaft station is 400 tons. Ore is hoisted in 12-ton bottom-dump skips.

The McDonald Shaft is served by Nord-berg double-drum 700-hp service hoist and a 1500-hp 13-ft-dia ore hoist.

Mine electrical staff and hoistman check delicate adjustments on control panels for ore and service hoists.

has been driven on the 1400 level to connect North and South portions of the orebody. Two units are in use on the 1400 level and two on the 1600; a fifth machine is ready to be lowered. Maximum economy is achieved on 400- to 600-ft hauls. Hence railheads with loading ramps and loading chutes will be installed to keep the Transloaders within these distances from working head-ings as much as possible. On short

hauls the Transloader will carry 60 tph and, on long hauls, 30 tph. (See photo for Transloader ramp in-stalled on 1600 haulage level.)

Capacity of the Transloader is 5 yd (6 1/2 to 7 tons). Two loads will fill a mine car. As mining pro-gresses, the Transloaders will dis-charge into chutes above the haulage level to achieve greater flexibility in loading ore trains.

Ore and muck are hauled in 10-

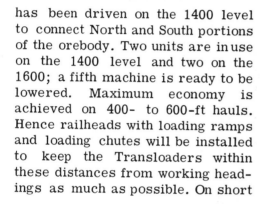

Engineering Data for Sand Fill Treatment [1]

Position	Dry sand tph	Water tph	Per cent solids	Dry sand sp gr	Pulp sp gr	Water gpm	Pulp gpm
A	157.02	549.3	22.2	3.15	1.179	2193.2	2390.6
B	57.02	199.3	22.2	3.15	1.179	793.2	870.6
C	100.00	350.0	22.2	3.15	1.179	1400.0	1520.0
D	40.00	74.0	35.0	3.20	1.32	295.0	345.0
E	60.00	338.0	15.2	3.10	1.12	1330.0	1400.0
F	40.00	120.0	25.0	3.20	1.21	480.0	530.0
G	4.00	104.5	3.6	3.10	1.04	418.0	422.0
H	36.00	15.5	70.0	3.20	1.94	62.0	108.0
I	150.00	65.0	70.0	3.20	1.94	260.0	445.0

[1] These data are based on the initial engineering design estimates and may vary some-what when the system operates at full capacity.

car trains pulled by an 8-ton GE or Goodman locomotive. Bottom-dump Sanford-Day cars, measuring 15 ft 7 in. from coupler to coupler, carry 15 to 16 tons each. Track on the 1600 level consists of 60-lb rail on 42-in. gage.

HOISTING

Ore trains discharge into either of two loading pockets extending from the 1600 sill to twin transfer gates 90 ft below the 1600 level. Ore can travel from either loading pocket to either or both control gates which discharge into measuring hoppers. (See drawing of shaft-loading installation.) Capacity of the pockets is 400 tons. Twelve-ton Jeto bottom-dump skips in counter balance hoist the ore to a surface bin at 1400 fpm. A complete hoisting cycle takes two minutes. Hoisting rate is 360 tph. The skip tender operating the loading gates actuates controls of the completely automatic hoisting system with a pull cord. The ore bin at the headframe is equipped with an air-operated deflection plate which can divert waste to an overhead conveyor discharging on the waste dump below the mine changehouse and office.

The man cage or service cage is counterbalanced by one weight which travels a 20-in. O.D. pipe cast in shaft lining concrete. The service hoisting system, designed by Westinghouse engineers, has a semiautomatic control which eliminates problems of transmitting control signals through trailing cables. Start, stops or destination control signals are sent by push-button from inside the service cage through the hoisting cable on high-frequency carrier waves. The signals are

taken off the rope by an antenna on the headframe where they are transmitted to the automatic hoist control room. The same system provides voice communication via two-way radio from the cage to the hoist room operator.

Both the Nordberg service hoist and the ore hoist are equipped with interchangeable 700-hp dc motors, one for the service hoist and two for the production hoist.

The production hoist has two 600-kw generators in its 1500-hp motor-generator set, and the service hoist has one 600-kw generator for its 700-hp set. Reactive kva compensation in the production hoist drive increases the field strength of the synchronous m-g set motor when pulling heavy loads. This eliminates need for a flywheel m-g set and improves the power factor.

Hoist controls have an electromechanical programming device that reproduces the conveyance travel through a Selsyn device with a moving replica advanced slightly ahead of actual position of the conveyance. This advance selector anticipates the conveyance position and programs slow-down at the selected levels. Operation of the hoist is electronically coded, and the use of interlocks and sequence switches prevents outside electronics ("Sputniks") from actuating the circuits accidentally.

The cage hoist drum is 10-ft x 84-in., rope diameter is 1 1/2-in. and sheave diameter is 10-ft. The ore hoist drum is 13-ft x 87-in; rope diameter is 2 in. and sheave diameter is 12 ft.

SAND FILL SYSTEM

Sand fill for the mine will be treated in a two-stage classification

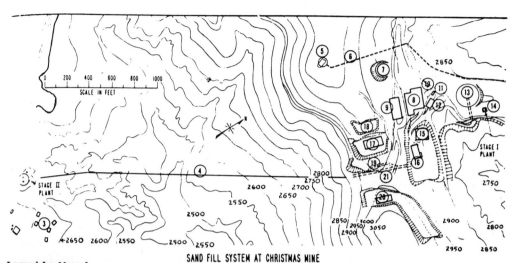

SAND FILL SYSTEM AT CHRISTMAS MINE

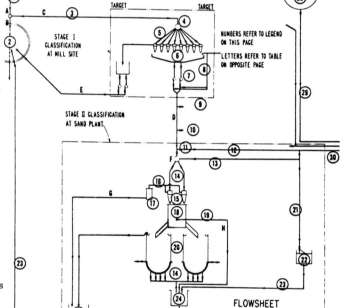

FLOWSHEET
OF SAND FILL PLANT
CHRISTMAS MINE
ARIZONA

Legend for Map of
Sand Fill System
1. Diamond drill hole No. 13 to transport sand to 800 level
2. Two 25-ft-dia x 62-ft storage tanks at Stage II plant
3. Old town of Christmas
4. Pipelines including 6-in. return slimes, 6-in. sand line from Stage I to Stage II plants, 6-in. compressed air line, 3-in. return water line, 2-1/2-in. fresh water line
5. 1-million-gal storage tank
6. 10-in. supply line from Dripping Springs
7. 100-ft rougher-scavenger thickener
8. Concentrator
9. Ore storage building
10. 50-ft concentrate thickener
11. Filter plant
12. Concentrate storage
13. 200-ft. tailings thickener
14. Stage 1 classification plant
15. Machine shop
16. Warehouse
17. Hoist and compressor house
18. Power substation
19. McDonald Shaft
20. Change house, safety headquarters and offices
21. Supply tunnel to McDonald Shaft

Legend for Flowsheet of
Sand Fill System
1. 14-in. Transite line
2. 200-ft tailings thickener
3. 10-in. Transite line
4. Distributor
5. Eight Model D10B Krebs cyclones, 4-in. valve, 3/8-in. rubber lining
6. Pump sump
7. Two Galigher 6x8 Vacseal pumps, 365 gpm at 70-ft head, 50 connected hp.
8. 3-in. flush-water line
9. Vent
10. Blowdown
11. Valves
12. 4-in. flush line

13. 4-in. new water line, 46 tph, 185 gpm
14. 6-in. 3/8-in. rubber-lined pipe
15. Two Model D15B Krebs cyclones
16. 6-in. slime overflow line
17. Overflow box
18. Cyclone underflow box
19. 4-in. pipe, 3/8-in. rubber-lined
20. Two 25-ft-dia. 62-ft-high, 1000-ton storage tanks
21. 2-in. water supply with float valve
22. 5000-gal flushing water line
23. 6-in. steel flushing pipe
24. Sand box

25. Diamond drill holes to 800 level
26. Pump sump
27. Two 450-gpm pumps, 310-ft head, 75 connected hp.
28. 40,000-gal tank
29. 2-1/2-in. potable water to Christmas
30. 4-in. dilution water from Christmas
31. Pump sump
32. Two Galigher 8x10 Vacseal pumps, 1400 gpm at 70-ft head, 75 connected hp.

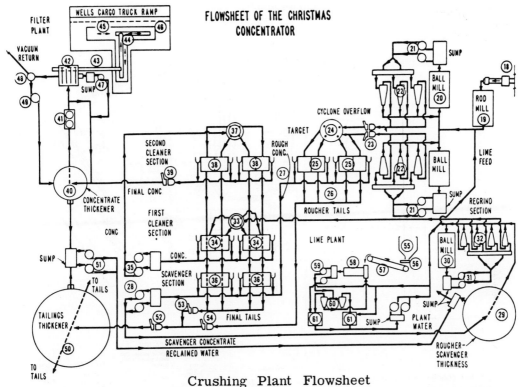

FLOWSHEET OF THE CHRISTMAS CONCENTRATOR

Crushing Plant Flowsheet
Christmas Development — Inspiration Comsolidated Copper Co.
Christmas, Ariz.

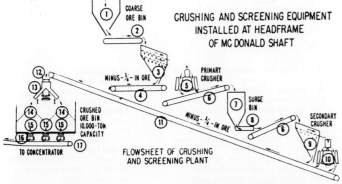

CRUSHING AND SCREENING EQUIPMENT
INSTALLED AT HEADFRAME
OF MC DONALD SHAFT

FLOWSHEET OF CRUSHING
AND SCREENING PLANT

LEGEND
1. Course ore storage bin, 1000-ton capacity
2. 54x22-in. Stephens-Adamson apron feeder, 400-tph capacity
3. 4x12-ft, two-deck Allis-Chalmers vibrating screen: with 4-in. square openings on top deck, 3/4-in. openings on lower deck between 1/2-in. loose rods
4. 30-in. conveyor belt takes minus-3/4-in. to crushed ore conveyor
5. 24x60 Allis-Chalmers gyratory crusher receives plus-3/4-in. and plus -4-in. from the screen. Discharge set is 2-1/2 in.

6. 30-in. belt conveyor
7. 100-ton capacity surge bin
8. 36x144-in. Hewitt-Robins vibratory feeder
9. 5-ft x 12-in. single deck Allis-Chalmers vibrating screen: minus-3/4-in. openings between 1/2-in. loose rods
10. No. 584 Allis-Chalmers Hydro-cone crusher, 1/2-in. discharge setting
11. 30-in. belt conveyor
12. 30-in. belt conveyor, perpendicular to feeder conveyor No. 1 ll
13. Self-propelled jeffry type

234B tripper
14. Minus-3/4-in. crushed ore storage building, 10,000-ton capacity
15. Three rows of seven draw-points in building floor
16. 21 Jeffrey No. 4DL vibrating feeders (beneath each draw-point) supply six 24-in. belt conveyors
17. 24-in. belt conveyor draws from feeder conveyors and conducts ore to rod mills in the concentrator building
18. Con-O-Weigh belt scales on 24-in. conveyor from crushed ore storage bin
19. 11x16-ft Allis-Chalmers over-flow rod mill
20. Two Allis-Chalmers 11-1/2x14-ft ball mills
21. Four 8x10-in. Vacseal R.L. pumps
22 Two sets of three Krebs D20B cyclones
23. Two 18-in Galigher H.D. samplers
24. 8-ft. Denver motorized distributor
25. Rougher flotation section: 96 units, Galigher No. 48 machines
26. Tails from roughers go through two samplers (No. 52 and 54), then to tailings thickener

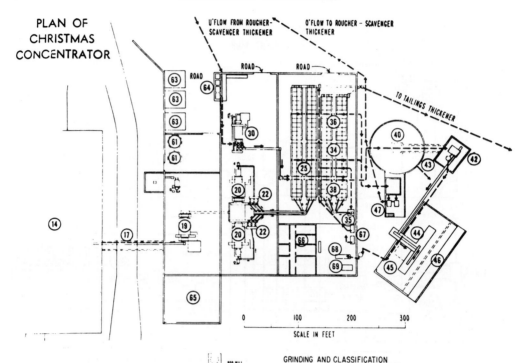

PLAN OF CHRISTMAS CONCENTRATOR

U'FLOW FROM ROUGHER-SCAVENGER THICKENER

O'FLOW TO ROUGHER-SCAVENGER THICKENER

TO TAILINGS THICKENER

SCALE IN FEET

GRINDING AND CLASSIFICATION

SECTION THROUGH THE CONCENTRATOR

27. Rougher concentrate travels to sumps
28. 6x8-in. Vacseal R.L. pumps move rougher concentrate to rougher-scavenger thickener
29. 100-ft-dia Process Engineering rougher-scavenger thickener
30. 9x14-ft Allis-Chalmers regrind ball mill (overflow)
31. 6x8-in. Vacseal pumps
32. Four Krebs D10B cyclones send underflow back to regrind ball mill. Overflow goes to 1st cleaner distributor
33. 5-ft Denver motorized distributor
34. 1st cleaner flotation: 32 Galigher No. 48 machines
35. 6x8-in. Vacseal pumps
36. 1st cleaner tails go to scavenger section: latter consists of 40 Galigher No. 48 machines, which send concentrate to sump and pumps (No. 28) and back through regrind ball mill
37. 5-ft. Denver motorized distributor
38. 2nd cleaner flotation: 16 Galigher No. 48 units: tails return to 1st cleaners, concentrate to samplers
39. 12-in. Galigher standard samplers
40. 50-ft-dia Process Engineers concentrate thickener
41. Two No. 3 Dorr-Oliver ODS slurry pumps
42. Eimco 8-ft-10-in.-dia four-disk Agidisc filter

43. 24-in. belt conveyor
44. 18-in. belt conveyor
45. Shuttle platform
46. Load-out platform. Front-end loader dumps into special Wells Cargo trucks for 37-mile haul to Inspiration smelter at Miami
47. 2-in. Hazelton pump for water return to thickener
48. 48x84-in. vacuum receiver with return to vacuum system
49. Kroga No. 55 filtrate pump
50. 200-ft-dia Dorr-Oliver tailings thickener (see No. 26)
51. 5-in. Hazelton VS pumps return water to plant system
52. 30-in. Galigher HD sampler
53. 18-in. Galigher HD sampler
54. 24-in. Galigher HD sampler

Lime Plant

55. 100-ton lime bin. Line is brought to Christmas on the return trip of the concentrate trucks

from Miami
56. Syntron F-21 feeder
57. 14-in. belt conveyor
58. 3x6-ft Denver ball mill, scoop feed
59. 2-in. Hazelton VN pumps
60. Two Dorr-Oliver 100A cyclones. Underflow returns to ball mill
61. 14-ft-dia x 14-ft Dorr-Oliver paddle agitators receive cyclone overflow
62. 2-in. Hazelton VN pumps move lime to rod mill at head of flowsheet
63. Rod storage
64. Ball storage
65. Mill office above, electrical equipment below
66. Bucking rooms and laboratory
67. Blowers
68. Vacuum pump
69. Air compressor

system shown on the accompanying flowsheet and map. In the Stage I plant at the mill area, part of the tailings from the concentrator are diverted to a bank of eight cyclones. Water is added as needed to the cyclone underflow to produce a pulp running about 35% solids. (Note: the pulp densities, etc., which are listed in the table of the flowsheet are based on initial engineering design and may be varied somewhat when the plant is in full operation.) Classified pulp is pumped through a 5000-ft 6-in. rubber-lined pipeline to the Stage II classification plant near Christmas. Here the pulp goes through two cyclones in parallel to two 25-ft-dia by 62-ft-high storage tanks which feed a sand box where make-up water is added as needed to deliver sand fill running about 70% solids to the diamond drill holes transporting the fill to the 800 level of the mine. The sand line connecting the two classification systems drops from about 3000 ft at Stage I to below 2550 ft in a dry gulch, and then rises to about 2700 ft at the Stage II plant. (See map.) This accounts for the 310-ft head on the pumps returning slimes from Stage II to the tailings thickener near Stage I.

Flowsheet-type panel in mill controls operations of equipment, and indicates and records critical data.

Primary grinding section houses 11 x 16-ft Allis-Chalmers rod mill, rod-charging deck, and reagent deck.

Harold Sorstokke, mill superintendent, at control console overlooking the flotation section of the concentrator.

Flotation section includes banks of roughers, scavenger, cleaner and second cleaner Galigher flotation cells.

Secondary grinding takes place in two A-C 1 1/4 x 14-ft ball mills. Grind is classified in six Krebs D20B cyclones.

Regrind section includes a 9 x 14-ft A-C overflow ball mill and a bank of four Krebs D10B cyclone classifiers.

Concentrates are hauled 27 miles to rail siding at Miami in this 25-ton Wells Cargo twin-kettle trailer unit.

Concentrate kettles are flipped over easily with overhead sling and crane at railside unloading ramp at Miami, Ariz.

CRUSHING PLANT
AND CONCENTRATOR

All equipment units and the flow of various products in the Christmas crushing plant and concentrator are identified and illustrated in accompanying flowsheets, sections, plans and photographs. Performance at the mill during initial operation has been satisfactory, exceeding the metallurgical results indicated by the pilot-plant which was refurbished to test Christmas ores in 1957.

Provisions for handling heavy equipment and supplies are unique at the Christmas surface plant. An 80-ton P&H rubber-tired crane is employed to replace heavy overhead bridge cranes normally installed in surface plants. The mobile crane, equipped with a 40-ton boom, can travel on roadways entering the hoist and compressor house, mill, and areas adjacent to the outdoor crushing equipment at the McDonald Shaft to handle heavy parts and supplies. In addition to saving the cost of heavy bridge cranes, the mobile crane permitted use of lighter steel sections in the construction of buildings and served during the actual construction. This item alone more than offsets the cost of the mobile crane.

The primary and secondary crushing flowsheet is designed to divert undersize to storage as soon as it is formed in various stages of the plant. Ore travels via conveyor to a 1000-ton surge bin and then to the 8000-ton live-storage (10,000-ton dead-storage) bin. Ore is discharged through 21 drawpoints arranged in three rows of seven each. The 8000-ton capacity is sufficient to operate the mill for two days if mine production should be scheduled on a five-day basis. The ore bin is emptied every week with the aid of a front-end loader, if necessary, to prevent oxidation.

Some 15 different types of flowsheets were tried on the Christmas ore during pilot-plant test work. The present flowsheet incorporates a high degree of flexibility. Designed by William Wraith Jr., the flowsheet closely parallels those at Inspiration and El Salvador in Chile. If the character of the mill feed should change in future mine production, the mill staff will merely have to change the "plumbing" and Victaulic fittings in the flotation plant to adjust the flowsheet to the new type of feed.

During initial operating period, the primary grind was 20% plus 200 mesh and the regrind discharge to flotation was 2% to 3% plus 200 mesh. Reagents included MIBC frother and some Dowfroth, 404 and Z6 collectors and lime about 3.5 lb per ton. Mill liners are chrome-moly. Addition rods are 4-in. dia, and addition balls are 2-in. cast and forged. Rods are charged with a specially built rod charger. Balls are loaded in to bins and then handled by crane in charging buckets.

CONCENTRATE TO MIAMI

Some 400 tons of concentrate (7% moisture) can be stored in the load-out building. A separate building contains an Eimco leaf filter. A traveling conveyor on horizontal rails lays the concentrate down on the smooth concrete floor, which is raised above the truck loading ramp.

Load-out arrangments were made to the specifications of Wells Cargo Inc., who asked for the smooth loading surface and supplied a John Deere 300 front-end loader to dump its 5/8-yd bites into the two unit "soup kettle" truck for the 37-mile haul to Miami. Wells Cargo designed the special truck, which has a total of 25 tons capacity in two kettles, and is loaded in about 30 minutes and 26 passes by the loader.

The red trucks are designed to be dumped by a clevis hook and P&H hoist arrangment at a rail siding in Miami (see figures) for the trip to Inspiration's smelter on the hill. The kettles make a 180 flip over the railroad cars. On the return haul to Christmas, the trucks bring lime for the concentrator.

Tailings from the concentrator move by gravity through a system of pipes, launders and ditches to three tailings disposal areas below the thickeners. An average 3 1/2% grade is necessary to keep the magnetite in the tails moving. The main tailings dams are constructed on solid foundations, and secondary slimes dams are constructed behind the main wall to protect the toe of the dam.

From the McDonald headframe looking north (left), the conveyor takes ore to the crushed ore building. Mill and load-out building step down to the tailings thickener. Building in foreground is the maintenance shop. Looking southwest (right)

the sand fill line in the foreground rises across the Christmas Basin to the sand plant. The No. 3 Shaft is at right and the old town of Christmas at left center. The new townsite is at lower left.

As the project progresses, water from the tailings ponds will be reclaimed for mill use.

COMPRESSED AIR

Compressed air at 110 psi is supplied to the mine by two I-R 3184 two-stage compressors of the PRE type, powered by 600-hp synchronous motors. The units installed in the hoist-house are completely automatic and are fully protected against damage by failure of valve, cooling water and lubrication circulation and bearing failure. See automatic control cabinet in accompanying photo.

WATER SUPPLY, WATER PROBLEMS

Inspiration is handling water from two sources: first, from its own fresh water supply; second, from its underground workings. The first source, Dripping Springs, is the site of two wells — one 800 ft deep, the

other 420 ft. The first well is tapped by a 720-gpm pump and the second by a 300-gpm unit, both of which fill a 120,000-gal tank. Two line pumps provide 1050 tdh to move the water through a 10-in. line from the tank at Dripping Springs to a 1-million-gal tank at the minesite, three miles away.

A 40,000-gal potable water tank at the minesite also serves the camp. The 1-million-gal tank supplies an estimated 1-million gpd process water to the mill and also serves as one part of the 8-in. fire loop which encircles the entire surface plant and originates in the 10-in. feed line from Dripping Springs.

Inspiration's second water source was originally a less welcome one. When the mine crews were sinking the McDonald Shaft, they encountered no water, but it did appear later. Subsequent pumping has reduced the flow, and some older workings in the mine now show signs of drying out. Underground water from the McDonald is now added to the process water tank via a 10-in. line to the surface. Three Barrett-Haentjens 1770 rpm, 600 hp, 950-gpm pumps provide 1750 tdh to move it to the 1-million-gal tank on the surface. The Barrett-Haentjens units draw from a sump 8 ft above the bottom pocket, which is fed by three 6-in. type MS Hazleton pumps, which drain the ditch in the haulage drift. The sump is raised 8 ft above the larger pumps to provide a positive suction head.

MINE VENTILATION

Both the McDonald and the No. 3 Shafts are downcast in the ventilation system designed by Inspiration's engineers. A 12-ft-dia shaft, the No. 6, provides upcast service for the system, which principally uses a 2300-v main fan at the surface of the No. 6, supported by auxiliary 440-v units underground. The former is a Joy Axivane 300-hp unit, providing 200,000 cfm on 2.3-in. water gage. The underground fans consist of a number of 38-in., 42-in., and 45-in. two-stage units, with two 4-ft single-stage fans.

Downcast air travels along the 1600 level between the two haulage shafts, goes through the mining areas and exhausts on the 1300 and 1400 levels to the No. 6 Shaft. A ventilation raise between the 800 and 1400 levels together with others between 1600 and 1400 completes the layout.

POWER FROM SALT RIVER

Inspiration purchases 115,000-v electric power from the Salt River Power District and brings it to a transformer substation located next to the hoist house. Redistribution control gear in the hoist house directs the transformed 4160-v power to underground workings, to the crusher plant, and to the mill. The fans are on 440 v underground and on 2300 v at the surface. The pumps are on 4160 v.

Underground, 150-kw silicon rectifiers at either end of the main haulage shaft (which is at 1600 ft at the McDonald Shaft end of the drift and 1400 ft at the No. 3 Shaft) convert the 2300 v ac to 275 dc for the trolley line.

BROKEN HILL — A LIVING LEGEND

by
JOHN V. BEALE

Conservatively, there are a half million square miles in Australia just like it, this spot near the western border of New South Wales. Space and distance are the elements. Mulga tree and salt bush, silvery under the sun, hug the ground too close to make welcome shade. To the east a wrinkle on the empty plain marks the line of lode, the Broken Hill bonanza.

Strangely, the outback stops at a cyclone fence close by the ridge. Beyond, the peculiar island continent vegetation flourishes with the same frosty patina of the mulga and the salt bush. A city of 30,000 people is hidden behind the screen of vegetation. Once, the city was ugly and the people miserable from marching, flying sand. Now with a protective screen of vegetation, it is an oasis in the outback. The secret of the oasis is the fence. All regeneration plans failed until it was built to keep kangaroo, rabbit, sheep and man from destroying the plantations.

There are no other secrets here because Broken Hill is known to every Australian. A medley of wonderful contrasts dot, the 80 year history; and even today new ones are born. Broken Hill, the source of sudden riches wrenched from underground perils, where market booms slumped to black depressions, where inventive genius thrived and sometimes management fumbled.

Range rider Charles Rasp pegged the first claim at Broken Hill in 1883 on what he thought was a tin deposit. His employer — station manager George McCulloch — and five other cronies jumped in for six more claims in the name of the Syndicate of Seven. In 1885, after long months of frustration, a specimen assaying 800 oz of silver per ton prompted the partners to float the Broken Hill Pty. Mining on the outcrop, the Proprietary was able to pay as it went. It was on the dividend list three years from discovery.

Australians of those days were great mine promoters and soon the line of lode was pegged by several different companies. In the beginning, only silver-bearing lead ore was mined, but with depth, the operators entered zones of partially oxidized ores and eventually the mixed galena-marmatite ore. There were serious mining difficulties in supporting the workings, poor ventilation and fires. At first the lead ores were smelted at Broken Hill but they speak of vast bulwarks of zinc-rich tailings which accumulated because they could not be processed. The Zinc Corporation and Amalgamated Zinc (DeBavay) Ltd. were formed

"Broken Hill — A Living Legend" by John V. Beall. Reprinted from Mining Engineering, *Vol.* 16 (*October* 1964) *pp.* 70-75, *with permission of the editor.*

in 1905 to attempt processing the zinc residues. In 1912, experimental work in flotation resulted in the first differential flotation process by which zinc could be separated from the lead by adding eucalyptus oil and aerating the pulp.

The companies came and went, and often sold blocks that became profitable to the purchasers as the structure of the lode was disclosed. Broken Hill Pty., in 1887, sold some of its blocks, and after 55 years of operation it abandoned its remaining leases at Broken Hill for lack of ore. It had made large profits from mining the center, near-surface portion of the deposit and had launched into the iron and steel business during World War I.

(North), Broken Hill South Ltd. (South), The Zinc Corporation Ltd. (Zinc) and New Broken Hill Consolidated Ltd. (NBHC), all that remain of the many companies. The latter two companies are part of the Conzinc Riotinto of Australia Ltd. (CRA) group (NBHC being 1/3 owned) and are under a single management.

Wealth created by the Broken Hill deposit has contributed materially to the industrial growth of Australia through these and other companies. Among the list of companies which have sprung from Broken Hill are: Broken Hill Pty. Ltd., iron and steel (BHP); Broken Hill Associated Smelters Pty. Ltd., lead smelting and refining (BHAS); E. Z. Indus-

Panorama of The Zinc Corp. surface plant shows the main shaft, administrative offices adjacent and the concentrator at left. Circular concrete structure in front of shaft houses two primary crushing units. Producing nearly 900,000 tons per year, The Zinc Corp. has greatest output of ore among the four producing mines.

Out of attrition and consolidation emerged the present day ownership of the Broken Hill deposit. The maps on pages 298 and 299 show the positions of North Broken Hill Ltd.

tries Ltd., zinc refining and chemicals; The Electrolytic Refining and Smelting Co. of Australia Pty. Ltd., copper; Commonwealth Aircraft Corp., Associated Pulp & Paper

Mills Ltd., Commonwealth Steel Co. Ltd., and the bulk of the CRA group. Broken Hill money has also helped finance Australia's two burgeoning aluminum complexes — Alcoa (through North and South) and Comalco (Zinc) and NBHC through the CRA group.

The great Broken Hill lode primarily consists of two long, thin, highly folded, ore-bearing strata in Precambrian quartzites and gneiss. The zones are arched in longitudinal, vertical projection, outcropping near the center and plunging toward the ends. The line of lode is continuous for 24,000 ft on strike and up to 500 ft wide. In 80 years of mining, it has produced 90 million tons of rich lead-silver-zinc ore. Present ore averages 23% metal, divided 11.3% Pb, 3.9 oz Ag, 11.8% Zn. Broken Hill engineers are inclined to capsulize grades as: "11-4-12." Ratios of lead : silver : zinc vary from place to place but it is not uncommon to have assays of 50% metal content.

At present mining rates, there are known to be reserves of 50 years at the southern end, 20 years in the north, and 7 or 8 years at Broken Hill South Ltd. At the North mine, the 42° pitch of the ore zone steepens to subvertical below the 2920 ft level. The bottom level of stoping is 3520 ft, deepest on the lode, and drilling has disclosed ore to an additional 1000 ft depth. The bottom of ore is not known.

The South mine, low in reserves, is doing extensive drilling and tunnel exploration to test the lode horizon as it dips steeply west below the town. Lead-zinc mineralization persists to depth in the deepest holes (6402 ft). A body of mineralization above the 1480 ft level has been defined but is not presently considered economic with average grade, 3-1-5. South is conducting negotiations with the unions for revised conditions to permit mass mining

New Broken Hill Consolidated Ltd. is most recent operation at Broken Hill although it began production in 1936. Back of the mine surface plant is the diesel power station of Southern Power Corp. Pty. Ltd. owned by Conzinc Riotinto. The Zinc Corp. operates NBHC in which Conzinc Riotinto has a one-third interest.

Table 1. Sample Data Broken Hill Mines

	North Broken Hill Ltd.	Broken Hill South Ltd.	The Zinc Corp. Ltd.	New Broken Hill Consol. Ltd.
Ore mined, l.t.	495,114	293,765	887,679	778,537
Assay: %Pb, oz Ag, %Zn	15.0-8.2-12.5	11.8-6.2-10.3	13.7-3.2-10.0	12.7-3.4-12.0
Lead concentrates, l.t.	97,032	46,057	155,929	124,366
Assay: %Pb, oz Ag, %Zn	74.9-38.9-4.3	72.9-37.3-5.4	75.9-16.7-4.0	77.1-19.6-3.8
Zinc concentrates, l.t.	105,251	49,899	149,761	157,782
Assay: %Pb, oz Ag, %Zn	0.6-0.8-52.8	1.1-1.0-52.1	0.9-0.7-52.6	0.7-0.6-54.0
Total ore mined, l.t.	19,568,879	18,229,618	20,226,224	7,625,359
Ore reserves, l.t.	10,000,000	1,270,000	6,000,000	5,200,000
Year of first production	1880	1888	1915[1]	1936
Power consumed, KWH	26.0 million	10.7 million	25.5 million	22.3 million
Compressed air, cu ft	1.9 billion	0.9 billion	1.4 billion	1.3 billion
Mine timber, super ft	4.0 million	2.2 million	5.8 million	3.2 million
Explosives, lb	214,445	189,000	316,100	290,100
Diamond drilling, ft	25,554	11,957	8,447	22,756
Number of employees	1,137	869	1,694	686
Surface	490	391	852	177
Underground	647	478	842	509
Wages & salaries, £A	£1,525,114	£1,077,561	£2,305,165	£1,026,013
Lead bonus, £A	£517,406	£274,396	£615,955	£249,991
Dividends, £A	£992,000	£533,333	n.a.	n.a.

[1] Mined prior to 1915 by Broken Hill South Blocks.

of this orebody at lower cost.

Zinc and NBHC, with the largest reserves, have six separate minable lodes. These plunge at 30° on Zinc Corp. property but are flatter at NBHC.

Mining and concentrating operations are performed at Broken Hill; the bulk of the concentrates are sent by rail to Port Pirie. The lead is treated at Port Pirie by BHAS; the zinc is transhipped to E. Z., Risdon, Tasmania; to the Sulphide Corp., Cockle Creek, New South Wales, or to other destinations. Some zinc and lead concentrates are also railed directly from Broken Hill to the Sulphide Corp. at Cockle Creek. Typical production data for the four mines are shown in Table 1.

MINING

The ore deposit is reached through vertical shafts ranging from a minimum depth of 1200 ft to a maximum at North of 4320 ft. The North No. 3 shaft is the largest; it is elliptical in cross section, 31 x 15 ft inside concrete, and fitted with steel buntons. Each mine operates more than one shaft for a combination of man, material and ore hoisting service. These

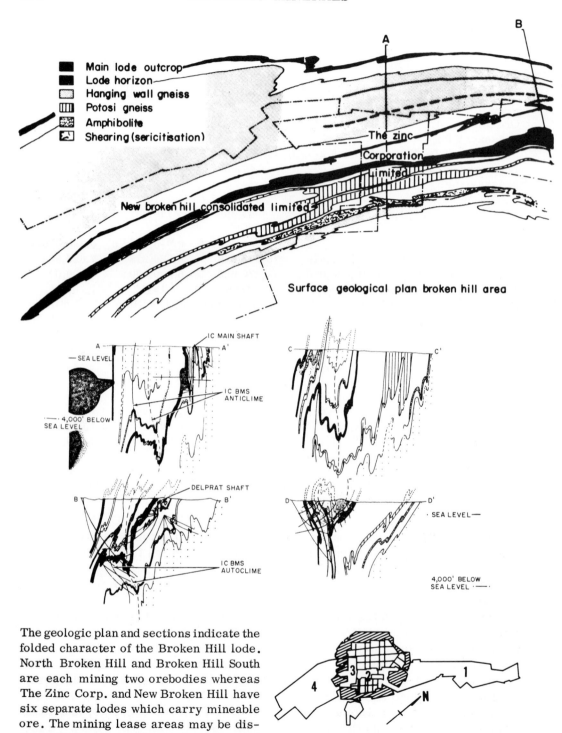

Main lode outcrop
Lode horizon
Hanging wall gneiss
Potosi gneiss
Amphibolite
Shearing (sericitisation)

The zinc
Corporation
limited

New broken hill consolidated limited

Surface geological plan broken hill area

IC MAIN SHAFT
A   A'
SEA LEVEL
IC BMS
ANTICLIME
4,000' BELOW
SEA LEVEL

C   C'

DELPRAT SHAFT
B   B'
D   D'
SEA LEVEL
IC BMS
AUTOCLIME
4,000' BELOW
SEA LEVEL

The geologic plan and sections indicate the folded character of the Broken Hill lode. North Broken Hill and Broken Hill South are each mining two orebodies whereas The Zinc Corp. and New Broken Hill have six separate lodes which carry mineable ore. The mining lease areas may be distinguished on the geologic plan. The diagram above shows the property relationships to each other and the town. 1) North Broken Hill; 2) Broken Hill South; 3) The Zinc Corp.; 4) New Broken Hill. Hatched area is the protective ring of plantations which surround the city and suppress the invasion of sand which at one time plagued the inhabitants.

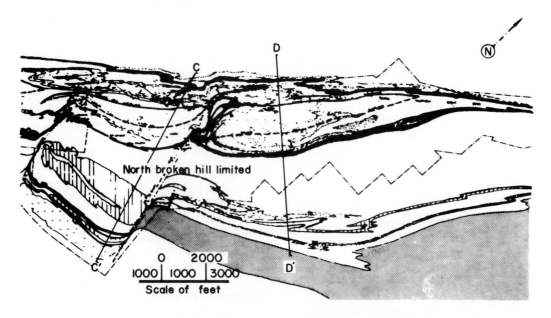

Relics of early day mining may be found along the lode in the form of pits, foundations, tailing piles and slag heaps. Here an old BHP headframe is seen with Mount Hibbard in the background.

are supplemented with two or more ventilation shafts.

Levels are spaced from 100 to 190 ft apart. The most common mining method is flat-backed cut-and-fill stoping with square-set timber supports where needed. Some shrink stoping is practiced. Mining is in three stages: vertical stope extraction, pillar removal, and crown pillar recovery. Considerable attention is being given to the possibility of employing trackless equipment for stoping.

Ground support is achieved with rock bolts, timber sets, and sand fill. The sand fill is stored on the surface and underground in a dry state and pulped at surface and underground mining stations and fed by gravity to the stopes.

Drilling is accomplished with airleg drills and stopers. Column and arm machines with coupled steel are used for long holes, which are required by law for raise development. Blasting has been with Gelignite AN 60 but there is a trend to AN-FO. Both electric and safety fuse detonation are employed.

Broken rock is moved by scrapers in the stopes and rocker-arm loaders on the levels.

Transportation is by 8-ton (maximum size) battery locomotives pulling 110 cu ft (maximum size) Granby cars.

Drainage is not a big problem. The average mine pumps about 1 million gallons per week.

The most extensive ventilation plant is at the Zinc and NBHC mines, circulating a maximum of 1 million cfm under winter conditions.

CONCENTRATION

Rated capacity of the four flotation concentrators pertinent to each mine is as follows: North, 102 tph; South, 70 tph; Zinc, 180 tph; and NBHC, 145 tph. Plants operate on a five-day or 120-hr week. No attempt is made to maintain coarse ore storage above ground, the average size crusher feed bin being about 120 tons capacity. All plants have primary jaw crushing and one stage of standard cone crushing except the newer NBHC plant which has underground jaw crushing followed by standard and short head reduction. The other plants employ roll crushing for the tertiary stage. From three to five roll units in parallel are required to achieve capacity.

Various grinding systems are used. At North, ball mills are in closed circuit with cyclone classifiers. Two stages of grinding composed of tube mills and ball mills with closed circuit cyclone classification in both stages are the practice at South. The Zinc mill has one stage of ball mill classifiers, and NBHC has a rod mill ahead of ball mills both discharging to the same rake classifiers. The flotation feed is from 40% to 50% minus 240 mesh BSS at 48% to 50% solids.

In general, a final lead concentrate may be taken from the first few cells of each machine or it may be cleaned. Middling or scavenger concentrates are classified and the coarse fraction is reground. Deleaded tailing is the feed for zinc flotation. Reagent consumption is shown in Table 2.

Zinc rougher concentrates are cleaned and in some cases recleaned. The rougher tailing is the final tailing used for sand fill. Cleaner tailing is returned to the head of the rougher section, and recleaner tailing to the head of the cleaner section. Reagents are shown in Table 3 and the tailing loss in Table 4.

Concentrates are filtered or thickened and filtered.

At the Zinc and NBHC mills, the plant is simplified to permit shutting down in 1 1/2 hrs. There are no primary thickening and no conditioning tanks prior to flotation.

The richness of the Broken Hill lode has had drawbacks as well as the many advantages. A special ambience affecting mining operations and community life has evolved. The population has remained steady at 30,000 for 50 years or more. A miner must have resided eight years of the last ten in Broken Hill before he can get a job underground. The union officers, because of the solidarity of the rank and file, pack the

Table 2. Lead Flotation Reagents

North		South		Zinc		NBHC	
Reagent	lb/ton	Reagent	lb/ton	Reagent	lb/ton	Reagent	lb/ton
Sodium ethyl xanthate	0.082	Sodium ethyl xanthate	0.106	Sodium ethyl xanthate	0.095	Sodium ethyl xanthate	0.102
Amyl xanthate	0.001	Sodium sulfite	0.635	Methyl iso-butyl-carbinol	0.003	Methyl-butyl-carbinol	0.004
Cresylic acid	0.018	Cresylic acid	0.015	Zinc sulfate	0.331	Zinc sulfate	0.229
Coal tar	0.002						

Table 3. Zinc Flotation Reagents

North		South		Zinc		NBHC	
Reagent	lb/ton	Reagent	lb/ton	Reagent	lb/ton	Reagent	lb/ton
Sodium ethyl xanthate	0.088	Sodium ethyl xanthate	0.140	Sodium ethyl xanthate	0.089	Sodium ethyl xanthate	0.113
Copper sulfate	0.946	Copper sulfate	0.823	Copper sulfate	0.818	Copper sulfate	0.909
Cresylic acid	0.036	Flotation oil No. 66	0.040	Cresylic acid	0.013	Cresylic acid	0.010
Coal tar	0.010			Lime	0.435	Lime	0.472
						Fortisol	0.0002

| Table 4. Tailing Assays | | | | |
Company	Weight %	% Pb	Oz/ton Ag	% Zn
North	59.3	0.45	0.47	0.79
South	67.4	0.4	0.3	0.9
Z Corp	65.7	0.39	0.21	0.69
NBHC	63.8	0.47	0.22	0.65

most weight in the community. The unions are not registered with and therefore not subject to the state or Commonwealth Industrial Courts although action of these groups does influence the trend of negotiations with the companies. Labor is said to be the highest paid in the mineral industries. Mines and concentrators operate a five-day week only, apart from essential weekend maintenance.

Lead-silver-zinc is among a se-lect group of minerals for which the 20% income tax deduction given mining companies is disallowed. A royalty on gross profit from the mines is paid to New South Wales based on a sliding scale percentage of profits — sometimes as much as 50%. It costs about $15.40 per ton of crude ore to produce concentrates at one mine and as a result mineralization that assays 4.5-1.5-9.5 is not economic there at present.

Broken Hill is an orderly community, it is a proud community and it is also one that is admired by Australians not so fortunate as to reside there. However, it is a working man's community and the authorities are inclined to overlook certain peccadillos of the residents such as a penchant for Two-Up School on weekends.

Broken Hill is a living legend.

It is sometimes difficult for the visitor to distinguish subsidence areas from old open-pit workings. Across the subsidence area here is an exposed section of the line of lode. D. F. Fairweather, manager, Broken Hill South, stands at the rim.

A PELLET GIVES IRON ORE
INDUSTRY A SHOT IN THE ARM

A little ball of upgraded iron ore is rolling the iron mining business through a revolution.

Called a pellet, and about half an inch in diameter, the ball has been the object of some $1.5-billion in worldwide investment over the past decade. By far the biggest chunk of this money, about $1-billion, has gone into the Mesabi area of Minnesota. The over-all investment is "more money than the iron ore industry spent for all its capital investments in its entire history prior to this," according to W. A. Marting, president of Hanna Mining Co.

And it's only the beginning. In the Mesabi range, some $500-million has been earmarked for new capacity in the past year. Worldwide, twice as much money will go into pelletizing in the next 10 years as in the past decade.

Thus by 1975, the iron mining industry will have run up a 20-year investment bill of some $4.5-billion — almost all of it for pelletizing.

MANUFACTURE

The story takes in much more than dollars; the entire character of iron mining has been changed by the little round ball. Mining, which once was essentially a matter of digging up ore and shipping it to a blast furnace, is now becoming something of a manufacturing operation. That's because the relatively iron-poor stuff left in the earth after 100 years of steelmaking has to be processed, enriched, and formed into the pellets that most blast furnaces now can take.

Even here, the revolution is just getting started. Today, the finished pellet contains about 64% iron. But developments already under way will take pelletizing at least one step further. That step is pre-processing — often called metalizing — which will raise the pellet's iron content to more than 90%.

For example, a process to produce metalized pellets containing more than 95% pure iron has been developed jointly by Hanna, National Steel Pellet Co., and Surface Combustion Div. of Midland-Ross Corp. The process is believed to be nearing the commercial stage.

DEPLETION

The reason for all this investment and interest in pelletizing is easy to explain. In many mining areas, notably the Mesabi, a century of mining has depleted the reserves of "good" ore, leaving mostly what was considered worthless rock 20 years ago.

Just before World War II, new processes were evolved for upgrad-

"A Pellet Gives Iron Ore Industry Shot in the Arm." Reprinted by special permission from Business Week (*December* 4, 1965), *pp.* 106-114. *Copyrighted* 1965 *by McGraw-Hill, Inc.*

ing this rock — which came to be generally labeled taconite. The stage was set for the revolution in iron mining, with the most important of the new processes those that produced iron-rich pellets to be fed directly into the blast furnaces.

Actually, "artificial" iron ore is even better than the natural stuff. The so-called direct shipment ore that used to be mined in the Mesabi had an iron content of 51% to 56%. Taconite, whose iron content is at best 40%, can be upgraded to form pellets in the 64% to 68% range. That means you are shipping more iron per carload of ore, and the richer ore is better for blast furnaces.

RISING STAKES

The business aspects of mining have undergone a major change, too, since the taconite pellet boom really got going around 1955. Before that, the business was simple. You bought or leased a tract of land, and you dug up the ore for shipment. Initial investment to get a mine operating ran to about $10 per ton of annual capacity.

The advent of pelletizing has vastly increased the stakes — in many cases more than tripling them. Even in places where transportation and housing for workers are already available, the ante in the U.S. runs as high as $30 per ton of annual capacity. In some remote foreign areas, such as Northern Canada and Australia, investment for setting up a pelletizing operation runs to an estimated $50 a ton.

The stepped-up investment rate, plus the fact that the minimum efficient capacity of a taconite plant is generally figured at 1-million tons

a year, has made iron mining increasingly a partnership business.

Among the investors currently carrying out major taconite expansions, only giant U.S. Steel Corp. is going it alone, building a 4.5-million-ton, $135-million plant from scratch in Minnesota. All the other projects are joint ventures involving anywhere from two to 10 investors. Thus Armco Steel Corp. and Republic Steel Corp. are spending $25-million to add 1.7-million tons of capacity for Reserve Mining Co., which they control. Up in Canada, nine steelmakers and a mining company have gone in together to build a plant.

HEAVY DEMAND

Even with the mining stakes so much higher, the companies still believe the odds are right, with a healthy supply-and-demand ratio. "Right now, if we had twice as many pellets, we could sell them overnight," says H. Stuart Harrison, president of Cleveland-Cliffs Iron Co.

It will take more than overnight to double production of pellets. Harrison says that Cleveland-Cliffs studies indicate that the present 30-million-ton capacity in the U.S. won't reach 71-million tons until 1975.

Miners call this U.S. growth spectacular — for worldwide expansion they reserve a stronger word: fantastic. Cleveland-Cliffs expects a fivefold increase outside the U.S. in the next decade. Among the expected increases are:

Canada, from 15-million tons up to 45-million.

Western Europe, from less than 3-million tons up to nearly 30-million.

Worldwide Growth in Taconite Plants

	Operating as of Aug. 15, 1965	Thousands of tons capacity	
		Under construction in 1965	Total est. capacity by 1975
U.S.	30,150	17,350	70,800
Canada	14,950	2,000	45,050
Western Europe	2,620	1,600	27,990
South America	1,000	300	12,400
Australia	None	1,000	12,100
Asia and Africa	1,000	550	9,500
Total	49,720	22,800	177,840

Asia, Africa and the Western Pacific area, from a nominal 1-million tons to a phenomenal 21-million — a more than 20-fold increase.

These present and future international developments are causing a lot of thinking and some action by mining and steel companies. One puzzler is the balance of ore production and shipments. For example, Japan's fast-growing steel industry now gets most of its ore from four sources — Canada, Africa, South America, and the U.S. But what will it do after taconite production gets going, as it will, in and just off the coast of Australia?

REACHING OUT

Actually, the U.S. mining companies are already reaching out into

Major Taconite Pellet Plants Under
Construction in U.S. and Canada

Owner or operator	New capacity thousands of tons	Investment $-million	Completion
U.S. Steel	4,500	135	1967
Hanna Mining	2,400	79	1967
Hanna Mining	2,000	56	1967
Oglebay Norton	1,600	45	1965
Armco and Reserve	1,700	25	1966
Pickands Mather	2,300	50	1967
Cleveland-Cliffs	1,800	45	1966
Hanna Mining	750	23	1967
Kaiser Steel[1]	2,000	119	1965
Hanna Mining (Canada)	1,500	5.5	1965
Inland Steel (Canada)	1,000	17	1967
Cleveland-Cliffs (Canada)	1,000	40	1967

[1] Includes some non-pelletizing investment
Data: American Iron Ore Assn.; BW est.

international areas. Only Western Europe — where local companies seem ready and able to handle their own taconite development — appears to be out of reach. Australia is already a major target for U.S. miners; one executive calls the fields there "the major mineral discovery in the 20th Century."

One of the biggest U.S. stakes in Australia is Pickands Mather & Co.'s share of a $70-million, 2-million-ton pellet plant in Tasmania off the southwestern coast. Pickands Mather and a group of Australian partners hold half of it; the rest is owned by five Japanese steel and trading companies.

Other U.S. companies with projects under way in the Southwest Pacific include: Hanna Mining, Cleveland-Cliffs, Oglebay Norton Co., Kaiser Steel Corp., American Metal Climax, Inc., Utah Construction & Mining Co., and Cyprus Mines Corp.

While the U.S. producers are thus moving calmly into the international picture, they are under a great deal of pressure to insure the competitiveness of the domestic ore industry. That pressure is behind much of the present expansion.

TAX GUARANTEE

It was with an eye to the future that the mining houses backed the four-year campaign that finally brought an amendment to the Minnesota constitution and a tax structure beneficial to the miners. The amendment freezes for 25 years 1963 legislation providing that special occupation and royalty taxes on taconite should not be increased above either their present levels or the levels of income taxes paid by manufacturing companies.

Before the amendment, mining investment in the state had dragged to a halt. With the new tax guarantee, the gates opened and some $500-million in investments poured in.

From the state's point of view, the tax guarantee and the expected taconite pelletizing expansion promised a badly needed economic shot in the arm. The state's economy and employment had been badly hit by the mechanization that goes with pellitizing, and the closing of less productive mines.

Mechanization of mining is still a bugaboo in Minnesota. Mining jobs are expected to climb up to 13,000 in 1975, but that's still far below the 1957 employment figure of 20,000.

EQUIPMENT

Taconite expansion means a lot of new business for the companies that make the processing equipment. But at least one executive of a major equipment builder says it has yet to prove itself profitable. Says M. M. York, general manager for process equipment and systems at Allis-Chalmers Mfg. Co.: "It's an expanding business, but an extremely competitive one." York's company will build about half the 14-million tons of capacity being added in Minnesota.

Other important suppliers of the equipment include: Dravo Corp., Midland-Ross' Surface Combustion Div., McDowell-Wellman Engineering Co., and Arthur G. McKee & Co., which works primarily under an Allis-Chalmers license.

In principle, at least, it's simple enough to make pellets. Pulverizers first grind up the taconite. Then the iron is separated from the unwanted silicon by methods ranging from magnetic separation to flotation.

BALLING

At this stage, the product is a powder rich in iron. But the powder is too fine to be charged in a blast furnace, whose high winds would blow it around. To beat this difficulty a process was developed for balling the powder into a clay-like material called Bentonite.

The resulting pellets have proved a boon to the steel industry in two ways:

1. They have eased the fears that steel production would be drastically curtailed by the exhaustion of the good iron ore in the Mesabi.

2. The pellets, being richer than good ore and also of constant quality and easier to handle, have boosted the productivity of blast furnaces, sometimes by as much as 50%.

As a further plus, the uniform quality of the pellets has removed one more obstacle to the ultimate automation of the blast furnace. Says a mining executive: "One of the biggest changes that we have seen in the blast furnace is that science has gotten into the act. The blast furnace operator was an 'artist,' ordering ore by feel rather than science. We used to sell an awful ore to a company, just because the blast furnace operator wanted it. When they switched to pellets, the improvement in production was spectacular."

MINERAL OBSOLESCENCE AND SUBSTITUTION

by
*CHARLES W. MERRILL**

Obsolescence in the mineral world is virtually nonexistent if the term is taken to mean that a mineral commodity, once established in commerce and industry, subsequently has fallen into disuse. We are living in an age of minerals. Each generation puts an increasing array of mineral-based commodities, in larger quantities, to more uses than ever before. Bastnasite, a museum mineral and a collector's item a few years ago, is now produced in quantity at Mountain Pass, Calif. Uranium, a minor by-product of vanadium mining in the Rocky Mountain plateau area before World War II, has grown to be a leading mineral product in several western States. And finally the total quantity and value of minerals both in the United States and in the World establish new records almost yearly. Surely the mineral industry as a whole is not obsolescent in our economy.

Nevertheless, there are particular uses for particular minerals that are obsolescent and some applications have been supplanted entirely. Tin does not occupy the prominent place in foil manufacture that it once did, and the schoolboy's slate left most

*C. W. Merrill, member of SME, is Chief of Division of Minerals, U. S. Bureau of Mines, Washington, D. C.

classrooms before the oldest of us were born.

It is encouraging to the mineral industry as a whole that much of the obsolescence to be noted represents the replacement of one mineral product by another and not the loss of markets to products of the vegetable or animal kingdoms. There is an endless competition among minerals to serve the economy better and at lower cost to the industrial consumer and to the ultimate user.

Although the word *substitution* is commonly used for the replacement of one raw material by another in an established use, the connotation that the substitute is somehow inferior to the obsolescent raw material usually is mistaken. Unlike the bench warmers who on occasion substitute for the first string players in athletic contests, substitution of minerals usually occurs when the new raw material demonstrates superior performance, lower cost, or both.

In considering the part that obsolescence may play among the uses of a particular mineral, it is essential that the influence of technical as well as economic factors on the competitive positions of the several uses be recognized. For one use, consumers will find a particular commodity so well suited that they

"Mineral Obsolescence and Substitution" by Charles W. Merrill. Reprinted from Mining Engineering, Vol. 16 (September 1964) pp. 55-59, with permission of the author and editor.

308

would continue to use it even at a much higher price. Another set of consumers putting the commodity to a different use treat the same commodity as marginal and subject to replacement by any substitute if a small commercial inducement appears. For example, silver and its halides have held a firmly established position in photographic use for over a hundred years. From the time of the daguerreotype until present films for motion picture theater and television use, no serious competitive substitute for silver has appeared. Perhaps some research laboratory has new visions of substitution now that silver's soaring price is only restrained by United States Treasury sales, but no public announcement of such an early prospect has been made. On the other hand, the die casters serving the automobile industry frequently switch between zinc- and aluminum-base alloys, depending on market quotations of these two important metals. Any study of obsolescence and substitution must focus careful attention on those economically marginal uses to which particular mineral raw materials are put.

With most mineral commodities, there seem to be growing uses that tend to counterbalance obsolescent applications. In addition, the growing relative importance of minerals in the world economy, as well as overall economic expansion, increases the demand for most mineral raw materials to an extent that obscures the areas of obsolescence for particular commodities.

There are, of course, some instances of aggressive substitution for a major use which may cause an over-all decline in demand for the obsolescent commodity. An example of unusual economic significance in the United States is anthracite where total consumption has experienced an 84% decline from the peak it established 45 years ago. Petroleum and natural gas have taken over most of the energy market supplied by anthracite, which lay principally in space heating. In addition, anthracite has lost ground in some of its important metallurgical applications.

Phenomenal changes have occurred in several uses for tin. In 1928, a peak year, almost 8000 long tons of tin were used for collapsible tubes and foil; and in 1941, before restrictions on use, almost 9000 tons were used for those purposes. Because of technologic advances and for economic reasons, most collapsible tubes and foil now are made from aluminum, which itself must compete with plastics. Despite recent large gains in population, only about 1000 tons of tin now are used annually for the production of tubes and foil in the United States. The decline in use of tin for pipe and tubing has been even more spectacular. In 1941, 1325 tons of tin were used for pipe and tubing. Adoption of plastics for these uses resulted in the consumption of only 65 tons in 1963.

Efficiency in consumption can rival substitution in decreasing the demand for a particular mineral commodity. Tin in its traditional leading use — tin plate — has lost ground in the United States despite population growth and a wider acceptance of canned goods, including beer and soft drinks. Here the obsolescent hot dip method of applying a relatively thick tin coating to steel sheets has given way to continuous electrolytic tin plating, which applies an equally protective but much thinner coating. As a result, tin plate production in 1963 increased 90% since 1939, while tin consumption for tin plate declined 23%. An insignificant but positive obsolescence of a metal was brought about by Public Law 87-643, September 5, 1962, which prohibited the use of tin in copper coinage in the United States.

It should be noted that the struggle for growth on the part of mineral commodities is not always carried out among just minerals — established mineral uses may be replaced with vegetable and animal products or, vice versa, minerals may displace non-mineral raw materials. In this area of competition, however, it is usually the mineral that is the substitute — for example, gasoline for hay; aluminum for lumber; petroleum base lubricants for vegetable oils and animal fats.

There are instances where minerals are eliminated without material substitutes through new techniques as where discharge of high tension electricity is used in forming hard objects which formerly were shaped with mineral abrasives.

Sometimes fashion intervenes to make a mineral application obsolescent, as was the case where the vogue for heavy, rustling silk weighted with tin chloride gave way to natural silk.

SPECIFIC CHANGES
IN MINERAL ROLES

The slates and slate pencils used by our forefathers have largely succumbed to easier-to-use methods which produce easier-to-read copy. The slate blackboards used by the schoolmaster for pedagogic instructions are disappearing from schoolrooms and new fiber boards with a special coating, usually green in color, or frosted glass, are taking over. Many of the new boards are less fragile, not as heavy, easier to write on, and easier to see. Slate, too, has been obsolescent in building construction largely because of the high labor costs of laying slate roof and partly because permanence of structures is less the builder's objective than in former times. Except for use in expensive dwellings and restoration of historic buildings, manufactured roofing materials, usually of mineral origin, have replaced the once highly prized roofing slate. However, in another form of roofing material, crushed slate continues to be an important raw material for composition roofing and roofing granules.

Block steatite talc for electronic insulators, another nonmetallic which, like slate, was shaped for use as it came from the mine, is obsolescent. It has been largely replaced by bodies manufactured from high-purity ground talc formed into useful shapes with a phosphate binder. Parts made of ground steatite talc and phosphoric acid have been found to be fully as serviceable as those made from block steatite talc.

Arsenical insecticides, which include lead arsenate and calcium arsonate, were used extensively until the end of World War II. At that time organic pesticides and insecticides became available, and the demand for inorganic materials waned. The use of arsenates declined from 77,000 tons in 1943 to about 10,000 tons at the present time. Arsenical

Table 1. Gypsum Building Plasters and Pre-Fabricated
Building Products Sold or Used in the United States,
selected years (thousand short tons)

	1916	1922	1939	1946	1952	1962
Building plasters	1,677	2,178	1,680	1,938	2,564	2,055
Pre-Fabricated building products	117	314	1,334	2,594	5,003	7,711
Ratio — Building plasters: Pre-Fabricated products	14:1	7:1	1.25:1	0.75:1	0.5:1	0.3:1

Source: Bureau of Mines Minerals Yearbook.

insecticides, however, have been called back into use in some instances where the pests have developed a degree of immunity to the newer organic poisons while losing their defenses against arsenicals.

Silver, which long has been obsolescent in the monetary systems of the world, presently appears to be losing further ground in the money of the United States. This metal is being progressively replaced by gold as the metallic backing for currency as silver certificates are retired to be replaced by Federal Reserve Notes of small denominations. In addition, proposals to either reduce the silver content of United States coinage or to replace silver coins with coins of some base metal or alloy are receiving serious consideration.

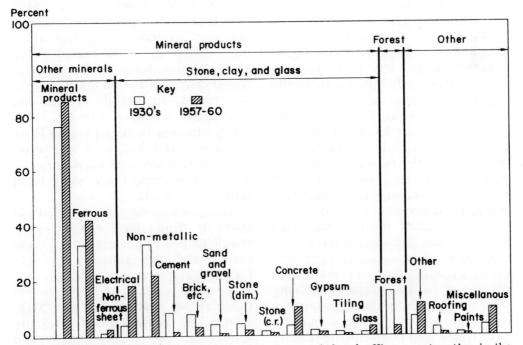

Percentage distribution of materials costs in new federal office construction in the late 1930's and in 1957-60.

Strangely, however, the pressure for freeing silver from monetary demand comes from a sharply rising price which has already given silver dollars a full face value for their metal content. This uptrend in price results from rising demand from use in the arts and industries. Thus, obsolescence in monetary use is being more than compensated by rising demand for other applications, and in a sense has been brought about as a result of these other demands.

In the general field of construction materials there are many examples of material obsolescence or substitution due to factors such as fickleness of consumer or architect tastes, technological innovations affecting construction materials, methods and costs, or even environmental changes as the rising atmospheric acidity due to sulfur.

One interesting case is that of gypsum building plasters versus prefabricated gypsum products. In 1916, tonnage of gypsum building plasters outsold prefabricated gypsum products by 14:1. But the cheaply installed prefabricated units rapidly overhauled plasters in popularity as shown in Table 1. In 1922 the use ratio had dropped to only 7:1 and by 1939, 1.25:1. By the close of World War II prefabricated products were in the lead, and by 1962 held a 3:1 advantage. Both classes of products increased sales due to a vastly expanded market, but from 1916 to 1926 gypsum plasters rose only 22% while sales of prefabricated gypsum products multiplied 65-fold. It is also interesting to note that the gypsum plaster industry is now fighting to regain advantage with time- and cost-cutting technical innovations such as metal lath-

ing and emplacement by machine blowing. Taste is also becoming a significant factor as our affluent society feels an increasing desire for the rich variety of grain and textured finishes and graceful contouring possible with plaster but not with wallboard.

Rising construction and urban land costs have generated requirements for maximum usable floor space in new office and apartment buildings and for economies in methods and materials wherever possible. Elaborate finishing such as involved in the use of columns, pillars, and ornate trim has declined. Use of manually placed building materials such as brick and stone has decreased, thus depressing cement and mortar consumption. Concrete, easily handled and poured into forms, has risen sharply. In the chart on page 311 changes in the distribution of materials used in new federal office buildings are presented. These changes probably are typical of large buildings in the United States as a whole. Some other mineral based commodities on the list have, of course, improved. Metals and glass, for example, are up. However, plastics in such uses as floor coverings and as tubes and pipes have taken a share of materials requirements completely away from mineral products.

Changes in consumer or architect taste at times have caused sharp obsolescence of certain materials in the construction industry. An extreme example would be the dimension stone used in the brownstone industry of eastern United States. In the 19th century brown Triassic sandstone was highly fashionable when New York and Boston gentry preferred brownstone fronts for their town houses. The stone was easy to quarry and convenient to markets but changes in taste to a preference for lighter colored stone, coupled with poor building practices, brought brownstone into disfavor. Some builders set thin sandstone sheets on end as a veneer over brick. Set that way, with bedding planes vertical, the rock spalled in frosty climates and produced a ragged, pocked surface. When properly used it is a handsome and durable construction material. Incidentally, it now appears that we may be entering a new fashion cycle as consumer tastes react to the monotony of the rectangular, light-colored concrete and glass megaliths that have recently been favored by architects. Richly colored facings of various materials, even including colored slates, are finding increasing application.

Modern metropolitan environment is also causing change. For example, 1 1/2 million tons of sulfur dioxide are exhausted into the atmosphere of New York City each year. The acids formed as a result attack building materials containing calcium carbonate, such as limestone or marble, reducing their appeal to architects. Even concrete is defaced to some extent by modern city atmosphere.

This review of changes, past and present, in building practices could go on and on; pre-stressed concrete replacing structural steel, increased use of lightweight and air-entrained concretes, increased use of concrete slabs instead of basements beneath new single-unit family dwellings, and even into the use of bronze plaques instead of memorial stones as markers in cemeteries. The point is clear — a producer of construction materials cannot afford to plan his future only by reviewing his past, but must devote effort to research in product improvement and utilization, constantly studying market developments, and making judicious use of advertising media so that architects will know the particular advantages and availabilities of the materials the producer has to offer.

Lead as one of the six metals available to prehistoric man found many uses because of the ease with which it could be reduced from its ores and worked. Properties such as density, fusibility, malleability, and resistance to corrosion fostered its use. As industrial techniques advanced, however, other raw materials tended to replace lead in some of its important applications as a construction material. On the other hand, lead's superior performance as a chemical material in the common storage battery and in internal combustion engine fuel in the compound tetraethyl lead has opened a huge 20th century market as automobile use expanded. The number of automobiles and trucks in use and being manufactured is a measure of the lead required for storage batteries, tetraethyl compound, solders, and alloys. In 1948, the use in batteries and tetraethyl in the United States was 438,000 tons — about 39% of the total. During 1963 this use had risen to 623,000 tons, 54%. At the present time there is no foreseen development which will counteract a continuing rise in use of lead in the automotive field.

The relationship of lead to the construction and household segments of the national economy is complex, incorporating many end products — pipe, sheet, pigments and compounds. In general, the use of lead in this area has declined as competitive materials presented advantages in comparison to the traditional construction material. Lead base pigments long noted as ingredients of weather- and corrosion-resisting paints have been supplanted significantly by titanium, barium and other metallic compounds as well as new alkaloid, resin base and zinc-rich paints. In addition new developments in construction and construction materials — aluminum, vitreous clad steel sheets, and galvanized steel — have decreased the need for anticorrosion lead-base paints. The decline is measured by a fall in the consumption of lead in white lead from 31,000 tons in 1948 to less than 9000 tons in 1963.

Perhaps the most significant change in the use pattern of lead is as cable covering. The rapid expansion of power and communication services required tremendous quantities of connecting cable for both surface and underground construction. Lead was the material with the properties and the availability that most effectively filled the requirements during the latter part of the 19th century and first half of the 20th century. As much as 200,000 tons of lead has been used to cover some 30,000 miles of cable in a single year.

The advent of improved insulation materials and especially plastics incorporating many of the advantageous noncorrosion properties of lead and offering other advantages in weight, bulk, lower temperatures application and greater flexibility have, during recent years, substantially reduced the use of lead in cable covering. In 1948, for example, cable covering required 172,-000 tons of lead while in 1963, only 58,000 tons were used. Cable covering has thus declined from 15% of the total use to 5%. Table 2 shows U.S. consumption data for lead in four important uses: rising figures for storage batteries and tetraethyl, and declining trends for cable coverings and white lead.

Bismuth illustrates a major shift in use pattern. To quote from the Bureau of Mines 1946 Minerals Yearbook (page 187) when domestic consumption was approximately 1,-330,000 pounds:

"The manufacture of bismuth pharmaceuticals which comprise principally antisyphilitic drugs, antiacid in stomach remedies and cosmetic powders — consumed about 831,900 pounds (63 percent) of bismuth in 1946, approximately the average quantity consumed for that purpose during the last decade."

During the following years advancement in medical technology and pharmaceuticals research has resulted in more effective remedies and methods of treatment of human disorders previously dependent on the medicinal qualities of bismuth and consumption for this purpose has steadily declined.

Counterbalancing this decline, research in metallurgy has expanded the use of bismuth as minor additives to aluminum and to malleable iron and steel to improve machinability without sacrifice of strength, corrosion resistance and toughness. Bismuth has found expanding use as a catalyst in the polymerization of acrylic acid derivatives to produce synthetic fibers and as a bending alloy for precision shaping of thin-wall tubing.

Reexamination of the over-all bismuth picture that has emerged after 17 years of applied research and technology indicates use of bismuth in pharmaceuticals has decreased to 257,000 lb during 1963 and represents only 12% of the 2.2 million lb of bismuth consumed in 1963.

from uranium ores millions of grams of uranium must be processed. For over 40 years most of the radium has been extracted from Congolese and Canadian ores which contain about 0.4 gram radium per ton of uranium. Historically, the price of radium has been as high as $135 per milligram during World War I, but in recent years

Table 2. United States Consumption of Lead in
Selected Uses and Total (short tons)

Year	Cable Covering	White Lead	Storage Batteries	Tetraethyl	Total
1948	171,654	30,970	354,405	83,809	1,133,895
1949	144,340	18,400	313,718	94,644	957,674
1950	131,989	36,181	398,409	113,846	1,237,981
1951	131,863	25,578	375,384	128,407	1,184,793
1952	142,571	22,943	350,930	146,723	1,130,795
1953	146,565	17,775	367,575	162,443	1,201,604
1954	127,939	17,704	337,272	160,436	1,094,871
1955	121,165	18,549	380,033	165,133	1,212,644
1956	134,339	16,951	370,771	191,990	1,209,717
1957	108,225	15,701	361,015	177,001	1,138,115
1958	74,981	13,589	312,725	159,412	986,387
1959	61,626	10,958	330,732	160,020	1,091,149
1960	60,350	8,432	353,196	163,826	1,021,172
1961	57,458	7,615	367,998	169,802	1,027,265
1962	56,676	11,091	419,906	168,926	1,109,635
1963	57,631	8,871	430,296	192,683	1,154,300

An account of the replacement of naturally occurring radium by manufactured radioactive isotopes of other elements illustrates the significant role of science and innovation in mineral use patterns.

Radium has been called the most important short-lived natural radioactive element. The radium of commerce, the isotope radium 226, has a half-life of 1620 years and is derived from uranium 238. For every gram of radium extracted

prices quoted for new radium have been from $16 to $21.50 per milligram, in the form of bromide, sulfate or chloride. This would be up to $21,500 per gram or curie.

On the other hand, the prices — as low as $2 per milligram — being paid for used radium indicate the increasing displacement of the metal by artificially produced radioactive isotopes. An excellent example is cobalt 60, now priced as low as 50¢ per curie in quantities of 100,000 curies, a radioactivity figure impossible with radium, which would require 100,000 grams. Another great disadvantage is that radium has a complicated radioactive spectrum, releasing radon gas as a daughter product which, with other gases, provides a pressure buildup in radium-bearing capsules, thereby requiring periodic checks for leakage.

In addition to cobalt 60, thulium is being used for industrial radiography. Irradiation facilities are being constructed that range from a few hundred curies to over a million curies to accomplish things that could never have been contemplated with the more costly and rare radium.

Radium compounds, in proportions of about 1:20,000 base pigment, have been used in luminous paint but are reported to have been replaced almost completely by tritium (hydrogen 3), considerable quantities of which have been shipped by the AEC recently.

Radium has been used in static elimination devices because of the high specific ionizing power of its alpha particles. The potential leakage of daughter product radon from thin walled capsules, through which alpha particles can pass, has led to adaptation of americium and polonium in these devices. Radium-bearing neutron sources have been replaced by polonium-, americium-, and plutonium-activated sources. Radioisotopes, principally cobalt 60, are being used in medical teletherapy. However, in other medical uses, a number of physicians, who have been trained in its use, retain a great respect for and continue the use of radium implants in medical applications. A factor which may lead to further substitution of radioisotopes is the recent transfer of certain regulatory authority, formerly exercised by the AEC, to several states. These controls ultimately will be administered by most, if not all, the state governments. Because many of the states' regulations require the licensing of radium for the first time as well as radioisotopes, the advantages of the radioactive substitutes will become more apparent to individuals previously able to procure unlicensed radium.

SUMMARY

At first thought, obsolescence may appear to be a depressing subject. A very little reflection, however, shows obsolescence to be the badge of progress. It is only in a static economy and society that nothing becomes obsolete. In a dynamic environment like that in the United States, invention, innovation and discovery are constantly unearthing new and better raw materials and processes which make the old obsolete. In fact there is a world revolution fostered by research in many fields led by the United States that makes widespread obsolescence and accompanying progress inevitable.

Fuel Minerals and Energy Production

To aid him in his labors man draws on many energy sources: his own muscle; the harnessing of animal, wind, water, and sun power; the mineral fuels; and, more recently, nuclear power plants. Both the sources of energy used and the amount of energy used per capita vary widely throughout the world. Commonly, the amount of energy consumed per capita is employed as a measure of the level of economic development that a nation has achieved, with the more advanced nations accounting for the lion's share of the world's total energy consumption.

The following articles, dealing primarily with the mineral fuels, illustrate several important factors influencing the generation and use of power, selection of power source, and trade in fuels.

Important energy-consuming nations may or may not have major resources of energy minerals, and major producers of these minerals may or may not be high per capita consumers of energy. Thus, some areas are major importers or exporters of fuels. The resulting trade in energy minerals between nations is greatly influenced by political conditions, as are the exploitation and development of such fuels petroleum and natural gas. Attitudes toward foreign corporations, tax rulings, trade agreements, and similar factors may encourage or discourage development of an energy source.

Even within nations the deposits of energy minerals may not be coincident in location with the energy market, or several energy sources may vie for the same market. Consequently, the forms of energy utilized in a region may reflect availability, cost advantage, or specific requirements of the consumer. In the case of metallurgical processes requiring coal, hydroelectric power or natural gas may not be competitive energy sources although they may be cheaper per unit of energy contained. In the case of electricity, it is the total cost per kilowatt that determines its competitive utility, regardless of whether it was generated at a dam, thermal plant, or nuclear plant.

Technological changes can modify significantly the competitive positions of various types of fuels. For example, the development of the Gronigen gas fields in the Netherlands may modify the present pattern of energy production and consumption in northern Europe. Technologic change may cause various consumers to change from one energy source to another. Thus, in the past twenty years railroads have declined as a major consumer of coal with the onset of dieselization. At the same time that coal lost this market, it gained in thermal electric generation, in part due to an expansion of that market, and in part due to technical changes such as improved thermal electric plant efficiency.

To be completely representative, this section should contain articles on nuclear power. However, this source has become important so recently that its literature remains scanty and technical with generally useful summary articles still to be written.

317

ECONOMICS OF POWER PLANT USE OF COAL

by
CARROLL F. HARDY and J. S. LAIRD*

Present-day electric utility plants are designed to burn a wide range of coals. Coal availability is usually considered in locating a plant; in addition, the relationship to electric load and other factors are considered. The characteristics of the seams and fields are surveyed.

The survey forms a firm foundation on which to design a plant. Once the fuel has been determined it is a relatively simple matter to design a plant on a guaranteed performance basis. Some utilities follow the once prevalent practice of building the plant first, and then trying to find the most suitable coal.

Mine mouth plants or plants with dedicated tonnage can be designed to burn a particular coal, although the difference in plant construction cost alone is usually not great enough to warrant deviation from a flexible design.

PLANTS DESIGNED FOR WIDE RANGE OF COAL SPECIFICATIONS

One example of the fuel specifications for boiler design is as follows:

The boiler shall be designed to burn pulverized coal as the primary fuel and shall operate satisfactorily when burning coal within the following ranges:

Moisture — 3-20%
Volatile Matter — 27-40%
Fixed Carbon — 40-63%
Ash — 4-20%
Sulphur — 0.5 to 5.0%
Heat content, as fired, 10,000 to 13,800 Btu per lb
Ash softening temperature — 2000 to 2600°F
Grindability (Hardgrove scale) 40 to 85

Pulverizer capacity guarantees and performance shall be based on the following:

Moisture Total — 10%
Ash — 12%
Grindability — 45
Heat content "as fired" — 11,000 Btu

The guaranteed performance of the boiler shall be based on a coal which has the following analyses:

Proximate analysis
Moisture — 8%
Volatile matter — 28.4%
Fixed carbon — 53.9%
Ash — 9.7%
Grindability — 53
Ash softening temperature — 2430°F
Size — 1 1/2 by 0

*Carroll F. Hardy is the Director of Engineering and Fuels Technology Department, National Coal Association. J. S. Laird is Manager of Fuels Services, Southern Services, Inc.

"Economics of Power Plant Use of Coal" by Carroll F. Hardy and J. S. Laird. Reprinted from Mining Congress Journal, *Vol.* 49 *(November* 1963) *pp.* 38-40, *with permission of the editor.*

Btu per lb — 12,600 "as fired"

Full load performance shall be maintained when the above fuel is burned with one pulverizer out of service.

Once the performance test is over and the plant accepted, coal selection may be left to the discretion of the purchasing department or a real effort may be made to take into consideration all the factors which have a bearing on the cost of operating the plant. Studies of various cost factors lead to a list of acceptable coals, graded as to availability, analysis, plant performance, freight rate and both delivered and "as burned" costs. Tests under operating conditions clearly indicate which are the best coals.

The above is fine until some coal operator calls up and explains — "I have a deal for you — distress coal." Of course it's high ash — but it's cheap on a delivered cost per million Btu basis. Then the specification and acceptable coals lists are out the window and the plant is burning a fuel that may or may not be within the specifications as listed. However, the cost per million Btu delivered to the plant does not take into account all the costs involved in handling, burning and disposing of the refuse.

COST OF ADDITIONAL ASH DETERMINED

Listed below are some of the plant factors to be considered and evaluated to obtain the "as burned" cost of a particular coal in a given plant:

1. Cost of unloading, crushing and conveying coal to plant.
2. Cost of operating pulverizers and accessories.
3. Collecting fly-ash.
4. Sluicing ashes — bottom fly-ash and pyrites.
5. Plant maintenance costs.

Ash content is indicative of the heating value of the coal. Ash, in the absence of or as a check on actual heating value, may be used as a primary factor. Table 1 indicates the additional fuel required with an increase in ash. Table 2 gives the increased cost for coal and freight when changing to a higher ash coal.

In Table 1 it is shown that 13.4 percent more cost will be required if a coal contains 20 percent ash than if it contains ten percent ash. This 13.4 percent increase will apply regardless of the coal price or freight rate. However, it is important to note that the increase in both coal costs and freight costs rises in direct proportion to the unit cost of either.

Thus, for the example given of 20 and 10 percent ash, if the freight rate is $2.50 per ton, an equivalent amount of 20 percent ash coal will cost 33.5 cents more for transportation, but if the freight rate is $5.00, it will cost 67 cents more. Thus, if the plant had been at a $2.50 rate from the mine, only 33.5 cents more could have been afforded for the ten percent ash coal before the cost of the two was equalized, but if the plant had been located at a $5 freight distance up to 67 cents could

Table 1. Percent Increase in Coal Required Due to Increased Ash Content (Based on actual heat value of coal at various ash percentages rather than upon mathematical relation alone)

Higher ash coal, percent ash content	Lower ash coal, percent ash										
	6	7	8	9	10	11	12	13	14	15	16
7	1.2										
8	2.5	1.2									
9	3.8	2.5	1.2								
10	5.1	3.8	2.5	1.2							
11	6.5	5.1	3.8	2.5	1.2						
12	7.8	6.5	5.1	3.8	2.5	1.2					
13	9.2	7.8	6.5	5.1	3.8	2.5	1.2				
14	10.6	9.2	7.8	6.5	5.1	3.8	2.5	1.2			
15	12.1	10.6	9.2	7.8	6.5	5.1	3.8	2.5	1.2		
16	13.4	12.1	10.6	9.2	7.8	6.5	5.1	3.8	2.5	1.2	
17	14.8	13.4	12.1	10.6	9.2	7.8	6.5	5.1	3.8	2.5	1.2
18	16.2	14.8	13.4	12.1	10.6	9.2	7.8	6.5	5.1	3.8	2.5
19	17.7	16.2	14.8	13.4	12.1	10.6	9.2	7.8	6.5	5.1	3.8
20	19.0	17.7	16.2	14.8	13.4	12.1	10.6	9.2	7.8	6.5	5.1

Example: If a 9 percent ash coal has been used and a 16 percent ash coal is contemplated, the chart shows that 9.2 percent more coal will have to be bought, transported, and handled to furnish the same heat value as formerly.

have been paid for the better coal.

For example a 12 percent ash coal, selling for $4.00 per ton f.o.b. mine, and a $2.50 freight rate, has its ash content reduced to eight percent by the installation of preparation facilities. Using Table 2, the value of the coal will increase 33.15 cents per ton. This must be weighed against the cost of the preparation facilities to give the four percent decrease in ash.

COST OF COAL PREPARATION EVALUATED

As to the pros and cons of preparation of coal for the utility market, there are several basic concepts which are worthy of mentioning. Of primary importance is the seam being mined and the method of mining.

A mine which produces a high-ash coal, say 30 percent, with a large share of this being fireclay may have to clean the coal to make it saleable to any utility plant. On the other hand, a mine may deliver 12 percent ash coal with fair consistency. Will it pay to wash this down to eight percent ash? The market will resolve this problem, but if coal can be sold at either ash content, may eight percent ash coal be sold for enough to warrant the cost of washing? Coal washing facilities may cost from $2000 to $8000 per ton hour of product and the simplest jig costs from seven to ten cents per ton of product to operate.

If the total cost of washing including fixed charges, reject and plant operation is 40 cents per ton what can the mine operator expect the utility to pay for the improved

Table 2. Increased Cost of Coal or Freight Due to Purchase of Higher Ash Coal
(Body of table in cents additional cost per ton replaced)

Percentage points difference in ash contents	Price of coal or freight (dollars/net ton)								
	2.50	3.00	3.50	4.00	4.50	5.00	5.50	6.00	6.50
1	3.0	3.6	4.2	4.8	5.4	6.0	6.6	7.2	7.8
2	6.25	7.5	8.75	10.0	11.25	12.5	13.75	15.0	16.25
3	9.5	11.4	13.3	15.2	17.1	19.0	20.9	22.8	24.7
4	12.75	15.3	17.85	20.4	22.95	25.5	28.05	30.6	33.15
5	16.25	19.5	22.75	26.0	29.25	32.5	35.75	39.0	42.25
6	19.5	23.4	27.3	31.2	35.1	39.0	42.9	46.8	50.7
7	23.0	27.6	32.2	36.8	41.4	46.0	50.6	55.2	59.8
8	26.5	31.8	37.1	42.4	47.7	53.0	58.3	63.6	68.9
9	30.25	36.3	42.35	48.4	54.45	60.5	66.55	72.6	78.65
10	33.5	40.2	46.9	53.6	60.3	67.0	73.7	80.4	87.1
11	37.0	44.4	51.8	59.2	66.6	74.0	81.4	88.8	96.2
12	40.5	48.6	56.7	64.8	72.9	81.0	89.1	97.2	105.3
13	44.25	53.1	61.95	70.8	79.65	88.5	97.35	106.2	115.05
14	47.5	57.0	66.5	76.0	85.5	95.0	104.5	114.0	123.5

Example: Assume that a 10 percent ash coal is being bought for $4.50 with $4.00 freight, and that a change is made to 13 percent ash coal with the same cost and freight rate. The percentage points difference is 3 (13 − 10) for which the table shows that the amount of coal which will have to be purchased to equal the former heat value will cost 17.1 cents more per net ton and that the freight will be 15.2 cents more, a total of 32.3 cents per ton more for the same heat value. To this must be added the increased cost of handling the higher ash coal at prevailing plant costs.

product? The relationship shown above is 33.15 cents. The utility plant operating force may be very happy to have a more uniform product with a lower ash. The purchasing department may be difficult to convince that this is worth 40¢ per ton, and plant accounting may prove that it isn't.

UTILITY MAINTENANCE COST BIG FACTOR

Looking at the problem from the utility standpoint, the measurable factors fall under the following five headings: Cost of handling, coal pulverizing and burning, collecting fly-ash, disposing of ash, and plant maintenance costs.

A cost comparison was made at one of the plants on the Southern Services, Inc., system. Costs were determined from plant data on the basis of the coal used in a year. This data was extrapolated to other ash percentages. At 12 percent ash the costs per ton were as follows:

1. Unloading, crushing and in plant coal handling .... 2.641¢
2. Operation of pulverizer and accessories 4.212
3. Collection of fly-ash 0.345
4. Sluicing ashes — bottom ash, fly-ash and pyrite 1.254
5. Plant maintenance costs 19.370
   Total costs, cents ...... 28.822¢

LONGWALL MINING, A BREAKTHROUGH IN UNITED STATES COAL PRODUCTION TECHNOLOGY

by
L. C. CAMPBELL *

The history of coal mining in the United States from its first mining to present day production and use would fill a volume. Only a short time ago every ton of coal was undercut with hand pick, shot down and loaded with the shovel of the miner of that day. The air puncher followed to relieve the hard pick work and to speed up the undercutting process. It took a lot of man to handle the air puncher, but it was a step towards increased production.

There followed the shortwall and longwall undercutting machines which vied for a place among the producing equipment, offered eventually by a number of manufacturers. A six to eight-ft undercut first drilled with man powered augers

*Industrial Consultant

"Longwall Mining, A Breakthrough in United States Coal Production Technology" by L. C. Campbell. *Reprinted from* Mining Congress Journal, *Vol.* 50 (*August* 1964) *pp.* 85-87, *with permission of the editor.*

and then with electrical augers was another step toward greater production, even though it still entailed loading coal by hand into mine cars, from entry, room, or pillar faces.

MECHANICAL LOADER DEVELOPED

Although these were but minor steps toward increased productivity at the working face, a long stride toward greater productivity was achieved about 45 years ago. At that time Joe Joy's dream of installing mechanical equipment to load coal with track mounted units into mine cars from prepared faces where the coal had been undercut, drilled and shot down, became a reality. This was, undoubtedly, the most radical change in coal mining procedure that had taken place to that time. A new highroad to production technology had been opened. It took the combined courage and cooperation of the coal operators and manufacturers and the unwavering support of mechanization by John L. Lewis of the United Mine Workers to carry forward so radical a production change. It required from five to ten years, together with a lot of money and heartaches, to develop mechanical mining as a major factor in the overall coal production of the country.

This type of mechanical equipment, produced by various manufacturers, gradually replaced the room and entry type conveyor mining which had been an intervening production step that started with hand loading onto conveyors.

The almost unbelievable ingenuity of the coal operator, the manufacturer, and the men of the mines, who operated the mechanical equipment and adapted it to local conditions to achieve high production and

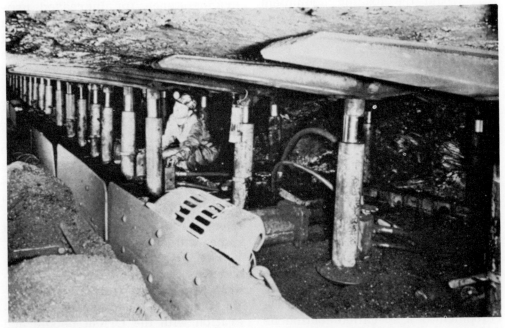

Longwall mining equipment was installed in Stotesbury No. 11 mine of Eastern Associated Coal Corp. at Helen, W. Va. in 1951.

low costs, is a tribute to the fact that United States coal mining has not tended to stand still in the face of competition.

LOADING MACHINES PUT ON TRACTOR TREADS

Various types of mechanical loading equipment on tractor treads were introduced to increase mobility and do away with the necessity of maintaining track in the working places. It was natural that this step should be followed by another improvement in production and cost technology with the introduction of shuttle cars, panel belts, and similar items. The producing technology was bringing tremendous changes, not only in the operator but in the approach of the manufacturer as well.

There were basic tests for all of this equipment which may be simplified into three categories:

1. Would the loading equipment dislodge the coal for loading regardless of how well the place was prepared?
2. Would the equipment load the coal into mine cars or to shuttle cars with a satisfactory clean up?
3. Would the equipment mechanically hold together to do a rigorous job?

These three equipment requirements, which were a measure for the initial loading machines, became even more important with the advent of the continuous miner.

When the operating people in any mine were introduced to the potentials of successful mechanical loading, they seemed to envision the development of a so-called continuous type of loading machine which would do away with the problems of under-

cutting, shooting, and preparing the working place for the loading machines available at that time. Continuous mining production as then envisioned introduced another long step forward in production technology.

McKINLEY ENTRY DRIVER WAS FORERUNNER OF CONTINUOUS MINER

The McKinley entry driver was a vision which has sparked the mechanical development in United States coal production technology throughout the years. It was an early attempt to accomplish what is now accepted as routine with modern equipment.

The coal industry put a considerable amount of money into research to increase production by attacking the coal face with new cutting and loading approaches. Out of producers insistence for increased production units and the research of the coal industry, as well as that of the manufacturer of coal mine equipment, came the development of such continuous units as the Joy Ripper. This, indeed, was another giant step forward toward increased production.

Eastern management looked to the possibility of a borer type continuous unit, not only for entry driving, but room and pillar production as well. George Harrington had pioneered in equipping the Orient mine with that type of machinery. It was considered for use at Eastern Gas and Fuel Associates' Federal No. 1 mine at Grant Town, W. Va. Continued investigation in cooperation with the Orient people and the Goodman Manufacturing Co. convinced Eastern management that it should go ahead with the Goodman 500 boring type continuous miner. It was an outstanding success in production, in cost reduction, and in safe operating conditions. This was a further breakthrough in United States coal production technology, and resulted in the introduction of a tremendous amount of this type of equipment in coal production, not only in the United States, but abroad.

The application of another type of continuous mining machine, initially in the Pocohontas Field, provided further progress when Chief Arentzen's Lee-Norse CM miner was put into successful operation.

LONGWALL MINING CAME TO U.S.

The longwall mining breakthrough in the United States coal production technology came about 12 years ago. The Bureau of Mines made repeated approaches to Eastern Gas and Fuel Associates to provide a location to introduce the Westfalia Coal Planer and its other longwall equipment and roof supports. The Bureau had been investigating this equipment in Europe to determine its applicability to mining in the United States. Negotiations resulted in the installation of the Westfalia Coal Planer, Panzer conveyor, and roof supports on a 340-ft face at Stotesbury No. 11 mine at Helen, W. Va., in November 1951. The equipment was supplied, installed, and its operation supervised by Mining Progress, Inc. The unit operated very successfully in the Pocohontas No. 4 seam until the area where it was installed was worked out. Eastern purchased the Planer and it was transferred in August 1953, to Stotesbury No. 8 mine where it also operated very successfully in the Pocohontas No. 4 seam until that mine was closed. Both the Stotesbury No. 11 and Stotesbury No. 8 longwall faces used manually set mechanical props.

The 340-ft longwall unit was transferred to Keystone mine where it was equipped with hydraulic jacks and later extended to a 600-ft length in the Pocohontas No. 3 seam. The results from the viewpoint of production, costs, and ability to hold the difficult draw rock were very outstanding. The rejects compared to continuous mining were reduced approximately 50 percent and the consistency of the coal greatly improved.

The results at Keystone prompted the installation of another coal Planer unit for a 340-ft face at Kopperston in the Eagle Seam. The equipment included the modification of the original type Planer to cut the entire seam as had been done at Keystone. This unit performed so successfully at Kopperston that the original 340-ft unit with hydraulic roof supports has been extended to a 600-ft face.

The very satisfactory experience at Kopperston prompted the opening of another 600-ft longwall face in the Eagle Seam. This installation is fully equipped with the improved Planer which cuts the full seam. It includes the Panzer conveyor and other auxiliary equipment. The longwall face is equipped with self-advancing hydraulic roof supports. Very satisfactory results are being obtained in spite of tender roof conditions and massive sandstone which overlies the seam. Results have been very gratifying since the first unit was installed more than ten years ago.

UNDERGROUND MINING WILL INCREASE

The operation of the coal plow permits a minimum of open space between the coal face and the first line of roof supports which is so essential to maintaining the face in a safe operating condition at all times. The result is the nearest to continuous mining operation possible in view of the fact that the coal planer produces coal on a full cycle basis.

Production is well in excess of 50 tons per face man and the cost into the mine car is better than 50 cents a ton lower than the best continuous mining operation under similar conditions.

This achievement in longwall mining in the mines of Eastern Gas and Fuel Associates was a definite breakthrough in United States coal production technology.

There will be available in the not too distant future, equipment that will cut coal of any hardness, produce it at an excellent cost under safe conditions and at a rate per man that will further revolutionize United States coal mining. The cost of coal production which has been held so well in line by previous mechanical operations, will be further reduced by longwall applications.

The time is not too distant when lack of available strip mining areas will force the mining of more underground coal. This is true, certainly, for the Eastern coal fields. Longwall mining methods could well be the production and cost answer.

IMPORTANCE OF MINERAL FUELS IN THE
CENTRAL UNITED STATES*

by
HUBERT E. RISSER

The Central United States is made of the four smaller regions of the nation commonly designated as the East North Central, the East South Central, the West North Central and the West South Central regions. Possessing a combination of favorable factors that enable it to contribute immeasurably to the economic and industrial strength of the nation, the area's activities can be indicated to some degree by the following:

1. Agricultural products from the area are valued at 60% of the national total.
2. Manufactures produced in the area in 1962 totalled 45.4% of the total value of all manufactures of the United States.
3. Mineral production value in the area in 1962 was 62.9% of the total value of minerals produced in the United States.

Especially notable is the contribution the Central United States makes in supplying the major portion of the energy requirements of the nation, and its tremendous reserves of mineral fuels. More than half of the nation's known reserves

*Based on a report by the author

of each of the three major fuels — oil, gas and coal — lie within the Central area.

CRUDE OIL

Recoverable reserves of crude oil in United States at the end of 1963 were estimated by the U.S. Bureau of Mines to be almost 31 billion barrels. Of this amount 77% lay in the oil fields of the Central United States, most of it (69%) in the West South Central states.

NATURAL GAS

Natural gas reserves in the continental United States at the end of 1963 were estimated at 276.2 trillion cu ft, of which 274.5 trillion were within the 48 contiguous states. Of this latter amount, 86.9% lay within the Central United States. As in the case of crude oil, most of the natural gas reseves (78%) lie in the West South Central Region.

COAL

Coal is somewhat more evenly distributed than either oil or natural gas. In 1960 reserves were esti-

"Importance of Mineral Fuels in the Central United States" by Hubert E. Risser. *Reprinted from* Mining Engineering, *Vol.* 17 *(June* 1965) *pp.* 67-70, *with permission of author and editor.*

mated by the U.S. Geological Survey to total 782 million tons of recoverable coal of all types within the 48 contiguous states. About 45% of the reserves is bituminous and 20% sub-bituminous, 27% is lignite, and the balance anthracite and semi-anthracite.

As estimated, 55% of the bituminous coal and 70% of the lignite reserves lie within the Central United States. The Central states contain 51% of the coal of all types.

Within the Central states, North Dakota reserves, consisting wholly of lignite, are estimated at 22.4% of the total coal reserves in the United States. Leading Central states with bituminous reserves are Illinois, Missouri, Kentucky, Ohio and Indiana. Large areas of other states are also underlaid by coal, mostly in relatively thin beds.

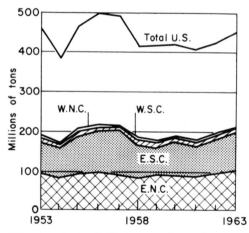

Fig. 1: Central States coal production, bituminous and lignite.

Coal has shown much wider fluctuations in production than either natural gas or crude oil. Figure 1 shows both the national and the Central United States production by region. As shown in Table 1, in 1963 the Central states provided 208.6

million tons, or 45.5% of the country's total production. Production for the Central states has held near the 200-million-ton level for the past ten years.

Table 1. Production of Coal, 1963

Region	Millions of tons	Pct. of U.S. total
E.N.C.	103.63	22.58
W.N.C.	7.97	1.74
E.S.C.	95.83	20.88
W.S.C.	1.23	0.27
Sub-total	208.66	45.47
Total U.S.	458.93	100.00

Source: U.S. Bureau of Mines Minerals Yearbook.

Although the West Central states provide most of the liquid and gaseous fuel of the United States, they are much less important in coal production. Most of the coal produced within the Central states comes from the two regions east of of the Mississippi River, which contribute almost equally. Of the East South Central Region, Kentucky is the principal producer with a 1963 output of 77 million tons. In the East North Central Region, Illinois with 51.7 million tons, Ohio with 36.8 million, and Indiana with 15.1 million were the principal producers.

As Figure 1 indicates, coal production in the Central states has been much more stable than that in the United States as a whole. One important reason for this is the fact that little or no coal from the Central states is exported to foreign nations. The effect of fluctuations in the export market is illustrated by the fact that exports increased from 35 million tons in 1961 to 47 million tons in 1963.

Another reason for stability of the Central states production is that a relatively minor portion of output goes into coke production. On Figure 1 a drop of 82 million tons in total national production may be seen from 1957 to 1958. During the same period, consumption of coal in the manufacture of coke dropped 31.5 million tons. While the failure to participate in both coke and export markets has somewhat reduced perhaps the production from coal mines of the Central United States, it has, at the same time, resulted in much greater stability of production.

CONSUMPTION

Coal consumption is shown in Figure 2. The Central states used 235.9 million tons in 1963, equal to almost 58% of the total United States consumption of 409.2 million tons for that year. Especially significant was the consumption in the East North Central Region, which was

Table 2. Consumption of Coal, by Use, in the Central U.S., 1963

Use	Millions of Tons	Pct.
Electric Utilities	124.58	52.81
Coke	36.74	15.58
Retail	18.86	8.00
Other Uses	55.71	23.61
Total	235.89	100.00

Source: U. S. Bureau of Mines Mineral Yearbook.

40% of the total United States consumption. At the other extreme was the West South Central Region where only 0.2% of the national total was used.

Uses of coal in the Central United States are shown in Figure 3 and in Table 2. Of the 235.9 million ton consumption shown for the Central region for 1963, 70% occurred in the industrialized East North Central Region and 20% in the East South Central Region.

Of 209 million tons of coal consumed by all United States utilities,

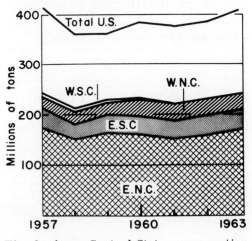

Fig. 2: shows Central States consumption vs. US consumption.

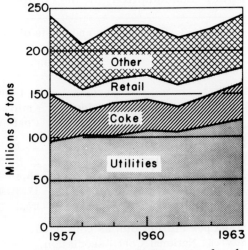

Fig. 3: shows Central States uses of coal.

124.6 million tons, or 60%, was consumed in the Central states. This amount was 52.8% of the area's total coal consumption.

The Central states, which in 1963 produced 54.7% of the United States pig iron and consumed 56.5% of the coke, used 47.2% of the coal consumed in coke-making.

Eighty percent of the nation's retail coal (exclusive of anthracite) was used in the Central United States. It constituted only 8% of the total coal consumed within the area.

General industrial use, 23.6% of the Central states total consumption, accounted for 21.8% of the United States total (see Table 2).

THE ROLE OF ELECTRIC POWER

Electric power consumption is the fastest growing segment of the energy market today, for both the Central United States and the nation as a whole. While total energy consumption showed an increase of 30% in the period from 1953 through 1963, the growth in sales of electric power was four times as great. Power consumption in the United States grew from 383.5 to 830.1 billion kwh during the period from 1953 to 1963, an increase of 120%. For the Central United States, the growth was from 172.1 to 402.4, an increase of 132%. In 1963 consumption by industrial, residential and miscellaneous uses in the Central states was 48.4% of the total national consumption.

Because low cost coal and gas are readily available, utilities in the Central states use very little oil as fuel. In the West South Central Region, natural gas is used exclusively. By contrast, 96% of the fuel consumed in the East North Central states in 1963 was coal (the other 4% was natural gas), and fuel in the East South Central Region also was predominantly coal. In the West North Central Region the market was shared almost equally between coal and natural gas.

Table 3 shows the costs of fuels consumed by utilities. A decline occurred in the cost of coal from 1953 to 1963 in all regions. In contrast, a very pronounced increase in price is indicated for natural gas. In the West South Central Region the increase in the 10-year period was

Table 3. Percentages and Costs of Fuels Consumed by Electric Utilities

	1953						1963					
	Percent provided			Cents per million Btu*			Percent provided			Cents per million Btu*		
Region	Coal	Oil	Gas	Coal	Oil	Gas	Coal	Oil	Gas	Coal	Oil	Gas
East North Central	93	—	7	26.1	52.3	19.7	96	—	4	24.8	69.8	24.9
West North Central	48	2	50	28.8	35.8	21.1	49	1	50	26.4	50.1	23.8
East South Central	73	—	27	20.4	45.4	16.1	92	—	8	20.0	47.5	24.5
West South Central	—	—	100	17.3	43.5	10.1	—	—	100	16.6	38.3	19.4
United States	66	11	23	27.3	32.3	16.7	65	7	28	25.0	33.5	25.9

*Cost per million Btu, as consumed.
Source: National Coal Association.

92%. The over-all average increase for the United States was 55%.

Table 4. Fuels Consumed by Electric Utilities in the Central U.S., 1963

Fuel	Tons of coal equivalent (thousands)	Pct.
Coal	123,469	69.23
Oil	326	0.18
Gas	54,567	30.59
Total	178,362	100.00

Source: U.S. Bureau of Mines Minerals Yearbook.

Trends in the percentages of the various fuels consumed reflect primarily the changes in relative prices. In some areas natural gas is used only to a limited extent even though it apparently has the lower cost. In such areas gas usually is sold to utilities only on an interruptible basis — when the available supply exceeds the amount required for residential and other specified uses.

SUMMARY

Possessing more than half the known United States reserves of each of the major fuels, the Central United States provides three-fourths of the nation's oil, 85% of the natural gas, and 45% of the coal. Two-thirds of the gas, almost 40% of the oil, and more than 57% of the coal are consumed within the area. In 1963, two-thirds of the total supply of energy from domestic sources in the United States came from within the Central United States. Forty-eight percent of this fuel energy came from the oil and gas fields of the West South Central states. Even more striking, three-fifths of the latter amount came from two states —Texas and Louisiana. They accounted for 29% of total fuel energy produced in the United States.

The extreme importance of the area, and especially the West South Central Region, with regard to fuel resources already has been pointed out. It seems that we can accurately say that a large portion of our fuel ergs lies in one basket. However, as any of us would be quick to point out, it is a rather large-sized basket.

BITUMINUOUS COAL ECONOMICS

by
GLENN E. SORENSEN*

One must be an optimist to be in the coal business today. Otherwise he would elect to be a shoe salesman, a filling station operator, or to pursue some equally unglamorous kind of occupation. However, there has been a rather encouraging upward turn which the coal business has taken in recent months. In 1962 about 423 million tons of bituminous coal and lignite were produced in this country. Production for 1963 was about 452 million tons — an increase of 29 million tons of coal or about 7.1 percent. This gives some reasonable basis for optimism, and to hope that there is still a future in the coal industry.

900 MILLION TONS PREDICTED FOR 1980

The experts' predictions for the future of coal cast a rosy glow. Many of these experts say the time is not far distant when the industry will be producing well over the record production of 630 million tons in 1947. For example, the U.S. Bureau of Mines has predicted that by 1980 the demand for coal will be pushing 900 million tons a year, or about twice last year's production of 452 million tons. Only time will prove whether this forecast is correct. This perhaps sounds high, but 1980 is a long way off. There is no question, however, that to achieve a market of this proportion will require every ounce of initiative, skill, perseverance and business know-how the industry can muster.

It is well understood that times have changed very rapidly for those engaged in coal mining. For many, the times have changed somewhat, painfully too. Today, coal furnishes more than one-third of the nation's competitive fuel supply, whereas 40 years ago it furnished more than two-thirds. Salesmen have to fight for every ton of coal they sell — not just against other coal companies, but against natural gas, imported residual oil, and now the newest threat to markets — subsidized atomic power plants.

Under the types of difficulties which eliminated the fainthearted early, the coal industry has had to face up to these challenges: Enormous sums have been invested in modern machinery, fights have been conducted for markets throughout the free world, and the cost of transporting coal, or the energy of coal, have been reduced.

WESTERN U.S. COAL MARKET HAS GREAT POTENTIAL

These were things that had to be done for survival. Now, one looks

*President, Kemmerer Coal Co.

"Bituminous Coal Economics" by Glenn E. Sorensen. Reprinted from Mining Congress Journal, *Vol.* 50 (*February* 1964) *pp.* 95-96+, *with permission of the editor.*

Coal sales to electric utilities continue to rise as the demand for electricity increases. The introduction of the integral train concept has enhanced coal's potential in this market.

supply — it is demand, or customers if you please.

Many eastern and mid-western operators are now showing considerable interest in the western reserves. One illustration is the Peabody Coal Co. which has announced that it is building a new mine near Craig, Colo. This mine will get into operation in 1965 to serve the utility market. Peabody also has said that it has large reserves in Arizona. Other companies have shown similar interest in developing

forward to the further improvement of markets, particularly in the West, since by 1975 the population of the western states will be around 40 million, with California alone having a population of 25 million. While California is a difficult area to reach and serve competitively, it nevertheless offers a great challenge to the coal industry.

The westward movement of population has brought renewed interest in western coal reserves, which make up about two-thirds of the nation's total reserves. More than one-quarter trillion tons of coal are west of the Mississippi River. At present rates of consumption, it is estimated that the U.S. has enough coal for national supply for almost 2000 years.

So the big problem is not one of

Large reserves of western U.S. coal offer a dependable supply of energy for California's rapidly expanding population.

some of the western coal deposits.

Although the cost of transporting coal has been reduced, particularly in the East, there is still a long way to go. This is especially true in the West, where distances are so great.

By working with those who deliver
the coal, particularly the railroads,
and those who consume large quantities of it, especially electric utilities, one hopes to be able to reduce
transportation costs so as to be able
to compete for a greater share of
the fuel market.

NATURAL GAS PRICES
ARE INCREASING

From a strictly competitive
standpoint, natural gas is still one
of the major problems in the West,
as it is in other parts of the country. As has been said many times,
at Congressional hearings and in
other forums, it is felt very strongly
that the limited supplies of such a
valuable natural resource as natural gas should not be wasted by using them under industrial boilers.
It has already been indicated that
the U.S. has more than enough coal
to meet these requirements.

In the fight against gas the coal
industry appears to be making some
headway. For example, just recently, Los Angeles took note of the
fact that the prices of natural gas
were constantly increasing. Los
Angeles authorities have shown renewed interest in coal as a boiler
fuel — not only for use in the metropolitan area, but via high voltage
lines to furnish power to the city.

Even though gas is coal's big
competitor now, nuclear power represents the threat of the future.
Again, this is particularly true in
the West. It is here, in this so-
called high fuel cost area, that
atomic power has the greatest attraction.

COAL INDUSTRY FIGHTS
NUCLEAR POWER INTERESTS

At the moment, the coal industry
is waging a determined fight to hold
down government expenditures on
subsidized nuclear power plants.
The Atomic Energy Commission,
in its report to the President dated
November 20, 1962, said: "Nuclear
power is believed to be on or near
the threshold of competitiveness
with conventional power for large
plants in areas of the country where
fossil fuel costs are high."

In other words, the Commission
says it is on the threshold of being
competitive in high fuel cost areas
after 1.3 billion tax dollars have
been spent.

Spending the taxpayers' dollars
on nuclear plants is a waste of
money when the principal objective
is merely to get the cost down so it
will be competitive with coal. On
several occasions, the coal representatives in Washington have appeared before the Joint Committee
on Atomic Energy and have even
discussed with the staff of the
Atomic Energy Commission the
views held with respect to continued
subsidizing of nuclear power. The
consensus is that some progress
has been made in getting the point
across, but the returns are not all
in yet.

An example of this kind of subsidy
is the proposed reactor for the city
of Los Angeles, which was the subject of hearings before the Joint
Committee on Atomic Energy in
July 1962. This provides for a waiver
of inventory carrying charges on
fuel in the amount of $8,200,000 over
a five-year period, which is an average of $1,640,000 per year. In
this installation, this represents a
subsidy of about 1 to 1 1/2 mils per
kwh during the first five years. Then
in subsequent years, the subsidy
arising out of government ownership
of the inventory would amount to
about 1/2 to 1 mil per kwh.

Government subsidy of nuclear power plants ultimately can destroy the conventional fuels industries, which must compete with nuclear power to survive. No private industry, coal or any other, can compete with government-financed industry.

ELECTRIC UTILITIES ARE ONLY REAL GROWTH MARKET

Coal's only real growth market at the moment is the utility market. Perhaps coal and nuclear power will grow together, side by side, but should coal's growth, if that actually comes to pass, be inhibited by the growth of a subsidized competitor? The entire power-consuming and taxpaying public has a vital interest in the answer to that question.

Another problem in the West is to stop government subsidy of competitive hydro-power projects, like that of the Burns Creek project which would eliminate a market for about 250,000 tons of coal.

A loss of tonnage of this magnitude would mean a loss of $275,000 in mine payroll, about $225,000 in the purchase of mine supplies, $18,000 in state and local taxes and $100,000 in annual payments to the United Mine Workers Health and Welfare Fund.

Furthermore, hydro-power is surplus in the West at the present time. The Bonneville Power Administration, which is now losing $15 to $18 million a year, is offering surplus power in southern Idaho at less than half the rates charged by the taxpaying private utilities.

RESEARCH HOLDS PROMISE FOR FUTURE COAL MARKETS

Even though coal must fight government subsidy on the one hand, and gas and oil adversaries on the other, there are glimmers of hope, as stated at the outset.

One of these hopes lies in the coal research program. It is pleasing to note that the Office of Coal Research has negotiated two contracts that bear specifically on western coals. One, with the University of Utah, calls for research on five separate processes for upgrading western coals. The contract provides for a three-year laboratory program under the joint sponsorship of the Office of Coal Research and the State of Utah. The federal government's allocation for this project is $150,000 and the state's $102,000.

The Office of Coal Research also has awarded a one-year $26,000 research contract to the Endowment and Research Foundation of Montana State College at Bozeman, Mont. The contractor will determine the yield and composition of liquid and gaseous products that can be obtained from carbonization of several high volatile non-coking bituminous coals.

It is evident that the coal industry, if it is to achieve the status that many predict for it in the future, has serious challenges that must be met, and obstacles that must be overcome. The challenges are real. The obstacles are all too obvious. They must be met with new ideas, new methods of mining and selling the product.

The millennium for the coal industry is not going to arrive automatically. Coal's competitors will see to that. United effort will be needed to keep subsidized atomic power from grabbing our markets.

A lethargic and divided coal industry would lose the struggle. But a vigorous, vigilant, united industry, working together for the common good, can carve out a prosperous future by putting its great reserves of energy into the service of America.

THE ROLE OF REGIONAL INTERTIES IN POSTWAR ENERGY RESOURCE DEVELOPMENT[1]

W. R. DERRICK SEWELL

University of Chicago

ONE of the most important features of the period since the Second World War has been the tremendous growth in the demand for energy in various parts of the world.[2] Not only has the rate of growth been rapid, but it seems to be accelerating. Accompanying this expansion in energy demands has been a trend towards, and an increasing proportion of, energy consumed in the form of electric power.[3] Electrical energy is regarded as a higher form of energy, and the volume of energy consumed in a country or a region is often viewed as a measure of its standard of living.

As the demand for energy in its various forms has increased, the geographic horizon of energy supply patterns has broadened. At the turn of the century most industrial areas relied on local sources of energy. The coal-field and the hydropower stream were major location factors. Advances in technology and the discovery of new sources of energy have increased locational flexibility *vis à vis* energy supplies. Energy now moves over thousands of miles in its various forms, and is transported by a wide variety of media. More-over, most centers of consumption now have several alternative sources from which to choose instead of only one.

As events such as the Suez crisis have amply demonstrated, the means of transporting energy from one area to another have become matters of crucial economic and political importance. Geographical research has devoted much attention to pipelines and to ocean transportation of oil and coal. So far, however, electrical transmission lines have been the subject of comparatively few studies. There have been a few studies of transmission systems within a single region,[4] but few studies have been focussed on inter-connections between regions.[5] No broad study has been attempted to examine the significance of regional interties as a factor influencing economic development.

This article discusses the role of regional interconnections in the development of energy resources since the war in three parts of the world: Europe, the Soviet Union, and North America. It notes the advantages of regional interconnections, and the factors which have

---

[1] The author wishes to acknowledge the helpful comments of the following people in the preparation of this article: Professor Marion E. Marts, Professor Edward L. Ullman, Richard Lycan, Guy Steed, and John Parr, all of the Department of Geography, University of Washington; Professor George W. Hoffman, University of Texas; Professor George Kish, University of Michigan; and Professor Ian Burton, University of Toronto.

[2] In 1937 world demands for energy in its various forms totalled 1,910 million metric tons of coal equivalent. By 1949 they had increased to 2,365 million metric tons, and by 1961 they had reached 4,418 million metric tons. See United Nations, *World Energy Supplies, 1929–1960* (New York: United Nations, 1962); and United Nations, *Statistical Yearbook, 1962* (New York: United Nations, 1963). Rates of growth vary considerably from country to country, being most rapid in those countries which are in what W. W. Rostow has termed a "take-off stage" of economic development. See W. W. Rostow, *The Stages of Economic Growth* (Cambridge: University Press, 1962). For an application of the concept of stages of economic growth to energy consumption, see John Davis, "The Market for Energy," *Transactions of the British Columbia Natural Resources Conference* (Victoria, B.C.: 1961), pp. 10–24.

[3] Electricity demands throughout the world have increased by over twenty times over the past forty years, whereas total demands for energy in its various forms has only tripled in the same period. Electricity now accounts for more than sixteen per cent of the energy consumed. See J. I. Bernard, "Electricity's Flexible Role," *Financial Times* (September 24, 1962), p. 27.

[4] See, for example, Martha Church, *The Spatial Organization of Electric Power Territories in Massachusetts*, University of Chicago, Department of Geography Research Paper No. 69 (Chicago: 1960); E. M. Rawstron, "Changes in the Geography of Electricity Production in Great Britain," *Geography*, Vol. XL (1955), pp. 92–97; and Chauncy D. Harris, "Electricity Generation in London," *Geographical Review*, Vol. XXXI (1941), pp. 127–34.

[5] A notable exception is George W. Hoffman, "Toward Greater Integration in Europe," *Journal of Geography*, Vol. 55 (1956), pp. 165–76.

"The Role of Regional Interties in Postwar Energy Resource Development" by W. R. Derrick Sewell. Reprinted from ANNALS — Association of American Geographers, *Vol. 54 (December 1964), pp. 566–581, with permission of the Association of American Geographers.*

encouraged their development in the postwar period. It examines proposals for future development and discusses some of the difficulties which will have to be overcome before these proposals can become a reality. The article concludes with some remarks about the implications of the development of regional interties.

MAJOR FEATURES OF POSTWAR DEVELOPMENT

The development of energy resources since the Second World War has been characterized by four distinct, but interrelated, features. These are the increasing interest of governments in development; growing international cooperation; increasing scale and scope of projects; and increasing volumes and distances of energy transfers.

Government Interest in Power Development

Governments have taken a growing interest in the development of energy resources in recent years. This interest stems largely from the fact that there appears to be a close relationship between energy consumption and economic growth. It has often been observed that the wealthiest countries are those which have the highest per capita consumption of energy,[6] and that industrial output tends to increase with a growth in energy consumption.[7] As a consequence, energy resource development has come to be regarded as a major requirement for economic growth.[8] Since the war

such development has assumed increasing emphasis in economic policies[9] as well as in investment programs of various countries throughout the world.[10]

Expression of government interest in energy resource development has taken a variety of forms. Sometimes it has been limited to the collection of basic data or the sponsoring of research. Sometimes it has extended to the regulation of development to insure that the "public interest" is adequately served. Increasingly, however, governments have participated directly in the actual harnessing of energy resources, through the construction and operation of power dams, transmission lines, thermal power stations, and pipelines. Coal has perhaps the longest history of gov-

---

[6] For discussions of the relationship between energy consumption and economic growth, see E. S. Mason, Energy Requirements and Economic Growth (Washington, D.C.: National Planning Association, 1953); and Nathaniel B. Guyol, "Energy Consumption and Economic Development," in Geography and Economic Development (Chicago: University of Chicago, Department of Geography Research Paper No. 62, 1960), pp. 65–77.

[7] A study by E. A. G. Robinson suggests that for every two per cent increase in energy consumption in the world as a whole, there has been a three per cent increase in industrial output. See E. A. G. Robinson, The World's Needs for a New Source of Energy (Geneva: Conference on the Peaceful Uses of Atomic Energy, 1955).

[8] Two points, however, need to be emphasized in this connection. First, per-capita income tends to be more closely associated with per-capita energy consumption than with per-capita energy production. Per-capita energy production is high in the Middle East oil states but per-capita income in many of them is very low. The second point is that, in common

with other natural resource development, the harnessing of energy resources tends to decline in relative importance as economies reach more mature stages of economic development. For discussions of this point see Joseph Spengler (Ed.), Natural Resources and Economic Growth (Washington, D.C.: Resources for the Future, Inc., 1960); and Sam S. Schurr et al., Energy in the American Economy (Baltimore: John Hopkins Press, 1960).

[9] Specific motivations, of course, vary from country to country. In some cases energy resource projects have been used as a tool to stimulate economic growth. This has been especially the case with some multiple-purpose water resources projects, in which the development of hydroelectric power is the principal purpose. National economic policy is also involved in instances where energy imports are so large that they may create currency exchange difficulties. On the other hand, a country may encourage energy export to help earn foreign exchange. The recently concluded agreement between the United States and Canada for the purchase of Canada's share of the downstream benefits of Columbia River development will provide Canada with much needed foreign exchange to help bridge the balance of payments gap.

[10] Investment in the development of energy resources accounts for a large proportion of total investment in some countries. It has been estimated that over $4,500 million was invested for this purpose in the OEEC countries of Western Europe in 1954. This amounted to about eighteen per cent of the total investment in that group of countries in that year. See Organization for European Economic Cooperation, Europe's Growing Needs for Energy: How Can They be Met? (Paris: 1956), p. 50. In Canada about fourteen per cent of total investment in that country is devoted annually to the development of energy resources. See John Davis, Canadian Energy Prospects (Ottawa: 1957), p. 325. In some of the lesser developed countries the ratio of investment in energy resource development to total investment is no doubt much higher.

ernment control in the energy resources field; but the oil, gas, and electric power industries are now government owned and operated in many countries as well. The trend seems to be towards increasing government participation in development, and especially in the lesser developed countries.[11]

Increasing International Cooperation

A second major feature of postwar energy resource development has been the growing international cooperation in the technical and financial fields. Considerable cooperation has existed in the technical field for many years, particularly through such organizations as the World Power Conference, the International Conference on Large Electrical Systems (CIGRE), and the International Union of Producers and Distributors of Electricity (UNIPEDE). Since the war, however, many more international agencies have been set up to foster exchange of technical information, including those agencies sponsored by the United Nations. These agencies complement and supplement the functions of those established before the war.

In addition to increasing cooperation in the technical field, there has been growing cooperation in the financing of power projects. Some projects have been constructed as joint ventures by the countries which would benefit most directly from them. The St. Lawrence Seaway and Power Project is an outstanding example. An even larger number of projects have been built, or are planned for construction, as a result of international cooperation between various countries through such organizations as the World Bank and the Colombo Plan. More than one-third of the loans of the World Bank since the war have been used for power projects.[12]

Increasing Scale and Scope of Projects

The third feature consists of increasing size of projects. Projects several times the size of those built before the war have already been constructed, and even larger ones are planned for development in the future.[13] Moreover, the scope and scale of projects has broadened considerably, often embracing several functions and extending their influence over a wide area.

Before the war there were very few dams over 600 feet in height. Today, however, not only are there dams over 700 feet high, but dams over 1,000 feet will soon be constructed in the Soviet Union. Before the war, Grand Coulee had by far the largest generating capacity of any power plant in the world. Its 1,944,000 kw. installation, however, has since been topped by several plants in the Soviet Union, and a number of plants to be constructed in North America will have installations several times that size.

Furthermore, comparable increases in scale have been achieved in thermal power development. Stations with capacities well over 1,000,000 kw. are becoming commonplace in North America and in the Soviet Union. Stations with capacities over 3,000,000 kw. are planned for the Soviet Union.[14]

There have been important advances in the development of the various means of transporting energy as well. Huge oil and gas pipelines, several hundreds of miles in length, have been built in several parts of the world. Coal slurry pipelines have been proposed for development, some to stretch almost a third the way across the North American conti-

---

[11] In most countries in Western Europe, and in the Communist bloc of Eastern Europe and the Soviet Union, the coal and electric power industries are under government control, and in many instances are government owned and operated as well. In most of the emerging industrial nations the trend appears to be towards direct government participation in development.

[12] In the period 1946–1961 loans amounting to $6,544 millions were advanced by the World Bank. Of this total $2,214 million was advanced for construction of power projects.

---

[13] Several projects being built in the Soviet Union will have installations of over 4 million kw. Even these are minute in comparison with the Ichang Gorge project which is planned for construction on the Yangtse River. This project would have an initial installation of 25 million kw., to be increased to 40 million kw. at a later stage of development.

[14] For discussion of progress in the fields of hydroelectric power and thermal power in the United States and the Soviet Union, see U.S. Department of the Interior, *Recent Electric Power Developments in the U.S.S.R.* (Washington, D.C.: December, 1962); and H. D. Lavrenenko, "U.S.S.R. Power Developments and International Co-operation," *Transactions of the World Power Conference* (Melbourne: 1962).

nent.[15] Huge conveyor belts have been built from coal mines to power stations. Oil tankers more than three times the size of those built before the war are now in use. Electric power transmission voltages have more than doubled since the war, making it possible to transmit much more power, and to transmit it over much longer distances.[16] The overall effect of these advances in technology has been to decrease the transport cost of various forms of energy, thereby increasing their geographic mobility. As a result, geographic variations in energy supply prices have diminished.

Increasing Volumes and Distances of Energy Transfer

The fourth feature is the vast increase in the volume of energy transferred between regions and between countries.[17] This, of course, is a reflection of the overall increase in the demand for energy. It also reflects the decline of local sources of supply, and the discovery of new, lower-cost sources of supply. The increase in energy transfers has been made possible by improvements on the technological front, and by the relaxation of trade barriers, such as the removal of embargos on the export of electric power.

THE DEVELOPMENT OF REGIONAL INTERTIES

The development of regional interties reflects these four major features of postwar

---

[15] The United States Bureau of Mines, for example, has undertaken studies of possible coal pipelines between Utah and Los Angeles (969 miles), southern Illinois and Chicago (344 miles), and West Virginia and New York (450 miles). See "Mines Bureau Compares Transportation Costs in Three Regions," *Electrical World* (August 20, 1962), pp. 54–55. Several coal companies have also been engaged in studies of coal pipelines of comparable magnitudes.

[16] Advances in transmission technology have led to considerable reduction in transmission costs. A 345-kv. line, for example, costs five times more than a 115-kv. line, but it can carry nine times as much energy, and the transmission cost per kw.-h. is roughly one-half that on a 115-kv. line. See "EHV Expanding at a Rapid Rate," *Electrical World* (February 25, 1962), pp. 139–42.

[17] International movements of energy have tripled since the war. Much of this increase has been due to the expansion of markets for oil, but international exchanges of electric power have also increased considerably, especially in western Europe.

energy resources development. The technical and economic advantages of interconnecting electric power transmission systems have been recognized for more than a half century, and interconnected systems have gradually evolved in various parts of the world. Before the war, however, interconnections were fairly limited in scale and in scope. There were only a few national grids, and only limited exchanges of electric power across international frontiers.

There have been dramatic changes in this picture since the war. Large-scale interconnections have been built between the major power regions in the Soviet Union, in Europe, and in North America. Several national grids have been completed, and there is even discussion of transcontinental super-grids. Many of the interties cross international boundaries, within and between countries. Such developments have facilitated major increases in international transfers of electrical power. Governments have played an active role in the development of interties, and it seems certain that this role will continue to increase.

Technical and Economic Advantages of Interconnection

There are five principal technical and economic advantages of interconnection. These stem from differences in the demand conditions or in the supply patterns of neighboring regions, and from differences in the stage of economic development in adjacent regions.

First, interconnection may make it possible to take advantage of the fact that peak loads in neighboring regions seldom coincide. The peak load of one system may occur one hour ahead of that of a neighboring system. The seasonal peak of one system may be in the summer, whereas, in another system it may be in the winter. Such differences in the time of occurrence of peak loads on adjacent systems are described as "diversity" in the electric power ultility business. The amount of peaking capacity required to serve the interconnected systems is less than the sum of the peaking capacities required to serve the systems operated in isolation. Therefore, considerable savings can be derived through interconnections; for example, diversity in the peak loads of the United Kingdom and France encouraged the construction of the cross-Channel cable.[18] Similarly, most of the benefits of the proposed California Intertie arise from the fact that California has a summer peak and the Pacific Northwest has a winter peak.

Second, interconnections make it possible to take advantage of differences in streamflow patterns in adjacent regions. Streams in one region may have a summer peak flow, whereas the streams in a neighboring region may have a winter peak flow. By interconnecting the two regions, therefore, the firm power capability of both regions can be increased.[19] France, for example, takes advantage of the fact that the Atlantic region (Massif Central and Pyrenees) has a winter peak, whereas the Alpine region's streams have a spring peak.

Third, interconnection makes it possible to complement thermal power production with hydropower production, and vice versa. Often it is possible to use thermal power capacity in the winter when streamflows are low and hydropower capacity in the spring when streamflows are high. In France the thermal power plants of the north carry most of the load in the winter, and the hydropower plants of the south service most of the load in spring and summer.

Fourth, interconnection makes it possible to reduce reserve capacity. All power systems have to carry a certain margin of spare capacity to cover such emergencies as breakdowns in generating equipment, and to make capacity available during routine overhauls and maintenance. By spreading the risk over a larger number of plants through interconnec-

tion, reserve capacity in the interconnected systems can be reduced. Considerable savings in costs of carrying spare capacity can be achieved as a result.

A fifth advantage of interconnection makes possible the enjoyment of the economies of large-scale production much earlier than would have been possible with isolated operation. Recently a number of electric power utilities in the eastern United States agreed to construct a huge thermal power plant as a cooperative venture. By connecting their systems to this station and by sharing its capacity, the various utilities will be able to share the resulting economies of large-scale production.

Recognition of the above advantages has led to the development of three types of interconnection:

1) Tie lines between individual power supply systems. These interconnections are mostly short-distance lines of moderate voltage. This type of interconnection is by far the most numerous.

2) Regional interties connecting neighboring regions of power supply. These interconnections are usually of high voltage, and high capacity, and sometimes are several hundred miles in length. In some cases they facilitate exchanges of energy between regions, whereas in others they transfer energy in only one direction.

3) National grids which link various regions into a national network. These are high-voltage, high-capacity lines, and are usually several hundreds of miles in length.

These three types of interconnection perform a variety of functions. In some cases they are used solely for the transfer of daily or seasonal supplies of energy from one system or region to another. In other cases they are part of an integrated network and are used as a vehicle for transferring energy from the most efficient units in the interconnected regions to the various load centers within those regions.

FACTORS ENCOURAGING THE DEVELOPMENT
OF INTERTIES SINCE THE WAR

The scope and scale of interconnections has increased tremendously since the war, and as

---

[18] The Cross-Channel Cable between the U.K. and France was completed in 1962. Its basic objectives are to take advantage of the diversity between the United Kingdom peak load and the French peak load in the winter; to facilitate the use of the most efficient capacity in either country; and to facilitate transmission of emergency supplies of energy between the two countries. For discussions of the Cross-Channel Cable see H. Boudrant, "Frontiers Go as Power Link-Up Grows," *Financial Times* (September, 1962); "DC Cable Fits Channel Exigencies," *Electrical World* (August 13, 1962), p. 45; and George Kish, "A British-French Electricity Grid?" *The Professional Geographer*, Vol. 15 (July, 1963), p. 35.

[19] Firm power is the amount of power a plant can be expected to deliver 100 per cent of the time. In a hydropower system it corresponds to the amount of water that can be made available to a power plant under minimum water conditions.

it has done so, the geographic horizon of interconnection has broadened as well. Several factors have been responsible for these developments: particularly, the rapid growth in power demands, the scarcity of capital, the increasing costs of local sources of power, improvements in technology, and the development of larger generating units.

Growth in Power Demands

Since the war the demand for electric power in Europe, in the Soviet Union, and in North America has expanded very rapidly. Demands in Europe and in North America have increased at an average rate of 8.5 per cent per annum, and those in the Soviet Union have grown at about twelve per cent per annum in the postwar period. The rapidity of these increases is emphasized when it is noted that seven per cent annum increase implies a doubling in demand every ten years.

If present trends continue, electric power requirements in Europe will reach 2,750 billion kw.-h. by 1980. It has been estimated that demands in the United States will reach 2,700 billion kw.-h. by that date.[20] These increases in power demands will necessitate large additions to generating capacity. In the United States it is expected that installed capacity will increase from 210 million kw. in 1962 to about 600 million kw. in 1980. In the Soviet Union it is anticipated that installed capacity will increase from 84 million kw. in 1962 to about 600 million kw. in 1980.[21]

Scarcity of Capital

This expansion will require huge amounts of capital. In the United States, annual capital expenditures in the electric power industry amount to over $3 billion per annum, or about ten per cent of total capital investment in the country. It has been estimated that by 1980 such expenditures will have increased to about $12 billion per annum.[22] Expenditures

of comparable magnitudes are expected in Europe and in the Soviet Union. Possibilities of capital savings, such as those obtainable through interconnections, are being actively sought.

Increasing Costs of Local Power

The problem of providing additional generating capacity is especially acute in regions where local sources of supply are declining. In some areas the more accessible coal has been worked out and mining costs have tended to increase. In other areas the nearby hydropower sites have been developed and it has become necessary to develop sites further afield. In such regions costs tend to rise quite steeply. Improvements in transmission technology, and in the development of large-size generating units, however, have helped to temper the effects of these changing circumstances.

Improvements in Transmission Technology

Much progress has been made in transmission technology in the past twenty years. Before the war the highest voltage transmission lines in the world were the 287-kv. lines used in the Hoover Dam project. Today, however, lines with voltages over 500 kv. are in use, and lines of over 700 kv. are being constructed. Such developments in transmission technology have made more sources of power available, they have expanded the scope of regional interconnections, and they have made continental supergrids at least a technical possibility.

Development of Larger Scale Units

The development of larger scale thermal power generating units has also helped to keep down power costs.[23] The largest generating units used in thermal power plants before the war were rated at less than 100,000 kw. Today, however, it is commonplace for orders to be placed for 500,000-kw. units, and development work is now proceeding on units of over 1,000,000 kw.

[20] U.S. Senate Committee on Interior and Insular Affairs, *Relative Water and Power Resource Development in the U.S.S.R. and the United States* (Washington, D.C.: 1962), p. 19.

[21] U.S. Department of the Interior, *Recent Electric Power Developments in the U.S.S.R.* (Washington, D.C.: 1962), p. 42.

[22] Edison Electric Institute, *The Investor-Owned Electric Utility Industry* (New York: 1962), p. 33.

[23] Moreover, costs per kw. tend to decline with increases in scale. For a discussion of this point see "American Power Conference Urges Drive for Larger Generating Units," *Electrical World* (April 8, 1963), pp. 64–67.

Of course, such large generating units are very costly. Their high cost, however, is more than offset by their superior thermal efficiency, thus reducing the cost of generation per kw.-h. Units of 500,000 kw. permit the achievement of efficiencies as high as thirty-nine per cent, whereas before the war the most efficient units did not reach efficiencies above thirty per cent.

Large units, however, often make far more power available than can be used locally. An arrangement is sometimes sought whereby a neighboring utility or region will purchase part of the capacity of the generating unit and participate in the construction of an interconnecting transmission line. In recent years several such arrangements have been established in North America; for example, project Keystone and Project VEPCO were established in the eastern United States. These projects involve the construction of huge thermal power stations on eastern coalfields, connected by high-voltage transmission lines to several utility systems.[24]

PROGRESS IN EUROPE

At the end of the Second World War several of the major industrial areas of Europe experienced rapidly increasing power costs, partly because of declining local sources of fuel. Capital for development was scarce. Interconnections appeared to offer one attractive solution, particularly in view of the great diversity in the energy resource base, and the diversity between the loads of the various regions across the continent.

The diversity of Europe's energy resources is illustrated in Figure 1 which indicates three broad zones: a hydropower zone to the north, a hydropower zone to the south, and a thermal power zone sandwiched between them. There is also great diversity within these zones. There are several types of hydro regimes within the hydropower zones, and within the thermal power zones there is a great variety of fossil fuels. In addition to the diversity of the resource base there is also great diversity in the pattern of electric power demands from one region to another across the Continent.

A number of interconnections between the thermal power zone and the hydropower zones were built before the war, and some countries laid the foundations of national grids. Some of the most attractive opportunities for the development of interties, however, remained as interesting possibilities only, largely because they would have involved the transfer of electric power across international frontiers. Some international interties were built before war, but most of them were fairly small in scale, and involved only small transfers of power.

There have been some dramatic changes in the growing European spirit of international cooperation in economic development. This spirit has been especially evident in the development of electric power. After the war, the Economic Commission for Europe, especially through its Committee on Electric Power, undertook a number of studies relating to the energy demand and supply situation in Europe.[25] Among its recommendations was one for the establishment of unions or groups of nations to coordinate power production and transmission.

In 1951 the Union for the Co-ordination of Production and Transmission of Electricity (UCPTE) was established, with eight countries in Western Europe as members: Belgium, West Germany, the Netherlands, France, Italy, Luxembourg, Austria, and Switzerland. Some of the members have interconnections with nonmember countries as well. Such interties include those between France and Spain, between France and the United Kingdom, and between Italy and Yugoslavia.

There are a number of other groupings besides the UCPTE. These are the Scandinavian group, composed of Norway, Sweden, Finland, and Denmark; the east European group, composed of Czechoslovakia, Hungary, Poland, East Germany, Bulgaria, Roumania,

---

[24] For discussions of the Keystone and VEPCO projects see "Eastern 500 kv Supergrid Begins to Take Form," *Electrical World* (November 26, 1962), pp. 40–42; and "New Route for 500 kv Line Eases R-O-W Tiff," *Electrical World* (July 1, 1963), p. 61.

[25] Reports of these studies include: United Nations, Economic Commission for Europe, Committee on Electric Power, *Transfer of Electric Power Across European Frontiers* (Geneva: 1952); *Some Technical Aspects of the Transmission of Electric Power* (Geneva: 1952); and *Prospects for Exporting Electric Power from Yugoslavia* (Geneva: 1955).

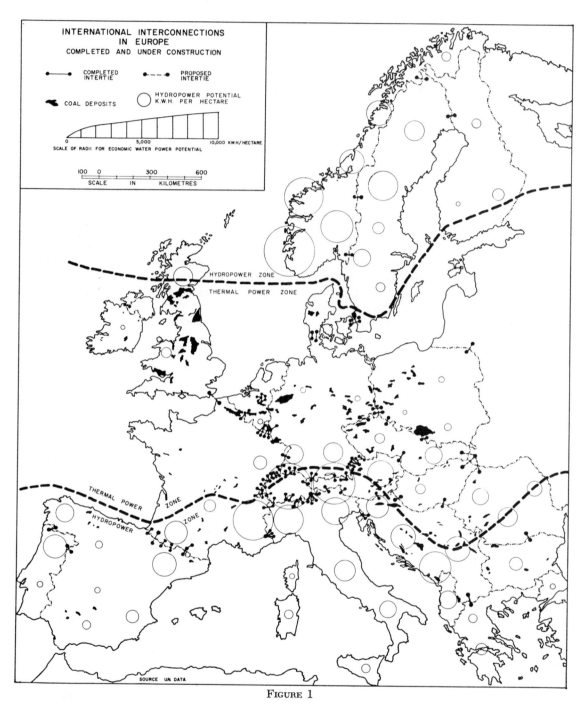

FIGURE 1

and the U.S.S.R.; and the southeastern European group consisting of Greece, Turkey, and Yugoslavia. The degree of interconnection and the volumes of energy exchanged are much greater in the UCPTE group than in any of the others. Several of the regional groupings are interconnected.

Formation of these groupings has been a major factor in fostering the tremendous increase in international power interconnections since the war. Today there are over eighty such interconnections in Europe, and many more interconnections are scheduled for construction in the next few years. As a result of these developments, international exchanges of electric power have increased fourfold in the past ten years. In 1960 over 11 billion kw.-h. crossed international boundaries in Europe, and international exchanges of electric power among UCPTE countries amounted to over 3.5 per cent of their total production, compared with 2.5 per cent of their total production in 1948.

International interconnections have made it possible for the various countries to make better use of their generating facilities and to enjoy savings from postponement of additions to capacity.[26] Interconnections have also made it possible to increase production more rapidly than generating capacity. In 1960–1961, output in the UCPTE countries increased by ten per cent whereas generating capacity increased by only seven per cent.

Although some countries, such as Austria and Switzerland, export a large part of their total production, and a few countries, such as West Germany and Hungary, import a large proportion of their total requirements, the tendency in most countries has been to reduce the dependence on external sources of power to a minimum. This seems to stem from a fear that supplies may be cut off in the event of an emergency such as a war. The major function of international interconnections in Europe, therefore, has been to facilitate seasonal and daily exchanges of energy, and to assist in the provision of emergency supplies of energy. Power systems in adjacent countries normally are not regularly operated on an integrated basis, and there is comparatively little joint planning of integrated development.

Nevertheless, there appears to be a growing enthusiasm for international interconnections. Many new interconnections are now under construction, and more are scheduled for completion in the next few years (Fig. 1). Future developments will include further interties within the various regional groupings, and further interconnections between these groupings.[27]

The matter of a Continental Supergrid has been actively discussed, and it is conceivable that such a network might eventually be developed. For the moment, however, it is still only a technical possibility. For such a grid to become a reality would require an even greater degree of international cooperation in the electric power field than has been achieved to date in Europe. It would require close integration of operations as well as a joint planning of development. Further studies are required to determine the overall advantages of a supergrid, and to determine the extent that each of the participants would benefit.

PROGRESS IN THE SOVIET UNION

There is a tremendous diversity of energy resources within the 8.7 million square miles of the territory of the Soviet Union.[28] There are several hydropower zones, each with different hydraulic characteristics. There are numerous fossil fuel zones, containing vast deposits of coal, oil, and natural gas (Fig. 2). There is also great diversity in the pattern of electric power demand, both within and between regions. Such diversity in supply and demand patterns suggests that considerable advantages could be derived from interconnecting the various regions.

Long-range plans in the Soviet Union call for the development of coordinated and integrated power systems, controlled from a central load-dispatching center. Initially a number of regional networks will be established in the European and Asian parts of the country. Subsequently, high-voltage interconnections will link these regions into a national network.[29]

Europe's Fuels and Inter-ties?" *Electrical World* (July 16, 1962), pp. 59–62.

[28] For an analysis and discussion of the Soviet energy resource base, see Jordan A. Hodgkins, *Soviet Power: Energy Resources, Production and Potentials* (Englewood Cliffs, N.J.: Prentice Hall, 1961).

[29] For discussions of Soviet proposals for development of regional power systems and interconnections, see K. D. Lavrenenko, "U.S.S.R. Power Developments and International Co-operation," *Transactions of the World Power Conference* (Melbourne: 1962); R. L. Lawton, "Power Development in the U.S.S.R.," *Power Apparatus and Systems* (October, 1962), pp. 385–99; G. Krzhizhanovsky and V. Viets, *A Single Power Grid for the U.S.S.R.* (Moscow: Foreign Languages Publishing House, 1957); and J. P. Hardt, *Economics of the Soviet Electric Power Industry* (Air University: Research Studies Institute, 1955).

---

[26] Spilled energy in UCPTE countries dropped from an equivalent of 534 million kw.-h. in 1952 to 242 million kw.-h. in 1958. See UCPTE, *Ten Years of Activity, 1951–1961* (Paris: 1962), p. 27.

[27] For a discussion of recent developments in Europe see C. Hochgesang, "What is the Trend of

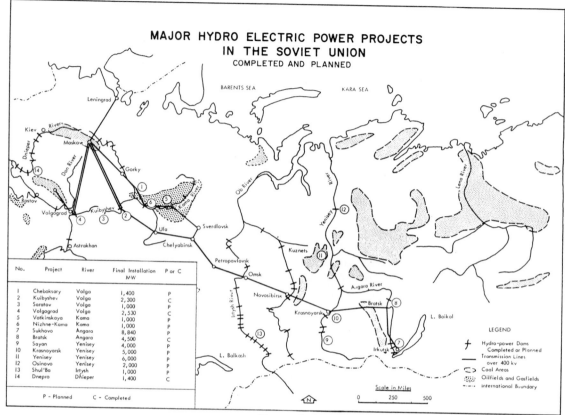

MAJOR HYDRO ELECTRIC POWER PROJECTS
IN THE SOVIET UNION
COMPLETED AND PLANNED

No.	Project	River	Final Installation MW	P or C
1	Cheboksary	Volga	1,400	P
2	Kuibyshev	Volga	2,300	C
3	Saratov	Volga	1,000	P
4	Volgograd	Volga	2,530	C
5	Votkinskaya	Kama	1,000	P
6	Nizhne-Kama	Kama	1,000	P
7	Sukhovo	Angara	8,840	P
8	Bratsk	Angara	4,500	C
9	Sayan	Yenisey	4,000	P
10	Krasnoyarsk	Yenisey	5,000	P
11	Yenisey	Yenisey	6,000	P
12	Osinovo	Yenisey	2,000	P
13	Shul'Ba	Irtysh	1,000	P
14	Dnepro	Dnieper	1,400	C

P - Planned   C - Completed

LEGEND
Hydro-power Dams Completed or Planned
Transmission Lines over 400 kv
Coal Areas
Oilfields and Gasfields
International Boundary

Scale in Miles
0   250   500

FIGURE 2

Considerable progress has been made towards the development of a consolidated power system in the European part of the Soviet Union. This has been accomplished by the construction of a number of major regional interconnections, and by the establishment of a central load-dispatching center in Moscow. This center controls 32 of the nation's 55 power systems, and a total capacity of 30 million kw.

Major regional interconnections in the European part of the Soviet Union include those between the Urals and Kuibyshev, between Kuibyshev and Moscow, and between Volgograd and Moscow. These interties are among the longest transmission lines in the world, each exceeding 500 miles in length.

Several major regional interties have also been built in the Asiatic part of the Soviet Union. For instance, 400-kv. lines have been built between Irkutsk, Krasnoyarsk, and Novosibirsk. These lines link the large hydropower installations on the Angara River and

on the Yenisey River with the large thermal power stations in the Kusbass region. An integrated grid is being developed in this part of the country, and in the near future it will link together generating capacity totalling nearly 50 million kw.

The European and Siberian parts of the country have been interconnected by a major link from Irkutsk to Moscow. Further trunk lines and major regional interconnections, some over 1,000 miles in length, are planned for construction in the near future. Trunk lines with voltages as high as 1,400 kv. are planned for construction between Siberia and the Urals. The objectives of these lines are to facilitate transmission of large blocks of power from east to west, and to take advantage of the time zones across the Soviet Union.[30]

In addition to regional interconnections being built within the Soviet Union, a number

[30] There are eleven time zones in the Soviet Union. There is an eight-hour time difference between Moscow and Vladivostock.

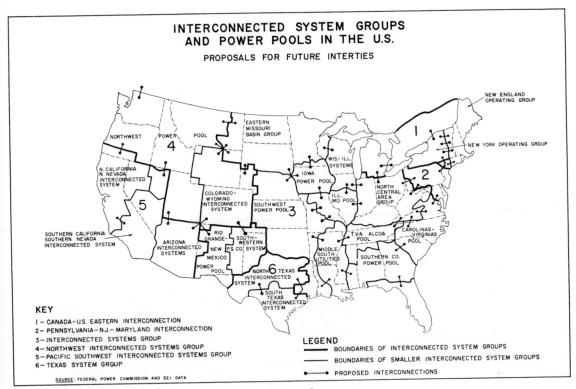

INTERCONNECTED SYSTEM GROUPS AND POWER POOLS IN THE U.S.

PROPOSALS FOR FUTURE INTERTIES

KEY
1 – CANADA–U.S. EASTERN INTERCONNECTION
2 – PENNSYLVANIA–N.J.– MARYLAND INTERCONNECTION
3 – INTERCONNECTED SYSTEMS GROUP
4 – NORTHWEST INTERCONNECTED SYSTEMS GROUP
5 – PACIFIC SOUTHWEST INTERCONNECTED SYSTEMS GROUP
6 – TEXAS SYSTEM GROUP

SOURCE: FEDERAL POWER COMMISSION AND EEI DATA

LEGEND
――――― BOUNDARIES OF INTERCONNECTED SYSTEM GROUPS
――――― BOUNDARIES OF SMALLER INTERCONNECTED SYSTEM GROUPS
•――• PROPOSED INTERCONNECTIONS

FIGURE 3

of lines are being constructed to link the U.S.S.R. with eastern Europe. A 220-kv. interconnection has been built between the U.S.S.R. and Hungary, and another is under construction between the Soviet Union and Poland. A 500-kv. interconnection between Czechoslovakia, the Soviet Union, and Roumania is planned for development in the near future.

Major advances in transmission technology have made transmission lines of this magnitude possible. Considerable success has been achieved with 400-kv. and 500-kv. lines, and work is now proceeding on lines of 750 kv. and above. So far, a.c. transmission has dominated the scene, but results of research at the Leningrad Direct Current Institute and elsewhere suggest that increasing use will be made of d.c. transmission in the future. An 800-kv. d.c. line from Volgograd dam to the Donbass region is the largest d.c. line in the world. This 275-mile line is regarded by the Soviets largely as an experimental venture, to provide data for much larger lines.

Implementation of plans for an integrated national network will call for a tremendous increase in transmission facilities. In the Soviet Union in 1958 there were about 35,000 miles of transmission lines with voltages over 110 kv. whereas in 1964 there are about 68,000 miles of such lines. The Soviets plan to increase this total to 178,000 miles by 1965. This will require an average annual increase in transmission facilities of about twenty per cent per annum. Obviously it will involve considerable capital investment. In the present 7-Year Plan Soviet expenditures on transmission facilities will amount to about 33 billion rubles.[31]

PROGRESS IN THE UNITED STATES

Considerable progress has been made in the United States in the development of inter-

[31] Soviet expenditures on electric power facilities in the period 1952–1958 totaled 75 billion rubles. Of this, some 8 billion rubles were spent on transmission lines. In the present 7-Year Plan the Soviets expect to spend 127 billion rubles on electric power facilities, with 33 billion rubles devoted to the construction of transmission facilities. See U.S. Senate Committee on Interior and Insular Affairs, *Relative Water and Power Development in the U.S.S.R. and the U.S.A.* (Washington, D.C.: 1960), p. 129.

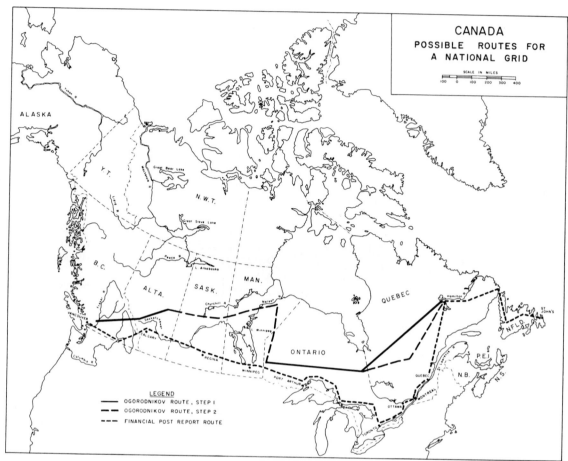

FIGURE 4

connected transmission networks in various parts of the country. Gradually seven broad regional groups have emerged, which together cover the whole of the contiguous United States.[32] These groups, or Interconnected Systems as they are called, have a total installed generating capability of 157 million kw. (Fig. 3).

---

[32] These Interconnected Systems are as follows: the Canada–U.S. Eastern Interconnection (popularly known as CANUSE); the Pennsylvania–New Jersey–Maryland Interconnection (PJM); the Interconnected Systems Group; the Pacific Southwest Interconnected Systems Group; the Northwest Interconnected Systems Group; and the New Mexico Power Pool. The largest group is the Interconnected Systems Group which has a total generating capacity of 85 million kw. For a detailed discussion of the operations of the various Interconnected Systems and Power Pools, see Edison Electric Institute, *Report on the Status of Interconnections and Pooling of Electric Utility Systems in the U.S.* (New York: 1962).

The coordination of operations between the members of the various regional groups varies from day-to-day barter arrangements, and various informal agreements, to elaborate constructual agreements. The more sophisticated contractual groupings are called "power pools." There are twenty-six of these pools in the United States at the present time. Some of the Interconnected Systems contain several pools. Others, however, contain no pools at all.

The various Interconnected Systems east of the Rockies are linked together by a number of interties. By 1966 it is expected that the systems east and west of the Rockies will be tied together, thus linking the various power systems from the Atlantic to the Pacific Coast, and from Hudson Bay to the Gulf of Mexico.

Many of the interties between and within the various regions, however, are fairly small in scale and have only limited capacity. The United States is still some way from having a national power grid which can take full advantage of the differences in the supply patterns across the country, and the diversity of power demands between one region and another.

The need for stronger links between the regions has been recognized both by the electric power utility industry and by the federal government, and plans have been announced for constructing several major interconnections in various parts of the country. The investor-owned utilities have announced an $8 billion construction program, in which over 100,000 miles of transmission lines will be built.[33] High priority in this program will be given to the construction of extra high-voltage lines.[34] A number of developments under this program are already under way.[35]

The federal government has also shown increasing interest in the possibilities and implications of the development of regional interconnections, and has undertaken studies of the possibilities of developing interties in several parts of the United States. It has announced plans for interconnecting some of the federal power systems, and has also called for a study of the possible advantages of a national grid.

The plans and proposals of the federal government have aroused considerable controversy in the United States. In particular, a question has been raised about the role of the federal government in the development of interties. On the one hand, the private power utilities oppose federal construction of interties on the ground that it would increase federal influence and control over the electric power industry. It is also claimed that some

of the interties proposed by federal agencies would duplicate lines planned for development by the private power utilities.[36] However, proponents of federal interties point out that the federal government has an important stake in the electric power industry, having invested several billion dollars in this field in the past three decades. The construction of interties, they suggest, would help to improve the operating efficiency of federal power facilities, thereby increasing the profitability of investment in them. The proponents of federal interties also suggest that these interconnections might be justified on other grounds as well. Some have proposed, for example, that investment in federal interties might be used as a counterrecessionary measure.

In addition to the problem of determining the role to be played by the federal authority in the development of interconnections, there is the problem of "regional preference." Often the legislation authorizing the construction of federal power projects has contained a clause which states that public agencies and cooperative electric power systems have priority in the purchase of power from federal projects. Once these public agencies and publicly owned power systems have been served, however, private power utilities are also able to purchase power from federal projects. In fact, many power utilities obtain a large proportion of their total requirements from such projects.[37]

So far transmission distances have limited the sale of federally produced power to the region within which the project is located. Long-distance interties, however, are now both technically and economically feasible. A major problem arises, however, because they would broaden the market area beyond the region in which the projects are located, and would thus increase the number of potential preference customers. It is probable that the public power agencies outside the region will

---

[33] *Electrical World* (September 11, 1961), p. 42.

[34] Extra high voltage in this paper is taken to mean voltages in excess of 345 kv., the highest voltage in use so far in the United States. There are at present 3,000 miles of 345-kv. lines in the United States. Several projects using 500-kv. lines, however, are now under construction. Projects planned for development in the next decade call for the construction of over 6,000 miles of 345-kv. lines, and over 3,000 miles of 500-kv. lines. See "Future EHV Apparatus Needs and Ratings in Profile," *Electrical World* (January 13, 1964), pp. 60–66.

[35] See, for example, "EHV Expanding at a Rapid Rate," *Electrical World* (February 25, 1963), pp. 139–42; and "Synchronizing the World's Largest Power Pool," *Electrical World* (December 11, 1961), pp. 57–72.

[36] For a discussion of the problem from the viewpoint of the private power interests, see "What Is Federal Role in Interconnections?" *Electrical World* (December 11, 1961), pp. 57–72.

[37] In the Pacific Northwest, for example, about fifteen per cent of the Bonneville Power Administration's sales are to private power utilities. Some of these utilities obtain as much as sixty per cent of their total requirements from BPA.

want to claim preference over private power agencies which are located within the region. For this reason, the private power utilities in the Pacific Northwest are firmly opposed to a California Intertie unless they are accorded a prior claim to power produced by federal power facilities in the Pacific Northwest.[38] The "regional preference" issue is being debated in the United States Congress and elsewhere, and the outcome is awaited with interest by all regions where federal interconnections are planned for development.

In summary, then, the advantages of interties have been recognized in the United States, and there now exists a major network of interconnections. It is generally agreed that stronger ties are required to take full advantage of the diversity of the energy resource base, and the differences in load conditions in the various regions of the United States. The major question that remains to be answered, however, is "who will build the interties?" The answer could have important implications for the future pattern of energy resource development in the United States.

PROGRESS IN CANADA

Canada is endowed with a great diversity of energy resources. From east to west across the country hydropower regions alternate with regions of rich deposits of fossil fuels. In addition, there are major differences in load characteristics and in power costs in the various regions of the country.[39]

So far, however, the development of interties in Canada has been limited. A few interconnections were built within some of the regions, notably the Maritimes Grid, and the interties between the power systems of Ontario and Quebec. A few international interconnections were also constructed. On the whole the interties are fairly small in scale and in scope, and exchanges of power are also relatively small. Interconnection is intraregional rather than interregional. The reasons for the lack of development of interties in Canada

are not hard to find. In most parts of the country sources of energy are abundant and there has been little need to look elsewhere. In addition, distances between established centers of population in many parts of the country have been so great that they could not be bridged technically or economically by transmission lines.

Recently, however, there has been a rapid awakening of interest in interties. Several factors have been responsible. First, some regions, such as southern Ontario, are beginning to experience rising costs of power as a result of exhaustion of local sources, and are therefore looking further afield. Second, there are attractive opportunities for developing power in some regions, such as Saskatchewan and Manitoba, but local demands are insufficient to justify development at the moment. Regional interties have been suggested as a means of facilitating the development of these resources.[40] Third, advances in transmission technology have made it possible to broaden the geographic horizon of electric power supply. In particular, they have led to a reappraisal of some of Canada's northern streams as potential sources of power for southern Canada, and possibly for the United States as well.[41] Fourth, the recent decision of the Canadian federal government to permit the export of electric power "where this is in the national interest" will no doubt stimulate the construction of many more international interconnections. An intertie between the West Kootenay Power and Light Company's plants on the Kootenay River in British Columbia and the Northwest Power Pool in the United States Pacific Northwest is one of the first fruits of this change of policy. Other major international interconnections contemplated for future construction are those relating to the development of the Columbia River, the Hamilton River, and the Nelson River.

---

[38] For a discussion of the regional preference issue and its implications, see "Will Preference Snag Interties?" *Electrical World* (December 11, 1961), pp. 68–69.

[39] For a detailed analysis of the Canadian energy resource base, see John Davis, *Canadian Energy Prospects* (Ottawa: Queen's Printer, 1957).

[40] D. M. Stephens, "Power Across International Frontiers." Paper presented to the Canadian Electrical Association (Banff, Alberta: June, 1961).

[41] The role of interconnections in the development of Canada's northern rivers is discussed in W. R. D. Sewell, "Power from the Yukon," *Water Power* (June, July, and August, 1964); and in "U.S., Canada Breaking Power Barriers," *Electrical World* (February 17, 1964), pp. 23–25.

In addition to the possibilities for the development of interconnections between regions, the advantages and implications of a national grid are being studied and discussed.[42] Proponents of the grid suggest that considerable savings could be derived from linking the various power regions across the country into a single network. In this way it would be possible to take advantage of the diversity in load conditions and the diversity in the resource base across Canada.[43] They also point out that savings would increase rapidly over time, as loads in the various regions are built up[44] (Fig. 4).

The development of a national grid in Canada is probably still some distance away. Some provinces, notably Saskatchewan and Manitoba, are extremely enthusiastic about the idea. Most of the others, however, have contemplated the notion with interest but not with great enthusiasn. There is general agreement that much more study is required before the potential advantages can be determined. In addition, the role that the federal government should play in the development of the grid is still to be settled.[45]

---

[42] A Federal–Provincial Committee has been established to investigate the possibilities of a national grid. All the provinces except Quebec are participating. A firm of consulting engineers has been commissioned by the federal government to study technical aspects of the matter.

[43] D. Cass-Beggs, for example, has estimated in a theoretical analysis of capacity and reserve requirements in Canada by 1965, that a national grid could result in savings of nearly $600 million. Of this, $430 million would be attributable to savings in capacity and the remainder of savings in reserve requirements. See D. Cass-Beggs, "Economic Feasibility of a Trans-Canada Electrical Interconnections." Paper presented to the Engineering Institute of Canada (October, 1959).

[44] V. E. Ogorodnikov of the Ontario Hydro Commission, for example, has estimated that savings of up to $1.3 billion could be realized by 1980 if a national grid were developed in the near future. See V. E. Ogorodnikov, "EHV Power Transmission in Europe and the Canadian Future," *Proceedings of the Canadian Electrical Association* (1959).

[45] For discussions of the possibilities and implications of a national grid in Canada, see A. R. Burge, "National Grid for Canada?" *Electrical News and Engineering* (November, 1960), pp. 55–57; and John Davis, "Is Canada Ready for a National Grid?" *Electrical News and Engineering* (November, 1960), p. 59.

CONCLUSIONS

Regional interties have become a major element in the energy supply structure of several parts of the world. Although the advantages of interties have been known for more than half a century, progress in developing interconnections was fairly slow until the Second World War. Interties built in the prewar period were mostly small in scale, locally focussed, and limited in function. In the past two decades, however, there has been a rapid broadening of horizons in the energy resource development field, necessitated by economic conditions on the one hand, and made possible by technological advances and relaxation of political barriers on the other. A consequence has been the development of many hundreds of new interconnections, some of them several hundreds of miles in length.

A heirarchy of types of intertie has emerged: small-scale, local interconnections between power systems within a region; regional interties linking two or more regions; national grids providing a backbone for the power systems of the country; and transcontinental supergrids. There are thousands of the local type of interconnection. Several hundred major regional interconnections have been built, and many countries now have national grids. The development of transcontinental supergrids, however, is still at the stage of technical contemplation.

Not only is there a heirarchy of types of intertie, but there is a heirarchy of functions as well. These range from the use of interconnections for emergency transfers of energy, to seasonal transfers, and finally to the operation of interties as an element in an integrated network. Occasional transfers, either on an emergency basis or on a contractual basis, are the most common. Integrated networks emerge only slowly.

There is a tendency for regions to become interconnected with several regions. As this happens the geographic horizon of a given source of energy broadens. It then becomes an element in a region of ever-increasing dimensions. A new set of relationships is established which tend to move like ripples in a pool. One illustration of this is the manner in which electric power moves from one time zone to another by displacement of capacity. The relationships stemming from the development of interties, however, are most intense and most direct in the regions closest to the intertie.

As the geographic horizon of energy supply has broadened, however, decision making has become more and more complex. Not only has the problem of economic choice become complicated as a result of the broadening range of alternatives, but institutional factors, such as government policy and political boundaries, have tended to become prime considerations in decision making. In some cases these latter considerations have been decisive factors. International boundaries in particular have tended to limit the boundaries of electric power supply regions.

From the standpoint of technical and economic efficiency, the next logical step beyond interconnection is the integration of the operations of electric power supply regions. Progress towards integration, however, has been fairly slow. In part this is a reflection of the fact that some systems have not yet reached the stage where it would be economically advantageous to integrate their operations. More often, however, institutional problems such as the existence of political boundaries, or considerations of national policy, have inhibited the evolution of an integrated network. Thus, although considerable progress has been made, the pattern of energy supply does not yet fully represent the pattern that would exist if economic considerations were the only determinant.

PRODUCTION DEPENDS ON ECONOMICS — NOT PHYSICAL EXISTENCE

by
RICHARD J. GONZALEZ*

The greatest cause of failures in forecasting the future stems from two related erroneous assumptions:

1. That events of the recent past serve as a guide for all future time.
2. That technology will never again undergo unpredictable changes such as those which have occurred many times in the past.

These assumptions account for many mistaken prophecies since the early days of the petroleum industry that domestic production would soon enter a period of permanent decline leading to early exhaustion. Some of these gloomy forecasts have been made by high government officials who were well informed about petroleum matters, such as David Day of the U.S. Geological Survey in 1909, and Secretary of the Interior Ickes in 1944.

Usually, fears about impending scarcity develop during periods when supplies seem short relative to rapidly growing demands. In recent years, however, some pessimism has been expressed despite a relative abundance of productive capacity and a rather slow rate of growth in demand. On the other hand, some very optimistic estimates have also been advanced about future production. In these circumstances, the question of future production deserves some thoughtful attention.

What is the role of economics in determining future production? What are the limitations of both the optimistic and pessimistic views? And what's the value of concentrating attention on the outlook for the next 20 years, rather than attempting to guess the entire future course of domestic petroleum production?

ECONOMIC FACTORS

Much of the recent discussion of future production has centered around measurement of the resource base, or the amount of oil and gas that may exist physically beneath the surface of our country. The theory back of this seems to be that determination of the quantity of petroleum in place will indicate how much will be produced and when all supplies will be exhausted. This basic assumption is only partially correct. Perfect knowledge about

*Director, Humble Oil & Refining Co.

"Production Depends on Economics — Not Physical Existence" by Richard J. Gonzalez. Reprinted from Oil and Gas Journal, *Vol. 62 (March 30, 1964), pp. 59–64, with permission of the author and editor.*

absolute physical existence, if it were possible, would set a limit on production, but would not necessarily establish how much will be produced or at what rate.

Physical existence vs. recovery. A few examples will serve to prove that production depends on economics rather than on physical existence. Chemical analysis reveals traces of gold in sea water which would be worth trillions of dollars in the aggregate from the vast volume of the oceans. Despite precise knowledge about this resource, no one has found an economic way of extracting gold from sea water at a cost less than its value. If some one were to invent a cheap process for doing so, the balance between supply and demand would be altered so greatly that the price of gold would drop sharply. In this case, even with complete certainty as to physical existence, no one can predict how much gold, if any, will ever be recovered commercially from the sea.

In the energy industries, large known resources not economically competitive up to this time are familiar to everyone. Known shale deposits of the Rocky Mountains are estimated to contain more than a trillion barrels of liquid fuels, far overshadowing known oil resources. Despite much research work by both the Government and private interests, however, no commercial production has yet been realized in this country from shale oil. The limiting factor has been an economic cost in excess of market value. Oil from shale may soon become commercial, but no reasonable estimate can yet be made of the rate or aggregate quantity of production in future years.

The same situation applies to the tar sands in Canada, which seem to be approaching commercial development. Coal deposits exist in great quantities at many different places throughout the United States, but the majority of them can't be developed profitably at current prices. If known physical existence determined production, coal would be many times more important than oil and gas in domestic energy output. Instead, because the petroleum industry has been able to supply energy at attractive prices, oil and gas are now much more important fuels than coal.

These examples show that production of a resource cannot be forecast on the basis of its physical existence. Many known resources may never be economically recoverable. Some may come into production, such as new coal mines and shale-oil deposits, but we will probably never exhaust these resources, because demand will be limited by availability of cheaper or better alternates.

Estimates of ultimate production may be defended by some on the ground that they are necessary in planning for the future. Judging by the past, however, they are much more likely to be misleading than helpful. Enough knowledge doesn't exist for anyone to measure with any degree of confidence how much oil exists or to say how much will be recovered. As new oil provinces are discovered, as technology improves, and as economic conditions change, estimates of recoverable reserves are constantly being modified.

Fifty years ago, the generally accepted geologic view was that the Permian basin would never produce oil. Nevertheless, it has become a prolific source of oil. No one can prove that this experience will not be repeated again in some other large sedimentary area. Better drilling and producing technology has commercialized large offshore and onshore accumulations that were submarginal before the days of fracturing. With the advent of large and efficient pipelines, wellhead prices for gas improved to an extent that fields previously considered noncommercial became worth developing. The increase in the price of crude oil from $1 to $3/bbl did not change physical existence, but it obviously had a profound effect on the discovery of commercial deposits and on economic recovery from all fields.

The impact of dynamic developments is evident in the rapid upward revision of estimates of recoverable reserves within a relatively short span of time. Whereas 20 years ago, 100 billion bbl was considered an optimistic estimate of ultimate production in the United States, a figure twice that high is about the minimum being considered now. In view of this substantial change, the usefulness of estimates of ultimate production as a basis for planning and policy determination is highly questionable.

Technology changes things. A major problem in predicting future resource production stems from lack of knowledge about the impact of future technological developments on interfuel competition. Consider first the developments affecting oil and gas. No one anticipated accurately the favorable results from progressive application of geology and geophysics. The industry is discouraged that no new technique has been devised for locating petroleum reserves; but much work is being done to improve geophysics with the objective of locating structures that have been passed over because of insufficient sensitivity in existing equipment. Should these efforts succeed, many new fields may be found in provinces already intensively explored. A direct method for locating petroleum beneath the earth's surface before drilling would have even more revolutionary results.

No one can say when or if such breakthrough will come to pass, but it would be equally rash to say that they are impossible and will never occur.

Technological developments in competing industries can also have great effect on future petroleum production. Mechanization of coal mining and reduction in the cost of moving coal by rail have already affected the demand for oil and gas by industry and by electric utilities. Transmission of electricity at extra high voltage will further improve the position of coal relative to oil. Atomic energy will also operate to limit demand and price for fossil fuels. Shale oil is already on the threshold of commercial feasibility, and ways may be found to lower its cost sufficiently to reduce the search for oil long before the prospect for locating new fields are exhausted. The use of solar energy is still in an experimental state, but could significantly affect energy markets in the future.

Government policies must not be overlooked in evaluating the economics of energy fuels. Federal regulation of gas prices, federal tax treatment of mineral production, and state conservation policies all bear on cost and profit factors that influence exploration, development, and recovery. If foreign oil continues to be available in large quantities at low cost, the import policy of the United States will be a major factor in determining the incentive to develop new domestic oil resources. Clearly, anyone who undertakes to predict how much oil will be produced in the United States must make some far-reaching assumptions about the future course of government policies relating to petroleum as well as about future technology in all fields of energy supply and demand.

Having established the point that future discovery and production will be determined by many complex economic and governmental forces entirely independent of the question of physical existence, let us now consider both the pessimistic and optimistic views about future domestic petroleum production.

THE PESSIMISTIC VIEW

Those who believe that the U.S. is at or near its peak of petroleum production and will soon enter a steadily declining phase base their views on various assumptions. One is that the industry has reached or passed the midpoint in cumulative discovery, so that by definition the amount remaining to be found is no more than discoveries to date. Another is that diminishing returns and rising costs evident since the end of World War II can be projected indefinitely into the future. It doesn't take any sophisticated mathematical analysis to see that these approaches must lead to pessimistic conclusions, since the answer is determined by the basic premises. It must be noted, however, that similar premises used many times in the past have consistently led to erroneous conclusions, leaving little basis for confidence that such techniques can provide reliable estimates currently.

Assumptions are questionable. Two major points should be noted about the pessimistic forecasts. First, they assume that trend lines or curves fitted to past data can be relied upon to predict the future. Second, they assume that no dramatic technological development will occur affecting the cost of finding and developing new reserves. Both of these are open to serious question.

Historically, costs have fluctuated instead of moving steadily in a straight line. New techniques have generally been the cause of a major downward reversal of costs. Geophysics and conservation regulations brought about a sharp decline in real costs in the period 1926-1940. For example, using the accepted figures for production and proved reserves estimated by the API in 1925, total wells drilled up to that time developed an average of only 20,000 bbl per well, compared with an average for all wells drilled from 1926 through 1951 of 81,000, and an average of 55,000 for all wells drilled since 1951. The figures demonstrate how significantly results can fluctuate with time, even though the numbers are subject to change because of revisions in the estimates of reserves attributable to past discoveries.

A line fitted to the data of the past 30 years should not be misinterpreted as a normal trend line. This may be as misleading as a projection of business conditions or stock-market prices arrived at by projecting a trend from the bottom of a depression to the top of a boom. The decrease in real costs experienced in the 1930's was followed by a rise in costs after World War II, but already evidence is developing that in recent years costs have tended to stabilize.

It cannot safely be assumed that costs will necessarily continue to rise or that they will never again show any significant reduction. On the contrary, costs should decrease as a result of recent progress toward wider spacing and better allocation of production. The continued application of improved recovery techniques will also have a favorable effect on costs, even in the absence of any major breakthrough in exploration or development.

One of the widely publicized projections places ultimate petroleum production in the United States at 170 to 175 billion bbl by the use of a logistic curve fitted to cumulative discoveries. While the S-shaped logistic curve which approaches a limit when projected indefinitely is often used in predicting the future of a time series, it has serious limitations in any dynamic situation. For instance, it is greatly influenced by the latest actual value used in the series of data and it cannot anticipate or cope satisfactorily with a resurgence in growth following a significant slowing down.

Predictions of 30 years ago by this method of the maximum population that would ever exist in the United States have already been surpassed because of changes that have occurred in life expectancy and in birth rates. The logistic technique is based on looking backward at historic data as a means of predicting the future without any effort to consider the effect of dynamic forces changing the picture. Therefore, it is not a dependable method for predicting the future.

No accuracy in oil. The logistic technique is even more questionable when used to predict ultimate petroleum production because of unsurmountable limitations of the basic data assumed to represent cumulative discoveries. Accurate information doesn't exist on actual discoveries by years, and the series used is deficient in two respects. First, it represents a reconstruction for many years prior to publication of any official estimates of reserves. Second, it uses gross additions to reserves due to discoveries, extensions, and revisions as reported by the API since 1936. These data do not attribute revisions and extensions back to the year of actual discovery. Consequently, a curve fitted to such unsatisfactory data is seriously deficient as a means of predicting ultimate discoveries. It is well recognized throughout the petroleum industry that a very long time is required to determine how much oil was found in past years, and that substantial upward revisions continue to be made for many years after a discovery.

Although cumulative discoveries are rated at 100 billion bbl at the end of 1962, everyone knows that future revisions will cause this figure to be increased greatly. Furthermore, the upward revision may be quite large, as indicated by the 1961 National Petroleum Council report that estimated production to be recovered from fields discovered through 1944 increased 50% between 1945 and 1960.

The significance of the deficiency in basic data is that the most recent values to which a curve should be fitted will tend to be progressively higher in the future than those now being used. This change will raise the estimate of cumulative discoveries by a logistic curve far above current levels, even assuming that such a curve is appropriate for the purpose.

Another indication of the limitations of the logistic technique becomes evident if it is applied to cumulative production data, which are far more accurate and reliable than the series on cumulative discoveries. Theoretically, the two series should both approach the same limit, since in the long run cumulative production must equal cumulative discovery of recoverable reserves. Actually, application of the same method to cumulative production indicates a much lower limit in the range of 85 to 100 billion bbl, or less than present estimates of cumulative discoveries to date. The conclusion from such calculation that we have already discovered more oil than will be produced is not compatible with the extensive expenditures being made by the industry to locate and develop new supplies.

Another approach. An attempt has been made to support the figure ascertained by using the logistic technique by means of an estimate of the number and size of small and large fields remaining to be discovered. This method is not an independent verification, but the use of another set of assumptions to arrive at the same answer. The assumptions used in this case are as follows:

1. That the total number of small fields to be found will be 20,000, or twice the number found by 1955.

2. That the crude-oil production from the average small field will be 3,100,000 bbl, based on estimates of recovery made in 1955.

3. That the total number of large fields will be 460, or roughly twice the figure of 240 recognized by the end of 1961.

4. That the crude-oil production from large fields will average 247,-000,000 bbl, based on estimates of recovery made in 1962.

The basic assumption in this approach is that half of all the fields to be found were discovered by about 1958 and that the average recovery from future fields will be the same as now estimated for those discovered in the past. The foregone conclusion dictated by this method is an estimate about twice the cumulative discoveries through 1958, or 175 billion bbl. The apparent agreement with the estimate of 170 billion arrived at by the logistic method is inherent in the assumptions made and cannot be accepted as proof that the estimate is correct. Since future revisions in estimated reserves will raise the average size of both small and large fields, a higher estimate of ultimate production can be justified by the latter method if the assumed number of future discoveries is correct.

The great weakness of this method is in the lack of adequate support for the estimate of the number and size of fields to be found in the future. In view of the large quantity of sedimentary deposits remaining to be explored intensively in the United States, which is considered to be much larger than the volume thoroughly tested so far, the number of fields to be found hereafter may be much greater than discovered to date. No one can say with assurance, however, how many fields will be found in the future or what their size will be. Therefore, we cannot rely on this approach to provide a reliable estimate of future production.

THE OPTIMISTIC VIEW

Several optimistic projections of future production of oil have been published in recent years. They estimate production ultimately recoverable as high as 400 to 500 billion bbl, including marginal reserves. Comparing this with cumulative production of 72 billion bbl through 1963, and present estimates of proved crude-oil reserves of about 32 billion bbl, one would conclude that the industry is far short of the midway point in discoveries and production. These views share assumptions that recovery from known fields will improve substantially and that large new discoveries will be made in sedimentary deposits remaining to be intensively explored.

Judgment as to the merits of the optimistic view may be separated into two parts. First, as to the anticipation of a higher recovery of oil in place from known fields than indicated by present estimates of proved reserves, there is good reason to believe that such achievement is technically feasible and will occur. The actual amount of recovery will depend on economics, however, rather than on technology alone. Once exploration and development costs have been incurred, operators have a great financial incentive to work diligently for the maximum recovery economically feasible in competition with new sources of supply. Whether recovery is low or high depends on the nature of each reservoir and on the price that can be realized for the production in competition with other sources of supply.

Through the years, great progress has been made in raising recovery levels, and further progress is confidently expected. In the absence of reliable statistics on the oil in place actually discovered to date, some analysts assume that present estimates of proved reserves reflect average recovery of not more than 30%, and that the recovery factor will at least double before production ceases. If these assumptions prove correct for fields already discovered, then ultimate production should exceed 200 billion bbl exclusive of the reserves to be recovered from new fields.

The main point requiring evaluation in the optimistic outlook for production relates to the quantity of new oil to be found and produced from fields not yet discovered. Clearly, evidence required to determine how much oil exists underneath the surface of the earth is not available. All estimates are only conjectures based on limited knowledge. One approach involves a comparison of the amount of oil found to date in the volume of sedimentary deposits thoroughly tested by drilling with the total volume considered favorable for accumulation of oil. So long as the cubic content of the sediments remaining to be explored far exceeds that already explored, as is still the case, this technique leads to higher estimates of ultimate production. The basic weakness of this approach is the absence of assurance that commercial occurrence of oil will be as favorable in further exploration as it has been to date, particularly since it must be assumed that the work done has been designed to test prospects that looked best according to present knowledge.

Several major questions can be asked about the optimistic forecasts of future production. One of these arises from the statistics of the American Association of Petroleum Geologists indicating a definite decline in the chances of finding a major field since the end of World War II. Since major fields have provided more than half of estimated recoverable oil discovered so far, such a development has serious implications if it continues as to quantity and cost of future discoveries. To the extent that sediments remaining to be tested are deeper than those tested in the past, costs may place a limit on the use of existing technology to discover and develop new resources. As for the provinces that have not realized significant production to date, the natural question arises whether they will ever prove as productive as the provinces already well tested and developed. These are all valid questions that must be weighed even though they cannot be answered now. Better technology may enable us to cope with these problems, but we do not know at what cost.

APPROACH TO FUTURE

Neither the optimists nor the pessimists are able to prove the superiority of their views to an impartial critic. Both depend on assumptions subject to question. There are probably only two points that can be made with certainty. First, the extent of commercial occurrence of oil has far exceeded earlier expectations, largely because scientific methods have steadily increased ability to locate, develop, and produce oil and gas at costs that have enabled these fuels to increase their position in the energy market. Second, petroleum production in the U.S. will be determined in practice by economic forces within the much larger limit of physical existence. Accordingly, we need to consider the economic outlook.

Since energy production will be determined by economic considerations rather than by physical limitations, we should quit wasting time in predictions of ultimate production and concentrate attention instead on the outlook for the next 20 years. Several factors suggest this period as appropriate. First, that span of years will cover much of the useful life of any capital outlays made currently for facilities to use or produce energy. Second, many of the forces that will determine developments for the next 20 years are already at work, providing some basis for accurate analysis. Third, such time is ample to allow for adjustment to changing circumstances as additional information and developments provide a basis for intelligent modifications of current forecasts and plans.

A basic starting point in planning for the future is that by any measurement the United States can count on sufficient supplies of total energy to meet requirements for a long time, well beyond the next 20 years. Widespread agreement exists that known and prospective supplies of oil, gas, and coal from domestic sources will be adequate for at least 20 years if government actions don't discourgage development of new resources. Even the pessimistic estimates of future production indicate that we will not come close to exhausting our resources that quickly. In addition, ample supplies of domestic coal and of foreign oil and the prospects for commercial production of shale oil will operate to stimulate greater efficiency in development and production of oil and gas. In these circumstances, no unusual rise in real cost or price of any fuel seems likely.

A second point of great importance is the increasing degree of interchangeability in the use of fuels. In the largest part of the energy market, consisting of electric-power generation and industrial use, all the major fuels are suitable in ordinary circumstances, except where limitations on the use of coal and fuel oil are imposed to reduce air pollution. For transportation uses, which account for less than one-fourth of all energy requirements, liquid fuels are still essential, but there is no danger of any shortage. It is already technically feasible to convert crude oil almost entirely into gasoline, although the current yield is less than 45%. Such adjustment could readily take place if, contrary to current expectations, any shortage of crude

oil should develop within the next 20 years and create an incentive to shift yields.

Another factor that should not be ignored is the interrelation of supply and demand for different fuels. We use oil and gas in large quantities because they have been available in ample supply at attractive prices. Demand cannot be projected independent of supply and price. Higher prices for petroleum products would lead to a shift over a period of years in the fuels used for home heating and in the miles realized per gallon of gasoline. No new technology is required to bring about such transitions. Electrical heating of homes is already growing and could become important.

As for automobiles, there is nothing to keep the public from switching from heavy cars loaded with power-driven equipment to light ones with four- and six-cylinder engines if that becomes economically desirable or necessary. The gasoline will do the same foot-pounds of work in either case, but this necessarily means better mileage per gallon for the lighter cars.

Lower demand, increased imports, and greater supplies of shale oil are among the major adjustments which would operate to maintain an economic balance between supply and demand should shortage of domestic crude ever materialize.

GEOGRAPHY OF THE WORLD PETROLEUM
PRICE STRUCTURE

Alexander Melamid

*Dr. Melamid is Associate Professor of Economic Geography in the
School of Commerce and Graduate School of Arts and Sciences of New
York University. For some years he has been specializing on the geog-
raphy of the petroleum industry.*

ON a world-wide average, omit-
ting tariffs and taxes, direct
transportation costs account for
about one-fifth of the delivered price of
crude oil and petroleum products in
international trade. Due to this high
freight element in the cost of oil, prices
differ significantly from place to place.
These local price variations concern the
economic geographer, and, in this article, it is proposed to describe the geographical structure of these variations
and explain their causation. Except
where stated, crude oil and petroleum
products will be considered together and
referred to as oil. This treatment is
permissible, as crude oil accounts for
about 70 to 75 per cent of the cost of
finished petroleum products in bulk at
the refinery regardless of refinery location; also contrasting trends between
crude oil and petroleum prices are only
short-term phenomena.[1] The latter
need not be considered here, as, due to
refinery and distribution requirements,
nearly all international trade in oil is
based on long-term contracts which tend
to level out short-term local fluctuations.
Because of the prevalence of long-term
contracts, historical perspectives are
essential in this as well as in other
geographical studies of oil industry
economics.[2] To avoid confusion resulting from the incidence of local tariffs
and taxes, only prices before the addition of these tariffs and taxes will be
considered. An exception has to be
made for United States import duties
and quotas which have direct repercussions on foreign prices. However, international prices, as described here, will be
compared with local prices (which include tariffs and taxes) in order to
evaluate the limitations of the effect of
geographical price differentials on consumer expenditures and price stability.

The Evolution of Geographical
Pricing Techniques

Until about the outbreak of World
War I, kerosene (then almost entirely
used for illumination) was the main
product of the oil industry. Although
international trade in oil commenced
immediately after the beginning of commercial oil production in Pennsylvania
in 1859, this trade did not reach modern
dimensions and diversity until the evolution of substantial gasoline and fuel oil
consumption. Even after the introduction of the pipeline and the tanker in
the 1870's and 1880's, much oil con-

---

[1] Melvin de Chazeau and Alfred E. Kahn:
*Integration and Competition in the Petroleum
Industry,* New Haven, 1959, p. 71 ff.

[2] See Alexander Melamid: "The Geographical Pattern of Iranian Oil Development," *Econ.
Geog.,* Vol. 35, 1959, pp. 199–218.

*"Geography of the World Petroleum Price Structure" by Alexander Melamid. Re-
printed from* Economic Geography, *Vol. 38 (October 1962), pp. 283–298, with permission of the editor.*

tinued to be transported long distances in barrels. Expenses for containers and freight usually exceeded the cost of oil at the source by substantial margins (Table I), and monopolistic practices were widespread and economically much more significant than in subsequent years. As a result, geographically separate markets were frequently not connected commercially, international price reporting was primitive and limited to a few places, and no significant worldwide price structure evolved. An outline of the then prevailing limited geographical price relations is given in the discussion of political prices before World War II. However, during this early period most of the modern trading techniques were developed in the United States.

As wells produce oil continuously and products flow or "run" continuously from refineries, and as both crude oil and nearly all products are liquids which are expensive to store, oil men found it unsatisfactory to trade in "certificates" or "contracts" requiring delivery at specific dates, the usual practice in commodity markets.[3] For this reason traders developed a system of "posted prices" and "nominations." Prices at which traders are transacting business are announced or posted after initial trading, and they apply until new prices are posted. Qualities or grades of oil, mainly defined by physical analysis, are specified for each posted price. Price scales, established in a similar way by trading and posting, permit adjustments for differences in quality. In addition to posting, the price traders announce or "nominate" the quantities which they will handle. "Nominations" are usually made on a per diem basis for a period of time or until the posted

[3] Petroleum products which are not liquid, such as waxes, also smaller quantities of liquid products, are still sold on a "contract" basis. This does not affect the following discussion.

TABLE I

COST OF CANADIAN PETROLEUM (GRADE UNSPECIFIED) DELIVERED TO A GERMAN PORT IN 1863*

	Per barrel of 40 Imperial gallons
Price in bulk f.o.b. Olica, Ontario...	$ .50
Cost of empty container f.o.b. Olica, Ontario......................	2.00
Freight Olica, Ontario to Montreal (St. Lambert), Quebec...........	1.65
Handling charges in Canada........	.24
Ocean Freight to Hamburg or Bremen (Germany).....................	2.13
Total cost for delivery to German port (excluding insurance)......	$6.52

*According to William Wagner: *Das Petroleum aus Canada bezogen in seinem Werthe fuer Deutschland*, 1863, summarized in Mineraloelwirtschaft, Hamburg, Sept. 5th, 1961, p. 181. According to this calculation the delivered cost was thirteen times the price of the bulk material at the point of origin. In subsequent years this ratio was substantially reduced which permitted the gradual evolution of a price structure.

price changes. Due to the evolution of this trading technique barrels per day (abbreviated b/d)[4] became the basic measure of the oil industry. Obviously, if the nominated quantities do not match the available quantities, the posted price will change according to the laws of supply and demand. To increase the quantities available at each posted price, the flow of oil from all wells within an oil field or a group of geologically and geographically related oil fields (oil region) is included in the posted price. For example, today one posted price covers all crude oil produced in West Virginia, or one series of posted prices graduated by quality covers all oil fields of Oklahoma and Kansas.

For petroleum products, and for crude

[4] As a measure a barrel equals 42 U. S. gallons. This measure developed when wooden barrels of smaller inside dimensions were used; however, a modern steel barrel holds 54 U. S. gallons. Some products are measured in gallons per day—gasoline for example. Many countries measure oil output in metric tons or cubic meters per year. For an approximate conversion of metric tons or cubic meters per year to barrels per day, divide by 50. When tons per year are used as a measure, specific gravity and temperature have to be considered for accurate conversion to cubic meters, respectively barrels per day.

oil and products for export, a similar system of publicly announced prices applying within specific regions also developed. The best known of the product-pricing regions today is called "Group 3" of the Midcontinent area. It is centered on Tulsa, Oklahoma, and covers the output of all refineries in the State of Oklahoma.[5] For export pricing the most outstanding region is the Gulf Coast of Texas and Louisiana. Its prices are referred to as U. S. Gulf prices. These product and export prices differ legally from posted prices, but the principle of their geographical application is the same. As some posted prices were not and are not publicly available (not published in the petroleum press), both posted and product and export prices will be hereafter simply referred to as "prices."

Within each region, prices also specify the method of delivery: for crude oil it is generally at the wellhead;[6] for products at the refinery or storage rack. Export prices specify delivery f.o.b. vessels (today almost always tankers) at ocean terminals (piers with pipeline terminals or floating off-shore pipeline terminals connected to the main pipeline system by flexible hoses). This pricing system is, in fact, a system of uniform prices for each grade of oil in a specific region. However, the detailed location of the point of delivery within the region is not stated. The system

therefore permits gathering large quantities of oil at the same price within a region. While these large quantities tend to favor the growth of large companies within the regions, the system also assures the same prices for lesser quantities to smaller firms. Occasionally, traders announce different prices for the same grade of oil in a region, or "premiums" or "discounts" on prices are reported in the press. For products and exports "Highs" and "Lows" and "Averages" are also sometimes given. Under competitive conditions these variations are frequent but transitory features of the price system. After its evolution in the United States, this system of pricing and its definitions spread to other countries actively engaged in the international oil trade. Although this system evolved in the United States in the kerosene age of the oil industry, its world-wide dispersal was mainly a phenomenon of the post-World War II era.

In the United States the early formative period ended generally in 1911 when gasoline production first began to exceed kerosene production. In the same year the Standard Oil Trust was dissolved resulting in a new pattern of competition. Simultaneously, oil production in Oklahoma, Texas, and later Louisiana began its rapid growth, the general area soon replacing California as the first ranking oil production region. This geographical shift of production further increased competition within the United States. It also favored the evolution of a geographically interconnected world market for oil, because the new production area was better located than its predecessor for transportation to world markets primarily situated near the Atlantic Ocean. This relocation of production also added to the significance of the export prices in the Gulf Coast region. The opening of the Panama

[5] This region was created by decision of the Interstate Commerce Commission which established equal rates for the movement of oil from all points in this region to Midwestern destinations. Originally, this region covered the whole Midcontinent oil producing area (Oklahoma, Kansas, Missouri, etc.). After 1915 this Midcontinent region was divided "into three groups for rate making purposes, Group 1 points having a Kansas City origin, Group 2 a Southeastern Kansas origin, and Group 3 an Oklahoma origin" (Ralph Cassady, Jr.: *Price Making and Price Behavior in the Petroleum Industry*, New Haven, 1954, p. 187).

[6] Definitions differ west of the Rocky Mountains without upsetting the geographical principles discussed here.

Canal in 1914 greatly facilitated connection of this export price center with Californian and other prices in the Pacific Ocean area (for example in the then Dutch East Indies).

Prices Before World War II

Internationally, the effect of all these developments did not become marked until after World War I. Competition in the United States had increased since 1911, but, in other countries, only a few companies produced, refined, or marketed oil, and little independent price formation took place. As a result, companies, consumers, and governments[7] looked to the United States for information. This information was available in the form of U. S. Gulf prices. As the United States was by then also the world's largest exporter of oil, U. S. Gulf prices became the world's basing prices. To determine the price of oil in any region outside the United States, freight from United States Gulf of Mexico ports to this region was added to the U. S. Gulf price at the time of shipment. This system of pricing, colloquially referred to as "Gulf-Plus," was applied, irrespective of the origin of the oil. Thus the price of Iranian oil delivered from Abadan to the Stockholm region of Sweden, equalled the U. S. Gulf price for the applicable grade of oil at the time of shipment *plus* freight from Gulf of Mexico ports to the Stockholm region. In theory, insurance for the oil while in phantom transit from Gulf of Mexico ports to the actual destination would have to be added to arrive at a complete c.i.f. price. However, for pricing purposes this insurance charge was neglected. Variations between the quality

of oil specified in U. S. Gulf prices and the delivered oil were adjusted according to price scales also available in the competitive American market. This method of world-wide pricing became general in 1921 but its beginnings can be traced to the period before World War I.

As American exports relied almost exclusively upon tankers, tanker freight rates from the Gulf of Mexico region to ports of destination were used in calculating world-wide prices.[8] Inland transportation rates from the ports of arrival were generally not added for international pricing. In countries without ocean ports, such as Switzerland or Bolivia, river or rail freight to the point of entry was added to tanker freight from Gulf of Mexico ports; for example, in Switzerland, Rhine River freight to Basle was added. For internal pricing most countries added inland freight to points distant from ocean ports. Due to the limited significance of inland freight rates in the world price structure and absence of detailed information, inland freight is largely neglected in the following discussion.

Within this world-wide price structure, prices fluctuated with changes in U. S. Gulf prices and tanker freight rates. The latter were periodically (in the 1930's usually half-yearly) determined by a panel of outstanding shipbrokers in London, the world's foremost freight market and a very competitive one. The panel determined only typical freight rates for the period preceding determination[9] as there were frequently

---

[7] Besides exercising general supervisory powers for the economies of their countries, governments are also most important buyers of oil (military and civilian). Price information is indispensable for governments who levy ad valorem import duties, or who today participate in oil company profits.

[8] Exceptions were land exports to Canada and Mexico, and lubricants, etc., shipped in drums, etc., by dry-cargo vessels. In the latter cases prices were determined by addition of the applicable freight rates to U. S. Gulf prices. Prices for land exports were usually related to Group 3 prices to which freight from Oklahoma was added. These methods of pricing for land exports, etc., are still applied today, although their scope is now very limited.

[9] Precise method of determination not disclosed. Some typical rates were not published. This includes inter-company rates which were

substantial fluctuations in rates, particularly for single voyages. For this reason there were often significant differences between the typical rate of the preceding period and actual rates paid. As a result of these differences, the price structure provided some leeway for additional competitive pricing outside the United States.

The prevalence of long-term contracts in the tanker market, and the quantitative significance of company-owned tankers not entering the freight market limited the effect of this leeway on most prices. In occasional price-wars competitors disregarded the price structure completely, as for example in India in 1926. Due to the large quantities of oil involved and the magnitude of freight charges, disregard of the price structure was rare, of short duration, and regionally localized. No alternative method of pricing was suggested during the period between the two world wars, and there was little substantial criticism of the then prevailing geographical price structure.

THE GEOGRAPHICAL PRICE STRUCTURE BEFORE WORLD WAR II

Neglecting these minor fluctuations, the world-wide price structure consisted of a single basing point region from where prices increased geographically outward with transportation charges. These increases were not proportional to distances from the basing point region. Distortion of proportionality resulted not only from the distribution of land-masses and shipping routes, but also from the incidence of special dues, such as port (Basra), lighthouse (Persian Gulf), canal transit (Suez), or other charges related to special risks (weather, delay, politics). Proportionality was

further distorted by the regional grouping of ports in freight rates. For example, in Europe, all ports capable of accommodating ocean-going tankers within the Bordeaux-Hamburg range were usually grouped together; in the United States, all ports north of Cape Hatteras were so grouped. As a result one freight rate covered shipment from all U. S. Gulf of Mexico ports to all ports within a regional group or between other regional groups (Table II).

Despite these distortions, prices increased gradually in both easterly and westerly directions from the basing point region. Land and ice prevented a continuation of this pattern in northerly and southerly directions through polar regions. As a result, an area of maximum prices was reached in a longitude approximately opposite that of the United States Gulf Coast region (90° to 97° West). Due to the bunching of ports into regional groups this maximum price area was not a line but a zone. By way of analogy to the terminology of physical geography, this line or zone is called "price-shed."[10] As lowest elevations decrease with increasing distances from water-sheds, so do lowest prices decrease with increasing distances from price-sheds. Before World War II the world price-shed was located in the Indian Ocean running north-south, east of Burma (Fig. 1). Due to the absence of large ports in this general area except Rangoon (longitude 95° East) this price-shed cannot be traced in detail. In theory, inland freights should have extended this price-shed in a northerly direction through Asia and in a southerly direction into Antarctica. This single price-shed was another characteristic of the world price structure before World War II.

---

usually separately determined. Today these rates are expressed in terms of per cent of standard rates (see Table II).

[10] Also analogous is the term "milk-shed" used in milk marketing. John M. Cassels: *A Study of Fluid Milk Prices*, Cambridge, Mass., 1937. p. 20 ff.

TABLE II

SELECTED UNITED STATES MARITIME COMMISSION (USMC) TANKER FREIGHT RATES*

In long tons (of 2240 lbs.)

The rates given below are some of several standard freight rates used in the oil industry. Actual or typical, etc., rates are calculated in per cent of these standard rates. For example during 1961 a rate of USMC minus 80 per cent was quoted from the Persian Gulf to Japan or $2.04 per ton.

Region	Northeastern United States	North France Great Britain Belgium Holland West Germany	ITALY excluding Adriatic ports	La Plata	JAPAN	BOMBAY
U. S. Gulf....................	$2.85	$7.65	$8.75	$9.65	$15.40	$15.90
Caribbean....................	2.70	6.55	7.05	7.20	14.20	14.20
Levant Coast..................	7.80	5.45	2.80	11.35	not available	6.65
Central Persian Gulf (Ras Tanura).	12.70	10.90	8.15	13.40	10.20	2.40
Northern Persian Gulf (Abadan)...	13.25	11.60	8.85	13.95	10.80	3.00

*These rates were used during 1942–1948 for the calculation of payments to tanker operators. Today they serve only as a standard for calculation. Other standards are "American Tanker Rate Schedule" (ATRS), the British "Ministry of Transport Rates" (MOT), and the "London Market Tanker Nominal Freight Scale" (SCALE). The use of these standards varies between companies and regions. The leeway on pricing by the use of these various standards has been very limited. (The above figures were obtained from oil companies and ship-brokers.)

EXCEPTIONS BEFORE WORLD WAR II:
CARIBBEAN PRICES

Exceptional prices occasionally found between the two wars in some regions can be related to the price structure emerging after World War II, or to the survival of some of the discontinuous price patterns dating from before World War I. None of the exceptions made the price structure of one world basing point region and one world price-shed inoperative.

In the late 1930's exports from the Caribbean region (crude oil from Venezuela, and products from the Dutch West Indies) began to exceed United States exports by a substantial margin. This was the result of both increasing Venezuelan production and growing United States domestic consumption. Due to lack of competition in the Caribbean region, no independent regional prices evolved. Instead, to accommodate the changed export pattern, Caribbean crude oil prices were equalized with U. S. Gulf prices less United States import duty of 10½ cents per barrel. For example, in 1938 the U. S. Gulf price for average crude oil (36° API gravity) was

about $1.38 per barrel. The Caribbean price was therefore $1.27½. Product prices were adjusted accordingly. Differences in quality continued to be allowed for as before. The new prices f.o.b. tanker at terminals in the Caribbean region (Dutch West Indies, Venezuela) were called Caribbean prices. In theory freight was added to both U. S. Gulf and Caribbean prices to determine prices elsewhere. However, lower base prices and lower freight rates to most destinations (Table II) resulted in lower "Caribbean-Plus" prices everywhere except to the Gulf of Mexico. For this reason "Caribbean-Plus" prices, although dependent upon U. S. Gulf prices, began to dominate nearly all world prices shortly before the outbreak of World War II. A new but minor price-shed between "Caribbean-Plus" and "U. S. Gulf-Plus" prices evolved west and north of Cuba and east of Yucatan.[11] Due to the relative prox-

[11] Tanker rates (see Table II for definitions) used for computation (per ton): United States Gulf ports to Havana $1.70, to Cienfuegos (South coast, Cuba) $1.95, to Antilla (East Cuba) $2.15; Aruba (Dutch West Indies) to Havana $2.05, to Cienfuegos $1.80, to Antilla $1.55. Havana is, therefore, located to the

imity of the United States Gulf and Caribbean regions, the geographical shift of world prices was not marked, and the world's major price-shed remained located to the east of Burma. Over-all, the geography of the world price structure was not much changed by this development which anticipates the trends of pricing after World War II.

EXCEPTIONS BEFORE WORLD WAR II: ROMANIAN AND RUSSIAN PRICES

Before World War II lower export prices quoted f.o.b. Romanian Danube or Black Sea terminals, or Russian Black Sea terminals, occasionally interfered with the world price structure based on U. S. Gulf prices. This interference was

sporadic, particularly as Romanian prices were "adulterated by constantly changing export duties."[12] In view of the progressive decline of Romanian and Russian exports in proportion to world consumption, the effect of these lower prices decreased in the 1930's compared with the 1920's. Before World War I, Romanian and Russian prices had been still more significant.[13] According to a United States Federal Trade Commission report, Romanian prices in the 1930's were also "not entirely independent of the United States Gulf price."[14]

[12] P. H. Frankel: *Essentials of Petroleum*, London, 1946, p. 146.

[13] Russian prices became important in 1889 after construction of a 78-mile pipeline to bypass the 3000-foot summit of the Baku-Black Sea Railroad (Harold F. Williamson and Arnold R. Daum: *The American Petroleum Industry*, Evanston, 1959, p. 635 ff). The outbreak of war in 1914 ended the permanent significance of Russian prices.

[14] *The International Petroleum Cartel*, Committee Print #6, 82nd Congress, 2nd Session, United States Government Printing Office, 1952, p. 354.

north of this price-shed and Cienfuegos and Antilla are to the south. In view of the limited consumption in Cuba this price-shed was not important. From the North coast of Cuba, east of Havana, the price-shed extended to the East coast of Florida north of Miami. Due to lack of freight rates for Mexican ports the western terminus of this price-shed cannot be calculated; theoretically its terminus should be in Eastern Yucatan.

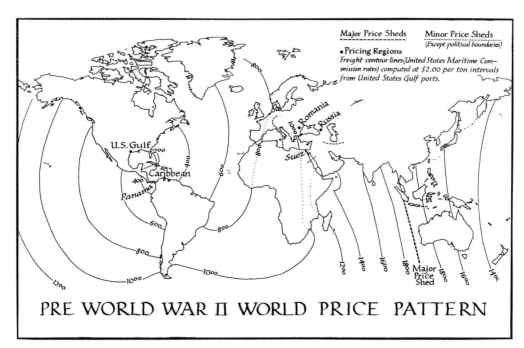

PRE WORLD WAR II WORLD PRICE PATTERN

FIG. 1. Prices before World War II: major exceptions.

Romanian oil was exported by sea from Constanta and up the Danube from the Danube river port Giurgiu. As Constanta exported far larger quantities than Giurgiu,[15] Constanta prices generally also applied in Giurgiu. Romanian export prices were therefore regional prices like Gulf prices.

To arrive at prices in the area surrounding Romania, freight was added to Romanian export prices upriver from Giurgiu, and across the Black Sea, Mediterranean, etc., from Constanta. During periods when Romanian export prices were lower than "Gulf-Plus" prices calculated for Constanta, a minor price-shed between "Romanian-Plus" and "Gulf-Plus" prices evolved. Due to the availability of Danube transportation up to Ratisbon (Germany), a frequent location of this price-shed was approximately along the water-shed between the Danube, and the Rhine, Elbe, and Oder river-systems. South of the Danube valley this price-shed frequently bisected Italy and the Mediterranean between the Adriatic and Tyrrhenian Seas. To the southeast this price-shed was sometimes located in the Red Sea or in the northwestern Indian Ocean. However, shifts in the location of this price-shed and even its complete disappearance were not unusual.

Soviet Russian prices were and are today established by government action. Like Gulf or Romanian prices, Soviet Russian export prices are regional in character and apply in all Black Sea oil ports (Batumi, Tuapse, Novorossiysk). Despite the different method of determining prices in Russia, geograph-

ical proximity generally made Russian and Romanian prices move together. As a result no separate price-sheds evolved. During the early 1920's, however, extremely low Russian prices, followed by Romanian prices, pushed the price-shed between these prices and Gulf prices several times as far west as Great Britain, and east as far as India. Due to the instability of both Romanian and Russian prices, many contracts in Eastern hemisphere countries specified that the lowest price calculated either according to the "Gulf-Plus" or "Black Sea (Romania or Russia)-Plus" formula should apply on shipment.

A COMPARISON WITH UNITED STATES DOMESTIC PRICE PATTERNS

This pattern of shifting minor price-sheds related to subsidiary basing price centers connected to a major basing price region was also found in the domestic market of the United States before the 1930's. At various times Oil City, Pennsylvania; Cleveland, Ohio; and Tulsa, Oklahoma, had been major base price centers, and many towns in the Appalachians, the Middle West, California, and the Southwest had served as minor centers. In the early 1930's Tulsa, Oklahoma (Group 3), became almost the sole basing price center.[16] Its prices were connected to Gulf

---

[15] For example, in 1936 Constanta handled 80 per cent of all Romanian petroleum product exports. Giurgiu handled only 17 per cent; the balance was exported by railroad. Crude oil exports were not significant. However, during World War II when no price formation took place, Giurgiu handled up to 56 per cent of Romanian oil exports. Date according to Constantin N. Jordan: *The Romanian Oil Industry*, New York, 1955, p. 284.

[16] This evolutionary change which resembles similar changes abroad was well described by Robert C. Gunness, Executive Vice-President of Standard Oil Company (Indiana): "There was a period in the earlier stages of Standard's development when the Company had as much as 80 per cent of the gasoline volume in the Middle West. We had less need then to consider the pricing policies of our competitors in setting our own prices. A price was established at each refinery, and the posted price in a given community was simply the refinery price plus the cost of all rail freight to the destination."

"This charmingly simple state of affairs failed to last. In the early 1930's new crude discoveries in the midcontinent area culminated in a flood of gasoline moving by rail from that area into our marketing territory. Standard was compelled to meet that competition by establishing its prices in conformity with the

prices by the addition of pipeline or rail freight from Group 3 to Gulf of Mexico shipping terminals. This freight was the same for all terminals in the Gulf of Mexico region; for crude oil, pipeline charges, and for products, rail tank-car freight was added. Thus throughout most of the 1930's nearly all the world possessed only one very simple geographical price structure due to the direct connection between internal North American (United States and Canada see Footnote 8) and Gulf prices. The absence of similar connections to domestic markets also made Romanian and Russian prices less significant among world prices.

POLITICAL PRICES

Another category of exceptions in the world price structure resulted from deliberate government action in oil producing countries. Already prior to the nationalization of its oil industry in 1938, the Mexican Government insisted on lower domestic prices than "U. S. Gulf-Plus" prices. Mexican export prices, which remained equal to "U. S. Gulf-Plus" prices, therefore, subsidized lower Mexican domestic prices.[17] Theoretically, this should have resulted in the establishment of a minor price-shed along Mexico's border. However, smuggling frequently made this price-shed ineffective. In Iran, an agreement between the producing company and the government established similar low domestic Iranian prices at Abadan to which freight within the country was

added. Exports from Baku (USSR) to which freight was also added sometimes competed with inland "Abadan-Plus" prices. As a result, a price-shed divided Iran along a line connecting Tabriz, Tehra, and Meshed in 1937.[18] Elsewhere this price-shed followed political boundaries.

All these exceptional prices were related either directly (for example by taking an agreed figure or percentage of "U. S. Gulf-Plus" prices) or historically (by not following "U. S. Gulf-Plus" price increases) to the world basing price, and did not invalidate the principles of the world price structure. Analysis of exceptional prices also emphasizes the significance of political boundaries within geographical price structures.

PRICES AFTER WORLD WAR II

The pre-World War II price structure of cumulatively higher prices with increasing distances from the United States Gulf Coast region encouraged a remarkably successful search for oil in other countries. The resulting expansion of exportable production outside the United States caused important changes in the price structure toward the end of World War II and thereafter. This change was gradual and commenced with, first, British, and then American Government objections to high prices for products supplied for military purposes in the Persian Gulf during World War II.[19] As costs of production in the Middle East are substantially lower than

current prices at Tulsa, Oklahoma, plus the cost of rail transportation to destination." (In Jules Backman: *Pricing Policies and Practices,* New York, 1961, p. 103.)

[17] This reduced investment in the Mexican oil industry. The nationalized Mexican petroleum industry continued this practice, and for many years suffered from a shortage of capital funds. W. J. Levy: *The Search for Oil in Developing Countries,* prepared at the request of the International Bank for Reconstruction and Development, New York, 1960, p. 88.

[18] According to the writer's observations, in Meshed trucking charges for products in drums from the port of inland delivery (Shatt-al-Arab, Persian Gulf, or Caspian Sea) were added to the reduced prices. As trucking charges varied virtually from day to day, the location of the price-shed changed frequently. Under these conditions shortages of oil and additional local premiums were not unusual. Presumably this state of affairs prevailed in many countries in the first decades of the oil industry.

[19] Federal Trade Commission, *ibid* n. 16, p. 355 ff., describes in detail the negotiations for the changing of Persian Gulf prices.

in the United States, the profits from oil production with "U. S. Gulf-Plus" prices were regarded as too high. Due to these objections all Persian Gulf prices were made equal to U. S. Gulf prices in 1945. This equalization followed the pattern of the earlier and continuing Caribbean price adjustment (in which governments played only a limited part), exclusive of the deduction of United States import duties. Persian Gulf prices therefore directly followed all changes in the Gulf prices of the United States.

To arrive at prices elsewhere, freight was added to both the new and the old basing prices. New price-sheds therefore developed which separated "Caribbean-Plus" from "Persian Gulf-Plus" pricing areas. A western price-shed was located in the Central Mediterranean, extended theoretically across Africa, and continued southward from Capetown. An eastern price-shed was located in the Pacific Ocean east of Japan and Australia. Due to restrictions on navigation near poles, both price-sheds ran generally in a north-south direction. As before, a minor price-shed, located west of Cuba, continued to separate the primary "U. S. Gulf-Plus" pricing area from the "Caribbean-Plus" pricing area.

The rapidly-growing volume of Middle East production and the simultaneous increase in U. S. Gulf prices soon induced further changes. In 1948, at the insistence of the American Government, which was then indirectly paying most of the free world's oil bills, the Western price-shed was deliberately shifted from the Central Mediterranean to Great Britain. Prices in the Persian Gulf were therefore calculated by adding to the U. S. Gulf price freight from the United States Gulf ports to Great Britain, and subtracting freight from the Persian Gulf to Great Britain. This method re-duced Persian Gulf prices below U. S. Gulf prices, as freight from United States Gulf ports to Great Britain is $7.65 per ton, and from the Persian Gulf to Great Britain $10.20.[20] Later in 1948 freight rates from the Caribbean to Great Britain ($6.55) were substituted for United States Gulf ports–Great Britain rates. This reduced Persian Gulf prices still further below U. S. Gulf prices without shifting the western price-shed. The eastern price-shed remained located in the Pacific Ocean and was little affected by either changes. About the same time prices at Iraq pipeline terminals on the Levant coast of the Eastern Mediterranean came to be determined in the same way, but only the freight from the Eastern Mediterranean to Great Britain was deducted from the price-shed in Great Britain.

In 1949 the western price-shed was deliberately shifted to the Eastern United States north of Cape Hatteras. Freight from the Caribbean continued to be added up to this price-shed. This change further lowered prices on the Levant and in the Persian Gulf. As the eastern price-shed remained in the Pacific Ocean, all delivered prices in the eastern hemisphere were also reduced which aided economic recovery, especially in Europe. With the opening of the Trans-Arabian pipeline from Saudia Arabia to Sidon in 1950, prices at this port were also included among Levant prices. In view of the deduction of freight from the western price-shed, the differential between Persian Gulf and Levant prices was therefore equal to tanker freight from the Persian Gulf to the Eastern Mediterranean and not to the cost of pipeline transportation between the two regions.[21] Separate lower prices evolved

[20] United States Maritime Commission rates. See Table I.

[21] Costs of pipeline transportation are lower than tanker freights from the Persian Gulf to the Eastern Mediterranean (including Suez

at oil terminals in the northern Persian Gulf (Kuwait, Iran) which are more distant from the price-shed than terminals in the central Persian Gulf (Saudi Arabia, Bahrein, Qatar). To compensate for very high port dues in the Shatt-al-Arab which are included in freight rates, prices at Abadan (Iran) and Fao (Iraq) were further reduced below the level of prices at northern Persian Gulf terminals. During the 1950's separate prices began to be published in the East Indies. These covered Indonesian, North Borneo (crude oil delivered f.o.b. Lutong, Sarawak), and imported oil (Fig. 2). These prices are calculated by the addition of freight to Persian Gulf prices, and are thus also ultimately related to the primary U. S. Gulf prices. No minor price-sheds en-

close the various separate Persian Gulf, Levant, or East Indian prices, as these prices are all directly determined by deduction of freight from the world's major price-sheds. None of these developments changed the dependence of prices outside the United States upon fluctuations in U. S. Gulf prices.

As before World War II, freight rates for pricing were periodically determined in London. Gradually more sophisticated methods of determination evolved. These methods neither increased proportionally to distances nor reduced the gap between typical and other rates of the preceding period and actual rates paid. These discrepancies had little effect on the new basing prices, except that occasionally some companies announced slightly different prices for the same grades of oil in the same region, as for example in the central Persian Gulf. The existence of such differential prices for any length of time primarily reflects a lack of competition outside the United

canal transit dues). The resulting profit on pipeline operations has now to be shared with the countries which are crossed by the pipeline. Profits on the operation of the pipelines from Iraq to the Levant coast are theoretically similarly calculated and then shared.

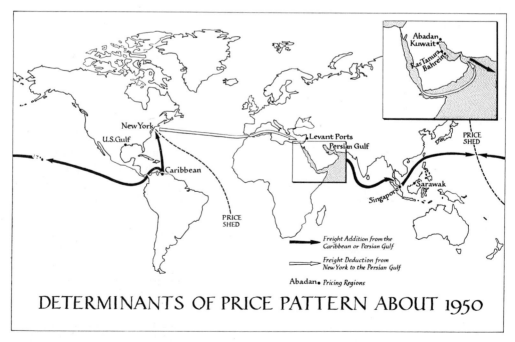

DETERMINANTS OF PRICE PATTERN ABOUT 1950

Fig. 2. Determinants of 1950 prices.

States. This lack of competition further explains why all the new basing prices continued to follow U. S. Gulf price changes.

Despite the many changes which lowered prices outside the United States in relation to United States prices, the governments of several oil producing countries, for example Iran, Ecuador, etc., made arrangements for even lower prices for their own markets in order to develop their local economy. In view of the political nature of these arrangements, all price-sheds enclosing these markets tend to follow political boundaries.

THE IMPACT OF THE SUEZ CRISIS

Price behavior during and after the Suez crisis (1956–1957) illustrates geographical aspects of the working of the price structure (Fig. 3). As a result of the closing of the Suez Canal and the severe diminution of pipeline deliveries to the Levant, demand in Europe could

not be satisfied from the Middle East. Supplies were, therefore, obtained in the United States, thus raising U. S. Gulf prices. Caribbean prices increased by the same amount. A shortage of tankers, due to the need of transporting as much Middle East oil as possible by the much longer route around Africa, raised freights substantially. Higher U. S. Gulf prices and higher freights raised prices at the price-shed in the Eastern United States; however, deduction of higher freight rates from the Persian Gulf to the Eastern United States reduced all Persian Gulf prices. During a period of generally rising prices this reduction was a strange phenomenon. It conforms, however, to the law of supply and demand, for during this period exports from the Persian Gulf to Europe were reduced, and no alternative buyers were available as the eastern price-shed did not shift. Levant prices increased slightly due to lesser freight deductions from the price-shed. As exports from

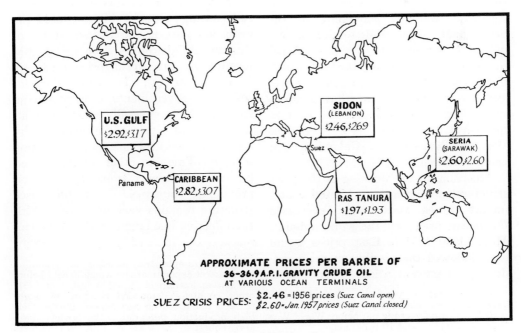

FIG. 3.   Suez crisis price changes.

the Levant were limited to nations not participating in the Suez campaign, this slight rise can also be explained in terms of supply and demand. With the restoration of normal conditions freight rates returned to lower levels; however, U. S. Gulf prices remained for some time at the high levels of the Suez crisis. As a result Middle East prices (Persian Gulf and Levant) increased.

Recent Changes

Successive increases in U. S. Gulf prices since World War II had made the unchanged import duty of $10\frac{1}{2}$ cents per barrel relatively unimportant.[22] Due to the shift of the western price-shed to the Eastern United States, foreign oil could effectively compete in the American market. The use of lower actual freights, rather than the rates determined in London for the purpose of pricing, gave additional encouragement to foreign oil imports. These low freights were the result of excessive tanker construction, the impact of the economy super-tankers (over 40,000 tons deadweight),[23] and the reopening of the Suez Canal. As a result foreign oil was delivered not only to the East Coast, but also to California and the Gulf Coast. Calculations using foreign basing prices and low freights indicate that theoretically, during recent years, the western price-shed was located as far inland as Western Pennsylvania (inland freight charges added).

According to the working of the price structure, an increase in United States import duties would have decreased Caribbean prices by the same amount. Most likely Middle East prices would have followed the Caribbean price reduction to prevent a loss of markets in

countries adjoining the North Atlantic. This price reduction would have adversely affected not only incomes in oil producing countries (through profit sharing in oil company operations), thus increasing their political instability, but would also have negated entirely the effect of higher import duties. For this reason, the Government of the United States first experimented with voluntary import restrictions, and in 1959 introduced severely restrictive import quotas. As a result, the American market is today very largely insulated against the effect of both low freights and any lowering of foreign prices. Although the western price-shed remained in the Eastern United States, and although fluctuations in U. S. Gulf prices still principally determine price fluctuations outside the United States, this country ceased to be the marginal market capable of absorbing increases in foreign oil production. These increases were substantial during recent years.

Already before the introduction of American import quotas, this economically strange state of affairs caused the evolution outside the United States of "unofficial" discounts from prices conforming to the world price structure ("official" prices). To protect their incomes the governments of oil producing countries have generally tried to maintain "official" prices, for example by means of a world-wide export restriction scheme. This and other schemes failed for lack of support from all major oil producing countries,[24] and the price structure remains very unstable. With the effective insulation of the American market, the increasing volume of com-

---

[22] During recent years the United States import duty was about 3 per cent of the value of 36° API gravity crude oil; before World War II it was usually about 10 per cent.

[23] Melamid, *op. cit.*, p. 215.

[24] For example Iran insisted on regaining the share of export markets which it held before the nationalization of its oil industry in 1951; other countries demanded a share of world markets not based on past exports but on their high production potential. The Soviet Union also requested the share of European markets which she had held in the early 1920's.

petition in Europe may now replace U. S. Gulf prices with European fundamental basing prices. This possible trend towards a "new spectrum"[25] of oil prices located in Italy, with its many competing refineries, was already considered shortly after the end of the Suez crisis. Alternatively the world price structure can be expected to break down into a series of geographically unrelated prices maintained by agreement between governments, as for example in the international sugar trade (Fig. 4).[26]

New Basing Points

In 1959 price instability was increased by the establishment of another basing point at Bougie (Algeria) for exports from the Saharan oil field of Hassi

[25] Platt's Oilgram News Service, New York, March 13, 1957.
[26] Until recently Cuba sold sugar at substantially different prices to the United States (highest price), members of the International Sugar Agreement (Sweden, Japan, etc.), and others (Soviet Union, lowest price).

Messoud. Bougie prices were quoted about 5 per cent below "Middle East-Plus (Persian Gulf or Levant)" prices. Due to the relatively limited quantities of Sahara oil so far available, the establishment of Bougie prices has not created any effective price-sheds in the western Mediterranean and its vicinity and the price was subsequently raised to conform more with "official" prices.

During 1961 an even lower price than that originally prevailing at Bougie was announced for Libyan oil f.o.b. Mersa el Brega on the Gulf of Sirte. Mersa el Brega is the terminal for the 30-inch diameter pipeline from the Zelten oil field of interior Libya, which is potentially a large supplier. For this reason Mersa el Brega prices may not only set regional price standards for other Libyan oils expected to enter world markets during the next years, but may also affect the prices of other Saharan and Middle East oils. As only test tanker loads have so far been shipped from Mersa el Brega,

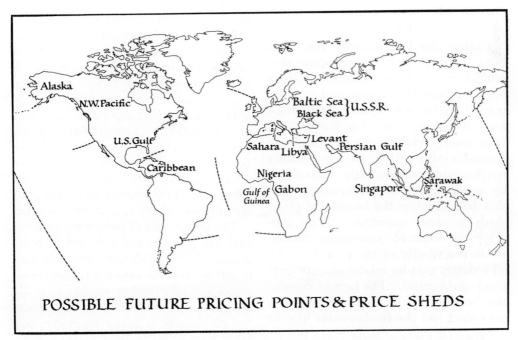

POSSIBLE FUTURE PRICING POINTS & PRICE SHEDS

FIG. 4.   Location of new basing points and price-sheds.

the full impact of the new price on price-sheds cannot yet be ascertained.

With increasing production in Nigeria and Gaboon, both on the Gulf of Guinea, Alaska and Northwest Canada, and other countries or regions in many parts of the world without consumption, new basing points may be established. Additional supplies from Russia are also entering world markets and are sold to destinations as far away as southern South America and Africa. Russian prices f.o.b. Black Sea ports vary with the destination of the oil. Generally prices for export to the free world are below "Middle East-Plus" or "Caribbean-Plus" equivalents, although prices charged to satellite countries of Soviet Russia appear to conform to such equivalents.[27] New pipelines reported to be under construction to new terminals on the Baltic Sea (either Kleipeda, Lithuania, or Schwedt, East Germany) are expected to increase the volume of Russian exports and thus may have repercussions on world prices and basing points.

Conclusions

During the last decades there has been a change from a single-base to a multi-base world price structure. However, only one base responds directly to market mechanisms, and its fluctuations are followed by the other bases. The fundamental relations between all bases (equalization, plus, or plus-minus freight) are independently determined by governments and companies. For this determination the location of price-sheds is most important. The geographical shifts of price-sheds demonstrate the vitality of the growth of the oil industry and its relationship to governmental control. The lack of correlation between the location of the major price-shed and the fundamental base of

TABLE III

Selected comparative international prices: may 1961[*]
In United States currency and measurements

Region	Crude oil per barrel (36.0–36.9° API gravity)	Gasoline per gallon (93 octane)
U. S. Gulf.........	$2.865	¢ 11.00/11.75
Caribbean.	2.76	10.625
Levant Coast......	2.21	not available
Central Persian Gulf.	1.84	9.9/10.125
Abadan...........	not available	9.7/9.9
East Indies	2.42	10.625/10.8

*The above prices are not strictly comparable as not all quality differentials are allowed for in trade publications. These prices were obtained or calculated from current publications (*Platts Oilgram*, New York; *Oil and Gas Journal*, Tulsa, Oklahoma; *Petroleum Press Service*, London) to give a measure of the world price structure. Due to unofficial discounts these figures do not completely reflect actual prices obtained in trading.

the price structure is a significant cause of instability today. Stability in a multi-base structure is aided, if the major price-shed is located in an active market capable of absorbing increases of production. Within any world-wide geographical price structure exceptional price regions may exist. These exceptions are the result of political arrangements, and their price-sheds tend to follow political boundaries.

Both the single and the multi-base price structure conform with the models of spatial economics.[28] In their evolution and patterns the world wheat markets resemble the geographical structure of oil prices.[29] Exceptional political prices with price-sheds following political boundaries are also characteristic of wheat markets. In many cases the effect of political boundaries on the location of price-sheds is also very similar.

The importance of geography in international prices is not reflected in retail prices. Tariffs and taxes create a lack of proportion between international prices and retail prices, so that virtually no evidence of basing points, price-

[27] Horton B. Connell: "Soviet Pricing Policy," *International Oilman*, July, 1960.

[28] For example in August Lösch: *The Economics of Location*, New Haven, 1954.
[29] *Ibid.*, p. 420.

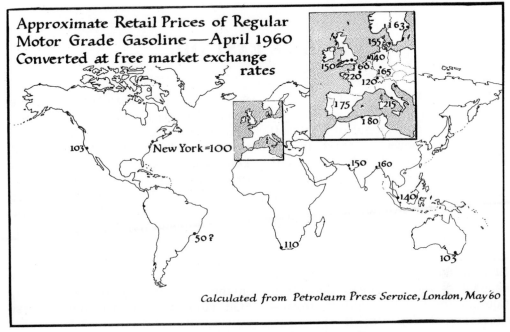

Approximate Retail Prices of Regular Motor Grade Gasoline — April 1960 Converted at free market exchange rates

New York = 100

FIG. 5.   Retail Prices: New York Index 100.

sheds, or freight addition or deduction remains. Differences in retail mark-up appear to be a minor cause of distortion. As a result, regions located on price-sheds do not have the highest retail prices, for example, prices in New York City (Fig. 5). According to the price structure, all European retail prices should be lower than New York City prices; in fact, they are not. Geographical distortions are most marked within Europe. Retail prices also differ significantly from state to state within the regions of the United States as for example between New York and New Jersey in the Northeastern United States region. These distortions of retail prices restrict many markets by severely reducing economic responses to international price changes, and are another significant cause of the instability of geographical price structure.

MIDDLE EAST OIL

THE PLAIN OF OIL

More than 60 percent of all the oil at present known to exist in the world lies under the Middle East. Count it more practically: of all the oil reserves presently being drawn upon for international trade to any significant degree, the Middle East possesses more than three-quarters. About two-thirds of the oil Britain uses comes from there; 60 percent of the European Economic Community's oil supplies; three-quarters of Japan's. If it were not for American protectionism, a sizeable chunk of the United States' consumption would be supplied from there, putting its own higher-cost wells out of business. As of today, the Middle East still deserves the name of the place where Reynolds first struck commercial oil there just 57 years ago last week — *Maidan-i-Naftun,* the Plain of Oil.

As of tomorrow, too, oil — and gas — will be found elsewhere, probably nearer to market. Nuclear energy is coming down to the costs of a practical, workaday fuel. Technology gets more and more production out of all kinds of fuel. Nevertheless, postulate the rates of economic growth continuing that

we all expect nowadays, and the world's energy needs grow almost alarmingly. Alarmingly, indeed, if it were not for oil. Over the next generation, energy demand may grow two-and-a-half times; and until say close to the end of those 25 years, oil will probably have to supply the biggest part of that increase. And as Mr. John Loudon, who is retiring as senior managing director of the Royal Dutch/Shell group, said in the Cadman Lecture last month, "On current evidence the largest

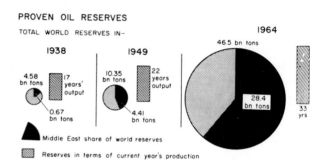

PROVEN OIL RESERVES

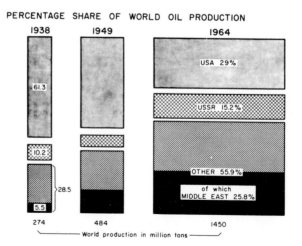

PERCENTAGE SHARE OF WORLD OIL PRODUCTION

"Middle East Oil." Reprinted from <u>The Economist</u>, *Vol. 215 (June 5, 1965), pp. 1151–1168, with permission of the publisher.*

proportion of the increase required will have to be supplied from the Middle East."

During the past five to ten years — since Suez, as it happens, but those politics are only part of the tale — the circumstances in which this prodigious flow of oil from the Middle East to the world's industrial countries takes place have been altering, with an accelerating rate of change. During the next five to ten, the structure of Middle East oil supply looks to be in for even greater change. Under increasing economic pressure and political temperature, established relationships are melting. The concession terms of companies that have long been producing oil in the area and exporting it have been modified, steadily but of late sharply, to give the host governments more oil income. New concessionaires have made deals on even more generous terms. Above all, the host governments' own oil companies are moving into the business.

This is not entirely a matter of money — though the comparably prodigious flow of oil royalties and taxes into Middle Eastern treasuries will swell in volume, and be supplemented by shares of profit, once the oil now being sought on these new terms is found, developed and sold. It is to some degree a shift of control: a little less in the hands of international companies that treat with governments of many kinds but behave on the whole commercially, a little more into the hands of producer governments that behave politically but may be obliged in future to think more commercially.

But these host governments too are possessing themselves of dilemmas. On the one hand, in a world of oil surplus, they want to get the highest value they can for the oil already exported from their countries — to keep up not only their own revenues, but oil prices too. This could, before long, bring them into positive conflict with the interests of western consumers. On the other hand, each wants the maximum oil development of its own country now, and by new oil companies, plus their own national companies. Make the concession agreements; draw the bonuses; get the national company seriously into business. Fine; but a few years down the road, if they find the oil as both parties hope, this new oil will be swelling the surplus.

This is the main economic dilemma of Middle East oil today (let alone the dilemmas of the companies). But there are political ones too. Arab socialism, as yet, does not have too much leverage on Middle East oil. But if this is still true in a few years' time, it will not be for want of trying.

The western oil consumer cannot do much about all this, and perhaps for the moment he does not need to. But he does need to watch it.

OIL ON NEW TERMS

Signature of an Iraq oil agreement if it can finally be achieved in Baghdad in the next few weeks, will put the seal on the second basic new deal agreed by the major international oil companies in the Middle East this year. This one has taken more than 18 months' patient negotiation, following on two years of deadlock under the late General Qasim's nationalisation Law 80 of 1961, punctuated only by occasional feelers from either side. The Iraq

Petroleum group will get back its rich known oilfield of North Rumeila; a joint exploration company with the Iraq National Oil Company will seek to develop oil in another 8-9 percent of the original nation-wide concession area; a long list of outstanding points at issue between the companies and the Government have been cleared up; and INOC will be free to make any other exploration deals that it chooses with all comers, from East perhaps as well as West.

This deal over Law 80, to which the companies are now asked to give some form of recognition after long having argued that it was *ultra vires,* may clear the way too for Iraq to follow the other Middle East member governments of the Organisation of Petroleum Exporting Countries in working out an acceptable formula for the expensing of royalties — the "OPEC settlement" of early this year. That settlement has cost and will cost the major companies a lot of money — perhaps steadily more per barrel over a period of years. Nevertheless, it did finally nail down any possibility of "unilateral action" by OPEC governments on three issues they had raised — marketing allowances; the expensing of royalties; and the restoration of posted prices for crude oil in the Middle East to the levels from which they were reduced in August-September 1960. (Iraq, too, had been the member that wanted unilateral action.) Formally, it lifted the state of dispute in which OPEC had been with the companies since June 1962.

Will congratulations on all sides soon be in order? Perhaps. But is this the beginning of period of relative tranquillity in this character-istically perturbed area, at least economically if not politically?

By no means.

Unfinished business with OPEC. First, there remains some unfinished business in the OPEC settlement itself. One of the countries whose government agreed to it at the end of last year, Kuwait, has still not ratified the agreement. Its National Assembly, set up by the country's Ruler only a short time ago, flexed its muscles and declined to approve the supplemental agreement on royalty expensing without lengthy and detailed scrutiny. The fact that Kuwait has not ratified yet will make it no easier for negotiators in Baghdad even to consider thinking later about the terms on which Iraq might be induced to drop its objections to the deal as an infringement of national sovereignty, and to accept the benefits that it would bring in higher revenue.

Libya, another member ready to accept a royalty expensing deal at the end of last year, has found it hard to do so for more practical reasons. Its present concessions relate income tax to "realisations" — i.e. the prices at which oil is actually exported, not the posted prices to which other OPEC governments in the Middle East have their taxes pegged. But the final OPEC settlement included, in order to moderate the cash effect of expensing royalties, a discount for tax purposes off *posted* price. Standard Oil of New Jersey, Libya's biggest producer, in fact exports most of its oil at posted price, and has offered Libya a deal comparable to those in the other countries — provided other companies operating in Libya are obliged to do the same.

But this would mean requiring the

companies of the Oasis group, second largest producer in Libya, also to pay tax related to posted price. They say they cannot; they are managing to export this oil only by accepting very large discounts. If they suddenly had to pay far more tax, they would be unable to cover it in their prices, and have to cut back exports; and Oasis is now providing Libya with most of its export growth. Libya would incidentally have to amend its existing petroleum legislation. But its dilemma is economic, not legislative. It cannot get the extra that Esso offers unless it makes the other companies pay as much per barrel; and if it were to make them pay as much, it might face cutting off its growth in production and total revenues.

Ask me a question? No. The major companies, moreover, in phrasing the terms of their supplemental agreements with Middle East governments this year, have neatly guaranteed themselves further dispute with these OPEC members. They agreed to consider a further reduction, in 1967 and after, of the discount for tax purposes written into this settlement for 1964, 1965, and 1966, taking into account such evidence of the state of the market as the member governments could put before them. This clearly invited said governments to find out what actual prices were being paid for Middle East oil, as distinct from posted prices. And where better to find it out than from these major companies who are producing the bulk of this oil? Predictably, therefore, the companies fairly rapidly received letters asking for details of the prices paid on their actual sales of oil during 1964, and for continuing data as 1965 and later 1966 go on.

Inviting the question did not mean that the major companies had any intention of answering it. Without quite conveying a flat "No," they have made it known to the governments and to OPEC headquarters in Geneva that they are not prepared to provide the price data that had been requested; indeed, they have not promised to provide any price details at all. This because it would be divulging commercial information that might be used commercially against them — for example, by the National Iranian Oil Company, which has already ventured into the world market with oil at cut prices. This argument, which will become tenable eventually, is tenuous as regards the next few years; at all events, the companies should have thought of it before inviting the OPEC governments to find out the state of actual prices. The dispute rumbles on, so far in low key. OPEC has other questions of prices, no doubt, to consider. But before long, if unresolved, this issue must inevitably produce trouble.

Phrasing any terms on which the Iraq government could accept the OPEC settlement — with due regard to its sensibilities and also to those of governments that were readier to agree last autumn — may also not be easy. Anything agreed in Iraq this spring and summer is guaranteed some quite hawk-eyed attention from neighbours such as Iran and Saudi Arabia.

Getting into the act. Terms of any joint exploration venture with INOC in Iraq, for most of the companies concerned, will represent their first acceptance of government participation as an equity shareholder in oil search and development. This form of concession — the national company need not come in until oil is found in commercial quantities, and its equity investment may be simply a matter of foregoing some of its oil revenues until the share is built up by installments, over years — has become almost de rigueur for new concessions in the Middle East in the last six or seven years. But up to now, of the seven international majors, five of which are Iraq Petroleum Company shareholders, only Royal Dutch/Shell has gone in for such deals in Middle East production; and some of them have hitherto set their face against any deals involving sizeable government participation.

From what one hears, the terms of the new exploration venture with INOC may not look quite as favourable to the government as the concessions that Iran granted to Shell among other companies offshore in the Persian Gulf early this year or that Saudi Arabia in April signed with a French state company, Auxirap. INOC will not necessarily come in as a partner for as much of the capital as Iran's 50 percent for the National Iranian Oil Company or Saudi Arabia's 40 percent (with 50 percent voting rights) for its own Petromin.

Much will depend on whether there is a royalty fully expensed, as it is in the Saudi Arabian deal; in the Iranian concessions offshore, no royalty is payable. Another key factor will be whether there are provisions obliging the private partners, if the national company does not manage to dispose of all the crude to which it will become entitled, to "buy back" the remainder at "halfway price" — i.e. a price half way between the production cost plus tax and the posted price. In Iraq, as the government at present sees it, there will certainly be no question of agreed discounts off the posted price which may reduce the private partner's tax liability, as there might be in these Iranian operations. Iraq, at any rate, argues that this particular part of its new deal will bear comparison with the best that its fellow member governments have been extracting (admittedly along with large cash bonuses) from newcomers and Shell. Mr. Watlan, Iraq's able oil minister, has called it a "75-25" deal.

Most favoured something or other. But these new participation deals will be compared not only with each other, but also, inevitably, with existing concessions, including the traditional big four in Iran, Iraq, Kuwait, and Saudi Arabia. If and when the Auxirap concession somewhere off Saudi Arabia's Red Sea coast ever produces oil (nobody knows, remember, and at best it will be a matter of some years yet), how will the government's take from this oil compare with what it gets out of Aramco, for example? As a rough and ready guess, assume that the oil produced can be sold for, or at any rate "posted" at, the same price as say Aramco's 34 degrees crude from Ras Tanura, $1.80; and that both have a production cost of say 20 cents. Then on present figuring, Aramco would be paying the government about 84 cents on such a crude; and from Auxirap the government and Petromin (with an investment of 40 percent of the capital involved) could get $1.20-$1.30.

Those assumptions are fanciful (for one thing, identical crudes with identical costs at these two places would probably have different prices posted, because the Red Sea one would be so much closer to market). But comparisons of this kind are going to become the currency of argument between governments and oil companies throughout the Middle East as soon as some of these new concessions start producing oil, and their costs become known. If the physical costs of production on these new concessions compare with the old (this is unlikely, because most are offshore, where costs are generally higher), then the governments will be quoting cents per barrel to their traditional tenants. If the costs are out of line and the comparison in cash terms less impressive, they will no doubt quote percentages of net profit paid on the new concessions to put pressure on the old.

This year's royalties settlement, too, incidentally, helped to strengthen the interest in such comparisons. The major companies, in agreeing to the increase of about 3-4 cents per barrel that this OPEC settlement involved, stipulated a "most favoured company" clause protecting them from being charged more than any other company would be if it applied the terms of its own concession to the circumstances under which they produce oil. In one way, this stipulation looked almost impossible to interpret on any agreed

basis; in another, it will further have stimulated the comparison of different kinds of concession relating to different basic circumstances. Some of the Middle East governments have "most favoured nation" clauses written into their own concessions — usually related to the cash amount per barrel of payments made by the same concessionaire company to any other Middle East government. These clauses never seem to have been invoked; they were in any case worded more restrictively than the most favoured company clauses that the major companies managed to get into their supplemental agreements this year. But they will no doubt be dusted off for inspection some time soon.

A quite different problem — and in some ways larger — posed by these deals on new terms, for Middle East governments as well as for established companies there, is that they promise, fairly soon, a lot more oil. Not all the new venturers off Iran are dogged by the bad luck that has forced Shell to go on bidding so high to try to find itself "cost oil" (i.e., its own, not other people's purchased at some margin above cost). These are slices of the most "prospective" oil area on earth; one must assume that by the early seventies they will be able to produce very large additional amounts of oil — if anyone can sell it.

Participation in price-cutting. Unless the market suffers some welcome sea-change in the next five years or so, one thing is certain: nobody is going to be able to sell this additional oil at posted prices. Already a sizeable proportion of the oil exported from the Middle East moves at discounted prices; as to the rest, invoiced at posted prices

OUTPUT: WHERE THE GROWTH IS GOING

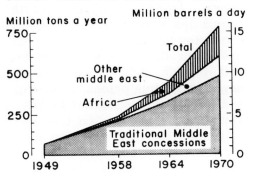

into integrated producers' own networks, the same effective discount has to be taken somewhere, and shown as losses on tankers, refining or marketing. And the newer producing areas and concessions, which over the last five years have been making up more and more of the growth in total exports from the Middle East and Africa, have generally had to accept the biggest discounts of all (like the 60 cents a barrel discounts by the Oasis group that are setting Libya such a conundrum at present).

Participation by national companies in these new deals has become popular in the Middle East not merely as a way of increasing the cash the government gets on each barrel of oil. It represents a genuine desire to gain experience in management and real decision-making in the market for these countries' most important product. This national aspiration is much more than a money-grubbing one. Nevertheless, it will be somewhat ironic for these national companies' initial experience in the oil business to involve them in undercutting the very prices that their governments, as OPEC members, are pledged to try to support and, if possible, to increase.

It would need deep political solidarity in this oil-producing governments' trade union to stifle the temptation — indeed the compulsion — to cut prices in order to get into the world oil market. After all, the governments' equity stakes are limited (and will have been subscribed painlessly over time as oil revenues from the concessions build up, to say nothing of the enormous cash bonuses most of them got to start with). If the choice is between

not cutting a cent or two more a barrel or not getting one's oil sold (hence no income whatever), it will need fortitude not to take the cash and let the political credit go. Participation ventures in which a national company did not manage to make an apparent commercial success might, after all, forfeit another kind of political credit, nearer home.

This promised further flood of fresh oil will present problems for the established oil companies — and for OPEC as well. At the end of last year OPEC committed itself to measures to bolster up the price of oil; yet the extra oil that its member countries hope to be in a position to produce in a few years' time must inevitably contribute to softening the market further. These concessions, certainly, are for the most part still years away from production; if OPEC has managed to think up practical ways of operating to harden prices, then it has a year or two in which to try to get them working. It probably hasn't, in which case the problem cannot get any worse; if something is impossible, nothing can make it more difficult.

By committing itself to this labour of Sisyphus, OPEC has, however, made itself rather vulnerable over the next few years to accusations of being ineffectual. It may well achieve something, via member governments, from arguments with the companies next year about royalty expensing for 1967; but that will follow from this year's settlements, rather than show anything really new. By tackling prices, it has chosen the big target: great kudos, if anything is achieved; if not, renewed criticism for biting off more than it (or possibly anybody) could chew.

OPEC has devoted critics; some

of them with ambitions to supplement (read "supplant") it. The Arab League continues to nurture hopes of forming an Arab Petroleum Organisation; its committee of "Arab oil experts" passed some more resolutions about it only a week or two ago. As an article looking at Middle East politics says, this organisation is unlikely ever to get off the ground. But Egypt, originally responsible for the idea, now has hopes of livening up OPEC in a different way — by qualifying as a petroleum exporting country. If you can't beat them, join them: Egypt was already at this year's Arab Petroleum Congress suggesting that OPEC was probably short of really qualified technicians and petroleum experts, and that its own graduates — who are competent — might be glad to help.

Egyptians have not yet made much contribution to serious economic discussion of the world oil industry. Their own policy, which unites concessions on pretty weak terms with large words about controlling companies and a probable readiness to nationalise any company whose parent company gets too kind to Israel, displays a certain amount of treblethink. But their main emphasis, clearly, is on the political possibilities of Middle East — particularly Arab — oil. And if they could get into OPEC without being blackballed, the Egyptians could perhaps be confident of making it, too, more politically oriented.

Breathing down OPEC's neck. So far, the Geneva organisation has shied off politics, sensibly enough; being in Europe may have helped it do so, instead of being in the overheated political atmosphere of some Middle Eastern capital. Politics do play their part already in Middle East oil bargaining; the dangers of instability in this state or that have to be taken into account by companies planning large-scale investment there. It may be, even, that concerted negotiations like those over royalty expensing can be advanced or retarded somewhat by the ebb and flow of political tides in the region generally. But of late they have receded from the discussions; lowering this element of the temperature has been one of OPEC's achievements. To reverse that — and bring "oil as a political weapon" back to the centre of things — would be a step back, replacing "ice-cold logic" by nationalist emotion. Middle East oil has enough rods in pickle for its own back without that.

Industrialised countries that have been growing steadily more dependent on oil for their own continued economic growth are naturally afraid that some of the Middle East rods may be in pickle for *their* backs, too. The common market, for example, would like an energy policy based on ensuring "security of supply": coal protection, diversification of foreign energy sources, and ventures by Community companies into the Middle East itself are some of its expedients. Coal doesn't protect enough and costs a lot. Diversification, except where it brings in nearer-by sources of cheap oil like Libya, is a debatable bet; and Libya long ago joined OPEC, and would probably be in any Arab alternative, too. Whether Community companies have any particular magic to charm Arabs remains to be seen. More dependable bets as insurance for security of supply — of which Middle East landlords, too, have to take note — are cheap nuclear power from stations like Britain's AGR and the chances of off-shore petroleum being found near markets by explorers like BP's Sea Gem drilling in the North Sea. Fuel — not just oil — is where you find it.

GETTING AND SPENDING

Rising two billion dollars a year, for a total population of around 35 million. That oil income alone averages out to a pretty comfortable income per head for any five underdeveloped countries, even if not all of these Middle East oil peoples are Kuwait-rich. Or it would, if the billions were averaged out.

Looking forward, oil exports from their main concessions will go on rising, with a probable growth rate from here to 1970 of 4-5 percent a year; and they can probably hope for some increase in their revenue from every barrel (which is more than the people who sell the oil can) to multiply their growth in total revenue. Even faster growth in exports — and total government revenue — can be expected for the newer Middle East concessions; some of this further money will come to the established producing countries, some of it to the smaller sheikhdoms.

In practice, the income never is averaged out — between countries, or within them. Iran, the oldest producing country in the region, possesses about two-thirds of the population but gets only about a quarter of the revenue; it feels that it has never been allowed to make up for the ground it lost in the production race during the two years of nationalisation under Mossadegh, and for years looked particularly jealously at Kuwait, where most of the balance of oil exports was made up. Of late, however, Iran has been able to put on a spurt.

These Middle East landlords have looked abroad, too, to see how some of the others are doing. Their own unit revenues in cents per barrel of oil — ranging from about 67 to 88 cents (Qatar) — never appear quite to have matched Venezuela's. Of late, they note that Libya's unit revenue, when oil is moved at posted prices, probably exceeds any of their own; but they can console themselves partly with the fact that a large and growing proportion of Libyan oil is sold at discounts deeper than any the Middle East has customarily to accept, and that the Libyan government revenue on such deals is not protected as their own would be. (The consolation is only partial; the chances are that this cheap Libyan oil is bought instead of oil from somewhere in the Persian Gulf.)

Within the countries, the oil benefits are spread unevenly too. This is no longer the tale of sheikhs squandering their royalties on palaces that Middle East travellers used to tell. There is a large amount of corruption still, particularly in some countries; probably still more waste. But these no longer happen so much for want of trying; it is because much of the trying to achieve commercial and fiscal virtue is pretty amateurish.

All the Middle East oil countries, nowadays, would subscribe to the doctrine first enunciated by one of Iran's earliest planners: "No Middle East country has the right to spend the income gained from selling a wasting natural resource simply as current income. It must be invested in development that will go on bringing in future generations income after our oil has gone." And following Iran's example, each of these oil-producing countries has gone in for plans and industrialisation programmes — reserving a large part of the accruing oil income, in theory at least, for capital investment to modernise their countries.

The Undeveloped Rich. This steady flow of current income that they feel they should turn into fixed capital gives them a different set of embarrassments from most developing countries. They have no lack of foreign exchange; but like the others, they lack trained people. Where they already possess a sizeable civil service, as in Iran, this tends to be an old-fashioned bureaucracy more afraid of the change that the planners may bring than even the private enterpriser.

Local private enterprise, again, usually rests on a tradition of trade and commerce, and may prove surprisingly reluctant to venture into industry, in spite of high tariff protection and fiscal baits. Local education is inadequate and, anyway, unsuited to instill the crafts of industrialisation. Send the students abroad, on the other hand, and apart from the fact that some never return, those who do may have picked up rather dangerous thoughts (witness the recall of students to Iran, after the implication of some of them in the latest attempt on the Shah's life). And reform measures based on widely differing ideologies may have the same result of alienating the moneyed classes: the Shah's "white revolution" of agrarian reform as much as Arab Socialism's nationalisation of most of the small, protected and probably inefficient private businesses in Iraq.

Direct Payments by Oil Companies to Governments					
($ million)					
	Iran	Iraq	Kuwait	Saudi Arabia	Qatar	Total
1951	50	43	18	165	4	280
1952	...	116	57	212	10	395
1953	...	162	169	226	18	575
1954	9	192	194	281	29	705
1955	91	207	282	275	34	889
1956	153	194	293	283	36	959
1957	213	137	308	303	45	1,006
1958	247	224	354	302	60	1,187
1959	262	243	409	294	53	1,261
1960	285	267	442	334	54	1,382
1961	301	265	465	378	54	1,463
1962	334	266	476	410	56	1,542
1963	385	308	535	609	60	1,897
1964	480	353	537 (est.)	515 (est.)	61	1,946 (est.)

So far as possible, exceptional bonuses are excluded, except for retrospective payments 1964 under OPEC settlement. Kuwait includes neutral zone except for 1959. Saudi Arabia, from 1960, includes revenue from neutral zone; for 1963, its total includes $152 million of back payments.

Communication, even, is hard to organise in the vast, thinly-peopled areas of some of these countries where neither literacy nor newspapers ever spread widely. At least, it was until the advent of the transistor, which is giving the remote countryman access to national news — and "guidance" — with the power of pocket batteries (until then, even getting accumulators charged for battery radio was too much).

Iran and Iraq have large layers of poverty of their own. Saudi Arabia is only now, under King Faisal, seriously being organised into anything resembling a modern state. Kuwait, richest of the lot because of its huge income and small population, has already run through most of the array of benefits any welfare state can give its citizens, and is lending more and more of its accumulating capital for development elsewhere in the Arab world. This is only prudent; tiny, it is vulnerable, and now beginning to have to toe the Arab socialist line. But whatever ideology its ruling family may find it convenient to flirt with, or its National Assembly to thunder about, Kuwait so far acts as the most enlightened of Arab oil capitalists. It hires the world's best banking and investment advice on the disposition of the government's own investments abroad; its Development Fund is lending at low interest for infra-structure projects throughout the Middle East, but on not wholly uncommercial terms. Its local industrial development is proceeding cautiously — focusing on the points where its location or its cheap energy really may make development commercial. No other Middle East government, admittedly, has it so good to start with.

CASH ON THE BARREL

One look at an oil map of the Middle East shows you the first outstanding difference between the traditional concessions in Iran, Iraq, Kuwait and Saudi Arabia and most of the newer ones there and in neighbouring, competitive, oil-producing countries. The old ones (dark-shaded on this map) are enormously bigger.

Originally, concessions of the Iraq Petroleum group covered virtually the whole area of the country; the Kuwait Oil Company, too, had the whole of the state. Aramco's concession originally covered 440,000 square miles in Saudi Arabia; the Consortium's operating area in Iran is 100,000 square miles. These "big four" traditional concessions have all been subject to sizeable relinquishment of unproductive acreage at one time or another. Even so, they are still huge, undivided areas, quite unlike the fragmented concessions, looking on a map like half-completed jigsaws, under which oil is sought and developed in Libya and Algeria. There are some small concessions in the Persian Gulf, too, but mainly in small sheikhdoms, offshore, or in areas relinquished earlier from the big four.

Right up to the end of the last war, all that the governments of these producing countries got out of their oil was a fixed, flat royalty — usually three rupees or four shillings a ton. In the thirties, with oil prices depressed, this was a little more than it sounds; the rupees and shillings were in gold. But by the late forties, this low royalty was out of date.

Percentage's Progress. Between 1950 and 1955, the traditional concessions were converted to "fifty-fifty" agreements. The phrase came from Venezuela, though the terms were never quite the same. Until this year, the traditional 50-50 agreement in the main Middle East concessions provided for a 12 1/2 percent royalty that was offset within the 50 percent income tax charged on the net profit — i.e., the published or "posted" price less the production costs. When the oil was actually sold at posted price, the host government's revenue thus did amount to half the net profit.

A key point about these traditional concessions is that the tax stays related to posted price even if, in fact,

the oil is sold for less; and in the last six or seven years, discounts have become general and quite large. So even the traditional 50-50 was giving the government more than half the net profit actually made.

In Algeria, Nigeria and Libya, on the other hand, taxes are related to "realisations," i.e., the actual prices that companies exporting oil from there get. The tax is 50 percent of the difference between the production cost and this "realised" price. When the realised prices are significantly lower than posted prices — like today — this kind of 50-50 deal based on realisations gives the government a smaller per-

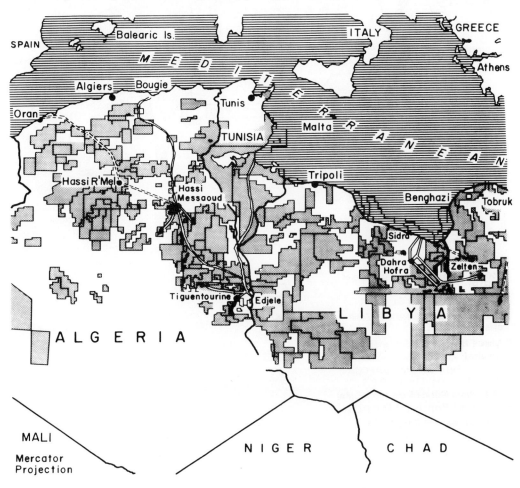

centage than in the traditional concessions.

The traditional concessions and
these others, as negotiated in the
fifties, were variants of 50-50 deals.
From 1957 onwards, Iran, Kuwait

and Saudi Arabia granted conces-
sions to some newcomers to the
Middle East on terms offering the
governments more than 50 percent.
Iran granted Italy's ENI and the
Pan-American company concessions

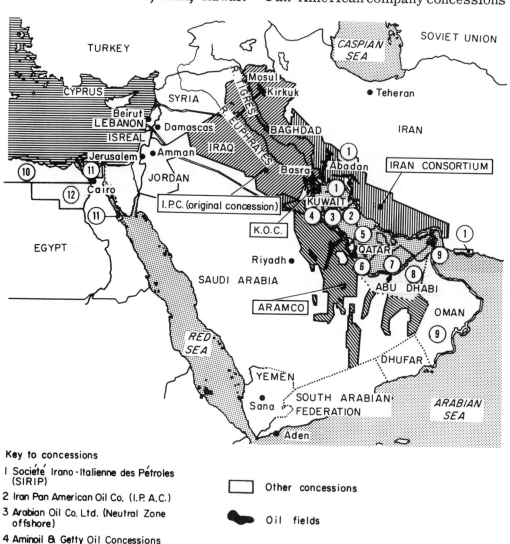

Key to concessions

1 Société Irano-Italienne des Pétroles
   (SIRIP)
2 Iran Pan American Oil Co. (I.P. A.C.)
3 Arabian Oil Co. Ltd. (Neutral Zone
   offshore)
4 Aminoil & Getty Oil Concessions
   (Neutral Zone)
5 Bahrain Petr. Co. Ltd. (BAPCO)
6 Qatar Petr. Co. Ltd. (Q.P.C.)
7 Abu Dhabi Marine Areas Ltd.(ADMA)
8 Abu Dhabi Petr. Co. Ltd (A.D.P.C.)
9 Petr. Development (Oman) Ltd.
10 Phillips
11 E.N.I.
12 Pan American

▢ Other concessions

⬤ Oil fields

═ Crude oil pipelines

═══ Projected pipelines

offshore in the Persian Gulf in which, once commercial oil was found, the National Iranian Oil Company would participate with 50 percent of the equity capital. In theory, at least, Iran would therefore get 75 percent of the profits; but it would also, eventually, have put up half the capital.

When governments participate. This was the first of the "participation" deals, which have since become customary. Kuwait and Saudi Arabia the next year granted Japan's Arabian Oil Company concessions offering them 57 percent of net profit. Saudi Arabia, but not Kuwait, later exercised its right to take a 10 percent interest in its Japanese concession — entitling it, in theory, to share refining and marketing profits made downstream, as well as the income realised on crude sales. So these deals could possibly bring the Saudi government 71 percent of net profits (for a 10 percent capital investment). Royal-Dutch/Shell, in 1960, gained a concession from Kuwait for offshore development in which the Kuwait government could take a 20 percent interest.

Egypt, too, has participation deals with Phillips and Pan American and ENI; its General Petroleum Company has a 50 percent interest with them. But these are on easier terms for the companies. The 50 percent tax, with royalty offset, is based on realised prices, not posted prices.

With this subsequent progress in government percentages, and following cuts in posted prices in 1959 and 1961, the big four concessions came under pressure to pay more. After 2 1/2 years' arguments with OPEC, they finally made supplemental agreements this year to do so in Iran, Saudi Arabia, Kuwait and Qatar. The method adopted was the reduction of some small marketing allowances against tax and also the "expensing" of royalties — i.e. counting them before tax and paying them in addition to tax. However, it was at the same time agreed to allow small (declining) discounts off the posted price when reckoning tax. The broad effect of this revision was to give the governments, in 1964, 57-58 percent of net profit reckoned at posted prices; if discounts are counted, the percentage is much higher.

While these negotiations were being completed, Iran granted a new set of 75-25 concessions offshore, to several groups including Royal Dutch/Shell. NIOC will come in as a 50 percent partner once commercial oil is discovered. Iran has claimed that these were the most advantageous agreements it had ever signed.

The only advance on 75-25 so far (for the government) is the RAP deal with Saudi Arabia, signed early in April. There is a royalty that can rise to 20 percent, and it is expensed, before tax. The income tax is 40 percent, but could rise later with any general change in Saudi taxation. The national company Petromin can come in as a 40 percent partner once oil is found; it will have 50 percent voting rights. The government calls this an 80-20 deal.

But there remain still some oddities among the concessions. In the Saudi-Kuwait neutral zone, Getty Oil has a concession with a big royalty of 55 cents a barrel, and also pays the governments 25 percent share of profits based on posted price. The company has said in recent years that this deal gives the governments the highest percentage revenue of any oil deal actually operating so far in the Middle East — as much as 84 percent.

Way out in the other direction are the Abu Dhabi and Oman concessions. These are survivals of the "four gold shillings" government payments system: the governments get simply the fixed royalty. The companies operating there have suggested a move to some 50-50 formula; but Sheikh Shakbut has long refused. When output gets to the level of Abu Dhabi's now, sticking to a low royalty might be described as a way of deliberately not coining money.

POLITICS OVER THE OIL SCENE

Political stormclouds are once again hovering over Middle East oil. This much would have been evident to even the most casual sign-reader at March's Arab Petroleum Congress in Cairo. One should not, on the other hand, be over-impressed by the exuberant invective directed against the major oil companies and their home governments at the congress, nor even by Sheikh Abdullah Tariki's fervent plea for nationalisation of the oil producing companies. If such a step really were feasible at the present time, the governments of the big oil producing countries — whose officials took noticeably little part in the Congress proceedings — would doubtless be quite prepared to take all the action they considered advisable without prompting from anyone else.

The real significance of the congress lay not so much in the rhetoric as in the relentless insistence with which the Egyptian delegates urged the formation of a pan-Arab petroleum organisation to direct regional oil policy. The idea was not new. But the way it was put over at this latest congress carried the suggestion of a twofold warning to both the oil companies and certain producer governments. First, that oil cannot forever remain a sort of sacred cow, divorced from the main political and economic trends of the Arab world as a whole; and second that the UAR now intends to play a leading role in the formulation of Arab oil policy.

Egypt's virtual exclusion from the major decisions affecting Arab oil — particularly since the creation of OPEC in 1960 and the consequent eclipse of the petroleum agencies of the Arab League — has always been a sore point in Cairo. In Egyptian eyes it is ridiculous that the United Arab Republic — which is by far the largest political and military power in the Arab world and which naturally has to bear the brunt of any confrontation with Israel or the West — should have no voice in the employment of the Arabs' main strategic weapon and international bargaining counter.

Oil Strategy and Israel. It is this strategic aspect of oil that Nasser is most interested in. He feels that the UAR is entitled to full backing from the Arab oil producers on any issue affecting vital Arab interests — something which has not always been forthcoming. The oil producers, understandably enough, have been very cagey about committing themselves to using their oil as a political weapon under any circumstances. Not, of course, that Nasser himself would ever play fast and loose with oil in this way; he is much too much of a realist for that. But in the event of a war with Israel

— which (*pace* President Bourguiba) is not such a remote possibility, considering Israel's commando raids and threats of military action at the first sign of a start of work on the projected Arab water diversion installations in Syria or Lebanon — oil could still be a factor in deterring Western intervention on Israel's side.

Apart from the strategic angle, it is difficult to pin down exactly how the proposed Arab petroleum organisation would work. In the recommendations of the Cairo congress it is merely stated that the organisation would "implement the agreement for co-ordination of Arab oil policy." However, this agreement, which was originally drafted back in 1959 and has been lying in suspended animation in the Arab League files ever since, is itself couched in extremely vague and general terms. Some people evidently envisage it as a kind of Arab OPEC (including the non-oil producing Arab countries), but with a tougher line vis-a-vis the oil companies — tending towards legislation rather than negotiation to achieve its aims.

However, the brute fact is that the organisation is unlikely ever to get off the ground. The idea of a unified Arab oil policy has always been something of a chimaera; for the past 20 years all efforts in this direction have foundered on precisely the same rocks of chronic inter-Arab discord as the attempts at political unity. In fact, part of the rationale behind the creation of OPEC was to permit the Arab oil producers to pursue their common economic interests — in concert with Iran and Venezuela — undisturbed by the rough-and-tumble of Arab politics. To a certain extent this

worked and still does. But politics inevitably crept back in again with the advent of the Cairo-Baghdad alliance in late 1963. There was profound dissatisfaction in both Cairo and Baghdad when, in the OPEC royalty negotiations with the oil companies, the Arab oil producers chose to follow the moderate line of Iran — Nasser's No. 1 political enemy in the Middle East — rather than the tough policy of Iraq. From then on it became part of UAR policy to remove Iranian influence from the Arab oil scene.

As the only non-Arab oil producer, Iran is rather an odd man out in the Middle East configuration. On one level, of course, Iran is very much part and parcel of the prolific oil basin centred on the Persian Gulf and has certain characteristics in common with some of her Arab neighbours like Saudi Arabia — the Islamic religion, a monarchical regime and a generally pro-western political orientation. On the other hand, a long history of racial antagonism and power struggles between Arabs and Iranians has left the Shah's regime (saddled as it is with a sizeable propaganda-prone Arab minority in the oil-rich province of Khuzistan) profoundly hostile to any manifestations of militant pan-Arabism on its borders — particularly when the pan-Arabism is dosed with a strong admixture of UAR-style socialism and neutralism. Translated into oil terms, this means that whereas the Iranians are prepared to co-operate with the producing Arab countries within an international organisation like OPEC, they would never come to terms with a politically motivated pan-Arab oil organisation. Nor would they then, if the occasion arose, feel any compunction about increasing their oil production at the expense of the Arabs (this would doubtless be regarded as tit-for-tat for Arab gains during the three-year shutdown of Iranian oilfields after Mossadegh's 1951 nationalisation). Conversely, the current Cairo line is to portray Iran as OPEC's "Trojan Horse," employed by Western governments and their oil companies to block any radical action by the oil producers.

Now there is a distinct split in the ranks of the Arab producers. Iraq, and Kuwait perforce, are with the UAR. (Algeria, though politically sympathetic to Cairo — on socialism anyway, whether or not on Israel — cannot really be counted in this line-up owing to its special relationship with France.) On the other hand, Saudi Arabia and Libya — both profoundly suspicious of Egyptian designs and both, incidentally, having close oil ties with Iran — have no intention of joining a Cairo-dominated Arab petroleum organisation. In the circumstances, therefore, as even Iraq seems to have recognised, OPEC remains the only really viable vehicle for dealing with the economic interests of the big oil exporters.

Nevertheless, Egyptian influence on Arab oil will undoubtedly grow with time. For one thing, it now seems quite on the cards, with Pan Am's recent oil discovery in the Gulf of Suez and the prospect of more to come, that Egypt may herself join the big oil league before long. For another, of course, there is the alliance with Iraq. The breakthrough here came in November 1963 when President Arif threw out the Baath party and installed a pro-Cairo government in Baghdad. For Nasser, this was an event of the utmost significance. Firstly, it smashed the power of the Baathists, his only rivals for the leadership of the Arab nationalist movement, confining them to the relative obscurity of Syria. And secondly, it gave him his first real opening to the oilfields. The drawback, for Nasser, is the chronic governmental instability of Iraq, which has made him extremely cautious about undertaking commitments in the direction of political union. The Iraqi regime is still an uneasy coalition of army officers and civilian Nasserites without, as yet, any really broad base of popular support. True, a settlement of outstanding issues with the oil companies may be nearly in the bag, but other difficulties remain; the intractable Kurdish problem and the danger of a Baathist comeback, to name only two. Nevertheless, provided the present regime can hang on, the Cairo-Baghdad axis could develop into a formidable power.

For tiny Kuwait, faced with the Iraqi-Egyptian combine, there is no alternative but to toe the line as far as general policy is concerned. Hence the somewhat incongruous spectacle of a traditional sheikhly amirate, with an oil-rich, laissez-faire economy, firmly yoked to the chariot of "revolutionary" Arab socialism. Moreover, the traditional rulers are now watched over by an independent-minded national assembly, whose vociferous minority of Arab nationalist deputies has been giving the government a very hard time of late. It was perhaps no coincidence that Iraq's rejection of the oil companies' offer should have been so swiftly followed by the refusal of the Kuwait assembly to ratify the royalty agreement concluded by its own government.

Between the Cairo-Baghdad axis and the rest of the Arabian peninsula stand Britain and Saudi Arabia, now forced into a shotgun alliance after many years of bitter border conflicts in southeast Arabia. Since the start of the Yemen war some two and a half years ago, the keystone of King Faisal's policy has been to combat, by all means short of risking a direct military confrontation, the spread of Egyptian power in Arabia, which he regards as an exclusively Saudi sphere of influence. With the sudden arrest of most of the leading political dissidents in Saudi Arabia last summer, following the final ousting of the ailing and incompetent ex-king Saud, Faisal's internal position is now about as secure as it could be. He is, of course, a confirmed autocrat who is unlikely to take any serious steps to democratise the regime. On the other hand, with his somewhat Gaullist personality he has succeeded in giving his country some sense of direction, particularly in the field of economic development. The regime will probably last his time, but after him — and his health is not exactly robust — the prospects for the House of Saud are most uncertain.

In many ways, Faisal has held the trump cards in his conflict with Nasser; up to now, all he has had to do is to keep the Yemeni royalists supplied with arms and money. Also, the extent of the conflict has been masked by the so-called "summit sprint" of the past 18 months, which has entailed a toning down of inter-Arab disputes in favour of solidarity against Israel. But there are now signs that Nasser's patience is becoming exhausted. He holds Faisal personally responsible for the fact that efforts to find an acceptable compromise solution to the Yemeni impasse have so far come to nothing.

Does Britain's presence pay? As far as Britain is concerned, a good hard look needs to be taken at the whole antique system of protection treaties and agreements stretching round the littoral of the Arabian peninsula from Aden to Bahrain. The purpose of the Aden base and its satellites, we are told, is to defend our oil interests in the Persian Gulf. But does this now apply to Kuwait, for example? Since its emergence from under the British wing only a few years ago, Kuwait has been taken so thoroughly into the Arab fold that it would be difficult to imagine any circumstances in which the ruler would now dare to invite British military intervention, as he did against General Kassem in 1961. The argument does, however, make more sense when applied to the new oil producing states of the lower Gulf such as Abu Dhabi and Muscat and Oman, where the oilfields are still subject to territorial claims — the former by Saudi Arabia and the latter by the exiled Imam of Oman.

However, the price, both politically and in hard cash, which Britain has to pay to keep this sort of protection going seems to be getting too much. In Aden and the hinterland the situation has degenerated into a hopelessly complex and highly dangerous muddle, where even the supposedly "tame" Arab ministers of the Aden administration are now demanding a speedy British evacuation. In Bahrain, the bloody riots that occurred last March had their roots in the political frustration of a fairly sophisticated populace

whose ruler has consistently refused, against British advice, to allow any form of representative government.

The problems for Britain of dis-
engaging from the interlocking series of commitments in Arabia
should not be underestimated. But
at least some consideration should
now be given to plans for a phased
withdrawal. It has been suggested
that the principalities of the lower
Gulf might somehow be put under
the protective umbrella of Saudi
Arabia. The rulers would assuredly
object, but there may be no other
alternative. For, in the final analysis, the survival of Western oil interests in the Middle East will depend on the commercial strength of
the oil companies, rather than on
military bases.

NEW GROWTH FOR NATURAL GAS

by
Charles W. Frey

Engineer James Murdock had a hobby that was considered a little unusual in Birmingham, England, in the late seventeen hundreds. In his spare time he roasted coal in a tightly closed iron oven, piped off the gas that emanated from the hot coal, and burned it. Other people had done this before, but Murdock, obviously braver than most, went them one better by illuminating his whole house with the gas he manufactured. Gas lighting was soon used in displays and factories. Early in 1807, Pall Mall in London became the first street in the world to be illuminated its full length by gas.

Less than a decade later, manufactured gas crossed the Atlantic to Baltimore, Maryland, to be displayed in a festival of illumination. So great was the public's enthusiasm that a Baltimore gaslight company was organized on June 13, 1816 — a date regarded as the birthday of the gas industry in America.

Gas was not entirely unknown before Murdock's experiments. The fire-worshipping religions that grew up on the shores of the Caspian Sea were inspired by numerous burning seepages of natural gas there. The Chinese were moving gas through bamboo pipes and using it for fuel 2,000 years ago. The journals of America's early explorers are full of references to "burning springs" in Ohio, New York, Pennsylvania, and elsewhere.

But in the beginning, gas lighting in Europe and America was strictly a manufactured gas industry, using the same basic methods that Murdock developed, only on a larger scale. By 1859 there were 297 manufactured gas companies — and only one natural gas company — serving almost 5 million American customers.

The natural gas company was in Fredonia, New York, where in 1821 William Aaron Hart had discovered a reservoir of natural gas. He began experimenting with it and by 1824 had installed natural gas light in several buildings in Fredonia including the inn, where the gas was also used for cooking. The Fredonians were a little more leisurely than the Baltimoreans had been. The Fredonia Gas Light and Water Works Company was not organized until 1858, when it became America's 298th gas company, the world's first natural gas company, and the forerunner of a great and important industry.

The industry was born slowly and grew up at a laggard pace. Natural gas did not begin to reach major

"New Growth for Natural Gas" by Charles W. Frey. Reprinted from The Lamp, *Vol. 48 (Spring 1966) pp. 24-25, with permission of the editor and Standard Oil Company (New Jersey).*

metropolitan areas in significant volume until the early nineteen twenties. The first 1,000-mile gas pipeline was completed in 1931.

World War II slowed the expansion, but since the war the industry has increased its production at an average rate of 7.7 percent a year. It is easy to see why.

People like the convenience of natural gas — there is no smoke or ash. They like its steady hot flame — which gives about twice as much heat per unit of gas as manufactured gas.[1] It is versatile enough both to heat and cool a house, and it can still be used for light. Not many families desire gaslight inside, but there has been a remarkable return to gas street-lighting in residential urban areas. People say that it's friendlier.

Industries, too, like natural gas and for the same reason that people do — controllable sootless and ashless heat. Industrial uses for gas range from the crisping of dry cereals to the tempering of missile nose cones, which must withstand intense friction heat. The body of a Polaris missile is hardened under three hours' exposure to gas heat at 1,600 degrees Fahrenheit. Gas is also a prime raw material in countless chemical operations where, alone or in combination with other substances, it is changed into plastics, fibers, medicines, detergents, and a host of other aids to mankind.

About one-third of the natural gas produced in America is found in conjunction with the search for and production of oil. Many oil producing companies are natural gas producers, too, selling their gas to public utilities which in turn supply it to homes and industries. Humble Oil & Refining Company, Jersey Standard's principal affiliate in the United States, leads the nation in gas production as well as gas reserves.

Natural gas accounted for about 30 percent of all U.S. energy consumption in 1965, a figure roughly equivalent to the energy in 7.5 million barrels of heavy fuel oil every day in the year. The oil producing countries in Latin America have vast gas reserves, and the utilization of these reserves is increasing steadily. To the north, Canada produces large quantities of gas, about 35 percent of which is exported to the United States, the remainder being used within Canada. A great deal of natural gas is produced in association with crude oil in the Middle East and North Africa. An Esso affiliate in Australia discovered gas in commercial quantities about a year ago, and plans to market it are under way.

In Western Europe a rapid switch to natural gas is taking place currently. In 1964 Western Europe's demand for natural gas was slightly more than the equivalent of 300,000 barrels of oil a day, or about 2 percent of the area's total energy supply. It is now galloping ahead at an average annual increase of almost 20 percent a year and is expected to maintain this rate for the next few years.

Natural gas occurs and has been commercially developed in various parts of Germany, in the Po Valley in Italy, and in southwestern France.

[1] Burning one cubic foot of the average natural gas is roughly equivalent to burning 1,200 common wooden matches all the way down. This amount of heat will make fifteen cups of coffee, starting with cold water, or bake two one-pound loaves of bread. It is almost impossible, however, to bake a loaf of bread with matches.

Italy, France, and West Germany each have reserves of about 5 trillion cubic feet of gas. None of these countries has enough gas to meet present demands from expanding industry, let alone to supply all prospective domestic users. And yet Europe's demand for energy has been increasing at a rate higher than in the United States.

Europe, in fact, was fast getting into a bind as far as convenient fuel was concerned. Then, in 1959, one of the largest natural gas fields of all time was discovered under the sugar beet fields near Slochteren in the Netherlands, close to the German border. It was found by a company owned jointly by Jersey and Shell — N. V. Nederlandse Aardolic Maatschappij, or NAM for short — at a depth of 9,000 feet. The discovery came after thirteen years of drilling and about 200 holes. A number of profitable, relatively small oil fields were discovered and developed. Then came the discovery well which established the presence of natural gas in commercial amounts and led to the development of the Groningen field. Today, based on current estimates, Groningen's reserves of gas appear to be about 39 trillion cubic feet. To put it another way, the energy content of Groningen is something like thirty times the present annual consumption of all forms of energy in the Netherlands. By 1975 Groningen should be furnishing about one-third of the steadily increasing energy needs of the Netherlands, with about the same quantity being exported to neighboring countries.

Plans to export Groningen gas to Germany and Belgium are already well past the drawing-board stage, and it would be relatively simple to export natural gas to France and the United Kingdom.

Jersey affiliates and their partners are presently active and busy in plans and arrangements to get Groningen gas into the local markets as fast as possible. No fewer than seven separate contractual or active-participation agreements to provide markets for Dutch natural gas have been signed or are near conclusion, and potential consumers in Europe are ready and eager for natural gas.

Individuals and families want it for cooking and, as dreams of a little more affluence come true, for home heating and for refrigerators and other appliances. Heavy industries, including public utilities, are eager to switch to natural gas for its caloric value and its easy use. New chemical plants, rising all over the Benelux and West German area, will use it not only for fuel but as the raw material for various chemicals, synthetic fabrics and rubbers, paints and insecticides. Ammonia-manufacturing plants that will use Groningen gas as a raw material are now under construction.

It is currently estimated that Groningen production may reach the equivalent of 750,000 barrels of oil a day in 1975. One thing is sure — a new day is dawning for energy users in the Benelux countries and West Germany, and perhaps for the United Kingdom and France as well, as a result of the Groningen discovery.

But what of the rest of Western Europe, especially the heavily populated and industrialized areas of Italy and Spain? Italy's Po Valley reserves of natural gas are not sufficient now, and they are steadily dwindling. Gas in any amount that even hints at commercial possibilities has not been discovered in Spain to date.

With the opening up of oil fields in North Africa, a great new source of natural gas has become available to these countries. Jersey affiliates this year signed contracts with Italian and Spanish firms to provide them with huge amounts of liquefied natural gas (LNG) by ship from North Africa. The natural gas will come from Esso Libya's oil sources in Libya, including the famous Zelten oil field, discovered in 1959 about 100 miles south of the Mediterranean Sea in the middle of a lifeless desert. A new pipeline will carry the gas to Esso Libya's seaside oil-exporting terminal at Marsa el Brega. When the gas gets there, it will be liquefied by refrigeration to a temperature of minus 260 degrees Fahrenheit in what will be the world's largest natural gas liquefaction plant. The liquid gas will be stored at Marsa el Brega and piped as a liquid into tank ships especially designed to carry it. Four such tankers will be built to Jersey Standard's specifications.

The Esso LNG project is scheduled to go into full operation toward the end of 1968. Ships on the Italian run will go from Marsa el Brega to La Spezia, southeast of Genoa, where the gas will be piped ashore for storage and distribution by SNAM, an affiliate of Italy's Ente Nazionale Idrocarburi (ENI). The amount of gas delivered over the life of the twenty-year contract will be about 235 million cubic feet a day, or the equivalent of some 55,000 barrels of oil daily.

Spain has long had a manufactured gas industry, but rapidly expanding industrial activity calls for more energy than present facilities can produce. In Barcelona, Catalana de Gas of Barcelona and Jersey Standard officials have agreed to organize a joint company that will own and operate an LNG terminal and facilities for the distribution of gas products to Spanish industry. Facilities costing about $20 million will be built in Barcelona. These include large storage tanks, fractionating towers to remove some of the heavier components of the gas (which will be sold separately), and a distribution grid. The facilities will be ready for operation when the first shipload of gas from Marsa el Brega is scheduled to arrive late in 1968 — at the same time deliveries to Italy will begin. Gas will be delivered to Barcelona, under the terms of the fifteen-year contract, at the rate of 110 million cubic feet a day — the equivalent of about 25,000 barrels of oil daily. The busy city will then be well supplied with natural gas for its thriving industries.

An interesting footnote to the development of natural gas in Barcelona, Spain, is that 1968 will be the 140th anniversary of the first use of natural gas to light the beacon of a lighthouse — in Barcelona, New York. The Barcelona-on-Lake Erie lighthouse, now maintained as a historical landmark, is still burning natural gas.

Whether for old lighthouses or the newest chemical complexes, the outlook for natural gas was never more auspicious. There is plenty of it, the need is growing, and the future of gas is even brighter than foretold by that dazzling display in Baltimore 150 years ago.

THE NETWORK OF WORLD TRADE

The world's oil requirements are now approximately doubling every ten years, and so is the production of crude. The largest increases in demand, however, are concentrated on areas such as Western Europe and Japan, which have no substantial indigenous resources and therefore depend primarily on imports from other regions, notably the Middle East, the Caribbean, and now the new producing countries of Africa. North America, on the other hand, which is at one and the same time a major producing and consuming area, is now moving ahead at a far more modest rate. A consequence of these unequal developments is that the inter-regional trade in oil tends to expand even more rapidly than the world's total production of crude.

TREBLING IN A DECADE

Some interesting statistical facts about trading developments in the last few years emerge from a paper, entitled "The International Petroleum Industry: Review and Forecast," which was prepared by Messrs. G. T. Ballou and W. J. McQuinn, of California Standard, for the recent Fifth Arab Petroleum Congress in Cairo. The world's crude oil production (including the estimated output of Communist countries) went up from about 19.5 million barrels daily in 1959 to close on 28 million b/d in 1964, or by about 43 percent over a period of five years. However, as is shown in the accompanying table, inter-regional oil movements, over the same period, expanded by as much as 75 percent, going up from about 7.1 to 12.6 million b/d. These trends, if continued, will indeed bring about a doubling in crude oil production within a decade, but this would then be accompanied by a trebling in the volume of oil involved in inter-regional movements.

The figures also indicate that some 45 barrels out of every 100 barrels produced last year entered the inter-regional trade, compared with only 37 out of 100 five years previously, and there is every reason to assume that a similar growth will continue. In addition, there are very substantial, and in some cases increasing, oil movements within the eight large regions into which the world has been divided for the purpose of these statistical comparisons. In particular, the "Far Eastern" region comprises the larger part of non-Communist Asia and Oceania, and Indonesian shipments to countries such as Japan, India or Australia thus count as intra-regional. The same, of course, is true of shipments within the U.S.A. (*e.g.*, from Texas to the East Coast) and within Latin America (*e.g.*, from the Caribbean to the main South American consumer countries). There is also a large-scale export trade with petroleum products within the European area.

"*The Network of World Trade*." *Reprinted from* Petroleum Press Service (*June* 1965), *pp.* 210-212, *with permission of the publisher.*

Inter-Regional Oil Movements
(Thousands of Barrels Daily)

To:	U.S.	Canada	Latin America	West Europe	Africa	Middle East	Far East	Total Exports	% of Total	Index (1959 =100)
1959 From:										
U.S.	—	67	24	48	6	4	62	211	2.9	
Canada	98	—	—	—	—	—	—	98	1.4	
Latin America	1,253	251	—	566	77	3	27	2,177	30.4	
Western Europe	6	—	20	—	109	15	11	161	2.3	
Africa	1	—	—	72	—	1	—	74	1.1	
Middle East	353	106	81	2,422	169	—	864	3,995	55.7	
Far East and Oceania	69	—	4	21	2	9	—	105	1.5	
Soviet Bloc	—	—	24	260	37	9	3	333	4.7	
Total Imports	1,780	424	153	3,389	400	41	967	7,154	100.0	
% of Total	24.9	5.9	2.1	47.4	5.6	.6	13.5	100.0		
1964 From:										
U.S.	—	21	37	52	5	1	77	193	1.5	95
Canada	302	—	—	1	—	—	—	303	2.4	309
Latin America	1,493	319	—	898	88	2	51	2,851	22.7	131
Western Europe	5	1	5	—	68	21	11	111	.8	69
Africa	50	1	16	1,498	—	—	6	1,571	12.5	2,110
Middle East	317	140	220	3,584	334	—	2,033	6,628	52.7	167
Far East and Oceania	62	—	2	21	—	1	—	86	.7	82
Soviet Bloc	—	—	115	595	30	2	108	850	6.7	255
Total Imports	2,229	482	395	6,649	525	27	2,286	12,593	100.0	175
% of Total	17.7	3.8	3.1	52.8	4.2	.2	18.2	100.0		
1964 Index (1959 = 100)	125	114	258	196	131	66	237	175		

Source: "The International Petroleum Industry: A Review and Forecast."

The question might be raised, however, whether the recent expansions in the volume of trade have not been accompanied by a contraction in average tanker hauls, in view of the growth in short-distance deliveries from North Africa to nearby Europe. Such reduction in average tanker hauls would, of course, moderate the expansion in the international oil trade, if measured in ton-miles, and would thereby affect the world requirements of tanker tonnage.

Messrs. Ballou and McQuinn do not endeavour to answer these special questions, but it appears from a study by the London oil economist, Mr. W. L. Newton, that there has been in recent years a strong counter-trend in the shape of increased oil deliveries over very long distances, *e.g.*, from the Persian Gulf to Japan, and *average* distances of tanker movements have in consequence been fluctuating around about 4,000 miles throughout 1959-64. There will undoubtedly again be conflicting influences in the future, but Mr. Newton suggests that, on balance, the distances will tend to increase rather than decrease, and may reach nearly 4,300 miles by 1970. An important factor by that time will be the haul of large quantities of oil (perhaps as much as 700,000 b/d) around the Cape to destinations West of Suez.

EUROPE IN THE LEAD

Among the world's main oil-importing regions it is not surprising to find that Western Europe is easily

1 "The Long Term Development of The Tanker Freight Market." Lecture given to the Tanker Owners Group of the Norwegian Shipowner Association in Oslo.

in the lead, followed at a considerable distance by the Far East and the U.S.A. In Western Europe imports from other regions virtually doubled over the five years and now account for well over half the world's inter-regional trade. In the Far East, Japan's inland consumption — which is mainly supplied from extra-regional sources — soared from about 320,000 b/d in 1959 to 1,350,000 b/d last year, and there have also been satisfactory, if less sensational, increases in Australia, New Zealand and the less developed countries of Eastern Asia. In the U.S.A., imports in 1959-1964 rose by only 25 percent, though it is pertinent that indigenous production, despite protection, went up over the same period at only about half this percentage rate.

The remaining regions of the world all contain highly significant producing areas and play only a relatively minor part as importers. It is true that deliveries from other regions to Latin America (mainly Brazil, Trinidad and Uruguay) have sharply risen in recent years, but deliveries to Canada and to Africa have only shown modest increases, and the small deliveries to the Middle East (mainly of products) have further declined. Nor are there any commercial deliveries of oil from the free world to the Communist bloc.

THE MIDDLE EAST'S
HALF-SHARE

Where do the imports come from? It will be noted that the Middle Eastern region has broadly maintained the dominating position it enjoyed in 1959, and still accounts for more than half the oil entering the world's inter-regional trade. It is true that

Middle Eastern oil now encounters strong competition from other sources in the all-important West European market, where its sales in 1959-1964 consequently went up by barely 50 percent, or considerably less than the over-all expansion of demand in that area. On the other hand, however, Middle Eastern oil gained further strength in the large areas east of Suez, with its sales in the Far East (chiefly Japan) rising by as much as 135 percent, and in Africa (mainly in Indian Ocean countries) by nearly 100 percent. Sales of Middle Eastern oil in the various parts of the Western Hemisphere went up, in the aggregate, by only about 25 percent, but these now account for little more than one-tenth of the region's total exports.

Latin America — which in practice means the Caribbean area — still takes second place, after the Middle East, among the exporting regions. However, oil shipments from there to other parts of the world went up over the past five years by barely one-third, and its share in the world's expanding inter-regional trade was therefore sharply reduced, from 30.4 percent in 1959 to 22.7 percent in 1964. The larger part of the area's oil exports goes to North America where the capacity of the market is limited, but a mitigating factor is the continued expansion of oil sales from the Caribbean to West European countries. These latter exports rose in 1959-1964 by 59 percent, and — while they did not maintain their share in the expanding European markets — they now account for nearly a third of all exports from Latin America to other regions. Heavy crude and fuel oil from Ven-

ezuela are still required in Western Europe in substantial quantities, largely as a counter to the growing use of light crudes from nearby sources.

Africa started its career as a significant oil-exporting region around 1959, and its shipments last year had reached nearly 1.6 million b/d, equivalent to 12.5 percent of the total inter-regional trade. There are now at least three major producing countries in Africa — Algeria, Libya and Nigeria — all of which have plans for further large-scale expansions. Virtually all the African oil — except for the quantities used inside Africa — is marketed in Western Europe, where much larger quantities will be absorbed in the future.

The Soviet bloc's exports of oil more than doubled over the past five years, and, including deliveries to Cuba, attained around 850,000 b/d in 1964, accounting for 6.7 percent of the world's inter-regional trade. The rate of expansion has lately, however, tended to decline and, except for year-by-year fluctuations, future rises may no longer be expected to be much in excess of the rate of expansion for the international petroleum trade as a whole. Western Europe remains the main target of the Soviet bloc's oil trading drive, but — apart from Cuba — there are now also substantial deliveries to Japan and to Brazil.

The world's main oil-importing regions — Western Europe, the Far East and the U.S.A. — also figure among the exporters, but the volume of these sales is relatively small and has tended to fall in recent years. Canada's exports have trebled during 1959-1964, though they all go to the nearby U.S.A., thus remaining within the North American continent.

This article, with its accent on regions rather than countries, unavoidably represents a somewhat simplified picture of the world's oil trade. Most of the regions, of course, comprise a large number of countries, and the world as a whole has now about 18 countries with an oil export trade of from about 100,-000 b/d upwards (not including the re-export of products from imported crude). Moreover, the emergence of Africa as an important producing/exporting region is but the most striking recent example of a continued trend towards an even greater diversification in the sources of supply. The world's importing countries are therefore assured of a wide choice of sources, and consequently of a fair measure of security — quite apart from the large energy-producing potential of North America which would be bound to make its presence felt in the event of a serious interruption of supplies from traditional sources.

SOVIET OIL EXPORTS

by
ALAN R. PLOTNICK

In the past few years a number of articles have been written on the dangers of Russian oil trade with the West. Their principal theme has been that oil exports from the Soviet bloc are a threat not only to the European Common Market, but also to all of NATO. In a recent address before the American Petroleum Institute in November, 1961, Senator Mike Monroney went so far as to say that the Russians have already declared war on the Free World and that their weapon is oil.

These Western oil experts have criticized the Russians for using price discrimination and barter to foster their oil trade. One would assume from the alarm that has been sounded that both these practices are recent economic inventions of Mr. Mikoyan's. In this writer's opinion, there is probably a much greater danger in accepting the opinions of these oil experts than in importing petroleum from the Soviet bloc. In an issue such as this, the logic of Big Business or the military mind can be deceiving. The danger of allowing the economics of restrictionism to replace the economics of welfare is a real one that

[1] Within the bloc as a whole, the USSR and Rumania are the two countries that can produce enough to sell to the Free World.

is inherent in the arguments of those who propose simple solutions in dealing with the "Soviet oil offensive."

The idea, for instance, that Soviet oil exports represent a planned attempt to weaken the economies of the Free World is a much-repeated theme in current articles on Communist oil trade. Through this type of "economic banditry" — as it has been described by Senator Hubert Humphrey — the Russians have transformed oil into a powerful cold-war weapon. Suppose we examine the trade situation.

The Soviet petroleum industry did not actually get started along modern lines until six years ago, when Premier Khrushchev decided that the entire energy-producing sector of the nation needed a complete overhaul. During the time that Soviet planners concentrated their efforts on coal, the opportunities for capital- and labor-saving innovations were limited. The lag that existed in the coal industry relative to the rest of the economy was serious; clearly, the fuel industry could not recover from its depressed state unless a shift were made toward an entirely different form of energy, namely petroleum. Russian planners also saw the potential value that a healthy oil industry would have in-

"Soviet Oil Exports" by Alan R. Plotnick. Reprinted from The Nation, *Vol. 196 (April 13, 1963) pp. 302–306, with permission of the publisher.*

ternally in enabling them to develop other industries, such as petrochemicals and plastics. Externally, it would enable them to trade oil for much-needed consumer and capital goods. It was the latter that held out the greatest promise, as subsequent events proved.

To implement their petroleum program, the Russians imported large amounts of materials such as pipe, pumps, electronic equipment and even entire petrochemical plants. Italy, West Germany, France and Sweden, to mention only a few, were among the European suppliers. Orders for new oil tankers were also placed in Japan, Yugoslavia and Finland. Examined from the exporter's standpoint, these sales involved substantial business for a good many firms throughout Europe. During the eighteen months ending in June, 1961, approximately $1.5 billion worth of industrial goods were exported from Western Europe to the Soviet bloc. Since there has been a shortage of foreign exchange in the Communist bloc, the Western supplier countries came under pressure of their own nationals to accept payment in Russian products, especially oil.

Had the Western European governments refused to accept this oil, their sales to the Communists would have been impossible. As long as the Soviet standard of living remains low compared to that of the United States and the other economically advanced countries of the Free World, one must expect the Soviets to have an oil surplus which they will try to barter for manufactured goods. Alternatively, as long as the rest of the world boasts that its standard of living exceeds that of Russia, it will undoubtedly have to

face up to the problem of deciding how much Communist oil it can afford to take.

Those who insist that the oil deals in Western Europe benefit the Russians at the expense of the oil-importing countries ignore the two-way nature of this trade. In any business transaction, both parties expect to benefit; otherwise they would not agree to trade in the first place. It is highly doubtful whether Western European exporters of petroleum equipment and pipe would be willing to stop selling to the Communists. The profitableness of the trade for them, and for their nations' economies, is in itself proof that Russian oil has not harmed Western Euope's economic growth. Many businessmen would also point out that it is Russia's loss, not her gain, when she gives up large quantities of non-replaceable natural resources to the Free World.

When the Russians recently told the British that they were in the market to buy fishing vessels, the oil experts came rushing into counsel the British on the deal. The original proposal was for Russia to place $56 million worth of orders if the British would accept about $5 million in fuel oil as part payment. The amount of oil involved was 1.5 million tons, which represents about 3 percent of total annual British oil imports. A number of British groups have lobbied on the matter. British shipbuilders naturally favor the deal; unemployment in that industry has been growing for several years. The major oil companies supplying Britain's fuel-oil needs are opposed, arguing that they have been good customers of the shipyards and will do more for them, in the long run, than the Russians. Competition in the British fuel-oil market has already reached a dangerous level, with large buyers getting considerable discounts and ex-refinery prices being maintained at uneconomic levels. If the Russians did enter the market, their ability to reduce prices could put the major companies to rout; they could probably undersell the majors by about 20 percent. So far, however, the Russians have denied that their prices will be reduced. In fact, they have stated that their main concern is not to dump oil in Britain, but to get fishing vessels they need at the lowest possible price.

The British coal lobby has stood with the oil companies on the issue, although usually it is in opposition. The National Union of Mineworkers has stated that any increase in oil imports threatens the domestic coal industry; they emphasize that their opposition is directed to *any* increase in oil imports, not just from Russia. (Even before the oil-for-ships question arose, the British Government was worried about the cutback in mining in Scotland and North England. The Government had already modified its program for oil-fired electric generating stations in favor of coal-fired ones.)

In considering the Russian deal, the British are also faced with the need to preserve a political equilibrium in the Middle East and Venequela, whose interests could be affected if Russian oil sales grew to substantial levels. Finally, the American Government has been edgy about the proposal; it would like to have British fishing vessels placed in the forbidden "strategic export" category. Washington has apparently also put pressure on the West Germans and Japanese to get them to embargo pipe exports to the Russians. By such actions, the United States exposes itself to the same kind of criticism of political manipulation which the oil experts argue will result from the purchase of Soviet-bloc oil.

In deciding what to do, the British should not let the Pentagon or NATO call the shots. It would be very shortsighted of their government to refuse an opportunity to reduce unemployment in the shipbuilding industry, assuming that other economic or political costs of a greater magnitude were not imposed on the economy through this decision. As to coal mining, this industry was depressed before the Russians ever talked about placing orders for ships. Then again, the level of the proposed oil imports from Russia is not large enough to make a serious dent in the major-company markets unless the oil is sold at very low prices.

The second criticism that has been made of the Communist petroleum trade concerns the effect it has had on world market prices. There is no denying that, relative to their size, Soviet-bloc sales have had a disproportionately large effect. Bloc exports have been growing rapidly; according to the U.S. National Petroleum Council, its sales to the West will grow to 50 million tons by 1965 compared to 30 million in 1961. While it is true that the crude-oil market has been marked by a certain degree of price instability and that this has been felt in Latin America and the Middle East, the careful observer will recognize that Russian oil has been only one among many contributing causes. The other factors that should be examined are:

1. The excess capacity in international oil production relative to existing market needs.

2. The increased competition from companies that were not previously operating in the international oil industry. There are also many new, small, independent companies active in various phases of the industry, such as refining and marketing.

3. The effect of import controls, such as those in the United States and in other countries. They place limits on the size of the market for petroleum imports in both unrefined and refined forms.

The combination of these pressures has led to widespread discounts and other allowances being offered on posted prices in the world's principal oil-producing countries.

As recently as 1956, one could explain the factors that determined the price of oil by reference to a world-market system. At that time, the posted price of crude oil in the Middle East plus average tanker freights was relevant for most of the refineries in Europe and only a comparatively small quantity of oil moved at more advantageous terms. Most of the sales of finished products throughout most of Western Europe (exceptions existed in parts of Scandinavia, Italy and Switzerland) were made on a basis approximating Caribbean posted prices plus average freight rates. These prices applied to the large quantities of products originating in European refineries, as well as to the comparatively small amounts imported from abroad.

Since 1959, however, posted prices for crude oil have departed significantly from current market conditions as a result of the factors I have mentioned above. The same thing has been true for finished products.

To speak of Russian oil prices being lower than those of the Western oil producers raises a number of interesting problems, one of which is the basis on which the comparison is made. Communist oil trade with the rest of the world is generally conducted on a C.I.F. (cost, insurance and freight) basis, with the sellers responsible for shipment. This complicates any meaningful comparison of Russian and Western basic oil prices. Even if Soviet F.O.B. (not including transport costs) prices were equal to Persian Gulf postings for comparable crudes, *the Russians would still have a competitive advantage in Western Europe* equal to about $.44 a barrel at current ocean-tanker rates. This is due to the location of the Black Sea ports, which are nearly 3,000 miles closer to the market. A second complication in making price comparisons is that we must consider not only the price which the buyer of Russian oil pays, but also the prices that the Russians pay for their offsetting imports.

The prices of the international petroleum companies have been undercut by the Soviet oil monopoly in many markets, though Soviet spokesmen are quick to deny accusations that they are "dumping." They are especially sensitive to Arab feelings on the subject and find it difficult to convince the Arab governments that they are merely in-

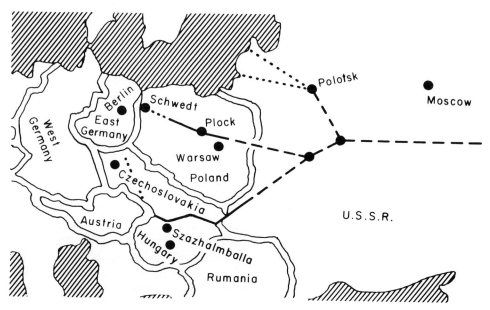

Solid lines indicate finished sections; dotted lines, under construction; barred lines, proposed.

terested in recovering their pre-war share of the world oil market.

Naturally, the international oil companies have sided with the Middle Eastern rulers in opposing Russian oil expansion, since price competition means price instability; its effects on government revenues and company profits are unwelcome. Anyone who studies present oil-market conditions in Western Europe knows that the real oil-price problem there lies in the ability of the large international companies to charge high prices to the consumer through an almost complete control over all supplies. Today's oil costs in Europe have become burdened by a complex system of prices that brings huge profits to a relatively small number of companies. On the basis of these conditions, the economic significance of Communist oil, especially in its price aspects, appears as an advantage for the European market, since low prices enhance consumer real income.

Oil prices have been a thorn in the side of the international oil companies especially since the formation of the Organization of Petroleum Exporting Countries (O.P.E.C.), an intergovernmental agreement designed to re-establish price stability throughout the world. Should a combination of petroleum-producing countries, through O.P.E.C., be able to determine the price at which oil is sold, it would mean, in effect, that oil-price decisions were reached in the political councils of government. This would create problems for the international oil companies, which are as willing to surrender their economic sovereignty to governments as they are to relinquish their markets to the Communists. In either case, the power of the private companies is at stake.

A third major criticism of Soviet

oil policy to be examined concerns the alleged threat it represents to the defense strength of NATO. A strong emotional fear underlies this complaint, since some of the largest importers of Communist oil are in the NATO group. Moreover, nearly two-thirds of all Soviet-bloc petroleum exports are destined for the Western European market. A closer examination of the facts bearing on this trade relationship may clarify the extent of the danger that is supposed to exist.

Today there are seventeen European countries that buy oil from the Communists. Ten of of them belong to NATO, but only two of these, West Germany and Italy, import any substantial quantity. In 1961 Italy, through its state-owned E.N.I., bought 6,500,000 metric tons, representing 22 percent of its total oil imports. West Germany imported 3,900,000 metric tons, or 10 percent of its entire foreign supply. On an overall basis, 1961 imports from the Soviet bloc represented only 10 percent of Western Europe's gross oil imports. What appears to make the Russian oil expansion look so menacing is that (1) Soviet oil production is already half as large as that of the United States and is growing rapidly, and (2) practically every country in Europe, with the exception of Britain and Portugal, appears on the list of Russian oil buyers. However, oil-trade statistics show that Western Europe still obtains over 90 percent of its oil requirements from the Middle East and Venezuela.

Fear of Russian oil led the NATO countries in November, 1962, to place an embargo on large-bore pipe exports to Russia. During the preceding three years, Russian purchases of this commodity had been large and West Germany, Italy and Sweden counted among the producers. The embargo has apparently been effective enough to slow down the Russian construction of the Comecon (Friendship) pipe line, which will be completed by about mid-1964. Counting spur lines, the system will cover a total distance of 3,600 miles, making it the longest pipe line in the world.

In placing this embargo, one may well wonder whether NATO is acting for itself or for the major oil companies. Could the Soviet Union complete its planned pipe-line system, the immediate effect would be a reduction in the cost of transporting crude oil. Estimates are that it would bring the cost down from $1.05 per barrel to $.29 per barrel. This could be reflected in a substantial lowering of crude prices for the refiner. Who would be endangered by such a price cut? The private oil companies or the military strength of NATO? Any NATO argument that its defense would be jeopardized because its members would be likely to become overdependent on Soviet oil implies that the major oil companies are going to bow out gracefully in the face of rising Russian oil sales. How likely is this? There is also no reason why the stream of oil imports into Western Europe must freeze into any particular pattern, whether it be from the Free World or the Soviet bloc.

The charge that NATO countries are endangering their military defenses by becoming dependent on suddenly terminable oil supplies fails to recognize the practical advantages of utilizing Communist petroleum resources. The lower prices that the NATO countries now pay for Soviet-bloc oil relative to other supplies allow them to release a certain amount of their financial and real economic resources into alternative uses. This suggests that lower oil prices would help NATO countries to meet their costly military requirements. For the first time, these countries could say that the Communists are actually helping them to pay for their defense bill!

There is no country in the world today that can depend completely on any other for its future petroleum needs. It is therefore absurd to speak of the "risk of accessibility" during a future war. The American government's present Mandatory Oil Import Program is evidence of this country's desire to look more closely at nearby sources to supplement domestic reserves. The fact that Canada and Mexico both enjoy quota exemptions on the basis of their national-security advantages to the United States does not prevent us from continuing to buy large quantities of oil from the Middle East. Yet there is no doubt that American defense planners are not placing their confidence in the Middle East as an oil source over the long run. The same considerations are also relevant in evaluating the present usefulness of Communist-bloc oil in the NATO area. The risks that exist in becoming dependent on the Communists for oil should not prevent the NATO countries from conserving their own limited reserves by importing from other countries.

What, then, is the real danger of Soviet-bloc oil in the world today? It would seem to be mainly the risk of failure to see that there are commercial gains to be had from accepting it. If we trade with someone whose political views we dislike, it does not necessarily follow that we must accept his views along with his trade. Yet from the doctrinaire studies of the "oil experts" we can only conclude that trading with the Communists is the first step, or perhaps the last one, before democracy is supplanted by totalitarianism.

In a study of Europe's energy position made several years ago by the Organization for European Economic Co-operation entitled *Oil — Recent Developments in the O.E.E.C Area*, a forecast was made that the Western European oil demand in 1965 would stand at between 200 and 240 million tons. It was also estimated that by 1975 the market would need between 300 and 390 million tons. Already the projected estimates for 1965 seem too low in view of the tremendous growth in market demand in several Western European nations during the past few years. The O.E.E.C. report stated that while the amount of oil obtained from the Middle East and Venezuela will rise in the future, "their share in total supplies is likely to fall as those from North Africa and possibly Russia increase." However, they pointed out that Russia's future market would depend on the manner in which they compete with established exporting areas, as well as on government policies concerning the acceptability of Russian oil. One might add that the nature and strength of the opposition from the international oil cartel will be the single most important factor in this regard.

For some time the large oil companies have stood in the way of a cheap energy supply in Western Europe through their control of the market and their resistance to imports from "uncompetitive, risky areas." To promote their interests, these companies have distorted the true facts about the economic importance and national-security significance of the Communist oil trade. Instead of worrying about the methods that the Communists use in selling oil to the West — of which there seems to be very little economic understanding — the West would derive much more benefit from a careful study of the methods and policies employed by the large oil companies. In order

to curb the power that has been wielded by the world oil cartel, it might be a good idea to consider the establishment of a buying cartel, composed of European governments, which could counteract the power of the world's largest oil producers.

The European Economic Community represents the most advanced stage of economic integration that has thus far been reached in any part of the world. This arrangement grew out of a desire to improve the conditions of life of the people of the region. It would be unfortunate if the "private government" of the oil cartel became the divisive force in the region's effort to reach the highest possible level of economic well-being.

Manufacturing

Some of the products of the primary production activities discussed in earlier articles are ready for immediate use. Many of them, however, require additional processing or fabrication. In many cases these commodities go through a whole series of intermediate steps before they are ready for ultimate use. In the manufacturing industries primary commodities or semifinished components are refined, fabricated, combined, or otherwise altered to achieve the form of product for which there is a demand. Manufacturing varies widely in its location and complexity, from simple handicraft industries carried on in the home to gigantic complexes producing automobiles and other intricate machines.

In the study of manufacturing geography — concerned with the location of manufacturing and the causes and implications of that location — geographers commonly examine various factors of location. These are elements in the cost of the productive process, such as raw materials, water, labor, site, transportation facilities, and market, which influence the location of various types of manufacturing. Not all factors have the same influence on different types of manufacturing, nor do all plants manufacturing similar products always respond to these factors in the same way. Nonetheless, the costs of accumulation of materials, processing, and product distribution are the primary determinants in industrial locational choices.

Because certain factors of location affect a number of industries in much the same way, several differing types of manufacturing with similar requirements and cost patterns may be located near one another. This combined with the fact that the product of one manufacturer may be the material of another, may lead to the agglomeration, or concentration, of manufacturing into distinct manufacturing regions.

This selection of articles from business and trade publications as well as from scholarly journals will demonstrate, using specific industries as examples, some of the problems of manufacturing. They describe various processes used, and illustrate the impact of changing technology, corporate structure, and the wide array of variables influencing the operation and location of manufacturing activities. For example, the article by Burck points out the impact of increasing growth and declining trade restrictions on the European chemical industry. Another article, "The Big Change Comes to Steel," describes the internal changes taking place in the steel industry in response to dramatic changes in processing methods. Articles from professional publications, such as those by Zelinsky, Hurley, and Alexandersson analyze in depth the patterns or structures of various industries, reasons for these patterns, and factors contributing to change.

The Automotive Industry: A Study in Industrial Location

By NEIL P. HURLEY*

THE geographical patterns which characterize different industries are a compound of economic considerations, socio-historical factors and happenstance. Especially true is this of the geography of automotive manufacturing in the United States. This study will attempt to dissociate the myriad threads in the intricate web of causal factors which have shaped, and are now re-shaping, the locational profile of America's automotive production.

The development of the industry in Detroit is a classic instance of how historical accident and socio-economic factors combine to determine industrial sites. The fact that Henry Ford, Ransom E. Olds, Elwood Haynes and Charles Duryea lived in Michigan undoubtedly had much to do with the state of Michigan, and particularly Detroit, becoming the cradle of auto manufacturing.[1] This accords with Piquet's observation in 1925: "A recent canvass of a 100 leading industries has disclosed the fact that in almost all cases the location of the plant was the founder's home town. That, and not industrial factors, was the reason for the location."[2]

There were nevertheless sound commercial reasons why automotive manufacturing succeeded in thriving in the Detroit area. First, the vigor of such industries as machine shops, tool and die makers, and parts manufacturing exercised an unmistakable attraction on car producers. Bankers in the east were less willing to furnish short-term credit to the infant industry's promoters than were the more progressive middle West financiers. An additional factor in favor of locating in and around Detroit was that gas engines were preferred in Michigan as opposed to the steam engine (favored in Massachusetts) and the electric motor (in Connecticut); Ohio had been experimenting with all three. Naturally Michigan had a decided advantage over the other states when the gas engine proved to be the most efficacious way to power an auto. Otherwise, New England could have

* Jesuitenkolleg, Innsbruck, Sillgasse, Austria.

[1] For early locational influences in the auto industry see E. M. Hoover, Jr., *Locational Theory and the Shoe and Leather Industries* (Cambridge: Harvard University Press, 1937), p. 247; Allan Nevins and F. E. Hill, *Ford: The Times, the Man, the Company* (New York: Charles Scribner's Sons, 1954), pp. 20-35; Alfred P. Sloan and Sparkes Boyden, *Adventures of A White Collar Man* (New York: Doubleday Doran & Company, 1941).

[2] J. A. Piquet, "Scientific Versus Haphazard Plant Location," *Industrial Management*, June 1925, p. 330.

"The Automotive Industry: A Study in Industrial Location" by Neil P. Hurley. Reprinted from Land Economics, *Vol. 35 (February 1959), pp. 1-14, with permission of the editor.*

easily become the motor region of the world.[3]

Other factors of varying weight played their part, too. Thus the importance of motor boats and commercial vessels on the Great Lakes resulted in an important marine-engine industry developing in the area; this lent impetus to the production of all types of engines, including those for autos as well. The horseless carriage, a hybrid product developed by crossing a buggy with a marine engine, would naturally be manufactured in a region such as that of the Great Lakes.[4] Moreover, Detroit, Cleveland and satellite cities were specialists in pressed steel, malleable iron, brass parts, springs, rubber tires, paints and varnishes, materials which were indispensable for the assembly of a horseless carriage.

The mid-West, with its sprawling land expanses and scattered trade centers, was more transport-conscious than was the East. Its flatland surfaces were ideal for experimentation inasmuch as the first autos lacked the extra horsepower to navigate hilly terrain. Besides, glacial gravels were sufficiently plentiful in the region to make road-building an easy matter. Lastly, an intense spirit of resourcefulness and enterprise, so characteristic of pioneer groups, flourished in the mid-West in contrast with the more conservative, tradition-bound East.

So much then for historical background. To understand the subsequent maturing of the industry it is necessary to recall some basic principles of locational economic theory. Every fabricating industry, such as auto manufacturing, lends itself to the combined pull of five vector forces: raw materials, fuel and power sources, market availability, the proximity of labor and capital pools, and transport arteries. Using these five rubrics, an attempt will be made to explain the geographical patterns which the American auto industry has historically assumed.

Locational Factors Peculiar to the Automotive Industry

The assembly line nature of the industry rules out its being oriented to raw materials; it does not consume raw materials directly but in the form of semifinished and finished components such as steering shafts, cylinder blocks, bearings, axles, etc. The auto industry is so dependent on diverse material sources that when its assembly lines stop for lack of sales "a tide of secondary idleness washes through hundreds of other cities across the nation." A Ford chemist stated before World War II that Ford cars used cotton from 433,000 acres, wool from 800,000 sheep, hair from 87,500 goats, 11,200 acres of corn, 12,500 acres of sugar cane, 61,500 acres of soy beans, not to mention a fifth of the nation's steel and staggering quantities of rubber, glass, and textiles.[5]

The auto industry is not linked to any invariable factor such as land in the case of agriculture, or climate and flat land in the case of aircraft plants,[6] or raw materials as in the extractive industries.[7] Extractive industries, such as mining, lumber and whaling, have little locational freedom; reproductive industries, such as tobacco, cotton and fruit growing, must conform strictly to the natural conditions of soil, climate and topog-

[3] For further details consult Paul M. Banner, *Competition in the Automobile Industry* (Unpublished Doctoral Thesis, Cambridge: Harvard University, 1952), pp. 22-27.

[4] Since an abundance of the supply of hardwoods was present in the area at the turn of the century, the Mid-West attracted more than sixty percent of the total carriage production in the United States at that time. *Loc. cit.*

[5] Ralph Woods, *America Reborn: A Plan for Decentralization of Industry* (London: Longmans, Green & Company, 1939), p. 274.

[6] William G. Cunningham, *The Aircraft Industry: A Study in Industrial Location* (Los Angeles: Lorin L. Morrison, 1951), pp. 25 ff.

[7] C. H. Cotterill, *Industrial Plant Location: Its Application to Zinc Smelting* (St. Louis: American Zinc, Lead & Smelting Company).

raphy, while service industries, such as retailers, brokers and barbers, are predominantly market- and therefore urban-oriented.[8] Fabricating industries, such as auto producing, generally seek that site which affords optimum access to all the materials ingredient in the final product. This necessitates a compromise location.[9]

Essential to an understanding of the locational policies in the auto industry is its oligopolistic and highly competitive nature. There are three giant producers (General Motors, Ford and Chrysler) and three smaller independent producers of note (American Motors, Kaiser-Willys and Packard-Studebaker).[10] Entry into the field is extremely difficult, if not virtually impossible, due to the large capital investments required to maintain a vertically integrated productive process, a nation-wide dealer system and the exorbitant costs attendant upon advertising and establishing company prestige and goodwill.[11] Indicative of the difficulty involved in offering more than negligible competition to General Motors, Ford and Chrysler is the fact that together these three firms control about 95 percent of the market.[12] The fact

that within a span of a few years six independent companies merged into three companies indicates the oligopolistic nature of the American auto industry. Because of the sensitivity of their product to the business cycle and because of the huge investment requirements in the annual model change-over, the auto producers are quick to exploit any advantages which sound plant site decisions may yield. Such advantages are linked with: (a) the assembly-line nature of the industry; (b) freight-rate practices; (c) the economies of specialization; (d) labor volatility; (e) the process of technical maturing; (f) the pyramidal nature of large-scale production in the auto industry; (g) managerial decentralization policies among the "Big Three"; and (h) the multiplier effect in regional expansion.

The Assembly-Line Nature of the Automotive Industry

It is a well-known fact that the auto industry pioneered in mass-production techniques and spawned the assembly-line, which today can turn out a finished car every minute.[13] The refined subdivision of labor, the endlessly moving belt, the concourse of sub-assembly lines feeding into the main belt, the logistical wizardry required to supply basic items without, however, maintaining large plant inventories, the minute detailing of "lead-time" production plans to harmonize a process extending from the blue-

[8] G. T. Renner, "Geography of Industrial Localization," *Economic Geography*, July 1947, p. 167.

[9] E. B. Alderfer and H. E. Michl, *The Economics of American Industry* (New York: McGraw Hill Book Company, 1950), p. 145.

[10] All three firms were the product of mergers. As of 1953 there were six independent auto producing firms: Nash and Hudson (which later merged into the American Motors Company), Kaiser and Willys (later combined into Kaiser-Willys) and Packard and Studebaker (subsequently merged into Packard-Studebaker).

[11] Harold G. Vatter, "The Closure of Entry in the American Automobile Industry," *Oxford Economic Papers* (New Series), October 1952.

[12] From 1946 to 1954 the share of the market that went to the so-called "Big Three" (General Motors, Chrysler and Ford Motor Company) rose from 85.5 percent to 95.6 percent. General Motors' proportion has been as high as 55 percent; in 1957 it fell to 45 percent but in 1958 rose again to 50 percent. Ford's share of the automobile market hovers between 22 and 28 percent while Chrysler's proportion ranges from 15 to 20 percent. "New Hands at the Wheel of an Auto Empire," *U. S. News & World Report*, September 5,

1958, p. 63. Also *cf.*, Banner, *op. cit.*, chapter II. Another characteristic of oligopoly in the industry is General Motors' traditional role as the price leader. "Has GM Lost Price Leadership?", *Business Week*, November 9, 1957, p. 171.

[13] E. G. Fuller, "Automobile Industry in Michigan," *The Michigan Historical Magazine*, April 1928, pp. 280-296; Philip Van Doren Stern, *Tin Lizzie: The Story of The Fabulous Model T Ford* (New York: Simon & Schuster, 1955); Allan Nevins and Frank Ernest Hill, *Ford: Expansion and Challenge: 1915-1933* (New York: Charles Scribner's Sons, 1957); Harry Barnard, *Independent Man: The Life of Senator James Couzens* (New York: Charles Scribner's Sons, 1958).

print stage to the display floor—all have captured the imagination of the world and elicited the laments of sociologists and industrial psychologists the world over.[14]

The creation of the "Model T" Ford[15] added to the two fundamental principles of standardization and inter-change-ability three other steps: (1) the orderly progression of the product through the shop in a series of planned operations arranged so that the right part always arrives at the right place at the right time; (2) the mechanical delivery of these and of the assembled product to and from the operators; and (3) a breakdown of operations into their simple constituent motions.[16]

The assembly-line permits larger integrated firms with annual sales volumes of tens of thousands of autos to offset the costly investment for machines, jigs, dies and tool fixtures by means of volume production of standardized parts. Only the "Big Three" can afford the burdens of a heavy automation program and the yearly re-tooling which accompanies model re-design. The assembly-line operation, in permitting a divorce among parts-manufacture, sub-assembly and final assembly, enables centralization of operations where component and semi-finished parts are concerned and a de-centralization of regional assembly plants. Consequently, the "Big Three" have centralized the assembly of component parts and units (e.g., chassis, pistons, transmissions) in and around Detroit, to take advantage of nearness to mid-Western suppliers and then have arranged to ship these assembled units to regional assembly plants for final assembly in order to reap the economies of proxim-

ity to local markets. This divorce between the parts manufacture and the final assembly phase enables sizeable economies; however, it leads to vulnerability in the event of civil or military disaster. This was demonstrated in 1953 when one of the nation's greatest industrial fires struck the General Motors hydromatic-transmission plant at Livonia, Michigan and crippled some twenty percent of the industry's auto production.[17]

One sees how geographically strategic is the location of Detroit, equidistant between both coasts and advantageously situated for shipment of parts to regional assembly plants in any part of the nation.[18] The economies which attach to the centralization of facilities manufacturing auto parts and accessories become obvious when one considers how dependent the early phases of auto production are on nearby industries. In the Great Lakes area are concentrated such vital industries as electric generating stations, electrical machine producers, foundry shops. Besides, the iron ore resources of the Lake Superior region and the proximity of steel centers such as the Chicago-Gary area, Pittsburgh-Cleveland area, not to mention Akron's rubber supplies and the area's rail and water transport facilities, are location factors of great moment. The early phase of parts manufacture and primary assembling is then distinctly materials-oriented and labor-oriented and as such seeks out urban locations near basic suppliers and pools of semi-skilled and skilled workers. The later phase of final assembly is market-oriented and is therefore decentralized to reduce transport costs to the dealer.

[14] Charles R. Walker and Robert H. Guest, *The Man on the Assembly Line* (Cambridge: Harvard University Press, 1952), p. 180 ff.

[15] Peter Drucker, *The New Society* (New York: Harper & Brothers, 1950), p. 1.

[16] Walker and Guest, *op. cit.*, pp. 10-11.

[17] William B. Harris, "The Great Livonia Fire," *Fortune*, November 1953, p. 132 ff. Also "General Motors Segregates Its Transmission Output," *Automotive Industries*, June 1, 1954, p. 33.

[18] J. A Quinn, "The Hypothesis of Median Location," *The American Sociological Review*, April 1943, pp. 148-156.

Freight Rate Practices in the
Automotive Industry

Prior to 1936 the industry's advertised price differed markedly from delivered price because of accessories, state and local taxes, and carrying charges on sales-financing contracts. In that year the Automotive Manufacturing Association published a list of agreed-price quotations. This led to the practice of including freight charges from the home plant (Detroit in the case of the "Big Three" and most independents) to the regional assembly plant in the final selling price. This meant that the customer paid freight on a fully assembled car shipped from Detroit even though the car was actually shipped unassembled from Detroit to a plant near the dealer. Whereas only four assembled cars can be loaded into a freight car, some twelve "knocked-down" (unassembled) cars can be shipped from Detroit and later assembled into final form for distribution.[19] In any event the customer pays the freight bill—f.o.b. Detroit. Supposing the car were assembled in New Jersey and marketed in New York, using 1955 prices, the differential between the shipping costs incurred by the producer and the freight bill paid by the customer would be $50 a model.[20]

By applying modern techniques of linear programming to determine the most profitable location of regional assembly plants in relation to earlier assembling phases and later marketing operations,[21] companies such as Ford and General Motors can, because of their nation-wide network of assembly plants, operate their own basing point system. The only difference between the method employed in the auto industry and basing point is that the customer absorbs the freight charge, not Ford or General Motors. The transportation charge, with its element of "phantom freight," has in the past swelled the profits of those auto producers who could avail themselves of the practice.[22]

The more common practice in American industry (e.g., steel) is freight absorption by the manufacturer even to the point of quoting a lower delivered price in more remote markets than in the home market. In the case of General Motors and Ford, however, there is the anomalous situation in which a seller has less competition from producers in a remote market than in the home market.[23] The apparently inflationary nature of freight policies of Ford and General Motors are understandable in the light of the industry's concentration in the Michigan area, the vertical structure of the industry's production process and the assembly-line nature of its operations. Other industries with different structures must follow other freight pricing policies;[24] one should not

dustry. The author is indebted to a pilot study done by John F. Kain, *Linear Programming—An Answer to the Automobile Distribution Problem* (Mimeographed Copy, Bowling Green College, 1957).

[22] It has been estimated that General Motors made $33 million in 1938 on "phantom freight"; the Federal Trade Commission announced that the corporation's profits for that year were $77 million. If the "phantom freight" profits were accurately gauged, then 42 percent of General Motor's profits in 1938 were from this single source. "Chevrolet," *Fortune*, January 1939, p. 108.

[23] Naturally, Chrysler and the independent auto firms sought to have the Interstate Commerce Commission stabilize the situation by lowering the Detroit freight rate and by increasing rates from branch assembly plants. "Auto Freight Row," *Business Week*, December 2, 1950, pp. 20-21; also, *Hearings Before the Subcommittee on Automobile Marketing Practice of the United States Senate Interstate and Foreign Commerce Committee. Statement of Mr. Frederic G. Donner, Vice-President of General Motors, 1956.*

[24] E. M. Hoover, *The Location of Economic Activity* (New York: McGraw Hill Book Company, 1948), p. 55.

---

[19] This figure is based on the estimate of industry experts who insist that it is unthinkable to give a figure of 40 "knocked-down" autos per freight car. The number 40 is the figure found in the 1950 edition of E. B. Alderfer and H. E. Michl, *The Economics of American Industry, op. cit.,* p. 165.

[20] Further savings are possible, obviously, when cars are transported from the assembly plant to the local dealers on specially designed two-story motor carriers. *Ibid.,* p. 165.

[21] The use of computers and linear programming are becoming widespread management tools in determining the most profitable distribution arrangements in the auto in-

forget that dealerships play a critical role in the auto business. As members of the service or tertiary segment of our economy, auto dealers are urban-oriented.[25] Where population density is heaviest, there are the dealers and where the dealers are close by will be found the regional assembly plants. At this phase of operations decentralization brings the greatest rewards.

The Economies of Specialization in the Automotive Industry[26]

In the earlier stages connected with manufacturing parts and accessories the auto industry reveals a nucleated pattern designed to reap the competitive advantages associated with (1) the principle of multiples, (2) the principle of the massing of reserves, and (3) the principle of bulk transactions.

The principle of multiples offers a major producer the opportunity to offset what is known as the imperfect divisibility of units of equipment and labor. An example will make this clear. In the Detroit Plymouth plant there are, say, four key pieces of equipment: (1) a 6-spindle boring machine which rough-bores cylinder blocks two at a time; (2) a multiple spindle drill press which drills 110 holes simultaneously; (3) a special automatic 6-spindle grinder which faces the hand valve seats at the rate of 90 motor blocks per hour; and (4) a milling machine which cuts pistons to specified dimensions.[27] Assuming that these machines are used in successive steps and that daily unit capacities for

these machines are respectively 1000, 1250, 1500, and 3000, then the plant's daily output should be 15,000 or some multiple of 3000 higher than 15,000 if all the machines are to be used at full capacity. It is this principle of multiples which is continually at work in auto centers such as Saginaw, Lansing, Pontiac and Detroit, where large scale economic concentration insures a minimum of waste, curtailed production and "downtime" for heavy equipment.

How does the principle of the massing of reserves operate in large auto producing units? A giant car manufacturer is in a position to dispense with the larger margin of inventory resources which smaller operators must maintain against demand fluctuations, production interruptions, accidents, etc.[28] With a far-flung system of branch assembly plants the "Big Three" can readily estimate the individual requirements of each branch more closely than a smaller competitor might since they know statistically that the fluctuations of requirements in each branch will cancel out. This is an obvious advantage at the concentrated stage of automotive operations where production is geared for a national demand and not just for a local demand as is the case with the regional assembly plants.

As for the principle of "bulk transactions," it is fairly obvious that large manufacturers enjoy considerable bargaining power in closing contracts for material purchases, advertising and dealer arrangements. A company such as Kaiser-Willys, with an average annual output of some 100,000 cars, could not

---

[25] "How to Build a Dealer Empire; Strategy of the Edsel Campaign," *Business Week*, June 22, 1957, p. 52 ff. This is an interesting account of the detailed market studies the Ford Motor Company made in order to introduce a new car onto the market.

[26] Henry Ford once said: "There is no point in centralizing manufacture unless it results in economies. If we, for instance, centered our entire production in Detroit we should have to employ about 6 million people." Cited in Lewis Mumford, *Technics and Civilization* (New York: Harcourt, Brace & Company, 1934).

[27] Alderfer and Michl, *op. cit.*, p. 158.

[28] For a discussion of the role of mass production economies in General Motor's operation, see, *Profit Margins at General Motors: A Background Study in Management Action*, The Corporate Director, American Institute of Management, July 1956. For a short treatment of the dimensions of risk and investment involved in predicting market demands and determining new car designs, see, Joseph C. Ingraham, "Detroit's Billion-dollar Gamble," *The New York Times Magazine*, June 29, 1958, pp. 16-17.

possibly sustain the tremendous overhead burdens which a General Motors must carry as a condition for its extensive plant expansion, automation programs, annual model change-overs and "hippodrome" advertising campaigns.[29] Not only are important items such as gas, electricity and water sold to industrial consumers at graduated rates, but a predictable and sizeable volume of business furnishes a safe margin for capital investment and bulk buying at propitious fluctuations of the market and the business cycle.[30]

Geared to volume production in order to avail itself of the triple advantages of the principle of multiples, the massing of reserves and bulk transactions, the industry seeks an expanding market. In doing so its aim is "to create both consumer satisfaction and consumer desire, and at the same time."[31] In executing its program of planned obsolescence, the auto manufacturers employ classy dealers' showrooms, mass-advertising and the annual model change to create consumer dissatisfaction within a relatively short time. The fact that some degree of success has been attained in this respect is borne out by statistics: more than 35 million families own almost 50 million cars; 35 million of these cars are postwar vintage and some 12 percent of all car owners in America own two or more vehicles.[32] Thus it becomes relatively clear how specialization and volume production go hand in hand. The result has been the entrenchment of three companies as production leaders with negligible rivalry from other producers, the geographic concentration of the early phases of manufacture in Michigan and the diffusion of assembly plants to handle regional demands of a national market.[33]

Labor Volatility in the Automotive Industry

The most unpredictable labor market in the entire economy is to be found in the automotive industry and the most mercurial labor center is unquestionably Detroit. Consider some essential facts. Work is seasonal; mass lay-offs invariably occur during the model change-over period. The greater part of the working force is not skilled; reliable estimates claim that 65 percent of the industry's total force of 900,000 is made up of assemblers, janitors, sweepers, stock shipping clerks, receivers, checkers and sundry unskilled employees.[34] The instability of the industry is further aggravated by the fact that the product marketed is one whose purchase can be deferred if signs of recession set in.[35] Consequently, both dealers and personnel lead uncertain lives.[36]

This uncertainty has led to the creation of the powerful United Automobile Workers' Union which has secured high wage scales for its members to offset the disincentives of assembly-line monotony and seasonal lay-offs. Few industries have had labor-management relations

[29] "Smaller Makers of Autos Hit Hard," *The New York Times*, April 18, 1954, pp. 1, 9. Also, Charles E. Egan, "General Motors is Subject for Case Study in Bigness," *The New York Times*, Sunday, *News of the Week in Review*, December 11, 1955, p. E 7.

[30] E. M. Hoover, *The Location of Economic Activity, op. cit.*, p. 80.

[31] A statement of Alfred P. Sloan, Jr., then Chairman of the Board of Directors for General Motors. Quoted in James C. Jones, "How They Plan the Car You Want," *The American Legion Magazine*, June 1954, p. 51.

[32] *Automobile Facts and Figures*, (37th Edition) Automobile Maufacturers Association, 1957, pp. 20-35.

[33] For a treatment of the incentives which exist in diverse types of business toward agglomeration into a relatively small number of clusters. *see*, E. M. Hoover, *The Location of Economic Activity, op. cit.*, pp. 120-121.

[34] *Employment Outlook in the Automobile Industry*, United States Bureau of Labor Statistics, Bulletin Number 1138, Washington, D. C., 1953; also, *Automobile Facts and Figures, op. cit.*, pp. 62-68.

[35] The industry is regarded by its representatives as being income elastic and not price elastic. Thus, it is believed, that annual income levels of the average American consumer affect car sales more than the price fixed by producers. Within limits, this is undoubtedly true.

[36] This was dramatically seen in the sharply curtailed payrolls, shortened work schedules and skip-weeks which the recession in early 1958 caused in the motor city of Detroit. A. H. Raskin, "Detroit: Focus of the Basic Duel," *The New York Times Magazine*, May 4, 1958, p. 7 ff.

which have been so marred by mutual bitterness and class anatagonism.[37] The nature of operations in the automotive industry is such that the union is ever seeking new claims; the "guaranteed annual wage" demand was a counterweight to the adoption of automation programs by car producers. Critically dependent upon a large urban pool of unskilled, semi-skilled and skilled employees, the industry has reluctantly yielded to union requests.[38]

The auto industry's labor situation has serious locational implications: it is a general principle of locational theory that a less costly center of labor diverts the industrial process from its cheapest transportation point at that moment when labor savings at a new site exceed the additional transportation costs.[39] Detroit labor costs are very high due to a combination of factors; the concentration of the industry in a single area making it vulnerable to strikes and work stoppages; the strength and quality of the union and its leadership; the uncertainty of income payments; the high cost of living in Detroit and environs; the repetitive nature of the industry's operations with concomitant psychic dissatisfaction which must be compensated for in a monetary manner.[40]

The result is a tendency to seek plant sites in areas where labor is cheaper, less troublesome and free from a tradition of hostile labor-management relations. Although industry-wide bargaining insures equality of payment throughout the nation, definite advantages nevertheless accrue to, say, a Southern location rather than one in the mid-West. Workers there will be much more satisfied with wage rates than those in a city with a high living standard. Secondly, no tradition of labor strife exists. Thirdly, management can install labor-saving machinery and automatic equipment more readily in such a branch plant than in an established one. This is not to say that automation eliminates workers over the long run but merely to assert an undeniable fact—namely, the resistance of workers and the union to automation. There has been a real decentralizing force at work in the industry; management cherishes harmonious relations with its labor force and will go to great expense to achieve this ideal. One manufacturer moved his plant 400 miles to insure continuous production, free from the frequent and violent labor disturbances he experienced at his original site.[41] The deviation in the industry from traditional patterns of nucleation is due in large measure to the desire to mitigate as much as possible the volatility and antagonism found historically in the Detroit region.

The Process of Technical Maturing in the Automotive Industry

Discussion of the auto industry's labor problems leads naturally into the question of tehnological advance. The working staff, which is trained for highly specialized operations even of an unskilled nature, has been highly paid as we

[37] The beginnings of the United Automobile Workers' Union are found in, Irving Howe and B. J. Widick, *The UAW and Walter Reuther* (New York: Random House, 1949), pp. 1-309.

[38] Here the principle of the "massing of reserves" applies in reverse inasmuch as labor, by use of the ritual strike, can force management's hand. The auto union, for example, protested in the winter of 1951 when Ford decided to decentralize the River Rouge plant in the name of national security without, at the same time, refusing to divert any of its billion dollar defense contract to its Iron Mountain-Kingston plant in upper Michigan, a site well outside the defined target area for urban localities. "Union Protests Sale of Ford Plant," *The Wage Earner*, December 1951, p. 6.

[39] Carl J. Friedrich, *Alfred Weber's Theory of Location* (Chicago: University of Chicago Press, 1929).

[40] Peter Drucker, *Concept of a Corporation* (New York: The John Day Company, 1946), pp. 176-208; also, Walker and Guest, *op. cit.*, pp. 156-163.

[41] An incentive to plant re-location also exists where labor and tax policies are influenced by local or state legislation. For instance, one Wisconsin firm, with an annual tax charge of $68,000, moved to another state where its tax liability was $16,000 (or 75 percent) less. Ralph L. Woods, *op. cit.*, pp. 341-343.

have seen. The labor pool has had a monopoly position due to the extreme degree of concentration of production in and around Detroit. However, with increasing scatter the industry's dependence on a central labor pool becomes concomitantly relaxed. The locational histories of most individual industries have typically involved an early stage of increasing concentration followed by a stage of redispersion.[42] The auto industry reflects this characteristic. As an infant industry with peculiar problems it succeeds in combining appropriate basic skills with managerial resourcefulness, financial support and enterprising engineers. With the introduction of standardization of parts and mass-production techniques the industry became rooted in the Detroit area where it could be close to independent suppliers.

Since 1940, however, the industry has been in a maturing stage. The war led to many government contracts and served as a catalytic agent in expanding the industry and in dispersing it geographically. The application of automatic controls and electronic devices, the new methods of marketing and distribution, the refinement of advertising techniques have all cooperated to bring the industry out of its period of industrial adolescence.[43] Competition and scientific advances have eliminated many of the crudities and accidental elements in car production. The overhauling of the monolithic Ford Empire in the mid-1950's has been dramatic proof of this fact.[44]

Maturity of the industry has brought with it what might be called an "hour-glass pattern." Flowing down from some 25,000 suppliers of independent parts and accessories through the concentrated plants of Ford, Chrysler, General Motors corporations and independent producers, America's autos gradually take shape and move outward toward the regional assembly plants and finally to some 45,000-odd dealers. The top half of the hour-glass is materials- and labor-oriented; the assembly plants in the early stages are dependent upon the basic suppliers in the Michigan area. These plants represent the stem of the hour-glass. From these Detroit-clustered plants are diffused the component parts and sub-assemblies which reach the decentralized branch assembly plants. These assembly plants, located near regional dealers, finish the assembly and send the finished product on to the 45,000-odd dealers, who represent the lower half of the hour-glass pattern. This pattern has been the result of years of integration, both vertical and horizontal as well as forward and backward. A brief history of the auto industry's integration reveals a stress on engineering and production in the early history of car production. Later, marketing became important and caused the disappearance of auto wholesaling. Forward vertical integration took place in the form of factory branches and dealerships controlled by the company. It was only to be expected that auto producers would want to exercise surveillance over car dealers where it concerned problems of financing, maintaining customer goodwill, "repeat" sales and institutional brand advertising. Vertical backward integration arose when Ford bought coal and iron ore mines, built and purchased steel plants, glass factories, rubber plantations, etc. In time, General Motors developed a refined system of horizontal

[42] E. M. Hoover, *The Location of Economic Activity, op. cit.,* pp. 174-176.

[43] An excellent treatment of the influence of automation on geographical patterns in industry is to be found in, David G. Osborn, *Geographical Features of the Automation of Industry* (Chicago: University of Chicago Press, 1953). "Detroit automation" (the mechanical counterpart of electronic feedback control) is explained in John Diebold, *Automation—The Advent of the Automatic Factory* (New York: D. Van Nostrand Company, 1952); also, Hans Roeper, *Die Automatisierung* (Stuttgart-Degerloch: Verlag Dr. Heinrich Seewald, 1958).

[44] Alderfer and Michl, *op. cit.,* p. 167.

integration, manufacturing such diverse products as diesel locomotives, electric fans, frigidaires, Allison engines, AC spark plugs, Delco radios and a host of other products (numbering in all over 40).[45] Over the years both Ford and General Motors have extended themselves forward, backward and laterally until the "hour-glass pattern" has emerged. Seeking to minimize costs and to maximize profits the large-scale auto manufacturers have concentrated where economic advantages dictated and decentralized to take advantage of market proximity at the final assembly stage. Since the finished product is bulky and susceptible to the weight-gain interpretation of locational economics, the market will always exert a strong locational pull on final assembly plants.[46] The f.o.b. Detroit pricing practice made this pull even stronger by making the consumer pay the all-rail-freight charge for a fully assembled car even when it is shipped more cheaply as a so-called "knocked-down" car.

Managerial Decentralization Policies Among the "Big Three"

Although managerial decentralization is a radically different concept from plant decentralization, both are not completely unrelated. It is common to find progressive firms with avowed managerial decentralization policies constructing modern one-story country plants away from congested urban areas. Divisionalization, as managerial decentralization is called in the auto industry, is a common practice among the "Big Three." Alfred P. Sloan first initiated the policy in his tenure as President of General Motors

from 1923 to 1937.[47] Both Ford and Chrysler, after many long years of remaining centralized in all levels of operations, followed General Motors' divisionalization program in the mid-1950's.[48] At the head of each division (e.g., Buick, Pontiac, Chevrolet in the case of General Motors) is a divisional chief who directs the affairs of the entire division as if it were an autonomous company in production and sales; moreover, a controller is charged with the financial supervision of each unit so that a closer check on costs may be maintained. Autonomy is so complete that divisions really compete with one another.

The significance of divisionalization for location, however, is that autonomy in divisional operations enables segments of the company's activities to seek sites outside of Detroit and away from the traditionally congested loci of auto production. Managerial decentralization reduces impersonal human relationships and as such enhances personnel satisfaction. Job satisfaction is difficult to measure empirically but it is a parameter which all management experts accept today for increasing plant efficiency. A moderate-sized community plant within an autonomous divisional unit can be placed in a semi-rural area, enabling an employee to ride from his bungalow-

---

[45] Ford's vertical integration and its historical origins are treated in Garet Garret, *The Wild Wheel* (New York: Pantheon Books, Incorporated, 1952), pp. 96 ff. Ford's tapering integration is described in Alderfer and Michl, *op. cit.*, pp. 162-163. For a brief, popular discussion of General Motor's horizontal integration, *see*, "The Battle of Detroit," *Time*, November 1, 1954, pp. 90.

[46] C. J. Friedrich, *op. cit.*, passim.

[47] Peter Drucker, *Concept of the Corporation, op. cit.*, pp. 41-71.

[48] The rapid growth of the American economy and its bellwether industry of auto production together with close competition among the "Big Three" have caused successive changes in organization structure in General Motors, Ford Motor Company and the Chrysler Corporation. General Motors' organizational development can be traced in Peter Drucker, *Concept of the Corporation, ibid.*; "New Hands at the Wheel of an Auto Empire," *op. cit.*, p. 60 ff. Ford's re-organization is described in: "An Auto Empire Decentralizes and Reorganizes," *Business Week*, October 17, 1953, pp. 130-4; "Ford's Fight for First," *Fortune*, September 1954, p. 123 ff.; James C. Jones, "The New Ford Drive," *The American Legion Magazine*, January 1955, p. 22 ff.; "Co-Captains in Ford's Battle for Supremacy," *Life*, February 28, 1955, p. 84 ff; "Ford Gets Full Line at Last," *Business Week*, June 22, 1957, p. 45 ff.; Chrysler's managerial posture has been set forth in "The Chrysler Situation," *Fortune*, April 1954 and "Chrysler Restyles Its Executive Structure," *Business Week*, November 3, 1956, p. 85 ff.

type home to a spacious parking lot near the plant, free from all the inconveniences of commuting. In addition, auto plants generally have high land-extensive requirements for in-line productive processes which cannot ordinarily be accommodated by city lofts or a crowded urban site. Detroit has consequently experienced the migration of many types of businesses, including automotive production, which are land-extensive.[49] Divisionalization serves to flatten out the organization chart and to dispose of a company's operations for that degree of physical plant decentralization which has been a notable phenomenon in the auto industry in the decade after the end of World War II.

The Multiplier Effect in the Regional Expansion of the Industry

Probably the greatest single force in mitigating the historical centripetal tendencies of the American auto industry is the growth of the broad middle-class suburban market. Constituting only 19 percent of the nation's population in 1953, America's suburban families accounted for 20 percent of the nation's spendable income. The automobile is not only a sought-after item in suburbia (with not a few families owning two cars) but the auto has made suburban and rural habitation possible.[50] With the establishment of new communities and new urban strips in the Pacific Northwest, the Old South, the Gulf Coast and the Pacific Coast, new markets will arise and prompt the auto industry to set up dealerships and regional assembly plants in the vicinity. The attraction of new, wealthy

markets will likewise precipitate the building of metalworking facilities, tool and die establishments, foundries, parts and accessories manufacturers, who will seek to supply the needs of the regional plants which the industry will have introduced. A glance at the new assembly plants erected by the "Big Three" in the decade from 1945-1955 indicates a trend toward such dispersed sites as Los Angeles (General Motors, Ford and Chrysler); Atlanta (Ford and General Motors); Louisville (Ford); San Jose, California (Ford); Metuchen, New Jersey (Ford); Arlington, Texas (General Motors); Wilmington, Delaware (General Motors); and Framingham, Massachusetts (General Motors).

There are several multiplier effects at work in this regional expansion of the automotive industry. Motor vehicles are serving to accelerate the phenomenon of suburban living; as higher income levels become fixed in these non-urban locales an attractive natural market area arises for goods and services. Thus, in contributing to nation-wide decentralization the auto industry is effecting *pari passu* its own decentralization. In addition to this consumer multiplier effect there is also a consumer-goods multiplier effect noticeable. This consists in the relocation in newer regions of the United States of major industries and corporations which are large users of motor vehicles.[51] Sufficient demand on the part of newly situated customers can exercise a strong geographical magnetism on the auto industry, even at the earlier productive stages. Conversely, the relocation of basic suppliers of the auto industry is an invitation to auto producers to locate plants to be nearer to sources of capital, and to processed and unprocessed ma-

---

[49] Paul M. Reid, *Industrial Decentralization, Detroit Region, 1940-1950 (Projection to 1970)*, Detroit: Regional Planning Commission, June 1951.

[50] "The Lush New Suburban Market," *Fortune*, November 1953, p. 131; Joseph C. Ingraham, "Auto, Multiplying Faster than Man, Rule, Inconvenience and Frustrate Urban Life," *The New York Times*, January 28, 1957; and Neil P. Hurley, "New Patterns in American Commuting," *Social Order*, September 1958, pp. 343-349.

[51] This was undoubtedly one of the significant locational pulls in General Motors' selection of a plant site at Arlington, Texas to fulfill government defense contracts during the Korean episode.

terials, thus to minimize transport costs.

Similar trigger effects are also evident in locational changes in the earlier stages of production. The gradual depletion of iron ore sources in the Mesabi Range in the Lake Superior area is affecting a modification of traditional geographic patterns in the steel industry and less immediately on dependent consumer industries, of which the largest is the auto industry. Take the example of the Fairless Works which United States Steel Corporation put up in 1952 at Morrisville, Pennsylvania in order to be close to imported Venezuela ore and Eastern markets.[52] In the wake of further decentralization of the steel industry a production-multiplier effect will influence the auto industry to locate near the relocated steel mills and the metalworking shops which spring up around them.

Capital equipment multiplier effects should also be mentioned since budding industrial opportunities in new regions such as Dallas, Texas and Los Angeles, California attract investors and financial interests. Mention has already been made of the readiness of mid-West financiers to invest in the infant auto industry as contrasted with the conservative Eastern banking houses. Certainly the postwar boom made it relatively easy to float reasonably sound business ventures. The experience of the Kaiser Company in attempting to achieve entry in the automotive field proved the availability of capital in an expanding market economy.

Obviously, the multiplier effects can cooperate toward centralization equally as effectively as toward decentralization just as it can confirm the economic anemia of "stranded areas" (e.g., mill towns in New England and coal towns in Pennsylvania). However, the post-war trend in the auto industry has been toward scatter and the multiplier effects with its tandem reactions and mutual causation have helped the process to gain momentum.[53] Since 1940 the profile of American industry has undergone a marked change.[54] Although it will be decades before the primacy of Michigan as the nation's auto state will be seriously challenged, there seems little doubt that Michigan is losing its historic position of dominance.[55] To mention but one highly significant factor, automation is working a revolution in the auto industry as profound as that of Ford's assembly-line techniques. Automation effects the locational factors of space and labor suchwise that the industry is growing more "footloose" than it was formerly.[56] The "Big Three" of the auto industry are in a position to keep astride of the tide of expanding markets, technological advance, managerial decentralization and geographic de-concentration which has swept the entire American economy in the years

---

[52] The long-standing basing point system gave way in 1948 to the f.o.b. ("free-on-board") mill freight pricing policy. Under the latter system, proximity to markets exercises a strong locational pull.

[53] Input-output analysis studies can contribute to a better understanding of the casual interactions involved in the multiplier effect. "Considered from the point of view of the input-output scheme any national economy can be described as a system of mutually interrelated industries or . . . . interdependent economic activities." Wassily Leontiff, *Studies in the Structure of the American Economy* (New York: Oxford University Press, 1953), p. 9; also, Walter Isard, "Distance Inputs and the Space Economy," *The Quarterly Journal of Economics*, May and June 1951, pp. 181-198; 373-399 of Volume LXV.

[54] Glenn McLaughlin, "Regional Problems of Industrialization," Chapter IX, *Economic Reconstruction*, Ed., by Seymour E. Harris (New York: McGraw Hill Book Company, 1945), pp. 163-179.

[55] George Katona and James Morgan, "The Quantitative study of Factors Determining Business Decisions," *The Quarterly Journal of Economics*, December 1952, p. 73; Rex Henrickson, *Trends in the Geographic Distribution of Suppliers of Some Basically Important Materials Used at The Buick Motor Division—Flint, Michigan*, The Institute for Human Adjustment, The University of Michigan, March 1953; H. H. Ormand, "How Ford Selects Plant Sites," *American Business*, June 1946, pp. 12 ff.

[56] For a discussion of possible economic effects in the American automotive industry due to automation, *see*, John Robert Summerfield, *Some Economic Effects of the Development of Automatic Process Controls in American Industry* (Unpublished Doctoral Thesis, Berkeley: University of California, 1954), pp. 1-180; also, David G. Osborn, *op. cit.*

following World War II. Nor is there any portent that these trends will reverse themselves.[57]

So much for the economic factors in the locational policies of auto manufacturers. Just a word about the attempts of the national government and private industry to minimize atomic vulnerability in the age of the hydrogen bomb by a conscious strategy of dispersal. The inauguration of the National Industrial Dispersion Program by President Truman in 1951 sought to use accelerated tax amortization privileges as part of the defense contract program to encourage industry to locate new plants outside of defined target zones. The significance of the auto industry as a prime defense industry and its highly vulnerable nature have led the industry's executives to consider industrial dispersal as good business insurance where dispersal does not openly conflict with predominating economic goals.[58]

Summary and Conclusions

While substantially sound economic reasons existed for the birth and growth of the auto industry in and around Detroit, certain happenstance factors such as the local presence of inventors and men gifted with engineering genius also played a role. With the development of highways and such dependent industries as petroleum and steel, the industry grew into an "hour-glass pattern" whereby the manufacture and assembly of component parts became decidedly centralized in and about Detroit while the later operations of final assembly and distribution were scattered in order to reduce transport costs on a product which gained substantially in bulk and weight in the ultimate assembly phase.

Mass-production methods have led to widespread division of labor and specialization of function in all phases of the productive process. This together with dependence upon a large supply of skilled and unskilled labor and ready access to semi-fabricated materials, parts and accessories dictated the nucleated patterns of the industry in the productive stages leading up to final assembly. The policy of charging the customer f.o.b. Detroit freight rates on a fully assembled car while shipping "knocked-down" cars to regional assembly plants confirmed General Motors and Ford in a policy of maintaining a vast network of branch assembly plants.

Furthermore, the economies attaching to the principles of multiples, massed reserves and bulk transactions enable large-scale auto producers to reap the advantages of spreading lowered fixed costs over a great volume of finished goods. Without the economies of mass-production, concentration in the earlier production stages and oligopolistic features, it is doubtful if the industry could have succeeded in bringing the auto within the price range of the average American family. Only a giant producer can afford a policy of nation-wide branch assembly plants near regional markets, expensive automation and re-tooling programs for annual model change-overs, extravagant advertising campaigns and a vast arterial system of dealers under agreement to the factory.[59] Helping decen-

[57] For future prospects, see, "New Era Coming in Autos," *U. S. News & World Report*, June 13, 1958, p. 51 ff.; "Autos: A Market So Big You Can Drown in It," *Business Week*, February 6, 1954, p. 50 ff.; "Industry Studies Auto Styling as Key to Sell New Engineering," *Business Week*, November 10, 1956, p. 123 ff.; "The Small Car—What Are the Facts?," *U. S. News & World Report*, August 15, 1958, p. 64 ff.; and "What's Next in Autos?," *U. S. News & World Report*, May 2, 1958, p. 38 ff.

[58] Neil P. Hurley, "The American Achilles Heel," *National Defense Transportation Journal*, July-August 1956, p. 38 ff.

[59] *An Engineering Interpretation of the Economic and Financial Aspects of American Industry: The Automotive Industry* (New York: George S. Armstrong & Company, 1955); *The Automobile Industry* (New York: Merrill Lynch, Pierce, Fenner & Beane, 1953).

tralization trends in the auto industry is management's desire to settle in new regions where no tradition of labor strife exists, where workers are more content with their wages and where resistance to labor-saving devices is minimal.

Since motor vehicles render suburban living possible, the industry is contributing to its own decentralization by marketing a product which encourages industrialization and population of new regions, thus creating markets which eventually will exercise a locational pull on the industry itself. The overall maturing of the American economy in all regions, the rapid technological strides in the fields of chemical, electronic, atomic and solar energy, the radial growth of transport and communication lines all involve multiplier effects and economic chain reactions which are dissolving the traditional, deep-seated concentration of auto production in the Michigan area.[60]

[60] Automobile Manufacturers Association, "What's Next in Autos?" *A Chronicle of the Automobile Industry in America,* 1952.

FINDING THE BEST PLANT LOCATION

ROBERT A. WILL*

You have just been handed the assignment of finding a 20-acre site for your company's new facility somewhere on the U.S. mainland. The 48 contiguous states have a total of nearly two billion acres, which means your company needs 0.000001% of this area.

You may not think of your assignment in quite this light, and stating the problem in this way may be a bit far-fetched. But it does show that a lot of real estate must be eliminated from consideration before you reach that final 20 acres.

In looking for a site, you want the maximum economic benefits that a location can contribute to the facility. It is probably not oversimplifying the plant location study to say that it is completed in just two basic steps: (1) establishing as accurately as possible those requirements of the facility that will be influenced by location, including a relative weighting of these requirements; (2) applying these criteria to the largest geographical area that can be considered logically, then continuing to eliminate unqualified locations until only the best site remains.

Both steps are essential. Without correctly establishing the "ground rules" (Step 1), the results of the screening process (Step 2) are, at best meaningless, at worst incorrect.

The importance of a systematic approach to eliminating locations cannot be overemphasized. This has been demonstrated to us time and again by clients who set out to make their own study on a hit-or-miss basis, but who end up turning the project over to us, together with reams of information collected — most of it irrelevant.

STEP ONE: SETTING UP THE SCREEN

Just as the number of possible locations for a facility is virtually unlimited, so are the criteria that can be used to evaluate these locations. The trick is to keep the important criteria from being eclipsed by minor considerations. This becomes progressively more difficult as the study moves along.

The criteria that govern the approach to the screening process in the initial stages are primarily tangible economics; the intangibles are applied later. The tangibles, as we consider them, are the measurable costs.

Measurable costs are basically of two types: (1) the continuing costs affecting operation and (2) the one-time costs of setting up shop. The continuing costs, in most cases, consist mainly of inbound and outbound freight, labor, utilities and taxes. One-time costs are largely those of site acquisition and preparation, construction, and business organization taxes.

It is usually possible early in the study to pinpoint the lowest-cost area for shipments to customers (outbound freight), since in most situations there is but one lowest-cost area for this item. At the other extreme, the costs attributable to real estate taxes and the site are so localized that it is usually impossible to consider them until the final stages of the study. The accompanying table categorizes the more-frequent cost criteria by geographical pattern of occurrence. The descending order of classification also illustrates a logical order of screening steps appropriate to most site searches.

Costs Associated with a Site
Can Be Classified by Area

AREA OF OCCURRENCE	TYPE OF FACTOR	
	Continuing	One-Time
National	Outbound Freight	—
National or regional	Inbound Freight	—
National, with many regional and local variations	Labor Power Fuel Climate (heating and air conditioning)	Construction
State variations	Business taxes	Business organization taxes; sales tax on equipment and materials
	{ Air and water Pollution control Financing programs }	
Local variations	Water Real estate taxes	Building site

Note: Some consideration frequently must be given to other influences that may be neither one-time nor long-continuing. Such factors are usually related to governmental procedures. Examples are tax forgiveness to new industry for a specified period, right-to-work laws and transportation regulations.

THE INTANGIBLES

Not all important location criteria can be assigned a value as readily measurable as most of the cost considerations listed in the table. Yet, the intangibles can be of great and even overriding importance.

In our experience, we have seen intangibles range from the valid to the ridiculous. For example, a valid reason for rejecting a location, even though the cost picture looks good, is that key personnel necessary to the operation's success may refuse to move to the area because of unattractive living conditions. An example of a questionable intangible, which we see with increasing frequency, is the restriction of possible locations to those within a few miles of a commercial airport, to lessen executive travel discomfort. We would have to place in the ridiculous category a requirement, in one site search we know of, that all communities below a certain elevation be rejected because of management's belief that those people were not as likely to be as industrious as their highland cousins.

We cannot enumerate the many intangibles that should be applied to a plant location search, since they vary considerably with each situation and even with each company's philosophy. It suffices to mark the importance of intangibles, and to caution against going astray in their application.

STEP TWO: BEGINNING
THE SCREENING PROCESS

With the selection criteria tailored and weighted for the specific operation proposed, the screening of potential locations can begin. It is axiomatic that the more stringent the requirements, the easier the second step and the more positive the results.

By its very nature, applied screening requires considering the largest geographic area within reason, whether international, national, regional, state or local. It becomes essentially a matching process: match and reject; match and consider further.

A classic example from our files illustrates how two billion acres was boiled down to 100,000. (Admittedly, we are not often called upon to find a 100,000-acre site, nor is anyone else.) In this particular case, we were looking for a remote test site, somewhere in the U.S., for the future use of a major space-age company.

The size of the needed property established two immediate screening requirements for the survey, even before our client furnished us the specific criteria: (1) the site had to be purchasable at a very low cost per acre; and (2) since our client was a private organization without the government power of condemnation, the property had to have relatively few ownerships, to make it feasible to assemble one parcel of 150 square miles.

Our client also had a number of other requirements. For one thing, the proposed installation could not afford to be shut down or harassed by long periods of inclement weather. Also, it had to be within a reasonable distance of a fair-sized city, to provide supporting services as well as the amenities necessary to attract and retain scientists and engineers. And, finally, the client wanted a site on a navigable waterway to permit barge transportation of large space hardware.

With these rules set up, the screening process began. Starting with the 48 contiguous states, areas were eliminated by a series of map overlays. Application of climatic restrictions to the base map resulted in the disqualification of large areas (Fig. 1b). Here, snowfall, snow cover and temperature were the criteria used.

Since the Federal government owns large areas of land — parks, monuments, forests and military installations — which would not be available, this also was a restrictive factor. The elimination of such properties by the screening process is shown in Fig. 1c. This does not show the location of government-owned grazing lands, whose availability for the intended use at the time of the study could not be firmly established. Fig. 1c also shows those areas eliminated because of distance from a large support city.

By using topographic maps (1: 250,000 scale), the logical remaining areas of the country were checked for terrain and cultural features. Farmland values also entered into consideration. Ultimately, 14 logical areas were pinpointed. It was possible to complete this first screening process without even going into the field to see the prospective site areas.

Once the optimum areas are defined, the screening of communities and sites can begin. Here again, the established requirements continue to govern the procedure. Such requirements as acceptable community size, large water demands, the necessity of water transportation, and the absence of a competitor are typical of the restrictions frequently imposed. These restrictions reduce the possible locations to a manageable number prior to the start of detailed field investigation.

THE FIELD SCREENING

The plant location task has reached the point where it is now feasible to begin visiting locations. The screening becomes finer, since "X" number of locations have now been narrowed down to not more than a couple of dozen potential sites most of which should come reasonably close to satisfying the requirements.

Even with pre-screening, some communities can be disqualified when they are visited in the field, and need not be investigated further. Some of the more frequent reasons why we have eliminated locations include:

Prevalence of unusually high wage rates that our client could not meet and still remain competitive in his industry.

Announcement of a new industry that would soak up a good portion of the available work force.

Local resistance to new industry (most often found in college communities).

Inadequate or marginal water supply.

Labor shortages reported by local manufacturers.

Inadequate or marginal municipal power source, with alternative suppliers excluded from the area.

Absence of a workable site (this is more likely to be true in the case of process or heavy operations than for light manufacturing).

APPLYING ECONOMIC FACTORS

Screening for the remote test site mentioned previously did not permit

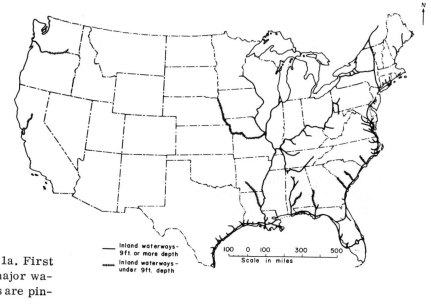

Figure 1a. First step: major waterways are pinpointed.

Inland waterways-
9ft. or more depth
Inland waterways-
under 9ft. depth

100 0 100   300   500
Scale in miles

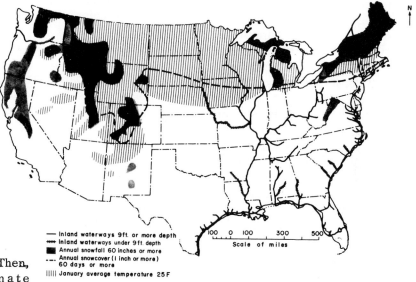

Figure lb. Then, cold climate eliminates some areas from consideration.

— Inland waterways 9ft. or more depth
⊦⊦⊦⊦ Inland waterways under 9ft. depth
■ Annual snowfall 60 inches or more
-·-· Annual snowcover (1 inch or more)
60 days or more
||||| January average temperature 25 F

100 0 100   300   500
Scale of miles

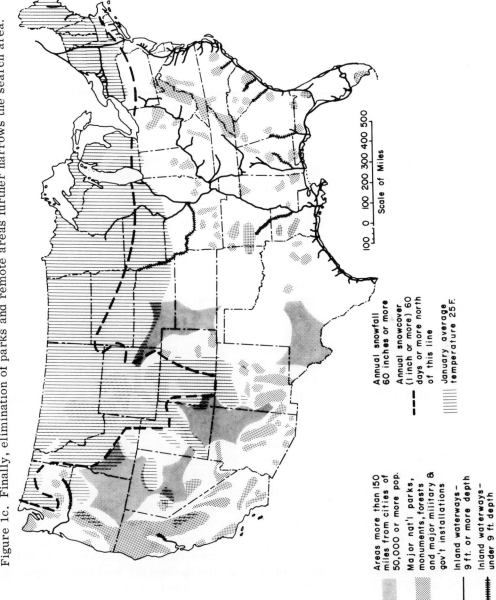

Figure 1c. Finally, elimination of parks and remote areas further narrows the search area.

Areas more than 150 miles from cities of 50,000 or more pop.

Major nat'l parks, monuments, forests and major military & gov't installations

Inland waterways – 9 ft. or more depth

Inland waterways – under 9 ft. depth

Annual snowfall 60 inches or more

Annual snowcover (1 inch or more) 60 days or more north of this line

January average temperature 25 F.

Scale of Miles

100 0 100 200 300 400 500

435

much application of operating-cost requirements in the first phase of the study. The result was that even after 14 widely scattered areas had been selected, we were not able to establish the most favorable region of the country. This could not be ascertained until specific sites within the 14 areas were checked out.

More typical, perhaps, is the location study for an operation with a high dependence on freight, labor and utility factors. A consideration of these basic requirements often quickly defines the optimum-cost region.

Although an early determination of the most favorable area is always comforting, it is not always possible. Witness the case of a flat-glass manufacturer, where opposing cost factors kept in suspense not only the exact site but also the region of the U.S. until near the end of the selection process. Gas and power costs, of major importance, were low in the middle South. The market center was in the Midwest. The result was a standoff between the two areas on combined utility and outbound freight costs. For a high-tonnage product like glass, we would expect that proximity to raw materials would then make the difference, since labor rates for the industry apply nationally and would not influence the cost picture.

The principal raw materials of glass (mainly sand, dolomite, limestone, soda ash and salt cake), plus packaging materials, were then checked as to availability and suitability within the survey area. For sand, the largest-tonnage material, locations of sources of supply were quickly established. Most of the

sand suppliers that could be considered were in the central Appalachian Mountain region. Further investigation soon revealed a number of underdeveloped sources, also within the favorable survey area. These included not only the Appalachian sandstones but midwestern sandstones, the unconsolidated sand deposits of central Tennessee and beach sands of the Gulf of Mexico. (We climbed several mountains and even rented a boat in the process of securing sand samples for testing.) Once a source was judged to be satisfactory, a cost for developing the supply and delivering it to the site also had to be established to make the picture complete.

Pinning down some of the other raw materials — particularly dolomite and limestone — proved to be nearly as difficult as sand. Here, we even considered the substitution of oyster shells for limestone in the Gulf area.

As with many process industries, availability of a large site was of major importance; the absence of such a site near a sand source was sufficient to disqualify some areas. If the location were to be in the Gulf Coast region and use beach sand and oyster shells, the site had to be accessible via barge transportation. For inland locations, situation on a navigable waterway also was desirable, since it offered some potential saving on soda ash transportation costs.

Adding all of the significant cost figures together showed that three of the potential locations, each in a different region, were nearly equal. Any one would have been a good location on the basis of meeting the tangible cost requirements established to guide the survey.

APPLYING THE INTANGIBLES

The glass-plant survey illustrates how the screening process continues to reduce the number of logical locations by application of cost criteria. At some point near the end of the screening, an impasse frequently occurs as the measurable cost differentials of the locations still in contention becomes less. This means that the intangibles will make the difference. It is time, then, for the final fine screening.

Some of the intangible criteria may reflect the corporate philosophy. Our experience is that the lighter types of industry are more likely to be influenced by the intangibles than the heavier ones because the easily measurable items of freight and utilities are relatively less important. One of the most extreme cases in our files is that of the space-age science company that requested that we compare an East Coast, a West Coast and a Gulf Coast location, to determine the cost of doing business in each. Our findings indicated a substantial advantage for the East Coast — with the West Coast running third. The company chose the West Coast location, despite the cost penalty, so it could be near the university that would contribute most to its technology.

The laboratory location problem is the epitome of the application of intangibles. Hardly anything about such a project can be assigned a dollar value. Yet the location of a laboratory should contribute to recruiting and retaining of the scientific personnel needed to ensure the operation's success. The presence of a major university (including access to the library) and "good living conditions" are widely proclaimed as essentials, but actually there are many cases where the absence of a university does not seem to be an insuperable handicap.

This is illustrated by a study we recently made for a chemical manufacturer headquartered in a moderate-sized city with no nearby major university. The problem was to determine whether another location might be more suitable for the laboratory — a move that would separate the laboratory from other company functions in the area. Investigation showed that qualified laboratory personnel were not recruited to the existing location as easily as they might have been in some of the major cities, but nevertheless could be attracted in adequate numbers. Once there, however, scientists were less likely to leave than would be probable in a larger metropolitan area. The company was overcoming the handicap of not having a major university by sponsoring special courses and cultural events, and by maintaining its own complete technical library — compensations that could be sustained indefinitely.

When all of the facts were evaluated, the company decided to retain its laboratories at the existing location. Had the laboratory been a newly conceived entity, it is likely that the important intangibles would have ruled out consideration of the community in which it was actually located. Superimposition of the advantages of remaining (also mostly intangibles, including easy intracompany liaison, general satisfaction of employees with community, reluctance of some to move, and a history of excellent labor relations) more than offset the probable advantages of another location in this case.

THE FINAL TOUCHES

We have seen how the location study begins with a large area, and by progressive screening, is narrowed down to several possibilities that are in close contention on a cost basis.

We are close to awarding the blue ribbon. Now is the time to be sure the school system has a high standard. Now is the time to meet local business leaders, to check further on labor conditions, to visit the country club, to talk with city of-ficials, and to form a general impression of the community.

Somewhere along the way, one of the locations will check out a little better than the others. Then is the time to option the best available site, negotiate a tax assessment, seek utility extensions, analyze soil conditions and do anything else necessary to bring the project to a successful conclusion. If all goes well, and everything checks out as hoped, the number one choice will get the new plant. If not, the final investigation can be transferred easily to an alternate location, secured by the knowledge that screening has provided a logical backup site.

WORKABLE COMPETITION IN THE SYNTHETIC RUBBER INDUSTRY[*]

CHARLES F. PHILLIPS, JR.

Washington and Lee University

For over twenty years students of business organization have been trying to define various concepts of workable competition. One of the most important questions remains unanswered: to what extent is the market performance of firms determined by the market structure of their industries? Or, to put the question in a slightly different form: in attempting to judge whether an industry is workably competitive, how should market performance and market structure be weighted?[1] This paper analyzes these problems with reference to the synthetic rubber industry.

The synthetic rubber industry was born during the early days of World War II, when the United States was cut off from natural rubber supplies. Then in 1955, after a long period of negotiations, the industry was sold to private enterprise.[2] It was delivered into private hands primarily through the "Rubber Producing Facilities Disposal Act of 1953."[3] Perhaps the major aim of this Act was "the development within the United States of a free, competitive, synthetic rubber industry."

The industry offers two unique features to the student of business organization. First, this was the first full-scale industry ever built by the Federal Government in the United States. During the war the Government financed fifty-one plants, representing a capital outlay of almost $700 million. From a meager production of 8,000 long tons of synthetic rubber in 1941, the industry was capable of producing more than a million long tons annually by the end of 1944.

Second, the transference of ownership of the rubber producing plants represented the first time in our history that Congress has had the final responsibility for establishing the structure of a private industry. It was against the background of our antitrust laws that Congress had to make its decision.

The first section briefly discusses the concept of workable competition. In the second section, the leading aspects of the synthetic rubber industry's market structure and market performance will be outlined. The final two sections will deal with workable competition in the synthetic rubber industry.

I

A purely competitive industry contains a large number of firms, none of which is able to exert a significant influence upon the market price of its products. A firm within such an industry accepts the price of its inputs, as well as the price of its outputs, as data.[4] Under these conditions, each firm selects an output level which maximizes short-run profits. As a consequence, long-run profit maximization is also assured. Competition among existing firms, together with the free entry of new firms and the free exit of existing firms, results in maximum economic efficiency throughout the industry and maximizes consumer satisfaction for the economy. Some of the more important results of pure competition are (1) the equality of prices and marginal cost, (2) the equality of factor prices and values of marginal physical products, and (3) the existence of zero pure profit levels.

No industry conforms exactly to all of the conditions and results of pure competition. Nevertheless, it is possible to examine the structure and performance of a particular industry against a background of explanatory hypotheses and to reach certain conclusions concerning the

---

[*] This paper is largely derived from the author's dissertation, "Competition in the Synthetic Rubber Industry," deposited in the library of Harvard University in 1959.

[1] See E. S. Mason, "The Current Status of the Monopoly Problem in the United States," *Harvard Law Review*, June 1949.

[2] R. A. Solo, "The Sale of the Synthetic Rubber Plants," *The Journal of Industrial Economics*, November 1953.

[3] Public Law 205, Act of August 7, 1953. (Hereafter referred to as the Disposal Act.)

[4] In addition to these necessary conditions, a perfectly competitive industry would require perfect knowledge and perfect factor mobility. See E. H. Chamberlin, *The Theory of Monopolistic Competition*, 7th ed. (Cambridge: Harvard University Press, 1956), pp. 6–7.

"Workable Competition in the Synthetic Rubber Industry" by Charles F. Phillips, Jr. Reprinted from Southern Economic Journal, *Vol. 28 (October 1961), pp. 154–162, with permission of author and publisher.*

degree to which they respond to market forces. Often evidences of competitive behavior can be found in markets in which competition is neither perfect nor pure. The question to be answered in the analysis of any industry, therefore, is how closely behavior satisfies the competitive norm. If the results are deemed satisfactory, the industry may be said to be effectively competitive.[5]

An industry may be designated as workably competitive in at least two other ways. First, an industry may be judged on the basis of the closeness with which the necessary conditions of pure competition are approximated in actual situations.[6] The main necessary conditions are: (1) a large number of buyers and sellers; (2) the absence of selling costs; (3) the acceptance of product and input prices as data; and (4) freedom of entry and exit. A judgment made on the basis of results might be different from one made on the basis of necessary conditions.[7]

Second, an industry might be judged workably competitive when, even in the absence of acceptable behavior under either criteria listed above, an alternative solution seems neither economically desirable nor legally feasible.[8] From an economic point of view, an existing market structure might well yield better market results than would any alternative structure. From a legal standpoint, an alternative solution might raise serious questions of "fairness" and "feasibility."[9] In either situation, public policy might support the status quo.

[5] J. M. Henderson, *The Efficiency of the Coal Industry* (Cambridge: Harvard University Press, 1958).

[6] J. W. Markham, *Competition in the Rayon Industry* (Cambridge: Harvard University Press, 1952); and D. C. Hamilton, *Competition in Oil* (Cambridge: Harvard University Press, 1958).

[7] "These analyses (of necessary conditions) provide valuable narratives which describe the nature of competition within particular industries, but tell little about results. The extent to which actual results deviate from those of perfect competition may not be directly related to the number of noncompetitive practices that can be listed, since the effects of one practice might offset those of another, and the same practice can cause quite different results under different circumstances." Henderson, *op. cit.*, p. 4.

[8] R. B. Tennant, *The American Cigarette Industry* (New Haven: Yale University Press, 1950); and Markham, *op. cit.*, p. 204.

[9] K. Brewster, "Enforceable Competition: Unruly Reason or Reasonable Rules," *American Economic Review*, May 1956, pp. 482–89.

II

The most important conclusions regarding the market structure and market performance of the synthetic rubber industry may be summarized as follows:

Market Structure

(1) In terms of production capacity the synthetic rubber industry is an oligopoly. The four-firm concentration ratio for the general purpose rubber[10] producers is 62 percent, representing a slight increase over the 1955–59 period. This overstates, however, the concentration of sales passing through the actual market, since the largest producers are also the most fully integrated. Nearly 51 percent of domestic SBR sales are "captive," representing either intercompany transfers or sales to affiliated or constituent companies (see Table I).

In the case of the three special purpose rubbers, concentration is high. Butyl is produced in two plants owned by Humble Oil & Refining Co., an affiliate of Standard Oil Co. (N.J.) Neoprene is made only at two plants of the duPont Co. Nitrile rubber is produced by five producers— the major rubber fabricators (Goodrich, Goodyear, U. S. Rubber, Firestone) and International Latex.

(2) The principal sellers in this market—a market which is segmented—are producers which have plants in three major areas: West Coast, Texas-Louisiana Gulf Coast, and the Northeastern belt. Buyers in the market include rubber fabricators, foreign purchasers, and jobbers. Most sales, however, are made either directly by producers to industrial users or through producer sales organizations. Sales contracts and partial requirements contracts are common.

(3) The market for nonintegrated shipments is not formally organized. Information on

[10] There are two major classifications of synthetic rubber. (1) General purpose rubber (Styrene-Butudiene Rubber: SBR), developed to replace natural rubber in major uses, accounts for nearly 82 percent of total synthetic production. (2) Special purpose rubbers (Butyl: IIR, Neoprene: CR, and Nitrile: NBR), developed to replace the natural product in certain uses, account for the remaining 18 percent. In the past three years a third major type, synthetic natural rubber, has been developed. This rubber has the same unit structure as the natural rubber hydrocarbon. To date, synthetic natural rubbers are not distributed on a wide basis.

TABLE I
SBR Capacity and Domestic Sales, 1959

	Percentage of capacity	Percentage of total domestic sales[a]	Percentage of domestic sales			
			Intracompany transfers	Affiliated or constituent companies	Big five rubber companies[b]	All other companies
Goodrich-Gulf	18.4	11.8	—	8.9	0.1	2.8
Goodyear	18.2	20.0	12.2	—	0.8	7.0
Firestone	15.6	17.9	10.4	—	0.2	7.3
Texas-U. S.	9.6	10.2	—	8.0	0.4	1.8
Phillips	8.2	7.2	—	—	1.2	6.0
Shell	7.0	7.1	—	—	3.5	3.6
Copolymer	6.4	9.0	—	6.0	1.4	1.6
A. S. R. C.	5.1	5.0	—	2.9	0.7	1.4
United Rubber	4.7	5.5	—	—	1.4	4.1
General	3.6	4.2	2.5	—	1.2	0.5
U. S. Rubber	2.2	1.8	0.5	—	0.1	1.2
All others[c]	1.0	0.3	0.1	—	—	0.2
Total	100.0	100.0	25.7	25.8	11.0	37.5

[a] Excludes domestic resale of purchased rubber.
[b] Excludes intracompany transfers and sales to affiliated or constituent companies.
[c] Includes Dewey & Almy Chemical Division, W. R. Grace & Co., and International Latex Corp.
Source: *Fifth Report of the Attorney General on Competition in the Synthetic Rubber Industry* (Washington, D.C.: U. S. Government Printing Office, 1960), pp. 14, 20.

prices is disseminated by individual producers and by way of trade journals. As a result, there is considerable scope for independent action on the part of competitors.

(4) Entry into the synthetic rubber industry is free from *artificial* restraints. Economies of scale are not so large relative to domestic market demand as to preclude the existence of a considerable number of optimum-size plants. The Disposal Commission was apparently successful in making sure that all SBR plant purchasers received needed patent licenses, and new entrants have experienced no difficulty in this connection.[11] No restraints on the access to raw materials have been uncovered. As for the channels of distribution and access to the final con-

[11] The one patent case, initiated in 1957, was recently settled in court. On June 9, 1960 the District Court for the District of Columbia ruled that General Tire & Rubber Co. was entitled to a product patent on tire treads made of high viscosity oil-extended synthetic rubber. Most SBR producers are now making such a product and are now foreclosed from purchasing and using this rubber for treads unless they enter license agreements and pay royalties to General. As General's claim is widely disputed in the industry, a series of patent infringement suits can be expected before the matter is finally resolved.

sumer, neither vertical integration nor the development of brand preferences has progressed so as to foreclose the market to the potential competitor. With entry free from artificial restraints, persistent and flagrant monopolistic behavior is unlikely. At the same time, the threat of rapid entry in response to short-term departures from competitive behavior is small.

However, for the nonintegrated outsider, entry is difficult. Within the past five years, three producers entered the industry. All three are large rubber industry producers. Two, Firestone and General, are members of the "Big Five" rubber companies and were the last of this group to enter into synthetic rubber production. The third, International Latex, is a large fabicator of latex rubber producers. These entrants had their own distribution channels, were fully integrated concerns, and even more importantly, had intracompany markets for their product.

(5) Rubber, being a producer's good, has a derived demand. Historically changes in rubber prices have had little effect upon the quantities of rubber consumed by industry. General economic conditions that influence the purchase of consumer goods, particularly automobiles, de-

termine how much rubber will be purchased annually.

In the rubber market, synthetics and natural rubbers are almost complete substitutes. The relative prices and qualities of these two materials are all important. During the past five years, synthetic rubber has enjoyed a marked advantage on both points. Synthetics can be made to meet precise specifications; natural rubber quality is far from uniform.[12] Since 1955, the price of synthetic rubber (SBR) has ranged from a low of 2½ cents to a high of 25½ cents a pound *below* the price of natural rubber. As a result of advantages both in quality and price, synthetic rubber now accounts for 66 percent of the domestic new rubber market.[13]

Market Performance

(6) By the usual definition synthetic rubber prices are administered—they do not move to equate short-run supply and demand conditions. Complete price stability has characterized the past five years, despite a change from a seller's to a buyer's market and a drop in output during 1958. Only one attempt has been made to change the base price structure. On May 1, 1956 Goodrich-Gulf increased its delivered base price for SBR. However, when other domestic producers failed to follow suit, the increase was promptly retracted and customers who purchased rubber at the increased price received refunds.[14]

(7) Seasonal and irregular fluctuations in monthly sales are absorbed by inventory adjustments. Production schedules lag demand changes by three or four months. Moreover, total unit costs increase sharply as output decreases below total capacity. A 25 percent reduction in SBR output for a plant with a 30,000 long ton rated capacity results in a rise of total unit costs of 14 percent.[15]

(8) The behavior of the price and output series strongly suggests that synthetic rubber producers place a higher premium upon short-run price stability than they do upon short-run profit maximization. And these facts, taken in connection with the industry's adoption of the Government's pricing policy based upon costs of production, indicate that the observed price behavior conforms to the kinked demand curve theory. This is reinforced by the small number of sellers, each selling an undifferentiated product, which suggests price uniformity. Throughout the period under consideration, no evidence of persistent deviations from published price lists have been found.

(9) There is no evidence that the industry is subject to chronic excess capacity. Synthetic rubber demand has experienced a rapid rate of expansion. Producers have shown no reluctance in expanding capacity or in building new capacity in line with demand increases. This also indicates that flexible prices are not too important for the maintenance of capacity utilization, which is fully consistent with the relatively inelastic nature of the industry's demand.

(10) Progressiveness has been persistent and improvements have not been noticeably retarded.[16] While prices have been held constant, buyers are receiving a higher quality product. Equally important synthetic rubber innovation has had at least three effects upon competition within the industry; the range of synthetic rubbers has increased, resulting in new markets; rivalry between the various types of synthetics has been intensified; and service competition heightened. These factors constitute a potential source of uncertainty within the industry and

[12] During the Korean War, when all natural rubber purchases were made exclusively by the Federal Government, it was possible to analyze all imports on a quality basis. After extensive analysis, it was found that 41.6 percent of all natural rubber imported into this country in 1951 was of a quality below the grade contracted. In addition to upgrading, sloppy packing by some overseas shippers has also represented a major point of contention between rubber importers and Far Eastern suppliers. Rubber Manufacturers Association, Inc., *Annual Report 1952.*

[13] C. F. Phillips, Jr., "The Competitive Potential of Synthetic Rubber," *Land Economics,* November 1960.

[14] Some price changes have occurred in various categories of synthetic rubber.

[15] *Chemical and Engineering News,* July 24, 1950, p. 2509, and House Committee on Armed Services, *Hearings on Disposal of Government-Owned Synthetic Rubber Producing Facilities,* 84th Cong., 1st Sess. (Washington, D.C.: U. S. Government Printing Office, 1955), p. 993.

[16] Polymer research has resulted in a continuous flow of new synthetic rubber types. Among these developments are urethane, fluoroelastomers, and synthetic natural rubbers. The range of synthetic rubbers also has increased, as over twenty new categories of the general purpose rubber have been put on the market.

make it impossible for any producer to take his market position for granted.

(11) Available data indicates that SBR producers have been earning a net return of 5 to 8 percent on their investment. In view of the growing nature of the industry this level does not seem excessive. Moreover, in connection with a lack of persistent rationing or excess capacity, the relative stability of these profit rates indicates a favorable rate of investment. Data on the growth rate of individual firms does not contradict the suggestion of independent action on the part of synthetic rubber producers.[17]

III

Do five years of private ownership indicate that the leading objective of the 1953 Disposal Act—"the development within the United States of a free, competitive, synthetic rubber industry"—has been achieved?[18] No definitive answer can, or will, be given. The period under consideration is too short to make any but tentative conclusions. But from the characteristics summarized in the preceding section, the author is of the opinion that workable competition is found in the industry.

The structure of the industry departs markedly from the necessary conditions for pure competition. There are a relatively small number of buyers and sellers; producers have control over their product prices and, to a lesser degree, over their input prices; selling costs, while small, are present; and entry (and exit) is difficult.

Market structure, in this industry, offers little basis for predicting market performance. Our examination of the latter leads to the conclusion that, with the noticeable exception of the lack of price competition, the industry's performance has been in accordance with the standards of

workable competition: profit rates have not been excessive; chronic excess capacity nonexistent; selling costs have averaged a small percentage of total costs; the scale of firms falls within the optimum range; and there has been no persistent lag in the adoption of product or process innovations.[19] On these counts, the synthetic rubber industry's market performance would probably be rated as workable.

Furthermore there are at least four offsets to the lack of price competition. First, there is evidence that producers have exhibited considerable independence in achieving the above mentioned performance results. The substantial growth in SBR rubber capacity has been accompanied by a broadening in the base of capacity in the industry. Market shares and positions have shifted during the past five years. While there has been some increased concentration in the collective share of the market held by the three leading producers, their share of production actually sold has remained relatively constant. Whatever increases these firms have experienced have been at the expense of other large companies, as the industry's smaller firms have generally strengthened their positions. This behavior is more readily associated with independent action than with collusion.

Independent rivalry is further indicated in the improvement and extension of technical services, the introduction of freight allowances or equalization, the improvement of existing grades, and the addition of new grades of synthetic rubbers. Competition for customers has continuously increased, aided by the transition to a buyer's market and the entry of new producers into the industry.

The second offset is closely related to the first: the conditions of entry. With entry relatively free from artificial restraints, monopolistic behavior is a priori unlikely, even in oligopolistic industries. Although entry into the synthetic rubber industry is difficult, the main barriers are economic in nature, closely related to efficiency and progressiveness. Entry has occurred and these new firms have successfully gained respectable shares of the market from existing producers. More importantly, there is no indication that these new competitors were con-

---

[17] From 1955–1959, SBR capacity rose 85.4 percent. Despite the facts that the top three firms in 1955 retained their position in 1959 and slightly increased their percentage of total industry capacity, shifting in relative standings among the other firms has continuously occurred and three new producers have entered the industry. Equally important, all producers have shared in the industry's expansion.

[18] The Disposal Act also contained a national security objective. With synthetic rubber now accounting for over 66 percent of domestic new rubber consumption and with total capacity of nearly 2 million long tons, it is here assumed that this objective has been fully met.

[19] See J. S. Bain, "Workable Competition in Oliogopoly: Theoretical Considerations and Some Empirical Evidence," *American Economic Review*, May 1950, p. 37.

fronted with either higher average costs or with retaliation by existing firms.

The rate of technological innovation provides the third offset. Mason has written that one should be cautious in attributing monopolistic significance to size of firm, share of the market, pricing formulae, and the like in markets subject to active innovation.[20] This is true because progressiveness is an end in itself, often requiring a measure of protection from a competitive forcing of prices to short-run marginal costs. In addition, progressiveness provides longer term fluidity within which oligopolistic rapport is difficult to establish and maintain. This seems to be true in the case of the synthetic rubber industry.

Moreover the industry's record of innovation has had beneficial results upon competition. While prices have remained stable, consumers have constantly received a higher quality product. In turn, producers have aggressively sought both new customers and new markets for their product. Nor is there any indication that the present rate of innovation will slacken in the foreseeable future. Rubber fabricators have a direct interest in maintaining and improving synthetic rubber quality. That this goal has largely been achieved is shown by the high degree of interchangeability which presently exists between synthetics and natural. The desire to be freed from dependence upon foreign sources of supply for natural rubber has also led to the rapid development of synthetic natural rubbers.

The demand for synthetic rubbers is closely geared to the price of natural rubber. Rubber experts state that efficient rubber estates can produce at a profit with a price between 12 and 15 cents per pound. Historically production costs have had little relation to natural rubber prices—world supply and demand conditions are controlling. But it is generally believed that the development of synthetic rubbers will tend to stabilize natural rubber prices. In addition, natural rubber producers are showing an increasing awareness of this situation and future technological developments are almost certain.[21]

Finally, there is a fourth factor which has

relevance to the industry. From a welfare standpoint there are definite advantages to synthetic rubber price stability. For rubber fabricators price instability is a cost. Prior to the commercial development of synthetic rubber these rubber buyers were at the mercy of a wildly fluctuating price for natural rubber and, in large measure, their gross profit margins were outside of their control. Under perfect competition hedging by speculators would tend to remove or reduce price fluctuations. Even with synthetic rubber, however, the lack of an organized market and varying product grades seem to prevent hedging. As a result price stability depends upon producer's actions.

Nor is there any indication that prices have been set unduly high by synthetic rubber producers. In fact, the opposite conclusion is warranted. Given that synthetic rubber is a relatively new product, producers are trying to develop new uses. The history of competition of natural products with synthetically derived products is replete with examples which show that the introduction of synthetic materials often expands the area of consumption and creates new markets. For synthetic rubbers, price stability is a major factor which makes this possible. Not only must man-made rubbers be able to withstand competition from natural rubber, but they must be competitively priced for enlargement of the twilight market which exists between rubber and plastic materials.

Therefore, the lack of price competition cannot be considered as a major factor in assessing the workability of competition within the industry. Rivalry has been aggressive, due in large part to the high rate of technological innovation which has characterized the industry.

Bain has suggested that within concentrated markets there may be an association between market structure and the workability of competition. He offers three hypotheses, of which the second is as follows:

2. Oligopolies with moderately difficult entry and moderate concentration—probably a common case. In general, markets of this sort promise the closest approximations to workability among oligopolies, provided that there is not persistently 'destructive' pricing, which seems theoretically unlikely as a long-run tendency. Efficiency should be reasonably good and prices and profits low or moderate. With product differentiation, however, selling costs may be excessive; thus standardized-product industries

---

[20] E. S. Mason, "Schumpeter on Monopoly and the Large Firm," *Review of Economics and Statistics*, May 1951, pp. 139–44.

[21] See D. M. Phelps, *Rubber Developments in Latin America* (Ann Arbor: Michigan Business Studies, XIII, 1957), especially chapter VII.

within this category get the best rating. Fewness of buyers may help, provided buying power is not overwhelming.[22]

Under Bain's hypothesis the synthetic rubber industry would come close to the most acceptable structural rating. Moreover this seems to summarize the workability of competition in the industry: entry is difficult, concentration moderate, and product differentiation minimal. Yet, market performance leaves little to be desired.

IV

Three tests of an industry were previously mentioned. They were: (1) Do the industry's results approximate the theoretical results of pure competition? (2) Does the industry approximate the necessary structural conditions for pure competition? (3) Does any alternative market organization seem economically desirable or legally feasible? Our conclusion is that the synthetic rubber industry meets the first, but not the second. As this is the case, we must necessarily consider the third.

Any type of market structure which might be set up in place of the present oligopoly would show some kind of imperfections. Three alternative market structures seem possible. The present firms might be consolidated into one to form a complete monopoly. The two multi-plant firms (Goodrich-Gulf, Texas-U.S.) might be split into somewhat smaller segments so that a few more firms appeared in the market. Or, finally, the industry might be returned to Government ownership. While pure competition is unattainable, the results of each of these alternatives differ and will be briefly discussed in turn.

The most serious drawback to a monopoly is a possible lack of incentive. It may be that a single enterprise deprived of the stimulus of competitive activity would be less efficiently run and would care for the wants of buyers less carefully than do the present companies. Our study has shown that rivalry presently exists in the synthetic rubber industry and that technological innovation has been high. Some of these qualities are more than likely to spill over into other parts of the firm's activities and lead to a better conduct of affairs than would occur in a full monopoly. Unless this doubt could be re-moved, there is no assurance that a full monopoly would be economically superior to the existing organization.

With a few more firms oligopoly relationships would persist and the current situation would be changed more in appearance than in fact. Oligopoly theory would indicate that as the number of firms within an oligopolistic industry increased, the opportunities for explicit (and tacit?) agreement would diminish. But given a kinked demand curve and the high degree of competition existing within the synthetic rubber industry at the present time, it is doubtful whether such a structure would result in different behavior.

At the same time it must be remembered that the two multi-plant owners included three big rubber companies. Such divestiture would thus add two strong buyers to the market by forcing these companies to purchase at least a part of their annual synthetic rubber supplies through the market. However, it is not obvious that this would result in improved performance. No price discrimination has been found and integration has not resulted in a foreclosure of the market. But again, this would be perhaps the most significant market structure alteration and would increase the necessary structural conditions for pure competition. Any public action, such as antitrust, aimed at forcing such an alteration, would face two problems: the industry's performance has been good and the pricing structure a direct inheritance of the period of Government operation. In this sense, the legal feasibility, at least for the present, of any public action would seem very small.

Of course, there is a third public policy available: nationalization. At the outset, one would hesitate to try to sell such a policy to the political and industrial leaders who went through the long period of negotiations during the postwar period. Even more serious, however, is the probable lack of incentive for research and development. At least one student of the industry has argued that the Government-sponsored research program during and following World War II left much to be desired.[23]

---

[22] Bain, "Workable Competition in Oligopoly: Theoretical Considerations and Some Empirical Evidence," *op. cit.*, p. 46.

[23] R. A. Solo, "Synthetic Rubber: A Case Study in Technological Development Under Government Direction," Study No. 18 of the Senate Subcommittee on Patents, Trademarks, and Copyrights (Washington, D.C.: U. S. Government Printing Office, 1959).

The present organization of the synthetic rubber industry thus appears in a favorable light when compared with possible alternative market structures. Pure competition is unattainable. A full monopoly might lack adequate incentives to maintain quality. Market forces indicate that the addition of two independent firms by divestiture would have little effect upon the industry's performance. And nationalization seems unfeasible. On economic grounds there does not seem to be a strong case for reform in the structure of the industry.

v

The lack of necessary conditions, however, raises serious questions about the future course of the industry. Past behavior contains no guarantee of the future. The industry possesses a relatively inelastic demand and an oligopolistic market structure. Such characteristics in other moderately concentrated industries have provided heavy pressure toward less independent action. To date the synthetic rubber industry has also been characterized by three other factors which have outweighed the above: a steady growth in demand, a rapid rate of technological innovation, and severe pressure from natural rubber producers. These seem to be necessary and sufficient conditions for workable competition in this industry.

It seems unlikely that the domestic rate of growth for synthetic rubbers will continue at its 1955–59 pace. However there are indications that a stabilized demand is still distant. The future of technology is even more speculative, but polymer chemistry seems to be far short of being an exhausted field. Moreover, present indications suggest that the pressure from natural rubber producers will increase, not diminish, to say nothing of competition from the plastics industry. On balance, it would seem very unlikely that the synthetic rubber industry would develop the type of performance commonly associated with other oligopolistic markets within the forseeable future.

The heavy emphasis upon performance raises two policy problems, both of which concern the disposal program of 1955. First, a more competitive market structure might have been achieved if Congress had been willing to accept a lower revenue from the sale of the producing plants.[24] While our study indicates that market

performance would not have been significantly affected by an alternative market structure, a more competitive structure would serve to insure a continuation of rivalry in the future. Second, and as a corollary problem, Congressional approval of two joint venture companies is open to question. All of the companies involved could have purchased plants alone. Moreover, those companies who were unsuccessful in buying Government plants might well have entered the industry at a later date via entry. From a competitive standpoint, the wisdom of joining together large industrial firms is always suspect. At least in the synthetic rubber industry the net effect seems to have been to increase market power without any offsetting factors, such as greater performance.

Returning to our earlier question, then, our study leads to the conclusion that the synthetic rubber industry is workably competitive. But in making this evaluation it must be stressed that a large element of personal judgment has been involved. On the basis of the evidence examined, others might well reach quite different conclusions.

One final consideration: These findings have some methodological implications for the study of industrial behavior. In recent years, economists have been concerned with the problem of how to weight performance as opposed to structural standards. In a number of cases, the choice is either structure or performance, but not both. In this industry it is clear that the findings depend upon the weighting system adopted. In part our preference for market performance is pragmatic—given our institutional constraints, no alternative market structure seems feasible.

Yet, from a political point of view, structural standards are to some extent more basic. Competition is desirable because it insures that the market will direct industry rather than give market power to individual firms and our society has always been concerned about uncontrolled private power. Others have argued that

---

[24] Conversely, this same result might have been achieved by postponing disposal for two or three years. Such a conclusion is warranted because the future of synthetic rubbers was still uncertain in 1955 and this accounts, in large part, for the lack of competitive bidding for some of the producing plants. See Rubber Producing Facilities Disposal Commission, *Report to Congress* (including *Supplement*), January 1955 (Washington, D.C.: U. S. Government Printing Office, 1955).

competition is a political as opposed to an economic concept. On this basis the synthetic rubber industry might well be rated as not workably competitive.

Given the highly desirable performance, however, combined with the high rate of technological innovation, and the entry of three new producers since 1955, the synthetic rubber industry does give reason for accepting the conclusion that the industry is workably competitive, despite its market structure. The industry stands on its own feet, receiving neither tariff protection nor subsidies. A workably competitive industry guarantees that the public interest will be served. Such results lead to the conclusion that Congressional intent has been realized.

CHEMICALS: THE RELUCTANT COMPETITORS

by
GILBERT BURCK

The chemical business is not only the most creative and one of the very biggest industries in Europe, it is also one of the most competitive. The last distinction, however, probably affords little pride and less joy to European chemical men. Although Americans believe justifiably that they have made competition work tolerably well, a lot of consequential Europeans still seem to regard it with fear and suspicion. When Stanley Chambers, chairman of Britain's Imperial Chemical Industries Ltd., recently deplored the "worship of the blind god of free competition," he doubtless spoke for thousands. Nevertheless, inexorable economic forces are compelling European chemical men to behave as if they too were worshippers of the blind god. And if being competitive may be defined as ferociously pursuing lower costs in order to meet the exigencies of a market that cannot be neatly allocated and boxed in, then they are probably doomed to become more competitive than they are now.

For one thing, the very nature of their industry compels them to. Producing chemicals is one of the oldest and at the same time one of the youngest of all of man's great enterprises. During the greater part of the nineteenth century it was a stable, plodding business devoted to the bulk production of standard industrial "inorganics" like alkalis and sulfuric acid. But profound change was on the way. A German chemist named Justus von Liebig began experimenting with "organic" chemicals or carbon compounds derived from once living matter. What he and his successors learned about them enabled William Henry Perkin to synthesize a mauve dye in 1856, and Johann Baeyer to synthesize indigo in 1880. To such men the earth's crust became a vast pile of chemical compounds, polluted by eons of geological change; it was their job to break these compounds down, rectify them, and recombine them into wholly new compounds with a wide variety of new uses. Gradually the chemical industry began to create new markets by creating new products. Bayer, for example, first produced artificial rubber, DuPont created nylon, and I.C.I. pioneered that ubiquitous plastic, polyethylene. Today probably more than half the industry's revenues come from products that did not exist twenty-five years ago.

To amount to anything at all, therefore, a chemical company must invest large sums in research to create new compounds and in developing a market for them. Once it has invested the money, it finds that the return on its investment will increase in almost geometrical ratio to production volume. To get the volume that will maximize return, it has no other course than to reduce prices. So even a chemical company with a monopoly in a new product finds itself behaving remarkably like a true competitor. No chemical company can monopolize a product for long because other chemical companies will have created something similar if not better. This is not all. The higher a company's profits on a new product, the more certain it can be that others will horn in on the market. The profitability of the industry, in Europe as in the U.S., has attracted many outsiders, particularly the oil companies, which in the process of refining crude oil find themselves with chemical raw materials. Naturally, they want to exploit such products.

Oil has made the industry more competitive in still another way. The shift from coal to petroleum hydrocarbons as a raw material occurred later in Europe than in the U.S., but it has been accelerated in the past few years by the discovery of immense gas reserves in France and now in Holland, an availability of cheap oil and gas in Italy, and the construction of great pipelines carrying African and Middle East oil north from the Mediterranean. This shift has called for the construction of large and costly "continuous" plants, whose economy depends on high volume. But like most huge plants, they temporarily endow companies with extra capacity that almost inevitably makes for extra-hard competition in the form of price shaving.

This tendency of today's chemical industry to behave competitively has been augmented and intensified by a number of postwar developments. The one that bothers many Europeans most is what they call "unfair" competition from the U.S., with its "protectionist" tariff structure; this contention will be discussed later in this article. But overshadowing everything else is the European industry's headlong growth, perhaps the swiftest in history, as chemical manufacturers have sweated to make up for wartime lags and to get their new markets established. The European chemical industry has recently been growing much faster than the American; during the years 1953-62, while U.S. chemical sales were expanding from $18.8 billion to $32.8 billion, Western Europe's more than doubled, from about $10 billion to more than $23 billion. If European chemical prices had risen as much as other industrial prices, the 1962 sales figures would have been much greater. Prices of some chemicals, indeed, have fallen sharply.

The West German industry lifted its sales from about $2.5 billion in 1953 to around $6 billion in 1962. It had regained its prewar position as Europe's No. 1 producer by 1956, but it does not dominate European industry to the extent it once did. Britain is not far behind, with 1962 sales of about $5 billion. And France and Italy came up even faster than the German industry. France increased turnover from around $2 billion in 1953 to about $4 billion in 1962; while Italy, by dint of recent increases averaging almost 20 percent a year, raised sales from around $1 billion in 1953 to around $4 billion last year. Together, Germany, Britain, France, and Italy account for more than 80 percent of Western Europe's chemical sales.

This expansion has been so precipitous that there has been little reason for companies to try to divide up the market. If they were alive today, such ardent and professional old-time monopolists as Carl Duisberg, who put I. G. Farben together, or William Ross, who built the modern Distillers Co. Ltd., would certainly shudder at the chaos about them. Moreover, the division of markets along national lines is fading fast. As tariffs go down in the Common Market and the European Free Trade Association, more and more chemicals are moving across European boundaries. Last year half the chemical exports of European nations, which amounted to about $5 billion, went to other European nations. This acceleration of intra-European trade is particularly noticeable in the six Common Market countries, whose exports account for about 65 percent of Western Europe's total exports. In these great fluid markets, no company knows yet exactly where it stands, much less where it is likely to stand a few years from now.

When tariff barriers are further dismantled, trade in chemicals is bound to be more quickly and deeply affected than trade in most other major products. As the first article in this series (FORTUNE, August, 1963) pointed out, European auto buyers are still somewhat nationalistic in their preferences. And much heavy electrical machinery (FORTUNE, September, 1963) is made to national specifications and bought by state railroad and electricity boards

that tend to favor domestic manufacturers. In man-made chemicals even the regional prejudices of the good European earth itself are wiped out. Since a ton of butanol made in France is the same as a ton made in Italy or Germany, what matters mainly is costs and prices.

Thus chemicals will probably be among the first commodities to reap the advantages as well as to suffer the stresses of being made and sold in the E.E.C., the world's second-largest free market. After World War II, Europe's more enlightened makers of economic policy began to realize, as Americans had years before, that cartels and monopolistic trade agreements tend to hamstring productivity growth and to play into the hands of advocates of government ownership. Above all, they reasoned, there would be little point in reducing tariffs in order to liberate international trade so long as cartels had the power to restrict that trade. So several countries passed laws against cartels and trade agreements, some of them very rudimentary; the main laggard is Italy, whose authorities drew up a model bill that lies buried in Parliament. Articles 85 and 86 of the Treaty of Rome of 1957, which set up the Common Market, contain sharp provisions against cartels and trade agreements, and in effect require member countries to adopt minimal antitrust laws. There doubtless still is some collaboration between companies, but many think the E.E.C. commission in Brussels will invoke the articles to eliminate such collaboration. It may, for example, radically change European marketing and distribution by prohibiting the appointment of exclusive distributors.

It would be very hard, of course, to find a European executive who is genuinely enthusiastic about such measures, but many seem ready to accept their consequences. European chemical manufacturers, in the main, seem to be tackling the problem of competition as good capitalists should. They often cut prices. They are forming mergers and combinations not to rope off markets, but to reduce costs by integrating, by increasing labor's productivity, and by eliminating duplicate or obsolete plant and equipment. The industry is also intensifying research that will enable it to introduce new and profitable products as the market for the older ones begins to crowd up.

COMPETITION IN THE LAND OF CARTELS

The most pleasantly ironic circumstance in the international chemical industry is that Germany, which once all but cartelized (and ruled) the whole chemical world, is legally more committed to free competition than any other European country. The gap between official policy and everyday behavior, to be sure, is probably even wider in Germany than in the U.S., and German businessmen surely complain about their government trustbusters as much as U.S. businessmen complain about theirs. But at least they are more competitive than they have been in the memory of man.

Accounting for nearly 40 percent of the Republic's approximately $6-billion sales in 1962 (the figure does not include sales of German-owned companies abroad) were the three well known companies that once constituted the bulk of the great I. G. Farben complex: Farbenfabriken Bayer of Leverkusen, with world sales of $1 billion (about half abroad); Farbwerke Hoechst of Frankfurt, with world sales of $865 million (nearly 40 percent abroad); and Badische Anilin-& Soda-Fabrik of Ludwigshafen, with world sales of $715 million (about 40 percent abroad). All three were founded about a century ago, and they played major roles in the German organic-chemical industry's great period of creativity, during which it dominated synthetic dyes and pharmaceuticals, and formed nitrogen compounds out of thin air. They were combined into I. G. Farben (*Interessengemeinschaft Farbenindustrie* — "community of interests in the dye industry") by Carl Duisberg, president of Bayer, the classic model of a man who passionately believed in combination because he considered competition destructive. Duisberg, incidentally, succumbed to this passion after a trip to the U.S. in 1903, where he observed the old-time trusts in all their glory. The great chemical complex he put together flourished mightily. I. G. Farben at one time accounted for more than half of Germany's chemical exports, which came to more than those of the U.S. and Britain combined.

Following World War II, I. G. Farben became the prime target of the Allied cartel-busters, who broke the colossus up into the Big Three and nine lesser companies. The Big Three have since absorbed several of the lesser companies, and have joint interests in two or three others. But they are doing so well separately that they have little economic or commercial incentive to combine further. Indeed, they have plenty of political reason not to merge; even now the German Parliament is investigating excessive concentrations of economic power, and may crack down on them.

"YOU GET LOADED WITH UNNECESSARY PEOPLE"

Some say that the Big Three go out of their way to avoid competing with one another and behave as if they were still parts of a bigger company; but officials of the Big Three say they *are* competing, more and more. Anyway, so far they have had little reason to harass one another. While the German chemical industry as a whole has been growing about 8.5 percent annually since 1955, the Big Three have grown about 50 percent faster. To them goes most of the credit for the fact that the Republic may be on its way to becoming once again the world's biggest chemical exporter. Last year German exports totaled nearly $1.5 billion.

The growth of the Big Three has been slowing down somewhat, but that was to be expected. The main problem facing them is the rapidly increasing cost of labor — wages were up 9.5 percent in 1959, 7.6 percent in 1960, 14.6 percent in 1961, 12.3 percent in 1962. Owing partly to these mounting costs, gross profits of Bayer and Badische dropped in 1961. The high cost of labor will probably be a relatively durable German phenomenon; indeed, thanks to the low wartime birth rate, the German labor force will decline a little in the next few years.

But all three, as well as other German companies, have already begun to take steps to reduce labor costs. Staffs are being thinned out. "In a period of quick growth," says Badische's financial director Rolf Magener, "you get loaded with all sorts of unnecessary people because you have not time to look at the details." More significant, the Big Three (and the rest of the German industry) have recently been increasing their investment much faster than sales. Much of this investment has been used to increase capacity, but a growing percentage of it, probably now about half, is going toward raising productivity. "It is now more interesting," says Klaus Franke, financial manager of Hoechst, "to increase profit margins than to increase sales." This new attention to costs has already been reflected in the statistics. In 1962, Bayer's domestic sales rose about 7 percent, but the number of employees rose hardly at all. In the same year Hoechst's sales rose 7 percent, but the number of employees rose only 3 percent, and Badische increased its sales some 10 percent with 3.5 percent fewer workers. And this is only the beginning; for wages per employee in all three were in 1962 rising faster than sales per employee.

The Big Three are also hitting the cost line in other ways. Badische, for example, has tightened controls and reduced inventory by $25 million over an eighteen-month period. Raw materials are probably more expensive in Germany than elsewhere in Europe. But the Big Three are gradually using less coal and more petroleum hydrocarbons, which are expected to account for two-thirds of the whole industry's organic production by 1972. Sooner or later, it appears, Germany's costs will be on a better competitive basis. And all three companies are plowing back about 4 percent of their domestic gross into research. Although they have yet to come up with great advances of the kind that distinguished them fifty years or more ago, observers from other countries have a good deal of praise for the quality of work they are doing, and certainly it is paying off handsomely.

Presumably, the Germans will eventually participate vigorously in ventures across national boundaries, a development that seems bound to come as Common Market tariffs continue to fall. Already Bayer has joined Progil and Ugine of France in setting up a small operation in Grenoble, France. But this sort of thing, on a big scale, seems some time away.

The German industry is likely to proceed with its expansion unbridled by government planning — at least so long as Ludwig Erhard and his kind are in power. It does not seem impressed by government planning in France. "We Germans have had some experience with planning," says Kurt Hansen, chairman of Bayer, in what is surely a masterpiece of understatement. "The trouble is that when you have a plan you have to fulfill the plan, and that leads to terrible regulations. The French may not take such things so seriously, but if we have a law we go to hell if we don't obey it."

"A BREATH OF FRESH LIFE"

The British industry, like the German, is legally constrained to be competitive. The Monopolies and Restrictive Practices Act of 1948 defines a monopoly as any business or combination of businesses doing a third of the national output of any product; and a later law has enabled a restrictive-practices court to crack down on some trade agreements. What is bothering the British chemical men, however, is not the law but competition itself. Having grown substantially all during World War II and having got back into the race earlier than the continental industry, the British industry lately has been confronted with increasing rivalry in the sluggish home market and with new competition in former colonies and in the Commonwealth. Its share of free-world exports has dropped from about 18 percent in 1953 to 13.4 percent. And now it is up against de Gaulle's refusal to let it compete equally in the rich Common Market.

The British industry is dominated by one company, Imperial Chemical Industries Ltd., whose 1962 group sales of $1.6 billion made it the largest chemical firm outside the U.S. The company has also performed better than the rest of the industry; between 1953 and 1962, while industry sales increased less than 60 percent, I.C.I.'s more than doubled. Some 17 percent of the $1.6 billion represents exports from the U.K.; thus I.C.I. accounts for about a quarter of all U.K. chemical sales including exports. For 30 percent of I.C.I.'s gross sales are made by its foreign subsidiaries.

Like I. G. Farben, I.C.I. was born in a merger; in 1926, when it became apparent that only size and power could stand up to I. G. Farben and the rapidly growing U.S. industry, Sir Harry (later Lord) McGowan created I.C.I. out of four companies. Sales and profits grew at a handsome rate in the early postwar period, but trouble began in 1958, when sales steadied, and return on capital employed, which had been above 11 percent, dipped to 8 percent. Sales and particularly profits recovered smartly in 1959 and 1960, but in 1961 competition and falling prices forced profits down almost 30 percent, and return on capital employed fell to less than 9 percent.

It was a tough time for Stanley Paul Chambers, the new boss. A brilliant but hardheaded economist, whom Lord McGowan had hired away from the Inland Revenue Board, of all things, Chambers had become deputy chairman in 1952 and succeeded McGowan as chairman in 1960. Chambers was undaunted. As one who had tried to make I.C.I. more commercially minded ever since he joined it, he had been a prime mover in shifting the emphasis from heavy low-profit chemicals into newer, faster-growing products like plastics and fibers. Now he launched an efficiency movement that scrapped old plants and processes and reduced the payroll from 99,000 to 94,000. He also hired McKinsey & Co., the U.S. management-consultant firm, to make a study of the company's business. Last year I.C.I.'s profits recovered some of their lost ground, and Chambers predicts that they will continue to improve.

Chambers was unsuccessful in one bold move — to acquire Courtaulds, the largest British rayon manufacturer. On the Continent, chemical and synthetic-fiber companies were merging to compete more effectively, and Chambers argued that only merger would enable the British industry to meet the competition. But Courtaulds' managers, raking up all kinds of embarrassing examples of I.C.I.'s past "mismanagement," fought hard to stay independent, and in the end I.C.I. was able to buy only 38.5 percent of Courtaulds' stock. Chambers' only solace is that the value of this stock has considerably appreciated.

Chambers was also dismayed at de Gaulle's summary exclusion of Britain from the Common Market. "Entry into the European Economic Community," he said in 1961, speaking like a true competitor, "will bring a breath of fresh life into the economic life of Britain." I.C.I. had increased its sales to E.F.T.A. countries from about $14 million in 1953 to more than $55 million, but it had been much less successful in exporting to E.E.C. countries; and it was Chambers' aim to raise both home and continental capacity enough to put I.C.I. in the Common Market in a big way. After de Gaulle's veto, he had to move fast and in several directions at once. In 1960 he had foresightedly begun to negotiate for a 300-acre site at Rozenburg, near Rotterdam, that could be developed into a full-scale petrochemical complex. Now he is beginning to develop it. But in the words of Douglas Bell, who heads I.C.I.'s continental operations, "All that's happened in the past two years makes us increasingly doubtful that a true single market in chemicals will be achieved in E.E.C."

So Chambers has been making haste slowly at Rozenburg, and has been quietly establishing I.C.I. in national markets by picking up small companies all over the Continent. Chambers has also raised I.C.I.'s research expenditures to some $50 million, or about 4.5 percent of its U.K. sales and exports. At the same time, he is vigorously expanding trade with the Communist-bloc countries, where I.C.I. is one of the leading Western suppliers of chemicals. Obviously, I.C.I. under Chambers knows how to compete. But he still has his reservations about competition as a way of life. Over the long run, he believes, governments and industries must work together to keep competition "orderly." "Industry," he told the American Chamber of Commerce in London not long ago, "must do better than present a spectacle of blindfolded giants blundering all over the place." The remark is typical of those Europeans who, seeing competition only in its most ruthless aspect, still hanker for the "security" of cartels.

THE ENGAGEMENT PARTY AT LACQ

For all its size, growth, and aggressiveness, the French chemical industry is commonly regarded as a prime example of the handicaps of too much fragmentation. There are about 2,500 chemical companies in France, and until very recently the ten largest firms together accounted for only 25 percent of national sales. To be sure, when all subsidiary interests are taken into account, actual ownership of French companies is somewhat more concentrated than this figure indicates. But such interlocking ownership, if unaccompanied by appropriate organization, doesn't help efficiency; on the contrary, it makes for inefficiency.

Nor is efficiency necessarily promoted by the French partiality to government planning. Thanks to the discovery of tremendous deposits of gas in France and oil in North Africa, the French industry found itself with very low raw-material costs and well endowed to expand faster than the economy as a whole. But the government's four-year plan is not content with merely setting a target growth rate for chemicals of 9 percent a year; it encourages companies to line up behind the plan by offering reductions in real-estate and income taxes, postponement of taxes, and various other kinds of indirect and direct aid. It can be argued that *Le Plan*, in effect, is a kind of national cartel. And whatever its subsidies may do for the national growth figures, they hide costs and tend to postpone the kind of cost cutting that abets true growth by improving productivity.

French chemical leaders have long been aware of their industry's deficiencies, however, and not long after the Common Market was set up they realized that the time had come for them to rationalize — to consolidate functions and companies wherever such consolidation would result in lower costs. In a sense, the actual merger movement began at Lacq, near Pau, close to the Pyrenees in the southwest corner of France, where one of the world's great gas strikes occurred more than a decade ago, and where some thirty wells are now producing nearly 250 billion cubic feet of gas a year. Some 1,300,000 metric tons of sulfur also came out of Lacq last year, enough to turn France from an importer into the largest European producer of that important chemical raw material. The field was exploited by gas and power authorities as well as by several chemical companies, which with government help built a joint complex called Aquitainechimie. Among the chemical companies was Pechiney, which is also France's largest aluminum producer, and Saint-Gobain, the country's largest glass producer. To make vinyl chloride from the gas at Lacq, the two companies set up a joint venture called Vinylacq.

They hit it off well. As Raoul de Vitry, chairman of Pechiney, remarks, "This was the engagement." After a decent interval, marriage followed. The two companies decided to merge most of their chemical interests in January, 1960. Two years later the new company, Pechiney—Saint-Gobain, took over the formal management of the chemical plants, and this year it published its first annual report as a producing and selling organization. Despite falling prices, the report says, the new company's sales last year came to $200 million, a 10 percent increase over the combined 1961 sales of the two companies' old chemical divisions. But the merger process still has some way to go. "It's still a two-headed monster that needs a lot more rationalization," says one observer.

The other big French merger occurred in 1961, when Rhône-Poulenc, which makes more than 3,000 different chemicals and excels in pharmaceuticals, took over the textile activities of Celtex. This gives Rhône-Poulenc a virtual monopoly in the French artificial-fiber market. The consolidated sales of the new company, including subsidies and affiliates, are probably well above $1 billion, more than those of any other European chemical company save I.C.I.; but the figure includes finished products that are not usually counted as chemicals.

It is generally agreed that the Rhône-Poulenc and Pechiney—Saint-Gobain mergers are a challenge to the "others" — i.e., companies like Progil, Ugine, and Kuhlmann, which has already strengthened its large position in the French dye industry by taking over two small companies. Says one business editor: "The horrible war hasn't taken place yet."

MATTEI'S LEGACY TO COMPETITION

The *enfant terrible* of the European chemical marketplace and the biggest threat to its future price stability is the Italian industry. Although Italy is still a net importer of chemicals, the Italian industry has elbowed its way into foreign markets by capitalizing on abundant supplies of cheap oil and gas. And how does Italy, of all the world's resource-poor countries, come by such raw materials? The answer is, or was, a single resolute and resourceful man, the late Enrico Mattei, who ran Ente Nazionale Idrocarburi (E.N.I.), the government's oil and gas monopoly. His big aim in life was to make energy cheap enough for all Italian industry to compete internationally. With a statutory monopoly on Po Valley natural gas, Mattei was able to sell the gas cheaply enough to force the international oil companies to cut fuel-oil prices; he also used barter agreements to import cheap crude from the U.S.S.R. To the chemical industry he sold natural gas at about 25 percent below the price to other customers.

The great beneficiary of this policy was, of course, Montecatini, Italy's largest chemical company, with sales of $550 million last year.

Montecatini has, for years, cut prices to make a place for itself in European markets, and was inordinately aggressive in selling plastics such as polyvinyl chloride and polyethylene. Recently the company is said to have grown "more conservative" in its marketing methods, but if so, there is no guarantee it will stay that way. Under sixty-three-year-old Piero Giustiniani, Montecatini expanded enormously into fertilizers, fiber polymers, and plastics; his great monument is a petrochemical complex at Brindisi, which will probably cost considerably more than $200 million when fully on stream. Brindisi was also Giustiniani's downfall. The bankers who controlled Montecatini's board thought Giustiniani had been too dynamically optimistic, and forced him to resign last April. The Brindisi complex will probably be able to produce more than the company's "normal" markets can absorb for two or three years, and other European producers finger their collars when they think about what Montecatini might do with that capacity.

Montecatini's aggressiveness is more than matched by other Italian companies. Indeed, its share of the Italian industry has declined steeply at the hands of other eager beavers. Società Edison, whose big electric-power complex in northern Italy was recently nationalized along with the rest of the Italian power business, has invested some $700 million in chemicals since 1950, and is now the second-largest Italian chemical company. It has been cutting prices right and left.

"LARGE COMPETITION, LARGE POSSIBILITIES"

But the fastest-growing and most dreaded of Italian companies is a creature of E.N.I. itself: Azienda Nazionale Hydrogenozine Combustibili (A.N.I.C.), which is 51 percent owned by the monopoly Mattei set up. Although A.N.I.C. didn't enter the chemical business until 1955, it has come along at a great rate. Some say A.N.I.C. gets natural gas at 40 percent below the price other companies pay, but A.N.I.C. stoutly denies that it is favored with more than the usual 25 percent discount. A.N.I.C. probably accounts for about a fifth of Italy's output of polyvinyl chloride, a quarter of its ethylene glycol, a third of its carbon black, nearly a third of its vinyl acetate, and more than 95 percent of its synthetic rubber.

"I remember when we had no coal, no gas, and we paid dear for coal from Germany," says A.N.I.C. Director General Angelo Fornara, with a sardonic smile illuminating his mobile face. "Now we are using oil, and we can do things too. Everybody says competition is nice, but when it comes, everybody does not like it." Fornara says that his company is expanding rapidly into non-European markets, and he hopes that Britain will join the Common Market, so A.N.I.C. can move in there too. "Enlarging a market increases trouble," he explains amiably, "but you have an advantage because size means economy. There is large competition, but also large possibilities. Tomorrow will be very good."

Italian rivalry would set much easier with the rest of the European industry if the Italians were not so dependent upon government. Yet the odds are not hopelessly rigged in their favor. The Italians are caught in the same cost squeeze that everybody in the industry wails about.

Italian labor, according to reports of visiting British productivity teams, is very productive, but skilled labor is growing scarce and therefore demanding and getting higher wages; labor costs in the chemical industry accordingly have risen 20 percent in the past two years, and show no signs of leveling off. Because Italian companies have cut prices so rashly, their profit margins are shrinking. And the rest of the European chemical industry, by one stratagem or another, should be able to force raw-material costs down too. Thus the Italian industry may soon be playing the competitive game with an appropriate sense of its own limitations.

THE "SHOCK" FROM THE U.S.

And so, all Europe hopes, will the U.S., which is a formidable competitor. For one thing, more than 100 U.S. companies, not only big ones like du Pont, Union Carbide, and Gulf, but small ones like Witco and Atlas, have gone into the chemical business in Europe, often in partnership with European companies. Last year U.S. companies invested some $105 million there, and in 1965, they will be investing more than twice as much.

More important, the U.S. is the world's largest chemical exporter; its foreign sales of nearly $2 billion are a quarter of all free-world chemical exports. Its potentialities as exporter were dramatically, not to say devastatingly, dramatized in 1961, after the American industry had installed more polyethylene and polystyrene capacity than it could use right away. The price of low-pressure polyethylene began to soften; early in 1960 the stuff was selling at 30 cents a pound in continental markets and by January, 1961, it was down to 26 cents a pound. About that time several American and Italian companies began to dump their excess production on the European market at prices below those prevailing in their home markets. Although the Stateside price declined, the price in Britain dropped much more, to below 20 cents, and on the Continent lower still. "We could have bought American polyethylene here, shipped it back to the U.S., paid the duty, and still sold it at a profit below the U.S. price level," says Dr. Hans Freiensehner, sales director of Badische Anilin-& Soda-Fabrik. But before any such thing could happen, both the British and French invoked their anti-dumping acts, and prices steadied.

European companies, to use their favorite phrase, were powerfully shocked. "The U.S. chemical industry," says Leslie Williams, deputy chairman of I.C.I., "completely wrecked the European price structure." And going on in the manner of a patient teacher, he explains, "Everybody dumps more or less. It's the degree of dumping that really matters. And it's the chaps who haven't been at school long enough to learn behavior who cause the problem."

WAILING AT THE "CHINESE WALL"

The basic trouble, Williams and other European chemical men argue, lies in the U.S. tariff, because it prevents Europeans from threatening to dump in return, which is the only effective way to forfend mass dumping in the first place. It also keeps Europeans from competing in the U.S. market to the extent that American companies compete in the European market. The U.S., Europeans admit, has a case. Some European tariffs discriminate against American goods; and moreover, American duties were originally erected neither arbitrarily nor whimsically. In the sixty or more years before World War I, when the U.S. industry produced mostly inorganic chemicals such as sulfuric acid, it enjoyed a sufficient but not immodest protection. But like the rest of the world, it found itself almost totally dependent on the Germans for organic products such as dyestuffs, intermediates, potash, and pharmaceuticals; just before World War I, in fact, Germany made no less than 87 percent of the world's synthetic dyestuffs. So during the war the U.S. had to develop its own organic industry from scratch, and despite the low-tariff policy of the Democrats, President Wilson and a Democratic Congress acted in 1916 to erect high tariffs against foreign chemicals. In 1922, when the Germans were striving to get their old markets back, U.S. tariffs on organics were again hiked, and in addition were based on U.S. "list" prices. Only such protection, many claimed, enabled the U.S. organic-chemical business, after World War I, to flourish against the superior forces of the Germans.

Now the shoe is on the other foot. The U.S. industry is not only the world's biggest exporter; it is the world's largest and perhaps best-developed industry. Though there is no longer an I. G. Farben, many U.S. chemical tariffs, particularly those based on list prices, in effect assume that there is. One E.E.C. official, denouncing U.S. tariffs as a "Chinese wall of protectionism," points out, relevantly enough, that in 1961 Common Market organic exports to the U.S. amounted to less than $30 million, while U.S. organic exports to the Common Market came to $112 million.

The European industry felt a lot better when Congress passed the Trade Expansion Act of 1962, which looked like a big step toward ending such protectionism. But one big stumbling block remains: the unevenness of the U.S. chemical-tariff structure, in which duty-free items alternate with items bearing a charge of 100 percent or more. The act authorizes the U.S. to bargain for broad across-the-board cuts. But European chemical men argue that such lineal reduction would still leave them with intolerable disadvantages in many products. To make international tariffs at all equitable, they say, Americans must make selective concessions in the GATT negotiations next year.

A FAIRLY EVEN MATCH

Their contention is reinforced by the fact that the U.S. and European chemical businesses, on the whole, are very evenly matched — which can be said of few if any other large industries. Most Americans, when they hear of European competition, promptly think of Europe's lower labor costs, and automatically conclude that Europe has an insurmountable advantage. This is not necessarily so.

To begin with, labor costs are only a small part of total chemical costs. A recent breakdown of cost factors in the U.S. chemical industry by Arthur D. Little Inc. for the U.S. Synthetic Organic Chemical Manufacturers Association indicates that labor accounts for only about 15 percent. Materials and supplies, including energy, demand about 50 percent of total costs. To be sure, this figure includes a great many chemicals themselves — i.e., products one segment of the industry sells to another. But apart from this duplication, there are significant raw-material categories in which the Europeans may be at a cost disadvantage. The industry is a large consumer of electric power, and electric power is by and large more expensive in Europe than in the U.S. because European coal can cost twice as much as U.S. coal. The price of coal is also a factor in the cost of raw materials, for about half of Europe's organic-chemical output is still derived from coal tar. But Europe, as already noted, is shifting to petroleum hydrocarbons. Although oil and gas are still more expensive in Europe, the difference should narrow as African oil flows into the Continent and new gas fields are exploited.

Capital accounts for about 6.5 percent of U.S. chemical costs; probably the same plant can be erected in Europe for 10 to 15 percent less than in the U.S. This means that European depreciation charges are correspondingly lower. Research and development accounts for about 4 percent of total costs in the U.S., and the same probably holds true in Europe. But European companies get more for their research dollar than the U.S. companies do; excellent researchers come a lot cheaper in Europe. The cost of advertising, about 4.5 percent of total costs in the U.S., is undoubtedly much lower in Europe.

Europe's labor costs per man-hour, when fringe benefits are counted in, are less than half those of the U.S. But its labor costs per unit of output, which are what count, are not much different from those of the U.S., because Europe uses more than twice as much labor per unit of output as the U.S. (Value added per employee in European chemicals averages much less than half the American figure.) This does not mean that the European industry is less efficient than the American; efficiency, as distinguished from productivity, consists of using labor, capital, and materials in the right proportion to minimize costs. When labor is cheap, you use more labor and less capital; by American standards, European companies, are profligate in their use of labor. But as wages rise, the European industry is gradually using less labor and more capital. In the past few years industry employment has increased only about a third as fast as output. Even so, the cost of labor appears to be going up faster than productivity, and this trend may well continue so long as overfull employment prevails.

Many modern European plants are fully automated, however, and turn out nearly as much per man-hour as similar U.S. plants; Europe's lower man-hour labor costs mean that *these* plants can produce goods more cheaply than similar U.S. installations. This worries some U.S. companies, and the Arthur D. Little study reinforces the concern. The study concludes that if all tariffs were abolished, European organic-chemical producers with new plants *could* export certain organics *on a marginal cost basis* (without taking full account of capital and other overhead costs) and land them in the U.S. cheaply enough to increase their tiny share of the U.S. market considerably.

The study says nothing about the advantages that might accrue to the U.S. industry from a tariff reduction and, above all, nothing about what might happen if U.S. tariffs stay up and the U.S. industry has to overcome the E.E.C. tariff wall. A protectionist U.S. policy could provoke a reaction that would set the clock back measurably. This is no flight of imagination. In the E.E.C. organization, Europe has a ready-made authority that could set up a combination strangely like a cartel. As a matter of fact, just recently ten European groups, without any objection from the E.E.C. anti-cartel authorities at Brussels, formed an organization called Nitrex. Its aim sounds reasonable enough — to rationalize and promote fertilizer sales in underdeveloped countries and to compete more effectively with U.S. manufacturers and Communist-bloc trading organizations. Nitrex, however, tries to stabilize export prices by fixing a price and fining members who sell in free markets below that price; the fine is a cent per pound for every cent they cut the price.

ALWAYS ROOM FOR EXCELLENCE

Competition has its paradoxes and downright contradictions, but nobody has shown how it can be eliminated without hurting productivity and encroaching on political freedom. The problem is to make competition work, albeit imperfectly. Even after some seventy years of antitrust laws, making it work in the U.S. is a hard job. The job will be harder in Europe, with its tradition of nationalistic wars, all-powerful government, and tendency to think in "logical" extremes — that competition leads to mutual extermination.

The fact is that, for the groaning about price cutting, competition in European chemicals has been a salubrious and rewarding experience for all concerned, producer no less than consumer. Any growing industry must build for the future and not just for the needs of tomorrow, and the European like the American chemical business is discovering that much so-called overcapacity is not a harbinger of doom but an accompaniment of progress. With perhaps the fastest secular growth rate of any big European industry, chemicals will doubtless learn to live with some overcapacity and like it. Once the industry has deployed itself in its markets, there should be plenty of room for the competitor who innovates consistently, watches costs sharply, and markets with vigor and imagination.

HAS AMERICAN INDUSTRY BEEN DECENTRALIZING? THE EVIDENCE FOR THE 1939-1954 PERIOD

Wilbur Zelinsky

Dr. Zelinsky is Professor of Geography at Southern Illinois University.

IN a previous article by the present writer[1] a relatively complex method for measuring change in the location of manufacturing activity was proposed and the technique applied in an analysis of relative shifts of industry among State Economic Areas for the period 1939 to 1947. The purpose of the present paper is to extend this study forward to the 1954 Census of Manufactures, to re-examine earlier findings and problems in the light of the newer data, and also to scrutinize another major aspect of change in the location of manufacturing—intra-metropolitan shifts.

In the initial study it was found that in the 1939–1947 period there had been "a significant relative dispersion of industrial activity out from the metropolitan areas into the adjacent, relatively unindustrialized regions, from the eastern to the western portions of the Manufacturing Belt, and from the Manufacturing Belt in general to the outer reaches of the nation." Even though an over-all pattern of decentralization from the industrialized core of the nation to various "sub-industrial" regions was discerned, whether gauged in terms of relative shifts of value added by manufacture or those in production workers (the V and the E factors[2]),

there was much divergence between the locational behavior of value added by manufacture and that of production workers, and there were also major local and regional deviations from the national pattern. The results were even less precise when shifts in the location of industry were related to the changing distribution of population through the use of the V:P and E:P factors.[3] When the population factor was introduced, the direction of change was reversed for some regions and the degree of change considerably modified for almost all, with the general tendency being to reduce greatly the amount of decentralization. In view of these facts and the quite unusual economic character of the 1939–1947 period, it was necessary to reserve judgment as to whether a slow, but significant decentralization of American industry since around the beginning of this century that had been detected in earlier studies had continued past 1939, or whether there had been some major qualitative change in the pattern of the relative movement of American manufacturing.

[1] Wilbur Zelinsky: "A Method for Measuring Change in the Distribution of Manufacturing Activity: the United States, 1939–1947," *Econ. Geog.*, Vol. 34, 1958, pp. 95–126.

[2] These factors, along with the P factor used to describe shifts in the relative location of population, can be defined as the change in the percentage of the total value in a universe (here the United States) to be found within the unit area.

[3] These factors can be most simply defined as the difference between actual change and that which would have taken place within the unit areas had there been a uniform rate of change in the given per-capita value throughout the nation during the period of observation.

"Has American Industry Been Decentralizing? The Evidence for the 1939-1954 Period" by Wilbur Zelinsky. Reprinted from Economic Geography, *Vol.* 38 *(July* 1962), *pp.* 251-269, *with permission of the editor.*

Fortunately, much of this uncertainty can now be removed with the admission of the 1954 evidence.

METHODOLOGY

Following the research design established for the earlier study, figures for the population,[4] value added by manufacture, and production workers were tabulated for each of the 462 State Economic Areas existing in the United States as of 1950, and the P, V, E, V:P, and E:P factors were computed for each of the SEA's and industrial regions.[5] Before commenting upon the results, we should take note of the general magnitude of change in American industrial activity occurring in the 1947–1954 as compared with the

[4] The tabulation of population and manufacturing data was carried on in 1958 and 1959 or well before the results of the 1960 Population Census could have been utilized. Consequently, it was necessary to fall back upon the best population estimates available at the time. The Bureau of the Census' *Current Population Reports* issues a series of population estimates for the nation and the individual states at frequent intervals; but in order to obtain county data it was necessary to apply to those various state agencies listed in *Current Population Reports*, *Population Estimates*, Series P-25, No. 116, Washington, D.C., June 6, 1955. The methods of estimation and reliability of results vary from state to state; but, in general, a rather high technical standard is maintained, and most of these figures can be used with considerable confidence. In the case of five states—North Dakota, Rhode Island, Texas, Vermont, and Wyoming—no official estimates were available, and it was necessary to make some simple extrapolations based upon 1940–1950 trends controlled only by the estimates of total state population furnished by *Current Population Reports*. The final 1960 population figures were issued only a few weeks before the time this article was written, and it was not feasible, with the time and facilities available, to obtain some presumably better 1954 figures by interpolation from the 1950 and 1960 statistics. I feel that it is highly doubtful whether more accurate population data would alter any of the findings presented in this paper.

[5] Minor discrepancies can be noted between the data in Table II, and the corresponding table in the earlier article. These changes can be attributed to the fact that the data for the 1939–1947 period were initially tabulated and computed by hand, while the same material was reworked by means of an electronic computer for the present tables. The minor errors that occurred in the previous tables do not in any way invalidate the conclusions derived from them.

1939–1947 period (Fig. 1 and Table I). The unprecedented rise in business activity from 1939 to 1947 continued until 1954, but at a distinctly slower pace. Instead of the tripling in total value added by manufacture that was registered in the earlier period, the amount for 1954 exceeded that for 1947 by only 57 per cent; but an absolute gain of 42.5 billion dollars certainly indicates a vigorously growing economy. Rather more disturbing was the fact that the number of production workers reported for 1954 was only 4 per cent greater than that for 1947, although there had been a 52 per cent rise from 1939 to 1947.

POPULATION SHIFTS, 1939 TO 1954[6]

Since the distribution of manufacturing is closely linked to the number and location of a nation's inhabitants in more ways than one, changes in the former cannot be fully appreciated without considering the changing population map. The impressive growth in the number of Americans from 1939 to 1947 accelerated markedly during the next seven years and was accompanied by unusually large shifts in the relative location of population. The long-term growth of metropolitan areas progressed vigorously, so that by 1954, 58.7 per cent of the aggregate population were residing in metropolitan areas as compared to slightly less than 51 per cent in 1939. There were strong upward and downward trends in various regions within both the industrial and subindustrial categories of SEA's, but they were so evenly balanced within each category as to eliminate any significant net change from 1939 to 1954 (Table

[6] The statistical table on which this discussion is based is not furnished here. Because of space limitations, it was possible to reproduce only three of the eight basic tables used in preparing the text and illustrations. The author will be glad to furnish a complete set of these tables to any reader upon written request.

VALUE ADDED BY MANUFACTURE
AND PRODUCTION WORKERS
1929 TO 1954

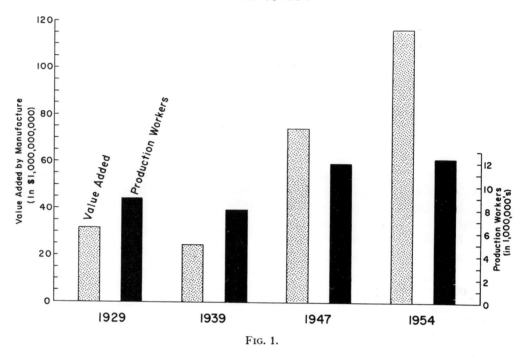

FIG. 1.

I). Thus we find the relative gains in population within the western part of the Manufacturing Belt cancelled out by the relative losses in the eastern segments; and the rapid growth of the Pacific, Mountain, and South Atlantic sub-industrial regions (the growth in the last largely within the Washington, D.C. area and southern Florida) compensated for the relative declines in other sub-industrial areas. In sum, then, the relative distribution of persons as between industrial and sub-industrial regions remained remarkably stable, with 50.0 per cent in the latter in 1939 and 49.8 per cent in 1954. Nevertheless, the relative population change within the individual regions should be taken into account in examining industrial change, not only in those instances where the two phenomena trend in

contrary directions but also in the more usual case where the two types of changes are parallel.

INTERREGIONAL SHIFTS
IN MANUFACTURING

A study of the indices of change in the relative distribution of manufacturing for the individual SEA's, which are summarized in Table II and Figure 2, reveals a predictable degree of variation from one area to another; but the overall pattern, as expressed in terms of regions and categories, is so clear-cut that tabular and diagrammatic representation is preferable to the use of detailed maps. We find for the 1947–1954 period an emphatic relative dispersion of industrial activity from all the closely clustered industrial regions, i.e., the Manufacturing Belt and the

TABLE I

SUMMARY TABLE: POPULATION, VALUE ADDED BY MANUFACTURE, AND PRODUCTION WORKERS—
BY LOCATION IN SMA'S AND INDUSTRIAL CATEGORY, 1929 TO 1954

A. Absolute Values

	Population (in 1,000's)					Value Added[1] (in $1,000,000)				Production Workers[2] (in 1,000's)			
	1930[1]	1940[1]	1948[1]	1950[2]	1954[2]	1929	1939	1947	1954	1929	1939	1947	1954
Metropolitan, total	61,990	67,127	79,088	85,485	94,556	24,964	19,179	55,982	88,358	6,305	5,601	8,517	8,716
Central Cities	39,491	41,522	46,194	49,225	--[4]	17,380	11,763	34,477	49,164	4,248	3,364	5,157	4,986
Rings, total	22,500	25,605	32,895	36,260	--[4]	7,584	7,416	21,505	39,194	2,058	2,237	3,360	3,730
Cities of 10,000 or more	9,662	10,297	11,939	--[4]	--[4]	4,433	3,839	10,200	17,046	1,172	1,095	1,566	1,669
Small cities and rural	12,838	15,308	20,955	--[4]	--[4]	3,151	3,577	11,305	22,144	886	1,142	1,794	2,061
Non-Metropolitan	60,785	64,542	66,957	65,212	66,626	6,921	5,500	18,440	28,561	2,534	2,283	3,418	3,656
Industrial[3]	--[4]	65,423 (1939)	71,640 (1947)	--[4]	80,927	--[4]	19,805	57,890	86,844	--[4]	6,155	9,124	8,955
Sub-Industrial[3]	--[4]	65,343 (1939)	71,874 (1947)	--[4]	80,255	--[4]	4,873	16,532	30,071	--[4]	1,728	2,812	3,417
U. S., total	122,775	131,669 (1940)	146,045 (1948)	150,697	161,182	31,885	24,678	74,422	116,915	8,838	7,883	11,936	12,372

B. Percentages of National Totals

	1930[1]	1940[1]	1948[1]	1950[2]	1954[2]	1929	1939	1947	1954	1929	1939	1947	1954
Metropolitan, total	50.5	51.0	54.2	56.1	58.7	78.3	77.7	75.2	75.6	71.3	71.0	71.6	70.5
Central Cities	32.2	31.5	31.6	32.4	--[4]	54.5	47.6	46.3	42.0	48.0	42.7	43.4	40.3
Rings, total	18.3	19.4	22.5	23.7	--[4]	23.8	30.1	28.9	33.6	23.3	28.3	28.2	30.2
Cities of 10,000 and more	7.9	7.8	8.2	--[4]	--[4]	13.9	15.6	13.7	14.6	13.3	13.9	13.2	13.5
Small cities and rural	10.5	11.6	14.3	--[4]	--[4]	9.9	14.4	15.2	18.9	10.0	14.5	15.0	16.7
Non-Metropolitan	49.5	49.0	45.8	43.9	41.3	21.7	22.3	24.8	24.4	28.7	29.0	28.4	29.5
Industrial	--[4]	50.0	49.9	--[4]	50.2	--[4]	80.3	77.8	74.3	--[4]	78.1	76.5	72.4
Sub-Industrial	--[4]	50.0	50.1	--[4]	49.8	--[4]	19.7	22.2	25.7	--[4]	21.9	23.5	27.6

C. Ratios among Population, Value Added by Manufacture, and Production Workers

	Per-Capita Value Added by Manufacture (in dollars and % of national average)				Production Workers as % of Total Population (in % of category pop. and % of national average)				Per-Worker Value Added by Manufacture (in dollars and % of national average)			
	1929	1939	1947	1954	1929	1939	1947	1954	1929	1939	1947	1954
Metropolitan, total	$403 (155)	$286 (152)	$708 (139)	$935 (129)	10.2 (142)	8.3 (138)	10.6 (129)	9.4 (12.2)	$3960 109.7	$3425 109.4	$6650 106.7	$10140 107.4
Central cities	440 (169)	283 (151)	746 (146)	--[4]	10.8 (150)	8.1 (135)	11.2 (137)	--[4]	4090 113.3	3495 111.7	6685 107.2	9860 104.3
Rings, total	337 (129)	290 (154)	654 (128)	--[4]	9.1 (126)	8.7 (145)	10.2 (124)	--[4]	3685 102.1	3315 105.9	6400 102.6	10510 111.2
Cities of 10,000 and more	459 (176)	373 (198)	849 (166)	--[4]	12.1 (169)	10.6 (177)	13.2 (161)	--[4]	3785 104.8	3510 112.1	6520 104.6	10215 108.1
Small cities and rural	246 (95)	234 (125)	539 (106)	--[4]	6.9 (96)	7.5 (125)	8.5 (104)	--[4]	3555 98.5	3130 100.0	6315 101.3	10745 113.7
Non-Metropolitan	114 (44)	85 (45)	275 (54)	429 (59)	4.2 (58)	3.5 (58)	5.1 (62)	5.5 (72)	2730 75.6	2410 77.0	5395 86.5	7810 82.7
Industrial	--[4]	303 (161)	808 (158)	1073 (148)	--[4]	9.4 (157)	12.7 (155)	11.1 (144)	--[4]	3215 102.7	6345 101.8	9695 102.6
Sub-Industrial	--[4]	75 (40)	230 (45)	375 (52)	--[4]	2.6 (43)	3.9 (48)	4.3 (56)	--[4]	2820 90.1	5880 94.3	8800 93.1
U. S., total	260	188	510	725	7.2	6.0	8.2	7.7	3610	3130	6235	9450

*Compiled, in part, from D. J. Bogue, Population Growth in Standard Metropolitan Areas, 1900-1950 and E. M. Kitagawa And D. J. Bogue, Suburbanization of Manufacturing Activity within Standard Metropolitan Areas.

1. SMA's defined as of 1940
2. SMA's defined as of 1950
3. Status defined as of 1947
4. Unavailable at present

Southeastern industrial region, to all the sub-industrial regions and to the Isolated Industrial SEA's whatever index is employed—with only a pair or so of equivocal cases. This decentralizing trend was so strong that the sub-industrial regions, which accounted for only 22.2 per cent of the nation's value added in 1947, reported 25.7 per cent seven years later. Or, expressed in another fashion, the total V, V:P, E, and E:P factors for these sub-industrial regions for the 1947–1954 period were all positive and ranged between 12.4 and 14.7 per cent of their 1954 totals of value added or production workers—a very healthy gain in every respect. This decentralizing trend was so pronounced in the years after 1947 that when we examine the V factor for the entire 1939–1954 period (Table II, Figs. 2 and 3), we note, as before, definite relative losses in the Manufacturing Belt and its Southeastern appendage and gains throughout the sub-industrial realm and the Isolated Industrial SEA's, excepting the minor losses in the New England and Middle Atlantic regions. When shifts in manufacturing activity are viewed against the background of changing population, as is done through the use of the V:P and E:P factors, the amount of disper-

sion is appreciably reduced (and in the solitary case of the East Lakes industrial region the dispersive trend gives way to centralization for the 1939–1954 period); but the general pattern of decentralization still remains quite strong for both the 1947–1954 and 1939–1954 periods.

Certain regions call for special comment. The Isolated Industrial SEA's, which at first glance would seem to represent an exception to the general trend toward decentralization, only confirm it after closer consideration. These are simply those scattered, outlying SEA's, presumably sub-industrial in character not too long ago, which have enjoyed an unusually large share of the industrial growth now being experienced by the better favored tracts of the nation lying beyond its older industrial core. These Isolated Industrial SEA's were defined on the basis of 1947 data; if our industrial regions were to be redrawn using 1954 criteria, it is more than likely that the number of

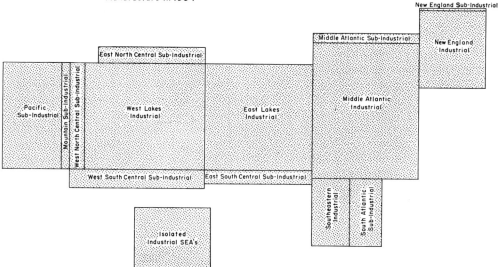

MANUFACTURING REGIONS

Areas Equivalent to Values Added by Manufacture in 1954

Fig. 2.

TABLE II

CHANGE IN THE RELATIVE DISTRIBUTION OF VALUE ADDED BY MANUFACTURE,
BY STATE ECONOMIC AREA AND MANUFACTURING REGION, 1939 TO 1954

Region	Value Added by Manufacture (in $1,000,000 and % of national total)			V Factor (in $1,000,000 and % of value of latter year)			V:P Factor		
	1939	1947	1954	1939-47	1947-54	1939-54	1939-47	1947-54	1939-54
INDUSTRIAL REGIONS A. New England	2366 9.6	6637 8.9	8858 7.6	-498 7.5	-1569 17.7	-2353 26.6	-258 0.1	-989 11.4	-1352 15.3
B. Middle Atlantic	5891 23.9	16704 22.4	24344 20.8	-1063 6.4	-1897 7.8	-3568 14.6	-337 2.0	-1424 5.9	-1874 7.7
C. East Lakes	4137 16.8	12213 16.4	19144 16.4	-262 2.1	-43 0.2	-455 2.4	+41 0.3	-69 0.6	+52 0.3
D. West Lakes	4844 19.6	14343 19.3	22147 18.9	-264 1.8	-384 1.7	-799 3.6	-462 3.2	-777 3.5	-1490 -6.8
Manufacturing Belt	17238 69.8	49897 67.0	74493 63.7	-2088 4.2	-3894 5.2	-7176 9.6	-1016 2.0	-3260 4.4	-4664 6.3
E. Southeastern	985 4.0	3278 4.4	4428 3.8	+307 9.4	-723 16.3	-239 5.4	+370 11.7	-582 10.7	-17 0.4
F. Isolated Industrial SEA's	1582 6.4	4715 6.3	7923 6.8	-53 1.1	+516 6.5	+431 5.4	-269 0.6	+126 0.4	-247 3.1
Total Industrial	19805 80.3	57890 77.8	86844 74.3	-1835 3.2	-4101 4.7	-6984 8.0	-915 1.6	-3716 4.3	-4928 5.7
SUB-INDUSTRIAL REGIONS New England	62 0.2	176 0.2	270 0.2	-9 5.1	-6 2.2	-22 8.1	-1 1.1	+4 1.4	+2 0.7
Middle Atlantic	358 1.4	1067 1.4	1624 1.4	-12 1.1	-52 3.2	-71 4.4	+94 3.7	+80 4.9	+208 12.8
East North Central	538 2.2	1738 2.3	2876 2.4	+114 6.5	+146 5.1	+327 11.4	+235 14.0	+327 11.4	+676 22.5
West North Central	494 2.0	1536 2.1	2672 2.3	+43 2.8	+260 9.7	+328 12.3	+201 13.1	+369 13.8	+680 25.5
Northeast	1452 5.9	4517 6.1	7442 6.4	+135 3.0	+347 4.7	+562 7.5	+531 11.8	+781 10.5	+1566 21.0
South Atlantic	677 2.7	2165 2.9	3773 3.2	+123 5.7	+372 9.8	+567 15.0	-20 0.9	+354 9.4	+260 6.9
East South Central	382 1.5	1557 2.1	2504 2.1	+406 26.1	+56 2.2	+695 27.7	+442 27.7	+202 8.1	+827 34.1
West South Central	603 2.4	2258 3.0	4218 3.6	+438 19.4	+670 15.9	+1359 32.2	+396 16.9	+629 14.9	+1222 29.0
South	1662 6.7	5980 8.0	10495 9.0	+968 16.2	+1100 10.5	+2622 25.0	+818 13.7	+1186 11.3	+2310 22.0
Mountain	274 1.1	835 1.1	1505 1.3	+8 1.0	+193 12.8	+206 13.7	-9 1.1	+70 4.7	+50 2.9
Pacific	1485 6.0	5200 7.0	10629 9.1	+721 13.9	+2459 23.1	+3592 33.8	-424 8.2	+1678 15.7	+1001 9.4
West	1759 7.1	6035 8.1	12134 10.4	+729 12.1	+2653 21.9	+3799 31.3	-433 7.2	+1749 14.5	+1051 8.7
Total Sub-Industrial	4873 19.7	16532 22.2	30071 25.7	+1833 11.1	+4101 13.6	+6983 23.2	+916 5.6	+3716 12.4	+4927 16.4
Metropolitan	19555 79.2	57244 76.9	90487 78.2	-1725 3.0	+558 0.6	-2154 2.4	-2448 4.3	-616 0.7	-4267 4.7
Non-Metropolitan	5123 20.8	17178 23.1	26428 21.8	+1724 10.0	-558 2.1	+2154 8.1	+2448 14.2	+616 2.3	+4267 16.1
GRAND TOTAL	24678 100.0	74422 100.0	116915 100.0	0	0	0	0	0	0

* SEA's defined as of 1950.

Isolated Industrial SEA's would be considerably augmented. Eventually, some of these rapidly developing areas may coalesce to form new and distinct industrial regions. Trends of industrial location indices within the clustered industrial regions roughly parallel population changes; relative losses are severe in the New England and Middle Atlantic industrial regions, but much less so in the East Lakes, West Lakes, and Southeastern regions.

Within the sub-industrial regions, changes in the New England and Middle

CHANGE IN PERCENTAGE OF NATIONAL VALUE ADDED BY MANUFACTURE, BY MANUFACTURING REGION, 1939-1954

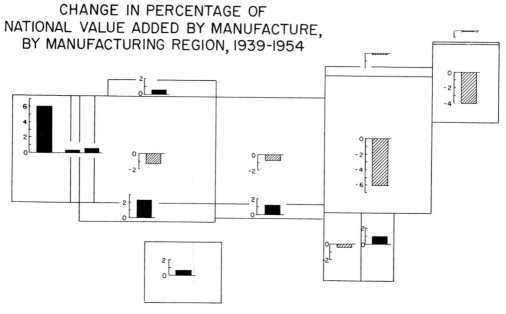

Fig. 3.

Atlantic are upward or downward, depending on the kind of index used, but unimportant in any case. Rather large positive changes are recorded for both North Central regions and for all the Southern regions, in spite of substantial relative losses in population (except in the South Atlantic region); and the gains are particularly impressive in the West North Central and West South Central sub-industrial regions. In the Mountain sub-industrial region, industrial growth more than kept pace with a sizable population increase from 1947 to 1954, even though it had barely succeeded in doing so during the previous period. The most spectacular change from the 1939–1947 period was, however, that experienced in the Pacific sub-industrial region. There rapid growth in industrial activity had been badly outdistanced during the earlier period by immense increments in population, so that large positive P and E factors were converted to strongly negative V:P and E:P factors. In the

years following 1947, accelerating industrial growth finally overtook a slackening, but still rapid, population upsurge, so that we find large V:P and E:P factors for the 1947–1954 period (and also for the entire 1939–1954 period). Here, then, we have what appears to be a major "breakthrough" in the economic development of the Pacific Coast; but only by analyzing the results of the 1958 and subsequent Censuses of Manufactures can we be certain that sufficient momentum has been generated to assure the long-term intensive industrialization of the Pacific region.

CHANGE IN METROPOLITAN LOCATION OF INDUSTRIAL ACTIVITY

One of the less predictable developments appearing in Tables I and II is the apparent halting or reversal of a trend of relative movement of industry from metropolitan to non-metropolitan SEA's—at least as measured in terms of value added by manufacture—that had prevailed up through 1947, though rather feebly after 1939 (Fig. 4). But the fact that there was an appreciable relative gain in production workers by the non-metropolitan areas from 1947 to 1954 indicates that the former trend still does persist after a fashion; and the slight gain of the metropolitan areas in terms of the V factor gives way to a large negative V:P factor when their large population growth is taken into account. The fact that the share of the total national value added by manufacture found in metropolitan areas increased from 76.9 per cent in 1947 to 78.2 per cent in 1954 can be attributed largely to the unusually vigorous development of SMA's having central cities

in the 250,000 to 1,000,000 class (Fig. 5), just those one would expect to identify as the major industrial centers of the more dynamic sub-industrial regions. A totally unexpected trend resulting from the contrary directions of change of value added and production workers as regards metropolitan location is the relative decline in per-worker productivity in non-metropolitan as opposed to metropolitan SEA's (Table I, Section C). This 1947–1954 development reverses a long-term trend toward the evening out of the differentials between the two classes of areas, and there is no ready explanation for this puzzling turn of events. In any event, we do see a continuation during the

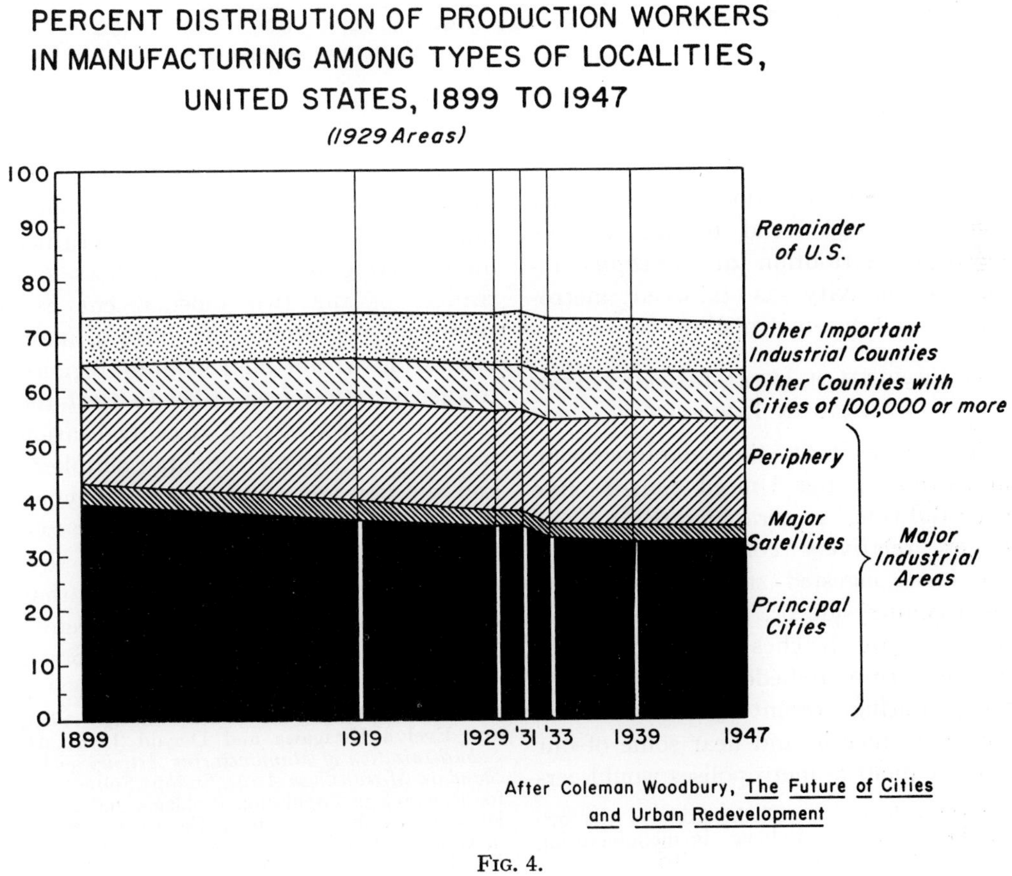

PERCENT DISTRIBUTION OF PRODUCTION WORKERS
IN MANUFACTURING AMONG TYPES OF LOCALITIES,
UNITED STATES, 1899 TO 1947

(1929 Areas)

After Coleman Woodbury, <u>The</u> <u>Future</u> <u>of</u> <u>Cities</u>
<u>and</u> <u>Urban</u> <u>Redevelopment</u>

FIG. 4.

DISTRIBUTION OF VALUE ADDED BY MANUFACTURE
BY LARGEST CITY IN SEA, 1939-1954
In Percent of National Total

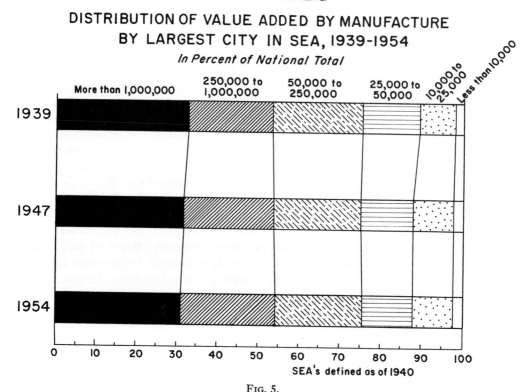

Fig. 5.

entire 1939–1954 period of the already well-established trend toward a more uniform distribution of *per-capita* industrial activity as between metropolitan and non-metropolitan areas.

The Problem of Intra-Metropolitan Shifts in Industry

The idea that the manufacturing industries of the United States have been diffusing[7] at a rapid rate from our larger, relatively congested cities to the less congested smaller towns and open countryside or, at the very least, to the outer reaches of suburbia has become firmly imbedded in the public mind during recent years. Casual reconnaissance in and near some of our larger industrial metropolises would cer-

tainly seem to confirm this popular impression. Consequently, it was rather disconcerting to both the authors and readers of the two most recent and thoroughgoing studies of shifts of manufacturing within metropolitan regions[8] to discover that from 1939 to 1947 the previous trend toward decentralization from large city to metropolitan periphery and the non-metropolitan areas beyond had been arrested and, in some respects, even reversed. These studies and several earlier ones leave little doubt that from 1899 to 1939 there had been a slow, but significant outward spread

[7] For a discussion and definition of the terminology of locational change in manufacturing activity, see Zelinsky, *op. cit.*, p. 108.

[8] Coleman Woodbury, ed.: *The Future of Cities and Urban Redevelopment*, Chicago, 1953; and Evelyn Kitagawa and Donald J. Bogue: *Suburbanization of Manufacturing Activity within Standard Metropolitan Areas*, Scripps Foundation for Research in Population Problems and Population Research and Training Center, University of Chicago, Studies in Population Distribution, No. 9, Oxford, Ohio, 1955.

of industry, a trend especially noticeable in the decade following 1929, so that the events of the eight years after 1939 represented a sharp departure from the historic pattern (Fig. 4).

In the course of this general study of locational changes in manufacturing from 1939 to 1954, it was decided to re-examine the 1939–1947 data on shifts in industrial activity within Standard Metropolitan Areas and, in particular, to chart the direction and extent of changes since 1947. The basic research design devised by Kitagawa and Bogue was adopted; and each of the 141 county-based SMA's, defined on the basis of 1940 population,[9] was subdivided into one or more central cities and the metropolitan ring lying beyond their corporate limits. The latter areal category was further subdivided into those suburban and satellite cities having a population of 10,000 or more, for which detailed figures are published, and the remaining smaller cities and rural tracts. Within the non-metropolitan SEA's, cities of 10,000 and more are again distinguished from the smaller cities and rural sections. In addition to the classification by region and level of industrial activity previously used in this paper, the SEA's have been assigned to six categories according to the size of their largest cities: more than 1,000,000, 250,000 to 1,000,000, and 50,000 to 250,000 for SMA's; and 25,000 to 50,000, 10,000 to 25,000, and less than 10,000 for non-metropolitan areas.

INTRA-METROPOLITAN DIFFUSION OF INDUSTRY AFTER 1947

The results of the subsequent analysis are most conveniently and meaningfully expressed in tabular and diagrammatic form. A glance at Table III or Figure 6 readily confirms the contention by earlier authors that decentralization was halted between 1939 and 1947. After 1947, however, the diffusion from the central city to the ring resumed with considerable vigor, even though there was no appreciable gain in non-metropolitan as opposed to metropolitan areas. This statement, like many that follow, refers to the aggregate pattern of all SMA's; but we should recognize a variability in the behavior of individual SMA's so great that no less than 44 were centralizing from 1939 to 1954 while 97 were decentralizing (Fig. 7). Within the metropolitan ring, there was a sharp difference between the record of cities of 10,000 and more, which barely held their own, and the small cities and rural areas, which gained considerably. It should be noted that there is a significant, but indeterminable, understatement of the relative losses in central cities and gains in the rings inasmuch as a number of central cities have annexed territory containing industrial enterprises during the study period. In any event, we can state that although the central city has contained the preponderance of industry within the SMA in the past—some 70 per cent of value added in 1929—the decline of its share to less than 56 per cent in 1954 indicates the strong possibility that sometime during the 1960's the metropolitan ring will be producing a larger share of the nation's manufactured goods than the central city. One paramount fact must be emphasized,

[9] The 1940 SMA's were used in Tables I and III, rather than the 1950 SMA's adopted in Table II, in order to ensure continuity with the Kitagawa-Bogue statistics. Despite the obvious discrepancies that result from the differences in definition, rough comparisons can still be made profitably between the metropolitan and non-metropolitan categories in the two sets of tables. For a discussion of the basis on which the 1940 SMA's were delimited see Donald J. Bogue, *Population Growth in Standard Metropolitan Areas: 1900–1950 with an Explanatory Analysis of Urbanized Areas* (Washington, Government Printing Office, 1953).

TABLE III

VALUE ADDED BY MANUFACTURE, BY LOCATION IN SMA'S, SIZE OF LARGEST CITY IN SEA, AND INDUSTRIAL
CATEGORY, 1939, 1947, AND 1954. (IN $1,000,000 AND PERCENTAGE OF CATEGORY TOTAL)

Largest City in SEA (1940 pop.)		Industrial SEA's (1947 definition)			Sub-Industrial SEA's (1947 definition)			Total		
		1939	1947	1954	1939	1947	1954	1939	1947	1954
1. More than 1,000,000	Total	7,242	20,564	29,767	886	3,103	6,715	8,128	23,667	36,482
	Central Cities	4,451	12,885	16,326	468	1,547	2,822	4,918	14,432	19,148
(6 SEA's)		61.4	62.6	54.8	52.7	49.9	42.0	60.5	60.9	52.5
	Rings, total	2,791	7,681	13,441	419	1,555	3,893	3,210	9,235	17,334
		38.6	37.4	45.2	47.3	50.1	58.0	39.5	39.1	47.5
	Cities of 10,000 and more*	2,051	5,049	7,786	160	634	2,284	2,211	5,682	10,070
		28.3	24.6	26.1	18.0	20.4	34.0	27.2	24.0	27.6
	Rural and small cities	740	2,632	5,655	259	921	1,609	999	3,553	7,264
		10.2	12.8	19.0	29.2	29.7	24.0	12.3	15.0	20.0
2. 250,000 to 1,000,000	Total	5,044	14,682	23,194	600	1,947	3,806	5,644	16,632	27,001
	Central Cities	3,103	8,890	12,650	488	1,593	2,871	3,592	10,483	15,528
(28 SEA's)		61.5	60.5	54.5	81.2	81.6	75.5	63.7	63.0	57.5
	Rings, total	1,941	5,792	10,544	112	354	935	2,053	6,149	11,473
		38.5	39.5	45.5	18.8	18.4	24.5	36.3	37.0	42.5
	Cities of 10,000 and more*	952	2,567	3,886	10	33	217	962	2,600	4,102
		18.9	17.5	16.8	1.6	1.7	5.7	17.1	15.6	15.2
	Rural and small cities	989	3,225	6,658	103	320	718	1,091	3,549	7,371
		19.6	22.0	28.7	17.2	16.6	18.9	19.3	21.4	27.3
3. 50,000 to 250,000	Total	4,565	12,961	19,837	840	2,721	5,037	5,404	15,682	24,875
	Central Cities	2,652	7,679	11,212	600	1,881	3,279	3,252	9,560	14,491
(107 SEA's)		58.2	59.3	56.6	71.5	69.2	65.1	60.2	60.9	58.2
	Rings, total	1,913	5,282	8,625	240	839	1,759	2,153	6,121	10,383
		41.8	40.7	43.4	28.5	30.8	34.9	39.8	40.1	41.7
	Cities of 10,000 and more*	636	1,829	2,601	30	89	273	666	1,918	2,874
		13.9	14.1	13.1	3.5	3.3	5.4	12.3	12.2	11.5
	Rural and small cities	1,277	3,453	6,024	210	749	1,486	1,487	4,203	7,509
		27.9	26.6	30.4	25.0	27.5	29.5	27.5	26.8	30.2
4. 25,000 to 50,000	Total	1,917	6,223	9,154	926	3,121	5,335	2,843	9,344	14,489
	Cities of 10,000 and more*	1,074	3,505	5,127	407	1,359	2,437	1,482	4,864	7,564
(96 SEA's)		56.0	56.3	56.0	44.0	43.9	45.7	51.7	52.1	52.2
	Rural and small cities	843	2,718	4,027	520	1,761	2,898	1,362	4,479	6,925
		44.0	43.7	44.0	56.0	56.1	54.3	48.3	47.9	47.8
5. 10,000 to 25,000	Total	928	2,993	4,238	1,250	4,347	7,176	2,178	7,340	11,414
	Cities of 10,000 and more*	227	875	1,276	335	1,075	2,092	562	1,949	3,367
(140 SEA's)		24.4	29.2	30.1	26.8	24.7	29.1	25.8	26.6	29.5
	Rural and small cities	701	2,118	2,962	915	3,273	5,085	1,617	5,391	8,047
		75.6	70.8	69.9	73.2	75.3	70.9	74.2	73.4	70.5
6. Less than 10,000	Total	110	463	654	372	1,291	2,002	482	1,753	2,656
	Cities of 10,000 and more*	3	8	60	2	11	96	6	19	156
(85 SEA's)		2.7	1.7	9.2	0.5	0.8	4.8	1.3	1.1	5.9
	Rural and small cities	107	455	594	369	1,279	1,906	476	1,735	2,499
		97.3	98.3	90.8	99.5	99.2	95.2	98.7	98.9	94.1
TOTAL	Metropolitan, total	16,850	48,209	72,798	2,328	7,771	15,562	19,179	55,982	88,354
		85.1	83.3	83.9	47.8	47.1	51.9	77.3	75.2	75.6
(462 SEA's)	Central Cities	10,204	29,454	40,188	1,557	5,023	8,975	11,763	34,477	49,164
		51.5	50.9	46.3	31.9	30.4	29.8	47.6	46.3	42.0
	Rings, total	6,645	18,755	32,610	771	2,748	6,587	7,416	21,505	39,190
		33.6	32.4	37.6	15.9	16.7	22.1	29.7	28.9	33.6
	Cities of 10,000 and more*	3,639	9,445	14,273	200	756	2,774	3,839	10,200	17,046
		18.4	16.3	16.4	4.1	4.6	9.2	15.6	13.7	14.6
	Rural and small cities	2,506	9,310	18,337	571	1,992	3,813	3,577	11,305	22,144
		12.6	16.1	21.2	10.8	12.1	11.9	14.1	15.2	19.0
	Non-Metropolitan, total	2,955	9,681	14,046	2,545	8,761	14,509	5,499	18,440	28,561
		14.9	16.7	16.1	52.2	52.9	48.1	22.7	24.8	24.4
	Cities of 10,000 and more*	1,304	4,388	6,463	744	2,455	4,625	2,050	6,772	11,087
		6.6	7.6	7.4	15.3	14.9	15.4	8.3	9.1	9.5
	Rural and small cities	1,651	5,293	7,583	1,801	6,306	9,884	3,449	11,668	17,474
		8.3	9.1	8.7	36.9	38.0	32.7	14.0	15.7	14.9
	GRAND TOTAL	19,805	57,890	86,844	4,873	16,532	30,071	24,678	74,422	116,915

*Category includes all cities indicated as having 10,000 or more inhabitants by preceding population census and a few cities of lesser population, including Virginia's smaller independent cities, for which data are tabulated by the Census of Manufactures.

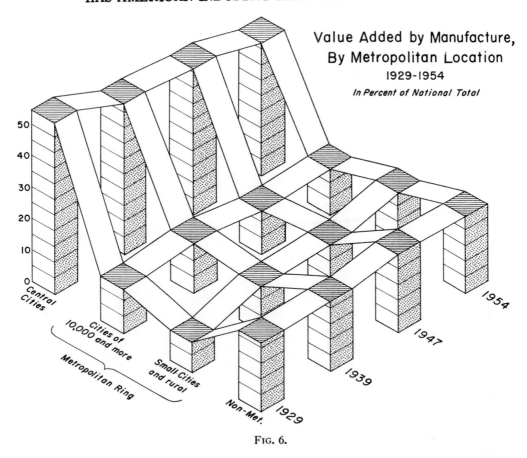

Value Added by Manufacture,
By Metropolitan Location
1929-1954
In Percent of National Total

FIG. 6.

however. Whatever the internal shifts within metropolitan areas or those among various parts of the nation, manufacturing remains an overwhelmingly urban phenomenon, if we use the term "urban" in its broader and ever more meaningful sense. By combining SMA's with the larger cities of non-metropolitan areas, we find that they account for more than 85 per cent of value added and more than 81 per cent of production workers, with no significant trend upward or downward in recent years.

INTRA-METROPOLITAN SHIFTS BY INDUSTRIAL STATUS

Thus far we have noted only the aggregate pattern of locational change;

but by separating industrial from sub-industrial areas, some striking divergences appear. Within the vigorously growing sub-industrial category, metropolitan areas have gained much more rapidly than the non-metropolitan, whatever the size of the central city concerned (Table III, Fig. 8). Furthermore, the relative losses of sub-industrial central cities have been relatively moderate as compared to the industrial central cities. Equally interesting is the sharp contrast in pattern within the ring and non-metropolitan sectors of the industrial and sub-industrial categories. The larger satellite cities in sub-industrial SMA's have reported rapid relative industrial growth; but the small city-rural sections of these

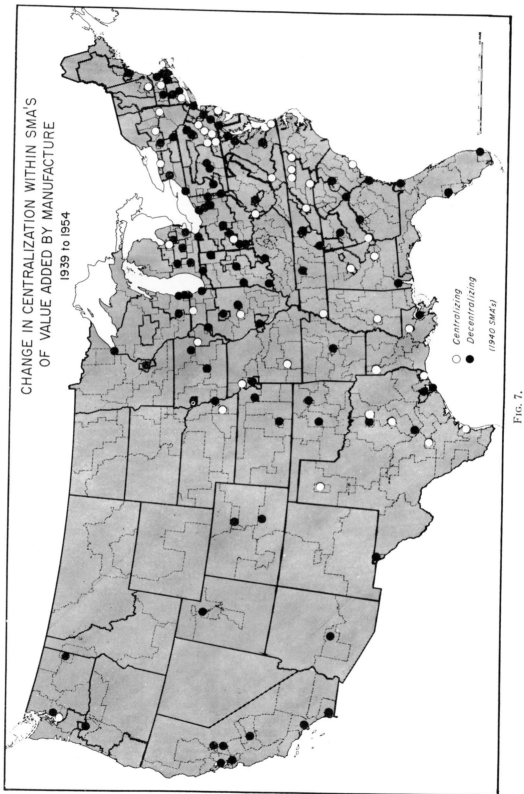

CHANGE IN CENTRALIZATION WITHIN SMA'S
OF VALUE ADDED BY MANUFACTURE
1939 to 1954

○ Centralizing
● Decentralizing

(1940 SMA's)

FIG. 7.

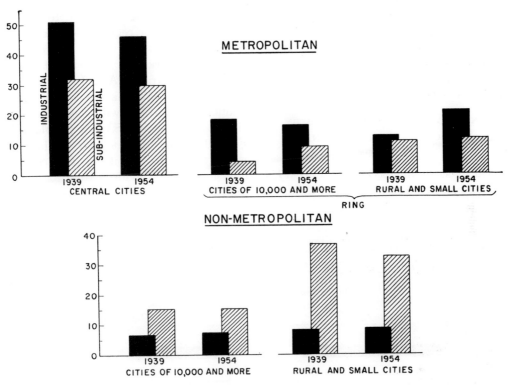

VALUE ADDED BY MANUFACTURE, 1939 AND 1954
BY INDUSTRIAL CATEGORY AND METROPOLITAN LOCATION
In Percent of Category Total

FIG. 8.

SMA's have barely gained, the larger cities of the sub-industrial non-metropolitan SEA's have lost slightly, in relative terms, and there has been a sharp drop in the small city-rural sections of these SEA's. The behavior of the industrial SEA's has been almost exactly the mirror image of these trends. Not only have there been sharp losses experienced by the central cities but also in the satellite cities, while there has been a notable expansion of activity in the small cities and rural sections of the rings; relative growth has been modest, but significant, in both urban and rural portions of industrial non-metropolitan SEA's. Much, but not all, of this divergence in pattern can be explained by the relatively large supply of good, undeveloped factory sites, the readier accessibility of other necessities for industrial expansion within the larger sub-industrial cities, and, hence, their superior ability to generate new or augmented industrial production.

It would be most instructive to observe intra-metropolitan changes in population alongside those occurring in industry; but at the time statistical compilations were being made for this study there was no way to obtain reliable estimates of the population size of individual cities in 1954 and thus carry the analysis past 1950. Nevertheless, it can be said that, at least until 1950, industry had been decentralizing even more rapidly than people, so that manufacturing, which was originally much more concentrated within the central city than population, is now somewhat less so (Fig. 9). The rural-small city sector of the ring still contains a larger fraction of total metropolitan population than of industry, but this differential may disappear shortly.

INTRA-METROPOLITAN SHIFTS BY SIZE OF CITY AND REGIONAL LOCATION

Our basic finding is that the 1947–1954 period has seen a resumption of diffusion from the central city to the metropolitan ring, but not significantly beyond the boundaries of the SMA. This is subject to major qualifications, however, when we view our unit areas in terms of population size or regional location and distinguish between value added and production workers. In terms of value added, the intra-SMA diffusion of industry since 1947 was much more pronounced in SMA's with large central cities than in other SMA's (Table III, Fig. 10). The tendency for production workers to disperse from the central city is much less evident than for value added; but, once again, the decentraliz-

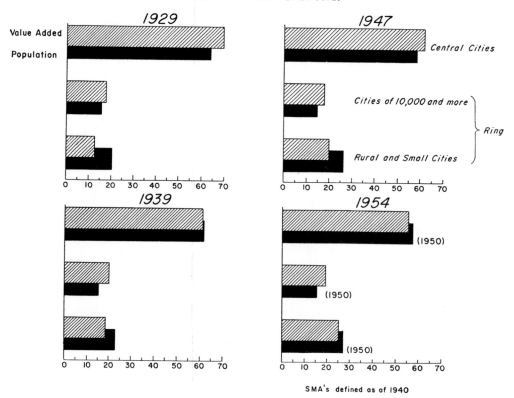

DISTRIBUTION OF VALUE ADDED BY MANUFACTURE AND POPULATION WITHIN SMA'S, 1929 TO 1954

In Percent of National SMA Total

SMA's defined as of 1940

FIG. 9.

PERCENTAGE OF VALUE ADDED BY MANUFACTURE
IN SEA'S ACCOUNTED FOR BY CITIES OF 10,000 AND MORE*
By Largest City in SEA, 1939 and 1954
In Percent of Category Total

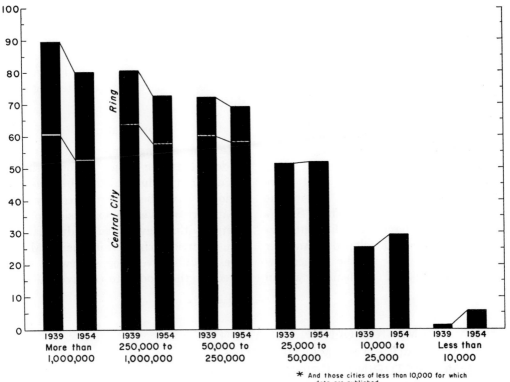

FIG. 10.

ing trend is positively correlated with the size of the central city. Within non-metropolitan areas, where industry has always been much less urbanized than in SMA's, the opposite trend prevails: cities of 10,000 and more are gaining much more rapidly than the rest of the category, and the rate of gain varies inversely with the size of the largest city in the SEA. It would appear, then, that centripetal forces weaken as size of city increases. At a certain level, probably cities of about 50,000 for value added or cities of about 200,000 for production workers, the forces of centralization and diffusion are in rough balance, while below this level the central tendency is the stronger one.

The 1939–1954 period has witnessed perhaps the most vigorous redistribution of industry in our modern history. It would seem worthwhile, therefore, to explore the possibilities that the aggregate pattern of intra-metropolitan diffusion represents a national average of widely disparate regional patterns and that these regional departures from the national norm might conceivably shed some light on the larger inter-regional shifts. Yet when we tabulate the industrial activity within each industrial region, in terms of central cities, metropolitan rings, and non-metropolitan areas, for 1939, 1947, and 1954, for both value added and production workers (Fig. 11), there is a surprising uniformity in their patterns of change. Almost everywhere there is the familiar growth of the ring at the expense of the central city and the slight or nonexistent expansion of activity within non-metropolitan areas. Only in the South Central sub-industrial and the Southeastern industrial regions did industrial growth within central cities outstrip that in the rings; and there the explanation may well lie in the predominance of relatively small SMA's in which, as we have seen, the centralizing trend is well developed. Another possible factor may be the rather low average density of settlement within

corporate areas in much of the South. Less clear is the explanation for the relative declines in the non-metropolitan industrial status of the Southeastern industrial region and the Mountain, Pacific, and West North Central sub-industrial regions or the sharp rise in the same category within the West Lakes industrial region; but these aberrations from the general trend have had little bearing on the larger inter-regional shifts.

Conclusions

In summarizing our findings, it seems evident that the major regional shifts, mainly from industrial to sub-industrial regions, have been generated by the greater than average expansion of industry within several sub-industrial regions, particularly within their SMA's. These shifts have been somewhat tempered by the moderate relative gains of

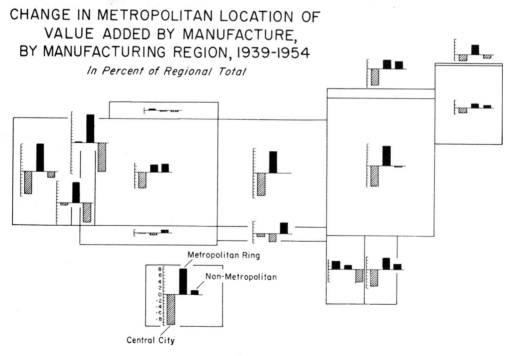

CHANGE IN METROPOLITAN LOCATION OF
VALUE ADDED BY MANUFACTURE,
BY MANUFACTURING REGION, 1939-1954
In Percent of Regional Total

Fig. 11.

PER-WORKER VALUE ADDED BY MANUFACTURE, BY METROPOLITAN LOCATION, 1929 TO 1954

In Percent of National Average

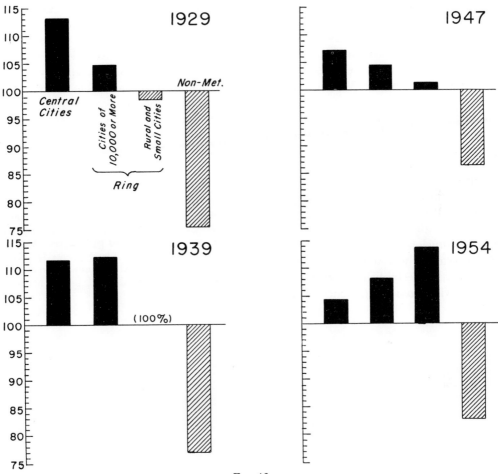

FIG. 12.

industry in much of the non-metropolitan sector within the Manufacturing Belt, and all these changes have evolved alongside a simultaneous national pattern (one that clearly transcends regional boundaries) of relative movement to or from the locally dominant city. Type of industrial index, size of the city, and degree of industrialization of the area appear as the major determinants of the direction and extent of the movement.

Since most manufacturing is centered in those highly urbanized and industrialized areas with the strongest tendency to decentralize from the dominant city, the aggregate trend toward diffusion of industrial activity within the SMA is unmistakable; but the centripetal tendencies of relatively rural and unindustrialized areas are also important and must not be overlooked.

It is important to note, in conclusion,

that despite strong basic similarities in the locational shifts of both value added and production workers, there are also significant divergencies in certain regions and categories and that occasionally these two measures of industrial activity trend in opposite directions. Within the SMA, the diffusion of value added has progressed much faster than that of production workers (except during the anomalous 1939–1947 period) with a consequent relative rise in per-worker productivity in the metropolitan ring (Fig. 12). This fact suggests, in turn, that much of the augmented production within the ring may be accounted for by newer plants with their greater efficiency and productivity. In view of these considerations and the virtual certainty that the halt of intra-SMA diffusion during the 1939–1947 period was only a temporary interruption of a well-established trend, we can accept with some confidence the conjectures by Woodbury and by Kitagawa and Bogue that this interruption was caused by the extraordinary seller's market of World War II and the immediate postwar period that favored the rapid expansion of output in existing, generally centrally located plants rather than the construction of newer, more efficient facilities in outlying areas. Even though it is hazardous to forecast such complex phenomena, it is reasonable to expect a continuation for some years of both the interregional and intra-metropolitan shifts in industrial activity described in this study.

Acknowledgments

The research reported in this study was made possible by a grant from the Association of American Geographers and by the assistance of Dr. H. N. Laden, Chief, New Systems Development, Chesapeake and Ohio Railway Company, Cleveland, Ohio, and his staff in the machine processing of statistics.

THE NEW WORLD OF MACHINE TOOLS

by
MELVIN MANDELL

"Our customers are so timid it's pathetic," complains a machine tool company executive. He has been caught in his industry's own private recession since 1958, and he puts at least a share of the blame for his troubles on the nation's metalworking companies. "They don't dare try a new process," he says. "They're just not interested in pioneering even when they can see a profit in it."

Every day, new evidence strengthens his indictment. Take, for example, the study of machine tool replacement just finished by Arthur D. Little, Inc., a Boston industrial research firm. The Little report shows that metalworking companies pay a lot more attention to what their competitors are buying than to their own needs when they are planning their machine tool purchases. So long as his competitor is not buying new equipment, the average metalworking executive is happy to make do with the tools already installed in his plant, no matter how old or obsolete they are.

This, it is plain, is a good part of the reason why the machine tool industry has been sinking into deeper and deeper trouble. The toolmakers' sales have been sagging ever since they reached a postwar high of $1,910 million in 1953. When their sales failed to swing up with the rest of the economy after the 1958 recession, the toolmakers first hoped that their own recovery had been postponed only a little. But the postponement went on and on. Now, while the 1960 recession comes to its end, machine tools stick stubbornly in their $500-$600 million slump. Says a veteran Wall Street analyst: "Here we are in the middle of a solid recovery and machine tools are hardly holding their own."

Other big factors contribute to the machine tool industry's doldrums. One is the heavy overcapacity in most lines of metalworking. This helps hold down orders from the toolmakers' potential customers. Another is the basic shift in defense production from large runs of airplanes and tanks to small, but high-priced, orders for missiles. This has made a change in defense contractors' machine tool needs. They no longer need large numbers of standard machine tools; instead, they want small numbers of highly specialized tools.

These are changes that the machine tool industry cannot hope to fight — they are quite beyond its control. But it can hope to drum up more business from many of its customers who are not affected by overcapacity or defense production.

And this is why the toolmakers are now engaged in an all-out effort to break down the barrier of timidity among their overcautious customers and build a new, more prosperous world for themselves. "One decent break in that wall might soon produce a steadily growing flow of orders," says one major toolmaker. "Once a few of the leaders in the metalworking business start modernizing, the others will probably have to step up their orders if they are to stay competitive."

THE BIG GAIN

To start the flow, the toolmakers are now building increasingly sophisticated, complex and adaptable machines. "We don't believe the great bulk of the metalworking industry can afford to ignore these new products and new techniques much longer," says the president of one leading tool company.

Of all the innovations in the toolmakers' array of new equipment, the most spectacular in terms of the gains in productivity they offer are tape-controlled machine tools. An operator working with a conventional machine can usually spend only fifteen minutes out of every hour actually cutting or grinding the piece of metal on which he is working. He spends the other 45 minutes measuring the cuts he makes, adjusting or replacing the cutting tools. But the tape-controlled machine is guided at its work by instructions punched on a paper tape or "fluxed" into a magnetic tape. Most of the stopping and starting, the adjusting and replacing, is skipped.

Some 1,200 tape-controlled machine tools are at work today in metalworking plants in the nation's industrial centers, and 71 different companies are making control equipment for these machines at prices ranging from $9,000 to $60,000. Scientists at Massachusetts Institute of Technology were the first to succeed in equipping a machine tool with tape controls that could guide the machine in a two-dimensional plane. That was in 1951. Since then scores of refinements have been added.

The most sophisticated today are the "five-axis," continuous-path, tape-controlled machine tools, which can carve out parts impossible to make in one piece by any other method. But it takes hours or days of computer programming to prepare the taped instructions for these machines. This can cost huge sums of money, and the initial price of the tools and their controls is enough to make even a prosperous metalworker wince.

So far only the Government has been able to afford these advanced machines, buying them for loan to the big defense contractors. To justify the investment, of course, a metalworker would have to keep the machines busy at least two shifts a day.

But one big potential saving in the cost of programming the machines is on the way. Late in June the International Business Machines Corp. put on the market its Autopromt system for preparing taped instructions for machine tools. This can help a manufacturer eliminate up to 90% of the cost of tape preparation. The heart of this system lies in a reel of magnetic tape that contains the skeleton of a machine program and into which can be fitted step-by-step instructions that will guide the machine as it tackles each job.

IBM guesses that Autopromt will generate much new business for its Service Bureau Corp. computer centers and so will let its customers use the Autopromt system at no cost.

Autopromt is the only simple systen generally available for guiding machine tools in complex, three-dimensional work. Many other standard programs for tape-controlled machines, it is true, are stored in libraries set up by the control equipment manufacturers. To match IBM's new move, the manufacturers are bound to expand the range of their tape libraries.

A NEAR-REVOLUTION

No less an authority than Warren C. Hume, president of IBM's data processing division, believes industry is on the verge of a near-revolution in tape-controlled machining. "Some day," says he, "the design engineer will simply tell the computer what the function of a part is to be. The computer will come up with the optimum design — and will then produce the control tape for the machine tool."

To the ever-hopeful makers of machine tools all this means that those versatile, super-accurate, numerically controlled tools may eventually come within the financial reach of many metalworking companies that have been sliding along so far with older machines and methods.

The toolmakers have been working, too, on simpler, less costly ways of boosting their conventional machines' productivity. They have:

1. Devised a system of quick-change tooling for conventional machine tools that make it unnecessary for the cutting angle to be set by hand. "In machining one complex part," says a user, "this switch has helped us cut time for tooling changes from eight hours to just ten minutes."

2. Redesigned the big transfer machines that are the workhorses of the U.S. auto industry. For instance, Detroit plants no longer must replace an entire line of machine tools at model change time. Their new machine lines are designed on the building-block basis so that one unit can be pulled out of the line and a new one fitted in without junking the rest of the machine.

3. Built up the talents of the big transfer lines so that instead of performing only one function, a single system can now mill, bore, turn, grind and broach, and provide heat treatments in between.

4. Improved accuracy to the point where ordinary grinding machines that not long ago could work only on specifications of thousandths of an inch now can grind to tolerances of millionths of an inch.

5. Cut prices and boosted quality, as, for example, in a bearing race grinder built by Van Norman Industries that takes up only half the usual floor space, needs only $5,000 worth of tooling *vs.* $15,000 worth for older machines, costs from 20% to 35% less than previous models and has 30% more productive capacity.

On the horizon are even more startling advances due from the toolmakers. Four companies are working now on machines that will drill metal parts by electrolysis. By a technique of reverse plating, these machines can carve today's super-hard alloys ten times faster than any steel or carbide tool. Another exotic technique, still a long way from use in industry, is machining by means of concentrated beams of electrons or streams of plasma — ionized gases hotter than the surface of the sun.

But all that is the promise of the future. The reality of the present is that the nation's metalworking companies are content to get along with machine tools that average, by the best surveys, well over ten years in age. The toolmakers, not unnaturally, put most of the blame for this on the timidity of their customers. But they reserve some of the blame for the Federal Government, on two separate counts.

First, they charge, the Government is in direct sales competition with them. During World War II, Washington acquired 25% of the nation's stock of machine tools. And lately it has been disposing of them at bargain prices. This, the toolmakers complain, takes a large bite out of their potential sales and breeds a price psychology among the buyers that has grown into a long-term danger for the machine tool industry.

"The buyer," says William J. Pinkerton, vice president of Detroit's Micromatic Hone Corp., "finds the immediate saving in buying government machines too tempting to resist. But he gets a dated concept of our machines. He judges us by equipment that is old and not backed by all the services and production know-how we give our customers."

The toolmakers' second count against Washington stems from the Treasury's depreciation allowance

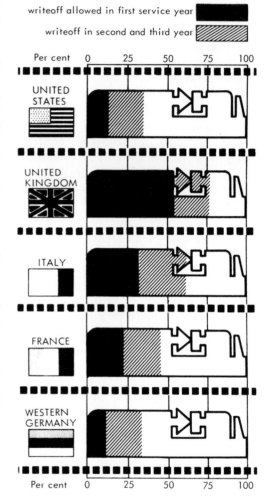

The Depreciation Gap

Toolmakers charge that slow depreciation on capital goods in the U.S. discourages new investment, slows national growth. Comparisons below are based on equipment given 15-year life for tax purposes.

writeoff allowed in first service year

writeoff in second and third year

Per cent   0   25   50   75   100

UNITED STATES

UNITED KINGDOM

ITALY

FRANCE

WESTERN GERMANY

Per cent   0   25   50   75   100

policy. With the solitary exception of West Germany, the U.S. permits a smaller write-off on a new machine tool during its first year of service than any other major industrial nation (see chart above).

"Look at the new British depreciation rules," says Francis J. Trecker, president of Kearney &

Trecker Corp. "They let a manufacturer credit 20% of the purchase price of a new machine against taxes immediately, and the full cost in just five years. That's the only way we could catch up here on undepreciation."

Even that tells only part of the problem. As the toolmakers readily admit, most of their smaller customers fail to take full advantage of the depreciation charges allowed by present tax rules.

"MEAT OF THE COCONUT"

Adding to the depreciation woes, the toolmakers do not believe that President Kennedy's proposed new corporation tax rules, touted as a means of stimulating capital investment, will have much benefit. "They just don't touch the meat of the coconut," says George H. Johnson, president of Gisholt Machine Co.

Adds another toolmaker: "What we need is tax laws that stimulate modernization — not just expansion."

However harsh, most of the toolmakers are facing up to the political realities; they do not expect liberalized depreciation rules this year or next. But there is growing awareness in Congress of the problems posed by the present rules, and the toolmakers are most optimistic about the chance for changes in the middle years of this decade. The question, though, is whether the metalworking industry can afford to stick with its old machines for that long.

Henry F. De Long, head of General Electric's Metallurgical Products Department, puts the question in sharp focus. "By neglecting to modernize," he says, "the metalworking industry is wasting $1 billion a year — twice the amount it is now spending for machine tools."

PROFILE OF AN INDUSTRY IN TRANSITION

You don't buy capital equipment the way you did a decade ago.

And because you don't, the machine tool industry is undergoing the most significant transition in its history.

The changes will affect the ways equipment is "sold" to you. They will affect the ways in which you "use" machine tool builders, and they already are affecting the kind of equipment you will use.

The change is turning nearly all builders from the role of inventor and seller of machinery to roles of customer consultant, process engineer, innovator, designer, as well as trainer of maintenance, operation, and management of new capital equipment and processes.

It used to be that one man in a plant did the equipment buying, and he often had a near carte blanche from management to spend what he needed to get performance. Now, this man is part of a buying team of both line and staff specialists.

The machines he bought in 1955 cost an average of $13,000. Today, the average metal cutting machine tool costs nearly twice that, and the small company that strained the coffers to buy a $50,000 machine may well be spending $250,000 for one today. Top management is directly involved.

When machines were selected, a basic choice most often was made between the flexibility of a standard machine, or the mass production capability of a single purpose special. Today, an increasingly large share of the machines bought fall in the wide gap between those two extremes. Standards are modified for special needs, specials are made so they can be rearranged to accommodate a variety of parts or design changes. And the "automated flexibility" of numerical control accounted for a full 20 percent of the backlog in metal cutting machines at the beginning of this year, and undoubtedly accounts for a higher percentage today.

Traditionally, you spent fairly heavily for new capital equipment whenever you had to expand production, or when you had a new product that wouldn't fit your existing facilities. Otherwise, you mostly just bought when one of your machines wore out and needed replacing. Today, you are more likely to have continuing analyses of manufacturing approaches, and the pace of new developments forces you to be almost always in the market for new equipment.

How important are the differences: One builder tells STEEL he feels: "Any company that continues to use the traditional approach to buying machine tools is going to be out of business within ten years."

WHY THE SWITCH?

The "old way" of machine tool buying encouraged substitution of a

"Profile Of An Industry In Transition." Reprinted from Steel, *Vol.* 157 (*September* 13, 1965), *pp.* 154-160. *Copyright* 1965 *by The Penton Publishing Co., Cleveland, Ohio.*

machine for another of the same type . . . or it allowed adding of machines without studying all of the proper alternatives. Consider the pitfalls in a situation that prevailed in one plant before the company decided to analyze its needs. The factory had 41 lathes. Fully 81.5 percent of the workpieces machined could have been handled on lathes having swing capacity of about 8 in. But no lathe in the plant had a swing of less than 10 in. And while 71.5 percent of the workpieces had lengths less than 8 in. only one lathe had less than a 59 in. center, the majority being 6 to 15 ft. The company's conclusion: The total lathe production could have been handled for half the capital investment, and savings from such things as floor space and electricity would have added to the economy.

The kind of buying that machine tool builders encounter today not only would have established a more judicial selection of lathes, it might also have turned up processes that eliminated turning on some parts, and could have automated other operations so that one automatic machine might replace three or four conventional ones.

The difference today is "systems buying," or "team buying," in which line and staff specialists work with suppliers to define a whole manufacturing problem to reach a total solution to the problem — and then make sure that all individual purchases fit the overall requirement. Commenting on the role of the machine tool builder, Paul Stanton, vice president, marketing, Pratt & Whitney Machine Tool Div., Colt Industries Inc., West Hartford, Conn., says: "In many cases, we become ad hoc members of our customers' process and manufacturing teams."

Philip O. Geier, Jr., president and general manager, Cincinnati Milling Machine Co., Cincinnati, asserts: We are becoming intimately involved with what the customers are doing and what they are planning for the next two or three years. And they should know what we are planning because it could affect their design and their costs. This kind of relationship requires the highest level of mutual confidence."

New Role? What does this mean? Mr. Geier continues: "We are less in the business of supplying hardware, and more in the business of trying to supply what the customer needs."

To the machine tool builder, this has meant a reshaping of his sales and service staffs. The traditional machine tool salesman knew his machine well, and was a superb mechanic and tooling expert. Today, he must also be able to analyze customer parts and their design, find new places where his machines can be used or adapted, talk about the financial justification of the method, discuss mechanics, electronics, hydraulics, and a dozen other subjects intelligently.

Machine tool distributors, who account for more than half the machines sold today, have launched a series of management workshops, numerical control seminars, and numerous other training aids through their American Machine Tool Distributors' Association.

Burnell A. Gustafson, executive vice president, capital equipment operations, Sundstrand Corp., Rockford, Ill., comments: "Selling machine tools today is more expensive than it has ever been. It includes

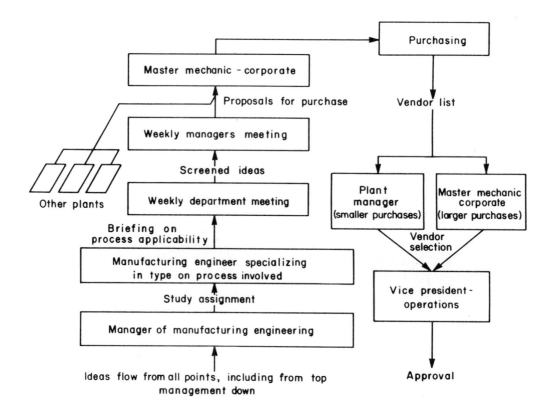

customer training, service booklets, follow-up. Users place a higher degree of reliance on us to provide a finished machine that's ready for production. In the old days, the customers had crews that could whip the machine into shape. Now, it takes a team of people selling allied areas rather than a single machine . . . service, maintenance, manufacturing methods, engineering, etc."

George Cassady, vice president, sales, Giddings & Lewis Machine Tool Co., Fond du Lac, Wis., agrees. "In our industry there has been more change in selling techniques in the last five years than there had been in the previous 25. In fact, the changes are coming so rapidly that some of the old-timers are simply giving up and turning over the reins to some of the younger men who are

not quite as frightened by the advent of such things as computers, committee buying, and payback analysis."

He adds: "In the last five years, our sales force has increased by more than 20 percent. More important has been the shift from the strictly mechanical expert to graduate engineers in either mechanical or electrical engineering." Further dramatizing his company's involvement in advanced equipment, including NC, Mr. Cassady emphasizes: "Our service force has gone up 185 percent in the last five years, and the electrical portion of that force has tripled."

Commenting on what it takes to back up sales of advanced machines, William Bentley, president, Cincinnati Lathe & Tool Co., Cincinati, says: "The builder must now train programmers. And to do this, we must become more and more involved in the user's operations. We must familiarize users with the new electronic controls. We must instruct users in the proper maintenance of NC machines. We must have our own service organization in the field. The total investment . . . is now at a remarkably high level. We now have three times as many service specialists in the field as we have engineers in the company."

Cost-Price Squeeze. The advent of all of the extra services as part of the marketing operation has put the cost of marketing machine tools into orbit. (Many builders bury these costs in overhead.) But many builders agree that the costs of such services are difficult to recover, and some are operating on profit margins under 5 percent, even during the record peacetime boom.

Many makers feel that the cost of machines that require this kind of support from the builder has to be covered. Some suggest that equipment prices must be increased.

A second approach is that used by Kearney & Trecker Corp., Milwaukee. J. Robert Jones, vice president, sales, explains: "We include in the basic price of our machines, such as the Milwaukee-Matics, the extras that we know should be a standard part of the package. This includes some basic instruction on maintenance and operation, for example. But if a customer desires added training or service, we charge for it. In addition, we charge when the customer wants us to furnish supervision for field erection."

This system permits the builder to recover his cost of providing the services — costs he might otherwise have to "eat." But also, many builders feel it has a direct user benefit, since the customer is charged only for those extra services he requires, and he does not pay (through higher machine prices) for the shortcomings or extra requirements of other companies.

RAMPANT TECHNOLOGY

Mr. Gustafson says: "In 1946, we introduced our 8-A lathe, and we're still selling it. Yet, we are now in the fifth generation — major change in concept or machine redesign — of numerical control; it was introduced in 1950."

And Julian C. Pease, president, New Britain Machine Co., New Britain, Conn., avers: "We used to feel that a new machine tool design had a product life of at least ten years. Today, we can't even be sure about a full year."

An industry that used to compare the price of a machine with its weight has come a long way in just ten years. But it has demanded a new approach to machine development. James A. D. Geier, vice president and group manager, machine tools, Cincinnati Milling, says: "Machine tools used to be invented. Today, they grow out of real needs that already exist in our customers' plants and that demand a solution."

The burden of detecting customer needs, translating them into solutions, and then engineering the solutions into hardware has been a heavy one for an industry that's made up mostly of relatively small companies, and it has taken its toll. Nearly two dozen of the machine tool companies that proudly showed their wares at the 1955 Machine Tool Exposition are no longer in existence as independent companies, and some have vanished.

Mr. Gustafson puts his finger on part of the reason when he opines: "You can't *follow* the trends in technology. They will eat you up. The only way you can hope to survive in the competitive technological race and to recover the investment it takes is to come out a leader."

New Order Of Capability. How much does it cost? Obviously there are no "averages" here, but take a couple of examples. Cincinnati Milling, which has always invested heavily in research, pours an increasingly large number of dollars into it. P. Willard Crane, vice president, research and development, tells STEEL: "In the last 12 years, our expenditures for research and product development of machine tools have increased seven-fold, and that does not include the cost of machine design."

At Ingersoll Milling, the engineering and technical staff has been doubled in the last five years. Giddings & Lewis reports similar increases, particularly in electronics capability.

Manufacturing. An old-timer could stroll through some of today's machine tool plants and not even recognize the industry. Parts of it are literally extensions of the electronics business.

The demands for precision have forced builders to spend heavily for new manufacturing facilities and equipment. Many numerically controlled machines and spindles are being put together in whiterooms — they're temperature, humidity, and dust controlled. Airborne Instruments Laboratory Div., Cutler-Hammer Inc., Deer Park, N.Y., has sold ten laser calibrators said to

be capable of calibrating linear distances within 0.000003 in. Giddings & Lewis is using one now for quality control. It permits extremely precise checkout of the movement and positioning of machine table, heads, and columns.

Why all the emphasis on precision? Customer demands. One builder tells STEEL: "We were asked to hold 50 millionths of an inch tolerance on piston pins. To guarantee that, we had to make the machine capable of holding within 25 millionths. The customers found that out, and today some are asking for the 25 millionths performance. The squeeze for precision still shows no sign of letting up."

WHAT'S AHEAD?

Beyond doubt, some of the builders who participate in the 1965 shows will no longer be corporate entities in 1970. The higher cost, and the more complicated, more demanding job of marketing, supported by service and technical backup, will make it impractical for some small builders to try to compete as independents. Further, the requirement for more technological capability and leadership in the home plant, the heavy expenditures for R&D, and the demands for new kinds of manufacturing equipment and facilities to produce some of today's equipment will be beyond the means of some builders. Turnover in the industry is a foregone conclusion.

Diversification. New Britain's Mr. Pease ranks diversification as one of the important trends in the business. He feels builders will continue to seek some lines outside the industry to keep their business cycle even.

But there is also diversification within the machine tool business for many builders. Fellows Gear Shaper Co., Springfield, Vt., has long been known as a maker of gear shapers. But, in line with the systems approach to marketing, the company now has a complete line of gear cutting and checking equipment. One spokesman tells STEEL: "Today, if the problem concerns gearing, we have the capability and equipment to solve it."

Then, too, the systems approach is leading some builders into other processes. James Geier points out: "As we get more involved with customers' needs, we tend to get involved with processes that augment and, to some extent, supersede our conventional metal cutting operations. Metal forming and electrical metal removal processes are examples."

Technology. There already is some indication that tomorrow's machine tools may have basic differences from those in use today. The Air Force's Ad Hoc Committee report cited some new demands in terms of rigidity and power (STEEL, May 17, p. 49).

One example: Giddings & Lewis is sponsoring research in vibration studies at the University of Wisconsin and at the University of Cincinnati. The purpose, says Mr. Cassady, is to produce the know-how that will permit the design of lighter, less massive structures that can be moved at relatively high speeds, with great precision, to withstand higher torques — in short, to have a lighter structure with no sacrifice in rigidity.

NC. The impact of numerical control, no matter how large, has just begun to be felt, many builders agree.

Mr. Gustafson comments: "NC is now going through the same growing pains that office automation did. The beginnings of both were in the large corporations, then they spread to nearly all companies. This spread is just beginning to take place, and ten years from now, all profitable companies will be using tape control and computer directed manufacturing control." Several other builders agree that smaller companies are now getting into NC, and that in a couple of cases, huge numerically controlled machines have been bought where the investment represents more than the company's previous net worth.

NC also is already influencing technology trends both up and down on the scale of sophistication. Mr. Crane comments that adaptive control is "already upon us." This is automatic control, probably NC, with feedback features from the cutting area that will assure some constant performance of surface finish, or of chip load, or of tool life, or of some other important factor.

But he adds: "We are also now producing standard, low cost, numerical control that will replace manual operations and cut costs — both in small and large shops. It is entirely possible that the standard machine tool of the future will have low cost, mass produced NC as a standard part of the package."

Marketing. The trend to team buying and selling is set. Graham Marx, president, G. A. Gray Co., Cincinnati, feels it may help even out the machine tool boom-and-bust cycle by continuously pointing up new needs. STEEL finds several other builders who agree.

NC may actually have a direct influence on over-all machine tool marketing. Ingersoll's Edson Gaylord, vice president, comments: "We think some of the gains with NC could have been made even without the control. It has come from the better planning and thinking that tape demanded. The greatest significance of NC may show up in the way it affects customers' thinking and evaluating, and planning, and solving."

And that change will affect the machine tool industry — no longer just builders of hardware, but suppliers of capability and know-how.

And that kind of organization at the customer level is already bringing new companies and new technologies into the "machine tool" business . . . and today's industry numbers among its ranks companies that were not machine tool builders five years ago. And it includes processes like EDM, ECM, electron beam, high energy rate forming, that have only recently been considered of the true machining family — and some conservatives still aren't sure.

CHANGES IN THE LOCATION PATTERN OF
THE ANGLO-AMERICAN STEEL INDUSTRY: 1948–1959

Gunnar Alexandersson

Dr. Alexandersson, Associate Professor of Economic Geography at the Stockholm School of Economics, is the author of "The Industrial Structure of American Cities: a Geographic Study of Urban Economy in the United States," published in 1956. He carried on the present study during 1959 while he was visiting professor at the University of Wisconsin.

IN empirical studies the location pattern of the iron and steel industry is usually approached through the assembly costs for raw materials at various actual and potential steel centers. This is a reasonable approach as assembly costs for raw materials make up a significant part of total costs for bulky and cheap products like the common types of steel. Most writers also emphasize that transportation costs for the finished product to market are a very important location factor.[1] However, since the freight rate structure for finished products is more varied and complicated than that for raw materials and the flow of steel products from mill to market is more complex than the flow of raw materials from mine to mill, no attempts have been made to evaluate nearness to markets in terms of dollars and cents. The strong pull of the market is a function not only of higher transportation costs for finished products than for raw materials but also of changing buying habits of steel users towards hand-to-mouth buying, especially since the 1930's.

About five-sixths of all steel is shipped from mills directly to users, the products often being made to the users' specifications.[2]

[1] Marvin J. Barloon: "Some Problems of Relocation Facing the Steel Industry," *Latin American Studies*, Univ. of Texas, No. 9, 1950, pp. 31–49; and "The Expansion of Blast Furnace Capacity, 1938–1948: A Study in Geographical Cost Differentials," *The Business History Review*, Cambridge, Mass., Vol. 28, March, 1954, pp. 1–23; H. H. Chapman: *The Iron and Steel Industries of the South*, University of Alabama, 1953; Richard Hartshorne: "The Location of the Iron and Steel Industry," *Econ. Geog.*, Vol. 4, 1928, pp. 241–253; Allan Rodgers: "Industrial Inertia, A Major Factor in the Location of the Steel Industry in the United States," *Geogr. Rev.*, Vol. 42, 1952, pp. 56–66; and "The Iron and Steel Industry of the Mahoning and Shenango Valleys," *Econ. Geog.*, Vol. 28, 1952, pp. 331–342; C. Langdon White: "Geography's Part in the Plant Cost of Iron and Steel Production at Pittsburgh, Chicago and Birmingham," *Econ. Geog.*, Vol. 5, 1929, pp. 327–335; C. L. White and G. Primmer: "The Iron and Steel Industry of Duluth: A Study in Locational Maladjustment," *Geogr. Rev.*, Vol. 27, 1937, pp. 82–91; Chauncy D. Harris: "The Market as a Factor in the Localization of Industry in the United States," *Annals of the Assn. Amer. Geogrs.*, Vol. 44, 1954, pp. 315–348; Arthur H. Doerr: "A Quantitative Analysis of the Locational Factors in the Integrated and Semi-integrated Iron and Steel Industry of the United States and Canada," *Journ. of Geog.*, Vol. 53, 1954, pp. 393–402.

[2] Douglas A. Fisher: *Steel Serves the Nation. The Fifty Year Story of United States Steel*, New York, 1951, p. 217.

"Changes in the Location Pattern of the Anglo-American Steel Industry: 1948–1959" by Gunnar Alexandersson. Reprinted from Economic Geography, *Vol. 37 (April 1961), pp. 95–114, with permission of the editor.*

Attempts have been made to forecast future changes in the location pattern of the iron and steel industry, based upon anticipated changes in assembly costs for raw materials, changes in the market for steel products, etc.[3] Some factors of importance for the location pattern have been considered and attempts have been made to quantify their influence. It has, of course, not been possible to take into account all influencing factors. So far no attempts have been made to present "the future locational pattern" of the American steel industry in map form.

[3] Cf. Walter Isard and William M. Capron: "The Future Locational Pattern of Iron and Steel Production in the United States," *Journ. of Polit. Econ.*, Vol. 57, 1949, pp. 118–133.

[4] Such a study may of course provide clues for forecasts of future changes in the distribution pattern of the Anglo-American steel industry: the time-honored method of extrapolating past trends into the future. This method could easily be applied to a detailed forecast in map form. In this period of revolutionary innovations in the steel industry the extrapolation method, however, should be used with greater circumspection than ever. Competition from other materials (aluminum, cement, glass, plastics, etc.) makes it hazardous even to forecast the total production of steel in, say, 1970.

Other factors also call for caution. Example: A vigorous and ingenious management has in the past played an important role in the expansion of individual steel companies and steel centers. It is impossible to forecast where such extraordinary personal endeavors will be made. For the 1948–1959 period Kaiser Steel, Detroit Steel, and Granite City Steel, the fastest growing of the 20 leading steel companies, all with growth rates exceeding 100 per cent, may be mentioned as examples. The fact that these three corporations with their widely different locations were the first to sign an agreement with the union after the long steel strike in 1959 is indicative of a vigorous management which the growth rate in itself suggests.

Recent changes in the distribution pattern of the Anglo-American steel industry should be of interest also to augurs dealing with the future European pattern. The same economic forces should be at work in both cases. The impact of two devastating wars and a depression and the compartmentalization of Europe into small national markets makes it reasonable to assume that the European pattern lags a few decades behind the Anglo-American. With a closer economic co-operation in Europe the European steel industry may start to catch up with the Anglo-American development and form a pattern more in agreement with its North American counterpart.

In this study a less ambitious goal is set. The goal is simply to observe, from the vantage point of the *ex post* situation, how the location pattern of the steel industry has changed in the last decade and to see if it is possible to arrive at some generalizations about the changes.[4] Since the national pattern is the sum of patterns for a small number of large companies with a large number of small companies just filling in and complementing the general pattern, it has seemed reasonable to approach the problem from an individual company basis. The companies are the decision making units, and their decisions are based on careful investigations, including a mass of data of which only part is presumably known to the general public.

It is probably unnecessary to point out that the differences in growth rates of companies observed in this study do not necessarily indicate differences in business success; that is measured by profits and not by growth rates. It should also be remembered that all large companies are more or less integrated vertically. Their activity may stretch from the iron and coal mines and limestone quarries all the way through transportation facilities, blast furnaces, coke ovens, steel mills (the only thing studied here), and finishing mills, to scattered warehouses supplying small steel users with products weighed in pounds. In the 1948–1959 period some companies may have emphasized the acquisition of raw material sources in their investment programs or they may have built up their finishing facilities proportionately more than their steel capacity. Two companies with the same "total" growth rates may thus have different expansion rates for their ingot capacity.

FIGURES 1 AND 2

The present study is focused on two maps, Figures 1 and 2, based on capacity

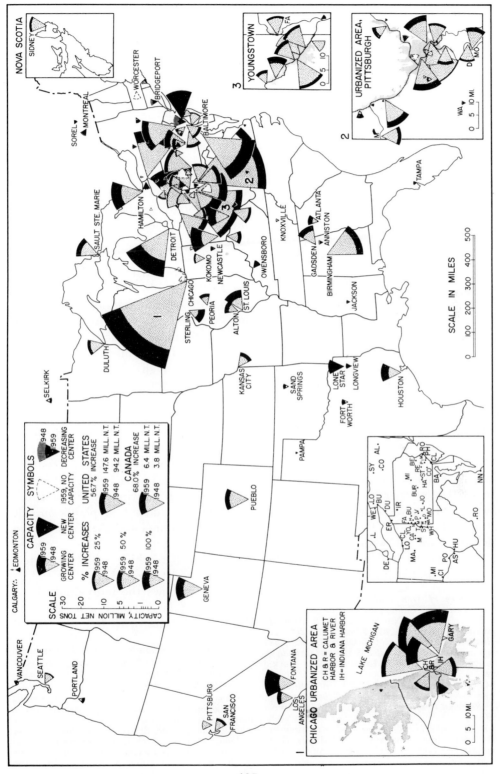

Fig. 1. Raw steel capacity in Anglo-America, 1948 and 1959.

495

data published annually by the American Iron and Steel Institute.[5] The same symbols, circle sectors with constant angles in which the surface is proportionate to quantities shown, were used by the author several years ago on three maps showing the oil refining centers of the world.[6] In the present study a new element, change, is introduced on the symbols, which makes them more complicated and difficult to interpret. The chief purpose is the same: to present the distribution pattern of an urban industry on a map scale that will permit a world-wide treatment of the industry on a few book pages without leaving out any production center. Even the small centers are part of the pattern, sometimes an important and always an interesting part, and should not be left out.[7]

With these ends in mind it is obviously not possible to use circles or squares as symbols. Sectors are superior to full circles, where either is possible to apply, in one important respect: they give a better indication of location by not covering so much of state boundaries, shore lines, and other orientation marks. In another respect they are inferior: they give a less harmonious picture. On Figure 1 Pennsylvania and Ohio are crowded with symbols, but each of them can be identified with the help of an inset map. (The full names

are given in Table I.) If necessary it would have been possible to squeeze in even more symbols by choosing a more acute angle or by using different map scales for eastern and western United States and an inset for Ohio-Pennsylvania.[8]

The symbol scale is the same on Figures 1 and 2. As shown in the legend of Figure 1, a growing steel center, the normal case, is represented by the dotted symbol for 1948 superimposed on the black 1959 symbol. The black margin thus represents increase in capacity. New steel centers which did not exist in 1948 have only the 1959 symbol. Centers which have disappeared from the map since 1948 are shown with a white sector. Those with unchanged capacity are represented by a 1948 symbol (a few centers with only a slight decrease were also shown this way). The symbol for decreasing centers is shown in the legend. On three inset maps are shown the location of individual plants in the leading steel centers: Chicago, Pittsburgh, and Youngstown. The term "center" refers to the urbanized area, which on the inset map is stippled. The Pittsburgh map includes four plants outside the urbanized area and the Youngstown map, two. Figure 1 should be compared with Table I in which the steel centers are grouped into *areas*.[9]

Figure 2 shows the individual plants of the eight largest steel companies in the United States, with 76.8 per cent of

---

[5] *Directory of Iron and Steel Works of the United States and Canada 1948*, American Iron and Steel Institute, New York, 1948; *Annual Capacities of Coke Ovens, Blast Furnaces and Steelmaking Furnaces as of January 1, 1959, by Companies and States* (*United States and Canada*), American Iron and Steel Institute, New York, 1959.

[6] Gunnar Alexandersson: "The Oil Refineries of the World—A Case Study," *Proceedings of IGU Regional Conference in Japan, 1957*, Tokyo, 1959.

[7] Both the refinery paper and the present study stem from the author's opinion that economic geographers, including textbook writers, do not give to urban industries a quantitative treatment which is on a par with the presentation of agriculture (crops) and mining.

[8] The latter solution was chosen by Gochman on his map of the American steel industry. See V. M. Gochman: *Geografija T'ažoloj Promyšlennosti SŠA*, Moskva, 1956, p. 139.

[9] A small, new steel mill (60,000 tons capacity) at Phoenix, Arizona, was not included on the maps as it could not be located at the time when the maps were drawn. It was listed under Helena, Arizona, which could not be found on any map and was unknown to the post offices of the state. According to a letter from the Phoenix Chamber of Commerce it is located at Tempe, a suburb of Phoenix.

TABLE I

STEEL CENTERS ARRANGED BY AREAS

Areas and centers	CAPACITY Thousand net tons		Increase 1948–1959	Percentage increase 1948–1959
	1948	1959		
I. COAL VALLEYS OF THE APPALACHIAN AREA				
A. *Pittsburgh (P; PI)*	14,734	18,345	3,611	24.5
B. *Other centers along the Ohio, Monongahela, and Allegheny*				
Rivers	8,368	13,218	4,850	58.0
Monessen (MO)	1,072	1,560	488	45.5
Donora (D; DO)	842	1,015	173	20.5
Midland (M)	998	1,362	364	36.5
Toronto (T)	136	136	0	0.0
Weirton (W; WE)	1,950	3,300	1,350	69.2
Steubenville (S)	1,073	2,400	1,327	123.7
Wheeling (WH)	336	.....	–336	–100.0
Huntington (HU)	.....	110	110	new
Ashland (AS)	828	1,022	194	23.4
Portsmouth (PO)	720	1,500	780	108.3
Cincinnati-Newport (CI)	413	613	217	52.5
Owensboro	.....	183	183	new
C. *Other centers in western Pennsylvania*	4,184	4,612	428	10.2
Johnstown (JO; J)	1,924	2,425	501	26.0
Latrobe (L)	103	145	42	40.8
Farrell (FA)	1,000	1,268	268	26.8
Harmony (H)	150	90	–60	–40.0
Irvine (IR)	25	25	0	0.0
Vandergrift (V)	500	.....	–500	–100.0
Washington (WA)	50	36	–14	–28.0
New Castle (N)	.....	66	66	new
Butler (BU)	432	557	125	28.9
D. *Other centers in eastern Ohio*	11,274	13,664	2,390	21.2
Youngstown (YO)	8,932	11,155	2,223	24.9
Massillon (M)	610	680	70	11.5
Canton (CA; C)	1,732	1,829	97	5.6
E. *Southern Appalachian district*	3,634	5,421	1,787	49.2
Birmingham	2,910	4,178	1,268	43.6
Gadsden	650	1,209	559	86.0
Anniston	74	34	–40	–54.1
II. SOUTHERN SHORES OF THE GREAT LAKES	29,490	50,512	21,022	71.3
Chicago	17,420	26,970	9,550	54.8
Detroit	3,473	7,942	4,469	128.7
Lorain (LO)	1,884	2,648	764	40.6
Cleveland (CL)	2,340	5,435	3,095	132.3
Erie (ER)	209	284	75	35.9
Dunkirk (DU)	33	33	0	0.0
Buffalo (BU)	4,131	7,200	3,069	74.3
III. ATLANTIC SEABOARD AND ADJACENT AREA				
A. *Atlantic Seaboard*	6,264	12,176	5,912	94.4
Newport News (NN)	8	15	7	87.5
Baltimore	4,746	8,382	3,636	76.6
Claymont (CL)	460	507	47	10.2
Philadelphia (PH)	549	173	–376	–68.5
Roebling (RO)	253	235	–18	–7.1
Morrisville (M; MO)	.....	2,687	2,687	new
Bridgeport	188	84	–104	–55.3
Phillipsdale, Rh.I.	60	93	33	55.0
B. *Inland centers, eastern Pennsylvania*	5,489	8,445	2,956	53.9
Harrisburg (HA)	389	588	199	51.2
Steelton (ST)	886	1,500	614	69.3
Milton (MI)	.....	90	90	new
Lewistown (Burnham, BUR)	149	189	40	26.8
Reading (RE)	75	88	13	17.3
Coatesville (CO)	624	930	306	49.0
Bethlehem (BE)	2,585	3,900	1,315	50.9
Phoenixville (P)	231	360	129	55.8
Conshohocken (Ivy Rock, I)	550	800	250	45.5
C. *Inland Centers, New England and New York*	403	192	–211	–52.4
Worcester	250	.....	–250	–100.0
Albany-Troy (AL, Watervliet)	25	77	52	208.0
Cortland (CO)	38	32	–6	–15.8
Syracuse (SY)	68	61	–7	–10.3
Lockport (LO)	22	22	0	0.0

TABLE I (*continued*)

STEEL CENTERS ARRANGED BY AREAS

Areas and centers	CAPACITY Thousand net tons		Increase 1948–1959	Percentage increase 1948–1959
	1948	1959		
IV. INLAND CENTERS, EASTERN OHIO, INDIANA, AND ILLINOIS...	3,337	6,919	3,582	107.3
Mansfield (MA)...................................	370	500	130	35.1
Middletown (MI)..............................	972	2,557	1,585	163.1
Fort Wayne.................................	38	38	0	0.0
Kokomo...................................	364	420	56	15.4
New Castle.................................	24	64	40	166.7
St. Louis (Granite City).........................	620	1,440	820	132.3
Alton.....................................	326	600	274	84.0
Peoria....................................	302	475	173	57.3
Sterling....................................	321	825	504	157.0
V. LAKE SUPERIOR ORE PORTS				
Duluth....................................	690	973	283	41.0
VI. THE SOUTH, OUTSIDE OF THE APPALACHIAN COAL FIELDS...	839	3,027	2,188	260.8
Tampa....................................	......	43	43	new
Atlanta...................................	165	400	235	142.4
Knoxville..................................	38	38	0	0.0
Roanoke (RO)...............................	......	25	25	new
Jackson (Flowood)...........................	......	45	45	new
Sand Springs...............................	54	120	66	122.2
Longview..................................	......	90	90	new
Lone Star..................................	......	800	800	new
Fort Worth.................................	22	132	110	500.0
Houston...................................	560	1,343	783	139.8
Pampa....................................	......	16	16	new
VII. THE WEST				
A. *Large coastal cities*	2,516	5,234	2,718	108.0
Fontana...................................	870	2,933	2,063	237.1
Los Angeles................................	463	801	338	73.0
Pittsburg..................................	363	380	17	4.7
San Francisco..............................	407	569	162	39.8
Portland..................................	66	150	84	127.3
Seattle....................................	347	401	54	15.6
B. *Inland centers*	2,981	4,868	1,887	63.3
Geneva...................................	1,283	2,300	1,017	79.3
Pueblo....................................	1,272	1,800	528	41.5
Phoenix, Arizona...........................	......	60	60	new
Kansas City................................	426	708	282	66.2
UNITED STATES, TOTAL...............................	94,203	147,634	53,431	56.7

the total capacity.[10] All plants of the remaining 74 companies are shown in the lower right corner of Figure 2. For the two leading steel companies the growth rate of individual plants and steel centers are compared with national and company rates (inset diagrams).

COMMENTS ON FIGURES 1 AND 2

Some generalizations can be based on Figures 1 and 2:

[10] The new Jones & Laughlin mill in Detroit is identical with the "disappeared" plant on the map in the lower right corner according to a letter from the Detroit Chamber of Commerce. The only new steel mill built by the eight big companies is the Morrisville plant of the U. S. Steel.

1. *Changes in the location pattern of the Anglo-American steel industry were caused almost entirely by differences in growth rate among existing steel centers and steel plants.* Almost all steel plants expanded their capacity. Few new plants were added and few plants were closed down. The eight largest corporations, with 76.8 per cent of the American capacity in 1959, built only one new plant and closed down only two. The other 51 mills expanded or had unchanged capacity. The small steel corporations added some new plants, most of them very small, scrap-

based electric-furnace-mills owned by local one-plant corporations.

2. The 1948–1959 period saw a steady increase in the size of American steel mills. *In a period of rapid expansion of the national steel capacity steel plants continue to grow in almost any location.* The rationale behind this fact seems to be the following: (a) The needed investment per ton of annual steel capacity may be as much as four times higher for a new plant on an undeveloped site than for the same capacity added to existing facilities.[11] (b) Multiplant corporations for technical-economic reasons usually have a division of labor between their plants; the plants to a certain degree specialize on different types of products. This may prevent restriction of the corporation's expansion to a single new mill in the most favorable location. (c) The policy of not putting all eggs in the same basket may also contribute to a spreading of a corporation's expansion to all its plants instead of a concentration in an optimum-located new plant. This may make the company better prepared to meet seasonal, cyclical, and long-term structural changes in the demand for steel, changes which may have geographical implications.[12]

A steel center with an obsolete location as far as transportation costs are concerned usually has compensating assets such as experienced labor and a community with schools, banks, and other service facilities geared to the steel

industry. It has, of course, buildings and machinery which may not be useful for any other purpose. The influence of these and other factors, which are difficult to measure, is often referred to as inertia. Inertia is a strong force working on all industrial location patterns.

3. *Steel mills with a coastal location had high growth rates.* Remarkably high rates of increase were noted for the following large steel centers: Chicago, Detroit, Cleveland, and Buffalo, all million-cities on the Great Lakes; Hamilton, the leading Canadian steel center; and Baltimore. Common characteristics of these centers are their coastal location, with consequent low transportation costs for iron ore and in some cases also for other raw materials (limestone, coal, and scrap), and their favorable market situation. Chicago, Detroit, and Cleveland rank among the leading North American metal manufacturing centers; Buffalo has a strategic location between the Lower Lakes market and the East Coast, especially New York City, which is the largest American steel market having no local steel capacity; Hamilton has a central location in the Canadian part of the Manufacturing Belt. The U. S. Steel's Morrisville plant, located on the Delaware River between Philadelphia and New York, one of the two large American mills built in the 1950's, also is a coastal mill with a good market location. Chicago, the world's largest steel center, with a capacity (27.0 million tons) exceeding that of the United Kingdom (26.2 million tons) and France (17.9 million tons) and approaching that of West Germany (30.9 million tons),[13] had a growth rate almost equal to the national average (Fig. 3). It grew more than twice as fast as the second and third largest American steel centers, Pittsburgh and Youngstown.

[11] W. B. Boyer: "Problems of Financing New Steel Capacity," *Iron and Steel Engineer*, Vol. 34, 1957, pp. 75–76; see also "The Siting of British Steelworks," *Steel Review*, July, 1958, pp. 26–35.

[12] The automotive industry in southern Michigan may work at a peak when the construction industry in New York City is in the doldrums and vice versa. This example illustrates both seasonal and cyclical changes. Structural changes, which may or may not be associated with geographic shifts, occur all the time. The switch in demand from locomotives and railroad cars to autos and trucks—produced in different cities—is just one example.

[13] *Steel Facts*, No. 153, February, 1959, p. 4.

4. *In the United States more than half of the steel capacity (54.3 per cent) is located in the outskirts of million cities:* Chicago, Pittsburgh, Detroit, Cleveland, Buffalo, Baltimore, Philadelphia, St. Louis, Los Angeles, and San Francisco. Only New York, Boston, Washington, and Minneapolis–St. Paul lack basic steel industries. Of these cities, New York, with an excellent location for integrated steel mills, is a notable exception to the observation that big cities have attracted a very substantial steel capacity.[14] Pittsburgh is the only example of a million-city having reached its size primarily because of its steel industry (which in turn has attracted metal manufacturing industries). It is the only city located close to either coal or iron ore.

The American million-cities increased their capacity somewhat faster than the national average[15] (61.2 and 56.7 per cent respectively), but the growth rate varied considerably from city to city (Table I).

By way of comparison, it may be mentioned that the steel industries of Western Europe and the Soviet Union still are overwhelmingly concentrated near coal, primarily, and iron ore fields, a location which has been "obsolete" in the United States for several decades, as indicated by lower growth rates for such centers (see Pittsburgh, Youngstown, and others).

5. *Even the largest American steel corporations are solidly planted in a limited region, the district from which they originated.* The world's largest free trade area is their market, but they have only to a limited extent ventured new producing facilities outside of the re-

gion where they were formed a few decades ago through mergers of many small companies. Bethlehem Steel has almost all its capacity at five steel centers within a small region in the eastern part of the Manufacturing Belt. U. S. Steel has 59 per cent of its capacity in two centers, Chicago and Pittsburgh, and 75 per cent in the Chicago-to-Pittsburgh region. There is a remarkably neat separation of location patterns between these two steel giants, of which U. S. Steel undoubtedly has had the best general location with the westward movement of the center of population and the center of steel manufacturing industries. For location patterns of these and other large companies, see Figure 2. It shows Bethlehem Steel by itself in the eastern part of the Manufacturing Belt and U. S. Steel competing in the central and western part of the Belt with the six companies that follow these in size.

All these patterns have run through the same development: merging of many small companies and their numerous mills, concentration of production in a few of the best located plants, expansion of capacity by additions to existing facilities. Plans to extend production into new areas have, when they have materialized, usually led to the acquisition of already established companies. The cases when big corporations have built new facilities outside of their "home areas" are rare, indeed. The possibilities for the largest companies to round off their location patterns by acquiring existing companies are hampered by institutional factors, as shown in 1958 when the overtures for a merger between Bethlehem Steel and Youngstown Sheet & Tube were stopped by the federal antitrust agency.

6. *There were great differences in expansion rates among the eight largest steel corporations.* U. S. Steel, the world's

[14] Lack of suitable sites? Are reasonably-priced tracts of land on tidewater and with large supplies of water for cooling purposes available in the New York area?

[15] Fontana was included in Los Angeles, but Morrisville was not included in Philadelphia in these calculations.

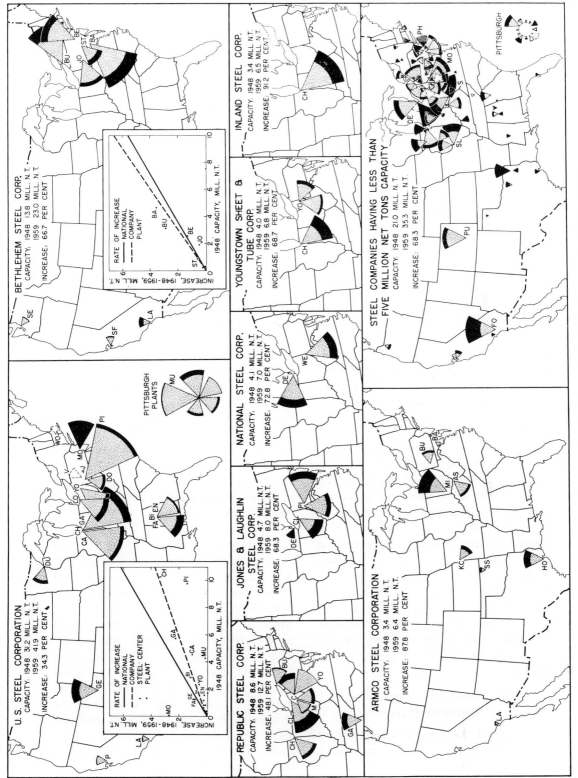

FIG. 2. Steel plant locations in the United States by individual companies, 1948 and 1959.

leading steel company, had a conspicuously low rate of increase. Six of the eight largest steel corporations in the United States expanded faster than the national average (Fig. 2).

7. *Both slow-growing and fast-growing multi-plant corporations had, with few exceptions, a higher expansion rate in fast-growing centers than in slow-growing centers.* The attractiveness of coastal-market locations at the million-cities on the Great Lakes and the Atlantic Seaboard was thus recognized by most of the large multi-plant corporations. This "recognition" materialized, however, in only one new plant (Morrisville). Other companies did not go so far. National Steel, for instance, has acquired plant sites in New Jersey and at Chicago and Bethlehem Steel owns one in the Chicago area, but no plants have yet been built on these sites.

8. *A steel center dominated by a slowly growing corporation may have a higher expansion rate than the company and still grow more slowly than the national average.* A case in point is Birmingham, dominated by the two U. S. Steel plants, Fairfield and Ensley. The former was second only to Geneva in expansion rate among the corporation's plants (see map and diagram, Fig. 2), giving an above-company growth rate to Birmingham. This was, however, not sufficient to match the national average. The example points up the necessity for taking corporation policy into account when various steel centers are evaluated. It is not sufficient to consider location only with regard to raw materials and markets.

REGIONAL VARIATIONS IN GROWTH RATE

In Table I the American steel centers have been arranged in districts or areas according to the principle that centers with similar location in respect to raw

material supply and markets should be grouped together. Location as regards waterways for the transportation of iron ore, limestone, and coal, as well as finished products, was considered to be more significant than the general geographic location. Thus Monessen and Johnstown, both located in western Pennsylvania, were referred to different areas, whereas Monessen and Owensboro, separated by much larger distances, were grouped together because they are both on the Ohio River system, which serves as a cheap transportation route. An attempt was made to make the names of the districts self-explanatory and thus imply the underlying principle for the division.

The Anglo-American steel industry is strongly concentrated in the Manufacturing Belt, stretching from the Atlantic Seaboard (southern Maine-Baltimore) to the Middle West (Milwaukee–St. Louis) and including a narrow Canadian strip along the St. Lawrence River and the northern shores of Lake Ontario and Lake Erie from Quebec to Windsor. The United States part of this region contains 86.8 per cent of the national steel capacity (1959). In Canada the corresponding share is smaller, 56.3 per cent.

The Manufacturing Belt of the United States had a somewhat lower growth rate than the national average (53 and 57 per cent), that of Canada a higher rate (94 and 68 per cent). Within the American Manufacturing Belt there were interesting regional differences. The Atlantic Seaboard and the Southern Shores of the Great Lakes had considerably higher growth rates than the national average. The "migration" of steel capacity to the latter area has been going on since the end of the last century. The Lake Shores now have more than one-third of the American steel capacity. The Atlantic Seaboard, with less than one-fourth as much capacity as the latter region, has grown rapidly in the postwar period with an increasing American dependence on imported ores. As is well known, new plants get much more publicity than additions of the same capacity to existing facilities. The widely published establishment of the large plant at Morrisville in the early 1950's may have left foreign observers with a wrong impression of the true importance of the Atlantic Seaboard area on the American steel map. The expansion at Baltimore (Sparrow's Point) actually represents a larger tonnage than the new plant at Morrisville.

The fastest growing area in the Manufacturing Belt, the only one to more than double its capacity, was the inland area from eastern Ohio to western Illinois.[16] This was in sharp contrast to

the development in other inland areas of the Manufacturing Belt, especially in the old districts of western Pennsylvania and eastern Ohio, which grew at very low rates. The inland centers of eastern Pennsylvania, even older as a steel district than western Pennsylvania and Ohio, kept their position fairly well with a growth rate close to the one of the Manufacturing Belt as a whole. The small capacity in inland New York State and New England was considerably reduced between 1948 and 1959.

If all steel centers along the Ohio River system outside of Pittsburgh are grouped together they form a district with a larger capacity than the Atlantic

[16] St. Louis is located on the Mississippi, but it receives its ores by rail from southeastern Minnesota and the Lake Superior area. Most of the coal also arrives by rail, but some of the finished products are shipped by barge.

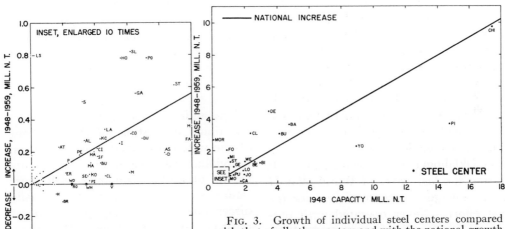

FIG. 3. Growth of individual steel centers compared with that of all other centers and with the national growth rate.

Centers growing faster than the national average: Baltimore (BA), Detroit (DE), Buffalo (BU), Cleveland (CL), Weirton (WE), Geneva (GE), Steubenville (ST), Middletown (MI), Fontana (FO), Morrisville (MOR); in the inset: Steelton (ST), Portsmouth (PO), St. Louis (SL), Houston (HO), Gadsden (GA), Sterling (S), Los Angeles (LA), Kansas City (KC), Alton (AL), Peoria (PE), Atlanta (AT), and Lone Star (LS).

Centers growing slower than the national average: Chicago (CHI), Pittsburgh (PI), Youngstown (YO), Birmingham (BI), Bethlehem (BE), Lorain (LO), Johnstown (JO), Canton (CA), Pueblo (PU), Monessen (MO); in the inset: Midland (M), Farrell (FA), Ashland (AS), Donora (D), Duluth (DU), Coatesville (CO), Conshohocken (I), Massillon (M), Claymont (CL), Butler (BU), San Francisco (SF), Cincinnati (CI), Harrisburg (HA), Mansfield (MA), Kokomo (KO), Pittsburg (PI), Seattle (SE), Erie (ER), and Phoenixville (P).

Centers which have disappeared in the 1948–1959 period (inset, dot and circle): Vandergrift (V), Wheeling (WH), and Worcester (WO).

Decreasing centers (inset): Philadelphia (PH), Bridgeport (BR), Harmony (H), and Roebling (RO).

Seaboard and with a somewhat higher growth rate than the national average. They grew more than twice as fast as Pittsburgh. The favorable development of the steel industry in the Ohio Valley outside of Pittsburgh paralleled a general expansion of construction work and manufacturing in this river system and to the south of it in the TVA region.

The largest steel district outside of the Manufacturing Belt, the southern Appalachian area, had a somewhat lower expansion rate than the national average, due chiefly to the dominance in this district of the slow-growing U. S. Steel Corporation. Duluth, the only American steel mill near the large ore deposits at Lake Superior, falls into the same category: it experienced an above-company but below national average expansion rate.

The highest growth rate for any of the areas in Table I was recorded for the scattered steel mills of the South outside of the iron ore and coal fields in Alabama. This part of the South has two medium-sized, integrated mills at Houston and Lone Star. The Houston plant was constructed during World War II by Armco with a government loan and based chiefly on scrap;[17] the Lone Star mill, based on local iron ore and coal from Oklahoma, was conceived and built during the last years of World War II as an emergency source of iron for the war effort. Never operated until purchased by a private company in 1948, it became an integrated steel mill in the early 1950's.[18]

The only integrated steel mill west of the Mississippi-Missouri before World War II was the plant at Pueblo. The

[17] Elmer H. Johnson: *The Industrial Potential of Texas*, Bureau of Business Research, The University of Texas. No date.
[18] *Facts Concerning Lone Star Steel Company*, Pamphlet, no date; Letter from Mr. Hal Kennedy, Director, Plant Public Relations, Lone Star Steel Company.

Geneva and Fontana mills were built during the war, the former by the government and the latter by Kaiser with a government loan. Both were built to supply the shipyards on the West Coast; they relieved the already overburdened transcontinental railroads which had to carry goods normally shipped through the Panama Canal, a route seriously hampered by shortage of tonnage and by enemy submarine attacks. The Geneva and Fontana plants, which might never have been built in peace time with a normal competitive situation, have expanded very rapidly in the postwar period. Geneva had the highest growth rate of any of the U. S. Steel plants (map and diagram of Fig. 2), and Fontana was the fastest growing major plant in the country (Fig. 2).

THE LEADING AMERICAN STEEL CORPORATIONS

Twenty American steel corporations with more than one million net tons ingot capacity account for 91.1 per cent of the national capacity. The remaining 8.9 per cent is divided among 62 companies.

The mills of the eight largest corporations, accounting for 76.8 per cent of the national capacity, are shown on individual maps (Fig. 2). The plants of the other 12 companies with more than one million tons capacity are easily discernible on the map in the lower right corner, Figure 2, as most of them are one-plant corporations.

The United States Steel Corporation was formed in 1901 through the merging of Andrew Carnegie's company, with all its steel mills in Pittsburgh, the Federal Steel Company, with main facilities in Chicago, and eight other corporations. This gigantic merger consolidated large companies which themselves had been formed through mergers in the sudden concentration movement, 1898–

1900. It was carried out by Judge Elbert H. Gary, president of the Federal Steel Company, and Charles M. Schwab, director of the Carnegie Company, with the financial backing of J. Pierpont Morgan. It was made possible by the fact that Andrew Carnegie wanted to sell his company, the leading steel producer in the world, and go down in history as America's greatest philanthropist.

U. S. Steel's capacity has increased from 10.6 million tons in 1901 to 41.9 million in 1959. But its share of the national capacity has decreased. It was 44 per cent in 1901, reached a high of 52 per cent in 1907, and amounted to 28 per cent in 1959. It was by far the slowest growing of the eight largest steel corporations in the 1948–1959 period. Employment grew from 168,000 in 1901 to 271,000 in 1957. No *country* except the Soviet Union has a larger steel capacity than U. S. Steel. The company has often appeared before the federal agencies handling the antitrust laws. Just before World War I the government even considered its dissolution as a violator of the Sherman Antitrust Act.

Among important changes affecting the location pattern of U. S. Steel since its formation in 1901, the following may be mentioned:

A large integrated steel mill was built on the sand dunes south of Lake Michigan, 1906–1911. The plant and city were named in honor of Judge Gary. The city is now part of the urbanized area of Chicago. The Gary plant was later enlarged and modernized and for a long time was the world's largest single steel mill. In 1959 it was a close second to the Sparrows Point Works at Baltimore, owned by the Bethlehem Steel Corporation, both with about 8 million tons capacity. The Gary works was the second large steel mill of the

U. S. Steel in the Chicago area; the first one had been established at Calumet Harbor in 1880,[19] thereby initiating the tremendous development of heavy manufacturing in southern Chicago on both sides of the Illinois-Indiana state line (Fig. 1, Inset 1).

In the financial panic of 1907, U. S. Steel acquired control of the largest steel company in the South, the Tennessee Coal, Iron, & Railroad Company, which after 1886 had started to make Birmingham an important iron and steel center. It was even competing north of the Ohio River with pig iron.

A steel plant was completed at Duluth in 1915 after threats by the state of higher taxes on ore shipped out of Minnesota. This plant, far away from the large steel markets, has experienced a very modest growth.

The greatest change in the Corporation's operations took place in a ten-year period from 1928 to 1938, with a concentration at the best located and most efficient plants.

In 1931 U. S. Steel purchased a steel company on the Pacific Coast with facilities in Los Angeles and near San Francisco (Pittsburg). During World War II the government built a large integrated steel mill at Geneva, Utah, to produce steel for the large wartime shipyards on the Pacific Coast. U. S. Steel was called upon to construct and operate the mill, which cost 202 million dollars. It went into operation in 1943. After the war it was sold to the highest bidder, U. S. Steel, for 47 million dollars (1946).

In 1951–1952, U. S. Steel built an integrated Atlantic Seaboard mill of 1.8 million tons capacity at Morrisville, Pennsylvania, across the Delaware River

[19] J. B. Appleton: *The Iron and Steel Industry of the Calumet District*, University of Illinois, Studies in the Social Sciences, Vol. 13, Urbana, 1927.

from Trenton, New Jersey. Named the Fairless Works, in honor of the president of the corporation, it was later enlarged to a capacity of 2.7 million tons. It is the only plant of the U. S. Steel east of Buffalo-Johnstown, an area dominated by the Bethlehem Steel Corporation. The latter company has acquired land near Gary on the southern shore of Lake Michigan—in U. S. Steel "territory"—but no steel mill has been built here so far.

The large U. S. Steel capacity is concentrated in a few plants in even fewer steel centers (Fig. 2). Its Morrisville plant has roughly the same capacity as the total steel industry of Sweden, and Gary equals the capacity of Belgium. About 59 per cent of the corporation's capacity is located in Chicago and Pittsburgh (see map and diagram, Fig. 2).

Bethlehem Steel Corporation. The first president of the U. S. Steel, Charles M. Schwab, resigned in 1903. His health broke shortly after the gigantic merger in which he had taken an active part. In 1904, after a long rest abroad, Schwab organized a new company which acquired shipyards and a steel mill at Bethlehem in the Lehigh Valley of eastern Pennsylvania. This area had been the leading American iron producing region for about two decades before the Civil War, based on anthracite coal and local ore deposits. The Bethlehem plant had an ingot capacity of 190,000 tons. From this small beginning Schwab built up a concern which for a long time has been second only to U. S. Steel among American steel companies. During World War I the company acquired a rail-producing steel plant at Sparrows Point, built in 1887.[20] This plant, favorably located to supply the large Atlantic Seaboard market, the growing West

Coast market, and foreign markets, was entirely redesigned to produce a wide and diversified group of products. Its capacity was expanded seven times in a decade to 1.75 million tons in 1926.[21] With a capacity of 8.2 million tons, it is now the world's largest steel mill. It is based on imported ores, especially from Latin America. In 1917, Bethlehem Steel bought a large steel mill in Johnstown, and in 1922 it acquired the Lackawanna Steel Company with its large plant on the outskirts of Buffalo. The latter mill had been moved from Scranton in the Anthracite Region of eastern Pennsylvania to Lake Erie about the turn of the century, to take advantage of low freight costs for iron ore and the growing markets along the Great Lakes while retaining its favorable location for supplying the Atlantic Seaboard market. In 1930, two small steel companies on the Pacific Coast were acquired with facilities in Los Angeles, San Francisco, and Seattle.

Republic Steel, a leading manufacturer of alloy steels, including stainless and high-tensile steels, is an important producer of steel for the automotive industry. It was incorporated in 1899 as a consolidation of 24 bar and forge iron manufacturing companies.[22] The present company was formed through a merger in 1930, which made it the country's third largest steel corporation with a capacity of 5.6 million tons. In the period, 1935–1937, Republic Steel acquired four steel companies. It bought the Gadsden plant in 1937. Since 1941, the company's electric furnace capacity has increased very much; it is now largest in the industry. Dur-

---

[20] P. Blood: "Factors in the Economic Development of Baltimore, Maryland," *Econ. Geog.*, Vol. 13, 1937, pp. 187–208.

[21] C. Langdon White and Edwin J. Foscue: "The Iron and Steel Industry of Sparrows Point, Maryland," *Geogr. Rev.*, Vol. 21, 1931, pp. 244–258.

[22] *Report of the Federal Trade Commission on the Merger Movement*, A Summary Report, Washington, D. C., 1948.

ing the war a new steel plant was built in Chicago.[23] Sixty-nine per cent of Republic Steel's capacity is located in northeastern Ohio.

Jones & Laughlin Steel Corporation is an old Pittsburgh company, its roots extending back to 1853. The present company was formed in 1902 when two firms on opposite sides of the Monongahela River merged. They had existed for about 40 years with substantially common ownership. The new company had a capacity of one million tons. Its mill is the only plant that can be seen from downtown Pittsburgh, the only one within the corporate limits of the steel city.

In 1912, Jones & Laughlin completed a new mill a few miles down the Ohio River at Aliquippa, which is now part of the Pittsburgh Urbanized Area. The assets of a steel company in Cleveland were acquired in 1942 and in 1958 a small steel plant was bought in Detroit. The last two acquisitions indicate a shift—even if it got a late start—to the lake metropolises.

National Steel was formed in 1929 by merging a steel company with a mill at Weirton and one with a plant at Detroit. Plant sites owned by National Steel at Chicago and in New Jersey have not been utilized so far.[24]

Youngstown Sheet & Tube, incorporated in 1900, got its present name in 1905. One of its Youngstown plants was acquired in 1923 and that same year the Indiana Harbor (Chicago) mill was bought.[25]

Inland Steel, largest of the American

one-plant corporations, was incorporated in 1893.[26]

Armco Steel has grown out of a sheet rolling mill at Middletown, Ohio, built around the turn of the century. Before entering the steel business, the founder, George M. Verity, had been manager of a steel roofing concern in Cincinnati. After having considered different locations, Verity in 1909 decided to build a new, large steel mill in his home town. The home plant at Middletown is the largest and most rapidly expanding of the eight steel mills of the company. Armco is the only steel corporation approaching U. S. Steel in the wide geographic distribution of its operations. It acquired several small companies in the 1917–1937 period. Its name was changed in 1948 from the American Rolling Mill Company to Armco.

The *Kaiser Steel* plant (Fontana, California) was built during World War II by Henry Kaiser, who built ships at seven shipyards and badly needed steel plates. It was originally planned for a tidewater site in Los Angeles, but the government, probably under the influence of the Pearl Harbor catastrophe, refused to lend money unless the plant was located some 50 miles inland.[27] About 1.4 of the 2.1 million tons added to the capacity in the 1948–1959 period were in the form of basic-oxygen or LD-capacity.[28] Coal is hauled 810 miles from Sunnyside, Utah, and some also from Oklahoma, a distance of 1300 miles. Iron ore comes from the Eagle Mountain mine, 164 miles distant. The company also owns other ore deposits in the Mojave Desert east of Los Angeles. Water is a critical factor for this plant; by recirculating the water it is possible

[23] C. M. White, President, Republic Steel Corporation, Address given by . . . , April 29, 1954. Published by Public Relations Department, Republic Steel Corporation, Cleveland, Ohio.

[24] *Moody's Industrial Manual*, New York, 1958.

[25] *Report of the Federal Trade Commission on the Merger Movement, op. cit.*

[26] *Ibid.*

[27] C. L. White: *Is the West Making the Grade in the Steel Industry?*, Stanford University Graduate School of Business, Business Research Series No. 8, 1956.

[28] For explanation of LD see p. 112.

to keep down the requirements to a small fraction of what is usually considered to be necessary. The LD-process has further reduced the low coal requirements which is of great importance as Fontana has to pay the highest freight charges on coal of any major steel mill. The trump card of this plant is its location close to Los Angeles which represents about one-half of the steel consumption of seven Western states. This advantage it would have had, of course, even if it had been located on tidewater.

Colorado Fuel & Iron (chief plant at Pueblo, Colorado; smaller plants at Claymont, Delaware; Buffalo and Roebling, New Jersey).[29]

Wheeling Steel (Steubenville, Ohio).

McLouth Steel (new mill in Detroit, LD- and electric furnaces).

Ford Motor (Detroit).

Sharon Steel (Farrell and Youngstown).

Pittsburgh Steel (Monessen).

Detroit Steel (Portsmouth, Ohio).

Granite City Steel (Granite City, suburb of St. Louis).

Crucible Steel Company of America (chief plant at Midland, Pennsylvania; smaller plants at Syracuse, New York and Harrison, New Jersey; the latter is smaller than 10,000 tons and is not shown on the maps. It is the smallest plant listed, the only one left out because of size).

International Harvester (Calumet area in Chicago).

Acme Steel (new LD-mill in Chicago, Cincinnati-Newport).

THE LEADING CANADIAN STEEL COMPANIES

Four companies dominate the Canadian steel production: the Steel Company of Canada (Stelco) and Dominion

Foundries and Steel Company (Dofasco), both with plants at Hamilton, Algoma Steel Corporation at Sault Ste. Marie, and Dominion Steel and Coal Company (Dosco) at Sydney.[30] They produce about 90 per cent of Canada's steel ingots. Almost all of the remainder is produced from scrap in electric furnaces at seven small mills at Hamilton and six other places (Fig. 1).

Stelco was formed in 1910 by merging five small Ontario companies. The company owns coal mines in West Virginia and Pennsylvania, and iron mines in Minnesota and Michigan.[31] It is the largest steel producer in Canada, accounting for almost 50 per cent of the total Canadian capacity. The first blast furnace was built in Hamilton in 1895, mainly because of tax concessions offered by the city, and two years later a steel mill was constructed. Now Hamilton has the same advantages as other steel centers with a coastal location and a situation close to the market. At least 60 per cent of the steel is sold south of a line from just east of Toronto to Sarnia, where most of Canada's automobiles, farm machines, and domestic appliances are manufactured. Dofasco, enjoying the same locational advantages as Stelco, was formed in 1917 and became a fully integrated steel mill in 1951. In recent years it has been the fastest growing Canadian steel company.

The two other steel corporations in Canada have peripheral locations.

[29] This plant is shown as unchanged on Figure 1, with small decrease on Figure 2.

[30] The discussion of the Canadian steel industry draws heavily on a paper by Donald Kerr, which has the same company-approach as followed in the present study. Donald Kerr: "The Geography of the Canadian Iron and Steel Industry," *Econ. Geog.*, Vol. 35, 1959, pp. 151–163.

[31] Raw materials for the steel industry move in both directions over the national boundary. The direction of shipments depends not only on transportation costs and c.i.f. prices, but also on ownership of mines. American companies own mines in Canada and Canadian firms have acquired mines in the United States.

Dosco is one of the great industrial empires in Canada, employing over 30,000 people. Its steel operations at Sydney are only one part of a complex including coal, iron and limestone mines, shipyards and shipping, as well as numerous steel fabricating mills. The present company was formed in 1928. It can be traced back through several mergers to some small companies which began smelting iron ore at the coal fields of eastern Cape Breton Island during the nineteenth century. Coal from nearby company mines makes a rather poor coke. Iron ore is hauled by company ships from company-owned mines on Bell Island (Wabana) off the east coast of Newfoundland. The steel plants at Sydney in the early years of this century specialized on rails (cf. Sparrows Point). After World War I the demand for rails fell off greatly. Subsidiary plants manufacturing various steel products were gradually acquired in the Canadian Manufacturing Belt, and these plants now absorb a large share of the production. Rails are, however, still very important, accounting for about 40 per cent of total production. The Sydney mill has the poorest location of any in North America as the domestic market is by far the most important for all mills. Sydney is the slowest growing of the "big four" Canadian plants. Because of its importance in the economy of the "underdeveloped" Nova Scotia it is unlikely that the government would ever permit this mill to be closed down.

Algoma's mill at Sault Ste. Marie is also off center and its location is similar to that of the Duluth plant. It was built in 1902 as a result of a personal initiative to develop electric power on the St. Mary's River. A pulp mill and a ferro-nickel plant had been built a few years earlier, and the ferro-nickel industry was stimulated by the discovery of ore at Michipicoten, 120 miles to the north, and the construction of the steel mill. The demand for rails on the prairies led to an expansion of the steel facilities. The mill now uses primarily American ores. The mine at Michipicoten was closed from 1921 to 1939 but then was reopened. Because of its high manganese content the ore commands a high price, and the company sells most of it on the American market and imports cheaper American ores. Rails are still an important item on the production program. The company has specialized on products which are not manufactured at Hamilton and can sell these products in the Manufacturing Belt and ship by water. The Mannesmann Tube Company recently built a plant at Sault Ste. Marie, the first large consumer to locate near the mill. This was a result of the postwar development in the Canadian oil industry in the Prairie Provinces.

In the future it seems that the Montreal area, now the largest deficit region for steel in Canada, will become a steel center. Stelco is building a small pipe mill at Contrecoeur, 30 miles northeast of Montreal on the shore of the St. Lawrence River. Dosco will build a rolling mill at the same place and, eventually, a steel plant.

SMALL STEEL COMPANIES IN ANGLO-AMERICA

Companies with less than one million tons capacity have 9 per cent of the capacity in the United States. Those of one-half to one million tons, most of them one-plant corporations, account for by far the largest part of this capacity. Plants of this size would be considered large in many countries in Europe.

The many small, scrap-based electric-furnace mills scattered over the continent, with capacities of 25 to 100 thousand tons, account for an insignificant share of the total capacity. The plant at Jackson, Mississippi, may illustrate the reasoning which underlies several such plants. Birmingham is the nearest competing steel center. The freight rate for steel from Birmingham is 8 dollars per ton. For scrap the rate to Birmingham is 6 dollars per ton. Electric power rates in Jackson compare favorably with rates in the surrounding states. A survey had indicated that Mississippi was using 60 to 70 thousand tons of steel a year, which could be produced on a small bar mill.[32] The economy of scale in Birmingham thus apparently was outweighed by savings in freight costs, at least for the Jackson market. The Jackson company was financed by the sale of common stock and debentured bonds to residents of Mississippi.

COMPANY SIZE AND INNOVATIONS IN STEEL TECHNOLOGY

In the United States the most striking technological innovations seem to have been introduced not by the gigantic U. S. Steel with its tremendous resources for research and experiments, nor by the second largest corporation, the expansive Bethlehem Steel, but by companies of second or third magnitude.

The most important innovation of the 1920's, the continuous rolling mill, was introduced by the American Rolling Mill Company, now Armco, at its Ashland (AS) plant in 1923 and perfected at its Butler (BU) plant in 1926 (Fig. 1 and Table I). It was immediately adopted by the industry under licenses from Armco. In 1954 about 40 wide continuous hot-strip mills were in operation in the United States, with an aggregate capacity of 40 million tons.[33]

Republic Steel became a leading

manufacturer of alloy steels in the 1930's by absorbing companies specializing in this rapidly expanding field. This company also pioneered "high-pressure smelting," an innovation that reduces the amount of fuel required in the blast furnace and increases the recovery of iron from the ore.[34]

In the 1950's the steel industry entered a new revolution in steel making techniques. For the first time since the end of the last century new steel processes have been developed. The basic-oxygen process, commercially put into operation for the first time in the small Austrian steelworks at Linz and Donawitz in 1952 after three years of experimental production, is the most important of these. Usually referred to as the LD-process, it is rapidly becoming a major steel making technique all over the world. The first LD-steel in Anglo-America was made at Dofasco's plant at Hamilton in 1952 and commercial production was started here in 1954. Dofasco is the smallest of the "big four" steel companies in Canada (see p. 110). The McLough Steel at Detroit started production without previous pilot plant operation the same year.[35] Linz, Donawitz, Hamilton, and Detroit were the only steel centers with LD-capacity in 1954. Five years later there were two Canadian (at Hamilton and Sault Ste. Marie) and four American (Detroit, Pittsburgh, Fontana, and Chicago) steel plants with combined LD-capacities of 1.1 and 4.0 million tons respectively. In 1959 the total world ingot capacity for LD-steel is over ten million tons.[36] Kaiser Engineers, the

[32] Letter from Mr. W. H. Stewart, President, Mississippi Steel Corporation.

[33] *The Making, Shaping and Treating of Steel*, United States Steel, Seventh Edition, Pittsburgh, 1957, p. 587.

[34] E. B. Alderfer and H. E. Michl: *Economics of American Industry*, Second Edition, New York, 1950, p. 60.

[35] C. R. Austin: "Oxygen Steel in the United States," *Iron and Steel Engineer*, Vol. 33, 1956, pp. 64–68.

[36] *L-D Process Newsletter*, Kaiser Engineers Division of Henry J. Kaiser Company, Oakland, February 27, 1959.

authorized licensor in the United States for the process, act under arrangements with Brassert Oxygen Technik of Zurich, Switzerland, which owns and controls the basic patents. They forecast that world LD-tonnage will account for 35 per cent of the total steel making capacity by 1965; it will approach 120 million tons.[37]

The Swedish Kaldo process, developed at Domnarfvet by Professor Kalling, and the German Rotor process, developed at Oberhausen, both similar to the LD-process, have not yet been introduced into Anglo-America.

In 1959, Jones & Laughlin was the only one of the eight largest steel companies making basic oxygen steel (at Aliquippa, Pittsburgh). This company had decided to start construction of the two largest basic oxygen furnaces in the world at its Cleveland plant in the summer of 1959. They are expected to produce 160-ton-heats and will have an annual capacity of 1.2 million tons. Eight adjacent 175-ton open hearth furnaces, constructed in 1924, will be deactivated.[38] Also other of the eight largest companies (e.g., Republic and Armco) are actively interested in building basic oxygen furnace capacity.[39]

What are the reasons for the rapid acceptance of the new process, which had to await the recent innovation of bulk producing methods in oxygen manufacturing? (Cheap oxygen is also used in conventional steel processes, but the new converters are specially designed for this technique.) The LD-converter seems to be more economical than conventional steel processes, both in construction costs and in operating expenditures, and it has a greater versatility than the open-hearth furnace prevalent in Anglo-America. For a capacity of 800,000 tons a year the investment in LD-furnaces has been estimated at 13 to 15 dollars per annual ton, in electric furnaces at 18 dollars a ton, and in open hearth at 33 dollars. This is exclusive of oxygen generating facilities for LD and power stations for electric furnaces. Comparisons between open hearth and LD are complicated by differences in charges. Oxygen furnaces operate with a maximum of about 30 per cent scrap and often much less, whereas open hearth charges have in recent peak periods averaged about half scrap and half hot metal. If the extra coke oven and blast furnace capacity needed for LD is considered, the overall investment for a completely new mill would be roughly the same for LD and open hearth.[40] But as found in this study, new mills are exceptions and additions to existing plants are the rule. For mills that can increase pig iron capacity at low cost the oxygen process offers clear-cut capital savings.

Republic Steel recently announced that it had an even more radical innovation, producing steel strip from iron powder and thus eliminating coke ovens, blast furnaces, steel furnaces, and blooming mills, on an experimental stage in its research center at Cleveland. A commercial plant will not be built for five or six years, but such a plant would cost only 40 to 50 per cent as much as installations used in the conventional melting process. Similar experiments have been under way in Europe (Domnarfvet, Sweden) for about five years.[41]

[37] Letter from Mr. R. A. Bateman, Manager, Public Relations, Kaiser Engineers, Division of Henry J. Kaiser Company, March, 1959.
[38] News Release, April 30, 1959, Public Relations and Advertising Department, Jones & Laughlin Steel Corporation, Pittsburgh.
[39] The New York Times, June 14, 1959.
[40] G. J. McManus: "Low Capital Cost Spurs Swing to Oxygen Steel," The Iron Age, Vol. 181, 1958, pp. 55–58.
[41] The New York Times, June 19, 1959.

The Future

It is too early to forecast the influence of these innovations on the future location pattern of the Anglo-American steel industry. It seems, however, that the pull of iron ore will increase, that of coal will continue to decrease. This does not mean that peripheral ore fields and shipping ports for ore will get most of the new steel capacity. It is more likely that the large urban agglomerations (large markets) with coastal location (cheap iron ore) will be the beneficiaries. The tendency of making steel to more and more exacting customer specifications, sold on a hand-to-mouth basis, will probably be strengthened by the great versatility of the LD-process, by which steel is made in relatively small heats in a very short time.

The "law" of industrial inertia will continue to work; it is not likely that the steel pattern will undergo any revolutionary changes in the next decade. It will probably continue to change primarily through differences in growth rate rather than by additions of new steel plants and closing down of old ones.

Acknowledgments

The present study was made when I was visiting lecturer at the Department of Geography, The University of Wisconsin, Madison, during the spring and summer of 1959. Mr. Randall Sale made the layout of the maps which were drawn by Miss Mei-Ling Hsu. Professors Arthur Robinson and David Shannon made suggestions which were incorporated in the text and the maps. Steel companies and organizations, too many to be mentioned, answered my inquiries and provided me with material.

ECONOMICS OF PROCESS SELECTION
IN THE IRON AND STEEL INDUSTRY

by
M. D. J. BRISBY, P. M. WORTHINGTON, B. Sc. (Eng.),
and R. J. ANDERSON, B. Eng., A.M.I.C.E.*

THE NEED FOR ANALYSIS

The motives for building a steelworks may be political, sociological, or strategic, but there is always an overriding requirement that the project should be financially sound and produce the highest possible profit within the given terms of reference.

Before working up a project in detail ready for board approval, it is necessary to make a series of interrelated business decisions concerned with the products to be made and the processes and raw materials to be employed. As there can be wide differences between the profitabilities of different schemes, it is important that the right decisions are made. Experience based on past usage is not always enough, particularly in a changed economic environment, or when there are new processes to consider.

The purpose of this paper is to discuss analytical methods of comparing the financial implications of different courses of action and of finding which course is likely to give the best results. There are in fact three recognizable stages in defining the company's forward plan: firstly the formulation of financial data for various technical and commercial possibilities, secondly the manipulation of these data to show the relative merits of different forward plans, and thirdly making the decision, taking into account the broadest possible assessment of all relevant aspects. The first of these is arduous and difficult and involves the skills of many specialists such as metallurgists, engineers, operators, market investigators, and accountants. The second stage, with which this paper deals, is relatively simple; it is concerned with the analysis and interpretation of these data to quantify as many as possible of the aspects involved in the decision. In this way the greatest possible help is given to those who have the responsibility of taking the final decision.

*Mr. Brisby is a partner in W. S. Atkins & Partners, Mr. Worthington is an associate partner and head of their Economics and Industrial Planning Department, and Mr. Anderson is head of their Business Economics Group.

"Economics of Process Selection in the Iron and Steel Industry" by M.D.J.Brisby, P.M.Worthington, and R.J.Anderson. Reprinted from Iron and Steel Institute Journal, *Vol.* 202 (*September* 1964), *pp.* 721–729, *with permission of the editor.*

COMPREHENSIVE
PRODUCTION COSTS

The economic merits of two or more methods of making equal quantities of the same product can be measured in terms of their capital costs and their annual production costs. When one of the schemes has both the lowest capital cost and the lowest production cost, it is clearly the most desirable. In most cases, however, the choice is not so simple; one scheme may have the lowest capital cost and another the lowest production cost. To compare schemes in general, therefore, it is convenient to express the costs for each scheme in terms of a single parameter. This can be done by regarding capital as a commodity which is hired for an annual charge. This annual charge may then be added to the annual production cost, giving a new annual figure which can be called the 'comprehensive production cost.' This concept of comprehensive costing is of great value in solving the more complex comparative problems.

A company will naturally choose those schemes which give it the best return on its capital. However, both the supply of money and the development of highly profitable schemes are limited so that the money is employed according to a natural law of supply and demand. If a company is short of money for the time being, it will only be prepared to implement the most profitable of schemes; but at the other end of the scale a company may have substantial sums of money available, and it is important in such circumstances to set the money to work, even at a lower rate of return. Thus, at any point in time, there is a value for the annual return r below which the company is not prepared to invest; r sets itself, by supply and demand, at the level where there are just sufficient superior schemes to keep the available money productively employed.

A discourse on the annual return r could really form the subject of a separate paper which would deal with such complexities as capital being invested some years before it starts earning profit, markets growing or declining during the life of the plant, and money being available from different sources. For most of the case-studies in this paper r is taken as 25% per year, after allowing for all running costs except depreciation. The 25% therefore has to cover provision for depreciation, taxation, reserves, and dividends. It also takes into account the effects of inflation and the absence of profit during the construction period.

COMPARISON OF COMPRE-
HENSIVE PRODUCTION COSTS

When comparing two or more methods of making the same product it is essential to include in the comparison all aspects which are different in the various schemes. The long computations involved in assessing capital and operating costs can be simplified by excluding all factors common to all the schemes, since at this stage the comparison is concerned with differences rather than with absolute values.

For schemes making the same quantity and quality of products, the income from sales is the same in all cases and does not enter into the comparison. The scheme with the lowest comprehensive production cost is thus the best. A method of making such a comparison for a

single production department is illustrated by the case-study given
below. The example is based on work
done overseas but is simplified to
some extent to present the method
without the detail. The conclusions
reached are only appropriate for the
assumed conditions. Other conditions in other parts of the world will
lead to different conclusions, and
there is no short cut to working up
in detail a comparison for each
particular different case.

*Case 1: Conversion of Ore to
Molten Iron.* This case examines a
proposed ironmaking plant in North
Africa required to make 100,000 long
tons of iron a year from a local lump
ore which can be supplied at the
works at £3 8s/ton. The processes
compared are:

(i) electric smelters charged with
    the cold lump ore
(ii) electric smelters, but with
    preheating of the burden using
    top gases
(iii) a blast furnace operated on
    simple practice, without oil
    injection or oxygen enrichment.

There are no suitable coals in the
area so coke has to be imported. The
delivered price for gasworks coke
for the electric smelters is £7 17s/
ton, and the price of metallurgical
coke for the blast furnace is £9 5s.
Electricity is available from local
oil-fired power stations at 1d/kWh.
Powerhouse facilities are not regarded as part of the department,
but any surplus top gas has been
credited at its appropriate oil-re-
placement value on the assumption
that it can be used elsewhere in the
works.

The burden per ton of iron for the
electric smelters charged with cold
ore is, tons:

lump ore	1.790
gasworks coke	0.424
limestone	0.076

The electricity consumption is 2500
kWh/ton. One furnace with a shell
diameter of 40 ft and a rating of 40
mVA will give the output. In assessing capital costs all equipment has
been included from the point where
the burden leaves the scale car to
the point where the molten iron enters the mixer. The capital cost of
the scheme and the comprehensive
production cost are summarized as
follows:

Capital cost for electric smelting:	£
One 40 ft furnace	250,000
40 mVA furnace electrics	350,000
Charging equipment	220,000
Gas-cleaning plant	180,000
Cranes, ladles, and other plant	109,000
Freight and erection	211,000
Mechanical services	38,000
Electrical services	82,000
Buildings	97,000
Civil engineering	84,000
Spare parts	30,000
Total	1,651,000

Comprehensive production cost:	£
Lump ore (179,000 tons)	609,000
Gasworks coke (42,400 tons)	333,000
Limestone (7,600 tons)	4,000
Electrodes (1,500 tons)	45,000
Refractories and other consumables	40,000
Electricity (250 × 10⁶ kWh)	1,042,000
Wages and salaries with overheads	32,000
Maintenance, including labour	45,000
Miscellaneous	15,000
Annual return (at 25%)	413,000
	2,578,000
Credit for top gas (6 × 10⁶ therms)	92,000
Total	2,486,000

One way of using the top gas is to burn it in the smelter charging-shafts to preheat the burden. This brings us to the second of the three processes to be compared. The temperature of the burden is then raised to about 800°C, which leads to a 20% reduction in the electricity required and slight reductions in the coke and limestone rates. For the stipulated output of 100,000 tons of iron a year the electrical rating of the furnace need only be 32 mVA, giving a substantial saving in its capital cost, although this is offset by the extra cost of the preheating equipment.

For the third scheme, a blast furnace with a hearth diameter of 12 ft 6 in will give the required output on a 100% Rice rating. Compared with electric smelting, the blast furnace requires more extensive coke storage and preparation facilities. The extra cost of these facilities, and the additional working capital for a three-month stock of the extra coke, must therefore be included.

The capital and comprehensive production costs have been worked up for the second and third schemes, and the comparative figures for all three schemes are as follows:

nored. It is permissible to do this because the purpose of the study is to compare production costs rather than to find their absolute values.

These calculations were based on an output of 100,000 tons/a, but they can be repeated for different outputs to show the effects of scale. This has been done for various outputs up to 500,000 tons/a, and the results are shown graphically in Figure 1a. It will be seen that scale effect is more important with the blast furnace than with electric smelters, particularly at small outputs. Indeed, for very small outputs, electric smelting with preheating becomes the most economic process. The crossover point of the two curves gives the output at which one scheme becomes preferable to the other.

The schedule of operating costs for the electric process shows that the greatest single element is the cost of electricity. The relative economics of the three processes therefore depend greatly on the relative prices of electricity and coke. Figures 1b and 1c illustrate the influence of electricity cost, Figure 1c giving the academic case where electricity is supplied free. As elec-

Scheme	Capital, £	Production, £/a	Comprehensive, £/a
Electric (cold ore)	1,651,000	2,073,000	2,486,000
Electric (preheated)	1,781,000	1,976,000	2,421,000
Blast-furnace	2,460,000	1,448,000	2,063,000

It is seen that the blast furnace scheme is the most economic. In fact it shows a saving of more than £3 10s/ton compared with either of the electric schemes.

The foregoing figures are comparative and are not intended to represent the total cost of making iron. Costs such as administrative overheads and laboratory costs are ig-

tricity becomes cheaper, two things happen: firstly the crossover points move towards higher outputs, and secondly the saving in cost by preheating the burden diminishes. In fact, where electricity is priced below about 0.5d/unit, preheating ceases to be an advantage.

Graphs have been drawn for intermediate electricity costs, and the

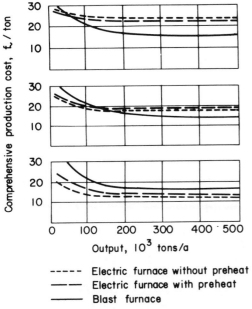

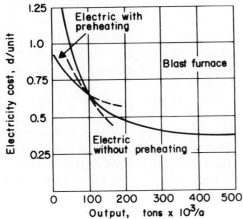

Figure 1: Ironmaking costs
Electricity costs: a 1d/unit; b 0.5d/unit;
c electricity free

crossover points on these graphs have been abstracted to make a plot of the economic zones for the three processes (Figure 2). As is now generally accepted, this shows that the rightful place of electric ironmaking is where electricity is cheap or where only small outputs of iron are required. Burden preheating only occupies a narrow zone between the other two areas. This illustrates how

Figure 2: Economic zones for ironmaking

the pursuit of thermal efficiency in a process is not always economic.

The comparison of ironmaking costs could have been widened to include a variety of refinements. For example, costs could be calculated for a blast furnace with oil injection, higher blast-temperature, or high top-pressure. For each practice being considered, the blast furnace size and other plant requirements are different and must be worked out in full. Different driving rates can also be studied to find the most economic balance between blower capacity and blast furnace size.

In the case-study, it was reasonable to restrict comparisons to a single indigenous ore. More usually a variety of ores are available and comparisons must be made of the relative costs of using them individually or in blends. The range of possibilities can be further widened to take into account the various methods of ore preparation and beneficiation. The operator of existing plant has such variables constantly under detailed review, since he is concerned with finding the optimum working conditions for plant he already has. However, in planning new capital developments the ultimate objective is to settle the choice of processes and arrive at their leading parameters so that plant-purchase specifications can be drafted. The operating studies are concerned with detailed comparisons of materials and practices, while the planning studies are concerned only with such detail as will affect the selection of plant or the viability of the scheme.

REPLACEMENT OF EXISTING PLANT

In selecting and building a plant the company bases its decision on its assessment of the markets and the relative prices of labour, materials, and services. So long as these remain stable and there is no relevant technical innovation, the process should remain unchanged. However, when any part of the economic or technical environment changes, the company needs to know whether it should change the plant. In such a case the problem is to compare a new process requiring additional capital with the existing process which requires no additional capital. The question now arises as to what value must be assigned to the existing equipment for the purpose of working out the annual return required. For comparative purposes, the second-hand or scrap value of the existing equipment should be used, plus the present value to the company of any tax allowances being made earlier than would otherwise be the case. Neither the original cost nor the present book value is relevant in making the decision, since neither figure represents the money which could be realized if the plant were replaced.

This point can be illustrated as follows. Let the book value of existing plant be E and its net sale value S; also let the capital cost of the new plant be N. Then the capital for the existing scheme may be said to be E, in which case the capital for the new scheme will be $N + E - S$. The term E is included for the new scheme as the company cannot escape from its commitments on the old plant. As E appears in both schemes, it is irrelevant for the purposes of comparison.

Case 2: *Replacement of Open-Hearth Furnaces*. A steelworks in North America has an OH shop operating on cold practice with a capacity of 500,000 tons of liquid steel a year. The problem is to find whether there is any merit in replacing the plant with either arc or fuel-oxygen furnaces.

The existing shop has four 200 ton furnaces operating without oxygen enrichment. The same production could be achieved with four 100 ton arc furnaces placed in the same building modified to suit the new plant. It is estimated that the output could also be achieved with four 50 ton fuel-oxygen furnaces, again placed in the same shop. In this case a 300 ton/day oxygen plant will be required and this equipment will be treated as part of the steel plant.

Taking return on capital at 25% a year, the comparative capital and comprehensive production costs are as shown in Table 1.

Thus, the best course of action is for the company to discard its present plant and introduce the fuel-oxygen process. By doing this the company would increase its gross profit by £420,000/a in addition to the 25% return on the extra capital involved. Even if the OH shop were brand new it should still be changed. Indeed the tax system in the UK and many other countries leads to the curious anomaly that a company is given greater inducement to replace new plant than old. This is because the balancing allowance depends on the extent to which the plant has been written down.

The comprehensive production costs show that the major reason for the superiority of the fuel-oxygen over the arc furnace is its thermal efficiency, the sum of the costs of fuel and electricity being low. It will be noted that the cost of oxygen does not appear in the schedule, as the oxygen plant is included in the capi-

Table 1. Steelmaking Costs

	Existing plant	Arc	Fuel-oxygen
Capital costs			
Steelmaking plant	—	1,550,000	880,000
Oxygen plant	—	—	1,900,000
Civils and services	—	184,000	170,000
Provision for development	—	—	200,000
		1,734,000	3,150,000
Sale value of existing plant	—	50,000	50,000
New capital		1,684,000	3,100,000
Comprehensive production costs:			
Scrap steel	5,530,000	6,950,000	6,950,000
Cold pig iron	3,265,000	847,000	847,000
Fuel oil	558,000	—	337,000
Electricity	24,000	732,000	170,000
Additives	450,000	428,000	420,000
Electrodes	—	405,000	—
Refractories	372,000	287,000	313,000
Wages and salaries	710,000	550,000	612,000
Other costs	170,000	135,000	135,000
Operating contingencies			100,000
Annual return		421,000	775,000
Total	11,079,000	10,755,000	10,659,000

tal; the department buys electricity to operate the oxygen plant. As the fuel-oxygen process uses such large quantities of oxygen it can be produced at very low unit cost.

In this case-study scrap was priced at £14/ton and cold pig at £19 10s/ton. However, the relative comprehensive production costs of the three processes are sensitive to changes in these prices. Quite a small change in one of them could produce a totally different result. It is therefore vital to base a decision on long-range forecasts.

Figure 3 has been drawn by putting different percentages to the return on capital required in the case-study. The graph shows how a company requiring a modest return should change to fuel-oxygen. How-

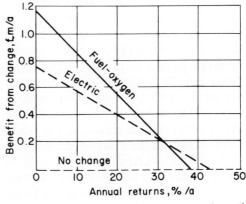

Figure 3: Benefit of replacing open-hearth furnaces

ever, a company may be requiring a higher return on new capital because of a shortage of money or an unusually good supply of high-return opportunities for investment. In such a case the higher capital cost of the fuel-oxygen process makes it less attractive. A company fixing r between 33 and 43% should adopt arc furnaces, and a company placing r at an unusually high figure should not change for the time being. A large part of the initial cost of the fuel-oxygen process is for the oxygen plant. The process can be made a low capital-cost scheme by calling on one of the oxygen companies to build the oxygen plant and supply tonnage oxygen under contract. If the oxygen company is satisfied. with a lower return on capital, the process could remain the most economic at values of r above 33%

In this study the ability of the arc furnace to make better steels was not taken into account. These advantages can only be quantified by considering markets and selling prices. These aspects are discussed later in the paper.

COMPARISON OF PROFITS

A statement was made earlier in the paper that, for a number of schemes making the same product, the scheme with the lowest comprehensive production cost is the most desirable. Schemes which make different products, or different quantities of the same product, obviously yield different incomes, so the analysis must go one stage further to assess the profitability of each. In such a case the comprehensive production cost can be deducted from the annual income to give the 'additional annual profit' for each scheme.

For the various schemes the additional annual profit Q can be expressed in the form:

$$Q_a = I_a - (P_a + rC_a)$$
$$Q_b = I_b - (P_b + rC_b)$$

and so forth, where I is the annual income, P the production cost, and C the capital required. As r includes the normal return on capital required by the board, the best scheme is the one with the biggest value of Q irrespective of the amount of capital involved. If Q is positive the scheme is economically worthwhile; if Q is negative the scheme falls short of the financial requirements.

This can be illustrated by considering two mutually exclusive schemes, A and B, with the following figures:

Scheme	Capital cost (C), £	Gross profit $(I - P)$, £	Profit, %
A	1,000,000	320,000	32
B	3,000,000	840,000	28

It might be thought that scheme A is the better since it offers the higher percentage return; but this is not sufficient evidence. By investing the further £2,000,000 to proceed with scheme B instead of scheme A, an extra profit of £520,000/a can be made. This can be expressed as follows:

Scheme	Capital cost (C), £	Gross profit $(I - P)$, £	Profit %
B—A	2,000,000	520,000	26

Thus if the company requires a return of 25%, the additional investment is worthwhile by definition. If the value of Q (the additional annual profit) is calculated, the right answer is given directly. Thus:

Scheme	Capital cost (C), £	Gross profit (I-P), £	Capital charges (r), £	Additional profit (Q), £
A	1,000,000	320,000	250,000	70,000
B	3,000,000	840,000	750,000	90,000

Scheme B is therefore better by £20,000/a.

Case 3: Sales Policy for Reinforcing Rods. Consider, for example, a works operating at full capacity producing reinforcing rods, ranging in diameter from 3/8 in to 1 1/4 in. At present the rods are cut into 180 ft

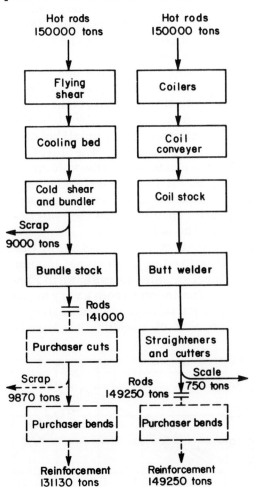

Figure 4: Methods of selling reinforcement

lengths by the flying shear and allowed to cool on a cooling bed in a commercially straight condition. The rods are then sheared into stock lengths, bundled, and kept in stock ready for sale.

The proposal is to offer a cut-to-length service to customers. To do this, the cooling bed and associated equipment would be replaced by two pouring reels, two laying reels, and a coil-cooling conveyer. Products would be stocked as coil, and each order made up by withdrawing coils from stock, straightening, and cutting accurately to scheduled lengths. In this way the customer can order exact numbers and lengths of bars to match his bending lists instead of ordering bundles of standard lengths by weight.

The two processes are illustrated in Figure 4. In both cases the mill produces its full output of 150,000 tons of uncut rods a year. In the present works 9,000 tons of scrap are unavoidably produced in the finishing department because of the short unsaleable ends left by the two shearing operations. In the proposed scheme there need be no such scrap, as coils can be butt-welded together to give, in effect, one continuous length of rod for straightening and cutting.

When the purchaser buys bundles of reinforcing rods in stock lengths, he has to cut the required lengths before bending, leading to a loss of 7% of the rod as scrap. (This figure is an average over the civil engineering and building industries.) By accepting the proposed new service he would avoid making this scrap and save his own cutting costs. Expressed in terms of money, the saving to the purchaser per ton of reinforcement used would be:

	£
7/93 ton of rods at £44	3.3
Cutting cost at £2.5	2.5
	5.8
Less sale of scrap at £10	0.7
Net saving	5.1

Once the service is properly understood, the purchaser should therefore be prepared to pay a premium of perhaps £3/ton for rods cut to scheduled lengths. It is now possible to find out whether the proposed scheme should be adopted.

	Existing scheme £	Proposed scheme £
Capital cost:	—	288,000
Less sale of existing plant	—	20,000
		268,000
Annual income:		
Sale of rods	6,204,000	7,015,000
Credit for internal scrap	90,000	—
	6,294,000	7,015,000
Comprehensive annual finishing cost:		
Operating cost	44,000	68,000
Capital charges (at 25%)	—	67,000
	44,000	135,000
Income less finishing cost	6,250,000	6,880,000

Thus, the benefit to the company in adopting the scheme would be

£630,000/a (after allowing for return on capital). This benefit comes from two principal sources: the output of the works is increased and the product fetches a better price.

Case 4: Production Level for a Strip Mill. In the foregoing case-study only two possible courses of action were considered. Each had its own clearly defined output and selling price. The present case study considers a proposal to build a strip mill in a country which is now importing all its requirements. In addition to the home markets the company could sell abroad. The problem is to find the most profitable level of production, and hence the type of plant to be purchased.

The sales department can be regarded as another works department whose duty it is to convert the product into money — be it by alchemy. The department has a small but definite operating cost, the level of which depends upon the volume of sales, but it has a correspondingly large income from its customers. The difference between the two constitutes the net income.

The market survey has shown that the relationship between net income and level of sales is as shown in Figure 5. The income from a very small level of sales is more than eaten up by the cost of running the depart-

Figure 5: Income from sale of strip

ment. For a large portion of the local market, the price per ton is relatively static as the company has simply to compete with the large reserve of existing world production. This condition prevails until all the easy local markets are satisfied. To sell more, the company must either bear the cost of transporting the product further afield, or force the market by reducing prices to enable the steel products to compete more favourably with alternative materials such as other metals, timber, and plastics. This causes the income graph to level out. Indeed, to force sales unduly would involve such large price reductions that the net income would decline as the sales increase; in the absurd limit, the product cannot be given away. The export market is large but at a lower net price. The ideal point to start exporting is where the slope of the forced home-market curve is equal to the slope of the export line. The export line is therefore tangential.

Before deciding the right level of output, the corresponding costs of making the product must be known. These are illustrated in Figure 6, which shows how the comprehensive cost of making the strip depends upon the output required. The costs are discontinuous; there is a sharp increase in cost when extra capital

is required for a larger mill. By subtracting the comprehensive production cost curve from the income curve, a new curve is produced which gives the additional annual profit to the company (Figure 7). In this particular case there would be no merit in being in the strip business at production levels below 270,000 tons/a (about three-quarters of the capacity of a Steckel mill). Above that figure it is worth having a Steckel mill, which becomes much more profitable as its capacity is filled. With outputs exceeding 350,000 tons/a a semi-continuous mill is required, but it is not as profitable as a Steckel mill on full production unless sales reach 420,000 tons/a. This leads to the interesting conclusion that works making between 350,000 and 420,000 tons/a should not be built. The best course of action is for the company to build a semi-continuous mill and aim at a production level of 500,000 tons/a. A fully continuous mill must be rejected. The graph shows that the size of markets to go for should not be decided first in isolation, leaving the works to be engineered to suit that market; the plant to be built and market to be sought should be decided together in the light of full financial information.

In the analysis the strip width was taken as 60 in and the coil weight as

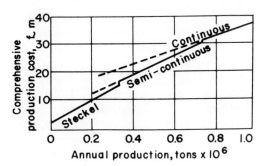

Fig. 6: Cost of making strip

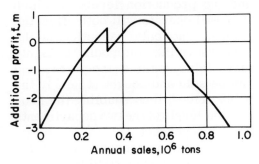

Fig. 7: Additional profit from a strip mill

20,000 lb. Many other combinations of strip width and coil weight could be adopted, all of which must be fully investigated before arriving at a final decision. It is also necessary to investigate whether the different qualities of strip produced by the three types of mill have any significant effect on the shape of the income graph.

INTERRELATED PROCESSES

In making calculations for a single department, values had to be assigned to commodities which were received from other departments of the works, or supplied to them. That is to say, interdepartmental prices were defined. For example, top gas was given a sale value per therm on the assumption that all of it could be used to replace oil elsewhere in the works. As another example electricity was ascribed a simple unit price although part of the electricity might be generated within the works and the remainder purchased outside at a complex tariff. To use such an interdepartmental price can often be misleading in making process decisions where more than one department is affected. This is because the bases for calculating the interdepartmental prices are themselves affected by the decisions yet to be made. The processes to be chosen and the production levels at which they will operate will both affect the prices. The only exception is the case where the commodity is highly marketable outside the works and can be sold and bought at nearly the same prices, thus enabling the production levels of the two departments to be independent.

When making economic comparisons in the broader field it is there-fore better to avoid the use of interdepartmental prices as far as is possible. This means linking departments together and considering the economics of the larger entity. In the ideal limit, the whole works should be regarded as one unit so that interdepartmental prices cease to be relevant because a debit to one part of the works is exactly offset by a credit elsewhere.

Case 5: *Production of Steel Blooms from Scrap.* A proposed new works in India is to make 300,000 tons/a of 6 in square blooms from purchased scrap. The question is whether ingot casting or continuous casting should be used. In both cases, steel is to be made in arc furnaces.

The flow diagrams for the two proposals are shown in Figure 8. They show how both the rolling mill and steel plant are substantially affected by the choice of casting method. Besides requiring a blooming mill with soaking pits, ingot casting requires a larger steelmaking plant because of its lower yield. For the ingot scheme the steelmaking shop could have, say, two 100 ton furnaces, while for the continuous-casting scheme it could have smaller furnaces, say four of 45 tons, to match the casting strands. The comparative capital and comprehensive production costs for the two schemes are briefly summarized as follows:

	Ingot casting £	Continuous casting £
Capital costs:		
Steelmaking	1,870,000	2,560,000
Casting	1,430,000	1,080,000
Rolling	3,460,000	—
General works	2,000,000	1,000,000
	8,760,000	4,640,000

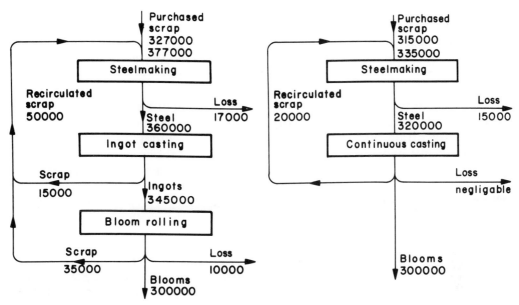

Figure 8: Flow diagrams for bloom production

Comprehensive production
 costs:

Purchased scrap steel	3,920,000	3,780,000
Steelmaking	2,260,000	2,010,000
Casting	720,000	560,000
Rolling	300,000	—
General works	800,000	650,000
Annual return (25%)	2,190,000	1,160,000
	10,190,000	8,160,000

Thus, the additional profit of the company will be £2,030,000/a higher with continuous casting than with ingots.

The steelmaking costs in the two schemes are radically different because they relate to different plants and different outputs. For ingot casting 360,000 tons/a of liquid steel have to be produced in 100 ton heats, but for continuous casting 320,000 tons/a have to be produced in 45 ton heats. The former has the lower unit cost, and the latter the lower absolute cost. Thus it would have been incorrect to assume a fixed price for liquid steel; to have done so would have favoured continuous casting unduly.

In the case-study, the end-product was defined as a 6 in square bloom to suit a specific market requirement. If the blooms are to be used for further rolling within the works, this dimension is not necessarily the most economic. The bloom size affects both capital and operating costs of all three departments. This is because the rolling facilities, the number of casting strands, the heat size, the cycle time, and the number of steelmaking furnaces all have to be matched to suit the bloom size. By setting down a range of alternative bloom sizes, and working up a full scheme for each, it is possible to arrive at the most economic size.

OVERALL OPTIMIZATION

When planning a new works, or re-planning an existing works, a whole series of business decisions has to be made. These include the choice of the raw materials, the markets to be sought, the process to be employed in each of the manufacturing departments, and the capacities of the production units. All of these decisions are interrelated, so ideally they should all be taken together in the light of full economic facts. The problem is to find which pattern of decisions is the best, i.e. the pattern which gives the most profitable venture. If the decisions are taken con-secutively there is no guarantee that the resulting scheme is the best.

Case 6: *Integrated Works for Producing Flat Products*. A new integrated works is to be built for the manufacture of flat products. The company could sell plate, coil, and sheet, or, by incorporating the appropriate cold rolling and finishing facilities, the company could also sell galvanized sheet, tinplate, or tubes.

For the purpose of analysing the problem, the works has been divided

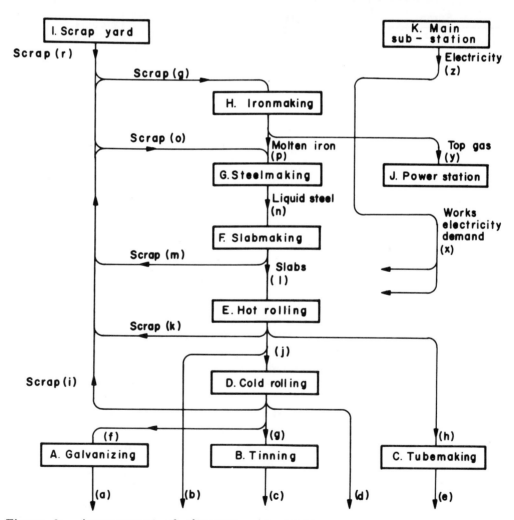

Figure 9:   Arrangement of alternative processes

into eleven basic departments as shown in Figure 9. In general, the work of each of these departments can be done by various alternative methods, and the likely possibilities can be set down for consideration. For example, the following steelmaking processes could be included:

G1 Arc (100% scrap)
G2 LD converters (17% scrap)
G3 LD with oil injection (30% scrap)
G4 LD with oil injection (50% scrap)
G5 Fuel-oxygen (100% scrap)

The alternatives for each of the other departments can be set down in a similar way, and for the purpose of this case-study it has been assumed that the numbers of alternatives are as follows:

Department	Number of alternatives
A Galvanizing	2
B Tinning	1
C Tubemaking	1
D Cold rolling	3
E Hot rolling	3
F Slabmaking	2
G Steelmaking	5
H Ironmaking	6
I Scrap yard	1
J Power station	2
K Main substation	1

There are thus 27 processes to be considered; these can be combined to give 1368 compatible alternative works:

Works 1
A1 B1 C1 D1 E1 F1 G1 H1 I1 J1 K1

Works 2
A1 B1 C1 D1 E1 F1 G1 H1 I1 J2 K1

Works 1368
A2 B1 C1 D3 E3 F2 G5 — I1 — K1

The ironmaking and power-generating departments are, of course, omitted whenever the steelmaking department operates on 100% scrap.

In addition to these different process combinations, there is a wide range of possible courses of action which the company can take in respect of the various markets. All must be considered. One way of doing this is to define a range of possible production levels for each of the different products. Taking tinplate as an example we may set down the following annual sales levels, tons:

c1	None	c6	200,000
c2	100,000	c7	225,000
c3	125,000	c8	250,000
c4	150,000	c9	275,000
c5	175,000	c10	300,000

Such a range of possibilities can sometimes be substantially reduced by inspection and experience. For instance, there is no point in including figures which are obviously outside the possible range. The figures for tinplate quoted above recognize that the output should either be zero or between 100,000 and 300,000 tons/ a. It is more important to divide the reasonable range of outputs into small intervals than to cover a wide field. The other four markets will have their own possible sales levels, and all these levels can again be combined into a large number of alternative product mixes, which can be expressed by the series:

Product mix 1   a1 b1 c1 d1 e1
Product mix 2   a1 b1 c1 d1 e2

and so forth. If product mixes and processes are considered together there could be several hundreds of thousands of possible courses of action for the company to take. Before attempting to compare these alternatives, the basic economic data must be collected and assembled in the most suitable manner.

Each of the five markets has its own characteristic curve of net income against annual sales. Also, each of the 27 alternative processes has its own curve of comprehensive production cost against annual output of the department's own particular product. This comprehensive production cost can include all the costs of running the department, including raw materials and services which it buys from outside the company (or to which a fixed value can be assigned). However, the process materials such as molten iron, and services such as electricity, which pass from one department to another, cannot be included in the costs without assigning arbitrary values which have already been shown to be unnecessary and misleading. These commodities flowing between departments (Figure 9) can be left unpriced and considered as the network of relationships between the departments.

Figure 9 shows a possible scrap flow into the ironmaking department. This is shown because a hot-blast cupola charged entirely with scrap is being considered as one of the ironmaking alternatives.

The scrap yard has been treated as a separate department; this is a device for summing up all the scrap required by departments, and all the scrap arising in other departments. The cost of operating the scrap yard consists mainly of the cost of buying the difference between the total requirements and the total arisings. The cost curve for this department can take into account the fact that the unit price of scrap may increase as the demand increases. This condition can arise, for example, when scrap requirements over a certain level have to be imported.

The main substation has also been treated as a department to enable electricity to be handled in the same way. The electricity demands of all the other departments are subtracted from the output of the power station, thus giving the quantity of electricity to be purchased from outside the works. The calculations can be refined to show separately the relevant electrical parameters such as units required and peak demand.

The relative flows of commodities passing in and out of a particular department can be expressed as sets of yield coefficients — one set for each alternative process which the department can use. For example, the coefficients for the steelmaking department are as follows:

Process	Scrap supplied (o/n)	Molten iron supplied (p/n)
G1 Arc (100% scrap)	1.087	0.000
G2 LD (17% scrap)	0.189	0.922
G3 LD with oil (30% scrap)	0.332	0.775
G4 LD with oil (50% scrap)	0.550	0.550
G5 Fuel–oxygen (100% scrap)	1.087	0.000

When all this information has been tabulated, it is possible to work out the annual flows of all interdepartmental commodities for any chosen product mix and set of manufacturing processes. With these flows it is then possible to read from the curves the net incomes from sales and the comprehensive operating costs of all the departments. The additional profit of the scheme can now be found by subtracting the sum of the comprehensive operating costs from the total net income.

In order to find the optimum course of action, the additional profit for every other feasible course of action must be found by similar calculations. Hundreds of thousands of such calculations are far beyond the limit of man's endurance, but they can be handled with comparative ease by a large high-speed digital computer.

Sufficient information to define all the net income curves, the comprehensive production-cost curves, and the yield coefficients has to be stored in the computer as basic data.

The programme is comparatively simple; it instructs the computer to operate on each course of action in turn, a course being defined as one of the possible product mixes and one of the possible works. The operation for each course of action is to determine the additional profit Q in an identical manner to that described above for manual calculation. All the answers are stored and it is possible to withdraw them for printing out in order of merit, starting with the scheme having the highest value of Q. The profitability, and the breakdown, of any other scheme can also be withdrawn for inspection.

The data and programme can be extended to handle refinements, and to present the information in other ways. For example, labour requirements could be added up and costed for the entire works instead of being incorporated in the departmental costs. The electrical demands and peak loads could be handled in a similar way. Capital costs could be kept separate from production costs and totalled separately for the whole works before being united into a comprehensive production cost, which needs to be done before the solutions are sorted into order. In this way it is possible to study other variables such as the effects on the order of merit of changing the required annual return r.

To deal with the larger problems associated with complete integrated iron- and steelworks it is necessary to use a computer having a large data-storage capacity and a high speed of operation. Some modern machines can handle on the order of 20,000 courses of action per hour, the exact number depending on the complexity of the network. In practice this imposes a limit on the reasonable number of alternatives that can be considered. For example, if ten hours of computer time is taken as a limit, only 200,000 courses of action could be considered. To introduce a new market or department with, say, ten alternatives could increase the number of courses of action ten-fold, which would call for an impracticable amount of computer time. Thus, even the most powerful present-day computers cannot handle, by this direct method, some of the more complex problems which could reasonably be posed.

To overcome this difficulty, more refined methods of analysis are being developed. Rational sub-optimization of major divisions of the works, successive relaxation of variables, and intermediate discarding in multistage calculations are examples of the more advanced methods under consideration.

ACKNOWLEDGMENTS

The authors wish to thank Mr. F. B. George for the encouragement he gave them to write a paper dealing with certain economic aspects of the iron and steel industry. They also wish to thank Mr. W. F. Cartwright, Mr. M. M. Zidi (President and Director General of Elfouladh, Société Tunisienne de Sidérurgie), Mr. I. M. D. Halliday, Mr. E. W. Voice, and Dr. R. Wild for their help and their valuable comments during the drafting of the paper.

Much of the material is based on planning studies made over the past few years by the Market Intelligence, Process Engineering, and Business Economics Departments of W. S. Atkins & Partners. The computer techniques have been developed by the firm's Research and Development Department. Members of all these departments have co-operated in preparing this paper.

BIBLIOGRAPHY

J. Astier: *J. Met.*, 1963, **15**, 619-626.

M. D. J. Brisby: *N. M. L. Techn. J.*, 1960.

W. F. Cartwright and M. F. Dowding: *JISI*, 1958, **188**, 23-35.

W. F. Cartwright and G. W. Thomas: *JISI*, 1962, **200**, 796-803.

F. C. Collin: *Tekn. Uke.*, 1960, 107.

P. Desfossez: *JISI*, 1962, **200**, 796-803.

G. B. R. Feilden and A. G. Raper: UN conf. on the application of science and technology for the benefit of less developed areas, 1962, Paper D. 7.1.

C. Goodeve: *JISI*, 1961, **198**, 117-123.

R. S. Howes and A. Jackson: *JISI*, 1960, **195**, 95-99.

J. R. Lawrence and A. D. J. Flowerdew: *Operational Research Quarterly*, March 1963, 31.

D. D. Moore: Iron Steel Eng. Yearbook, 1954, 177-191.

K. G. O'Brien and S. Robinson: BISRA Report OR/9/57, 1958.

T. F. Pearson *et al.*: *JISI*, 1964, **202**, 1-10.

J. W. D. Pictor and P. A. Young: *Steel Times*, 1964, 246-251.

J. Savage: *Steel and Coal*, 15 Feb. 1963, 320-329.

'Comparison of steelmaking processes,' U.N. Economic Commission for Europe, 1962.

W. S. Walker and G. R. Wieland: *Steel Times*, 17 April, 1964, 504 ff.

P. M. Worthington: *JISI*, 1962, **200**, 849-857.

THE BIG CHANGE COMES TO STEEL

The American steel industry is in the midst of a mammoth and costly job — rewriting the book on how to make its products.

On any other scale, the vast changes that are taking place might be described simply as evolutionary. But in the steel industry — which makes most of its pig iron in the blast furnace, a device invented 600 years ago — the changes add up to out-and-out revolution.

The basic oxygen furnace (pages 532 and 533) is the symbol of this revolution. It can make steel better and cheaper and five times faster than it ever was made before. Most steelmen believe no more open hearth furnaces — the steelmaking standard since the turn of the century — will be built in the U.S.

A CHANGING CLIMATE

The cost of this revolution comes high. This year, the steel industry will spend an estimated $1.8-billion for new plant and equipment. Much of the new capacity eventually will replace existing facilities. This, alone, once was a nightmarish prospect to steel management. The $1.8-billion expenditure is equivalent to over 20% of the present $8.8-billion total net fixed worth of the industry's plant and equipment.

The steel management that today accepts the realities of costly innovation exists in a vastly different environment from that of 20 years ago. The industry is riding high and is headed toward record production.

Pressures. But the cost of doing business in the steel industry, as in every other industry, follows an ever upward curve. Furthermore, competition — both from abroad and within the domestic industry, and from other materials — grows greater every year. Aluminum and plastics alone buffet the steel industry with ever greater force as time goes by.

In addition, steel customers are demanding higher quality, lower prices, and faster deliveries. It has become increasingly clear that the seller's market the steel industry enjoyed in the early and mid-1950s probably is gone forever.

Answers. Part of the answer to these new challenges is a move toward greater marketing consciousness — the present all-out attempt by U.S. Steel Corp. to sell the building trades, for example — as well as research aimed at more new products.

Another part is a broad program of expansion and modernization, and of adopting technological advances — some of them first developed in Europe — as soon as they can be made economically feasible for this country's vast steel industry.

Two trends. In one sense, this story is one of new processes — oxygen steelmaking, continuous

"The Big Change Comes to Steel." Reprinted by special permission from Business Week, (*August* 15, 1964), *pp.* 78–81+. *Copyrighted* 1964 *by McGraw-Hill, Inc. Illustrations with permission of the artist.*

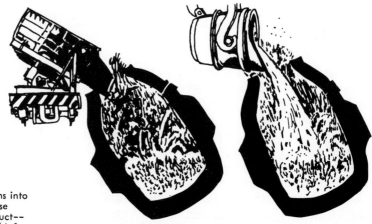

Oxygen furnace

Steel is putting billions into new technology to raise the quality of its product-- and lower its cost. Chief among the modern mill's new equipment is the basic oxygen furnace, which replaces the open hearth. Here's how it works:

1 Furnace, tilted on its side, is first charged with steel scrap. This can constitute up to 28% of the total charge.

2 In goes a load of molten iron produced in a blast furnace and kept hot until it's added to the oxygen furnace's charge.

casting, vacuum degassing. But it also involves an unstoppable trend toward more computer controls, both for processes and for management.

A number of huge rolling mills now turn out steel by computer control. It's better steel because its quality is more uniform and it is less costly to produce. But on the way, also, are computer controls for more complicated processes. U.S. Steel has a big blast furnace running under a computer's electronic thumb.

More of this is inevitable. In addition, there is a move toward tying together in a data processing network the whole business of making steel — from the initial order to the bill of lading.

More ahead. Equally significant is that steelmen are saying this is only the beginning. According to

T. F. Patton, Republic Steel Corp. chairman, and chairman of the American Iron & Steel Institute, the industry has been putting about $1-billion annually into capital improvements for several years. "Still," Patton said at the annual AISI meeting in May, "it was not enough. This year we will invest about $1.8-billion. And we face the prospect of having to continue to spend for capital improvements at a high rate for some time."

Conservative estimates place this projected spending at about $1.4-billion next year, and $1-billion in 1966. Others say this year's $1.8-billion will be equaled — or bettered — in 1965 and 1966.

GOING ON OXYGEN

This year has been a turning point for the most dramatic of the steel

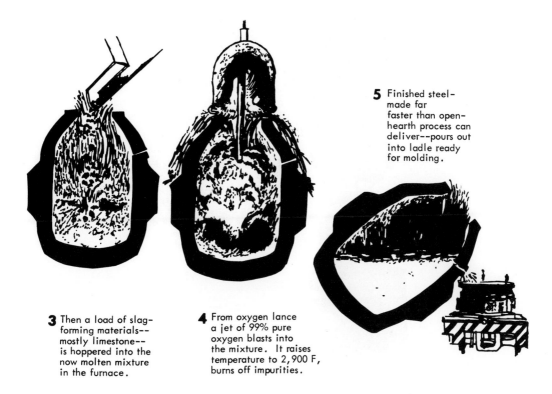

5 Finished steel—made far faster than open-hearth process can deliver--pours out into ladle ready for molding.

3 Then a load of slag-forming materials--mostly limestone--is hoppered into the now molten mixture in the furnace.

4 From oxygen lance a jet of 99% pure oxygen blasts into the mixture. It raises temperature to 2,900 F, burns off impurities.

industry's new processes — the basic oxygen process. Figures for the first six months of 1964 show that basic oxygen has become the second most important steelmaking process, passing the electric furnace for the first time.

Basic oxygen furnaces produced 6,623,153 net tons of steel during the first half of this year, as compared with 6,023,106 net tons from electric furnaces. The production increase appears to mark the beginning of the end for the open hearth, although open hearths produced a massive 48,179,029 net tons of steel in the same six-month period.

Speed and efficiency. Basic oxygen is a sharp departure from the relatively slow cooking that goes on in an open hearth. The oxygen sets off thermo-chemical reactions that refine the iron and scrap charge into

high-quality steel. But what enthralls steelmen most is that the basic oxygen furnace can turn out a heat of steel, from loading to tapping, in less than 50 minutes.

Depending on the size of the vessel, tonnages range from 60 to 300 tons per heat. Even the most modern open hearth, equipped with an oxygen lance that raises conventional production some 30%, can't do better than about 400 tons in from six to eight hours. Thus a big basic oxygen furnace can out-produce the best open hearth by up to four or five times. The savings are as much as $5 a ton.

Austrian development. The basic oxygen process first was developed some 12 years ago in Austria. Initial capacity was small, in the 30-to-50-ton per heat range. Americans give the Europeans their due, but they

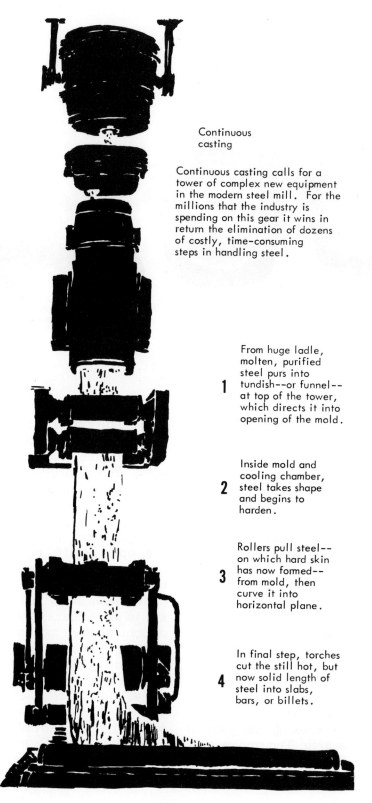

Continuous
casting

Continuous casting calls for a
tower of complex new equipment
in the modern steel mill. For the
millions that the industry is
spending on this gear it wins in
return the elimination of dozens
of costly, time-consuming
steps in handling steel.

1 From huge ladle,
molten, purified
steel purs into
tundish--or funnel--
at top of the tower,
which directs it into
opening of the mold.

2 Inside mold and
cooling chamber,
steel takes shape
and begins to
harden.

3 Rollers pull steel--
on which hard skin
has now formed--
from mold, then
curve it into
horizontal plane.

4 In final step, torches
cut the still hot, but
now solid length of
steel into slabs,
bars, or billets.

Degassing
process

To meet its customers' ever
more stringent demands—
and the needs of its own
new technology — steel
must spend millions to
raise the quality of its
product. One major cost
item: the vacuum degasser.

1 Ladle of molten
steel, holding up to
350 tons, rolls into
place atop movable
platform that can
be raised or lowered
by jacks.

2 "Snorkel" attached
to base of degassing
vessel dips into
molten metal each
time platform is
raised. For a 350-ton
load "snorkel"
makes 40 "sips".

3 Molten steel,
sucked up into
evacuated chamber of
degassing vessel,
boils off gases
and impurities.

contend that the process had to be scaled up to be economically attractive in this country — a technological feat in itself. In contrast to the early European units, Great Lakes Steel Corp., a division of National Steel Corp., now operates two 300-ton basic oxygen furnaces, presently the world's largest.

The scaling up process has, with some U.S. help, gone full circle. Italsider, Italy's huge steelmaking complex, soon will begin operating two 330-ton basic oxygen furnaces at Taranto. The units were designed by Koppers Co., Inc.

Leaders. Among the first U.S. companies to go into basic oxygen steelmaking were McLouth Steel Corp., which started up its 60-ton vessels in 1954, and Jones & Laughlin Steel Corp., which followed three years later with two 85-ton vessels.

Once the parade got under way, it could not be stopped. Now U.S. Steel has two basic oxygen furnaces at its Duquesne, Pa., works, and is building three more in Gary, Ind. Bethlehem Steel Corp. is building two vessels in Lackawanna, N.Y.; Republic Steel Corp. has two in Gadsden, Ala., two in Warren, Ohio, and two in Cleveland; Inland Steel Co. has two vessels under way at its Indiana Harbor Works, East Chicago, Ind.; Wheeling Steel Corp. is installing two vessels at Mingo Junction, Ohio; Allegheny Ludlum Steel Corp. has announced plans to build two at Brackenridge, Pa., near Pittsburgh.

Adding it up. In total, some $450,-million to $500-million worth of basic oxygen capacity either is completed or under way in the U.S. That adds up to about 30-million tons of annual capacity. Estimates are that another $500-million to $600-million worth of capacity will be added

within the next 10 years. A typical installation, having two vessels of 150 tons to 200 tons capacity each, represents an investment of about $20-million.

For some time it was feared that legal difficulties might halt the parade. Kaiser Engineers Div. of Henry J. Kaiser Co. has taken McLouth to court over ownership of the North American licensing rights for the group of patents covering the original basic oxygen process work done at Linz and Donawitz, Austria. The suit now is pending in U.S. District Court, Eastern District of Michigan. Also, Inland says it was granted a patent on basic oxygen steelmaking in 1954 that covers the essentials of the facilities it will install.

No slow down. But the rush toward building oxygen process vessels indicates that legal troubles — with the possibility in them that some users will wind up paying licensing or other fees — has not seriously slowed progress. Installations completed and under way will add up to a minimum of 27.8-million tons of annual basic oxygen capacity by December 1965.

The basic oxygen furnaces are not the only users of huge quantities of oxygen for steelmaking. Open hearths equipped with oxygen lances account for half again as much oxygen usage as the basic oxygen furnaces. But an official of the Linde Div. of Union Carbide Corp., major producer of industrial gases and a builder of oxygen plants for steel works, contends it will not be too long before the situation is reversed.

Indication. Linde's estimates of figures for oxygen usage in steelmaking show just how fast this development has grown. One of Linde's biggest oxygen customers 17 years ago — not a steel company — used about 15-million cu. ft. a month. Today, Linde reports, some big steel plants use four or more times that amount every day — almost all of it for basic oxygen or oxygen-equipped open hearth production.

One other important basic oxygen process is in use in the U.S., the so-called Kaldo method developed in Sweden. Sharon Steel Corp. is the only U.S. user. The vessel, instead of standing still and vertical during the oxygen "blow," is horizontal and rotates continually.

NEW WAYS, NEW MEN

Just as oxygen steelmaking is an all-new way to make steel, so the men who operate the oxygen furnaces are an all-new breed of steel worker. Their talk is peppered with such words as "process control," "computer," and "data processing."

At U.S. Steel's Duquesne works, for example, a workman uses a computer to determine what raw materials should go into the furnace to produce a given order. Until the temperature and make-up of the iron charge is known, the computer holds the order specification in its memory. It then calculates how much iron, steel scrap, flux, and other additives should be loaded into the furnace. It also determines the amount of oxygen to be "blown" during the heat.

Smoothing the steps. The semi-finishing of steel — turning the output of open hearth, basic oxygen, and other furnaces into slabs, billets, and bars for subsequent rolling into sheet and other finished products — is today a batch process. The furnace output is cast into ingots. Later, these ingots are heated

in what are called soaking pits. Then they are rolled on a primary rolling mill into slabs, billets, or bars.

But a process used for some years by nonferrous metal producers and European steelmakers — continuous casting (page 534) — is now proving that these batch-type steps can be smoothed into a continuous production line.

In and out. Molten metal from the open hearth or other furnace goes into one end of the continuous casting line; slabs, billets, or bars come out the other. This eliminates ingot molding, soaking, and primary rolling — along with their costs.

The process also results in a tremendous increase in yield over the traditional way of making slabs, billets, and bars.

Savings. In conventional processing, one ton of molten metal will produce 80% to 86% of its weight in semi-finished product. Most of the remainder is accounted for in trimming and scaling of the ingot. While this scrap eventually goes back into the furnace, it does represent a lot of wasted motion, time — and money.

Continuous casting, on the other hand, yields 94% to 98% of molten metal in semi-finished product. The savings to the producer are about $5 per ton of semi-finished steel.

Billets and bars. While it appears in principle to be beautifully simple, continuous casting has, in fact, required the solution of many engineering problems. Most of the big problems associated with continuous casting of billets and bars have been solved. Roanoke Electric Steel Corp., which owns the first commercial continuous caster, has been making billets successfully since last year.

The making of slabs, however, has

presented some tougher problems, especially for rimmed steel, the most commonly used variety for rolling into plates and sheets, the industry's bread and butter products. In conventional steelmaking, the gas and other impurities in so-called rimmed steel collect at the top of the ingot. This end is cut off before the ingot is rolled into slabs. But in the continuous caster, there's no place for the gas and impurities to go. Because of this, bubbles often form inside the cast pieces. The resulting steel contains holes that make rolling smooth sheets impractical, if not impossible.

Degasser. The answer so far appears to be another process called vacuum degassing, which uses a vacuum vessel to suck the gas impurities out of molten steel.

Aside from its probable use in making continuous casting more workable, vacuum degassing possesses a tremendous potential for making better and more uniform steel. It has been used by specialty steelmakers for some time. Latrobe Steel Co. is a veteran at it. The difference now is that it is being used more and more widely throughout the industry, and it has been adapted to big scale operations.

New demands. Steel customers are asking for — and more sophisticated end products demand — higher quality and more uniformity in steel. Highly automated production equipment also makes new demands on steelmakers.

One veteran steel operations man believes that in 20 years, 75% of all steel produced will be vacuum degassed. "There isn't any question that vacuum degassed steel is a purer steel," he says, "and if the quality of the end product demands it, you're going to use it."

Many ways. There's more than one process for vacuum degassing of steel — "stream degassing," the D-H (for Dortmund Hoerder-Huettenuion) process, ladle degassing, and a Republic Steel process called "induction stirred ladle vacuum degassing." But the principle, in each case, is essentially the same (page 535).

The biggest vacuum degassing unit in existence is a D-H unit at J&L's Pittsburgh works. It is twice as large as any other unit in use in the U.S. The installation has been in production since March, but J&L still considers it too early to talk about results. The company does say the monster can degass a 350-ton load in 20 to 25 minutes. Youngstown Sheet & Tube Co. last week announced it will build a 200-ton capacity unit at a cost of "several millions of dollars."

Teaming up. The joining of the vacuum degassing process with continuous casting recently has assumed the dimensions of an industry march. National Steel Corp. announced in March that it plans to build a four-strand continuous caster at its Weirton Steel Co. Div., capable of making slabs up to 9-in. thick and 40-in. wide. Armco Steel Corp. also will team up continuous casting and vacuum degassing at its Butler works.

U.S. Steel has scheduled for operation in 1966 a continuous caster to make slabs up to 76-in. wide. Bethlehem Steel plans a full-size pilot plant to make slabs 10-in. thick and 40-in. wide. McLouth is reported to have an experimental setup that uses vacuum degassing in conjunction with a continuous caster, but the company will say nothing about it. Crucible

Steel Co. of America last week said it plans to build a continuous caster at Midland, Pa., to make specialty and stainless slabs.

Expenditure. Thus far, an estimated $35-million to $40-million has been committed to building continuous casting facilities in the U.S. The majority of the plans are for relatively small units that turn out billets, which cost about $2-million to install.

However, as more companies decide to go into slab casting, which requires much greater capital outlay, investment is expected to climb. For example, F. L. Byrom, president of Koppers, estimates that the industry over the next two decades will spend at least $1-billion to install some 135-million tons of continuous casting capacity. Koppers, which has been working on the process for 15 years, also predicts that within two decades 60% of all steel will be made in continuous casting lines.

Question of capacity. Discussions about continuous casting's future usually center around the place it could have in a truly continuous steel producing plant. The ability to match its capacity to the output of a basic oxygen furnace frequently is cited as the basic reason for continuous casting's bright prospects. But, so far, continuous casting lines have been built with capacities of only about 100 tons per run, while bigger basic oxygen furnaces — 300 tons and up — are going into operation. It is expected that the capacity of continuous casting will be greatly improved.

PUTTING IT ON AUTOMATIC

The flood tide of change that is moving through the steel industry has affected more than the making of semi-finished steel. The finished processes — chiefly rolling — are undergoing a revolution, too.

Steel customers would like to buy larger and longer weld-free sheet and plate. Steelmakers are building ever bigger rolling mills to meet this demand. The sizes and total capacities of new rolling mills planned or under way in the steel industry are, according to one observer, "staggering."

Giants. U.S. Steel, for example, says it will build an 84-in. rolling mill that can turn out weld-free coils up to 76-in. wide, and holding enough rolled-up steel to weigh in at better than 37 tons. Other tons include 80-in. hot strip mills under construction at J&L, Inland Steel, and Bethlehem.

But far more significant than size alone are the computerized controls that are operating some of the new hot strip mills. Thus, like National's Great Lakes Steel Corp.'s new 80-in. hot strip mill that went on full computer control last year, the rolling mills are getting brawnier — and brainier.

Eliminating error. Computer control is moving swiftly toward the day when it will be an inseparable partner of the steel rolling mill. As the speed of the rolling mill increases, one General Electric Co. expert points out, so does the likelihood of error by human operators. Eventually a point is reached where manual operation becomes uneconomical. A little further on is the point where manual operation is impossible.

At one hot strip mill, the computer seems to do everything but vote at union meetings. As the strip moves through the mill at varying speeds of 200 ft. to 3,000 ft. a minute, the computer continually adjusts roll openings to maintain the gauge, takes X-ray readings of the moving strip, changes rolling pressures to accommodate new rolling slabs of different chemical composition — all automatically, and at such lightning speeds that errors are corrected before the steel can get out of tolerance.

Dollar saver. Computer control of a hot strip mill also saves money. GE gives what it says is a typical example: A computerized hot strip mill working at its million-ton annual capacity can save the operator over $800,000 in a year. A major part of this — about $500,000 — results from closer tolerance controls by the computer that decrease loss from scrap and rejects.

Chmn. Charles M. Beeghly of J&L sums up the way the industry views the advantages of computerized process control: "Computer control makes an optimum operation repeatable and allows you to apply remedial operations while a process continues."

On the furnace. The industry also looks forward to application of computer control to more complex processes — for example, the blast furnace, a device so cantankerous that two of them built side by side according to the same designs probably never will work exactly the same. Steelmen often give blast furnaces women's names for that reason.

A number of companies are tackling the problem of computer control of blast furnaces, but only U.S. Steel publicly claims being close to its target. At U.S. Steel's Homestead District Works a 2,000-ton-a-day blast furnace has been on partial computer control since January.

One step to go. The computer reads the furnace's condition continually, makes judgments on the settings for two of the furnace's three key functions, and then makes sure the furnace follows the computer's directions. The only big step between this and full computer control of the furnace, a U.S. Steel official says, is getting the computer tuned up to the point where it will operate without need of servicing. As it it, he adds, since the end of January "the computer has been in control 85% of the time."

But aside from computer control, blast furnace technology has been making tremendous advances. In 1954, the best blast furnaces produced 2,000 tons of iron a day. Now the most efficient ones produce 3,000 tons daily.

In 1948, the steel industry's 200 blast furnaces produced 60-million tons of pig iron. Last year, just 138 blast furnaces turned out 72-million tons of pig iron.

More than mere size. Higher capacity is partially a matter of size. But even more important are increases brought about by new ways of running the furnaces and new raw materials to feed them with. It takes about 15% less ore, limestone, and coke to make a ton of iron in a blast furnace today than it did six years ago.

In a way, the steel industry has improved on nature in handling its blast furnaces. Depletion of many of the rich ore pockets in the Mesabi range, together with the discovery that upgraded ores gave better blast furnace performance, led to increasing use of beneficiated ores. By 1957, about 60% of the ore loaded into blast furnaces was beneficiated.

Last year, some 87% of the ore used was beneficiated.

Sinter clinkers. Today, the most important beneficiated ore is "sinter." Fine ore is heated and caked together to form a clinker. Last year, 36% of total ore consumption was of these clinkers.

But destined to become even more important than sinter are iron ore pellets made from taconite, a relatively low-grade ore. From about three tons of taconite rock, the user gets a ton of pellets containing 60% to 65% iron. Most estimates are that pellets made from taconite will at least equal the consumption of sinter by 1970. One executive thinks taconite pellets eventually will constitute approximately 70% of the total iron ore input for blast furnaces.

The industry has spent an estimated $2-billion in the last 10 years to build pelletizing facilities. Inland, for example, has one pelletizing plant in production, two under construction, and two more almost ready for the drawing board.

Opportunities. In addition to the major advances in the way it makes its product, the now highly market-oriented U.S. steel industry is expanding its efforts to find out what new uses steel can be put to. The new tin-plated steel foils — first announced as a commercial venture by U.S. Steel this year — are prime examples of this development. In addition, new alloys, such as Inland's "alphatized" steel, whose surface is enriched with chromium and which is billed by an Inland official as the "poor man's stainless steel," are presenting the industry with new opportunities and new challenges.

Perhaps one of the most potent forces responsible for the present remaking of the industry was the emergence of a foreign competition that, rebuilding virtually from scratch its war-torn facilities, could compete on both quality and price. The revolution now sweeping the industry is taking place just 100 years after the U.S. turned out its first commercial batch of Bessemer process steel.

TECHNOLOGICAL CHANGE IN THE TEXTILE INDUSTRY[1]

CLIFFORD D. CLARK

New York University

AND

BERNARD M. OLSEN

North Carolina State College

INTRODUCTION

The question of how technological change can be measured led to the empirical study of a segment of the textile industry described below. A technique developed for comparing costs of production over a period of several years was applied to six textile mills. The conclusion reached from this study was that productivity had increased by an average amount of 1.6 per cent a year. This percentage change is less than the increase experienced by the aggregate of manufacturers in the United States, and the increment was found to be consistent with other measures of productivity changes in the textile industry.

The literature of economic change reflects considerable ambiguity in the usage of the terms: innovation, productivity change, and technological change. Not only are the terms sometimes used interchangeably which does little to promote clarity, but when distinctions are made they are seldom made in accord with fact. Though these difficulties are not surprising in view of the nature of the phenomena described, nevertheless they present the empirical investigator with the added problem of setting up a working definition. For example, one distinction that frequently occurs equates innovations with changes in production functions on the one hand and productivity changes with improvements in the quality of productive factors

on the other hand. But if we accept the fact that advances in efficiency result from simultaneous and interdependent changes in the characteristics and combinations of resources, particularly of capital resources, then this distinction becomes more artificial than real. Consequently, for the purposes of our investigation, we propose to use the term "technological change" to include both shifts in the production function and improvements in the quality of capital resources but to exclude changes in the quality of labor.

This investigation of technological change in the textile industry is limited to a small number of observations made of actual firms. As a result, the conclusions drawn from the investigation are less general than could be hoped for, but are nevertheless suggestive for the entire textile industry. The data support an estimate of the annual rate of technological change of 1.6 per cent from 1949 to 1955, a rate well below the long term average for most industries.

With the exception of an additional adjustment for variations in the utilization of plant capacity, the procedure used for measuring technological change is the same as the procedure employed by other investigators to measure total factor productivity.[2] Some troublesome variables were avoided by selecting the sample of firms from the segment of the textile industry that produces cotton sheeting and print cloth. These are the two staple products of the industry, and the mills that produce them often have a long-uninterrupted history of producing a homogeneous cloth product. Restricting the investigation to firms producing standard products avoided the need for adjustments in the measure of output that would have been re-

[1] The authors wish to acknowledge their indebtedness to the National Science Foundation and the Division of Research of the School of Textiles of North Carolina State College for support given to this project. Grateful appreciation is also due to the many who provided counsel and assistance including Clark Lee Allen, Solomon Fabricant, Earl O. Heady, George Morton, and William A. Newell. Without the information furnished by the officers of the unnamed firms there would have been no study.

[2] For example, see John W. Kendrick, *Productivity Trends: Capital and Labor*, National Bureau of Economic Research, Occasional Paper 53 (Princeton: Princeton University Press, 1956).

"Technological Change in the Textile Industry" by Clifford D. Clark and Bernard M. Olsen. Reprinted from Southern Economic Journal, *Vol. 26 (October 1959), pp. 125-133, with permission of authors and editor.*

quired if the characteristics of output, or product-mix, varied through the period studied. This limitation of output groups does not fully solve the problem of expressing output in comparable units over time, but it does minimize errors on this account. Further, producers of staple commodities are less likely to experience variations in the rates of change of output than producers of fancy or quality products.

All six mills studied are in North Carolina and South Carolina and together they produce a little more than one per cent of all domestic, broadwoven, cotton goods, and nearly four per cent of all bleached and white finished cottons. These mills may have undergone a degree of technical change somewhat greater than other mills of the industry producing the same commodities. Despite reassurance that individual mills could not be identified in the published results of the study, some mill managers chose not to cooperate in this investigation. It is not unlikely that some of the managers refused to avoid risk of a bad showing because they had made few alterations in methods or changes in equipment in recent years. It is even more likely that the main deterrent to participation was the revelation of confidential cost data, a factor that may have been either constant or randomly distributed among companies. Firms producing other cotton fabrics may be expected to show both greater and lesser degrees of change than those producing sheeting and print cloth, depending in some degree on whether the commodities are of finer or of inferior quality. Discussions with textile producers indicated that there was a tendency for fewer changes to be made in the mills producing lower quality fabrics.

PROCEDURE AND FINDINGS

The method used in this study is a straightforward comparison of real costs in two years. There are five elements other than technological change that affect unit costs. They are: (a) changes in the continuity of output; (b) fluctuations in the rate of output; (c) changes in scale of plant; (d) changes in quality of factors other than fixed capital; and (e) general and relative price changes for factors.

The four influences on unit costs that are the most difficult to remove are the effects of scale of operation, degrees of utilization of plant, changes in the quality of labor, and changes in relative prices of factors. General price changes are readily removed by appropriate price deflators. The problem of scale is often avoided by the assumption of long run constant costs or its equivalent, a production function homogeneous to degree one. Although such an assumption, which is also used here, may seriously distort measurements extending over long periods it is unlikely to bias short term results.

The second influence on unit costs is variation in unit output. Some understanding of the effect of variation in rate of output may be seen in the scatter diagram in Figure 1 showing the variation of total unit costs with output for each mill in every quarter of 1949.[3]

The regression equation for the data used in the construction of Figure 1 is: $y = 127 - .27x$, where x is output expressed as a percentage of average quarterly output by mills in 1949, and total unit costs, y, is expressed as a percentage of average annual unit cost in mill. The data withstood a test of curvature; to depart significantly from a linear regression with seven and seven degrees of freedom, F must be 3.79 or greater, and in this case $F = 1.12$.

Tests were made of the closeness of fit for similar equations relating the various classes of cost to output. Those for cotton, labor, and power reveal significance at the one per cent level, and the remaining equation for all other costs was significant at the five per cent level. Although the equations are statistically significant, their economic significance must be established on other grounds. For example, if general economic conditions caused each firm to operate at an output below maximum efficiency, the results obtained would be consistent with a U-shaped curve. There is good reason to believe that such a condition existed, for it is likely that all firms were affected by the July, 1949, trough of the cycle in cotton textiles.[4]

Production of the six mills was compared for the years 1949 and 1955, with two exceptions. The need for adjustments for fluctuations in the rate of output is emphasized by the comparison of the two years in different phases of the industry cycle. The year 1949 was the trough of one cycle and 1955 was a year of cyclical ex-

---

[3] The lag of costs behind output in the recording of data is about two weeks.

[4] T. M. Stanback, "The Textile Cycle: Characteristics and Contributing Factors," *The Southern Economic Journal*, October 1958, XXV, p. 175.

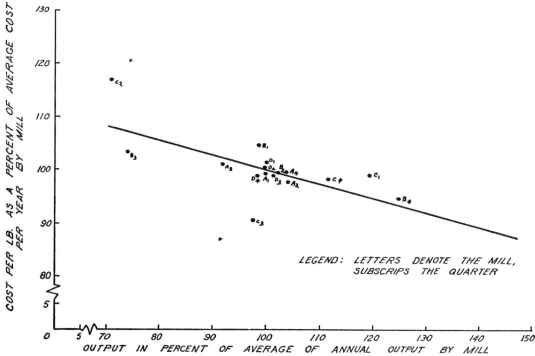

FIG. 1. VARIATIONS IN UNIT COSTS IN RELATION TO VARIATIONS IN THE RATE OF OUTPUT FOR SIX TEXTILE MILLS IN 1949.

pansion.[5] The actual variations in quantities of real output for the mills are shown in Table 1.

Clearly the relevant comparison is that of the last column, but since this figure may also reflect differences in scale the variations by quarter suggest the extent of fluctuation in utilization of capacity. Mills B and C increased their capacity between the years by about one-fifth and one-half respectively.

Base year output in Table 2 is adjusted to express the same ratio of output to plant and equipment that prevailed in terminal year. The adjustments for cost are made on the basis of the regression equation. This adjustment is made to answer the question: what would have been the unit costs if output in 1949 relative to the stock of plant and equipment then in place, had been the same as the ratio of output to plant and equipment that existed in 1955? These unit costs, in 1955 prices, are then compared to actual 1955 costs for a measure of technological change that excludes the effect of changes in utilization of capacity.

The actual terminal year unit costs and the

average yearly percentage reductions attributable to technical change are shown in Table 3. The unweighted averages of the unadjusted and adjusted reductions in unit costs are the same, 1.6 per cent annually.[6]

The third problem, that of removing effects of quality changes in factors other than fixed capital, was solved by adjusting for quality changes in the labor input. When quality changes occur in managerial ability they would appear as changes in the production function and accordingly would be accounted for as technical changes. Further, there are virtually no difficulties in comparing raw cotton fiber and electric power in the two years. There is some possibility of changes in the quality of cotton, but these are known in each instance and appeared to be unimportant.

---

[6] The equality of adjusted and unadjusted percentage reductions would necessarily be the same if adjustment had been made on the basis of deviations of each firm's base year output from the average output of all firms taken together. Otherwise there is no such necessity and the equality obtained is a matter of chance.

---

[5] *Ibid.*

TABLE 1
INDEXES OF OUTPUT IN 1949 AND 1955 FOR SIX TEXTILE MILLS[a]

	1949 (1st Qtr. = 100)				1955 (1st Qtr. = 100)				Total 1955 as a per cent of Total 1949
	Quarter				Quarter				
	1	2	3	4	1	2	3	4	
Mill A	100.0	102.6	94.0	104.4	100.0	101.9	94.4	97.2	83
Mill B	100.0	103.5	75.0	126.5	100.0	99.3	57.9	96.7	139
Mill C_1, C_2, C_3	100.0	59.0	81.9	93.6	100.0	92.9	91.5	91.3	89
Mill D	100.0	99.7	101.4	98.2	100.0	94.7	94.3	86.2	132

[a] Indexes are uncorrected for differences in number of weeks per quarter as reported by mills. Mills C_1, C_2, C_3 are treated as one. For Company D the years compared are 1950 and 1956.

TABLE 2
BASE YEAR OUTPUT AND UNIT COSTS ADJUSTED TO THE RATIO OF PLANT AND EQUIPMENT TO OUTPUT PREVAILING IN THE TERMINAL YEAR (IN 1955 PRICES)

Mill	Base year		Adjusted	
	Output (Mil. lb)	Unit Costs (¢/lb)	Output (Mil. lb)	Unit Costs (¢/lb)
A	13.4	72.4	11.7	75.0
B	21.9	80.3	25.3	76.9
C_1, C_2, C_3	47.4	78.3	47.2	78.4
D	43.1	84.3	41.9	85.0

TABLE 3
TERMINAL YEAR COSTS AND AVERAGE YEARLY REDUCTIONS (1955 PRICES)

Mill	Unit Costs (¢/lb)	Number of Years	Average Yearly Reduction (%)	
			Unadjusted	Adjusted
A	67.6	6	1.1	1.6
B	72.7	6	1.6	.9
C_1, C_2, C_3	71.2	6	1.5	1.5
D	74.9	5	2.2	2.4

The raw data supplied by the mills included the money payments to labor in the two years, the numbers of employees in each job category, and the wage rates paid to each job classification. A wage-price index that merely expresses the percentage change in wage-rates per man was inadequate to reduce the monetary wage bill to a reflection of identical labor units in both

years. It was obvious from the data that a shift in the quality of labor hired occurred between 1949 and 1955, appearing as an increase in the proportion of employees with more highly rated skills. Not only had the distribution of labor in job classes been changed, but wage rates of the several classes had changed in different ratios.

To incorporate all of the changes in the labor forces into one deflator an index was constructed that incorporated changes in distribution as well as in rates of payment. This was done in the following way: Let s stand for skilled labor in the initial year and S for skilled labor in the terminal year; and, similarly ss and SS for semiskilled in the first and terminal years; u and U for unskilled labor; L for the quantity of labor in man-weeks; and W for hourly wage. The index for expressing the 1949 labor input in 1955 prices and in comparable units would be:

$$\frac{L_s W_S + L_{ss} W_{SS} + L_u W_U}{L_s W_s + S_{ss} W_{ss} + L_u W_u} = \text{Index of Labor Costs.}$$

An implicit assumption in this index is that job specifications were unchanged in the two years, and assurances were received that this was the case. Relative wage rates between classes may differ because: (a) supply conditions change, (b) changes occur in the rate of output that may require different combinations of skill classes, and (c) production techniques may change. The adjustment for qualitative changes in the labor input is not wholly independent of the process of change since the weights used to combine the several skills into a homogeneous unit is partially affected by the technical change being measured. A particular change in techniques would need to be widespread to cause a significant change in the demand for the various skills. If a change of the production function is of the kind initiated internally by management rather than by a dramatic development from without, such a condition is not likely to be satisfied and this interdependence can safely be ignored.

Hourly wage rates rather than weekly wages or earnings were used in constructing the indexes in Table 4 for two reasons. The hourly data were more readily available, and were in a form that allowed classification by skills. If there had been a variation in the amount of overtime worked by the several classes or by the entire labor force in the two years the index of hourly earnings would have been correct. A comparison of observed wage bills for the two years with the wage payments implied by the independently derived, weighted, wage indexes yielded almost identical quantities. From this result it is evident that the amount of overtime in both years was not significantly different.

The indexes of Table 4 multiplied by the number of workers employed in 1949 gives a wage bill that would have been incurred in 1955 had these same workers, taking into account their enhanced abilities, been employed in 1955. This procedure was used to compute the unit costs, in 1955 prices, as shown in Table 2.

These indexes compared to an index based simply on average hourly rates for the two years, weighted by the quantity of labor in each year by class, would tend to show the extent of upgrading of labor, or quality improvement of input. Indexes of average hourly earnings are as shown in Table 5.

Comparison of these indexes with those in Table 4 indicate that the degree of quality improvement is about 2 per cent.

The fourth major factor impeding isolation of technical change is the effect of changes in the relative prices of productive factors. In the statistical cost function and the full input-output or total productivity approaches, factor prices have usually been expressed at base period levels. This procedure manifestly leads to an overstatement of costs in every period except the base period.[7]

---

[7] H. Staehle, "The Measurement of Statistical Cost Functions," American Economic Association,

TABLE 4
WAGE INDEX AS CORRECTED FOR QUALITY IMPROVEMENTS OF LABOR

	1949	1955	1956
Mill A	100.0	113.8	
Mill B	100.0	110.4	
Mills C_1, C_2, C_3	100.0	125.0	
Mill D[a]	100.0		117.2

[a] For Mill D a census of job descriptions and wage rates was obtainable only for 1949, cost data and output for 1950. Wage-hour data were declared to be identical for the two years 1949 and 1950.

TABLE 5
INDEX OF AVERAGE HOURLY EARNINGS 1949, 1955, 1956 (1949 = 100)

	1949	1955	1956
Mill A	100.0	116.5	
Mill B	100.0	111.6	
Mill C_1, C_2, C_3	100.0	124.1	
Mill D[a]	100.0		122.9

[a] See Note to Table 4.

TABLE 6
PRICE CHANGES OF STANDARD ITEMS OF TEXTILE EQUIPMENT SELECT YEARS, 1951 (BASE YEAR = 100) TO 1956[a]

Year	Revolving Flat Card, "40L, Whitin	X_2, "40 Loom Draper	Unweighted Average of Eight Pieces of Whitin Equipment
1951		100.0	
1952	100.0		100.0
1955		106.2	
1956	110.0	112.4	119.2

[a] Information supplied by Draper and Whitin Corporations.

Before discussing the procedure used to cope with changes in relative factor prices, and in order to complete accounting for costs, it is necessary to consider measurement of the capital input. There are two issues involved: (1) price movements, and (2) estimation of magnitude.

Readings in Price Theory (Homewood, Ill.: Richard Irwin, 1952), p. 274.

TABLE 7

COSTS BY CATEGORY IN 1955 PRICES AND OUTPUT FOR SIX MILLS, QUARTERLY FOR TWO YEARS.
(Amounts are in thousands)

	Labor	Capital	Cotton	All Other	Total	Output (in lb.)	Cost per lb. (cents)
Mill A							
1949							
1Q	$672	$174	$1,367	$200	$2,413	3,342	72.2
2Q	679	190	1,402	206	2,477	3,479	71.2
3Q	624	177	1,265	203	2,269	3,078	73.7
4Q	694	195	1,422	209	2,520	3,475	72.5
Total	$2,669	$736	$5,456	$818	$9,679	13,374	72.4
1955							
1Q	$508	$144	$1,183	$201	$2,036	2,969	68.6
2Q	521	141	1,213	199	2,074	3,074	67.5
3Q	473	139	1,112	197	1,921	2,817	68.2
4Q	508	141	1,130	199	1,978	2,983	66.3
Total	$2,010	$565	$4,638	$796	$8,009	11,843	67.6
Mill B							
1949							
1Q	$1,593	$242	$2,199	$514	$4,548	5,409	84.1
2Q	1,474	247	2,236	523	4,480	5,597	80.0
3Q	1,108	228	1,527	496	3,359	4,052	82.9
4Q	1,837	259	2,557	539	5,192	6,841	75.9
Total	$6,012	$976	$8,519	$2,072	$17,579	21,899	80.3
1955							
1Q	$1,727	$315	$3,305	$707	$6,054	8,590	70.5
2Q	1,733	312	3,172	704	5,921	8,531	69.4
3Q	1,261	280	1,901	658	4,100	4,973	82.4
4Q	1,873	315	3,133	706	6,027	8,306	72.6
Total	$6,594	$1,222	$11,511	$2,775	$22,102	30,400	72.7
Mills C₁, C₂, and C₃							
1949							
1Q	$3,543	$765	$5,791	$888	$10,987	14,163	77.6
2Q	2,394	631	3,828	837	7,690	8,407	91.5
3Q	3,008	629	3,745	878	8,260	11,594	71.2
4Q	3,497	626	5,168	898	10,189	13,252	76.9
Total	$12,442	$2,651	$18,532	$3,501	$37,126	47,416	78.3
10/54–9/55							
1Q	$3,312	$1,026	$6,021	$968	$11,327	15,747	71.9
2Q	3,299	1,102	5,870	964	11,235	15,684	71.6
3Q	3,291	968	5,246	965	10,470	14,340	73.0
4Q	3,272	1,051	6,100	963	11,386	16,632	68.5
Total	$13,174	$4,147	$23,237	$3,860	$44,418	62,403	71.2

TABLE 7 *Continued*

	Labor	Capital	Cotton	All Other	Total	Output (in lb.)	Cost per lb. (cents)
				Mill D			
9/50–8/51							
1Q	$3,672	$656	$4,166	$720	$9,214	10,791	85.4
2Q	3,596	645	4,132	764	9,137	10,761	84.9
3Q	3,500	660	4,197	768	9,125	10,947	83.4
4Q	3,363	656	4,091	726	8,836	10,601	83.4
Total	$14,131	$2,617	$16,586	$2,978	$36,312	43,100	84.3
10/55–9/56							
1Q	$2,602	$657	$4,235	$795	$8,289	11,491	72.1
2Q	2,523	690	4,078	790	8,081	10,676	75.7
3Q	2,540	726	4,068	795	8,129	10,511	77.3
4Q	2,343	669	4,024	792	7,828	10,492	74.6
Total	$10,008	$2,742	$16,405	$3,172	$32,327	43,170	74.9

If there were only one basic unit of equipment with deterioration characteristics of the one-horse shay, the magnitude of capital could be expressed either in physical or monetary units. If expressed in monetary units a pure deflator for price changes would be required to give the same comparison as would be given by the physical measurement. To approximate this ideal the stock of capital equipment in 1949 is revalued to assign to it the worth it would have had, had it been purchased in 1955 in its condition of the earlier year. To compare this figure to the actual amount of equipment in 1955, the latter is also expressed in 1955 prices. The best data available for such a price index are prices of models of textile equipment which have undergone little or no change between the two years compared. Some of these are shown in Table 6.

Properly weighted, such individual prices yield a price index of textile equipment as follows:

1949	85.6
1951	100.0
1955	104.0
1956	110.2

These indexes are appropriate for valuing similar stocks of capital in the prices of a single year given consistent base year appraisals. Some of the firms had valued their equipment in the prices of a single year. Use of these calcula-tions greatly facilitated base year appraisals. If such calculations had not been made, data were obtained for the characteristics of equipment specifying the date of construction and brand name, for major items of equipment so that an appraisal consistent with equipment in other mills could be made. As in any capital stock estimate there are deficiencies in this procedure, such as the assumption of similar physical conditions for every piece of equipment of a specified year and model. Nevertheless, these estimates are clearly superior to net or gross book values or even to used equipment estimates which were also available.[8]

To continue with this accounting for costs, some portion of capital values must be attributed as costs of the output for each quarter or unit of output. Theoretically, these costs are the returns to fixed capital determined as the residuum and need not be proportional to the amounts sunk at any time. They are treated here, however, as though they were a linear function of time only.

Expenditures for repair and alteration or improvement of the basic equipment also may be considered as capital costs. Expenditures for repair items, however, are not necessarily made at the time of consumption, they are more likely made when stocking the supply room.

[8] Estimates of resale value were kindly provided by Ben Davis of Charlotte, North Carolina.

Repair expenses were judged to be proportional to usage, or wear and tear. For this reason outlays for repairs are allocated among quarters, not as reported for accounting purposes, but in proportion to consumption of electric power. With expenditures for repairs included in capital costs, the major categories of cost are shown in Table 7.

All expenditures for factors have been expressed in 1955 prices. In the first, or base year the cost per pound of cloth ranged from a quarterly low of 71.2 cents in Mills A and C, to a high of 91.5 cents in Mill C in the second quarter. The second highest was 85.4 cents per pound in Mill D. In the later year, cost per pound ranged from 66.3 cents in Mill A to 82.4 cents in Mill B. The next high was 77.3 cents per pound in Mill D. These data have already been summarized in Table 2. There it was shown that, when adjusted for variations in the degree of capacity utilization, the average annual rate of technological change was 1.6 per cent. If allowance is made for changes in relative factor prices this conclusion is not changed.

A comparison of the various price indexes in Table 8 shows some change in the relationship

TABLE 8

Price Changes for Cotton, Labor, and Capital in Terminal Year as a Per Cent of Base Year for Six Mills

Mill	Cotton	Labor	Repairs	Capital equipment
A	110.5	113.8	127.6	104.0
B	113.8	110.4	127.6	104.0
C_1, C_2, C_3	119.3	125.0	125.1	104.0
D	88.2	117.2	126.1	110.2

TABLE 9

Unit Costs for Six Textile Mills in 1949 Prices, Unadjusted for Changes in Rate Output

Mill	Base Year Unit Costs		Terminal Year Unit Costs (¢/lb)	Average Yearly Reduction	
	Unadjusted (¢/lb)	Adjusted (¢/lb)		Adjusted (¢/lb)	Adjusted (%)
A	64.5	66.8	60.6	1.0	1.8
B	71.1	68.1	64.3	1.6	.9
C_1, C_2, C_3	64.6	64.7	59.4	1.3	1.4
D	74.1	74.7	66.6	2.0	2.4

between prices of the inputs. The change in relative prices would seem sufficient to cause some substitution among factors. The greatest variation in price movement, the price of cotton from Mill D, was the result of a single purchase. This occurrence would not have affected managerial decisions about factor combinations since general market trends were in the opposite direction.

To determine whether the relative factor price changes were important, inputs are weighted by 1949 prices rather than 1955 prices. The resulting estimates of technological change are shown in Table 9. These estimates average 1.6 annually, the same as the estimates based on 1955 prices.

When factors are expressed in 1949 prices, the resulting measure of technological change tends to set a lower limit for the actual change; just as an upper limit is approximated by expression in 1955 prices, as in Table 8 above. The rationale is straightforward. If relative factor prices have changed, and actual quantities of inputs employed in both years are valued in 1949 prices as in a Laspeyre's Index, terminal years' costs would be overstated. Theoretically, the entrepreneur would have used different proportions of inputs in 1955 than those observed because relative factor prices in 1949 differ from those which influenced his decisions. As a result, he would have succeeded in reducing costs in 1955 below the levels computed and technical progress would be greater than measured. The opposite would be true when both years' inputs are expressed in 1955 prices as in a Paasche index. Had relative factor prices been the same in 1949 as in 1955, the entrepreneur would have combined his resources in different proportions than those observed in 1949, and costs would have been lower than those computed. Technical change would therefore be less than estimated. This conclusion is inescapable for the case of neutral technical change, that is, for changes which do not affect marginal rates of substitution among factors. In the event of technical change which affects marginal rates of substitution valuation of factors in their base year prices continues to set the lower limit of change, but terminal year pricing does not set the upper limit.[9]

---

[9] V. W. Ruttan, *Technological Progress in the Meatpacking Industry, 1919–1947*, U. S. Department of Agriculture, Marketing Research Report No. 59 (January, 1954), pp. 15–20.

An alternative procedure of correcting for relative price changes of productive factors, and at the same time, of correcting for changes in the degree of capacity utilization is the use of a statistical production function. Although this procedure has the advantage of simplicity, the requirement of large quantities of data is an overwhelming disadvantage in this instance. Quarterly observations for the six mills were apparently insufficient for even a two factor production function.[10]

CONCLUSIONS

To the extent the mills included in the study are representative of the textile industry, the derived estimate of technical change can be generalized. The possibility of generalization is supported by a comparison of the results of this

analysis with productivity changes of yards per man-hour in the basic textile industry including producers of cloth from all fibers. The comparison is expressed in simple, unweighted, annual averages of percentage change. Increases in labor productivity in the six mills from 1949 to 1955 were: 2.9, 4.4, 4.1, and 8.3 respectively from Mills A, B, C, and D. The average of these changes was 4.9 to compare with a change of 31.3 over the same period for the whole industry, an annual average of 5.2 per cent.[11]

For the private domestic economy John Kendrick estimates that total factor productivity, a measure somewhat similar to the measure of technical change above, has increased by 1.7 per cent per year for the long period, 1899 to 1953. The unweighted average rate of increase for 33 industry groups has been 2.3 per cent for the same period. For the years 1919 to 1953, the respective rates were 2.2 and 2.9 per cent.[12]

In conclusion, the degree of technical change experienced by the six textile firms studied, and probably by the entire basic textile industry, has not been as great as the long term rate of change in other industries. Reasons for the disparity are probably due to such diverse causes as the low income elasticity of demand for textile products and the market conditions of the textile machinery manufacturers. The characteristics of the textile machinery market appear to be those of an oligopoly. An oligopolistic market for capital equipment would suggest that research and development would be directed toward minor modifications rather than radical new designs.[13] This, in turn, would at least partially explain the slight degree of technological change experienced in the textile industry.

[10] Production functions of the Cobb-Douglas form were derived for each mill from quarterly capital costs, C, defined as "user costs" and including repairs only; quarterly constant dollar expenditures on labor, L; and quarterly output, Q, in pounds. The exponents b_1, and b_2 of the functions of the general form $aL^{b_1}C^{b_2}$, for both years are as follows:

Firm	1949		1955	
	b_1	b_2	b_1	b_2
A	1.1134	.0806	−.9608	−.2039
B	.3212	.8936	−.6708	2.1446
C_1, C_2, C_3	1.2528	.0844	−3.8060	.5020
D	.2127	.3178	.7142	−.3792
Combined	.8458	−.0412	.6610	.1730

The combined function for 1955 takes on a familiar shape, but as an aggregate it obscures the unacceptable nature of the individual functions on which it is based. Nevertheless, use of this aggregate function to correct for changes in factor proportions yielded an estimate for technical change of 1.25 per cent annually.

[11] Estimates of the Textile Workers Union of America, Solomon Barkin, Director of Research.

[12] J. W. Kendrick, *Productivity Trends, op. cit.,* Tables 1 and 3.

[13] W. H. Brown, "Innovation in the Machine Tool Industry," *Quarterly Journal of Economics,* August 1957, LXXI, Pp. 406–425.

Transportation and Trade

The movement of goods and people from place to place — transportation — differs from the activities discussed to this point. In transportation no product is created, formed, or processed. Yet, it is an activity of interest to economic geographers for several reasons. First, there are distinct spatial patterns generated by transportation media — trails, roads, bridges, rails, pipelines, docks, airports, and others. Second, the transportation industry is itself an important activity in terms of such measures as number of people employed, capital investment, and value added. Third, and perhaps most important, is the impact that transportation has on other forms of economic activity — in the assembling of various materials entering the production process, in the process itself, and in the distribution of products.

Although the three articles included here cannot summarize the field of transportation geography, they reveal its important and integral relationship to other aspects of economic geography. The first two articles in this section, by Alexander and Weigend, reveal the intricacies of transportation and its impact on other activities. Alexander's article illustrates variations within the transport industry and the resulting impact on the location of related economic activity. Weigend's article also shows the impact of transport on other activity, but is important in showing the reciprocal impact of various activities on the location of transport facilities. The third article discusses a special type of transport — airline passenger traffic — and some variables modifying its location.

It is readily apparent from earlier articles that some regions tend to specialize in the production of certain goods, export their surplus, and meet their needs for other goods by importing them. The result is a pattern, or set of patterns, of world trade. Alexander's article on international trade indicates some of these patterns, the relative importance of trade to various nations, as well as the importance of trade to the individual economies.

FREIGHT RATES: SELECTED ASPECTS OF UNIFORM AND NODAL REGIONS*

John W. Alexander, S. Earl Brown, and Richard E. Dahlberg

Dr. Alexander is Associate Professor of Geography at the University
of Wisconsin. Dr. Brown is Assistant Professor of Geography at The
Ohio State University. Mr. Dahlberg is Acting Assistant Professor of
Geography at the University of California, Los Angeles.

IN a commercial economy having specialized transportation, the movement of goods is influenced by several forces, one of which is the freight rate structure. The spatial differences in transport charges is not only a geographic factor influencing the circulation of goods but also a geographic element in terms of which the character of a region may be expressed. "Mankind is not spread evenly over the face of the earth but tends to cluster in certain areas, which vary from each other. . . . Within such areas relationships arise. . . . It is through the means of transportation and communication that these interrelationships are set up and maintained. . . . But the cost of its use is often as great an element in the importance of a transportation line as its actual presence. Hence freight rates are of greatest value in outlining regions and in affecting their organization. This is seen in the practice of zoning rates and of offering special inducements for the movement of certain commodities. . . . If transportation facilities serve to consolidate regions, it must also be observed that freight rates are to regions and to cities what tariffs are to nations. They form a part of the cost of connections with other regions and may be manipulated to the advantage or disadvantage of a given region in almost exactly the same way."[1]

Thus, as a geographic element lending character to regions and as a geographic factor influencing the location of economic activities freight rates have significance for the regional analyst.

OVER-SIMPLIFIED GEOGRAPHIC CONCEPTS OF FREIGHT RATES

Unfortunately, some geographic concepts of freight rates have been oversimplified. As a result, there are spatial differences in such costs which either are not known or are not generally

*This study is based in part upon a research grant from the Graduate School of the University of Wisconsin for the 1952–1953 academic year. Mr. Brown and Mr. Dahlberg carried the entire burden of copying and mapping all the statistics pertaining to Wisconsin's freight rate structures presented herein. They also participated in drafting the manuscript.

[1] Harry E. Moore: *What is Regionalism?* Southern Policy Papers, No. 10, University of North Carolina Press, Chapel Hill, 1937, pp. 2–4.

"Freight Rates: Selected Aspects of Uniform and Nodal Regions" by John W. Alexander, S. Earl Brown, and Richard E. Dahlberg. Reprinted from Economic Geography, *Vol. 34 (January 1958), pp. 1–18, with permission of the editor.*

recognized in many geographic studies. This prevents the regional analyst from clearly understanding the relationships between regional economies and the flow of goods both within a region and between regions.[2] In general, there seem to be two misconceptions: (1) From any given point, freight rates (assessed by the same form of transport) increase similarly in all directions; i.e., the rail rate on a carload of coal from Milwaukee to a point 100 miles northwest is the same as the rail rate on a similar carload of coal from Milwaukee to a point 100 miles southwest. (2) The second misconception is that freight rates always increase with distance. The extreme expression of this fallacy is that rates increase *directly* with distance; i.e., it costs twice as much to ship a commodity 1000 miles as 500 miles. Less erroneous is the idea that rates increase with distance but always at a diminishing rate.[3]

It is difficult to document these two criticisms. In most geographical treatises dealing with economic activity, scarcely any but the most cursory mention is made of transport costs. Without so stating (and therefore not quotable) such studies apparently assume the two concepts expressed above. In any case, the very absence of recognition of freight rate analysis in geographic studies supports the conclusion that geographers are rather uninformed on spatial variations in such costs. On the other hand, a few studies do recognize the role of

transport costs but, for want of evidence, assume that freight rate structures are concentric around transport centers. For example, Harris employed this expedient in his analysis of the American market[4] but frankly raised the question "How nearly does the actual freight-rate structure approximate the generalized transport bands used in the calculations of this paper?"[5]

Geographers have made comparatively few investigations of spatial variations in freight rates probably because of rate complexity. "Rate structures are so complex that to generalize them into significant geographic patterns is extraordinarily difficult. . . . In spite of all these difficulties, it would be worth while to attempt some geographic generalization of rate patterns. . . . Rate structures can be studied from a geographic point of view."[6] Nevertheless, in view of the fact that freight rates are fundamentally important in the geography of flow (which in turn is the dynamic aspect of transport geography), because they are spatial variables contributing to regionalism, and because of misconceptions easily drawn regarding freight rates, this article will consider freight rates from two regional viewpoints: uniform regions and nodal regions.

UNIFORM FREIGHT RATE REGIONS

A uniform region, as defined by Whittlesey, is homogeneous because all parts of its area contain the feature or features by which it is defined, in this case,

[2] "As an example, under the system of freight rates prevailing before 1925, it cost less to ship fruit from California to New York than from the Ozark fruit region to the same city, while the cost of shipping fruit from California to New York was less than twice that of moving it from Florida and California . . . ." Harry F. Moore, *op. cit.*, p. 3.

[3] For more detailed discussion of these misconceptions, see E. F. Penrose: "The Place of Transport in Economic and Political Geography," United Nations' *Transport and Communications Review*, Volume V, Number 2, April-June, 1952, p. 4.

[4] Chauncy D. Harris: "Market As a Factor in Localization of Industry," *Annals Assn. Amer. Geogrs.*, Vol. 44, 1954, p. 323.

[5] *Ibid.*, p. 348.

[6] Edward L. Ullman and Harold B. Mayer: "Transportation Geography" in *American Geography, Inventory and Prospect*, Preston E. James and Clarence F. Jones, edits., Syracuse, 1954, reference on pp. 326–327.

FIG. 1. United States Freight Rate Territories, 1937. (Source: United States Government, 75th Congress, 1st Session, House Document No. 264, *The Interterritorial Freight Rate Problem of the United States, 1937.*)

similar freight rates.[7] An example of uniform freight rate regions is the structure of railroad class freight rates which prevailed for years in the United States. Since 1887 the rates charged by the nation's railroads have been regulated by the federal government's Interstate Commerce Commission (I.C.C.). It has not been a case of the Commission prescribing rates but rather of either approving or disapproving rates which the railroads proposed. For years the Commission recognized different regions within which the railroads had decided to charge characteristic prices. The five major regions, as mapped by a congressional committee in 1937, appeared in an official House Document

[7] Derwent Whittlesey: "The Regional Concept and the Regional Method," Chapter II in *American Geography, Inventory and Prospect,* references on pp. 36 and 39.

and is reproduced as Figure 1 in this article. Table I shows the *average* rate prevailing in each of the five regions. In such a rate structure, a shipment of any given commodity moving X miles in Official Territory was priced, on the average, at a lower freight rate than a shipment of the identical commodity moving the same distance in any other

TABLE I

LEVELS OF FIRST-CLASS FREIGHT RATES

Index numbers indicate the *average* levels of applicable class rates mile for mile in other territories in relation to Official Territory for shipments of up to 1000 miles.

Territory	Index of rate
Official or Eastern....................	100
Southern............................	139
Western Trunk Line.................	147
Southwestern.......................	175
Mountain-Pacific....................	171

Source: United States 75th Congress, 1st Session, House Document No. 264 *The Interterritorial Freight Rate Problem of the United States,* 1937.

rate region, so long as *class rates*[8] applied in both cases. It must be emphasized that the figures presented in Table I and portrayed graphically in Figure 1 are *averages* for all such movements within the region.

The reasons for this regional variation in class rates are exceedingly complex and comprise a sizable body of literature in transportation economics.[9] In general they reflect (a) the principle that efficiencies in mass movement warrant lower rates where heavy traffic occurs, and (b) the influence of competitive forms of cheaper transportation such as waterways along the Atlantic, the Pacific, and the Gulf coasts. In any case, division of the United States in terms of this geographic element produced clearly defined regions of the uniform type.

As a geographic factor, this regionalism in the nation's freight rate structure had a profound impact upon the nation's economic geography. It gave the Northeast a definite rate advantage making it less expensive, on the average, to ship goods in that region than in any other part of the nation. In recent years the I.C.C. received increasing protest from other portions of the country, especially the South, whose leaders complained that the rate structure was regionally discriminatory in favor of the

economy of the Official (or Eastern) region. Beginning in the 1940's the I.C.C. reviewed these regional discrepancies in the class rate structure[10] and, in a series of decisions spaced several years apart, gradually erased most of the regional differentiations. By 1952 uniformity had been achieved from the Atlantic Coast to the Rocky Mountains. Nevertheless, the effect of the regional differences in class rates which prevailed from 1887–1952 will be observable in the regionalization of the American economy for many years to come.

NODAL FREIGHT RATE REGIONS

"Nodal regions are homogeneous with respect to internal structures or organization. This structure includes a focus, or foci, and a surrounding area tied to the focus by lines of circulation. . . . Hence the nodal region is bounded by the disappearance or differential weakening of the tie to its own focus in favor of some other focus. Its boundary lines tend to run at right angles to the lines that tie it together."[11] Nodal freight rate regions are delimited in terms of rate structures to/from transport foci. The remainder of the present article is essentially a study of nodal regions[12] discernible in a case study area: the State of Wisconsin.

The specific objectives of the research reported in the following pages are (a) to

[8] Where the movement of a commodity is particularly heavy between any two points, the railroad may publish a reduced rate termed a *commodity* rate. By law, railroads are required to file each new rate with the Commission 30 days before its effective date. Unless protested at least 12 days before the effective date, it becomes an official rate. If protested, the new rate is suspended by the Commission pending investigation at the end of which time it may be disallowed or approved.

[9] For example, Roland B. Eutsler: *Transportation in North Carolina, A Study of Rate Structure and Rate Adjustment*, University of Pennsylvania, 1929; William H. Joubert: *Southern Freight Rates in Transition*, University of Florida Press, 1949; D. Philip Locklin, *Economics of Transportation*, 1947; D. A. MacGibbon, *Railway Rates and the Canadian Railway Commission*, 1917.

[10] F. L. Barton: "The Interstate Commerce Commission Considers The Class Rate Structure," *Journ. of Land and Publ. Utility Econs.*, Vol. 17, 1941, pp. 10–16.

[11] Derwent Whittlesey, *op. cit.*, p. 37.

[12] Examples of other studies in which freight rate regional nodality is implicit, although not always identified as such are: John W. Alexander: "Freight Rates As a Geographic Factor in Illinois," *Econ. Geogr.*, Vol. 20, 1944, pp. 25–30; Stuart P. Daggett and John Carter: *The Structure of Transcontinental Railroad Rates*, University of California Press, Berkeley, 1947; Olaf Lindberg: "An Economic-Geographical Study of the Localization of the Swedish Paper Industry," *Geografiska Annaler*, Arg. XXXV, 1953, Hafte I, pp. 28–40.

present facts with some analysis of freight rate structures in a case study area and (b) to consider problems of methodology in the study of freight rates from the geographical viewpoint.

This is a progress report in a study of Wisconsin's freight rate geography which is still in the descriptive stage. As yet little has been done in interpreting these rate structures or correlating them with other phenomena. The report is issued at this stage with the thought that it will be of interest to specialists concerned with the spatial variations of transport costs.

All maps are of Wisconsin's rate structures during the period 1952–1953.

The State of Wisconsin was selected for study because: (a) At least some types of spatial differences in transport costs prevailing over the earth were assumed to be discernible in an area the size of Wisconsin; (b) transport costs frequently are assessed on a "state" basis; a political state is a meaningful area in the consideration of transport charges;[13] (c) data on transport charges applicable to this political unit are on file in a central place (the Wisconsin Public Service Commission) which is easily accessible in Madison.

Procedure

Maps were constructed of several different freight rate structures: (a) *class* rates on *rail* shipments to/from all points in Wisconsin from/to Chicago, Milwaukee, Green Bay, Superior and Duluth (the first being the major out-of-state shipping center on the southeast and the last being a major out-of-state shipping point on the northwest); (b) *class* rates on *truck* shipments to/from all points in Wisconsin from/to

the same five shipping centers listed above; (c) commodity railroad rates on *coal* to all Wisconsin points from the southern Illinois-Indiana coal field, from Milwaukee, from Green Bay, and from Superior.

Data Sources

Data were procured from the State Public Service Commission which has on file in the Capitol all rate tariffs which apply to the movement of freight in Wisconsin.[14]

Mapping Techniques

Rates were plotted on base maps (provided by the Public Service Commission) which show the location of all railroads and shipping points in the State. Plotting of truck rates required interpolating from the State's official highway map for location of points not on railways.

Isarithms, herein termed *isophors*,[15] were constructed as lines connecting the innermost points of equal freight rates. "Innermost" has significance because in the structure of any nodal rate region it is possible for consecutive places on a radiating transport artery to have the same rate to the transport center around which the rate structure is oriented. In such a case the isophor is drawn through the place nearest the transport center

---

[13] Rates on an *intrastate* flow of goods to a major terminal, or rate-breaking point, are often different than rates on an identical flow of goods destined via that same terminal for another state.

[14] The authors gratefully acknowledge the cooperation of the personnel in the Wisconsin Public Service Commission office, especially Mr. Ivan A. Sherman, Transportation Rate Analyst, and Mr. Harold Hueblein. "Tariffs" are tables of freight charges or transport prices published by the carriers.

[15] The term isophor is derived from the Greek "isos" (equal) and "phora" (charge for carrying freight). Scandinavian scholars have used different terms. Tord Palander employs the term "isotim" defined as a line connecting points of equal delivered price. See E. H. Hoover's discussion of terminology on page 8 of his *Location Theory and the Shoe and Leather Industries*, Harvard University Press, Cambridge, Massachusetts, 1937. Olaf Lindberg uses the term "isovecture" defined as a line joining points of equal transport costs, *op. cit.*, p. 28.

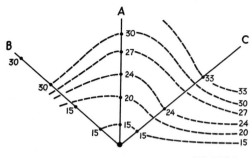

RATES IN CENTS PER 100 POUNDS
TO/FROM A TRANSPORT CENTER
FIG. 2.

which serves as the focus of the nodal region.

Several problems arise in the drawing of such isarithms. How should they be drawn where a sequence of shipping points along one radiating transport artery has a sequence of rates ascending in several small increments while a neighboring radiating line has rates ascending in a few large increments (Fig. 2)? Can the isophors be continuous lines located as per the quoted rates on line A and interpolated on lines B and C? This requires isophors to cross a transport line (thus indicating rates of a given value) where no such rates exist. Figure 3, a portion of a Wisconsin rate structure, illustrates this problem. The rail first class rate per 100 pounds to Chicago is 143 cents from Klevenville and 126 cents from Riley. Rates from all other shipping points (for which rates are published) are plotted on Figure 3. Isophors are drawn for only those rates which are quoted for places which are located in the area mapped. Between Klevenville and Riley there is no shipping point; no quoted rate exists. Yet three isophors (133, 136, and 140) run between the two. Is this realistic? Should isarithms be drawn in locations where there are nonexistent values?

A second problem is a visual one.

Closely spaced isarithms give the impression of steeper gradients than do isarithms farther apart. Figure 4 illustrates this problem by showing the first class rate structure on rail shipments between Chicago and all Wisconsin points. It has been constructed according to the "interpolated isophor" technique: viz., drawing isophors for rates which are quoted for specific stations, and extending them across all rail lines (even where no such rates are quoted) in order to give form to the rate structure. Thus, there are isophors for values 129, 133, and 136 but none for 130, 131, 132, 134, or 135 because there are no stations in Wisconsin for which such rates are quoted. The visual impression is one of a steep gradient extending through Wonewoc and Kiel because isophors are close together. Actually the rate contrast through this belt is only 10–11 cents.

One solution to these mapping problems could be the construction of isophors at selected constant intervals. However, this might hide important

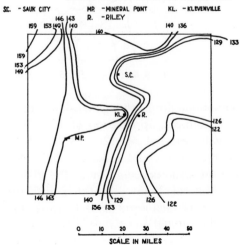

FIG. 3.

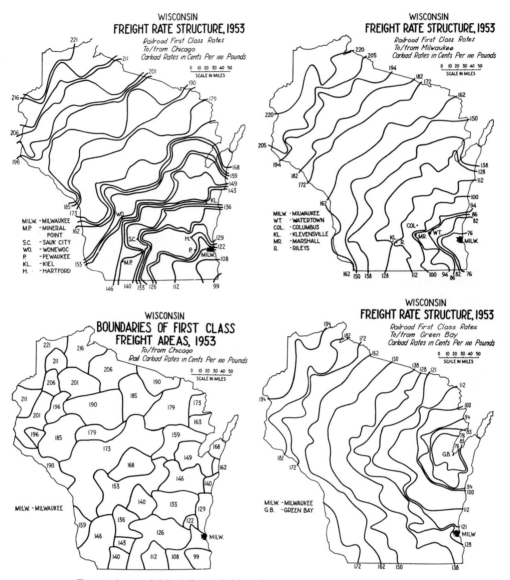

FIGS. 4 (upper left), 5 (lower left), 6 (upper right), and 7 (lower right).

deviations from the general structure. For example, application of 10-unit intervals selected at 126, 136, and 146 on Figure 4 would fail to reveal rather abrupt structure changes in the vicinity of Mineral Point. Another difficulty with this technique is that rates may not be quoted for values fitting into a regular interval; for example, there is no 156 rate and no 116 rate anywhere

in Wisconsin to continue the sequence proposed in the foregoing illustration.

An alternative mapping technique abandons the use of isarithms in favor of rate area boundaries. Each line would encompass all contiguous places with the same rate. Figure 5 has been constructed on this basis for rail first class rates to/from Chicago. Cartographically this is more accurate than the isarithmic technique, i.e., no rate is represented in any place if it does not exist there. On the other hand, the selection of adequate symbols is a problem since there are 26 different categories (from the area having a 99 cent rate in the extreme southeast to the area having a 221 cent rate in the extreme northwest). Also, this does not give a clear visual impression of the relationship between rates and distance nor does it give an easily grasped view of a rate structure.

In any case, there is need for improving the technique of mapping freight rate structures.

Railroad First Class Freight Rate Structures

Figures 4, 6, 9, 10, and 11 employ the interpolated isophor technique, showing Wisconsin's structure of rail first class freight rates to/from five major transport centers as of 1952–1953.

Figure 4 shows the rate structure between all Wisconsin rail stations and *Chicago*. Only very broadly is the pattern one of concentric circles, which should prevail if rates increased uniformly in all directions from Chicago. The capricious path of isophors is illustrated by numerous examples. For instance, the rate between Milwaukee and Chicago is 108 cents per 100 pounds. Just north of Milwaukee (on the rail routes along the lake shore) the rate increases abruptly to 129. Between these two values rates of 112, 122, and 126 are quoted elsewhere in Wisconsin. Though closely spaced just north of Milwaukee, these isophors diverge to the west; the 126 and 129 isophors are parallel to a point beyond Hartford where the 129 isophor bends sharply *northwest* while the 126 isophor bends sharply *southeast*. Similar variation involves other pairs of isophors: e.g., 146 and 149, 153 and 159, 185 and 190. Obviously, in this

particular structure, rates increase differentially in different directions from the focal city.

The complexity of a freight rate structure is illustrated by the profusion of isarithms on Figure 4 on which every existing rate quoted for any place in the State is represented. For the sake of simplicity, most maps to follow are not, in this respect, complete replicas of Wisconsin's rate structure. Only selected isophors will appear, in order to present more clearly the essence of the structure. The total visual impression of subsequent maps therefore cannot be compared directly with that of Figure 4; however, the complexities of isophor patterns are comparable.

Figure 6 shows the structure of rail first class rates between all Wisconsin shipping points and *Milwaukee*. There is some tendency toward a concentric pattern, yet sharp irregularities in many isophors indicate that increase with distance apparently is not consistent in all directions. Profiles of freight rate gradients to the north, west, southwest, and south of Milwaukee show marked variations (Fig. 8).

It might be supposed that places on a direct route to the focal city of the structure would have lower rates than neighboring places not on such routes. This is not true. For instance, Figure 9 shows Fort Atkinson to have a lower rate to Milwaukee than does Eagle, which is not only on a direct route but also closer to Milwaukee. Figure 9 also reveals sharp structure contrasts between two places on separate direct routes. For example, Columbus and Marshall are on direct routes to Milwaukee, in fact their routes converge at Watertown. Yet the Marshall rate to Milwaukee is 86 cents while that of Columbus is 100 cents. Note the steep gradient between Riley and Klevenville on Figure 8 as well as Figure 3.

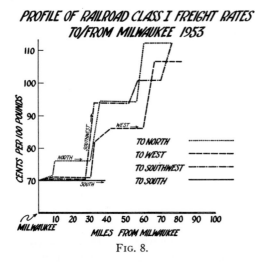

PROFILE OF RAILROAD CLASS I FREIGHT RATES TO/FROM MILWAUKEE 1953

FIG. 8.

The structure of rail first class rates around *Green Bay* (Fig. 7), *Superior* (Fig. 10), and *Duluth* (Fig. 11) reveals the same general arrangement: a tendency toward concentricity but strange deflections in and congestions of isophors. There is an anomaly in the Superior structure north of Milwaukee where nine stations on two different railroads have a 186 rate, in sharp contrast to the 214 rate prevailing around them. This actually represents an error in the published tariffs.[16] In the Duluth rate structure the 159 and 196 isophors are particularly distorted.

Inspection of the foregoing rail rate structures around five focal points reveals the structures of isophors to be very asymmetrical. Rates do not increase consistently with distance in any one direction, or similarly in different directions.

To understand what appears to be capriciousness on the part of rail first class rates one needs to consider three

[16] Since determining the exact rates to Superior for all Wisconsin points required several computations, it was first thought that an error had been made in computations; however, Mr. Ivan A. Sherman checked the computations, found them to be correct, and verified the conclusion that the tariffs quoted rates for this small area out of harmony with the general rate structure.

principles which apply in the philosophy of rate making adhered to by the railroads in this nation: (a) the "grouping" principle, (b) the "short line distance" principle, and (c) the "rate step" principle.

The *grouping principle* enables railroads to simplify the publication of class rates. Theoretically, if all rates were assessed on the mileage basis, a separate rate would have to be published between every pair of shipping points in the nation. As a result, each freight agent in the country would have to refer to volumes of tremendous size to determine rates on shipments to/from his depot. By treating several proximal stations as one, the railroads greatly simplify their rate tariffs. In essence, the grouping principle declares that all the stations in a group take the same rate to any other group of stations. The group's specific rate is computed in terms of the group's "control point" which often is the largest settlement in the group's area. Figure 12 shows the location of the 67 areas of station groups which the railroads proposed

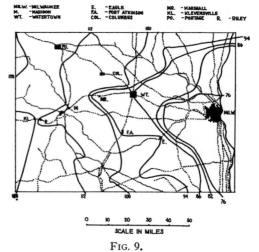

SE. WISCONSIN
FREIGHT RATE STRUCTURE, 1953
Railroad First Class Rates
To/from Milwaukee
Carload Rates in Cents Per 100 Pounds

FIG. 9.

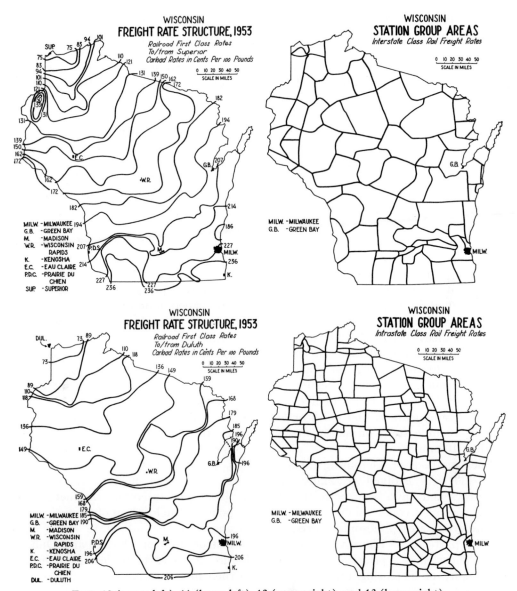

FIGS. 10 (upper left), 11 (lower left), 12 (upper right), and 13 (lower right).

(and the Interstate Commerce Commission approved) for the *interstate* class freight rate structure. The major dimension of each group's area is approximately 40 miles although some are longer and a few are shorter. Figure 13 shows that for *intrastate* rail shipments, Wisconsin's class freight rate structure comprises many more (180 to be exact) group areas.[17] Group areas are smaller on Figure 13 than on Figure 12 because intrastate shipments tend to be shorter than interstate.

The "*short line principle*" prescribes that rates shall be computed on the basis of the mileage of the shortest route over which carload freight can be

[17] Figures 12 and 13 are copied from manuscript maps prepared in the Tariff Section of the Wisconsin Public Service Commission, courtesy of Mr. Ivan A. Sherman.

transported without transfer of lading. In application this means that a shipment needing to move from one railroad to another would have to move through interchange points which the railroads have established, analogous to "transfer stations" on a city's rapid transit system. For this reason alone, rate structures could not be expected to be concentric around a transport center unless numerous railroad routes extended outward from it radially.

The third principle followed by the railroads is the *quoting of rates "in steps."* For instance, no *interstate* rates are quoted on shipments of less than 40 miles, but from 40 to 100 miles the rate increases in steps of five miles and is computed in terms of the distance between the control points of groups. For distances between 100 and 240 miles the steps are 10 miles in length; they are 20 miles long for distances over 240 miles. *Intrastate* rates in Wisconsin are quoted in terms of five mile steps on shipments of 100 miles or less and of 10 mile steps on shipments exceeding 100 miles.

Such methods of computing rates by railroads have evolved gradually over the years and have been permitted by the government commissions.

The group-area philosophy portrayed by the patterns of Figures 12 and 13, the "short line" principle, and the philosophy of increasing rates in steps are fundamental to the understanding of the isophor maps of class rates presented in this study, and are excellent examples of a cultural geographic factor (philosophy of rate-making) operating to influence the locational pattern of a geographic element, the freight rate structure of Wisconsin.

Truck First Class Freight Rate Structures

Maps of Wisconsin structures of common carrier truck rates are shown in Figures 14–18. Admittedly, more traffic probably moves by *private* truck and by *contract* truck, but it is impossible to construct rate maps for such flow. The structures of rates to/from *Chicago* (Fig. 14) are represented by selected isophors and reveal more irregularities in the nearer rather than the distant portions of the State. By contrast, the structures of rates to/from *Milwaukee*, *Green Bay*, and *Superior* (Figs. 15, 16, and 17) show surprising concentricity. The Milwaukee structure (Fig. 15) is shown in its entirety; i.e., all isophors are drawn. For the sake of simplicity, alternate isophors have been omitted on Figures 16 and 17.

A different philosophy of rate making has prevailed in determining truck rates. The trucking authorities, in contrast to the railroad men, proposed to the commissions that truck rates be computed generally in terms of *airline* distances rather than the "short-line-involving-no-transfer-of-lading" principle. This is the main explanation for Wisconsin's truck rate structures being more symmetrical than the rail rates. Nevertheless, the fact that truck rates, like rail rates, increase in shorter steps for short hauls and, on interstate shipments, also respond to the location of control points means that the interstate truck class rate structures for Chicago and Duluth, Figure 20, tend to be less symmetrical in their inner areas.

Class Rate Nodal Regions

Synthesis of rail rate structures and truck rate structures just presented enables the delimitation of nodal regions around the five focal centers, Figure 18. The nodal region for each focus was constructed by delimiting all shipping points linked by a lower rate to that center than to any other. For example, the first class rail rate per 100 pounds from Madison is 126 to Chicago, 107

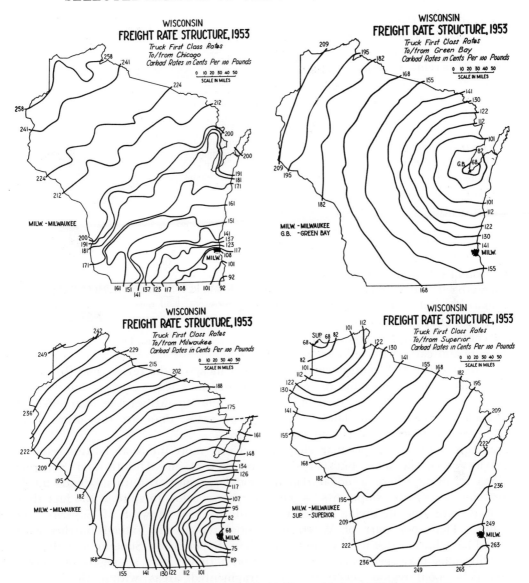

FIGS. 14 (upper left), 15 (lower left), 16 (upper right), and 17 (lower right).

to Milwaukee, 138 to Green Bay, 211 to Superior, and 190 to Duluth. Therefore, Madison is in the Milwaukee nodal region of rail rates. Where truck rates are lower than rail rates a solid black symbol is employed.

Two broad observations can be drawn from the map of nodal regions. First, over most of Wisconsin, first class rail rates are lower than first class truck rates.[18] However, in the immediate hinterlands of each focus the truck rates are lower. Chicago and Duluth have no such "truck advantage regions" in Wisconsin, and Superior's is small. The Milwaukee nodal area in which truck

[18] The reader is reminded that the areas delimited on Figure 18 as having lower truck rates are delimited in terms of common carrier rates, it being impossible to procure data on private truck movements and contract truck movements.

rates are less than rail rates exceeds Green Bay's which, in turn, exceeds Superior's. At least in the structures mapped herein, it appears that the larger the transport center, the more extensive the area in which truck transport has a favorable rate differential over railroads. Whether this principle is true or not for other transport centers in the State and in the nation is yet to be investigated.

The extent of the truck nodal regions within the rail nodal regions noted above relates to the well-known fact that on short hauls the truck is more efficient than the train. Recognition of this division of talent is demonstrated in the "piggy-back" development in which trucks accumulate loads in the hinterlands of major rail centers, assemble at the center, are loaded bodily onto rail flat cars and carried by rail over a long haul to another rail center where the truck disembarks, finishing its movement in short hauls to distributing points in the center's hinterland.

The second observation is that nodal rate regions can have peculiar shapes and locations, the most unusual situations resulting where a nodal region involving intrastate shipments is enmeshed with one involving interstate traffic. That any part of Wisconsin should have lower rates to Chicago than to Milwaukee may seem surprising, yet Chicago's nodal region penetrates the extreme southwestern corner of the State which is served by the Chicago, Burlington and Quincy Railroad's main line between Chicago and the Twin Cities. Milwaukee's nodal region blankets most of southern Wisconsin and actually reaches the Mississippi River at two places: (a) in the vicinity of Prairie du Chien where rates via the Milwaukee Railroad's direct line to Milwaukee are lower than the Burlington's rates to Chicago, thus fragmenting

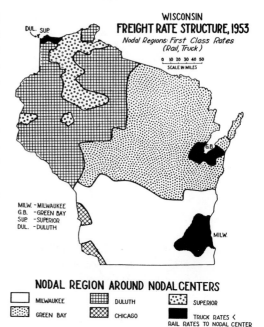

FIG. 18.

the Chicago nodal region, and (b) in the vicinity of LaCrosse where another direct line to Milwaukee has effected lower rates than to the other four centers.

Even more unusual is the relative location of the Duluth and Superior nodal regions. Duluth's extends much farther south. In spite of the fact that Duluth itself is west of Superior, its nodal region also extends farther east than Superior's. Superior's nodal region actually is an aggregate of several fragmented areas within the Duluth nodal region. Incongruous as it may seem, Figure 18 reveals that shippers and consignees in most of northwestern Wisconsin have lower first class rates on shipments to/from Duluth, Minnesota than to/from Superior, Wisconsin. Comparison of Figures 10 and 11 reveals that, even outside the Duluth nodal region, rates from Wisconsin to Duluth are generally lower than to Superior. For example, comparative rates for selected points are presented

TABLE II

RAILROAD FIRST CLASS RATES

(per 100 pounds)

From	To Duluth, Minnesota	To Superior, Wisconsin
Eau Claire.............	$1.36	$1.39
Wisconsin Rapids.......	1.53	1.62
Green Bay.............	1.79	1.99
Prairie du Chien........	1.90	2.07
Madison..............	1.90	2.11
Milwaukee............	1.96	2.27
Kenosha..............	2.06	2.36

in Table II. A graphic view of this information is presented in Figure 19, a comparative profile of the Duluth and Superior rate structures along the rail routes connecting Superior with Eau Claire, Portage, Milwaukee, and Kenosha. In the northern half of this route the two profiles intersect eight times, indicating that there are four segments where lower rates to Superior prevail alternating with four segments of lower rates to Duluth. The route's southern half sees the Superior structure climbing high above Duluth's. The differential reaches 30 cents in the vicinity of Oconomowoc, shrinks to 26 cents in the Milwaukee area, and expands again to 30 cents between Racine and Kenosha. Similar intertwinings of profiles would result if the Duluth and Superior structures were compared along other routes. At first glance, such a relationship of structures would appear illogical unless one remembers that the dotted graph portrays an interstate structure of rates, whereas the solid line represents intrastate structure which both result from rate computation methods which differ in terms of (a) size of group areas of stations and (b) length of steps by which rates increase.

Commodity Rate Structures: Coal

Figures 21, 22, and 23[19] show Wisconsin's freight rate structures as of 1952–1953 on movement of a selected commodity, coal, chosen because it moves between more points in larger tonnage than any other commodity.

Figure 21 portrays the structure on coal rates from the southern Illinois bituminous coal field from which most Wisconsin localities receive coal. The original map showed a confusion of isophors in the southern part of the State; for simplicity of reproduction 10 isophors have been deleted between the 344 and 437 rates. North of the 437 isophor only three have been deleted. The map reveals clearly the rate advantage enjoyed by southeastern Wisconsin. Most places have rates of 388 or 420 cents per ton. Northward the

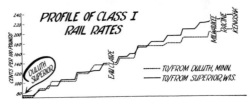

FIG. 19.

rates increase at rather long intervals, but the increases are abrupt. Figure 21 illustrates one of the mapping problems discussed earlier. A steep gradient is implied by the congestion of three isophors between Waukesha and Sussex, separated by a 25 cent differential (between 395 and 420). By contrast, a gentle gradient appears to prevail across the central portion of the state through Blair, Wisconsin Rapids, and Green Bay, where there is no close spacing of isophors. Yet here the rate increases sharply in a single step from 445 to 475, a differential of 30 cents per ton.

The lowest rates on Figure 21 occur, not along the Lake Michigan shore, but 60 miles westward along the Rock River Valley. Beloit's rate of 341 is the lowest

[19] These maps are based on coal rates filed with the Public Service Commission and recorded also by Mr. W. F. Ehmann for the Wisconsin Coal Bureau, Inc., who provided the data for this portion of the study.

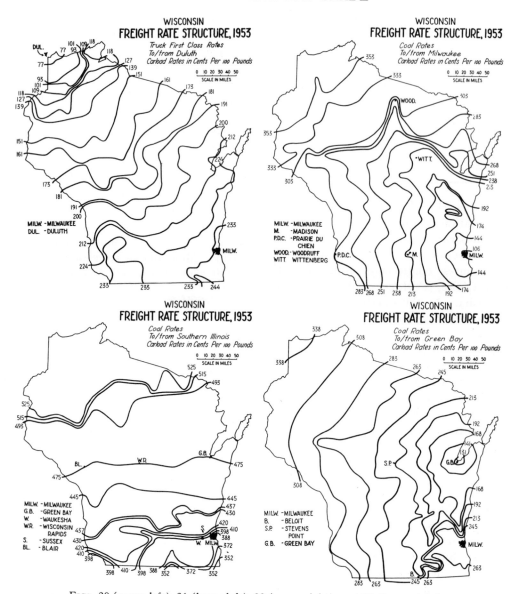

FIGS. 20 (upper left), 21 (lower left), 22 (upper right), and 23 (lower right).

in the State, 47 cents lower than Milwaukee's, 12 cents lower than Racine's. This concession was granted the Beloit area by the I.C.C. in response to vigorous persuasion by manufactural interests in the Rock River Valley, and is of significance in perpetuating this small industrial belt as one of the nation's more intensely developed industrial nodes.[20]

The complexity of the structure on rates from *Milwaukee* almost defies description (Figure 22). The original map was so intricate as to be illegible in reduced form. The map reproduced here omits two-thirds of the isophors in

[20] For further analysis of this adjustment on coal rates see John W. Alexander: *Geography of Manufacturing in the Rock River Valley*, University of Wisconsin School of Commerce, Bureau of Business Research Service, 1949, pp. 163–164.

an effort to portray the major structural characteristics which reveal an asymmetrical arrangement of rates very low to the northwest. For instance, the rate from Milwaukee to Madison, a distance of 90 miles, is 208 cents per ton; but in a northerly direction the 208 rate carries 200 miles to Wittenberg. Two hundred miles west of Milwaukee the rate is 278 at Prairie du Chien. A 278 rate in a northwesterly direction carries as far as Woodruff, almost to the Michigan border. It is difficult to explain all such idiosyncracies in the freight rate structure. However, certain factors can be identified. For example, the northward looping of isophors in the eastern portion of Wisconsin (e.g., the 213 isophor) is due to the competitive position of other coal gateways such as Green Bay. The railroads, with the approval of the Commission, have given Milwaukee a favorable competitive rate in Green Bay's hinterland. The result is that some communities in eastern Wisconsin enjoy lower rates on dock coal from Milwaukee than do communities closer to Milwaukee but located in southwestern Wisconsin. The strange pattern of isophors in north-central Wisconsin, like a prong pointing northward, is the result of what rate analysts term "holddowns" to give manufacturing firms in the Wisconsin River Valley competitive rates as compared to industry in the Fox River Valley to the east.[21] The same principle has been observed already in the case of the Rock River Valley on Figure 21.

Another unusual aspect of a rate structure portrayed by Figure 22 is the "negative anomaly" 50 miles north of Milwaukee. This is one result of the "equalization clause" which, in the words of Ivan A. Sherman of Wisconsin's Public Service Commission, "permits railroads to equalize without undue discrimination the rates to destinations from more distant ports, or to reduce the spread in rates from more distant ports over those from nearer ports; but such equalization or reduction in rates shall be to a level not lower than the rate that would be produced by the scale at 50 per cent of the rate-making distance from the more distant port." This equalization clause has been in effect for decades, ever since Appalachian coal began moving through Wisconsin's ports. This clause states another philosophy of rate making which, as a spatial variable, is both a cultural geographic factor and a geographic element.

The coal rate structures portrayed in Figures 21–23 are unique in the United States, according to the Wisconsin Public Service Commission. In no other state is there the overlapping of so many rate structures on coal movements.

To the absolute rate values on Figure 22 should be added $3.45, the rate on coal from the Appalachian field via rail and water to Milwaukee. Appalachian coal moving via the Great Lakes to Milwaukee, Green Bay, Superior, and other Wisconsin ports is termed "dock coal." The rate on "dock coal" to Madison would be $3.45 plus $2.08 equalling $5.53 which has a differential of $1.58 above Madison's $3.95 rate from southern Illinois. This is a major reason why inland consumers who do not require the higher quality Appalachian coal prefer the Illinois product.

Wisconsin's major nodal regions in terms of "*dock* coal" commodity rates are shown in Figure 24 which is based not only on Figures 22 and 23 but also on individual rate structures constructed around all other important coal ports (Racine, Port Washington, Sheboygan,

---

[21] Mr. Ivan A. Sherman in personal interview.

Manitowoc, Marinette, Ashland, and Superior). In every case the transport charge from Appalachian coal fields to lake port was added to the charge from lake port to Wisconsin points. Nodal regions then were delimited in terms of over-all rates from coal fields to destination.

The large blank area on Figure 24 indicates that the pattern of dock coal rate nodal regions is more complex than the construction of class rate nodal regions. Figure 18 reveals no areas of overlap; every place in the State can be ascribed to a single nodal region. This is impossible for dock coal rates. Nodal regions involving no overlap are outlined in Figure 24 and, in the aggregate, comprise less than half of Wisconsin. In most of southern Wisconsin a station is likely to enjoy equally low rates on dock coal from at least two, and often more, of the coal receiving ports. This appears to result from at least two causes: (a) Transport charges from the Appalachian coal producing fields are quoted for groups of Wisconsin ports rather than on a distance basis. Table III illustrates this point with data on shipments from Pittsburgh. (b) The equalization clause (mentioned earlier) enables railroads to quote equal rates between a point and two or more ports.

However, when rates on Illinois coal are considered, all of Wisconsin is in the Illinois nodal region excepting the

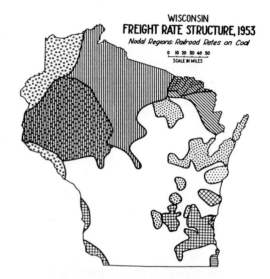

WISCONSIN
FREIGHT RATE STRUCTURE, 1953
Nodal Regions: Railroad Rates on Coal

0 10 20 30 40 50
SCALE IN MILES

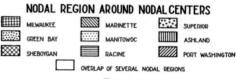

NODAL REGION AROUND NODAL CENTERS

▦ MILWAUKEE	▨ MARINETTE	▧ SUPERIOR
▩ GREEN BAY	⋯ MANITOWOC	▥ ASHLAND
▩ SHEBOYGAN	▤ RACINE	▨ PORT WASHINGTON
☐ OVERLAP OF SEVERAL NODAL REGIONS		

FIG. 24.

extreme north (i.e., northernmost portions of the nodal regions ascribed to Green Bay, to Marinette, to Ashland, and to Superior) and the seven communities having ports receiving dock coal (Racine, Milwaukee, Port Washington, Sheboygan, Manitowoc, Green Bay, and Marinette).

Summary Comments

1. Maps of selected components of Wisconsin's freight rate structure, on both *interstate* and *intrastate* shipments, reveal that rates vary markedly with distance. Isophors are not spaced at regular intervals.

2. The maps reveal that rates vary greatly with *direction*. Isophors twist and bend; they do not follow circular paths.

3. The explanation for these patterns or locational arrangements of rates is found, in part at least, in the philosophy of rate making which the railroads follow. Five important aspects of this

TABLE III

Transport charges per ton on coal from Pittsburgh to Wisconsin docks

Superior............................	$3.31
Ashland.............................	3.31
Marinette...........................	3.38
Green Bay..........................	3.38
Manitowoc..........................	3.38
Sheboygan..........................	3.38
Port Washington....................	3.38
Milwaukee..........................	3.45
Racine..............................	3.45

Source: Mr. W. F. Ehman, Wisconsin Coal Bureau, Inc.

philosophy have been shown to be: (a) the grouping principle, (b) the short line principle, (c) the rate-step principle, (d) the equalization principle, and (e) the hold-down principle. All five policies help effect spatial differences in transport charges.

4. Freight rate structures can be used to define nodal regions which may be useful in analyzing functional regions of the more important transport centers. Such nodal freight rate regions may be based on class rates or on commodity rates.

5. Many problems posed in mapping isophors remain unsolved. Should an isophor be constructed in only that part of the state where its value is quoted as a rate, thereby "dangling" in other parts of the state or terminating against other isophors? Or should an isophor once plotted in the area of its rate's occurrence be constructed continuously across the state maintaining its position relative to the other isophors? Should isophors be constructed for every value of rate quoted, or should only selected intervals be represented? The latter alternative often leads to the predicament where a consistent interval cannot be maintained, where no rates exist for some values which would appear in a consistent scale of intervals.

6. Logical steps in further research on freight rate structures include (a) an investigation of causes (other than the five cited in No. 3 above) behind the strange structural patterns and deviations of the isophors from concentricity, (b) a study of the actual movement of goods to determine the degree of conformance with the nodal regions as defined in terms of freight rate structures, (c) research into the influence of freight rate structures on the location of economic activities, and vice versa, (d) additional commodity studies to appraise their similarity with the class rate structures and the coal rate structures, and (e) experiments with techniques for mapping freight rate structures.

SOME ELEMENTS IN THE STUDY OF PORT GEOGRAPHY*

GUIDO G. WEIGEND

THE literature of port geography has become more abundant in recent years both in the United States and in Europe. The subject matter has been concerned chiefly with certain functions of ports or with the geography of specific ports, but there have also been methodological discussions. In this article the author would like to bring into focus some of the basic elements of port geography—port, carrier, cargo, hinterland, foreland, and maritime space—and analyze them systematically as they apply to seaports.[1] This is not a final and all-inclusive statement but is intended to be another step in the formulation of more definitive general principles in port geography.

THE PORT

The port is the place of contact between land and maritime space, and it provides services to both hinterland and maritime organization. It is, therefore, a knot where ocean and inland transport lines meet and intertwine. Its primary function is to transfer goods (and people) from ocean vessels to land or to inland carriers, and vice versa. Traffic means life and prosperity not only for the port but also for the city and region around it. Thus it is inevitable that a dynamic port will seek to attract as much traffic as possible from wherever it can, and will frequently come into competition with other ports. The origin and evolution of a port and its ability to attract traffic of any kind at a particular time are based on a complex of physical and human factors, which can be categorized but which must be studied carefully in each case.

---

* This is the final article in a series on port geography deriving from a project sponsored jointly by the Office of Naval Research and Rutgers, The State University of New Jersey. Reproduction in whole or in part is permitted for any purpose of the United States Government.

[1] The reader is referred to the following earlier articles by the writer, in which various elements of port geography are discussed: "Bordeaux: An Example of Changing Port Functions," *Geogr. Rev.,* Vol. 45, 1955, pp. 217–243; "Les notions d'arrière-pays et d'avant-pays dans l'étude des ports," *Rev. de "La Porte Océane,"* Vol. 11, No. 113, February, 1955, pp. 5–10; "The Functional Development of the Port of Hamburg," *Tijdschr. voor Econ. en Sociale Geogr.,* Vol. 47, 1956, pp. 113–120; "The Problem of Hinterland and Foreland As Illustrated by the Port of Hamburg," *Econ. Geogr.,* Vol. 32, 1956, pp. 1–16.

➤ DR. WEIGEND is chairman of the Department of Geography at Rutgers, The State University, New Brunswick, N. J.

"Some Elements in the Study of Port Geography" by Guido G. Weigend. Reprinted from Geographical Review, *Vol. XLVIII (April 1958), pp. 185–200, with permission of the editor.*

Among the physical factors, site is obviously of outstanding significance. Ideally a port, aside from sufficient space for its operations, should have among its attributes easy entrance, deep water, a small tidal range, and a climate that will not hamper port operations at any time of the year. Rarely can all requirements be met, because maritime services may be needed in locations where human considerations outweigh physical. Sites can be modified by man if the need is great enough. For example, in Saudi Arabia crude oil is loaded by means of pipelines in open roadsteads, and ships have no protection against wind and sea. One might even mention the construction of temporary port facilities on the Normandy beaches, where military necessity overbalanced all considerations of cost.

The "World Port Index"[2] recognizes eight types as sufficient to classify all ports of the world. Coastal ports and river ports can each be divided into "natural" and "tide gate" types, the latter being provided with locks or other devices that isolate the port area from the tidal effects of the open sea. Moreover, coastal ports may be of the "breakwater" type and river ports of the "basin" type, both of which have protective constructions or excavations that do not close off the port area. Finally, there are the "canal or lake" type and the "open roadstead," the former having a situation on the interior part of a canal or lake connected with the sea by a navigable waterway.

"Situation" is a concept that may have either physical or cultural implications. It is one that has been significant throughout the development of ports. The term "situation" implies a relationship to other factors, of which there may be a large number. Because many of these factors are not static, the relationship, and therefore the meaning of "situation," may be under constant change. For example, the situation of a port is related to the physical landscape; it may be an "interior" port, away from the open ocean, or an "exterior" port, directly on the coast.[3] Historically, most of the great ports have been interior ports, because sailing vessels needed protection from the weather and a few days' difference in travel time was not important. Moreover, ships were small, and estuaries were deep enough to be no hindrance to ocean traffic. Most important, before the building of railroads and adequate roads land transport was difficult and slow, so that a seaport located as far inland as possible was at the same time a regional capital that not only provided maritime and land transport but possibly performed political, economic, and social functions as well.

---

[2] U. S. Hydrogr. Office Publ. No. 950, 1953.

[3] Marcel Amphoux: Ports intérieurs et ports extérieurs, Rev. de "La Porte Océane," Vol. 6, No. 61, May, 1950, pp. 5–7.

Modern navigation, however, has brought grave problems to ports not on the seashore.[4] Ships are larger, and operating costs are constantly increasing. Shippers want fast and easy access to ports and a rapid turnaround. Many interior ports are plagued with inadequate depth of channel, sedimentation, and fluctuating water level; often approaches and departures can be made only at high tide, and delays are costly. Thus a port such as Le Havre, at the mouth of the Seine estuary, has attracted more ocean traffic than older ports upstream.

It is, however, the never-ending and constantly changing patterns of human activity that have had a continuing influence on situation. In the seventeenth and eighteenth centuries Bordeaux was ideally located for trade and traffic between France and its possessions in the West Indies. Port life flourished, as did the entire region. Yet in the twentieth century Bordeaux finds itself in the backwater of ocean transport. There are many reasons for the change, largely beyond the control of the port and its administration. For example, Napoleon decided to encourage the growing of sugar beets in northern France, in order to reduce the country's dependence on cane sugar, importation of which was threatened by the British blockade. Bordeaux had been a principal importer of cane sugar, and many refineries were located in and near the port area, most of which were eventually liquidated. Moreover, the Industrial Revolution had its greatest impact in Northwestern Europe, and the Channel and North Sea ports became the chief terminals and ports of call for the important sea routes connecting Europe with other continents. The situation of Bordeaux, therefore, is no longer favorable with respect to the major world patterns of ocean trade. The port, once of national importance, has become purely regional.

It appears to be the human factor, then, that is paramount in the rise and decline of ports. This factor may range from world activity over which the port has no control to decisions of local administrators and port planners. Between the eleventh and fifteenth centuries ports on the shores of the Mediterranean became prosperous through shipping and commerce, chiefly as intermediaries between the Orient and Northwestern Europe. In the fifteenth century, however, the rise of the Ottoman Turks and accompanying piracy made the traditional trade routes hazardous if not impossible to use. Moreover, the discovery of the route to Asia round the Cape of Good Hope created a safer and easier seaway connecting Northwestern Europe directly

---

[4] See, for example, G. G. Weigend: River Ports and Outports: Matadi and Banana, *Geogr. Rev.*, Vol. 44, 1954, pp. 430–432.

with the Orient. As a result, ports in the Mediterranean found themselves in the backwater of world ocean trade and traffic for more than two centuries and a half. An era of rejuvenation began with the opening of the Suez Canal, together with the advent of the steamship, continued industrialization in Northwestern and Central Europe, and French colonization in North Africa. The Mediterranean again became one of the world's principal ocean highways, benefiting ports located on its shore. Thus, in the case of Mediterranean ports, neither hinterland nor foreland nor the port itself has been able to influence or determine its destiny; rather, the totality of expansion and development in the world at each stage has narrowed or broadened its field of economic activity.

Similarly, policy decisions of national governments may influence ocean trade and transport. As has already been pointed out, the desire for national self-sufficiency in certain imported products may curtail port activity; the reduction or prohibition of export of other goods may have the same effect. Wheat exports from Russia ceased after the Bolshevik revolution, and Odessa lost its principal function; port life and city growth stagnated while many other cities in the Soviet Union doubled and trebled in size under the new regime.[5] Preferential railroad freight rates may favor some ports and cause traffic to flow over lines it would not normally follow. Finally, the movement of a commodity may come under the absolute dictate of the government, so that economically determined patterns of flow are erased. For example, the present French government decides how much coal is to be imported, where it is to be purchased and at what price, which ships are to carry it, and to which ports it will be shipped.

In the narrowest sense, the human factor in development operates at the local level. Although the port may attempt, often successfully, to influence governmental policy in its favor, it is within the port's own realm of activity that greatest influence can be exerted on its economic well-being. In other words, the aggressiveness and imagination of the port administration and commercial interests are vital to successful port operation. The port must find ways and means of providing services and facilities that will induce maritime interests and shippers in the hinterland to use it in preference to another port. The port and city of Rotterdam were severely damaged by the Germans during World War II. Although the city urgently needed restoration, port facilities were reconstructed first because port traffic meant life, and delay in restoring the flow of ships would have resulted in loss of

---

[5] C. D. Harris: The Cities of the Soviet Union, *Geogr. Rev.*, Vol. 35, 1945, pp. 107–121.

traffic to competing ports, traffic Rotterdam might not have been able to recapture. Extreme caution and conservatism may have the opposite effect and stagnate the life of a port and its tributary area. Failure to provide certain facilities, perhaps because of overreliance on established reputation, is likely to divert traffic to competing ports that can provide the services and are probably eager to do so.

The study of the human factor in port development can also be approached systematically. Economic, political, and social forces can be distinguished, all operating individually or simultaneously in conjunction. For example, the exceptional enterprise of the merchants and shippers of Hamburg, who early established commercial contacts throughout the world, and who succeeded also in local operations, contributed immeasurably to the continued success of the port despite such political setbacks as the two World Wars. Politically, the wars were only temporary, though severe, setbacks to Hamburg's development, but other political factors had longer-lasting effects. The fact that Hamburg enjoyed for many centuries a quasi-independent status and later complete political freedom as a city-state made possible full economic exploitation of city and port.

Frequently the economic and political factors are interlocked, as, for instance, in the growth of Marseilles into the largest seaport of France. In the nineteenth and twentieth centuries French colonial expansion in Africa, and especially in Algeria, created close economic and political ties between the two French shores of the Mediterranean, and Marseilles became the principal gateway for French-Algerian traffic. Moreover, the construction of the Suez Canal was motivated by both political and economic considerations of a scope far beyond the local interests of Marseilles. Yet because of the favorable location of Marseilles with respect to French sea transport to Asia by way of the Suez Canal the port benefited enormously when the canal was opened. In addition to being the chief contact point of France with Algeria, it soon became France's threshold to Asia and French colonial possessions there.

Social forces acting on port development can be as decisive as economic and political forces, but their influence may not be as continuous. Energy and foresight had much to do with Hamburg's evolution as a port, but at certain periods progress was hampered by difficulties emanating from the guild system. Quarrels, jealousies, and intrigues among the guilds postponed or slowed down the growth of manufacturing, even in such basic port industries as shipbuilding. A hostile attitude toward industrialization in the nineteenth century on the part of the policy-making class of merchants and shippers further delayed a general planning scheme for a Greater Hamburg, finally realized in the twentieth century.

Because the analysis of a port can be based on a great variety of criteria, many classifications have been devised and employed. The site factor is the basis for such terms as "river port," "coastal port," or "lake port." World, national, or local patterns of human activity yield a classification of ports as international, colonial, national, regional, or local. With respect to the port's radius of activity, such a classification is based on the extent of its hinterland and foreland. It is economic activity, however, that provides the widest variety in the nomenclature of ports. The name of the principal commodity handled may be applied, such as petroleum, ore, coal, or fish; or what is done with the greater part of the cargo may determine whether the port is industrial, commercial, transit, or transshipment; finally, ports have been named according to the type of carrier that predominates in their traffic patterns, such as passenger, liner, tramp, or tanker. Each of these classifications is based on specific criteria that presumably characterize the port according to a predominant function. However, the same port can be put into more than one classification. Thus an ore port may also be a local or regional port, and a liner port may be composed of an industrial port, a petroleum port, a lumber port, and a section where commercial activities predominate, perhaps within a free port or foreign-trade zone.[6]

Since the primary function of a port is to transfer goods (and people) from ocean vessels to land or to inland carriers, and vice versa, the classifications discussed above apply to variations of the primary function. As yet it has been impossible to assign a fixed order of importance to the various criteria employed, and no universal classification of ports has been formulated.

THE CARRIER

The carrier must be considered in port geography so far as its size or special construction affects port operation—characteristics that also reflect distinctive types of commodity movements and physical conditions of sea lanes. The classical division into tramps, liners, passenger liners, and so on is of limited value at present, but it is important to note that oil tankers of more than 100,000 dead-weight tons are now under construction. Only a handful of ports, San Francisco among them, can accommodate ships of that size. Although this does not mean that small tankers will disappear from

---

[6] For a recent study of free ports and foreign-trade zones, see R. S. Thoman: Free Ports and Foreign-Trade Zones (Cambridge, Md., 1956).

the oceans, large crude-oil importing ports will be forced to modernize their facilities either by deepening the channel approaches or by providing pipelines to stations where the water depth will allow such supertankers to discharge cargo. Thus the port is faced with solving a problem that includes both size of vessel and special equipment needed for loading or unloading. The supertanker is an extreme case, but the problem of larger ships and deeper channels has been with ports for decades. The principal question is whether dredging to certain depths is economically feasible in view of actual or potential flow of traffic through the port.

The evolution of specialized ships has also had to be taken into account by port planners in connection with the provision of specialized equipment. The petroleum tanker is but one of many kinds of vessels for which special facilities must be provided. Bordeaux lost most of its banana imports to Nantes because no unloading facilities were available, and it was in danger of losing part of its vegetable imports until the decision was made to provide the port with an air-conditioned transit shed and modern unloading equipment for fruits and vegetables. Subsequently the port recaptured its importance in this specialized traffic: banana imports rose from about 1000 tons in 1954 to more than 6000 tons in 1955, and imports of other fruits and vegetables from 20,000 tons to nearly 24,000.[7]

THE CARGO

Three aspects of cargo are of basic concern in port geography: volume, nature, and direction of flow. Generally, two large classes of merchandise are recognized. Bulk cargo moves unpacked and can be rapidly transferred from one carrier to another with a minimum of handling if appropriate machinery is available. Such bulk cargoes, therefore, as grain, ore, crude oil, and coal represent the largest tonnages of goods handled in ports, but they are much less significant than general cargo in giving the port viability. For example, in 1955 Hamburg imported 4.3 million tons of crude oil, which was somewhat more than one-fourth of all imports; although this large tonnage boosts the traffic statistics of the port and thus its competitive standing, it affects only a small part of the labor force because of the highly mechanized unloading.

It is the general cargo moving in and out of a port that requires a diverse labor force. This category comprises everything that is not carried in bulk and thus encompasses a multitude of commodities packed or unpacked,

---

[7] Statistics issued by the Port Autonome de Bordeaux.

which must be handled individually. It is the desire of every port to handle as much general cargo as possible, in order to maximize local employment. This achievement, however, may not result in the maximizing of local or regional income, but the proportion of general cargo to total tonnage is a much more valid measure of port prosperity than total tonnage.

The geographer is also interested in the origin and destination of the cargo, both incoming and outgoing. A port which is a terminus for incoming merchandise obviously has much narrower functions and opportunities for expansion and development than one through which goods move to and from interior areas. Merchandise moving through the port on the landward side can be categorized geographically as (1) goods originating in the port or city or destined for consumption or processing there; (2) goods passing through the port in transit to or from an interior destination; and (3) incoming goods marketed both in port or city and inland and outgoing goods coming both from port or city and inland. On the seaward side no such differentiation can be made. All cargo arrives or leaves the port in vessels, and attention must thus be focused on types of carriers and forelands.

In applying these three categories to a port analysis it is essential to distinguish between imports and exports and, more specifically, between types of merchandise. For example, in the traffic of Bayonne, in southwestern France, none of the major imports belongs in category 2; that is, none is shipped exclusively to an interior destination. The bulk of the imports remains in the immediate port area, where it is consumed by a few large port industries. These imports include phosphates and pyrites for a chemical factory, iron ore for a metallurgical plant, and coal for both these plants and for other local industries. The exports of the port, on the other hand, fall chiefly into the second category. They are products from the Landes pine forests to the north, which move through Bayonne to overseas destinations. Thus the port of Bayonne is a terminus for most of its imports and a transit point for its principal exports; or, in other words, the import hinterland is restricted largely to the port itself and its immediate surroundings, whereas its export hinterland extends into the Landes about halfway to Bordeaux.

The Hinterlands

The cargo classification brings our attention to the great variety of hinterlands of a port. A "hinterland" can be described as organized and developed land space which is connected with a port by means of transport lines, and which receives or ships goods through that port. A port does not necessarily have exclusive claim to any part of its hinterland, and an inland area may be the hinterland of several ports. For example, ports on the Mediterranean and on the North Sea have competed vigorously for Austria's overseas export. Trieste traditionally has been the sea outlet for Vienna, but between the two World Wars, and again since World War II, German North Sea ports have attempted to capture the traffic. They have met with considerable success. In spite of the fact that Hamburg is more than twice as far from Vienna as Trieste, freight takes as much as five days to move from Vienna to Trieste, and only six days to Hamburg, which has better and more frequent maritime connections with all parts of the world and port fees half those of Trieste.[8] The German policy of attracting goods traffic to German ports by granting preferential railroad freight rates has also been successful and has diverted Austrian merchandise away from Trieste and other Mediterranean ports. Furthermore, industry in Austria has been gradually decentralized. Some industries have moved westward, and many new industries have arisen in western Austria and have increased urban population there. Since western Austria has better transport connections northward than toward Trieste, more of its overseas exports now move toward the North Sea.

A different hinterland problem is presented by the port of St. John, N. B.[9] In winter the port has within its hinterland, in competition with other Atlantic-coast ports, most of the populated areas of Canada from the Atlantic to the Pacific and certain areas of the United States north of the Ohio and Missouri Rivers. In summer, however, the St. Lawrence and Great Lakes ports take over St. John's interior hinterland, and the tributary area of the port shrinks to the Maritime Provinces, which are economically less important and therefore stimulate much less traffic.

Yet another example is the port of Lobito, on the west coast of Africa, which until the end of 1956 was unable to attract the copper exports of Northern Rhodesia even though the ocean route from Lobito to the main markets is some 3000 miles shorter than that from Beira and Lourenço Marques, the area's sea outlets on the east coast.[10] The copper companies

---

[8] Herbert Paschinger: Triest als wirtschafts- und verkehrsgeographisches Problem, *Verhandl. des Deutschen Geographentages*, Vol. 29 (Essen, 1953), Wiesbaden, 1955, pp. 240–246.

[9] M. H. Matheson: The Hinterlands of Saint John, *Geogr. Bull.*, No. 7, Ottawa, 1955, pp. 65–102.

[10] W. A. Hance and I. S. van Dongen: The Port of Lobito and the Benguela Railway, *Geogr. Rev.*, Vol. 46, 1956, pp. 460–487.

of Northern Rhodesia .had signed an agreement for shipping all copper by way of the Rhodesia Railways to the east coast; in return the railroad had granted low freight rates for taking copper out and for bringing coal into the Copperbelt from mines it services.

It may be that no area can be claimed as the exclusive hinterland of a port except where special arrangements have been made, as in Northern Rhodesia. It can generally be assumed, however, that the ties of a hinterland with one specific port become closer as the distance from the port decreases. On the other hand, the extent of the hinterland varies with each commodity exported and imported through the port, and the geographical analysis of port traffic becomes more meaningful if totals are broken down into imports and exports, and even into individual commodities.

Thus we speak of import hinterlands as the areas of destination for goods imported through the port, and of export hinterlands as the areas where outbound shipments of the port originate. The terms "import" and "export" in this sense do not refer in any way to the foreign trade of the country in which the port is located. They refer simply to commodities arriving at the port, or moving out of the port, by sea regardless of whether its foreland is in the same country or continent.

The great range in the areal extent of import hinterlands is well illustrated by the imports of crude oil and fruits and vegetables in Bordeaux. The entire crude-oil import of Bordeaux, about 60 per cent of the import tonnage, in 1955 was discharged at the oil refineries in the Gironde Estuary, and the petroleum hinterland of Bordeaux is the port itself. Fruit and vegetable imports, on the other hand, are distributed throughout southwestern France, and occasional railroad shipments go to distribution points in all parts of the country in direct competition with other large fruit and vegetable importing ports such as Marseilles, Rouen, and Dunkirk. These other ports also have all of France as their fruit and vegetable import hinterlands, among which the urban concentrations, and especially Paris, are the most important. Marseilles markets Algerian fruit and vegetables even in Bordeaux when the prices are lower than those of the Moroccan products. The fruit and vegetable import hinterland of Bordeaux is therefore interwoven with those of other French ports, in which the details of movement depend largely on season, demand, prices, and, not least, the competitive spirit of the importers.

The export hinterland of a port can be similarly simple or complex. For example, in 1953 refined sugar exported through Hamburg originated in sugar-beet areas of Czechoslovakia and Eastern Germany. The petroleum export hinterland, however, was not only the oil-refining area of Hamburg and western Schleswig-Holstein; petroleum products also came to Hamburg for export by sea from as far as North Rhine–Westphalia and Hesse, and even from a refinery in Bremen, Hamburg's chief competitor. Although those petroleum products which originated in the Hamburg area were shipped to all parts of the world, those which came from refineries in Western Germany had their destination largely in Scandinavia, especially Denmark and Sweden. In order to find reasons for such a seemingly illogical pattern, one must analyze carefully an interrelated complex of factors.

It is evident that both "organization" and "development" of a hinterland are of great importance. The ease and rapidity of connection with the port, freight-rate structure and policy, the economic structure of the hinterland, the facilities of the port and the efficiency of its operations, the maritime organization in relation to the port and its forelands, and the forelands themselves all bear on the selection of the port or ports that are to serve as the hinterland's maritime links.

THE FORELANDS

Forelands are the land areas which lie on the seaward side of a port, beyond maritime space, and with which the port is connected by ocean carriers. The concept of "foreland," as opposed to "hinterland," can be applied to all situations provided traffic is viewed from the port. Cargo that arrives and leaves by ocean vessels comes from, or is sent to, forelands. If cargo arrives at a port and is transshipped to another ocean vessel, it has come from a foreland and leaves again for another foreland. In this case the port itself is the hinterland for the cargo—it never goes farther inland than the transit shed or warehouse in the port.

If, however, cargo is transferred from an ocean vessel to a coastal craft that cannot operate on the open seas, and is taken to another coastal port, that port must be regarded as being in the hinterland of the port where the cargo transfer was made. In the study of port geography there is no difference between this type of shipment and the transport of cargo from the seaport to an inland port by way of inland waterways. Inasmuch as most ports on or near the seashore handle both kinds of shipments, sea and coastal traffic are bound to overlap. The basic distinction between hinterland and foreland lies therefore in the type of carrier in which the merchandise arrives or leaves—coastal craft or seagoing ships.

The significance of forelands in port analysis has already been suggested. A striking illustration is offered by Iran, which, as a chief producer of crude oil in the Middle East, has been a foreland of many ports, particularly those of Europe. In Marseilles more than 9 per cent of the total import tonnage in 1950 came from Iran, most of it crude oil. In 1951 the percentage decreased to less than 5, and in 1952 and 1953 only a fraction of the port's import came from Iran, none of it crude oil. Then a recovery began, which became pronounced in 1955 (Table I). The reason for this peculiar pattern was the conflict between the Anglo-Iranian Oil Company and the Iranian government. The oil industry was nationalized in 1951, all British staff were withdrawn in the fall of that year, and exports of crude oil from Iran ceased for more than two years. The dispute was settled in 1954, the petroleum industry was reactivated in October of that year, and oil began to flow again.

The study of a foreland can be approached either in terms of the port's shipping connections as expressed by number of shipping lines, number of departures, or net tonnage moving in a certain direction, or in terms of the origin and destination of cargo moving through the port. These approaches do not necessarily yield similar results, and it is clear that net tonnage is least satisfactory. In 1955[11] more than twice as much net tonnage left Hamburg for French Mediterranean ports as for Finnish ports (respectively 603,570 and 240,712 net register tons), yet Finland received 50 times as much cargo (2784 metric tons exported from Hamburg to Mediterranean France; 141,343 metric tons to Finland). Also, to judge from the smaller number of departures to Mediterranean France (160; to Finland, 272), ships leaving Hamburg for that foreland were larger on the average than those leaving for Finland. In other words, most of the southbound ships probably used French ports merely as ports of call, delivering an insignificant amount of cargo from Hamburg, and perhaps loading additional cargo for farther destinations.

Similar relationships can be established for arrivals and imports or for the total traffic between the port and a foreland. In view of the primary function of the port, cargo tonnages are more meaningful in analyzing the port-foreland relationship than the number of departures or arrivals either of ships or of net register tonnages. A breakdown of cargo data by type (bulk, general) or nature (ore, oranges, and the like) will contribute further to comprehension of the problem.

For detailed analysis, a division of forelands is desirable. Genoa, in generalizing for its foreland traffic, uses a classification that is appropriate and

---

[11] *Handel und Schiffahrt des Hafens Hamburg 1955*, Handelsstatistisches Amt der Freien und Hansestadt Hamburg, 1956.

TABLE I—IMPORTS OF MARSEILLES AND ANNEXES FROM IRAN, 1950–1955*

(In metric tons)

IMPORTS	1950	1951	1952	1953	1954	1955
Crude oil	674,419	437,139	....	....	34,416	578,984
Other	12,219	2,359	2,255	4,184	5,681	16,100
TOTAL	686,638	439,498	2,255	4,184	40,097	595,084

*Source: *Activité Économique de la Circonscription,* Chambre de Commerce de Marseille, annuals for the years 1950 to 1955. The Annexes are the oil ports that belong to Marseilles administratively.

TABLE II—THE FORELANDS OF GENOA, 1938 AND 1955*

(In metric tons)

	1938	%	1955	%
1. Other Italian ports	1,142,822	20.1	2,292,461	21.9
2. Western Mediterranean	82,483	1.5	347,198	3.3
3. Eastern Mediterranean and Black Sea	263,985	4.7	2,313,256	22.1
4. Ports beyond Suez				
East and South Africa	89,577	1.6	239,866	2.3
Persian Gulf–India–Pakistan–Ceylon–Indonesia	171,563	3.0	931,106	8.9
Far East–Malaya–China–Japan–Philippines	46,809	0.8	139,108	1.3
Australia and New Zealand	43,387	0.8	110,302	1.1
5. Ports beyond Gibraltar				
Spain and France (Atlantic)–Portugal–				
Great Britain–Northern Europe	2,629,402	46.3	856,397	8.2
West Africa	121,953	2.1	419,321	4.0
North America (Atlantic)	577,224	10.2	2,170,784	20.8
North America (Pacific)	30,118	0.5	46,763	0.4
Central America	253,062	4.5	162,417	1.6
South America (Pacific)	40,254	0.7	69,610	0.7
South America (Atlantic)	182,025	3.2	355,719	3.4
TOTAL	5,674,664	100.0	10,454,308	100.0

* Source: *Traffic in the Port of Genoa during 1955,* Genoa Port Authority, Statistical and Traffic Promotion Office, 1956, p. 14.

useful for a port on the central section of the northern Mediterranean coast (Table II). Further refinements can be made, of course, particularly in the categories "Ports beyond Suez" and "Ports beyond Gibraltar." Table II shows a great increase in traffic from 1938 to 1955 between Genoa and the "Eastern Mediterranean and Black Sea" and "North America (Atlantic)." Also evident is a striking decrease in the ties with European ports beyond Gibraltar. It is apparent that changes in the world flow of fuels are largely the reason for Genoa's reorientation with respect to its forelands.

Other ports will devise different groupings of forelands, best suited for their traffic patterns at a particular time. For Japanese ports a division of forelands into those on the "Near Seas" and those on the "Far Seas,"[12] together with their subdivisions, was the most practical before World War II

[12] N. S. Ginsburg: Japanese Prewar Trade and Shipping in the Oriental Triangle (Dissertation, Ph.D., University of Chicago), Chicago, 1949, pp. 6–7. (Also published as *Univ. of Chicago, Dept. of Geogr., Research Paper No. 6.*)

in relation to the then prevailing trade and traffic patterns; but a reorientation of these patterns with the many postwar political and economic changes throughout Asia necessitates re-evaluation and regrouping. Still other ports may find it suitable to distinguish among national forelands, forelands on the same continent, and transoceanic forelands. Whatever classification is devised and in whatever detail, the basic concept of "foreland" remains valid and useful in port geography.

MARITIME SPACE

Between port and foreland lies maritime space. This space has been organized, not for itself, but as a reflection of economic activity in adjacent

TABLE III—TRAFFIC OF MARSEILLES AND ANNEXES THROUGH THE SUEZ CANAL, 1955*
(*In metric tons*)

FORELAND	IMPORTS	EXPORTS	TOTAL	% OF TOTAL TRAFFIC
France overseas and Indochina	313,759	276,637	590,396	3.3
Africa (east coast)	80,677	25,306	105,983	0.6
Asia	5,011,962	177,533	5,189,495	28.6
TOTAL	5,406,398	479,476	5,885,874	32.5

* Calculated from statistics of the Chambre de Commerce de Marseille in *Activité Économique de la Circonscription en 1955*, 1956.

land areas. Ships ply the waters of some parts of this space more regularly and with greater frequency than others. They thereby create a pattern of sea lanes that become avenues of traffic; these in turn attract traffic from adjacent land areas and promote economic progress. Ports on or near these avenues have an advantage over ports in "backwaters." Port competition is keenest in regions of converging sea lanes, where large expenditures for improvement of port facilities and deepening of channels can be justified by expected gains in traffic and trade; in fact, if such outlays are not made, traffic might be lost that could never be regained.

The distribution and nature of shipping lanes have been repeatedly discussed in geographic and economic literature. Suffice it to say here that oceanic ties are strongest among areas economically most advanced unless political doctrine or expediency outweighs economic considerations. Blockage of an important ocean highway has repercussions on the economic well-being of all states participating directly or indirectly in ocean traffic. The closure of the Suez Canal in 1956–1957 is an outstanding example, though it is not yet possible to make a statistical analysis of the consequences. However, we may take the port of Marseilles as an example (Table III). In 1955 more than 44 per cent of the imports of Marseilles and 8 per cent of the exports, or about one-third of the total seagoing traffic,[13] moved by way of the Suez Canal. The bulk of the imports from Asia was crude oil from the Persian Gulf producing regions. Four million tons of crude oil also came into the port from Baniyas, Tripoli, and Sidon, the three chief pipeline terminals in operation on the Levant coast. When this flow too was discontinued during the crisis, Marseilles lost 77 per cent of its imports, or more than half of its total traffic. Before the crisis France—and, in fact, all of Europe—depended on the Middle East for most of its crude oil; even the United States imported petroleum from that area. However, when this vital ocean highway was severed, the oil movements of the world had to be temporarily readjusted, and once again tankers began to move eastward from the United States, and also around the Cape of Good Hope, in an attempt to fill the fuel gap in Europe.

Improvement of sea lanes such as the Great Lakes–St. Lawrence route has far-reaching effects on the shipping and economy of land areas on these lanes. Ocean transport is expected to grow considerably[14] after completion of the St. Lawrence Seaway. Lake ports that heretofore have been chiefly inland shipping ports handling bulk cargo will have to expand port facilities to accommodate more and larger ships and to make possible efficient handling of general cargo and rapid turnarounds. New vessels will be designed to carry a possible maximum cargo tonnage within the draft limits of the enlarged seaway, and manufacturing and trade are predicted to grow in industrialized areas on the United States and Canadian shores. Even the Port of New York, which stands to lose traffic at first, hopes to gain in the long run because of the expected general upswing in economic activity.

It has been demonstrated that in port geography the human factors predominate. Ports have been founded and have evolved despite physical obstacles when economic advantage and political expedience were of overriding importance in surmounting such difficulties. In a free economy port traffic normally flows according to the best economic advantage, but in nearly all ports the political factor enters into the pattern in a varying degree. Political influence may, in fact, be so dominant that a port may be created and may flourish at the expense of a nearby port in a neighboring

---

[13] In 1955, Marseilles imported 12,181,687 metric tons and exported 5,975,163 tons, a total traffic of 18,156,850 metric tons.

[14] H. M. Mayer: Great Lakes–Overseas: An Expanding Trade Route, *Econ. Geogr.*, Vol. 30, 1954, pp. 117–143.

country on which traffic and trade for the entire region would focus were it not for political boundaries.

It is clear that ports must be studied and analyzed not as isolated phenomena but within the framework of relational patterns. A close relationship exists between port and hinterland on the one hand and port and maritime organization and foreland on the other. Effective organization and utilization of the land exert a powerful influence both on the evolution of ports and port functions and on the organization of maritime space, and the character and growth of a port play a leading role in the development and prosperity of the hinterland and maritime organization. Also, the sea lanes of maritime space have a direct bearing on the economic development of ports and land areas at each end. A change in the organization and function of any or all of these elements affects the entire structure.

TRENDS IN AIRLINE PASSENGER TRAFFIC:
A GEOGRAPHIC CASE STUDY[1]

EDWARD J. TAAFFE

Northwestern University

TO an ever-increasing extent air transportation is becoming a vital element in the complex pattern of inter-connections among large United States cities. The dynamic nature of this form of transportation in recent years is shown by the fact that between 1949 and 1955 the total number of passengers carried by the domestic trunk airlines increased 154 percent (Table 1). During the same period, air passenger-miles increased nearly 300 percent. It is also apparent from a comparison of the air and rail figures in Table 1 that a fundamental change in the nation's travel habits was in process. Air passenger-miles went from a position below the rail Pullman passenger-mile total to a position well above it during the study period.

In this study, attention will be focused on a series of maps depicting trends in the air passenger traffic of Chicago during this critical growth period. The maps will be examined for evidence of a relation between growth rates and possible growth-promoting characteristics of individual routes, such as resort travel, length of haul, and low coach fares. The implications of these and certain less obvious relations will then be discussed in the context of over-all air traffic trends. In its relation to geography, the study represents an example of

the functional or organizational approach to regional study as articulated initially by Platt and later by Whittlesey.[2] Air travel provides a partial expression of the linkages between Chicago and other cities which are, in turn, an aspect of the over-all spatial organization of the United States. A consideration of differential growth rates should therefore provide some insight into the changing nature of these linkages.

THE MAPS

Figure 1 is the map upon which most of this report is based. It illustrates the specific question to be examined: What has been associated with the variation in growth rate of Chicago air traffic from March 1949 to March 1955 among the 91 cities of Chicago's air passenger hinterland?[3] The area of each circle on Figure

---

[2] One of the earlier statements of this approach is contained in Robert S. Platt, "A Detail of Regional Geography: Ellison Bay Community as an Industrial Organism," *Annals*, Association of American Geographers, Vol. XVIII (1928), pp. 81–126. Derwent Whittlesey attached the term "nodal" to this approach in "The Regional Concept and the Regional Method" in Preston E. James and Clarence F. Jones, *American Geography: Inventory and Prospect* (Syracuse University Press, 1954), pp. 36–40. Some of the more explicit examples are to be found in the works of Ullman, Brush, Philbrick, and Hans Carol. It could also be said that recent work in central place theory represents an extension of this point of view.

[3] March 1949 was chosen as a base period for two reasons: (1) the author had previously conducted a detailed investigation of Chicago's traffic characteristics as represented by that month; (2) 1949 was the year before the Korean War and the initiation of low-fare coach services accompanied a great upsurge in air travel. March 1955 was the last survey period before the addition of competition to certain important routes further complicated the growth pattern. The maps are based on the two-way traffic data in Civil Aeronautics Board, *Airline Traffic Survey* (U.S. Government Printing Office. Washington, D.C.), and Air Transport Association, *Origination–Destination Airline Revenue Passenger Survey* (Airline Finance and Accounting Conference, Washington, D.C.). The fourteen-day passenger totals in the latter source were expanded by a factor of 2.21 to make them comparable to the 31-day totals in the former source. Most of the city abbreviations used are from the 3-letter airline code as listed in the *Official Airline Guide*.

TABLE 1.—SELECTED AIR AND RAIL STATISTICS FOR THE UNITED STATES, 1949 AND 1955 (IN THOUSANDS)[1]

Travel item	1949	1955	Percentage change
Air passengers	14,699	37,408	+ 154
Air passenger-miles	6,705,000	19,741,000	+ 293
Rail pullman passenger-miles	9,349,000	6,440,000	− 31
Rail coach passenger-miles	20,310,000	17,329,000	− 15

[1] Air Transport Association, *Air Transport Facts and Figures,* 1959. Figures refer to United States domestic trunkline and local service carriers only.

---

[1] The author wishes to thank the Transportation Center at Northwestern University for research funds and assistance. Mr. Frank H. Thomas and Mr. John T. Hoare, graduate students in geography, provided valuable assistance in computational and cartographic work, respectively.

"Trends in Airline Passenger Traffic: A Geographic Case Study" by Edward J. Taaffe. Reprinted from ANNALS — *Association of American Geographers*, Vol. 49 *(December* 1959), *pp.* 393–408, *with permission of the Association of American Geographers.*

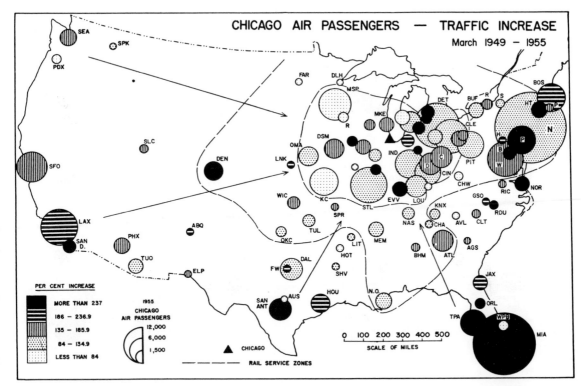

FIG. 1.   Chicago air passenger traffic increase, March 1949 compared with March 1955.

1 is proportional to the number of air passengers travelling in both directions between Chicago and the city represented by the circle in March 1955. Thus, each circle represents a route between Chicago and the city in question. The shaded patterns within the circles are graded in intensity according to the percentage increase in Chicago air traffic between March 1949 and March 1955. The vertical line pattern is centered approximately on the average growth rate of 156 percent for the Chicago routes represented on the map. The darker patterns represent clearly above-average growth rates and the lighter patterns represent clearly below-average growth rates.

In order to reduce the possible distortions inherent in such restricted time periods as the two survey months, several types of additional data were checked for some of the measures employed. Figure 2 represents one such secondary basis for the consideration of variations in air traffic growth rates. The 99 highest density routes or city pairs in the United States are represented on the four inset maps.[4]

[4] The degree of concentration of air traffic is such that 87 of the 99 leading city pairs had as one terminal

These insets differ from the Chicago map in the following respects: the areas of the circles represent passenger-miles rather than passengers; the circles are categorized into three magnitude groups rather than graduated; March and September figures are used rather than March figures.

Other supplementary sources of growth information consulted regarding conclusions drawn from Figure 1 included growth rates between other selected years, and the percentage of Chicago's traffic accounted for by each city during various survey periods.

one of four major centers (New York, Chicago, Los Angeles, and Miami). These city pairs could then be represented on four inset maps in a manner analogous to the Chicago traffic on Figure 1. The twelve remaining city pairs are represented by squares. On the Chicago inset, the squares represent Washington traffic; on the Los Angeles inset, they represent San Francisco traffic; and on the Miami map they represent Tampa traffic. For a thorough discussion of this map and the 99 city pairs, see Edward J. Taaffe, "A Map Analysis of Airline Competition: Part I—The Development of Competition," *Journal of Air Law and Commerce*, Vol. 25, No. 2 (Spring, 1958), pp. 121-47; "Part II—Competition and Growth," *Journal of Air Law and Commerce*, Vol. 25, No. 4 (Autumn, 1958), pp. 402-27.

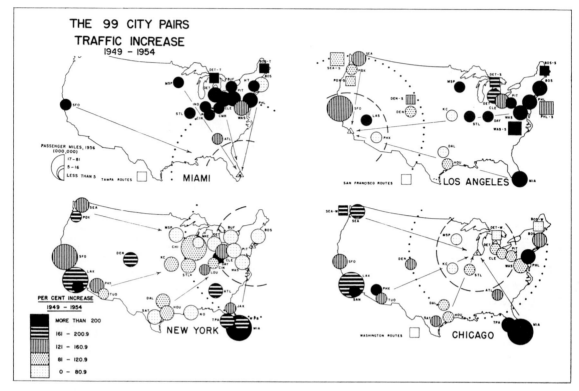

F<small>IG</small>. 2 Traffic increase, by passenger miles, for four major centers of 99 leading city pairs in air traffic, March and September 1949 and 1954.

The major portion of this paper will consist of the examination of several hypotheses as to reasons for the growth rate variations shown on Figure 1. This examination will consist of: (1) a discussion of the high growth rates noted at winter resort and long-haul cities; (2) a discussion of the impact of low coach fares on growth; (3) a discussion of apparently secondary growth characteristics, such as those associated with the high growth rates at many small-volume, short-haul cities and at many traffic shadow cities; (4) a discussion of the future prospects of air transportation in the light of the evidence presented on the various maps.

FLORIDA RESORT TRAVEL AND LENGTH OF HAUL

Many of the high Chicago growth rates on Figure 1 are at resort cities and long-haul cities. The concentration of high growth rates on the Chicago–Florida routes is particularly striking. Chicago–Miami traffic, for example, increased by nearly 400 percent between March 1949 and March 1955 as compared to

an increase in total Chicago air traffic of only 149 percent. The five Florida cities on Figure 1 increased their share of Chicago's total air passenger traffic from eight percent in March 1949 to 13 percent in March 1955. Figure 2 provides additional evidence of the widespread nature of this change. Most of the circles on the Miami map fall into the highest growth category as do many of the Florida circles on the other three inset maps. The magnitude and consistent nature of these increases indicate that a basic change in the nation's travel habits is in process. Many people who formerly took brief vacations a few hours' drive from the largest metropolitan areas now travel by air to Florida. The growth rates of the Chicago–Florida traffic are so markedly above the Chicago average that it seems reasonable to assume that the growth curve for Florida traffic differs from the growth curve for other Chicago air traffic. The Florida routes have therefore been excluded from most of the measures employed so as to provide a clearer view of growth rate variation other than that associated with this conspicuous change in recreational travel habits.[5]

The relation between rate of growth and length of haul is a considerably more elusive one. In view of the increase in average length of haul, one might expect a tendency for growth rates to vary directly with distance from Chicago. As Figure 1 indicates, however, the over-all tendency for growth rates to increase with distance is a weak one. The correlation is statistically insignificant if one considers *all* Chicago routes (with the cited exceptions). The principal disturbances are the high growth rates of many small-volume, short-haul routes (small circles close to Chicago). Saginaw–Bay City, Michigan, provides an extreme example of this with a 739 percent increase in Chicago traffic.[6] When the group considered is restricted to the 35 cities which generated enough traffic to warrant coach service in 1955, the relationship improves but is still weak. Approximately seven percent of the growth rate variation is statistically associated with length of haul.[7] The chief sources of disturbance in these instances are the small-volume, long-haul routes, which did not participate in the intensive growth of the large-volume, long-haul routes. This is apparently due to some variation on the traffic shadow

theme, as in the case of Spokane, Portland, and Birmingham.[8]

If the routes considered are restricted to the 30 leading passenger generators, the small-volume, long-haul cities also drop out, and some 30 percent of the growth-rate variation is seen to be associated with length of haul. A similar although weaker relationship (16 percent) is obtained when the 99 leading passenger-mile generators in Figure 2 are considered (with the exception of the Florida pairs). This is evident visually from the noticeable tendency for the darker patterns to predominate on each inset map in Figure 2 as distance increases from the city concerned. This tendency is emphasized by the curved lines on the map which represent the 500- and the 1,000-mile zones. The dotted lines representing the 1,000-mile zone serve as a rough boundary between the high and low growth rates. Thus, a relation between length of haul and rate of growth does seem to exist, at least on the large-volume routes.

This relation between growth and length of haul might also be examined as it is expressed in two important types of rail service. The outer dashed line on Figure 1 represents the limits of rail overnight service from Chicago; the inner dashed line represents the limits within which rail coach service from Chicago is most competitive with air service.[9] Although visual inspection reveals no well-delineated drop-off in growth rates at the margin of the overnight zone, there does seem to be a concentration of low increases among the large-volume routes within the rail coach zone. Table 2 lists the proportion of total Chicago

---

[5] Also excluded from most measures are the military travel centers of San Diego and Norfolk as well as Dayton, where heavy military air travel to and from Wright Field has a distorting effect.

[6] In some respects it is misleading to compare the high percentage increases of many of the small-volume routes (the smaller circles) with those of high density routes. Percentage increases among items of widely differing magnitudes may be deceptive. It should be noted, however, that not all the low density routes had high percentage increases. Many long-haul, low-density routes experienced below-average growth rates.

[7] Some caution must be exercised in interpreting the results of the statistical analysis in this paper. Certain biases introduced by the exclusion of data and certain defects in the data used render questionable the extrapolation of the computed relations. What inferences there may be regarding larger populations must be justified logically rather than statistically. The coefficient of determination (r^2) or percent of "explained" variation used above is derived from a least squares regression analysis in which rate of growth is treated as a dependent variable and length of haul is treated as an independent variable. It should be regarded as a measure of the closeness of an observed relation between two variables, useful for fundamentally descriptive and comparative purposes.

[8] The traffic shadow effect in air transportation exists when the largest city in a cluster of cities acts as a receiving center for traffic to other cities in the cluster, thereby depressing their air traffic levels. This effect is most noticeable within a range of 120 highway miles from the largest center. As the distribution of cities becomes less dense, however, the range of the shadow seems to increase. It is possible, therefore, that Seattle's presence depresses the traffic levels of Portland and Spokane, and that Atlanta depresses the traffic of Birmingham. See Edward J. Taaffe, "United States Air Transportation and Urban Distribution," *The Geographical Review*, Vol. XLVI (April, 1956), pp. 219–38.

[9] Rail overnight service was defined as service which is within one hour of a 4:30 p.m. departure and a 10:00 a.m. arrival; coach service was defined as a departure after 8:00 a.m. and an arrival before midnight with a trip duration not in excess of 8 hours.

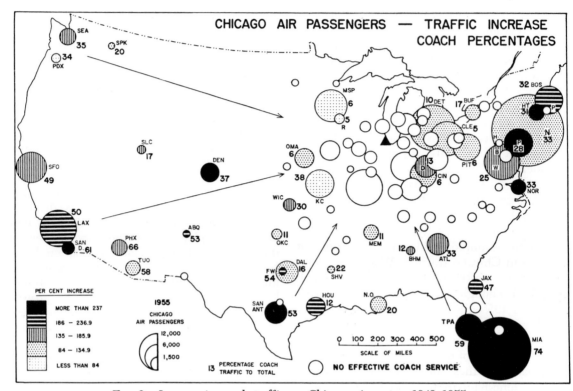

FIG. 3. Increase in coach traffic on Chicago air routes, 1949–1955.

TABLE 2.—PERCENTAGE OF TOTAL CHICAGO
AIR TRAFFIC BY RAIL SERVICE ZONES

Rail service zone	Percent of total traffic		Percentage change
	1949	1955	
Within coach zone	43	34	− 9
Between coach and overnight zones	29	27	− 2
Beyond overnight zone	28	39	+ 11

passengers accounted for in 1949 and 1955 by the cities in these zones. Note how the rail coach-zone cities decreased in their share of total Chicago passengers from 43 percent in 1949 to 34 percent in 1955.

AIRLINE PRICE GEOGRAPHY

Another possible growth-promoting factor is to be found in the offering of coach services by the airlines. These low-fare services, considered by some to be the major factor in the recent boom in air traffic, developed rapidly during the early fifties until, by 1955, they accounted for 35 percent of total passenger-miles.[10] Initially, air coach services were set

up at inconvenient hours (between 11 p.m. and 4 a.m., for instance) so as to encourage traffic on mail-oriented schedules which usually carried few passengers. They proved so popular that competitive pressure soon forced them up to convenient hours. Coach offerings over individual routes still vary widely, however, both in total flights scheduled and in number of convenient-hour coach flights. These variations are reflected in Figure 3. Growth-rate categories and circle sizes are identical with Figure 1, but the large numbers next to each circle represent the percentage of coach passengers over the particular route in March 1955. Thus, fully 74 percent of the Chicago–Miami passengers used coach services as compared with only 6 percent of the Chicago–Minneapolis passengers. The many blank circles on the map represent Chicago routes without effective[11] coach services in March 1955. Coach services are largely absent from small-volume routes and short-haul routes; they are particularly prominent on

[10] *American Aviation*, Annual Air Transport Progress Issue, April 23, 1956, p. 28.

[11] Effective coach service is considered to exist only if five percent or more of the passengers over a given route are coach passengers.

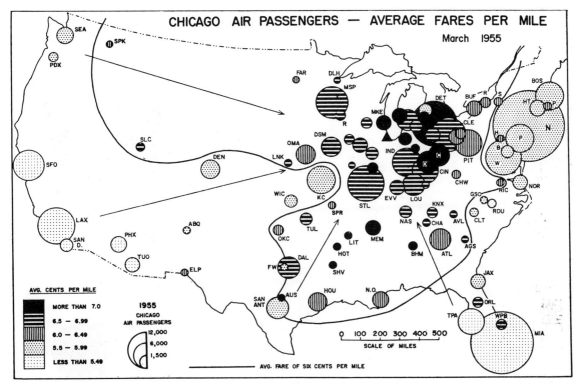

FIG. 4. Average fares per mile for Chicago air routes, March 1955.

large-volume routes, long-haul routes, and resort routes. In general, growth rates tend to increase as coach percentages increase. About 17 percent of the growth rate variation among the 35 non-Florida coach cities is statistically associated with coach percentages.

The apparent relationship between growth and the amount of effective coach service is complicated, however, by the fact that it is extremely difficult to separate coach and length-of-haul effects. Although, on Figure 3, high growth rates seem to bear a closer relation to coach percentages than they do to distance, this relationship is reversed in the case of the 99 leading city pairs (Fig. 2), where the relation between growth and length of haul is considerably closer than that between growth and coach services. In both cases, however, about 20 percent of the growth-rate variation is statistically associated with length of haul and coach percentage when the effects of both are considered simultaneously.

Another effect of the relationship between distance and coach percentages is to be found in the spatial structure of airline fares. Since coach percentages increase with distance, the

average fare decreases with distance. In order to construct Figure 4, an average fare was computed for each hinterland city by weighting first-class and coach fares with the actual percentages of first-class and coach passengers. The resulting average fare was then divided by the length of haul so as to give an average per-mile fare. Since low average per-mile fares are due chiefly to large coach percentages, this map is merely a way of portraying the air fare tendencies noted on Figure 3 for the coach cities in the map context of the average fares for the noncoach cities.[12] Thus, despite the fact that there are only two fare levels (approximately 6.5 cents per mile for first-class, four cents per mile for coach), it is clear from Figure 4 that the selective application of coach services by the airline has resulted in a fare structure which shows a reasonably consistent taper with distance. The

[12] Other factors contributing to variations from uniform per-mile fares are the grouping of fares and the flat $1.00 increase added to all airline tickets between 1949 and 1955. This latter would have a greater upward effect on short-haul routes than on long-haul routes, as witness the many cities near Chicago with an average fare of seven cents per mile.

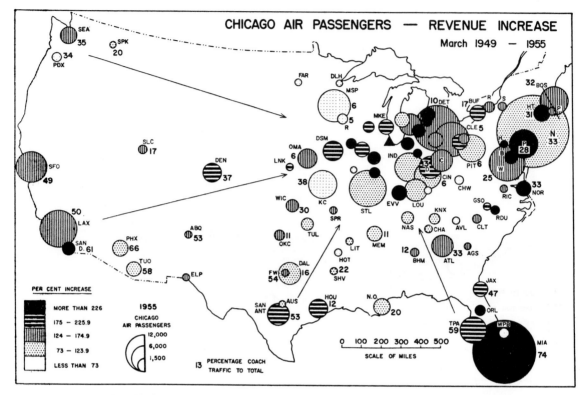

FIG. 5.   Total revenue increases for Chicago air routes, March 1949 to March 1955.

black line on the map represents an approximate isopleth for an average fare of six cents per mile.[13] Within this line nearly all average fares are greater than six cents per mile; beyond it nearly all average fares are less than six cents per mile. The selectivity of the taper is associated with the tendency for effective coach services to be concentrated on large-volume routes (note how Denver and Kansas City pull in the six-cent line, and how Omaha and Atlanta have low average fares for their distance zone). The taper in per-mile fares with distance is, of course, economically logical. Per-mile costs of carrying passengers tend to decrease with distance in view of relatively fixed terminal costs.

In a sense, Figure 4 represents price change. Since there were few coach services offered on Chicago routes in 1949, it may be assumed that 1949 per-mile fares were relatively uniform. Thus, it might be considered that the low average per-mile fares in Figure 4 represent a sort of decrease in average fare. The relation-

ship between such "lowered" price and traffic increases is a difficult one to evaluate. If the traffic is quite sensitive to price changes, then one might expect the routes with the lowest average per-mile fares ("reduced" from 1949 averages) to register the highest growth rates. The visual impression of a weak relationship which may be obtained by comparing the per-mile fare map (Fig. 4) with the growth map (Fig. 1) is supported by a statistically insignificant relationship.

Thus, there is conflicting evidence as to the price sensitivity of air travel. The relation between growth and coach percentages for the 35 coach cities noted on Figure 3 suggests price sensitivity; the lack of relation between growth and average per-mile fares noted on Figure 4 suggests an insensitivity to price. In order to examine price effects more critically, it is useful to refer to the economic concept of elasticity of demand. The demand for air travel over a given route is considered elastic if a given decrease in price is accompanied by a proportionately greater increase in traffic. The net result of this will be an increase in

[13] The isoline of six cents per mile was chosen arbitrarily so as to emphasize the decline of average fares with distance.

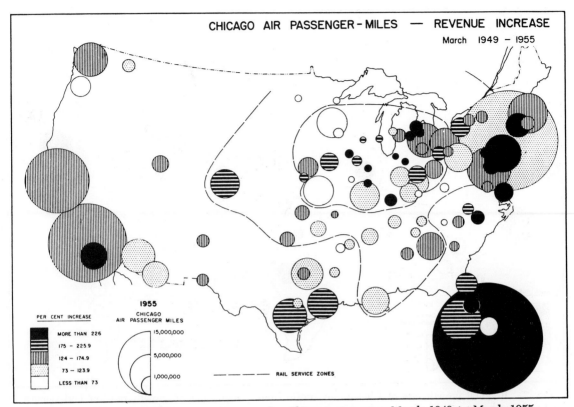

CHICAGO AIR PASSENGER-MILES — REVENUE INCREASE
March 1949 — 1955

PER CENT INCREASE

MORE THAN 226
175 — 225.9
124 — 174.9
73 — 123.9
LESS THAN 73

1955
CHICAGO
AIR PASSENGER MILES

15,000,000
5,000,000
1,000,000

RAIL SERVICE ZONES

FIG. 6.   Passenger-mile revenue increases for Chicago air routes, March 1949 to March 1955.

total revenue. If the traffic increases were proportionately less than the price decrease, the total revenue would decline. In order to examine relationships between any possible price sensitivity and price-elasticity of demand, therefore, it is helpful to consider differential changes in total revenue over individual routes.

Figure 5 presents the increases in total revenue among Chicago's hinterland cities. Nearly all instances of "lowered" fares (high coach percentages) are seen to have accompanied revenue increases. It is obvious that these increases cannot be attributed to an essentially elastic demand for air travel since virtually all other routes also increased in response to an apparent change in national travel habits. It is possible, however, to examine Figure 5 for evidence of a *relatively* elastic demand for air travel in the form of a consistent relationship between high coach percentages and above-average revenue increases. Initial inspection of the map reveals little consistency in this relationship. Many of the

cities with little or no effective coach services showed average or above-average increases in Chicago revenue; many cities with much effective coach service experienced below-average increases in Chicago revenue.

The above-average increases and the high coach percentages at the Florida resorts provide some initial evidence that the demand for resort travel might be relatively price-elastic. Further investigation of Miami traffic with other centers was carried on, however, and it was observed that the high rate of growth of Miami traffic seemed to vary independently of the percentage of coach traffic. Thus, it is the high general rate of growth in Florida travel rather than the high coach percentage which seems to be closely associated with the high Florida growth rates noted on Figure 1. Similarly, it is not justifiable to point to other individual instances of high revenue growth rates accompanying high coach percentages (or the converse) and attribute them to an essentially elastic demand for Chicago air travel to that particular city. Only if the entire map were to provide evidence of an over-all consistency of

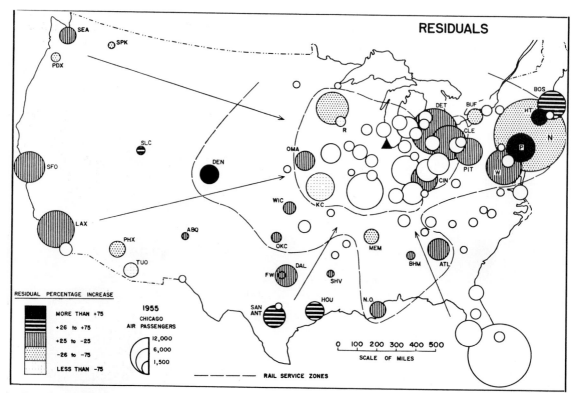

FIG. 7. Residual growth rate of Chicago air traffic from a regression of growth rate on both length of haul and coach percentage. See text fn. 17.

relationship would such a premise warrant further investigation.[14]

There is some suggestion on Figure 5 of a relatively inelastic demand for short-haul air travel. Despite slight fare increases and the general absence of effective low-fare services at such cities as Detroit, Cleveland, and Columbus (as well as numerous small-volume, short-haul cities), they experienced revenue increases comparable to those at such large-volume, long-haul cities as Los Angeles and San Francisco.

A final aspect of airline price geography is illustrated by Figure 6. The shading represents revenue-increase categories just as on

Figure 5, but the city circles are graduated according to passenger-miles rather than passengers. Since passenger-miles are roughly proportionate to revenue, this map provides a more realistic perspective from which to view the revenue percentage increases. Despite the very high percentage increases of the small-volume,[15] short-haul routes within the rail coach zone, their absolute magnitude is seen to be negligible. Although they nearly doubled their share of Chicago's traffic during the study period, they accounted for only two per-cent of the total revenue in March 1955. Conversely the high percentage increases of the Florida resorts are considerably more impressive in view of the large revenue totals involved. Florida traffic increased from 15 percent of Chicago's total revenue in March 1949 to 21 percent in March 1955.

OTHER FACTORS IN GROWTH OF AIR ROUTES

Both statistically and cartographically, it is clear that there is much variation on the

[14] The Florida case should serve to underline the fact that this section does not constitute an attempt to analyze the price elasticity of demand for air travel. The isolation of the price effect from such important determinants of demand as income, prices of substitutes, etc., is obviously a task for an economist. Consideration of this economic concept, however, does sharpen the description of some of the tendencies noted on the coach-service maps, and points up the importance of considering changes in total revenue provided by individual Chicago routes.

[15] Small in this instance is defined as fewer passengers than those on the Toledo route (901).

growth rate map which is not associated with variations in length of haul or variations in the pricing of airline services. Judging from the results of the regression analysis in which growth rate was treated as a dependent variable and both length of haul and coach percentage were treated as independent variables, more than three-fourths of the variation in non-Florida growth rates on both Figure 1 and Figure 2 remains statistically unexplained.[16] As a first step in detecting some of the many remaining factors associated with the growth of specific routes, this residual variation has been plotted on Figure 7 for the 35 coach cities.[17] The line pattern is centered on the regression line. The light patterns are clearly below the line; the black patterns are clearly above the line. Thus, the black pattern at Philadelphia indicates that Philadelphia–Chicago traffic increased more rapidly than would be expected from the average relation between rate of growth, on the one hand, and both length of haul and amount of effective coach service, on the other. The light shading at Minneapolis represents a rate of growth which is less than would be expected from length of haul and coach percentage. Examination of the residuals on Figure 7 should therefore stimulate speculation as to possible less obvious growth characteristics, those not associated with long-haul or low-fare routes. For the cities without Chicago coach services, Figure 5, the revenue increase map, should serve

a similar purpose in suggesting additional growth factors.

One interesting feature of Figure 7 is the tendency for such Eastern Seaboard traffic-shadow cities as Boston, Hartford, and Philadelphia to register high residual growth rates. Two other traffic-shadow cities without Chicago coach services, Providence and Baltimore, also recorded high growth rates on Figure 5. To a considerable extent these are associated with improved services scheduled in 1955 but not in 1949. This association, in turn, may reflect a tendency for direct Chicago air linkages to be expanded to the secondary centers after an initial phase of disproportionate concentration on the very largest centers, such as New York. Traffic shadow in general, however, is still noticeable on the map. Although the Eastern Seaboard traffic-shadow cities experienced a slight increase in their share both of Chicago's total traffic and of total revenue from 1949 to 1955, the other traffic-shadow cities[18] experienced a slight decline in these respects.

There is also some weak evidence on Figure 7 that the large-volume, short-haul routes east of Chicago have higher residual growth rates than do those west of Chicago (see Detroit, Cleveland, Pittsburgh, and Cincinnati as compared with Minneapolis and Kansas City). In part, this is related to the generally increased importance of long-haul flights, which in turn may be associated with the decreased importance of regional ties in the generation of air traffic. Comparative Chicago and New York growth rates, plotted on work maps, lend some support to this generalization. For the western group of cities, low Chicago growth rates were matched by high New York rates; for the eastern group, low New York growth rates were matched by high Chicago rates. Minor fluctuations in the fortunes of individual airlines also seem to be reflected in the map of residual variations. High growth rates at such cities as Denver and Salt Lake City may be associated with the presence of United Air Lines, which recorded relatively low traffic levels at these points in 1949. It is also possible that the unusually low growth rates at Minneapolis and Kansas City may be associated with difficulties experienced by Northwest and TWA,

---

[16] It is probable that some of this residual variation is associated with such haphazard factors as bad weather, conventions, strikes, etc. In the absence of precedents, it is difficult to evaluate the apparently low r^2 figure of 20 percent since cross-section analyses of growth rates on individual routes based on two-week periods might be expected to be quite erratic.

[17] The mapping of regression residuals in terms of point symbols is analogous to the same procedure in terms of areally more continuous phenomena as discussed in Arthur H. Robinson and Reid A. Bryson, "A Method for Describing Quantitatively the Correspondence of Geographical Distributions," *Annals*, Association of American Geographers, Vol. XLVII (1957), pp. 379–91. Strictly speaking, these are residuals from the least squares line (or plane) of best fit to a formulation in which rate of growth is treated as a dependent variable, and both length of haul and coach percentage are treated as independent variables. In this study, the mapping of residuals is regarded as a descriptive device whereby the departures from a weak general relationship may be examined on a map for purposes of suggesting additional relationships.

[18] Using the previously cited criterion of a larger standard metropolitan area within 120 highway miles.

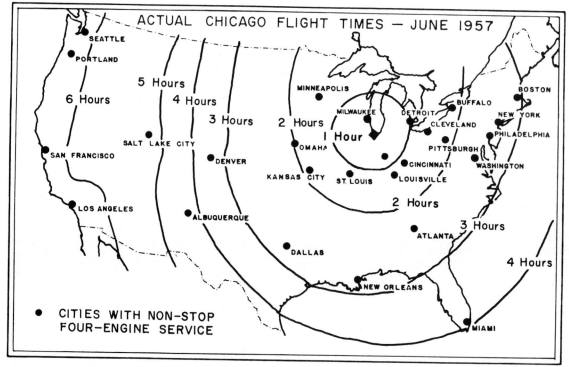

Fɪɢ. 8. Actual Chicago flight times with piston-engine aircraft, June 1957.

respectively, rather than with an east–west differential.[19]

On the revenue-increase map, another group of cities seemed to have experienced increases in Chicago traffic despite apparently unfavorable length-of-haul and coach-fare conditions. These are the short-haul, small-volume cities referred to previously. Although the revenue accounted for by these cities was negligible (Fig. 6), the total did increase somewhat, and there were a number of impressive individual growth rates among them. As is shown on Figure 1, the distribution of high growth rates among the inner-zone cities was quite erratic. Such cities as Saginaw-Bay City, Evansville, and Fort Wayne experienced particularly great growth, while cities such as Peoria, Grand Rapids, and Muskegon experienced below-average growth. Meager evidence suggests the presence of branch plants of large corporations as one possible traffic generating factor. The fact that Saginaw–Bay City has

unusually poor Chicago rail service suggests still another (note its position with respect to the rail coach zone on Figure 1).

FUTURE PROSPECTS

Any consideration of the implications of the traffic maps for the future development of air travel must be preceded by a consideration of probable future pricing and technological change within the airline industry as well as the over-all size of the travel market. A continuation of fare decreases comparable to those associated with the initiation of coach services is quite unlikely. It is more likely, in fact, that there will be fare increases.[20] In terms of improved services, however, the widespread introduction of domestic jet services will have a pronounced technological impact on travel time, as is shown on Figures 8 and 9. The isochrones in Figure 8 represent airport-to-airport flight time from Chicago to all cities with four-engine, non-stop services in 1957. On Figure 9, the isochrones are drawn

---

[19] Northwest Airlines, which is particularly prominent at Minneapolis, experienced a great deal of equipment difficulty during the study period; TWA, which is prominent at Kansas City, had management and administrative difficulty.

[20] In recent years, the airlines have been requesting permission from the Civil Aeronautics Board to increase fares. The Board's general passenger fare investigation is an outgrowth of these requests.

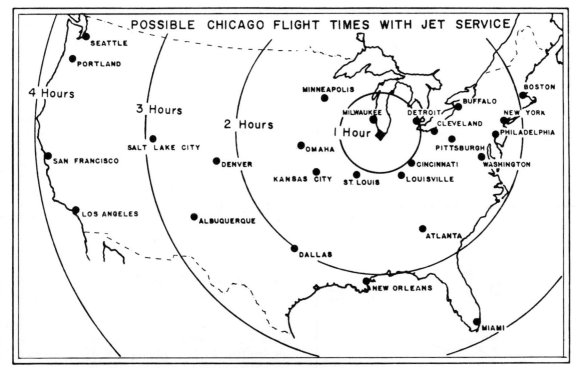

Fig. 9. Possible Chicago flight times with jet service.

for estimated jet flight times to the same cities.[21] Obviously the time or technological friction of distance will be reduced to a position of minor significance. California flights will consume between three and four hours as compared to six hours with piston-engine aircraft.

Faster, more comfortable service, however, is not necessarily a guarantee of a continuation of the rapid growth noted in the 1949–1955 period. The growth implications of the traffic maps must be evaluated against the over-all size of the United States travel market.[22] As shown on Figure 10, total passenger-miles per capita for the entire country have shown a steady increase. Much of this, however, has been due to an increase in private automobile passenger-miles per capita, and common-carrier passenger-miles per capita have actually declined somewhat. Thus, much of the airlines' increase must have been associated with the railroads' decrease. It would seem from Figure 10 as well as from the high growth rates of the long-haul routes (Figures 1 and 2) that the process of penetration of the rail first-class market does not have much further to go. To a considerable degree, therefore, continued rapid growth in air travel must be associated with induced common-carrier traffic. This may consist of traffic which now does not exist, or traffic which is now dominated by the private automobile. It is for evidence of possible sources of new travel, therefore, that we now consider the implications of the traffic maps.

[21] It is interesting to note that the greater speed of the jet has no appreciable effect on travel time within the one-hour zone. This is due to the relatively fixed time losses involved in taxiing, takeoff and landing, and the flying time necessary to attain airspeeds greater than those of piston-engine aircraft. Figure 9, the jet map, is based on generally conservative figures for 575 m.p.h. jet aircraft including a figure of 18 minutes for airport time and block speeds which increase with stage length as contained in Lord Douglas of Kirtleside, "The Economics of Speed," *The Journal of the Institute of Transport*, Vol. 27 (May, 1957), pp. 115–34. No headwinds or tailwinds are included in these estimates so that actual schedules will differ from the isochrones. Figure 8 was based on schedules for July 1957, as published in the *Official Airline Guide*.

[22] For some recent expressions of airline industry concern over this problem, see "Watch the Highways," *American Aviation*, October 6, 1958, p. 7, and "Things Won't Be the Same by 1962," *American Aviation*, September 22, 1958, p. 7.

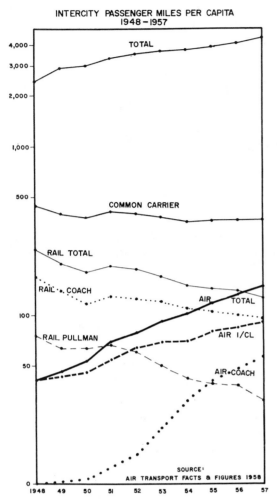

INTERCITY PASSENGER MILES PER CAPITA
1948–1957

FIG. 10. United States intercity passenger-miles per capita, 1948–1957.

First, increased common-carrier travel might result from the fact that linkages are becoming increasingly tight among the very largest centers irrespective of distance. In particular, California traffic to Chicago and other large centers of the American Manufacturing Belt seems to be increasing more rapidly than would be expected merely from continued penetration of the long-haul rail passenger market (Figures 1 and 2), partly because of population shifts. This type of traffic should also derive the most benefit from the initiation of jet services as discussed above. The high growth rates at the Eastern Seaboard traffic shadow cities may be another indication of intensified interaction between the largest centers. It is probable that some of this traffic

could be considered as having been induced. Most Chicago–Eastern Seaboard travel is business travel, and studies have indicated that a remarkably large percentage of such traffic comes from the repeat traveler.[23] The cumulative time penalties associated with repeat surface travel provide evidence that this is probably another respect in which air transportation has altered the nation's travel habits. Here too, the jets's advantages may bring about further changes in travel and business habits. The same small group of executives might be able to carry on an increasingly large share of their activities in the form of personal contacts, meetings, etc.

A second possible source of induced travel is the short-haul market, now dominated by the private automobile. Some idea of the potential size of this market may be obtained from an examination of Figure 11, on which city circles are graded in size according to Chicago phone calls.[24] Phone calls are an evidence of linkages between cities just as is air traffic. In fact, phone call data are used by airline research departments in attempts to estimate expected traffic between any two points. In a sense, therefore, this map represents a relative potential of each city as a market for Chicago air travel. With the availability of fast, convenient air travel, individuals will more and more frequently find themselves choosing between a plane trip and a long-distance phone call. The huge potential for travel within the zone of rail coach service is evident from the map as are the generally low ratios between Chicago passengers and Chicago phone calls. Such cities as Indianapolis and Moline had approximately one Chicago air passenger for every 20 Chicago phone calls as compared to an over-all average of one air passenger for every ten phone calls and a

[23] Port of New York Authority, *New York's Air Travelers*, Eno Foundation for Highway Traffic Control (Saugatuck, Connecticut: 1956), p. 49.

[24] The phone call data were compiled by the Illinois Bell Telephone Company. Among possible weaknesses in the data are the following: (1) 1956 phone-call figures were used as compared with 1955 air passenger figures; (2) no attempt was made to delimit and equate the differing air-passenger and phone-call tributary areas of the 91 cities; (3) the phone-call data were available only on a sent-paid and received-collect basis for a 10-day period (excluding Saturday and Sunday) and therefore had to be expanded to approximate monthly two-way figures.

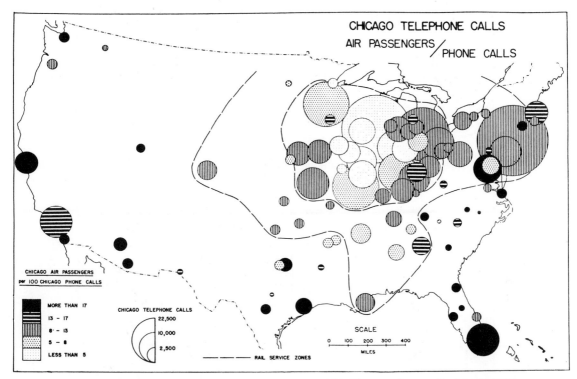

CHICAGO TELEPHONE CALLS

AIR PASSENGERS/PHONE CALLS

CHICAGO AIR PASSENGERS
per 100 CHICAGO PHONE CALLS

MORE THAN 17
13 - 17
8 - 13
5 - 8
LESS THAN 5

CHICAGO TELEPHONE CALLS
22,500
10,000
2,500

SCALE
0   100   200   300   400
MILES

RAIL SERVICE ZONES

FIG. 11.   Number of Chicago air passengers per 100 Chicago phone calls, March 1955.

California figure of one air passenger for every five Chicago phone calls. The airlines' failure to exploit the short-haul market is, of course, associated with the superiority of private auto, bus, and rail transportation within the zone of rail coach service. Prospects for increased penetration of the huge travel potential within this zone will not be aided greatly by jet aircraft. The comparative time saving is of negligible absolute magnitude, and the jet is not economically suitable for short-haul operations. Development of economical helicopter service would have far more impact on short-haul, large-volume routes. Nonetheless, there is evidence on the maps that the airlines may have had some success in diverting traffic from the private automobile within this zone. For example, fairly high ratios at certain large volume cities, such as Detroit and Cleveland, may be another indication of the importance of the repeat business traveller. High growth rates at some of the small centers within the rail coach zone (Fig. 1) provide another indication that some diversion may be in process, although passenger totals and phone-call ratios are still quite low.[25]

Finally, induced air travel could result from a continued increase of recreation travel. One of the most striking developments of the 1949–1955 period was the growth of the Florida resort traffic not only with Chicago but with the other large Manufacturing Belt centers (Figures 1 and 2). As discussed earlier, air transportation has apparently helped alter United States travel habits in this respect. Jet service, however, will probably have a greater impact on international than on domestic recreation travel. Figures 12 and 13 show the contrast between present schedules and estimated jet schedules. On the 1957 map, most of Africa and Asia is beyond the 24-hour zone.[26] Only the Caribbean centers fall within the ten-hour zone. On the jet map, the ten-

[25] It is also possible that the airlines will reduce losses on these uneconomic routes by raising fares, in view of the apparent insensitivity of short-haul traffic to price increases.

[26] Schedule and coach fare figures are from the *Official Airline Guide*, July, 1957. Traffic figures are from Air Transport Association, *op. cit*. They refer only to passengers ticketed through from Chicago to a foreign destination via an American flag air carrier. The jet isochrones include a one-hour stopover every five hours.

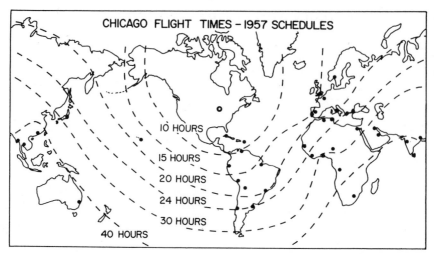

FIG. 12.   Actual Chicago international flight times, July 1957.

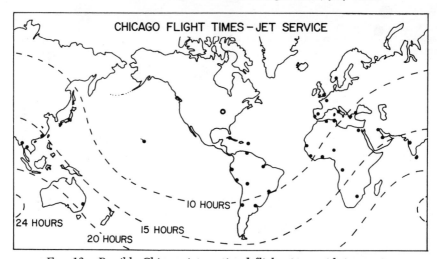

FIG. 13.   Possible Chicago international flight times with jet service.

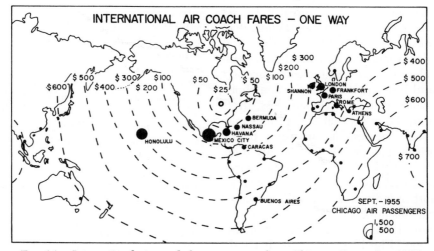

FIG. 14.   International air coach fares, one-way from Chicago, September 1955.

hour zone has expanded to include Western Europe, the Western Mediterranean, much of South America, and Hawaii. Most of the world will be within 24-hours' flight of Chicago.

On the basis of these maps, and in the light of air transportation's impact on domestic recreation travel, one might expect a virtual explosion of international recreation traffic. As is illustrated by Figure 14, however, there remains an appreciable cost-friction of distance. Note how the circles indicating Chicago passenger generation are clustered in the Caribbean, inside the $100 line for one-way coach fares. The absolute amounts involved are substantial enough to constitute a serious problem to the two-week vacationers who must necessarily form the majority of the much-discussed mass market for international recreation travel. Prospects of international fare reductions are problematic. On the negative side are such factors as the dubious operating economies of jet aircraft and the rigidities of international fare agreements. On the positive side are the recent development of a third and lower level of international fares and the tapering fare structure noted on the map of average per-mile fares (Fig. 4). Extension of this closer relation between fares and operating costs to international travel would result in sizeable reductions.

SUMMARY

Inspection of traffic maps, chiefly depicting changes in Chicago's air passenger traffic between March 1949 and March 1955 has led to the following findings:

(1) *The effects of recreation travel.* The spectacular growth of Florida resort travel to Chicago and to other Manufacturing Belt centers is associated with a basic change in recreation travel habits. Initiation of jet services should make this traffic increasingly important with a probable stress on international travel if domestic trends in fare adjustments are reflected on international routes.

(2) *The effects of length of haul.* Length of haul is also associated with high growth rates although the relationship is somewhat weaker and more variable than in the Florida resort traffic. The effects of length of haul have been particularly noticeable on large-volume routes and in traffic to cities beyond the rail overnight zone as compared to cities within the rail coach zone.

(3) *The effects of low coach fares.* The selective application of coach fares by the airlines has resulted in an average per-mile fare structure which decreases with distance. Although this inter-weaving of the distance and price effects renders difficult the precise isolation of either as a growth factor, there does seem to be a certain sensitivity to price evident on long and medium-haul routes. In the case of short-haul traffic, however, high growth rates at many small cities without coach services indicate a lack of sensitivity to price.

(4) *Other effects.* Improved services and repeat business travel are apparently associated with the tendency for air traffic between Chicago and Eastern Seaboard traffic-shadow cities to increase more rapidly than would be expected from the length of haul and the amount of coach traffic. A weakening of regional as opposed to national ties may be associated with the low growth rates at certain large-volume, short-haul cities west of Chicago. With jet services, tighter linkages and more repeat business travel are probable between Chicago and other Manufacturing Belt cities, as well as between Chicago and California centers.

Airline penetration of the large market within a roughly 400-mile zone wherein private auto and rail coach are most competitive has not been markedly successful and jet services promise little help. However, the high growth rates at certain small cities close to Chicago and the high phone-call ratios at a number of large nearby cities indicate that some of the conventional generalizations as to the weakness of short-haul air traffic might well be re-examined.

INTERNATIONAL TRADE: SELECTED TYPES OF WORLD REGIONS

John W. Alexander

Dr. Alexander is Associate Professor of Geography at the University of Wisconsin. Several previous articles by him have appeared in this magazine.

ECONOMIC geography endeavors to understand regions of the earth's surface in terms of production, exchange, and consumption of wealth. Comprehending such knowledge is expedited by classifying information about economic activities on a regional basis. Classification systems themselves are not the goal; at best they are merely "filing systems" for informative material. They expedite the understanding of a large number of items by grouping similar ones into classes, resulting in a smaller number of groups more readily comprehended. But the number of categories must be large enough to recognize significant differences between items else the very purpose of classification is defeated. To that end the scholar who applies geography's method of analysis to the topic of international trade must decide which characteristics of each country's trade enable the distinguishing of *types* of countries. These *variable characteristics* serve as the measurements by which categories are quantified. The present article proposes a few classification systems for regionalizing data on international trade and is predicated on the philosophy that no one system is "best" but that, depending on the objective, each system makes a contribution to understanding areal differences of international commodity exchange.

DATA SOURCE

The *United Nations' Yearbook of International Trade Statistics* presents data on exports and imports by commodities, by source of imports, and by destination of exports for approximately 100 reporting units (mostly nations) responsible for 98 per cent of the world's international trade. This study is based on the 1954 Yearbook.

AMOUNT OF INTERNATIONAL TRADE BY NATIONS

The general pattern of world trade (Fig. 1) is well known, has been mapped by others,[1] and needs little elaboration at this point. In 1954 there were two major regions, western Europe and

[1] Andreas and Lois Grotewold: "Some Geographic Aspects of International Trade," *Econ. Geogr.*, Vol. 33, 1957, pp. 257–266; W. S. and E. S. Woytinsky: "World Commerce and Governments Trends and Outlook," The Twentieth Century Fund, New York, 1955, pp. 59, 61 and 107.

"International Trade: Selected Types of World Regions" by John W. Alexander. Reprinted from Economic Geography, *Vol. 36 (April 1960), pp. 95–115, with permission of the editor.*

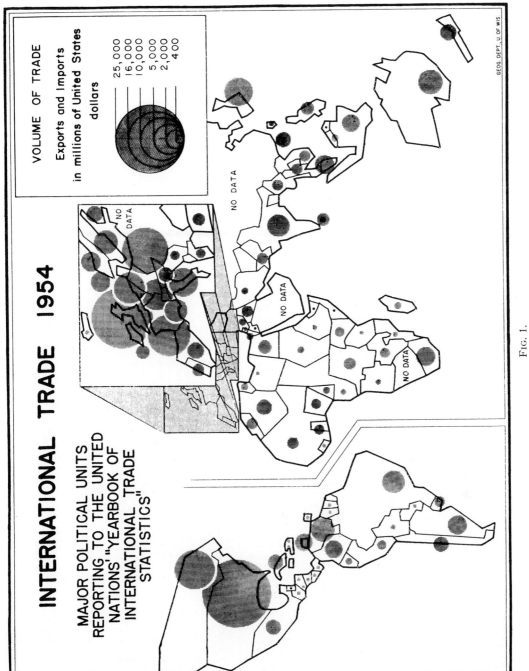

FIG. 1.

TABLE I

INTERNATIONAL TRADE BY REGIONS AND NATIONS

DATA SOURCE: UNITED NATIONS YEARBOOK OF INTERNATIONAL TRADE STATISTICS, 1954

(For explanation of symbols, see footnotes at end of table)

	(1) Exports Millions of United States dollars	(2) Imports Millions of United States dollars	(3) Exp./imp. %	(4) Sum of imports and exports	Regional classification (5) by exports	(6) by imports	(7) Proximity %	Commodity classification (8) by exports	Major item	(9) by imports	Major item
WORLD TOTAL.......	76,250**	78,650**	...	154,900	......	.....	....	...		...	......
ANGLO-AMERICA											
Canada*.........	4,055	4.204	96	8,259	N'u'E	N'u'	67 Y	mc	paper	my	machy.
United States*....	14,967	10,312	144	25,279	E-c	M-c	27 Y	my	vehicles	mf	coffee
MIDDLE AMERICA											
(North America)											
Br. Honduras*....	6	8	75	14	EkNM	EkN	s N	c'	wood	mf	textiles
Costa Rica*.......	81	80	101	161	N'u'E	N'u'E	s N	f'	coffee	m'	textiles
Cuba...........	640	489	131	1,129	N'u'	N'u'	68 Y	f'	sugar	my	textiles
Dominican Rep.*..	119	82	145	201	N'u'E	N'u'	s N	f'	sugar	m	steel
El Salvador*......	105	86	122	191	N'u'	N'u'	s N	f'	coffee	m'	textiles
Guadeloupe.......	33	36	91	69	E'f'	E'f'	s N	f'	sugar	m	textiles
Guatemala........	96	86	112	182	N'u'E	N'u'	s N	f'	coffee	m^w	textiles
Haiti...........	54	47	115	101	E'Nu	N'u'	s N	f'	coffee	m	textiles
Honduras*.......	56	51	110	107	N'u'	N'u'	s N	f'	bananas	m'y	textiles
Jamaica*.........	95	104	91	199	E'k'N	EkN	s N	f'	sugar	m	textiles
Mexico*.........	563	723	78	1.286	N'u'	N'u'	77 Y	c'	cotton	ym	vehicles
Nicaragua........	54	58	93	112	NuE	N'u'	s N	f'	coffee	m	textiles
Panama*.........	17	72	24	89	N'u'	N'u'	s N	f'	bananas	m'	misc.
(South America)											
British Guiana....	48	42	114	90	EkN	E'k'N	s N	f'c	sugar	m'y	vehicles
Colombia*........	644	650	99	1,294	N'u'	N'u'E	s N	f'	coffee	my	vehicles
Neth. Antilles*....	771	818	95	1,589	NuE	M'v	41 Y	m'	petrol.	c'	cr. oil
Surinam.........	28	27	104	55	N'u'	N'u'E	s N	c'	bauxite	m	machy.
Trinidad*........	152	145	104	297	E'k	EkM	12 N	m'	petrol.	mc	cr. oil
Venezuela........	1,689	819	207	2,508	M'e'N	N'u'E	35 N	c'	cr. oil	ym	vehicles
SOUTHERN HEMI-SPHERE AMERICA											
Argentina*........	1,062	954	111	2,016	E'k	Eu	20 N	f'c	grains	m	steel
Bolivia...........	142	92	154	234	N'u'E	NuS	12 N	c'	tin	fm	wheat
Brazil*..........	1,561	1,631	96	3,192	ENu	NuE	10 N	f'c	coffee	m'y	petrol.
Chile............	404	343	117	747	N'u'	N'u'	13 N	c'	copper	ym	machy.
Ecuador*........	99	86	115	185	N'u'	N'u'E	s N	f'	cocoa	m	vehicles
Paraguay*........	31	33	94	64	NuES	ENu	15 N	c'	cotton	m'	textiles
Peru............	245	249	99	494	NuES	N'u'E	s N	c'f	cotton	my	vehicles
Uruguay.........	248	274	90	522	E'k	E-u	14 N	c'f	wool	m	petrol.
EUROPE											
Austria*.........	609	653	93	1,262	E'g	E'g	53 Y	m'c	wood	cm	coal
Belgium-Lux.*....	2,299	2,534	90	4,833	E'n	E'g	48 Y	m'	steel	mc	wool
Denmark*........	948	1,163	82	2,111	E'k	E'k	35 N	f'	meat	m	textiles
Finland*.........	680	656	104	1,336	E'k	E'k	22 N	c'm	wood	m	steel
France*..........	4,188	4,215	99	8,403	EFr	EFr	26 N	m'	steel	c'f	cr. oil
Germany, W.*.....	5,247	4,570	114	9,817	E'n	Eu	38 Y	my	machy.	cf	grains
Greece*.........	151	330	45	481	E'g	E'g	16 N	f'	tobacco	m	petrol.
Iceland*.........	51	69	74	120	E'-u	E'-u	20 N	f'	fish	m	petrol.
Ireland*.........	322	503	64	825	E'k'	E'k	70 Y	f'	meat	m	machy.
Italy*...........	1,636	2,401	68	4,037	E'g	Eg	30 N	m'	textiles	c'	fibers
Malta*..........	8	56	14	64	Ek	E'k	13 N	c'f	minerals	fm	grains
Netherlands*......	2,413	2,857	85	5,270	E'g	E'g	42 Y	mf	eggs	mc	misc.
Norway*.........	582	1,018	57	1,690	E'k	E'k	39 N	mf	fish	my	ships
Portugal*........	253	350	72	603	Ek	Ek	s N	mc	textiles	m	misc.
Spain*..........	464	614	75	1,078	E'k	E-u	s N	f'm	fruit	cm	cotton
Sweden*.........	1,587	1,777	90	3,364	E'k	E'k	32 Y	cm	pulp	m	vehicles
Switzerland.......	1,228	1,303	94	2,531	E'g	E'g	39 Y	m'	clocks	m	misc.
Un. Kingdom*.....	7,489	9,179	83	16,668	E-a	E-u	15 N	m'y	misc.	fc	meat
Yugoslavia*......	240	339	70	579	E'g	E'Nu	19 N	fc	wood	ym	mach.

TABLE I—Continued

INTERNATIONAL TRADE BY REGIONS AND NATIONS

DATA SOURCE: UNITED NATIONS YEARBOOK OF INTERNATIONAL TRADE STATISTICS, 1954

(For explanation of symbols, see footnotes at end of table)

	(1) Exports Millions of United States dollars	(2) Imports Millions of United States dollars	(3) Exp./imp. %	(4) Sum of imports and exports	Regional classification (5) by exports	(6) by imports	(7) Proximity %	Commodity classification (8) by exports	Major item	(9) by imports	Major item
AFRICA											
Algeria............	400	622	64	1,022	E'f'	E'f'	s N	f'	wine	m	vehicles
Anglo-Eg-Sudan...	116	137	84	253	E'k	E'k	12 N	c'f	cotton	mf	textiles
Angola...........	102	95	108	197	E'Nu	E'p	s N	f'	coffee	m	textiles
Belgian Congo....	396	369	108	765	E'b	E'b	s N	c	copper	my	machy.
Br. Somaliland*...	3	6	50	9	A'd	EkA	37 Y	f'c	animals	mf	textiles
Cameroons.......	87	92	95	179	E'f'	E'f'	s N	f'	cocoa	m	misc.
Egypt*...........	397	458	87	855	E'fA	E'k	s N	c'	cotton	m	petrol.
Ethiopia-Eritrea...	64	64	100	128	NuA	E't	25 N	f'	coffee	m	textiles
Fr. Eq. Africa.....	71	95	75	166	E'f'	E'f'	s N	c'	cotton	my	textiles
Fr. W. Africa.....	332	379	88	711	E'f'	E'f'	s N	f'	coffee	m	vehicles
Gold Coast*......	294	200	147	494	E'k	E'k	s N	f'	cocoa	m'	textiles
Kenya-Uganda....	178	239	74	417	E'kA	E'k	s N	f'c	coffee	my	petrol.
Liberia*..........	31	18	171	49	N'u	N'u'	s N	c'	rubber	m'	misc.
Libya*...........	10	31	32	41	E't	E't	s N	c'	hides	mf	grains
Madagascar.......	92	137	67	229	E'f'	E'f'	s N	f'	coffee	m	textiles
Mauritius*.......	53	45	118	98	E'k'	EkA	s N	f'	sugar	mf	grains
Morocco.........	286	479	60	765	E'f	E'f'	s N	c'f	grains	m	sugar
Mozambique......	56	80	70	136	E'p	E'p	s N	c'f	cotton	my	misc.
Nigeria*..........	417	319	130	736	E'k'	E'k	s N	c'f	cocoa	m'	textiles
Reunion..........	36	37	98	73	E'f'	E'f'	15 N	f'	sugar	m	misc.
Rhod.-Nyasa*....	411	350	117	761	E'k'	EkF	23 N	c'	copper	m'y	misc.
Sierra Leone......	31	37	84	68	E'k'	E'k'	s N	c'	iron ore	m'	textiles
It. Somaliland*....	8	10	80	18	E't'	E't'	s N	f'	fruit	m'f	textiles
Tanganyika.......	103	89	116	192	E'k	E'kA	s N	c'	sisal	m	misc.
Tunisia..........	129	169	76	298	E'f'	E'f'	s N	c'f	grains	m	textiles
Un. S. Africa......	890	1,241	71	2,131	E'kA	E'k	12 N	c'f	wool	m	textiles
ASIA											
Brunei*..........	89	36	247	125	......	....	....	c'	cr. oil	m'	misc.
Burma*..........	240	203	118	443	A'j	AEk	25 Y	f'	rice	m'	textiles
Camb.-Laos-Vt. N.	96	394	25	490	ANu	E'f	s N	f'c	rice	m'	textiles
Ceylon...........	350	293	120	643	Ek	AEk	s N	f'c	tea	fm	rice
China: Taiwan....	93	115	81	208	A'j'	A'j'	60 Y	f'	sugar	m'	chemicals
Cyprus*..........	47	66	71	113	E'g	E'k	s N	c'f	copper	m'	textiles
Hong Kong*......	423	601	70	1,024	A'h	AhE	18 Y	m'	textiles	m'f	textiles
India...........	1,182	1,255	95	2,437	Ek	EkA	12 N	mf	tea, jute	m	petrol.
Indonesia........	856	629	136	1,485	AmE	AjE	20 N	c'f	rubber	m	textiles
Iran^w...........	111	223	50	334	Ek	E-u	s N	c	cr. oil	m	sugar
Iraq^w	429	203	210	632	En	E'k	s N	c	cr. oil	my	vehicles
Israel...........	88	289	31	377	EkN	ENu	s N	f	fruit	m	grain
Japan*..........	1,629	2,399	68	4,028	A-u	Nu	s N	m'	textiles	c'f	cotton
Jordan..........	6	38	16	44	A'l'	E'kA	46 Y	c'f	olive oil	mf	textiles
Lebanon.........	43	173	25	216	AsE	EAs	25 Y	f'	fruit	mf	textiles
Malaya*..........	1,015	1,025	99	2,040	E-u	AiE	27 Y	c'	rubber	cf	cr. oil
North Borneo*....	25	24	104	49	AEk	AEk	s N	c'	rubber	mf	textiles
Pakistan.........	358	324	110	682	E'kA	E'k	s N	c'	jute	m	textiles
Philippines.......	412	451	91	863	N'u'	N'u'	12 N	c'f	copra	m	textiles
Sarawak..........	138	129	107	267	A'm	A'x'	47 Y	c'	cr. oil	c	cr. oil
Syria...........	210	174	120	384	E'f	E'-u	s N	c'f	grains	m	petrol.
Thailand*........	272	313	87	585	A'j	AjE	24 N	f'	rice	m'	textiles
Turkey*..........	334	478	70	812	E'g	E'g	s N	f'c	tobacco	m'y	machines
AUSTRALIA*........	1,658	1,685	99	3,343	E'k	E'k	s N	c'f	wool	m'y	textiles
NEW ZEALAND......	683	687	99	1,370	E'k'	E'k'	s N	f'c	dairy prods.	my	textiles

**World total imports exceed total exports because of added value of transport charges.

*Nation reporting as per "Standard International Trade Classification."

^w Data from 1955 edition of the Yearbook of International Trade Statistics.

Columns 5, 6—Regional classification by exports and imports

    First capital letter: leading *region* receiving the nation's exports or originating the nation's imports.
    An Apostrophe (') indicates a proportion of **50** per cent or more.

      E   Europe
      N   Anglo-America
      M   Middle America
      F   Africa
      A   Asia including Indonesia
      S   Southern Hemisphere America

    Other capital letters: other major *regions*, each accounting for 25 per cent of the nation's trade in order.
    Lower-case letter: single leading *nation* regardless of its percentage. Apostrophe (') indicates it receives at least 50 per cent of the nation's exports or provides 50 per cent of that nation's imports. Letter is positioned after the trade region in which it is located. (-) Hyphen indicates the nation is not in the region represented by the capital letter.

a	Australia	g	Germany	l	Lebanon	s	Syria
b	Belgium	h	China	m	Malaya	t	Italy
c	Canada	i	Indonesia	n	Netherlands	u	United States
d	Aden	j	Japan	p	Portugal	v	Venezuela
e	Netherlands Antilles	k	United Kingdom	r	Algeria	x	Brunei
f	France				

Column 7—Percentage is share of a nation's total trade accounted for by neighbors.
    s   less than 10 per cent
    Y   Leading trading partner *IS* a neighbor
    N   Leading trading partner is *NOT* a neighbor

Column 8—Lower-case letter indicates 25 per cent or more of nation's total exports:
    f   Foods   c   Crude materials   m   Manufactures   y   Machinery
    Apostrophe (') indicates 50 per cent or more of total exports.
    ᵂ Data from 1955 Yearbook of International Trade Statistics.

Column 9—Same as for Column 8 but applied to imports.

Anglo-America, which, respectively, generated $65,000,000,000 worth of trade (43 per cent of the world total) and $33,000,000,000 (22 per cent of the world total). National leaders were United States, United Kingdom, West Germany, France, and Canada.

1. Regions by Balance of Trade

Balance between exports and imports is quantified in Table I, Column 3, by means of an *export/import index*. Value of exports is divided by that of imports; the quotient is expressed on the basis of 100 for perfect balance. Thus, an index exceeding 100 indicates excess of exports; an index of 99 or less indicates excess of imports.

Most places import more than they export. Of the 99 political units reporting, 63 are in this *debtor* category. A "favorable" balance is "enjoyed" by 36 *creditors*. Notice that *debtor* and *creditor* as used herein refer only to the net debits or net credits resulting from international exchange of *commodities*. Table II lists the major creditors and debtors. Figure 2 shows the location of four types of nations in terms of *trade balance* and suggests six areas of *creditors:* (1) from the United States southeastward through Surinam; (2) southern South America; (3) middle Africa between Liberia, Rhodesia, and Ethiopia; (4) southeast Asia; (5) the Near East (Iraq and Syria); and, (6) two European nations (West Germany and Finland). All told, these creditor areas have an aggregate differential of $7,744,000,000 in exports over imports. Almost 80 per cent of this differential is credited to nations in the Western Hemisphere, and an astonishing 60 per cent of it ($4,655,000,000) is the credit of just one nation—the United States. No student of international relations can miss the fact that three-fifths of the free world's debt incurred for commodities in 1954 is owed to one creditor; and no United States citizen can think constructively about foreign policy without realizing that his country must either write off this debt as foreign aid or be willing to participate in ventures whereby the debtors can redeem themselves.

Major regions of debtors are (1) Europe (every major nation except West Germany and Finland), (2) Africa's northern, eastern, and southern portions, (3) eastern and southern Asia, (4) Australia–New Zealand, (5) middle part of South America, (6) Canada, and a few Middle American countries. The largest deficits are those of United Kingdom, Japan, and Italy. But the lowest export/import indexes appear in Jordan, Panama, Lebanon, Cambodia, Israel, Libya, and Greece, countries in which the economy depends heavily on other income such as that from military establishments of outside powers, transport charges on traffic through the country (as oil pipelines crossing Jordan), and outside investments. The fact that the largest debts from trade imbalance occur in Europe helps explain the intense advertising campaigns in America sponsored by European countries to lure tourist dollars. Analysis of spatial variation in methods whereby debtor nations augment their incomes would be an interesting line of geographic research.

TABLE II

MAJOR COUNTRIES BY BALANCE OF INTERNATIONAL TRADE IN MILLIONS OF UNITED STATES DOLLARS, 1954

Excess of exports over imports		Excess of imports over exports	
ANGLO-AMERICA		ANGLO-AMERICA	
United States	$4,655	Canada	$149
MIDDLE AMERICAS		MIDDLE AMERICAS	
Venezuela	870	Mexico	160
Cuba	151	Panama	55
SOUTHERN HEMISPHERE AMERICA		SOUTHERN HEMISPHERE AMERICA	
Argentina	108	Brazil	70
Chile	61	Uruguay	26
EUROPE		EUROPE	
Western Germany	677	United Kingdom	1,690
Finland	24	Italy	765
		Netherlands	444
AFRICA		Norway	436
Nigeria	98	Belgium	235
Gold Coast	94	Denmark	215
Rhodesia-Nyasaland	61	Sweden	190
		Ireland	181
ASIA		Greece	179
Indonesia	227	Spain	150
Iraq	226	Yugoslavia	99
		Portugal	97
		Switzerland	75
		Austria	44
		France	27
		AFRICA	
		Union South Africa	351
		Algeria	222
		Morocco	193
		Egypt	61
		Kenya	61
		ASIA	
		Japan	770
		Cambodia-Laos-V. N.	298
		Israel	201
		Hong Kong	178
		Turkey	144
		Lebanon	130
		Iran	112
		India	73

Source: Computed from data in United Nations *Yearbook of International Trade Statistics,* 1954.

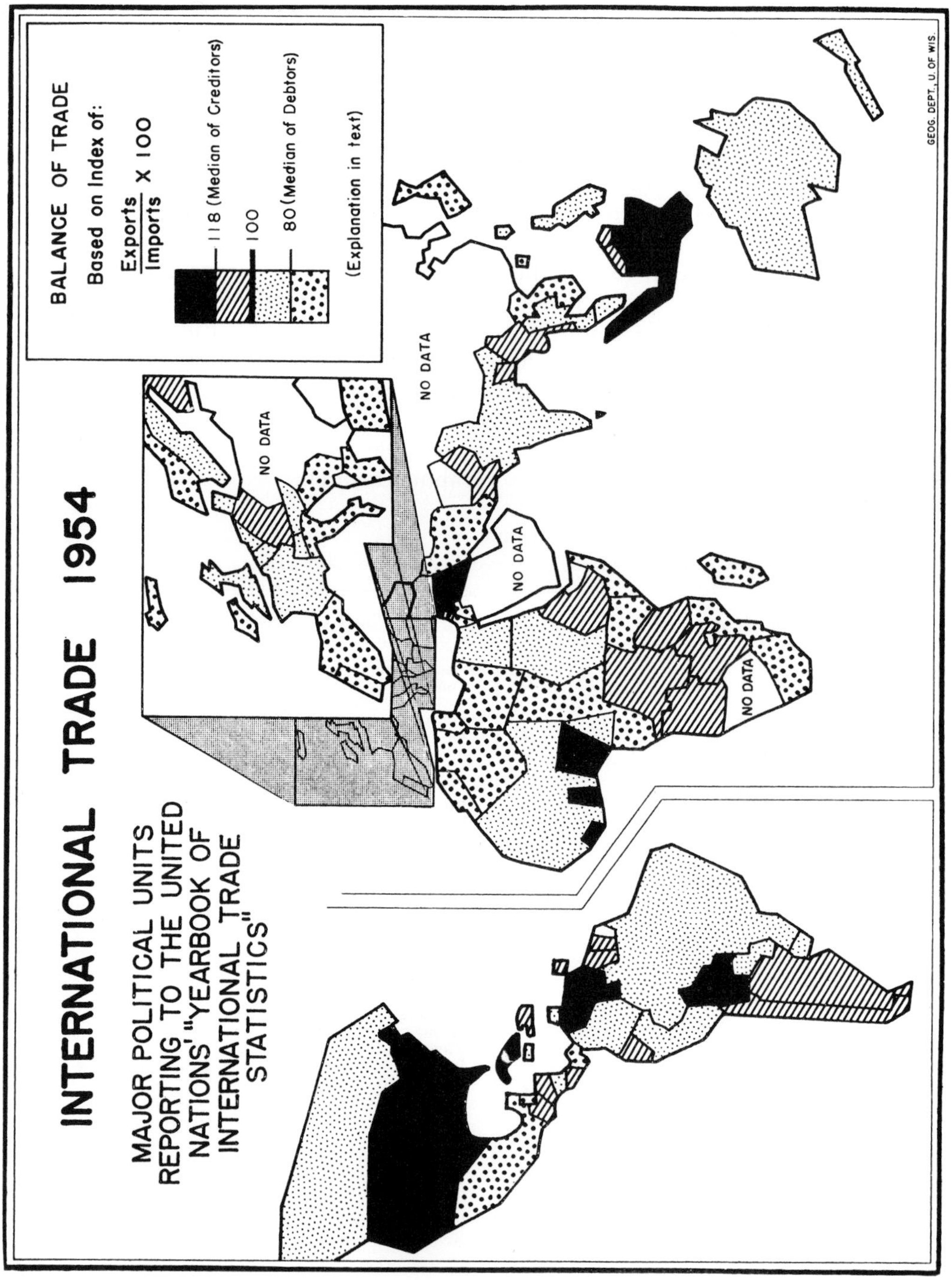

INTERNATIONAL TRADE 1954
MAJOR POLITICAL UNITS REPORTING TO THE UNITED NATIONS' "YEARBOOK OF INTERNATIONAL TRADE STATISTICS"
BALANCE OF TRADE
Based on Index of:
Exports / Imports X 100
118 (Median of Creditors)
100
80 (Median of Debtors)
(Explanation in text)
NO DATA
NO DATA
NO DATA
NO DATA
GEOG. DEPT., U. OF WIS.

FIG. 2.

2. Regions by Destination of Exports

Percentages were computed for each nation's exports destined for every major trade region and for leading nations.

Seven major trade regions were delimited: Anglo-America, Middle America, Southern Hemisphere America, Western Europe, Africa, Asia, and Australia–New Zealand. A coding system portraying the destination of each nation's exports was devised (Table I, Column 5) whereby the initial capital letter indicates the leading *region* receiving the nation's exports (e.g., Guatemala's first capital letter is *N*, indicating that her leading customer is Anglo-America). An apostrophe (') indicates that a proportion of 50 per cent or more of that nation's shipments are consigned to that region. Subsequent capital letters indicate other major *regions*, each accounting for 25 per cent of the exports, in order of rank (e.g., British Honduras ships mainly to Europe, *E*, but Anglo-America, *N*, and Middle America, *M*, each receives at least 25 per cent of British Honduras' exports). The lower-case letter indicates a single leading *nation*. An apostrophe (') after the lower-case letter indicates receipt of at least 50 per cent of the classified nation's exports (e.g., Guatemala sends over half of its exports to the United States as shown by the entry *u*').

Column 5 of Table I indicates the destination of exports as reported by each nation, and Figure 3 is an attempt to map these nations in terms of major consignees. Most extensive is the region linked to western Europe. This area contains every nation in Europe, extends eastward as far as Pakistan, and southward over Africa; it covers much of South America, a few small nations in Middle America, and the

United States. Its most remote section comprises Australia and New Zealand. In all, the European region contains 63 nations, with 29 in the *Ek* category (United Kingdom leading consignee). France was first buyer from 11 nations.

Regions exporting mainly to Anglo-America occupy much of North America, the western fringe of South America, and a few detached places: Surinam, Liberia, Ethiopia, and the Philippines. Sixteen nations identify the United States as their foremost customer.

The export-to-Asia region includes Japan and southeast Asia.

Venezuela alone reported Middle America as leading recipient. But most of her exports are crude oil shipped to Netherland Antilles which processes the oil and exports the products to the United States and Europe. Thus, one might contend that Venezuela should be classified the same as Netherlands Antilles.

There is no country having either Africa or Southern Hemisphere America or Australia–New Zealand as leading destination region for exports.

3. Regions by Sources of Imports

Each country was appraised in terms of the proportion of total imports ascribable to each of the seven trade regions and to its leading source nation. Exactly the same methods for classifying nations in terms of imports (Table I, Column 6) were used as for exports (Column 5).

Regions distinguished in terms of leading import sources are portrayed by Figure 4. Most expansive is the area receiving from Europe. It occurs on every continent, covering all of Europe, all of Africa (excepting Liberia), southern Asia, and Australia–New Zealand. In the Western Hemisphere the import-from-Europe region contains only Argentina and a few smaller nations. The

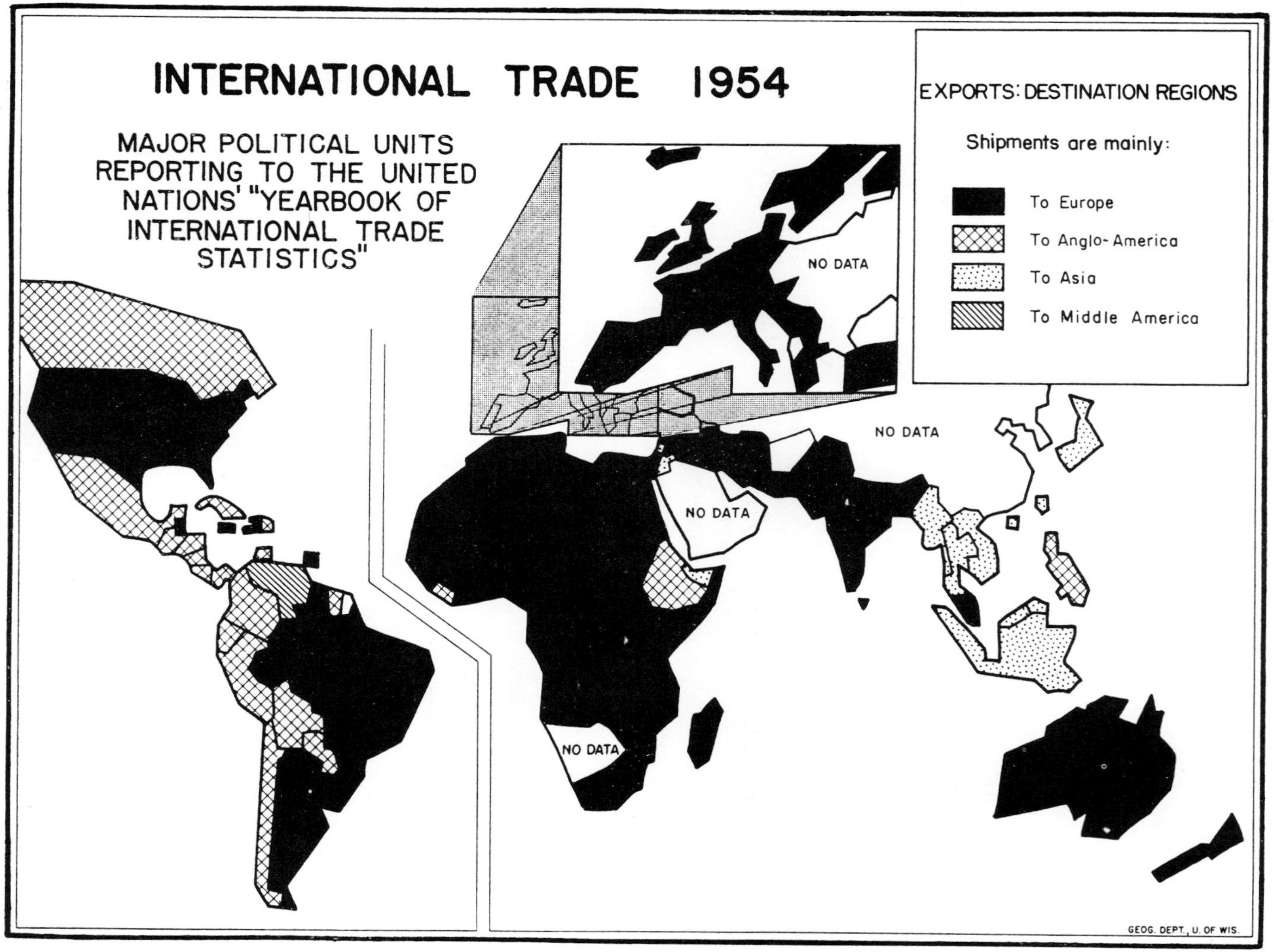
INTERNATIONAL TRADE 1954
MAJOR POLITICAL UNITS REPORTING TO THE UNITED NATIONS' "YEARBOOK OF INTERNATIONAL TRADE STATISTICS"
EXPORTS: DESTINATION REGIONS
Shipments are mainly:
To Europe
To Anglo-America
To Asia
To Middle America
NO DATA
NO DATA
NO DATA
NO DATA
GEOG. DEPT., U. OF WIS.

Fig. 3.

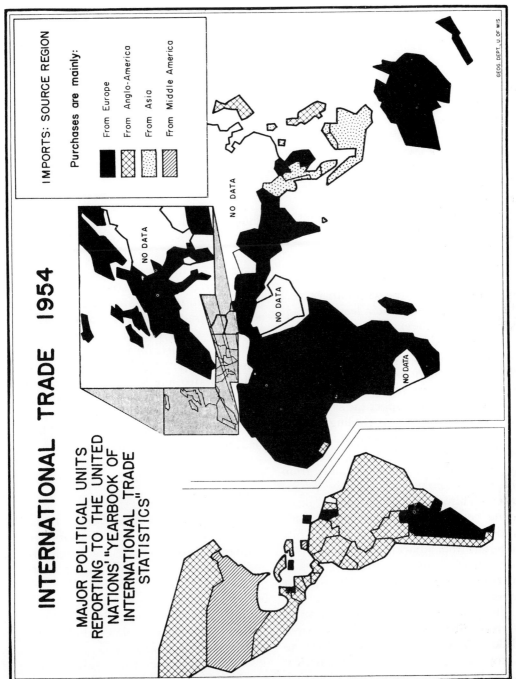

INTERNATIONAL TRADE 1954

MAJOR POLITICAL UNITS REPORTING TO THE UNITED NATIONS' "YEARBOOK OF INTERNATIONAL TRADE STATISTICS"

IMPORTS: SOURCE REGION

Purchases are mainly:

From Europe
From Anglo-America
From Asia
From Middle America

NO DATA

GEOG. DEPT., U. OF WIS.

FIG. 4.

611

United Kingdom is leading source for 29 nations.

Anglo-America is the main shipper to most countries in both North America and South America. Anomalous connections to distant regions involve Liberia, Japan, Philippines. Asia is leading source for several political units located in southeast Asia. The United States imports more from Middle America than from any other region.

Not a single country reports either Africa or Southern Hemisphere America or Australia–New Zealand as leading seller.

Perusal of Columns 5 and 6 in Table I indicates that 73 of the 98 countries have the same nation as their leading trade partner for both exports and imports. The United Kingdom, leading recipient of 29 nations' exports and leading supplier of 29 nations' imports, is the world's leading trading partner.

Eleven countries report the same trading region, but different trading nations as their leading export and leading import partners. One out of every six nations, however, imports mainly from one region and exports largely to another. This group includes some "processing countries" such as Netherlands Antilles and Malaya which import raw materials from adjacent nations and perform initial manufacturing processes in materials destined for Europe or America.

The United States exports most to western Europe yet buys most from Middle America; Brazil sells most to Europe, buys most from Anglo-America; Japan buys mainly from Anglo-America, sells mainly to Asia.

Figures 3 and 4 indicate that the world's major trading regions are related mainly with Europe for both exports and imports. Yet regions importing from Europe are less extensive than those exporting to Europe (especially in

TABLE III

FREQUENCY OF NATIONS BY PROXIMITY OF TRADING PARTNERS

Percentage of foreign trade accounted for by neighboring nations	*Number of nations reporting their leading trade partner to be*	
	A neighbor	*Not a neighbor*
50 plus...............	7	0
25–49................	12	7
10–24................	1	20
Under 10.............	0	52

South America). Conversely regions importing from Anglo-America are greater than those exporting to Anglo-America. This is a major feature of the geography of international trade, fundamental to understanding the large negative trade balances noted earlier for Europe and the large excess of exports over imports for the United States. Similarly, Japan buys largely from the United States but is unable to reciprocate with equal sales of her surpluses. This, concomitant with Japan's severe export deficit (Table II), is a problem for American-Japanese diplomacy.

4. Regions by Proximity of Trading Nations

Proximity can be appraised in terms of (a) percentage of each nation's foreign trade accounted for by its neighbors and (b) whether or not its leading trade partner is a neighbor. Table III shows frequency of nations according to this twofold classification. (See Table I, Column 7 for classification of individual nations on this basis.)

One might expect countries to trade considerably with neighbors even though their major shipments were to and from Europe. But over half the nations report that less than 10 per cent of their trade is with neighbors, and only 20 say that their leading trading partner is a neighbor. Only seven nations do even half of their business with neighbors.

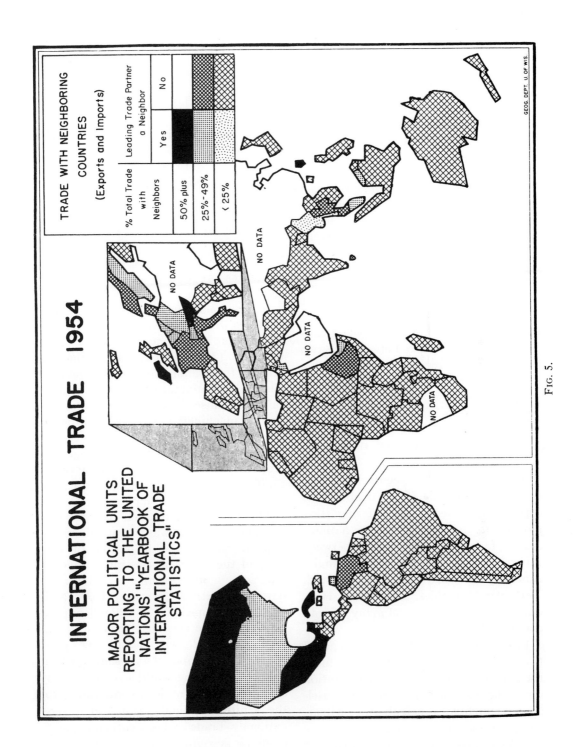

FIG. 5.

Figure 5 shows that parts of North America, much of west-central Europe, and a few states in southeast Asia comprise three regions where nations trade considerably with those adjoining them. The rest of the world has a low proximity rating.

This leads to a fundamental geographic principle: *complementarity* is more powerful than *transferability* in the realm of international trade. *Complementarity* exists between two nations if one has a commodity surplus needed by another which *desires* and has the *purchasing power* to buy it from the surplus producer. *Transferability* is the cost (measured in time or money) of transporting the commodity between the two complementary regions.[2] Two striking examples of this principle are Australia and New Zealand which, farther than any other nations from Europe, still are linked to that region for 60 per cent and 74 per cent respectively of their international trade.

The power of complementarity is augmented by the role of political ties, of capital investments, and of migration movements in linking remote nations. Notice, for example, the linkage between Liberia and the Philippines with Anglo-America; of Australia, New Zealand, Netherlands Antilles, and British Honduras with Europe; and of many African states with Europe.

Interesting as Figure 5 and Column 7 (Table I) may be, however, one must use the proximity index with caution lest it be confused with *distance*. Belgium, though not a neighbor of Switzerland, is closer to that nation than are the developed portions of Brazil and Venezuela which are neighbors.

[2] The terminology "complementarity" and "transferability" for these concepts was suggested by Edward L. Ullman in *American Commodity Flow*, University of Washington Press, (Seattle, 1957), pp. 20–24.

5. Regions by Commodities Exported

Commodity data for 55 countries are organized by the United Nations as per the Standard International Trade Classification (SITC) adopted in 1952 recognizing ten major categories: food, beverages and tobacco, crude materials, mineral fuels, animal and vegetable oils, chemicals, manufactures, machinery, miscellaneous manufactures, and others. Information on commodities for remaining nations is listed in heterogeneous sequences preventing uniform comparison.

For regionalizing in this study, commodities were grouped into four classes: (1) foods (including beverages and tobacco), (2) crude materials (including mineral fuels, animal oils, and vegetable oils), (3) manufactures (including chemicals, and miscellaneous manufactures), and (4) machinery. The reason for such grouping is that foods and crudes typify exports from nations in early stages of economic development, manufactures typify a more complex stage, and machinery a still more complex stage.

The percentage of each nation's exports in each group was computed. Subsequent classification of nations on the basis of these percentages raised several questions. Suppose the exports from nation X were 37 per cent foods and 21 per cent machinery. Should nation X therefore be classified primarily as a food exporter? Or should her percentages be compared with some central value such as the world average? For example, the 55 nations comforming to the United Nation's Standard International Trade Classification, report foods as accounting for 38 per cent of all exports, machinery for 7 per cent. Compared to these central values, nation X exported three times as much machinery as the average but was actually below average in food export.

Should she therefore be classified primarily as a machinery exporter? Since, in her own economy, revenues from food shipments surpassed machinery sales, the author decided to appraise exports in terms of support of each nation's economy.

On this basis, each nation's category is identified in Table I, Column 8, by a series of lower-case letters, one for each commodity group (exceeding 25 per cent) listed in order of percentages. The code system is: *f*—foods, beverages, and tobacco; *c*—crude materials, mineral fuels, animal and vegetable oils; *m*—manufactures, chemicals; *y*—machinery. An apostrophe indicates at least 50 per cent of exports.

The cartogram (Fig. 6) reveals four broad types of regions, distinguished by exports of: (1) foods, (2) crude materials, (3) manufactures, (4) manufactures and machinery.

Several areas are mainly *food* exporters. Middle America and eastern South America report the highest percentage of food exports in the world, climaxed by Costa Rica's 98 per cent; bananas, sugar, coffee, and grains are major commodities moving out from this region. In smaller European countries foods comprise over 75 per cent of exports: Iceland (fish), Ireland (animals and meat), Denmark (meat and dairy products). Equally high percentages occur in the Far East: Burma and Thailand (rice) and Taiwan (tea). Several African countries on the western and eastern portions of the continent are in this category. Wherever foods are the leading export, two principles prevail: (a) they invariably exceed all other exports combined (i.e., rarely do foods rank first without rating 50 per cent) and (b) the runner-up invariably is crude materials. Examples are Brazil and Argentina (coffee and meats followed by cotton and wool), eastern

Mediterranean countries (fruit, wheat, cotton), and New Zealand (dairy products, meat, wool).

Sales of *crude materials* dominate commodity revenues in three general areas. From South Africa northward through the middle of the continent and eastward to Pakistan is an arcuate region from which flow minerals (copper, petroleum) and fibers (cotton, jute). From Mexico through Venezuela and southward to Chile is a similar belt generating surplus minerals (e.g., petroleum, bauxite, tin, copper) and cotton. A third general area is southeast of Asia: Malaya, Philippines, Indonesia, and Australia. Many countries depend upon crude materials for an extremely high share of their exports: Venezuela, Surinam, and Bolivia, all above 95 per cent; Egypt, Tanganyika and Rhodesia, above 75 per cent. Wherever crude materials rank first, two principles appear: (a) they tend to comprise over half the exports, and (b) where a second commodity ranks as high as 25 per cent, it invariably is foods. Examples of such areas are Australia (wool, meat, grains), Indonesia (rubber, tin, copra, coffee), the Philippines (copra, sugar), South Africa (wool, fruit).

Manufactures rank first in three familiar regions: western Europe, Anglo-America, and Japan. India is now in this category: although her leading item is tea (25 per cent), the combination of two lesser manufactures (jute and cotton textiles) gives manufactures a slight margin.[3] In regions where manufactures are the leading export, they never attain the maximum percentages reached by foods and crude materials; the highest percentages occur in United Kingdom (88 per cent), West Germany (86 per cent) and Japan (85 per cent). Fre-

[3] If copper concentrate be considered a manufactured item, Rhodesia and Belgian Congo qualify.

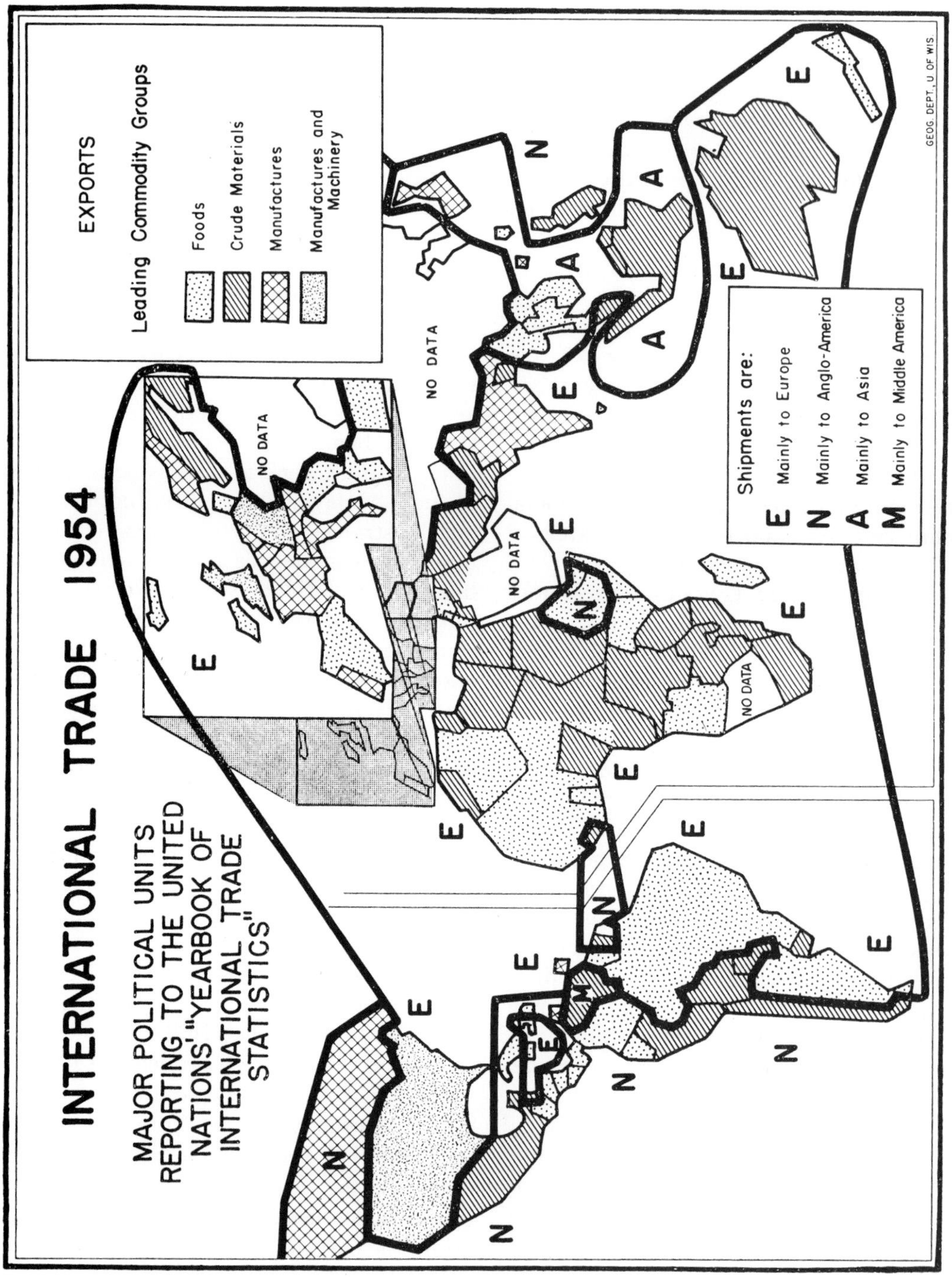

INTERNATIONAL TRADE 1954

MAJOR POLITICAL UNITS REPORTING TO THE UNITED NATIONS' "YEARBOOK OF INTERNATIONAL TRADE STATISTICS"

EXPORTS

Leading Commodity Groups

Foods
Crude Materials
Manufactures
Manufactures and Machinery

Shipments are:
E Mainly to Europe
N Mainly to Anglo-America
A Mainly to Asia
M Mainly to Middle America

GEOG. DEPT., U OF WIS

FIG. 6.

quently, manufactures rank first with less than 50 per cent of exports: United States 38 per cent, Canada 40 per cent, Netherlands 40 per cent, Norway 41 per cent. Also, there is not a close correlation between manufactures and the "runner-up" as was found for foods and crudes; sometimes the second ranking export is crude material (wood, second to paper from Canada), food (fish, second to pulp and paper from Norway), or machinery (second to general manufactures from United States, and United Kingdom). Another principle is that large volumes of trade correlate with exports of manufactures; all nine nations participating in $4,000,000,000 or more of trade (Table I, Column 4) have manufactures as the leading export (Column 8).

There is no region where *machinery* is the leading export. In three nations it ranks high (40 per cent Germany, 37 per cent United Kingdom, 35 per cent in United States) but in each case it is exceeded by other manufactures. A principle seems to hold that if machinery is a major export (representing at least 25 per cent of the outbound flow) it will be exceeded by other manufactures, and foods and crudes will be relatively minor exports.

The heavy lines on Figure 6 show regions in terms of leading consignees based on Figure 3. The "food-to-Europe" region is widely distributed through South America, Africa, and peripheral nations of Europe itself. New Zealand, half way around the globe, belongs to this type. Almost as widespread is the "crudes-to-Europe" region which occurs mainly in Africa, southern Asia, and Australia. Finland and Sweden belong. The area distinguished by "manufactures-to-Europe" is restricted to European nations except for the United States, Trinidad (petroleum products), and India (jute).

Fully two-thirds of the world's free countries belong to the foregoing triad of European regions.

The "food-to-Anglo-America" area occupies Middle America with an outlier in Africa (Ethiopia—coffee). More extensive is the "crudes-to-Anglo-America" region of western South America, Mexico, Liberia, and the Philippines. Canada is the sole nation tied to Anglo-America mainly by manufactures (paper) shipments.

In the Far East, mainland nations tend to be "food-to-Asia" shippers while the islands are in the "crudes-to-Asia" class. Japan and Hong Kong are the only units in the "manufactures-to-Asia" region. Malaya and the Philippines are anomalies: both are in the crude material group, but the former sells mainly to Europe, the latter to Anglo-America.

6. Regions by Commodities Imported

The classification system explained above for exports was applied to import traffic (Table I, Column 9) which is mapped on Figure 7. Four general regions are discernible. Most extensive is that receiving *manufactures:* much of Africa, southern Asia, the United States, several units of Central America, and peripheral European nations (e.g., Ireland, Portugal, Greece, Sweden). Notice the prominence of textiles in Column 9 of Table I; 37 countries report it as the leading item purchased abroad. Regions classed as receivers of *manufactures and machinery* include much of North America, South America, central Africa, and Australia–New Zealand. Might there be a correlation here between present rate of economic advancement and this type of import structure? *Crude materials* comprise the major inflow to only a few countries, most of which are manufacturing countries of Europe, and Japan. The absence in

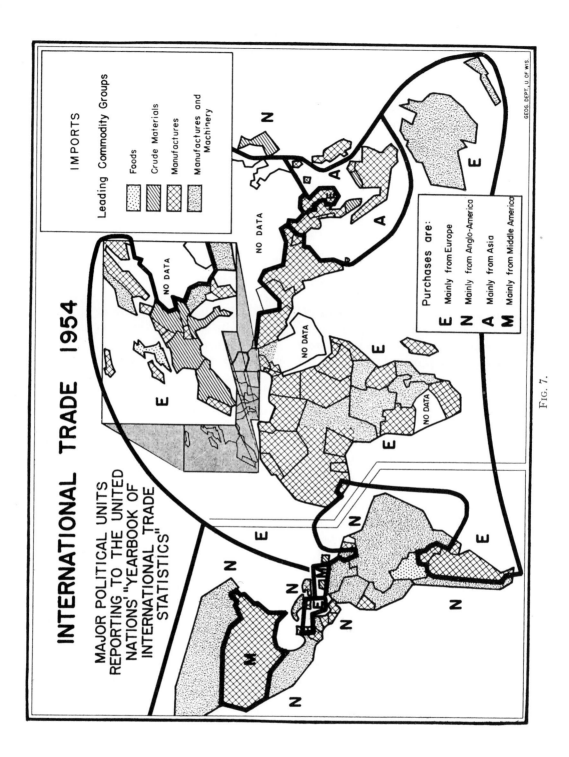

FIG. 7.

this category of the United States is somewhat surprising. Very few areas are primarily *food* importers.

Commodity groups never attained as high maximum percentages of imports as of exports; the highest proportion attained by inbound food was 40 per cent (United Kingdom), crudes 82 per cent (Netherland Antilles—crude oil from Venezuela), manufactures 70 per cent (Burma), and machinery 43 per cent (Mexico). Thus, the international trade picture of 1954 was distinguished by import structures much more diversified than those of exports.

The heavy lines on Figure 7 show regions in terms of leading source of imports. The dominant region ("manufactures-from-Europe") occurs on every continent, covering practically all of Africa, southern Asia, fringing nations of Europe itself, and a few countries in the Americas. Included are 46 of the 98 trading units. The "machinery-manufactures-from-Europe" region contains 12 countries, mostly in Africa and Australia–New Zealand. The "crudes-from-Europe" category has five entries, all in central Europe. A dozen units comprise "manufactures-from-Anglo-America" type and are mostly in Middle America. The "machinery manufactures-from-Anglo-America" region comprises much of South America, Mexico, and Canada. The "import-from-Asia" region is entirely within southeast Asia where imports are largely manufactures from Japan.

Comparison of Columns 8 and 9 in Table I enables construction of a frequency tabulation (Table IV) which indicates that two well-known principles continue to operate: (1) if a nation's export category is foods-crudes (*f*, *c*, *fc*, *cf*) its *import* category is likely to be manufactures (*m*, *my*, or *ym*); 66 of 80 countries conform with this rule. (2) If a nation's *import* category is manufac-

tures (*m, my* or *ym*) its *export* category will be foods-crudes (*c, f, cf, fc*); 66 of 73 places support this generalization. Notice the frequency with which textiles, as the leading import, correlates with bananas, sugar, coffee, cotton, wood, as leading export (Table I, Columns 8 and 9).

The novice might think that the opposite principle would hold; viz., that if a nation's *exports* are manufactures (*m* or *my*) its *import* classification will be foods or crudes. However, only six of 11 countries support this theory. The generalization does hold for United Kingdom, Germany, France, Italy, Japan, and Netherlands Antilles. But there are almost as many exceptions: United States, Belgium, Switzerland, Hong Kong, and Trinidad.

Table IV indicates that there are several nations with a rather unusual export-import structure. Two places are in the crude-food category for *both* exports and imports: Malaya imports oil, rubber, and food and exports tin and even more crude rubber. Sarawak's imports are mostly crude oil; her exports are largely crude oil and pepper. At the other extreme is Switzerland which is in the manufactures category for *both* exports and imports; in-movements of steel and machines are countered by out-movements of clocks, watches, and textiles. Many nations

TABLE IV

FREQUENCY OF NATIONS BY COMMODITIES: EXPORTS AND IMPORTS, 1954

Import classification	Export classification				
	c, f, cf, fc	cm, fm	mc, mf	m, my	Totals
c, f, cf, fc..........	2	0	0	6	8
cm, fm............	3	1	1	0	5
mc, mf............	9	0	0	4	13
m, my, ym........	66	2	4	1	73
Totals..........	80	3	5	11	99

report a "mixture" of commodities (i.e., both manufactures and foods-crudes appear in the classification symbol). Twelve countries have a mixed flow of imports while exporting foods and crudes. In general, these are rather sparsely populated areas where the economy is in the early stages of development (e.g., Bolivia, Libya, North Borneo, Lebanon, Jordan, and the Sudan). Four countries have a mixed flow of imports countered by outflows of manufactures (United States, Belgium, Trinidad, and Hong Kong). Six countries have diverse exports, while importing manufactures: Norway, Sweden, Finland, Portugal, India, and Canada. Mixtures in both inbound and outbound flows distinguish Netherlands and Austria.

The generalization seems to hold that a mixture of commodities is more typical of imports (18 countries in Table IV) than of exports (eight countries).

7. Regions by Exports (Destinations and Commodities) and Imports (Sources and Commodities) and Balance

Figure 8 is an attempt to regionalize nations by a single system combining several criteria: commodities exported, consignees, commodities imported, sources, and net balance. Four major regions appear: *A* (linked to Asia by both inflow and outflow), *E* (involved with Europe in both flows), *N* (receiving from and shipping mainly to Anglo-America), and *X* (linked by exports to one region and by imports to another).

Region E is by far the most expansive, appearing on all continents and covering the entirety of Europe, practically all of Africa, southern Asia, Australia–New Zealand, portions of South America, and a few units in North America. Moreover, every country in Region X (except Japan) is involved mainly with Europe. Most of this European region

is of the "colonial" type, i.e., exporting foods and crudes in return for manufactures; however, India and most countries of Europe show manufactures as the ranking export. Within Europe, an "inner core" of United Kingdom, France, Italy, and Germany exemplify the traditional exporter of manufactures in return for crudes and foods. The few small nations in this ring (Belgium, Netherlands, Switzerland) report manufactures leading in both receipts and shipments. Does this support a hypothesis that small nations with large numbers of skilled people but limited natural resources tend toward a trade pattern featuring imports of semi-processed manufactures which are processed to a higher form and then exported? An "outer ring" (Ireland, Iceland, Sweden, Finland, and Yugoslavia) are "colonial" with a surplus of foods-crudes but a deficit in manufactures.

Most of Region E is a "debtor" area insofar as visible trade is concerned; i.e., imports exceed exports. This does not mean that a debtor nation is en route to bankruptcy, but it does mean that she must devise other means of augmenting her income (e.g., tourism, foreign investments) to pay for the debt incurred through her unfavorable balance in commodity trading. Indeed, all European nations themselves (except Germany and Finland) have a trade deficit, with the United Kingdom's deficiency (an astounding $1,600,000,000) exceeding by far that of any other nation (Table II). The combined deficits of Japan ($770,000,000) and Italy ($765,000,000) do not equal the United Kingdom's.

The Anglo-American Region, *N*, is restricted to the Western Hemisphere (except for Liberia and the Philippines) and includes every North American country except the United States, Jamaica, Haiti, British Honduras, and Guadeloupe. This is another "colonial"

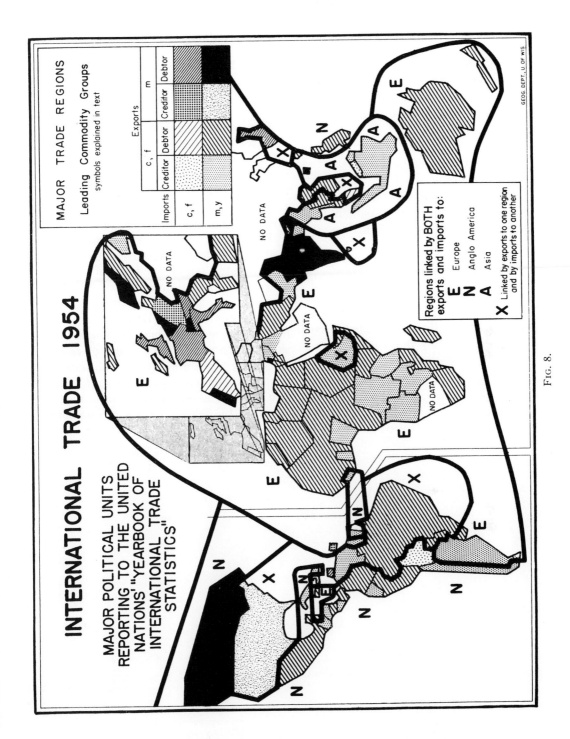

INTERNATIONAL TRADE 1954

MAJOR POLITICAL UNITS
REPORTING TO THE UNITED
NATIONS' "YEARBOOK OF
INTERNATIONAL TRADE
STATISTICS"

MAJOR TRADE REGIONS

Leading Commodity Groups
symbols explained in text

Imports	Exports				
	c, f			m	
	Creditor	Debtor	Creditor	Debtor
c, f					
m, y					

Regions linked by BOTH
exports and imports to:
E Europe
N Anglo America
A Asia
X Linked by exports to one region
and by imports to another

GEOG. DEPT., U. OF WIS.

Fɪɢ. 8.

621

trade region excepting Canada (with mixed exports) and Bolivia (whose imports are dominated by foods). Many nations in this region have a "favorable" balance.

The Asian Region, *A*, is another "colonial" trade area, and is restricted to small traders of southeast Asia. All but one have "favorable" balances and do major business with Japan, a fact which sheds additional light on the problem of that nation.

Two large traders of the Far East, Malaya and Japan, are in Region *X*, the former buying from Asia and selling to Europe (another factor in the European deficit) while Japan sells mainly to Asia and purchases from the United States (a factor in the United States problem of excess exports and Japan's problem of excess imports).

A major reason for Europe's trade problem is that the United States is in Region *X*, selling to Europe but buying mainly from Middle America.

FURTHER QUESTIONS

The present study has been based on data for only one year. Were its methods applied to a longer time period, would different findings result? That is, are annual fluctuations in international trade so capricious that a one-year glimpse produces fallacious conclusions?

To what extent would Figures 3 and 4 show a different pattern if they had been constructed on the basis of leading source *country* of imports and leading destination *country* for exports?

What would be the pattern of a world map of trade imbalance constructed to show debtor nations in terms of countries they owed and creditor nations in terms of countries owing them? Are any regions discernible in terms of methods used by debtor nations to augment their incomes?

Services and Urban Activity

The preceding articles have dealt with primary and secondary activities (the production and processing of commodities) and with commercial activities (the movement of goods to different locations.) Still another group of occupations are the service industries (which, with commercial industries, are often called tertiary activities). These usually include banking, education, insurance, wholesale and retail sales, personal and professional services, and similar activities.

The proportion of the population engaged in service activities varies greatly in relation to the general level of economic activity in a country. In the United States, for example, a majority of employed persons now works in service industries. In countries with largely subsistence economies, the proportion is very much less. Regardless of the level of these activities, however, those who are engaged in service industries are usually found in areas of concentrated population. These are essentially urban activities. Cities and other concentrations provide a market for the sale of these services, and conversely, the availability of services in urban areas may further stimulate the concentration of population. Some cities are characterized by specialization in particular services, and may be known as insurance or banking centers, just as some cities are known as manufacturing or trade centers.

These final articles are concerned with two major ideas: first, the nature of the service industries and how they are related to other activities; second, the factors which influence the generation and expansion of urban agglomerations. Fullerton investigates the first consideration by examining the pattern and concentration of several service activities in England and Wales. He relates variations in these activities to varying levels of employment and to varying types of employment found in several urban areas. Gibbs presents a theory for the development of urban centers and shows generalized trends in the growth of population agglomerations. He also indicates some of the problems found in population analysis. Gottmann's paper is an excellent study analyzing the historic growth, the present functions and problems, and future possibilities of a major conurbation of coalesced urban areas. This last is the original statement of the now-familiar concept of Megalopolis.

THE LOCALISATION OF SERVICE INDUSTRIES IN ENGLAND AND WALES

by
*B. FULLERTON**
Newcastle (U.K.)

The contribution of service industries to the employment structure of states and districts is becoming increasingly important and is of particular importance in areas subject to a changing distribution of population. U.N.E.S.C.O. figures[1] show that the proportions employed in service industries in England and Wales are similar to those in other West European countries. In 1956 England and Wales had, on this calculation, 46 pct. of the working population in service industries including 14 pct. in commerce, 8 pct. in transport and 24 pct. in other services. The Netherlands had 45 pct. and Denmark 41 pct. in service industries although West Germany (32 pct.) and France (35 pct.) had lower proportions.

The publication of the Industry Tables of the Census of England and Wales 1951, in 1957[2] provided more detailed information on the distribution of employment in service industries than has been available before. There is a companion volume[3] for Scotland which shows less geographical detail. In the previous Census of 1931 the classification of service industry published for the smaller local authority areas was too broad to be really useful and employees were located at home and not at work. The 1961 figures, to be published in a few years' time are based on a 10 pct. sample only.

It is possible to establish general patterns of service industry localisation in England and Wales from the Industry Tables of the 1951 Census. Of particular importance are the levels at which different service industries are concentrated in the capital and in regional and local centres and the tendency to regional differences in the levels of service provision.

In 1951 8,800,000 people, 45 pct. of the total employed population, were employed in the service industries in England and Wales.

The Industry Tables of the Census recognise 36 service industries giving statistics of employment in 23 service industries for each local

*Lecturer in Geography, King's College, University of Durham.
[1] United Nations, Demographic Yearbook 1956, Table 12.
[2] General Register Office, Census 1951, England and Wales, Industry Tables, 1957.
[3] General Register Office, Census 1951, Scotland, Vol. 4, Occupations and Industries, 1957.

"The Localisation of Service Industries in England and Wales" by *B. Fullerton.* *Reprinted from* Tijdschrift voor Economische en Sociale Geografie, *(May* 1963*), pp.* 126–135, *with permission of author and publisher.*

authority area, and in all service industries in towns of over 50,000 population, county boroughs and administrative counties.

The 12 service industries which employ a sufficiently large labour force in each local authority area to make analysis of their proportionate contribution to general employment valuable, are discussed below. These industries are italicised in Table 1 where figures for the two wholesale distribution industries have been combined. They account for 78 pct. of the employment in all civilian service industries. The smaller service industries not analysed below account for 15 pct.

The figures for local authority areas combine "other government service" (the civil service) with "defence" (the armed forces). Defence services were abnormally large in 1951 owing to disturbed international relationships following the Second World War. Their distribution was related to national needs and showed a marked concentration in certain rural areas of southern England. The presence of army camps and airfields in many rural districts and of naval bases at ports causes considerable difficulty in the interpretation of local and even regional employment statistics. All workers in National government (including

Table 1: Service Industries in
England and Wales 1951.

Industry	No. employed	Perc. civilian employed pop.
Retail distribution of non-food goods	913,217	4.8
Catering, hotels, etc.	807,213	4.3
Defence	710,787	
Retail distribution of food and drink	696,497	3.7
Medical and dental services	562,338	3.0
Local government service	546,499	2.9
Railways	463,120	2.4
Education	461,012	2.4
Private domestic service	453,753	2.2
Insurance, banking & finance	402,504	2.1
Other government services	316,585	
Postal, telegraph and wireless communication	301,627	1.6
Road passenger transport	284,786	1.5
Wholesale distribution of non-food goods	260,199	1.4
Sea transport, port services etc.	232,577	1.2
Entertainment and sport	197,649	1.0
Goods transport by road	173,207	0.9
Dealing in coal, builders' material etc.	160,346	0.8
Wholesale distribution of food & drink	150,726	0.8
Dealing in other industrial materials	120,049	0.6
Laundries	118,718	0.6
Retail sales of sweets, tobacco, papers	100,245	0.5
Hairdressing and manicure	81,801	0.4

the civil service) have therefore been excluded from calculations in Tables 1-4 where the total employed population has thereby been reduced to the *civilian employed population.*

There are at least a few employees of the large service industries analysed here in every local authority area. But the personnel of some service industries are characteristically widely dispersed amongst the population and in other service industries concentrated into a limited number of places. In many of these places concentrated sectors of service industries make a significant contribution to the local industrial pattern. The most important factor leading to local variations in the percentage in services is the pattern of local concentration of service provision. Contact with the consumer is important in all service activity and in many cases it is necessary to meet the customer personally. The degree of personal contact and the frequency at which the products of a service industry are bought, help to determine the numbers employed, their density on the ground, and their patterns of distribution. The classification of service trades, professions and occupations into 23 service industries involves considerable simplification and so makes distribution patterns less easy to recognise, but the geographical concentration of services whose contact with the individual consumer is indirect or infrequent and the dispersal of services where contact is frequent and direct may, however, still be appreciated.

Concentrated service industries may be servicing either a national or regional market, and are "basic" to the towns in which they are located. In some parts of the country there are clearly recognised regional capitals. In other areas such as the East Midlands there is a choice between a number of equally accessible centres.

SERVICE INDUSTRIES AND THE NATIONAL MARKET

London has exerted a very strong attraction on services catering for the national market and only strong geographical, historical or economic reasons locate these elsewhere. Services associated with resorts avoid such a large and inland concentration of population and national transport services are also found at provincial ports and transport nodes. It is important in this connection that the great majority of the population of England and Wales have lived within five hours' journey of London since the development of express rail services in the middle of the nineteenth century. There are a number of specialised service industry areas in London lying within an inner zone comprising the City of London and the five adjacent boroughs of Finsbury, Holborn, St. Marylebone, St. Pancras and Westminster. The resident population of these boroughs was 225,000 in 1951, but they provided for the employment of almost 1,250,000. This area employs 6 pct. of the total employed population and 9 pct. of the service population of England and Wales. Employment in the largest service industries in Inner London, Insurance and Wholesale distribution (food and non-food goods combined) is so highly concentrated there as to be poorly represented in the local authority areas of the Provinces.

Inner London employed 33 pct. of all workers in Insurance in England

and Wales, 31 pct. in Accounting, 29 pct. in Law, 21 pct. in Wholesale distribution and 17 pct. in Postal services. Other services, such as Retail food distribution, are markedly under-represented in the Inner London area owing to its relatively small population.

Although Industrial Census figures do not allow a fully accurate assessment of the numbers employed in service industries supplying national needs from the Inner London area it is possible to arrive at an estimate by calculating the proportion by which each service industry in Inner London exceeds the average proportion found in the rest of England and Wales. Such a calculation suggests that about 450,000 people, 5 pct. of the service employment of the country and half that of the Inner London zone, were employed in these "national" basic services in 1951. This figure includes employment in the civil service. Excluded are the headquarters and office staff of many manufacturing concerns whose main labour force is employed in provincial industrial areas. Despite the absence of mines or farms in these five boroughs they employed 1,657 in mining and 609 in farming. In contrast to the Inner zone of London the service industries in the remainder of the Greater London conurbation are present in about the same proportions of total employment as in south-east England in general.

IRREGULAR CONCENTRATION OF SERVICE INDUSTRY

The concentration of some service industries is not only related to local population numbers but to the presence of port or resort facilities or some other local geographical advantage of national importance. The major ports of Britain all had over 12 pct. of their industrial employment in transport services. Other towns developed as route centres or were chosen as headquarters of former railway companies and so had locomotive building and repair shops (which in Britain are owned by the railway administration). Such are the important rail centres of Carlisle, Chester, Exeter, Gloucester and York, each with percentages in transport services over half as great again as the average for county boroughs. Other services looking to national markets have developed in the south and east of England and Wales. The larger private boarding schools, as an example, show a distinct concentration in these areas.

LOCAL CONCENTRATIONS OF SERVICE INDUSTRY

An analysis of the distribution of employment in service industries in county boroughs and in other local authority areas[4] showed that of the larger service industries listed in Table 1, Railways, Road passenger transport, Postal communication, Wholesale, Retail (non-food) distribution and Insurance are predominantly concentrated into district service centres. Retail food distribution, Local government, Education, Medical services and Catering are *dispersed*. As an example the percentages employed in Retail food in county boroughs and in other Local Authority areas were 3.8 and 3.9

4 FULLERTON, B., The pattern of Service industries in northeast England. Dept. of Geography, King's College, Newcastle upon Tyne, Research Series No. 3, 1960.

respectively. Retail (non-food) provided 5.7 pct. of employment in county boroughs but only 3.9 pct. in other Local Authority areas. Private domestic service is another dispersed service industry but is rapidly declining in numbers (by 67 pct. since 1931) and is of greatest significance in rural districts. Figure 1 illustrates different patterns of service industry distribution in a characteristic strip of England extending eastward from the Pennines to York and southward from Morpeth across the Northumberland-Durham coalfield and the vale of York to include the West Riding conurbation and the northern section of the Yorkshire coalfield.

Regionally concentrated service industries show rather different *patterns* of concentration. Insurance, for example, has a limited number of regional concentrations in the provinces. Table 2 shows the concentration of Insurance in Inner London and, as an example, in the five north-eastern counties of England (Northumberland, Durham and the Yorkshire Ridings) where Leeds and Newcastle are the major regional centres. Outside these centres of regional concentration and a few towns like Bradford which provide specialist service for specific industries, other urban areas have low but regular proportions of their employed population in the Insurance industry. In rural areas there is a distinct concentration of employees in Insurance in the rural service centres. The distribution pattern of the Insurance industry is thus dominated by that of its concentrated elements. The concentration takes place at three levels: na-

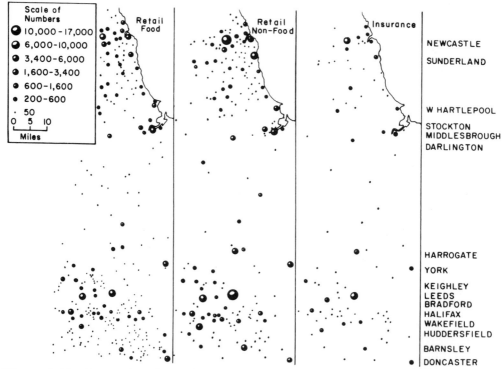

Figure 1: Employment in three characteristic service industries in northern England, 1951.

Table 2. Distribution of Insurance,
Banking, and Finance

	Population	Pct.	Insurance	Pct.
England and Wales	43,757,888	100	402,504	100
Inner London	378,750	0.9	130,448	32.5
County Boroughs	13,728,600	31.2	126,748	31.3
All other areas	29,650,538	68.0	145,308	36.2
Five N. E. Countries	6,884,951	100	40,274	100
Newcastle	291,724	4.2	4,419	11.0
Leeds	505,880	7.3	5,915	14.7
Other urban areas[1]	4,563,406	66.2	23,101	57.4
Rural service centers	135,992	2.0	1,079	2.7
"Agricultural" rural districts[2]	467,015	6.8	1,369	3.4

[1]Resorts and rural service centers excluded
[2]Those with significant mining population excluded.

tional, regional and, where settlement is dispersed, local. Wholesale distribution has a similar pattern to Insurance. The pattern of concentration of Retail (non-food) differs from that of Insurance in that service centres for Retail (non-food) are more frequent than those for Insurance. In Figure 1 it should be noted that three times as many people are employed in Retail (non-food) in the area shown as in Insurance.

Railways, Postal communication and Road passenger transport show distribution patterns like that of Retail (non-food) with, apart from specialised transport centres of national importance, employees concentrated into the same district service centres. In these towns the presence of workers in the concentrated service sectors, with their dependants, increases the total population and so provides a local market for increased numbers of workers in the dispersed services in that centre.

Retail food is shown as an example of dispersed service distribution in Figure 1. As the numbers employed in the area are about the same as those in Retail (non-food) the differences in degree of concentration may be appreciated. Retail food numbers correlate closely with the numbers of total population. In terms of employment Retail food comprises 3.8 pct. of the labour force, and shops extend into suburbs and villages. All small villages and general stores are included in this classification just as all large departmental stores are classified as Retail (non-food).

In those rural agricultural areas where the majority of the population live in villages of 3,000 people or less and in the rural mining areas (where villages associated with twentieth century pits may have populations of over 12,000), Retail food shows some degree of concentration into rural service centres.

LOCAL LEVELS OF SERVICE EMPLOYMENT

The degrees of concentration discussed above are reflected in Table 3,

Table 3. Service Industries in Rural Districts 1951

	Pct. civilian employed population		
	Agricultural R.D.s (10 pct. sample of 423)	Mining R.D.s (52)	Provincial England and Wales
All Services	32.1	19.2	41.3
Railway	4.6	1.5	2.4
Road passenger	0.5	0.5	1.6
Postal etc.	0.9	0.4	1.4
Wholesale	0.7	0.2	1.8
Retail food	2.9	2.3	3.9
Retail non-food	1.2	1.4	4.8
Insurance	0.8	0.4	1.5
Local govt.	2.2	1.5	3.1
Educational	2.6	1.9	2.5
Medical	2.5	1.7	3.0
Catering	3.9	2.6	4.1
Private domestic	6.3	1.6	2.3

which is based on a 10 pct. sample of the 423 rural districts of England and Wales without significant coalmining activity *(agricultural rural districts)* and on returns from the 52 rural districts with over 5 pct. employed in coalmining. Service industries accounted for an average of 32 pct. of employment in the agricultural rural districts, all of which contain some manufacturing industry.

The representation of Transport and the dispersed services was similar to the national pattern. The six large dispersed services totalled 18.9 pct. of the civilian employed population of England and Wales and 18.4 pct. in the rural districts. The proportions in the major Transport services were 5.4 pct. in England and Wales, 6.0 pct. in the rural districts. Concentrated services however accounted for only 2.5 pct. of the employed population of rural districts: 8 pct. in provincial England and Wales. Small service industries not listed in Table 3 employed 3.1 pct. in rural districts but 9 pct. in England and Wales.

The low proportion of the rural population employed in services reflected the concentration of Retail (non-food) distribution and similar services into rural service towns and district service centres. Some concentration of Retail food, Local government, Medical services and Catering is also indicated in Table 3. Only Private domestic and Railway service were better represented in rural districts than in the country at large. Employment in other forms of transport was not so well developed in rural districts. The progressive concentration of railway services in Great Britain which has led to the closure of many rural stations and lines had hardly begun to take effect in 1951. Although not shown in Table 3, National government service then comprised 15 pct.

of the total employed population of the rural districts reflecting the rural distribution of army camps and airfields.

Just as "dispersed sectors" of concentrated services are found in rural districts the concentrated elements present in small numbers even in dispersed services are often also located there owing to their need for space, low rents or isolation. Some rural districts contain large hospitals originally built in the late nineteenth century for infectious, tubercular or mental illness, or private boarding schools.

The local service centres of rural areas are descended from mediaeval market towns and market villages. After the development of railways in the middle of the nineteenth century some centres retained their importance but many others sank into obscurity. The development of automobile transport may lead to further developments in this direction but in 1951 the number of private cars in rural areas was still limited and public transport by road and rail played a significant role in the maintenance of rural service centres. These towns provide the concentrated service industries for rural areas but most have attracted some manufacturing industry such as the processing of local raw materials, minor engineering or the small scale manufacture of highly specialised products for a national market. Generally rural service centres have over 55 pct. in service industries. Where little other industry exists this proportion may rise to 75 pct. and the "basic" function of the town is purely local in character.[5]

[5] STEVENS, A., The distribution of the rural population of Great Britain. Transactions of the Institute of British Geographers, Vol. 11, 1946.

Figure 2 shows as an example the employment structures of towns and rural districts respectively, in a typical area of rural England lying immediately east of the area portrayed in Figure 1 and extending from Tees-side across the East Riding of Yorkshire to the outskirts of Lincoln. Manufacturing is only of major importance in Hull (whose size precludes it, being shown on the scale used for other local authority areas on the map), in Scunthorpe (south-west of the Humber estuary) and Loftus, (steel manufacturing centres), and in Gainsborough and Beverley (engineering). In the rural districts agriculture is the predominant non-service industry except in Beverley and Grimsby rural districts where new industrial plants have been sited outside the towns. Of the towns 24 are small and 19 have at least 55 pct. of their population in service industries. The coastal towns which have not been industrialised have developed as seaside resorts or dormitory towns. The 22 rural districts of this area have proportions in service industry ranging from 23-41 pct. but 20 have between 25 pct. and 30 pct. in services.

Figure 3 illustrates conditions in part of south-east England where the "normal" rural picture is overlain by service industry in the resorts of the south coast and those catering for the demands of commuters working in Greater London. A different symbol is used to show the variations in individual service industries in this area. Proportions in services in the rural districts range from 25 pct. to 59 pct. so that the minimum levels of servicing found in those rural areas with poorer accessibility to the capital

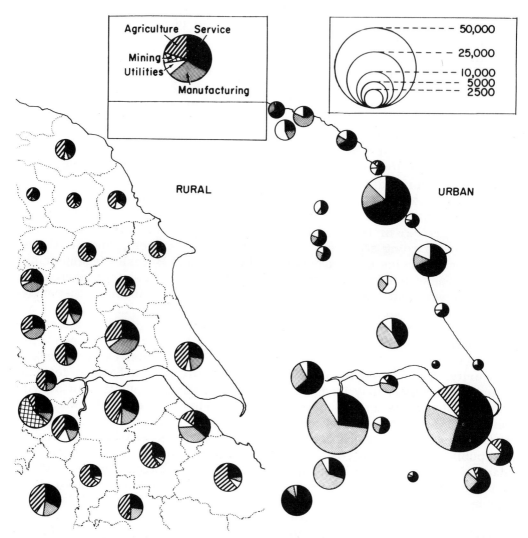

Figure 2: Employment in part of eastern England, 1951. Hull and its suburb of Halt-emprice have been excluded from the urban map owing to their large size in relation to other centers.

are similar to those in the East Riding and the northern part of the area shown in Figure 2. Maximum proportions are higher in residential rural districts near London or in good communication with it. The importance of Private domestic service in some rural areas and the significance of Catering on and near the south coast should be noted.

In south-east England many towns have a variety of functions, acting as rural service centres, as dormitories for workers in Inner London, and as residential towns for people no longer in employment. In both resorts and dormitory settlements high proportions of the employed population are engaged in services. A distinction may be made between Dormitory towns where the high proportion in services reflects the

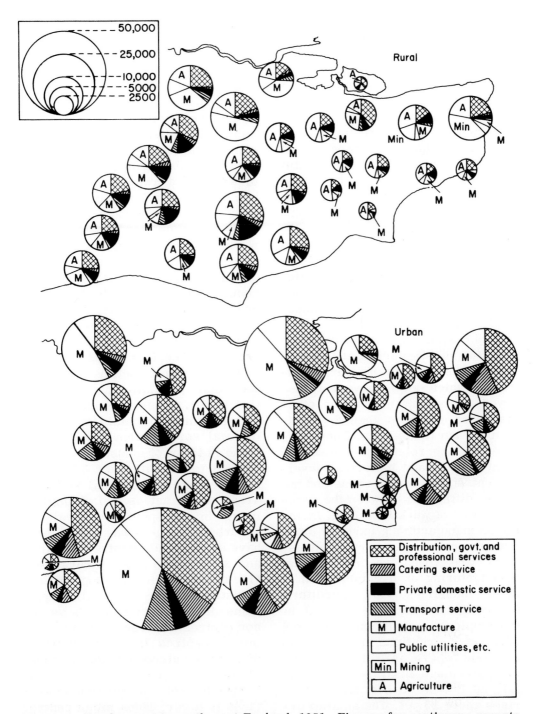

Figure 3: Employment in south-east England, 1951. Figures for contiguous resorts in Brighton conurbation, on Thanet and at the Medway towns have been combined into one symbol on the urban map.

daily outflow of workers and in relation to the *resident employed population* proportions in services are not abnormal, and resorts, however, which are "basic" service towns with high proportions of both resident and working population in service industry. The census is taken in April. In summer, numbers in the Catering industry are considerably augmented.

A different pattern of local service provision is found on the coalfields and on the periphery of the industrial conurbations of northern and midland England and south Wales. Here the pattern of settlement has evolved by the superimposition of several cycles of industrial or mining development.

Table 3 shows that Railway and Private domestic service are of small importance in mining rural districts, which also show a rather lower representation of the other dispersed services than the agricultural rural districts. These differences are related to the settlement pattern and historical development of the mining areas and not to the difference between the earning power of work in mining, farming or manufacturing industry since low proportions in service industries are found whether mining, manufacturing or a combination of these industries with agriculture forms the non-service element in the employed population.[6] Figure 4 illustrates conditions in the Durham coalfield where in rural districts the percentage in all services may fall as low as 15 pct. and seldom rises above 25 pct. The smaller urban districts of the industrial and coalfield zones also have percent-

ages in service industries as low as 15. Proportions fall below even this figure in a few single industry towns drawing large numbers of workers daily from other local authority areas. Billingham upon Tees (8 pct. in services) may be taken as an example. Established in 1923 to house some of the labour force of the Teesside chemical industry the number of workers drawn into the Billingham area daily from adjacent local authority areas in south Durham and Tees-side equalled the number of workers resident there in 1951.

In the Northumberland-Durham coalfield and the West Yorkshire conurbation and south Yorkshire coalfield, for example, 74, out of the 94 urban areas with under 50,000 people had 15-35 pct. employed in services. The four towns with proportions under 15 pct. had large inward daily population movements so that 15 pct. in services may be taken as a minimum in Britain for the level of local service provision whether found in towns or industrial villages. The 16 towns with over 35 pct. in services are small local authority areas which act as foci of employment in transport, the wealthier suburbs of large towns where these have separate administrative status, and some of the original rural service centres which developed before industrialisation and still supply some district service needs as minor centres. In these rather frequent minor centres the ratio between dispersed and concentrated services is similar to that in large towns although the total proportion in services is lower. These minor centres grew up when local communications were less well developed and now have a range of services intermediate between those of a mining village

[6] FULLERTON, B., op. cit., p. 21.

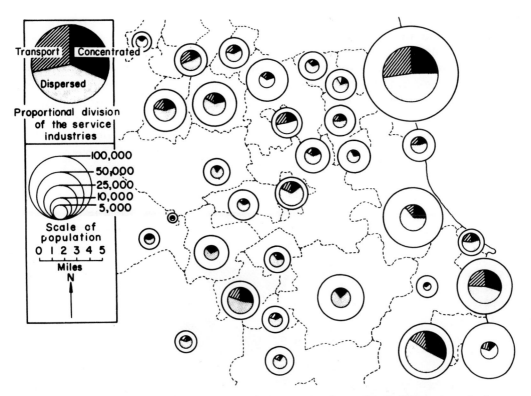

Figure 4: Service industries in central County Durham, 1951. The outer circle represents the total civilian employed population, the inner, divided circle the number in service employment. Sunderland lies in the north-east of the map, Tees-side towns to the south-east.

and factory town on the one hand, or those of a large or even rural service centre on the other. This is especially reflected in higher proportions in Retail (non-food) since shops are more highly specialised than in the rural industrial districts. The larger pre-industrial centres (Preston 43 pct., Wigan 43 pct. or Burton-on-Trent 38 pct.) for example have retained some centralised service functions despite attracting many industrial plants and so also have a similar employment structure to the national average. Other towns, like Manchester (48 pct.) and Bradford (47 pct.) by dint of a large regional concentration of services or of restricted extension of bound-

aries show a higher than average proportion of their industrial population employed in the service industries. Really large towns tend to approach the national average proportion by virtue of their size alone, since the extent of the market makes representation of all service industries economic. The smaller and more peripheral county boroughs within each industrial area and those experiencing very rapid growth in the nineteenth century still have low proportions of their working populations employed in service industries. Although manufacturing industry dominates the employment structure of these towns, they are sufficiently large to require

concentrated services within their
boundaries and may act as service
centres for shopping, entertainment,
and specialised medical and educational services for small settlements in their neighbourhood.

Three characteristic levels of
servicing may, therefore, be recognised in industrial areas. Small
industrial towns and rural mining
areas have a minimum level of servicing at 15 pct. of their employed

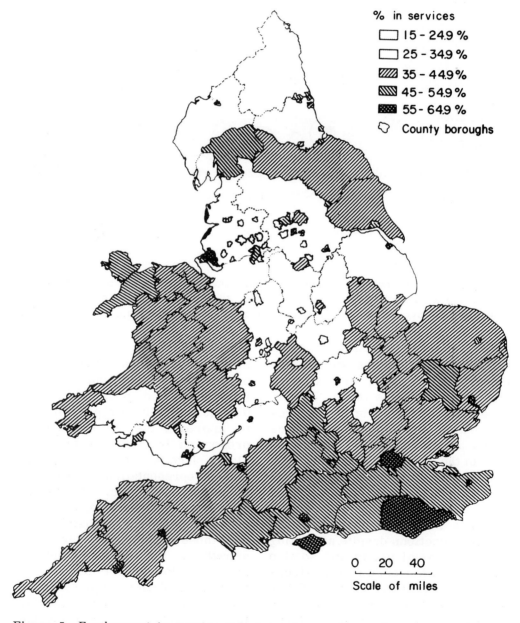

Figure 5: Employment in service industries in counties and county boroughs of
England and Wales, 1951.

population in service industries. Some of the small or medium sized towns act as local service centres, often as a legacy of their pre-industrial function. Here concentrated service industries are found and over 30 pct. of the population is employed in service industries. District and regional servicing is concentrated in much larger towns where proportions employed in service industries are about the national average.

REGIONAL PATTERNS OF SERVICE PROVISION

Differing patterns of rural and industrial servicing lead to marked regional variations in the proportion of the population employed in service industries in England and Wales. Figure 5 shows the percentage in service industries in county boroughs, generally the larger or historically more important towns, separately from that of *administrative counties* i.e. the geographical counties outside the county boroughs, in order to minimise the effect of local concentrations of service population. It is clear that the percentage in services is twice as high in some counties as in others. Within the class intervals chosen however the counties fall into recognisable geographical groups.

In the eastern counties (apart from Lindsey and West Suffolk) Warwickshire, the greater part of Wales and the south-western peninsula the percentage in services is near the national figure (excluding Inner London) of 41.3 pct. Services are poorly represented in the northern counties and the north Midlands. South and east of London services dominate the employment structure

to an extent only found elsewhere in north-west Wales, Westmorland and West Suffolk.

The adherence of one or two counties to the groups shown in Table 4 and Figure 5 may be explained by local administrative accidents. If the boundaries of Bristol were extended to the limit of its built-up area Gloucestershire would join the counties with over 35 pct. of their population in services, as would Bedford if Luton had been granted county borough status. These counties are geographically and statistically marginal to the group. *Mackinder* regarded Gloucestershire as a transitional county in 1907.[7] The marginal alteration of county boundaries or the use of a different class interval (as experiments have shown) would not disguise the fact that large areas of the north of England and the Midlands have a service provision well below the average for the county, while that in the south-eastern counties is well above it.

The county boroughs show a broadly similar regional pattern of service provision to that of the counties. It should be noted that county borough status is not based entirely on size or function and that few county boroughs have been created during the twentieth century. There are, therefore, few county boroughs in the south and east of England where population growth has been more recent. Canterbury is the only county with less than 50,000 people. Luton (110,000) is the largest non-county borough outside the conurbations. Most county boroughs have higher proportions of their populations in services than

7 MACKINDER, H. J., Britain and the British Seas. 1907. p. 232.

Table 4. Service Provision in Counties 1951

Pct. in services	Average pct. in each group of counties				
	25-34.9	35-44.9	45-54.9	55	Provinc. England & Wales
No. of counties	(18)	(29)	(12)	(3)	(62)
Railway	2.2	3.0	2.3	2.2	2.4
Road passenger	1.1	1.1	1.5	1.7	1.6
Postal etc.	0.9	1.7	1.7	2.2	1.4
Wholesale	0.9	1.2	1.1	3.2	1.8
Retail food	3.5	4.0	4.4	4.2	3.9
Retail non-food	3.4	4.1	4.6	5.4	4.8
Insurance	0.9	1.3	1.6	3.3	1.5
Local govt.	2.5	3.4	3.4	3.4	3.1
Educational	2.4	3.1	3.3	2.8	2.5
Medical	2.1	2.7	3.4	3.8	3.0
Catering	3.2	4.8	5.0	7.0	4.1
Private domestic	2.2	4.2	5.6	6.0	2.3
All services	30.1	40.5	48.0	57.6	41.3

The distribution of the counties in each group is shown in Fig. 5.

the surrounding administrative counties since they supply "basic" services to the latter. In the Midlands and north of England, however, many county boroughs have a similar proportion in services to that in the neighbouring county. Coventry and Smethwick in the west Midlands have a lower proportion. Eleven of the 12 county boroughs south of the Thames and Bristol Channel have over 55 pct. in services. Further north only Gloucester, Chester and six coastal towns attain this proportion, each with significant "national" functions as transport centres or resorts.

Transport services as a whole (road, rail and sea), Catering and Private domestic service show the widest percentage variations among services in county boroughs. All the county boroughs containing major port facilities have over 12 pct. in transport services. A percentage in Transport of over 12 only "explains" the inclusion of seven county boroughs in the group with over 55 pct. in services (Liverpool and Bootle, East and West Ham, Southampton, Cardiff and Grimsby). Administrative counties are too large and varied in structure to develop proportions in Transport far away from the national average of 8 pct.

The percentage distribution of Catering and Private domestic service in the administrative counties has been ranked and the percentage by which these services exceed the level of the upper quartile of the distribution deducted from the total percentage in services in the relevant counties. The high proportions of employment in the counties of Westmorland, Wight and East Sussex (over 55 pct.) may be explained by percentages in Catering (Westmorland 7.5 pct., Wight 9.4 pct., E. Sussex 5.3 pct.) and in Private domestic service (Westmorland 5.3 pct., Wight 5.1 pct., E. Sussex 11.1 pct.) well above the national averages for Catering of 4.1 pct. and Private domestic service of 2.3 pct.

These are the only counties where high proportions in the service group of industries may be explained by marked concentration in one or two service industries. Normally high proportions in several service industries are found in the same counties. The percentages employed in each service industry in each county were ranked and the quartile values of each rank distribution found. E. and W. Sussex had percentages within the upper quartile distribution of seven service industries, Caernarvon of six, Kent and the East Riding of five, Dorset, Hampshire, Berkshire, Devon and Westmorland of four. Of the counties with over 45 pct. employed in all service industries, only Oxford, Anglesey and W. Suffolk had less than four services in the top quartile of their respective ranges. The level of provision of individual services shows a close relation to the percentage employed in all services. This ratio is an important general guide to the level of service provision.

Consideration of figures at national, regional and local levels showed that the proportional distribution of employment in service industries was not simply related to employment in manufacturing and other industries. Several industrial counties, and county boroughs had proportions in services only slightly below the national average. The proportions in manufacture and service were respectively 48 pct. and 42 pct. in Middlesex, 38 pct. and 37 pct. in Warwickshire, 42 pct. and 42 pct. in Essex for example. The link lies rather in the economic history of England and Wales, for although the majority of the industrial and mining settlements grew up between 1840 and 1880 their characteristic industrial and social structure is clearly recognisable in the 1951 figures, prolonged by recurrent depression in coal, textile, steel and associated industries during the inter-war period and by the demands of total war. National policies for diversifying industrial life and raising the standards of servicing in such areas had not yet made a major impact, for the immediate post-war years were spent in repairing the physical destruction suffered in 1939-45.

The spread of manufacturing industry away from the coalfields since the fall in the relative costs of transporting fuel and power, has involved different industries from those of the coalfields and been associated with a more generous pattern of service provision. Low service provision is associated with the motor vehicle industry (Coventry 23.6 pct., Luton 25.8 pct.) and with certain inter-war industrial estates, (Slough 25.1 pct.), attracting a large daily influx of workers. A recent study of the larger British towns, however,[8] shows a positive correlation between percentage in services other than Transport and recent population growth in towns.

[8] MOSER, C. A., and W. SCOTT, British Towns. 1961.

THE EVOLUTION OF POPULATION CONCENTRATION

Jack P. Gibbs

Dr. Gibbs is Associate Professor in the Department of Sociology, the University of Texas, and Acting Director of the Department's Population Research Center, in which this article was prepared.

STUDIES of urbanization typically view population concentration in strictly quantitative terms, namely, as an increase in the proportion of the population who reside in cities. Urbanization is in fact the major factor in the process of population concentration,[1] but the process involves more than an increase in the proportion of city residents. Specifically, there is evidence of a particular order of stages in population concentration. This paper sets forth suggested major stages and reports a test of their applicability to the demographic history of the 48 coterminous states of the United States up to 1960.

STAGES OF POPULATION CONCENTRATION

The following stages of population concentration are suggested:

I. Cities come into being, but the percentage increase of the rural population equals or exceeds the percentage increase of the urban population at the time cities first appear.

II. The percentage increase of the urban population comes to exceed the percentage increase of the rural population.

III. The rural population undergoes an absolute decline.

IV. The population of small cities undergoes an absolute decline.

V. There is a decline in the differences among the territorial divisions with regard to population density, that is, a change toward a more even spatial distribution of population.

The stages are not mutually exclusive; consequently, it is logically possible for a society to be in two or more of the stages simultaneously. For example, during a given period both the rural population and the population of small cities may be declining. In such a case, the society may be said to be in both stages III and IV. However, the central question in such a case would be concerned with whether the rural population declined before the small cities began to lose population. This question could not be answered *a priori*, because it is logically possible for a society to reach stage IV before stage III; but the prediction is that stage III precedes stage IV. Thus, the theory states that population concentration occurs through the five stages set forth above and that each stage is reached in the order indicated.

Stage I

Little is known about population growth in the first cities, but it appears likely that it was not of any great

[1] See, for example, Hope Tisdale, "The Process of Urbanization," *Social Forces*, Vol. 20, 1942, pp. 311–316.

"The Evolution of Population Concentration" by Jack P. Gibbs. Reprinted from Economic Geography *, Vol. 39 (April 1963), pp. 119–129, with permission of the editor.*

magnitude[2] and may have been less than in the rural areas. The growth of a nation's population is largely dependent, at least early in the history of the nation, on an increase in the food supply. Accordingly, an increase in food production is likely to generate both rural and urban growth. This appears to be generally true, but it is more problematical for the urban population. An increase in food production is almost certain to benefit rural residents, because they have immediate access to the increase, whereas the influence of the same increase is less certain as far as the urban population is concerned. Whether or not the increase actually reaches the urban population depends largely on transportation technology; and, to the extent that efficiency of transportation is not improved relative to the increase in the food supply, the increase will not stimulate as much growth in the urban as in the rural population. For example, imagine a rural population which is producing 1,000,000 units of food per day, with each unit sufficient to support one person under the prevailing consumption standard. If the technology permits the transportation of only 10,000 food units from farms to cities, the urban population would number about 10,000 and the rural population would number about 990,000. Now suppose that some agricultural innovation (or the acquisition of new land) raises food production to 1,500,000 units. If the transportation technology remains unchanged, the urban population will not grow as a direct result of the increase in food production, whereas the rural population could conceivably increase more than 50 per cent. Some improvements in transportation would be likely

to occur eventually; but initially they follow advances in food production. It is also in the period of an inefficient transportation technology that rural-urban migration is most likely to be at a minimum.

Stage II

This stage of the concentration process begins when the rate of growth of the urban population exceeds that of the rural population. The immediate cause of a higher urban growth rate is rural-urban migration,[3] but advances in per capita food production and improvements in transportation are the major underlying factors. Improvements in transportation make increases in food production available to urban residents and reduce the friction of space as an impediment to rural-urban migration.[4] Stage II also reflects the accumulation of several generations of slow urban growth in stage I and the eventual appearance of fairly large cities. This concentration of population makes possible a high degree of division of labor,[5] and through it the appearance of new functions which offer opportunities for

[2] See Kingsley Davis, "The Origin and Growth of Urbanization in the World," *Amer. Journ. of Soc.*, Vol. 60, 1955, pp. 430–432.

[3] Conrad Taeuber, "Rural-Urban Migration," *Agric. History*, Vol. 15, 1941, pp. 151–160; Robert I. Crane, "Urbanism in India," *Amer. Journ. of Soc.*, Vol. 60, 1955, p. 466; Ana Casis and Kingsley Davis, "Urbanization in Latin America," *Milbank Memorial Fund Quarterly*, Vol. 24, 1946, p. 299; Harold F. Dorn, "Migration and the Growth of Cities," *Social Forces*, Vol. 16, 1938, p. 329; Harley L. Browning, "Recent Trends in Latin American Urbanization," *Annals of the Amer. Acad. of Polit. and Soc. Science*, Vol. 316, 1958, p. 118; United Nations, *The Determinants and Consequences of Population Trends*, New York, 1953, pp. 109–111.

[4] Stated in the way of a generalization: a high urban growth rate through rural-urban migration is a product of economic development and related advances in transportation and communication. See Kingsley Davis, "Internal Migration and Urbanization in Relation to Economic Development," *Procs. of the World Population Conference*, 1954, Vol. 2, New York, 1955, pp. 783–799; and United Nations, *op. cit.*, p. 126.

[5] Amos H. Hawley, *Human Ecology*, New York, 1950, pp. 122–123.

employment and a higher standard of living to potential rural-urban migrants.[6]

Stage III

As the volume of rural-urban migration reaches a high level, the number of migrants exceeds natural increase in the rural population which, therefore, undergoes an absolute decline.[7] This decline, which marks the beginning of stage III, is not altogether a product of an increase in the number of migrants from farms to cities; it also reflects a decline in rural natural increase, brought about by the fact that rural-urban migration is selective of individuals in their reproductive years.[8]

Stage IV

As the volume of rural-urban migration increases in stage III, the number of potential migrants becomes less and less,[9] but the "pull" factor is still present. Just as the large centers offer opportunities not present in rural areas, so do they offer opportunities that far exceed those in the small towns. Accordingly, migration to large cities continues, but it is now primarily a movement from small centers to larger ones, with the ultimate outcome being a decline in the population of small places.[10] This decline marks the initiation of stage IV in the concentration process. It results from: (1) the same factors which produced the earlier decline in the rural population; and (2) a loss of functions

in small centers that offer services to a now declining rural population.

Stage V

It might appear that stage IV would continue to the point where virtually all of the national population is located in one huge urban center,[11] but such is not the case. Even if the transportation and agricultural technology could support such concentration, it would not take place. Continued improvements in transportation and communication make it possible for a population to obtain services and maintain existing socio-economic relations without a high degree of concentration and, consequently, there is a movement from high density areas.[12] Persons who work in

[6] United Nations, *op. cit.*, pp. 124–126.
[7] See, for example, Conrad Taeuber, "Recent Trends of Rural-Urban Migration in the United States," *Milbank Memorial Fund Quarterly*, Vol. 25, 1947, pp. 203–213.
[8] United Nations, *op. cit.*, p. 149.
[9] Kingsley Davis and Hilda Hertz Golden, "Urbanization and the Development of Pre-Industrial Areas," *Econ. Development and Cultural Change*, Vol. 3, 1954, p. 11. England is a classic illustration of the process by which the pool of potential rural-urban migrants comes to diminish. See A. K. Cairncross, "Trends in Internal Migration, 1841–1911," *Trans. Manchester Stat. Soc.*, 1938–1939, pp. 21–29.

[10] A connection between small population size and loss of population is suggested by the findings of several studies. See, for example, Edmund de S. Brunner and T. Lynn Smith, "Village Growth and Decline, 1930–1940," *Rural Sociology*, Vol. 9, 1944, pp. 103–115; S. C. Ratcliffe, "Size as a Factor in Population Changes of Incorporated Hamlets and Villages, 1930–1940," *Rural Sociology*, Vol. 7, 1942, pp. 318–328; William Fielding Ogburn, "Size of Community as a Factor in Migration," *Sociology and Social Research*, Vol. 28, 1944, pp. 255–261; C. C. Zimmerman, *Farm Trade Centers in Minnesota, 1905–1929*, Univ. of Minnesota Agric. Experiment Station, Bull. 269, 1930. As the small places decline, the large urban centers grow; both trends contribute, of course, to population concentration. See, for example, Floyd and Lillian Dotson, "Urban Centralization and Decentralization in Mexico," *Rural Sociology*, Vol. 21, 1956, p. 44.
[11] Application of Stewart's formulas to trends in the United States yields a forecast of an eventual disappearance of the rural population and a population decline in small urban places which progresses up the size scale to a point where all of the national population reside in one urban center. See John Q. Stewart, "Empirical Mathematical Rules Concerning the Distribution and Equilibrium of Populations," *Geogr. Rev.*, Vol. 37, 1947, pp. 461–485.
[12] Edward Gross, "The Role of Density as a Factor in Metropolitan Growth in the United States of America," *Population Studies*, Vol. 8, 1954, pp. 113–120; Noel P. Gist, "Developing Patterns of Urban Decentralization," *Social Forces*, Vol. 30, 1952, pp. 257–267; J. Douglas Carroll, Jr., "The Relation of Homes to Work Places and the Spatial Pattern of Cities," *Social Forces*, Vol. 30, 1952, pp. 271–282; Henry S. Shryock, Jr., "Redistribution of Population:

(*Continued on next page*)

THE EVOLUTION OF POPULATION CONCENTRATION

or otherwise depend on large cities come to live at a distance, in small towns or in settlements that have low population densities. The result is eventually stage V, which is characterized by a change toward a more even spatial distribution of population.[13] This is the final stage in the concentration process, and one that could conceivably continue to the point where the population is more evenly distributed than in the case of stage I. However, unlike the situation in stage I, the basis of population distribution in stage V is residential dispersion and not a decline in interdependence; this means that the deconcentration does not result in widely-scattered communities that have virtually no economic

1940 to 1950," *Journ. of the Amer. Stat. Assn.*, Vol. 46, 1951, pp. 417–437; Leo F. Schnore, "The Growth of Metropolitan Suburbs," *Amer. Soc. Rev.*, Vol. 22, 1957, pp. 165–173; Leo F. Schnore, "Metropolitan Growth and Decentralization," *Amer. Journ. of Soc.*, Vol. 63, 1957, pp. 171–180; Donald J. Bogue, *Metropolitan Decentralization: A Study of Differential Growth*, Oxford, Ohio, 1950; Donald J. Bogue, "Changes in Population Distribution Since 1940," *Amer. Journ. of Soc.*, Vol. 56, 1950, pp. 43–57; and Homer Hoyt, "Forces of Urban Centralization and Decentralization," *Amer. Journ. of Soc.*, Vol. 46, 1941, pp. 843–852.

[13] Deconcentration involves, but should not be confused with, the expansion of urban boundaries, decline in urban population densities, or what is often referred to as "decentralization" within urban areas. (See Colin Clark, "Urban Population Densities," *Journ. Royal Stat. Soc.*, Vol. 114, 1951, pp. 490–496; and Henry S. Shryock, Jr., "Population Redistribution Within Metropolitan Areas: Evaluation of Research," *Social Forces*, Vol. 35, 1956, pp. 154–159.) Deconcentration *within* urban or metropolitan areas may take place at the same time that concentration is taking place at the regional level. (See Hans Blumenfeld, "On the Growth of Metropolitan Areas," *Social Forces*, Vol. 28, 1949, pp. 59–64.) The type of deconcentration which characterizes stage V occurs only through an increase in the relative population density of territorial units which are far removed from the major centers of concentration. It involves, in addition to population redistribution within urban areas, the appearance of new centers and shifts in the size hierarchy and spacing of urban centers. See Charles T. Stewart, Jr., "The Size and Spacing of Cities," *Geogr. Rev.*, Vol. 48, 1958, pp. 222–245; and Otis Dudley Duncan, "Population Distribution and Community Structure," *Cold Spring Harbor Symposia on Quantitative Biology*, Vol. 22, 1957, pp. 357–371.

relationships with one another. Stated otherwise, stage V is not a product of the "force of diversification" postulated by George K. Zipf, even though it may eventually involve industrial decentralization at the regional level.[14]

SOME QUALIFICATIONS

Considered as a theory, the sequence of stages of population concentration bears some resemblance to nineteenth-century evolutionary ideas. In recent decades, the notion of an evolutionary course in socio-cultural change has been sharply questioned. Evolutionary theories have suffered from at least two defects, namely, a vagueness in terminology and inadequate qualifications. The vagueness has precluded rigorous tests, while the absence of qualifications made it possible for isolated exceptions to invalidate the theory in question.

The present theory has been formulated with a view to avoiding the glaring errors in grand evolutionary schemes. For one thing, the theory is so stated that it can be subjected to systematic empirical tests. Of greater importance, however, are the qualifications attached to the theory. It is not suggested that all populations inevitably move through the specified stages. On the contrary, a population may remain indefinitely in stage I or a later stage. Furthermore, a population may regress to an earlier concentration stage, and the process may then start over again from that stage. Thus, there is no suggestion that change is inevitable or irreversible. The theory holds only that if concentration takes place it will follow the stages in the order specified.

A second major qualification relates to types of human populations. It is not

[14] See George Kingsley Zipf, *Human Behavior and the Principle of Least Effort*, Cambridge, Mass., 1949, Chap. 9; and George T. Renner, "Geography of Industrial Location," *Econ. Geog.*, Vol. 23, 1947, pp. 187–189.

suggested that the concentration process follows the specified sequence of stages in all populations. The hypothesized sequence will appear without exception only in indigenous and isolated populations, that is, populations that have always been ecologically closed systems.

The necessity for the qualifications is obvious. The migration of contemporary Europeans to unoccupied lands would in all probability never result in stage I; the population might well be in stage II at the outset. Moreover, contacts between the two populations may substantially alter the sequence of stages of concentration. For example, with a steady stream of immigrants there is no necessity for urban growth to result in rural depopulation. The immigrants may either move into cities or replace rural persons who have moved to cities. In general, then, to the extent that contact between populations takes the form of migration or an exchange of food or technology, there is no necessity for the specified stages of concentration to hold.

The qualifications immediately suggest a major criticism of the theory. At present there are no populations that meet the qualifications; and, therefore, it might be argued that the theory is neither testable nor useful. But this ignores the fact that the validity of any theory is contingent upon the qualifications imposed. Moreover, even if the qualifications of a theory create a null class, the validity of the theory can still be assessed indirectly. To the extent that conditions approximate those specified in the qualifications, predictions based on the theory should be correct. For example, the stages of population concentration should hold more consistently for nations than for small territorial divisions (such as counties in the U.S.A.). Small territorial divisions are least likely to approximate an ecologically-closed system, because there is usually a steady stream of migration, technological devices, and food from one division to the next. Finally, a theory does have utility even when applied to conditions that do not meet in all respects those specified in its qualifications. If predictions are to be made, if some kind of order in events is to be sought, then any generalization is better than none.

A TEST OF THE THEORY

Of all existing populations, those delimited by national boundaries most nearly satisfy the qualifications imposed on the theory. However, current international statistics are not suited for a test of the theory. In only a few countries do demographic statistics extend over long periods, and even in these cases the information necessary for determining stages is often not available, particularly with regard to the distant past. Furthermore, in some countries the census definition of urban and of rural has changed from time to time, thereby making historical comparisons difficult if not impossible.

Considering the present nature of demographic statistics, the most feasible approach is to test the theory on large territorial divisions of nations that have population data suitable for long-range historical comparisons. The United States provides such an opportunity, since the individual states are large and their demographic statistics extend back, in some cases, to the first census year, 1790. Moreover, the census classifications of urban, rural, and city-size ranges can be made comparable through each of the past eighteen decennial censuses.

This does not mean that the states are ideal territorial units for a test of the theory. On the contrary, in no state is the population indigenous and isolated; and, since colonial times, there has been an appreciable interstate and international flow of migrants, technological devices, and food. Nevertheless, the states do provide a basis for assessing the utility of the theory. If its predictive power is reasonably high, this would indicate that populations may deviate considerably from the conditions stipulated in the qualifications and yet still conform approximately to the theory.

The Determination of Stages in the Demographic History of the United States

Increases in the urban and rural population cannot be compared *for the time* the first city came into existence, because at least one urban place (defined by the census as a place of 2500 or more inhabitants) was already present in 18 states when their first census was taken.[15] However, some observations concerning stage I can be made. Of the 30 states with no urban place at the time of the first census, six states[16] had a percentage growth of rural population exceeding that of the urban population for the first census decade after an urban place had come into being; 24 of the 30 states had an urban growth rate higher than that for the rural population. These facts suggest that most of the states by-passed stage I, and that this stage is particularly dependent on the conditions specified in the qualifications of the theory. However, the experience of six states indicates that stage I is a possibility, and this is rather important since we are accustomed to the notion that urban growth uniformly exceeds rural growth. It is also of some signif-

icance that, whereas in six states the rural growth rate exceeded that of the urban population in the first decade after urban centers came into existence, this was true for only two states in the second decade.[17] A comparison of the differences between rural and urban growth in the first and second decades after the appearance of urban centers is also instructive. For the 30 states without an urban center at the time of the first state census, the average percentage increase in the urban population during the initial decade was 253 as compared with 108 for the rural population in the same decade. Corresponding figures for the second decade are 142 and 43. The average percentage increase in the urban population was 2.35 times that of the average percentage increase in the rural population in the first decade, but 3.30 times in the second decade.

In the absence of adequate historical data pertaining to stage I of the concentration process, the test of the theory is concerned with the remaining four stages. The major question is, thus, the extent to which the 48 states have passed through stages II, III, IV, and V in the predicted order.

To answer this question it is necessary to determine for each state at each decennial census: (1) the rates of growth for the rural and urban population, (2) the population of small cities, and (3) a measure of population movement toward concentration or deconcentration at the state level.

The most feasible way to determine urban and rural growth is to accept the inter-censal percentage increase for the two populations in each state as reported by the Bureau of the Census.[18] For the period 1790–1940,

[15] The 18 states are: New Hampshire, Massachusetts, Rhode Island, Connecticut, New York, Pennsylvania, Kansas, Maryland, Virginia, South Carolina, Louisiana, Oklahoma, Texas, Montana, Colorado, New Mexico, Arizona, and California.

[16] North Dakota, Nebraska, North Carolina, Georgia, Mississippi, and Utah.

[17] Maine and Wyoming.

[18] United States Bureau of the Census: *United States Census of Population: 1950*, Vol. I, Table 15.

these figures are based on a definition of urban which, for all practical purposes, encompasses only incorporated places of 2500 or more inhabitants. For purposes of comparability, this definition was extended to the 1940–1950 and 1950–1960 decades, even though the Bureau of the Census applied a new urban definition in the 1950 and 1960 censuses.[19] These data make it possible to determine when the percentage of urban growth first came to exceed that of the rural (stage II), and when the rural population first declined (stage III).

To determine when a state has reached stage IV, it is necessary to compare the number of inhabitants of small cities, at each census year, with a decline in the number marking the onset of the stage. In the present test of the theory, the size range 2500–4999 was selected as representing small cities. This size range was selected because the minimum corresponds to the definition of urban as employed by the Bureau of the Census and because the population of smaller places (less than 2500 inhabitants) is not consistently reported in census publications.

The historical statistics in the 1950 census publications show the number of inhabitants of places 2500–4999 for only the census years 1900 through 1950,[20] and the latest census extends this series up to 1960.[21] Thus an inter-censal decline in the population of small cities has been determined over only the years 1900–1960. This ignores the possibility that the population of small cities declined in some states before 1900, but

the over-all sixty-year trend indicates otherwise.

The identification of stage V presents the greatest difficulty of all. Deconcentration at the state level is a movement toward a more even distribution of population throughout the state. This movement can be expressed numerically by determining, for each census year, what percentage of the state's population would have to move from one component territorial division to another to bring about an even distribution of population. When this percentage figure begins to decline, deconcentration has commenced.[22]

For purposes of illustration, a direct measure of population concentration has been applied to Texas and Rhode Island for each census year from 1930 onward, using counties as territorial divisions. The results are shown in Table I. The figures in Table I show that a continuous increase in concentration has occurred in Texas during the past 30 years, whereas exactly the opposite is true for Rhode Island.

Two comments on this method of assessing deconcentration should be made. First, the value of such a measure is always relative to the territorial divisions employed; in general, the smaller the divisions the better. In the case of Texas, for example, it is possible that deconcentration has been going on *within* certain counties, whereas *among* counties the process has been one of concentration. Second, although the measure of population concentration

[19] Urban and rural population for 1950 and 1960 are reported by the Bureau of the Census under both the old urban definition (1940) and the new (1950) definition. 1960 census figures were obtained from reports on individual states as they were released.

[20] United States Bureau of the Census, *op. cit.*, Table 3 in each state part.

[21] From reports on individual states.

[22] This is not true for countries or regions with an expanding frontier of settlement. See Edgar M. Hoover, Jr., "Interstate Redistribution of Population, 1850–1940," *Journ. of Econ. History*, Vol. 1, 1941, pp. 199–205. Where population movement involves principally the settlement of unoccupied territory rather than redistribution, the measure must be adjusted so as to reflect only the relative decline of density in territorial units that were above average in the ratio of inhabitants to land at the start of the period.

TABLE I

COMPARISON OF TWO INDICATORS OF POPULATION CONCENTRATION
FOR RHODE ISLAND AND TEXAS, 1930–1960*

Year	Rhode Island		Texas	
	Increase of urban population over preceding decade minus increase of rural population during same decade (%)	*Measure of population concentration***	*Increase of urban population over preceding decade minus increase of rural population during same decade (%)*	*Measure of population concentration***
1930.................	8.8	39.65	49.0	44.99
1940.................	−12.4	38.47	19.8	46.33
1950.................	−66.3	34.03	70.0	51.35
1960.................	27.7	28.25	66.6	57.73

*Source of data: Census reports for 1930, 1940, 1950, and 1960. Old definitions (1940) employed in determining rural and urban growth.
**Percentage of the state's population that would have to move from one county to another to bring about an equal population density for all counties.

applied to Texas and Rhode Island could be applied to all states at each census year, it would require over 120,000 computations. The use of this direct measure of concentration is accordingly not feasible for an investigation with limited resources for research.

The percentage increase of the urban relative to the rural population provides one basis for gauging deconcentration indirectly. Just as an excess of the percentage urban growth over the rural indicates concentration, so the reverse is indicative of deconcentration. Some support for treating a higher rural rate of growth as indicative of deconcentration is found in a comparison of Texas and Rhode Island.

The percentage of the population that would have to move from one county to the next to bring about an even distribution of population is shown for both states in Table I, along with the difference between the percentages of urban and rural growth during each census decade. Note that for each of the four census years the measure of population concentration is greater for Texas than Rhode Island, and the excess of the urban growth rate over

the rural is also greater for Texas. Note also that in Rhode Island, between 1920 and 1950, the percentage growth of the rural population exceeded that of the urban, and that the values of the measure of concentration have declined since 1930. The exception in the case of Rhode Island is the decade 1950–1960; the measure of concentration declined, but the percentage growth was greater for the urban than the rural population. In Texas, population concentration increased over the past decades; this is in line with the fact that since 1920 the percentage increase of the urban population has been higher than the percentage increase of the rural population. However, as is witnessed by the exception in the case of Rhode Island, this does not mean that the difference between the rural and urban growth rates is a perfectly adequate substitute for a direct measure of population concentration. The difference between the rural and urban growth rates was used to identify the appearance of stage V only because limitations in resources for research precluded direct measures of population concentration. To sum up, when the percentage growth of the rural population comes to exceed that of the urban population, the state is considered to be in stage V. But this criterion cannot be applied without qualification. Although the test of the theory cannot incorporate a consideration of stage I, there is evidence of a tendency toward this stage in some states. If such a tendency did exist, then the earliest period in which the percentage rural growth exceeded the percentage urban growth represents stage I and not stage V. But stage I should occur very early in the history of the state, if it appears at all. Accordingly, the final criterion for the identification of stage V is a percentage increase of the rural population which exceeds that of the urban population *after* the first three census decades in which an urban population was present.

The application of the above criterion is based on the old (1940) urban definition for all census years, including 1950 and 1960. The extension of this definition to 1950 and 1960 can be questioned, despite the fact that it is the *only* way to achieve comparability over time. It could be argued that a higher percentage increase in rural population merely reflects the expansion of urban territory beyond municipal limits. This is doubtless true but the areas of expansion represent, on the whole, low residential densities. Thus, although the higher rate of rural growth may be a product of the failure of municipal boundaries to expand in accordance with population movement, the movement nonetheless suggests deconcentration.

Sequence of Stages for Individual States

Table II shows the decade in which each of the 48 states reached stages II, III, IV, and V of the concentration process. According to the theory, each decade within the rows of Table II should be later than the decade to the

immediate left. Where two adjacent dates are the same, there is no way of determining which stage was reached first during the decade, and such cases constitute evidence neither for nor against the theory.

On the whole, the states conform to the theory. Disregarding cases of adjacent dates that are the same, it is found that stage II appeared before stage III in 45 or 98 per cent of 46 comparisons, that stage III preceded stage IV in 23 or 58 per cent of 40 comparisons, and that stage IV preceded stage V in 28 or 70 per cent of 40 comparisons. Altogether, 96 or 76 per cent of the 126 comparisons indicate that the stages succeeded one another in the order specified by the theory. Such a proportion, or a greater one, would occur on the basis of chance in less than one out of every 100 cases.

Deviant Cases

Inspection of Table II reveals that, in 16 states, the percentage rural growth came to exceed that of urban growth between 1930 and 1940. It might be argued that this is largely the consequence of the economic depression and not a stage in an evolutionary concentration process. This may be partially true, but in 11 of the 16 states the percentage rural increase was greater than the percentage urban increase during both the periods 1930–1940 and 1940–1950.[23] The fact that some of the states reached stage V between 1930 and 1940 (on the basis of the rural-urban differential growth) actually produces several cases of error in

[23] States in which the percentage rural increase exceeded the percentage urban increase in both 1930–1940 and 1940–1950: New Hampshire, Massachusetts, Rhode Island, Connecticut, New York, New Jersey, Pennsylvania, Ohio, Michigan, Oregon, and California. States in which the situation held for 1930–1940 but not for 1940–1950: Indiana, Illinois, West Virginia, Kentucky, and Washington.

TABLE II

Stages of population concentration in the forty-eight coterminus states of the united states up to 1960*

State	Stage II Earliest census decade in which percentage urban growth exceeded percentage rural growth	Stage III Earliest census decade in which rural population underwent a decline	Stage IV Earliest census decade, 1900–1960, in which population of urban places of 2500–4999 underwent a decline	Stage V Earliest census decade (30 years after appearance of 1st urban place) in which percentage rural growth exceeded percentage urban growth
Maine	1800–10	1860–70	1910–20	1950–60
New Hampshire	1800–10	1850–60	1900–10	1930–40
Vermont	1850–60	1860–70	1920–30	1960–70b
Massachusetts	1790–00a	1860–70	1910–20	1930–40
Rhode Island	1790–00a	1790–00a	1900–10	1930–40
Connecticut	1790–00a	1890–00	1910–20	1930–40
New York	1790–00a	1860–70	1930–40	1930–40
New Jersey	1810–20	1960–70b	1960–70b	*1930–40*
Pennsylvania	1790–00a	1960–70b	*1930–40*	1930–40
Ohio	1810–20	1880–90	1910–20	1930–40
Indiana	1840–50	1900–10	1900–10	1930–40
Illinois	1840–50	1880–90	1960–70b	*1930–40*
Michigan	1840–50	1910–20	1940–50	*1930–40*
Wisconsin	1850–60	1920–30	1920–30	1960–70b
Minnesota	1860–70	1920–30	1930–40	1960–70
Iowa	1850–60	1900–10	1900–10	1960–70b
Missouri	1830–40	1900–10	1910–20	1960–70b
North Dakota	1890–00	1930–40	*1920–30*	1960–70b
South Dakota	1880–90	1930–40	*1900–10*	1960–70b
Nebraska	1880–90	1930–40	*1920–30*	1960–70b
Kansas	1860–70a	1890–00	1920–30	1960–70b
Delaware	1840–50	*1830–40*	1940–50	*1920–30*
Maryland	1790–00a	1880–90	1940–50	*1920–30*
Virginia	1790–00a	1830–40	1940–50	1960–70b
West Virginia	1840–50	1940–50	*1920–30*	1930–40
North Carolina	1830–40	1960–70b	1960–70b	1960–70b
South Carolina	1800–10	1860–70	1900–10	*1830–40*
Georgia	1810–20	1920–30	1960–70b	1960–70b
Florida	1860–70	1960–70b	1960–70b	1960–70b
Kentucky	1810–20	1940–50	*1920–30*	1930–40
Tennessee	1830–40	1910–20	1920–30	1960–70b
Alabama	1830–40	1940–50	*1900–10*	*1870–80*
Mississippi	1840–50	1910–20	*1900–10*	*1870–80*
Arkansas	1860–70	1940–50	1940–50	1960–70b
Louisiana	1820–30	1940–50	*1930–40*	*1840–50*
Oklahoma	1890–00a	1930–40	*1920–30*	1960–70b
Texas	1850–60a	1940–50	1960–70b	1960–70b
Montana	1870–80a	1920–30	*1900–10*	1910–20
Idaho	1900–10	1960–70b	*1950–60*	1960–70b
Wyoming	1880–90	1940–50	1960–70b	*1910–20*
Colorado	1870–80	1960–70b	*1920–30*	*1910–20*
New Mexico	1860–70	1860–70	1930–40	1960–70b
Arizona	1890–00	1950–60b	*1920–30*	1920–30
Utah	1870–80	1960–70b	1940–50	1960–70b
Nevada	1870–80	1880–90	1900–10	1900–10
Washington	1880–90	1960–70b	1960–70b	*1930–40*
Oregon	1860–70	1960–70b	1910–20	1930–40
California	1850–60a	1960–70b	1920–30	1930–40

*Source of data: United States Bureau of the Census, *United States Census of Population: 1950*, Vol. I, and individual state reports for the 1960 census. Statistics based on old (1940) urban and rural definitions. Italics indicate errors in prediction—cases in which the decade is earlier and not later than the preceding one.

ᵃ No earlier census data.
ᵇ Earliest possible decade.

prediction. Had they entered stage V after 1940 or 1950, the order of stages would have been more consistent with the theory.

The majority of errors in prediction involve stage IV. Whether this is true because this particular stage is more sensitive to the conditions specified in the qualifications of the theory or whether it is due to a failure to employ a lower size range for small cities (under 1000 or 1000–2499, rather than 2500 or more) is a question for further study. However, since the populations of places of less than 2500 inhabitants are not consistently reported in United States census publications, research on lower size ranges will have to be conducted for other countries.

CONCLUSIONS

The results of the test of the theory suggest a tendency for population concentration to occur through a certain order of stages. But the evidence suggests nothing more than a tendency, as several states in the United States have not moved through the stages in the sequence predicted by the theory. Whether this merely reflects the fact that the states do not meet the conditions specified in the qualifications of the theory or whether it means that the theory is inherently deficient can be determined only through further investigation. If it can be shown that the stages hold better for countries (or intra-national territorial units) that have not experienced an appreciable amount of international trade, immigration, or emigration, then the argument for the theory would be strengthened considerably. Tests of the theory at the international level will be difficult, largely because of the problems involved in obtaining the necessary data; but the results of the present investigation, while by no means conclusive, would seem to justify further research.

Further research on the subject should go beyond observations on the order of stages and consider variables related to the rationale for each stage. For example, is it true that a decline in rural fertility (as measured by the crude birth rate) typically occurs before the rural population declines in absolute numbers? Answers to this and to other questions pertaining to the dynamics of population concentration might well be more significant, particularly for underdeveloped countries, than the order of stages.

MEGALOPOLIS
OR THE URBANIZATION OF THE NORTHEASTERN SEABOARD

Jean Gottmann

Dr. Gottmann, Professor at the School of Political Science, University of Paris, is on leave to direct for The Twentieth Century Fund a research project, "A Study of Megalopolis." He is also a member of the Institute for Advanced Study, Princeton, N. J.

THE frequency of large urban units scattered along the Atlantic seaboard in the northeastern United States was a striking realization to the foreigner who first visited the area, even 15 years ago. In February, 1942, after a first trip from New York to Washington, the writer, being asked by Isaiah Bowman in Baltimore what was the most striking impression he had had as a geographer in his first months in this country, answered: "The density of great cities along this coast, from Boston to Washington."

In 1950, on the basis of the new census, the Bureau of the Census prepared a map, later published as an illustration to a booklet of statistics on *State Economic Areas*, which showed clearly the continuity of an area of "metropolitan" economy from a little north of Boston to a little south of Washington, more precisely from Hillsborough County in New Hampshire to Fairfax County in Virginia. This seemed to be a first statistical demonstration on the map of the existence of a continuous stretch of urban and suburban areas, the main NE-SW axis of which was about 600 miles long, and within the frame of which dwelt even in 1950 some 30 million people.

In the geography of the distribution of habitat this was a phenomenon unique by its size not only in America but in the world. It resulted obviously from the coalescence, recently achieved, of a chain of metropolitan areas, each of which grew around a substantial urban nucleus. The super-metropolitan character of this vast area, the greatest such growth ever observed, called for a special name. We chose the word *Megalopolis*,[1] of Greek origin, and listed

[1] The term *Megalopolis* was preferred to others after careful consideration of various possibilities. We wish to express our appreciation for the help received in this matter from several distinguished classicists at the Institute for Advanced Study, especially from Professors Harold Cherniss, Benjamin Merritt, and the late Jacob Hammer. "Megalopolis" was used by various authors in connection with quite different meanings: ancient philosophers described sometimes by it the "world of ideas"; recently Lewis Mumford used it to describe the whole trend towards large cities. We have felt it appropriate to describe a unique geographical region, characterized more than any other by enormous urban and metropolitan growth, and to assess the present status of a vast region in the northeastern seaboard section of the United States. Our statistical definition as on the maps is based on the map accompanying the Bureau of the Census publication: *State Economic Areas* by Donald J. Bogue, Washington, 1951.

"Megalopolis or the Urbanization of the Northeastern Seaboard" by Jean Gottmann. Reprinted from Economic Geography, *Vol. 33 (July 1957), pp. 189-200, with permission of the editor.*

in Webster's dictionary as meaning "a very large city."

Indeed, the name "Megalopolis" appears on modern maps of Greece, designating a plateau in the Peloponnesus. A city was established there in ancient times, the founders of which dreamt of a great future for it and of an enormous size. But the Greek town of Megalopolis never grew to be much of a city. What has developed now in the northeastern seaboard surpasses everything dreamers of the past may have visualized. Aristotle, however, wrote in his *Politics:* "When are men living in the same place to be regarded as a single city? What is the limit? Certainly not the wall of the city, for you might surround all Peloponnesus with a wall. Like this, we may say, is Babylon and every city that has the compass of a nation rather than a city." (III, 3, 1276a, 25.)

A few years ago the reviewer of a book on the history of eastern railroads referred to the stretch of land along the tracks of the Pennsylvania and Baltimore and Ohio Railroads from New York City to Washington, D.C., as the "Main Street" of the nation. To be quite correct, such a "Main Street" ought to be prolonged along the rail tracks from New York City to Boston. There is, however, some truth in this symbolical expression. This section of U.S. 1 has come to assume within the American nation a special function, or a whole group of intertwined functions, which is hinted at in less urbanized areas by the concept of Main Street.

WHAT IS THE MEANING OF A STUDY OF MEGALOPOLIS?

Geographers are of course convinced of the value of a study describing a given geographic region endowed with some unity and originality, and thus differentiated from neighboring areas. Although such a region may be unique in the world, investigating its features, problems, and structure has generally been recognized as a worthwhile enterprise. As the data describing unique cases piled up, the endeavor developed in the geographical profession to look for general principles and for studies of cases, the outcome of which would be more immediately valuable because they are applicable to some extent in more than one area or place.

Although unique today, *Megalopolis* obviously has been and still is an extraordinarily interesting laboratory *in vivo* where much of what may well be accepted as the "normalcies" of the advanced civilization of the latter part of the twentieth century is slowly shaping. It still is too early to assess the full meaning of a study of Megalopolis in the frame we have outlined. The study must first be carried out. The many questions it involves could not be listed, let alone discussed, in such a brief article. A few hints may be given, however, of what such a survey could mean and of the main problems it could tackle.

By its size and mass, Megalopolis is both an exceptional growth and a pioneer area; exceptional, for nowhere else could one find another concentration of population, of industrial and commercial facilities, of financial wealth and cultural activities, comparable to it. However, in several other points in America and on other continents growth of continuously urbanized spaces may be observed. More of such enormous "metropolitan" bodies can be expected to arise as the evolution, already well advanced in and around New York, Philadelphia, Boston, Washington, reaches other cities and their environs. In this sense Megalopolis is a pioneer area: the processes which develop therein will help toward an understanding of, and will forecast ways and obstacles to, urban growth in various other parts.

In fact Megalopolis has already been pioneering in the organization of urban life for quite some time. Such features as skyscrapers, building elevators, city and suburban networks of trains, traffic lights, and one-way streets started here on a large scale to gain later world-wide adoption. Megalopolis grew up from the network provided by the early mushrooming of sea-trading towns along the coast from Boston to New York and then, along the Fall line, from New York to Washington. The size of its principal urban nuclei, especially New York and Philadelphia, caused the subsequent mushrooming of suburbs filling in the spaces between the larger cities. James Madison defined New Jersey as a "barrel tapped at both ends"; that this state's function was essentially to link the area of New York and Philadelphia was apparently understood by such a clever observer at the end of the eighteenth century. But the polynuclear origin of Megalopolis is beginning to be repeated in other regions. A vast urban and suburban area is rapidly expanding around Los Angeles, for instance; inland it has already reached, in fact, San Bernardino; it may unite with San Diego on the coast. Around Chicago, on the shore of Lake Michigan, another impressive urban continuity is shaping. The metropolitan areas stretching in Ohio between Cleveland and Pittsburgh are close to coalescence; and the St. Lawrence Seaway, once opened, may accelerate and expand these trends in the area south of Lakes Erie and Ontario. And as more metropolitan areas are pushing forth suburban tentacles one towards another throughout the nation, additional but smaller Megalopolis-like clusters will be formed. This is a process involving considerable changes in the American modes of living.

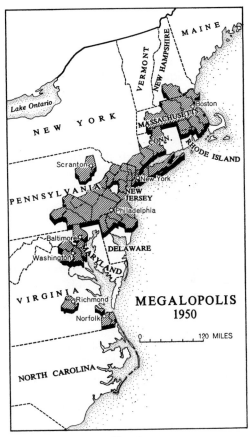

FIG. 1.

The trends may become better understood once the case of the largest and most advanced of these areas, the present Megalopolis, is thoroughly analyzed.

WHAT ARE THE PROBLEMS OF MEGALOPOLIS?

Within such a vast area the problems are, of course, many and diversified. It may not be necessary, nor very useful, to survey all of them, in their local variety, in the different parts of Megalopolis. A few basic questions must, however, be asked: How did Megalopolis happen to arise and with such a shape? What are the present main functions of this area, its role within the American economy and the North Atlantic system of relations? What are the present problems of internal organizations, and what solutions have been attempted?

Here are three sets of questions, each of which requires detailed consideration, involving a great deal of research.

Megalopolis' growth in the past sums up a good part of the economic history of the United States. It has not often been examined as to how the sequence of events and trends in the past growth of the nation affected local developments. Although it is, in area, only a small section of the Northeast, Megalopolis had a crucial part in determining national trends; on the other hand, the main swings of its own history were usually the consequence of shifts in national policies.

Why was Megalopolis' growth throughout its history more rapid and continuous than that of many other urban areas in the world? This question leads into an examination of the factors motivating or determining urban expansion in a given area. In a first inquiry concerning the matter conducted by this writer a few years ago were listed some forty-odd factors that in different ways and at different periods helped the upbuilding of Megalopolis. The two major among these factors appear to be, on the one hand, the polynuclear origin and the part played by the series of northeastern seaboard cities as a *hinge* of the American economy. The federal organization of government and the division of the Atlantic seaboard into so many states (each with access to Tidewater) that engaged in a fruitful rivalry made all nuclei compete one with another until their growth joined them together.

The role of the "hinge" is more difficult to perceive, but is easily demonstrated by the material accumulated in regional economic history. This seaboard had from the inception of the United States the opportunity and the responsibility of serving both as an oceanic façade for relations abroad and as a springboard for the settlement and development of the continent inland. At different periods the main weight of the northeastern interests oscillated from sea trade to continental development and back again; in New England one of these oscillations in the beginning of the nineteenth century was defined as the period when the main interest shifted "from the wharf to the waterfall." In many towns which, on the Fall line, were later integrated with the area of Megalopolis, wharf and waterfall were very close to one another. Whether the general trends of the American economy threw the door open towards the outside or closed it to turn the main endeavors inland, the hinge remained fixed at the series of eastern cities, extending from Boston to Washington, which alone had the geographical position, the authority, the capital, and the skill to elaborate such policies and put them into application.[2]

The inheritance of the past still influences heavily present situations and trends. Whether the eastern seaboard will keep the monopoly of the "hinge" advantages after the St. Lawrence Seaway is completed remains a burning question. However, the faculty of direct access to the sea was only one of many factors which favored Megalopolis and the others may still operate in the future. The relative part played by these various factors in shaping the present would be an important and suggestive aspect in the study of Megalopolis' historical background.

The present functions of Megalopolis

[2] See the historical sketch of the "hinge" function in J. Gottman: "La région charnière de l'economie americaine," *Revue de la Porte Océane*, Le Havre, VII, Nos. 71 and 72, March, 1951, pp. 9–14, and April, 1951, pp. 11–20.

would be the next step in the proposed research. These functions are several; there is, of course, a residential one expressed in the total figure of the population; but how do the inhabitants make a living and why do they have to be concentrated in this area?

Megalopolis arose as a grouping of the main seaports, commercial centers, and manufacturing activities in the United States. To a large extent the *maritime façade function* still is carried on: most of the seaborne foreign trade of the country goes through Megalopolis' harbors. The *manufacturing function* never stopped developing within the area, although many industries have been brought into operation in other sections of the United States. Megalopolis seems to specialize rather in the more delicate finishing industries and in those involving a great deal of laboratory work and research. However, a good number of large plants (iron and steel, chemical and metallurgical industries) have been erected within the last 20 years in this same area. What the balance is and how much specialization is really shaping up would be interesting to ascertain.

The *commercial and financial functions* remain extremely important for Megalopolis. Despite decentralization trends many times stressed and advocated, this area remains a decisive one for the American economy as well as for international financial relations. If New York City is no longer the financial capital it was earlier in the century, it is because much of that function migrated to Washington, with the increasing role of federal authorities in the management of the nation's business. As a market, for goods as well as for money, Megalopolis as a whole still dominates the rest of the national territory. Not only does it comprise one-fifth of the nation: this fifth is obviously the best paid and

the wealthiest. Though other centers of concentrated wealth have arisen and developed elsewhere, especially on the West Coast and along the Great Lakes' shores, none can yet boast a mass approaching that of the Boston-Washington region. Nor has any had such a traditional grouping of financial and social activities as that suggested by some of New York's thoroughfares: Wall Street, Park Avenue, or Fifth Avenue, all fractions of the national Main Street.

Whether or not related to the social stratification and the abundance of money in the area, Megalopolis acquired and retained a quite remarkable *function of cultural leadership*, despite the American endeavor at decentralization. Here are found the best-known universities, the better-equipped laboratories, the greatest density of learned institutions and large libraries in North America, and probably in the present world. The vast majority of nationally-read periodicals and important publishing houses have their editorial offices in Megalopolis; some newspapers from this area have even a nationwide distribution, especially for their Sunday editions. The concentration of cultural leadership makes it difficult for institutions such as the Ford Foundation or the R.C.A. Research Laboratories to operate from headquarters located far from Megalopolis. This leadership is even more evident in the arts: whether theater, music, or galleries, the concentration attained in this area has no match elsewhere in America.

Finally, the question may arise, and would be more difficult to answer, as to the actual weight of Megalopolis in the political life of the country. Although the national capital is part of it, this region is only one-fifth of the nation and its votes do not necessarily make the

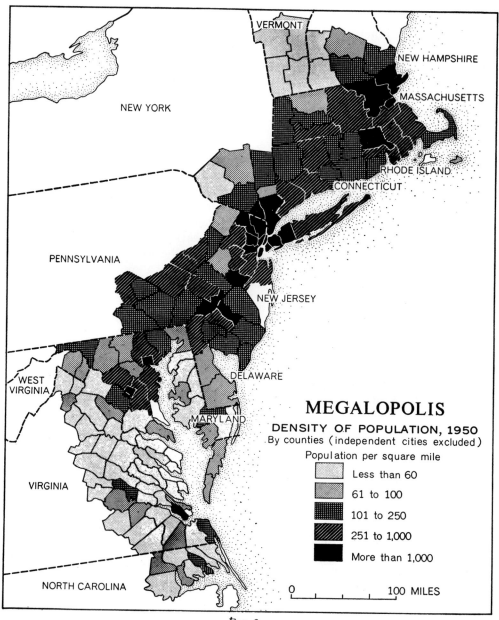

MEGALOPOLIS

DENSITY OF POPULATION, 1950
By counties (independent cities excluded)

Population per square mile

	Less than 60
	61 to 100
	101 to 250
	251 to 1,000
	More than 1,000

0   100 MILES

FIG. 2.

decision of major states, parts of which are megalopolitan, such as New York and Pennsylvania. Nevertheless, Megalopolis has a definite political pattern which differs from that of the surrounding northeastern country.

Having thus analyzed the past growth and present functions of Megalopolis,

we come to its actual problems. These are many. Two categories of problems, particularly pressing in all downtown sections of modern cities, have attracted attention and have been given much study: the traffic difficulties and the slums. Two other problems are nowadays receiving increasing attention in

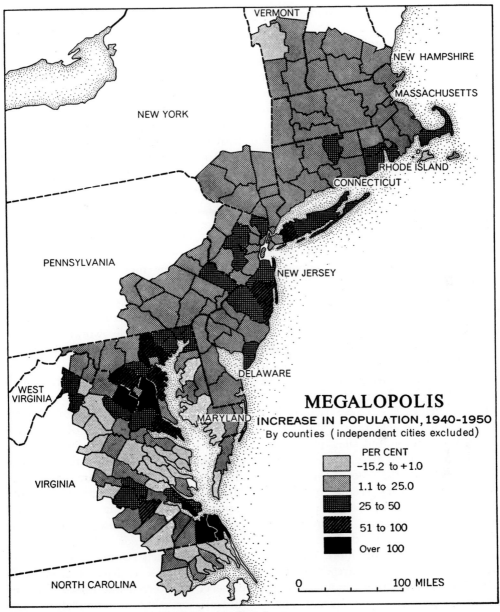

FIG. 3.

competent quarters: water supply and local government. Both appear inadequately set to answer the present needs of the huge cities and their quickly expanding suburbs. The rapidly mushrooming metropolitan commissions and committees seem to herald already deep changes forthcoming in the traditional concepts and practices of local government. Interstate compacts may arise to help solve transportation problems (such as the Port of New York Authority); experiments in metropolitan government may be more difficult to start in parts of Megalopolis because of the mass and variety of interests at stake—

but the very difficulties make every attempt more significant.

Megalopolis as a unit has taken shape only within the last few years. Its laws and customs will take much longer to evolve into new forms better adapted to the needs and resources of such an enormous urban territory. A survey of the new problems, in their variety, should nevertheless be of some help even at this time. While legislation and institutions change slowly, modes of living evolve far more rapidly. Novelists have satirized certain aspects of megalopolitan life: a quarter century after the "cliff-dwellers" were strongly established on Fifth and Park Avenues, we hear about the "exurbanites." The basic fact is the double trend of the large cities: part of the population moves out and commutes from an "outer suburbia" which often extends 50 miles beyond; and parts of the cities are converted into immense apartment house groupings (paradoxically sometimes called "villages"). These two trends are particularly clear in Manhattan and in Washington, but they are gaining other big nuclei of Megalopolis as well. The threat of the recent spread of juvenile delinquency seems to increase the migration of families to the periphery of metropolitan areas. The new mode of life involves more daily traveling, more traffic jams, and more highways outside the downtown areas; a redistribution of marketing channels (illustrated by proliferating suburban shopping centers and department store branches); some changes in the type of goods needed; an increasing interest in zoning, gardening, and nature conservation.

Because more megalopolitan, the way of life of an increasing proportion of the population becomes more country-like although not really rural. The Bureau of the Census has had to revise several times its standards for the definition of metropolitan areas; the criteria of integration with the central urban district include such measurements as the proportion of commuters and the average number of telephone calls per subscriber from a suburban county to the central county of the area, etc. In 1950 the Bureau even had to revise its definition of "urban territory" and introduced the term "urbanized areas" to provide for a better separation between urban and rural territory in the vicinity of large cities, especially within metropolitan areas. New suburban types of farming are also developing, consisting both of a few highly mechanized and specialized large enterprises (such as the truck farming on Long Island) and a scattering of numerous small farms inhabited by people working in the cities and deriving their income from nonagricultural occupations.

The city, in the days of yore, was a well-defined, densely settled territory, often surrounded by walls or palisades. Some time ago it broke out of such rigid frames and developed outlying sections, *extra-muros*. In its most recent stage of growth, already characteristic of Megalopolis, it extends out on a rapidly expanding scale, along highways and rural roads, mixing uses of land that look either rural or urban, encircling vast areas which remain "green" (and which some wise endeavors attempt to preserve as recreation space for the future), creating a completely new pattern of living and of regional interdependence between communities.

The coming of age of Megalopolis thus creates, besides problems in legislation, traffic, engineering, marketing, etc., also new psychological problems: people have more difficulty thinking along the traditional lines of division into states when megalopolitan sections of different states are much more integrated in daily life than they could be with up-state areas of the same "Common-wealth"; people have also some difficulty adapting themselves to such a scattered way of life; and officials are often lost when trying to classify according to the traditional categories of urban, rural, rural non-farm, farming, etc. Such are, too briefly reviewed, the various problems of Megalopolis. They are worth analyzing for the conclusions that may follow.

Lessons from an Analysis of the Megalopolitan Process

A detailed analysis of Megalopolis, as it appears today, seems a worthwhile enterprise despite the present unique character of this region. Its trends acquire immediate national, and some-times international, significance by the sheer size and weight of Megalopolis in economic and social matters. But it is also, as has been shown, a pioneering area in terms of urbanization. What is observed and experimented with here may serve, though on a smaller scale and in many cases only after some time, to avoid delays and errors in other growing urban areas. It may help improve our management of the intricate process of urbanization.

This process is an old one and has greatly contributed, as many authors have shown, to the growth of western civilization. Far from having reached its optimum, in the middle of the twentieth century, the process of urbani-zation accelerated its pace. The United States has demonstrated that enough agricultural commodities of all kinds can be produced for a populous nation, enjoying a high standard of living, by the work of only one-eighth of the total population. This proportion of the farmers within the nation may and probably will be further reduced. Thus 90 per cent of a prosperous nation must live from nonagricultural pursuits, but not in congested slums. This momen-tous evolution, one of the major Ameri-can contributions to this century, lead-ing to semiurbanized status, is most advanced in Megalopolis.[3]

The new forms thus attained, the intensity of the problems, the solutions attempted, must be compared to what happens in all these respects in other principal metropolitan areas in the United States and perhaps in Canada. A clearer mode of classification for both problems and possible solutions may thus be worked out, based on factual observation rather than generalized theory. The whole survey may help to evaluate this new expanding frontier of the American economy: the urbaniza-tion of the land.

Outside the North American continent many other countries are already faced with a similar acceleration of the process of urbanization. Their policies could greatly benefit from a full analysis of Megalopolis today and its comparison with other urban growths in America. None of the continuous chains of metropolitan areas or conurbations shap-ing now in other parts of the world is indeed comparable in size or shape as yet to the American Megalopolis. The one most nearly approaching it, which may perhaps coalesce sometime within the next 20 years, would be in our opinion in northwestern Europe, from Amsterdam to Paris, including perhaps a bulge eastwards as far as the Ruhr and Cologne along the Rhine and Meuse rivers.

Another possible super-metropolitan system of this kind could well be forming in England. A giant U-shaped urban

[3] See J. Gottmann: *L'Amérique*, Paris, Hach-ette, 1954, 2nd ed. revised, pp. 170–177 and 244–246; also "La ville americaine," in *Geographia*, Paris, No. 48, September 1955, pp. 9–14; and *Virginia at Mid-Century*, New York, 1955, pp. 473–479.

chain surrounds the southern Pennines, extending from Liverpool and Manchester to Leeds and Bradford, via Birmingham and Sheffield. This U may some day unite southwards with the expanding suburbs of Greater London. Then the whole system may enter the megalopolitan family. It would remain, nevertheless, quite different from Megalopolis on the northeastern seaboard. Each large area of such kind will long keep its originality, resulting from its own past and its relation to a given zone of civilization. Large urbanized areas do not need, however, to grow up to megalopolitan size to be able to profit by the lessons in metropolitan organization obtained in Megalopolis.

How Far Could Megalopolis Grow?

Several important studies of the metropolitan areas around New York City, Philadelphia, etc., are now in progress. These surveys will attempt to forecast future growth, by projecting curves for the next 10 to 25 years. Urban and suburban territory is expanding at a fast pace in the United States, and this pace has been notably accelerated in recent years. A vast area like Megalopolis would not have arisen without it. The time has perhaps come to ask once more the question: How far could Megalopolis grow? And in which directions?

In 1955, a group of city planners at Yale University began to speak about a citylike, well-knit system extending from Portland, Maine, to Norfolk, Virginia. Such may be the impression provided by road transportation maps. This writer's observations on completion of a study of Virginia by January, 1955, did not seem to warrant as yet the absorption into Megalopolis of more than a few counties in northern Virginia. Richmond and the Hampton Roads area

had not yet been consolidated with the Washington-to-Boston more intensely urbanized system. Beyond eastern Massachusetts northwards, urbanization was felt mainly in the summer as a seasonal migration of vacationing or semi-vacationing people from Megalopolis. However, there could be no doubt that Megalopolis is daily expanding its territorial scope. Our definition (see Fig. 1) based on the census of 1950 is certainly an underestimation in area for 1957.

Expansion proceeds in many directions, of course, all around the outer fringes. Consolidation of the urban land use within the 1950 limits goes on at the same time. The existing densities of population (see Fig. 2) and the trends of increase of this density by counties in the recent past (see Fig. 3) concur in stressing a relative saturation of most of the areas within Megalopolis between Philadelphia and Boston. Although a great deal of new construction still goes on even in those parts, the more striking increases appear in the southern section of Megalopolis and an expansion in the Virginian Tidewater and northern Piedmont seems unavoidable.

Thus Megalopolis is pushing southwards and southwestwards. It may indeed reach Richmond and Norfolk some day in the foreseeable future. Another set of directions, this time inland, and breaking away from the fateful axis of U.S. 1, may be inferred from an attentive examination of the distribution already in 1950 of the metropolitan areas in the northeastern section of the United States, between the Atlantic seaboard, the Great Lakes and the Ohio Valley (see Fig. 4). A rather impressive density of such metropolitan areas is found inland along the route of the New York Central Railroad up the Hudson-Mohawk route and the southern shores of Lakes Erie and Ontario. Then from Cleveland south-

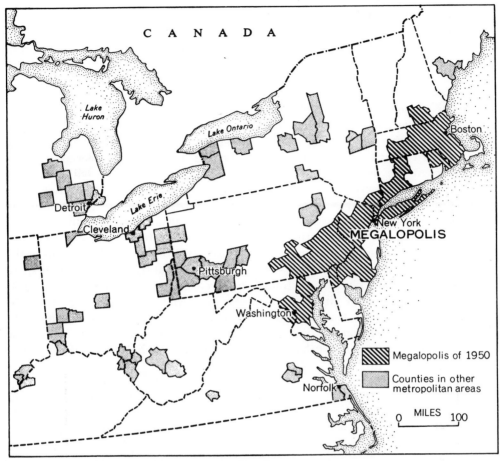

FIG. 4.

wards a little interrupted chain extends towards Pittsburgh, Pennsylvania. Between Megalopolis on one hand and the trans-Appalachian urbanized and industrialized areas, the valleys and ridges of the Appalachian Mountains cause a clearcut break. But if the Pittsburgh-Cleveland-Syracuse-Albany chain would come to be consolidated, even mountain ranges could be overcome and an enormous sort of annular megalopolitan system could arise; the St. Lawrence Seaway, if it developed into a major artery of navigation, could precipitate such a trend.

A much smaller but curiously "annular" urban system is already shaping in the Netherlands, as after the coalescence of the cities along the main seaboard axis of Holland, from Amsterdam to Rotterdam, urbanization is gaining inland, along the Rhine from Rotterdam to Arnhem, and along roads and canals from Amsterdam to Utrecht. The coalescence between Arnhem and Utrecht is on its way. In England the U-shaped chain of the metropolitan type outlined above from Manchester to Leeds has not been filled up in between these two cities along the shortest line into another annular formation because of the topographical obstacle of the Pennine range, still an empty area. This obstacle is comparable, though it is on a much smaller scale, to the Appalachian ridges back of Megalopolis.

Other trends of megalopolitan expansion in territory could be discussed either inside the mountainous obstacle itself or northeastwards in the seaboard area. But these trends are definitely seasonal. In the past Megalopolis has in fact *emptied* the neighboring mountains, northern New England, and even to some extent the province of Québec in Canada by attracting millions of people from difficult rural areas, less rich in opportunity. Now, with the rise of the standard of living, with more people taking longer summer vacations, the cooler New England seashore or hills, the Appalachian plateaus, attract a sort of *transhumance* of city folks to summer pastures. This transhumance seems to be constantly on the increase and creates for the summer months long-range commuting problems. If the contiguous areas, where the majority of the permanent population lives from the proceeds of summer residents and tourists, were to be included in the territorial concept of Megalopolis, the limits of our area would have to be rapidly and substantially enlarged.

Urban land utilization is indeed devouring land fast, in many ways. The old habit of considering it as a minor occupant of space will soon have to be revised. Our modern civilization has found the means to grow more and more agricultural products, to raise more and more livestock, on less space; but industrial, commercial, and residential uses are constantly increasing their space requirements. Our generation is probably witnessing the beginning of a great revolution in the geography of land use. Megalopolis heralds a new era in the distribution of habitat and economic activities.